Introduction to Financial Accounting

A USER PERSPECTIVE

CANADIAN EDITION

Introduction to Financial Accounting

A USER PERSPECTIVE

CANADIAN EDITION

Kumen H. Jones
Arizona State University (Retired)

Michael L. Werner
University of Miami

Katherene P. Terrell
University of Central Oklahoma

Wayne Irvine
Mount Royal College

David Allwright
Mount Royal College

PEARSON

Prentice
Hall

Toronto

To my wife, whose love and support made the publication of this book possible.

WAYNE IRVINE

National Library of Canada Cataloguing in Publication

Introduction to financial accounting: a user perspective/
Kumen H. Jones...[et al.]. – Canadian ed.

Includes index.
ISBN 0-13-035596-8

    1. Accounting. 2. Financial statements. I. Jones, Kumen H.

HF5635.I578 2004   657   C2003-901413-4

ISBN 0-13-035596-8

Vice President, Editorial Director: Michael J. Young
Executive Editor: Samantha Scully
Executive Marketing Manager: Cas Shields
Senior Developmental Editor: Paul Donnelly
Copy Editor: Anita Smale
Editorial Coordinator: Marisa D'Andrea
Production Coordinator: Andrea Falkenberg
Page Layout: Heidi Palfrey
Art Director: Mary Opper
Interior Design: Jennfier Federico
Cover Design: Alex Li
Cover Image © Walter Hodges/CORBIS

1 2 3 4 5   08 07 06 05 04

Printed and bound in Canada

Contents

Preface

As we enter the twenty-first century, we who are involved in accounting education at the collegiate level have reassessed the way we prepare our students for the business world. Technology changes more quickly than most of us can comprehend, complicating accounting education. Yet one constant remains: Business people must be prepared to perform tasks that only people can perform—in particular, communicating, thinking, and making decisions. Decision making is *the* critical skill in today's business world, and *Introduction to Financial Accounting: A User Perspective*, Canadian Edition, helps students to better use accounting information and improve their decision-making skills.

This text provides an introduction to accounting within the context of business and business decisions. Readers will explore accounting information's role in the decision-making process, and learn how to use various types of accounting information found in financial statements and annual reports. Seeing how accounting information can be used to make better business decisions will benefit all students, regardless of their major course of study or chosen career.

We believe an accounting course should be a broad introduction *to* accounting, rather than introductory accounting as it has traditionally been taught, and it should be taught from the perspective of the user, not the preparer. It should emphasize *what* accounting information is, *why* it is important, and *how* it is used by economic decision makers.

As you work with this text, you will find it focuses heavily on the uses of accounting information rather than the preparation of the information. This, however, is only one characteristic which distinguishes *Introduction to Financial Accounting: A User Perspective*, Canadian Edition, from other texts you may have used in the past.

Support for the Interactive Classroom

We believe this text provides tools to actively involve students in their learning processes. The conversational tone of the text, its user perspective, and the logical presentation of topics all contribute to the ability of this text to meet that goal. However, several features are particularly important in developing a classroom atmosphere in which students share ideas, ask questions, and relate their learning to the world around them.

Throughout each chapter of the text, you will find Discussion Questions (DQs) that challenge students to reach beyond the surface of the written text to determine answers. Far from typical review questions, for which the students can scan a few pages of the text to locate an answer, many of the DQs provide relevant learning by relating students' personal experiences to the knowledge they gain through the text.

The DQs provide a variety of classroom experiences:

- Many DQs provide the basis for lively classroom discussions, requiring students to think about issues and formulate or defend their opinions.
- Some DQs are springboards for group assignments (in or out of the classroom) to put cooperative learning into practice.
- DQs may be assigned as individual writing assignments to allow students to practice and develop their writing skills.
- Combining individually written DQ responses with follow-up group discussions leading to group consensus can spark lively debate!
- Having students keep a journal of their responses to all DQs (regardless if they are used in another way) encourages solitary pondering of accounting concepts.

The DQs comprise a critically important part of the text's pedagogy designed to emphasize important points that students may skim across in their initial reading. Even if they are not formally part of the required work for your course, students will gain a greater understanding of the concepts discussed when they take time to consider each question as part of the text.

- Students get enthused about accounting when working with real companies. Chapter 1 and its appendix provide students with information on how to use library and Internet resources to research companies, and introduce students to annual reports.
- We included the 2001 Sobeys Inc. annual report with our text and use it to demonstrate financial analysis. We added a term-length annual report project to further involve students in the business world that begins in Chapter 1 and continues through Chapter 11.
- Financial Reporting Cases, at the end of the chapters, encourage students to use the Internet to link to real businesses and explore their financial statements.

Adventures into *real* information about *real* companies always raises student interest! In addition to these features which help to foster an open, interactive environment in the classroom, a major distinction of this text is its total separation of the *use* of accounting information and its preparation.

Separation of Accounting and Bookkeeping

The text approaches accounting totally from the user perspective. Most chapters contain no bookkeeping. Is this an indication we believe that a knowledge of bookkeeping skills is unnecessary? On the contrary, bookkeeping is the nuts and bolts that holds our accounting systems together. What we have learned, though, is that bookkeeping procedures without a conceptual understanding of the uses of accounting information are meaningless. Beginning accounting students cannot digest the use of financial statements, the role of accounting information, the world of business, and the details of bookkeeping simultaneously. Once students have a basic knowledge of the other topics, however, learning details of the recording process becomes effective and efficient.

Separating accounting and bookkeeping makes both subjects easier to grasp and more enjoyable to learn. This approach also allows instructors and institutions to select an appropriate time and degree of bookkeeping coverage for their program. Some schools choose to have all students learn basic recording procedures; others may only require accounting majors to acquire these skills.

To facilitate the separation of accounting and bookkeeping, we introduce the accounting cycle in Chapter 6 and complete its coverage in appendices to Chapters 7, 8, and 9. We placed the accounting cycle coverage in Chapter 6 because this is the point when students have enough basic knowledge of the use of accounting information to be ready for accounting procedures. Some schools leave this material until the end of the semester, at the beginning of the second semester, or in a separate course for accounting majors. For this reason, no references are made to Chapter 6 in the remaining chapters except in the appendices.

Chapter 6 and the appendices in Chapter 7 through 9 cover the complete accounting cycle from analyzing transactions through post-closing trial balance, including debits and credits, journals, general ledgers, worksheets, and financial statement preparation. Chapter 6 contains a number of long problems and three Accounting Cycle Cases that are condensed practice sets.

In addition to the decision to focus on the uses of accounting information rather than the details of accounting procedures in this text, we have made several other deliberate and important choices about topical coverage.

Topics Covered

We carefully considered the inclusion or exclusion of topics from this text consistent with our pedagogical goals of building foundations that support effective student learning. Because our focus introduces students to accounting information and its uses in decision making, we could not simply follow the traditional coverage of topics. As we considered individual topics, we continually explored whether their inclusion would enhance a student's ability to interpret and use accounting information throughout his or her personal and professional life. The result is that *Introduction to Financial Accounting: A User Perspective*, Canadian Edition, covers those topics that every accounting student should leave the course understanding well. In short, we sought quality of learning, not quantity of minutiae.

For example, we cover the calculations of only two amortization methods—straight line and double declining balance. By limiting the coverage of detailed depreciation calculations, we have the opportunity to focus on the concepts of cost allocation, expense recognition, financial statement differences between the two methods, and the distinction between gains and revenues, and losses and expenses. Students will not only know how to calculate amortization expense, but also understand *why* they are calculating it and how to use those calculations in making business decisions. In the chapter, students learn how to properly interpret gains and losses. Most of them are surprised to find out that two companies buying identical assets for the same price can sell them later for the same amount and have different results—one company can have a gain and the other experience a loss.

Another example of building foundations to learning is the introduction to the concept of the cost of borrowing. Instead of sending students straight to the present value tables, we take time to measure the cost of borrowing—an important foundation for intermediate accounting and learning how to account for interest costs in long-term liabilities.

We also include some topics that traditional books omit. Chapter 1 includes discussions of each major type of business organization. As we discuss various topics, students learn to view the financial statements of each type of organization throughout the book. Chapter 1 and its appendix introduce students to library and Internet research on real companies and start students on a term quest to apply accounting concepts to at least one publicly traded firm. We pay particular attention to students' understanding of the difference between *reality* and the *measurement of reality* and the need to find both the *reality of cash* and the *reality of performance*.

From our classroom experience with this text, we believe that the content is appropriate for college sophomores to embrace and take forward to additional courses. The carefully chosen sequence of topics helps to make them more understandable by establishing firm conceptual foundations.

Sequence of Coverage

To effectively present the user perspective, we developed a logical flow of topics so that each chapter builds on what the student has already learned. Students can easily understand how the topics fit together logically and how they are used together to make good decisions. Moreover, students can see that accounting and the information it provides is not merely something that exists unto itself, but rather it is something developed in response to the needs of economic decision makers.

If you could read the entire text before using it in your classroom, you would have a very clear picture of the experience awaiting your students. However, even a short tour through the material covered in each chapter will show you how we have structured our presentation of the topics to maximize student learning.

Chapter 1 provides a brief overview of business and the role of accounting in the business, setting the stage for the introduction of accounting information. In the appendix, we provide students with information about public reporting of accounting information and research sources. In the world of business, there is a great need for accounting information and for increasingly sophisticated accounting professionals.

Chapter 2 presents an introduction to economic decision making. Because the stated purpose of financial accounting information is to provide information to be used in making decisions, we believe an understanding of the decision-making process is not only appropriate, but essential. We explore some of the characteristics crucial to making accounting information useful in that process. In this chapter we also introduce the concepts of cash basis and accrual basis of accounting, as well as the concepts of revenues and expenses. There is also a limited discussion of the income statement and the measurement of economic reality.

Chapter 3 introduces the balance sheet as one of several financial tools developed to present accounting information in a useful form. In this chapter we focus on how equity financing affects businesses and how its results are reflected on balance sheets.

Chapter 4 continues the exploration of the balance sheet, this time examining the impact of debt financing. We present notes and bonds as financing options for businesses and introduce the cost of borrowing.

Chapter 5 delves deeper into the income statement and introduces the statement of owner's equity as financial tools. Now that students have been introduced to the first three financial statements used by economic decision makers, they can see how the statements relate to one another.

Chapter 6 introduces the eight steps of the accounting cycle, including the process or preparing a trial balance. We discuss the chronology of the accounting cycle and walk the students through each step. Additionally, we introduce the concepts of the debit and credit, accounts, journals and journal entries. This comprehensive chapter also includes the process of reconciling the company's bank statement to its accounting records.

Chapter 7 explores issues surrounding the acquisition, amortization, and disposal of long-lived assets under accrual accounting. Also examined are the effects of choosing different types of amortization methods. We also show how to properly interpret gains and losses. The appendix demonstrates how to record the acquisition, amortization, and disposal of assets.

Chapter 8 explores another challenging issue arising from the use of accrual basis accounting—merchandise inventory and inventory cost flow methods. Students learn how to calculate amounts under FIFO, LIFO, and average cost methods for both periodic and perpetual inventory systems. They also learn how choosing one of these methods can affect the accounting information provided on income statements and balance sheets. This chapter has two appendices. The first appendix covers inventory purchasing issues and presents a discussion of freight terms and cash discounts, and how they alter the cost of purchasing. The second appendix presents the accounting cycle for periodic inventory systems and perpetual inventory systems including all recording, adjusting, and closing entries.

Chapter 9 returns to the balance sheet and income statement, taking a closer look at the way these two financial statements are organized. We explore the information provided in a classified balance sheet and an expanded multistep income statement in detail.

Chapter 10 introduces the statement of cash flows as another financial tool. After using the information provided by the other three financial statements, prepared under accrual accounting, students see the need to refocus their attention on cash. With an understanding of the purpose of the statement of cash flows at hand, students find its creation using both the direct and indirect methods easier to understand. More importantly, students learn how to read and interpret the information provided on the statement of cash flows.

Chapter 11 explains the importance of gathering various types of information to make the results of financial statement analysis most useful. Ratio analysis is the featured technique; information from Sobeys Inc. 2001 annual report illustrates the computations, comparisons, and analyses throughout the chapter. The 2001 annual report rather than a later year was chosen to illustrate the effect that non-recurring items can have on earnings and share prices.

Other Important Features of This Text

In addition to the Discussion Questions and the inclusion of the Sobey's Inc. Annual Report, discussed in detail above, our text offers other features that will enhance the learning process.

- Learning Objectives—Previewing each chapter with these objectives allows students to see what direction the chapter is taking, which makes the journey through the material a bit easier.
- Marginal Glossary—Students often find the process of learning accounting terminology to be a challenge. As each new key word is introduced in the text, it is shown in bold and also defined in the margin. This feature offers students an easy way to review the key terms and locate their introduction in the text.
- Summary—This concise summary of each chapter provides an overview of the main points, but is in no way a substitute for reading the chapter.
- Key Terms—At the end of each chapter, a list of the new key words directs students to the page on which the key word or phrase was introduced.
- Review the Facts—Students can use these basic, definitional questions to review the key points of each chapter. The questions are in a sequence reflecting the coverage of topics in the chapter.
- Apply What You Have Learned—Our end-of-chapter assignment materials include a mix of traditional types of homework problems and innovative assignments requiring critical thinking and writing. Many of the requirements can be used as the basis for classroom discussions. You will find matching

problems, short essay questions, and calculations. Assignments dealing directly with the use of financial statements are also included. Many of these applications also work well as group assignments.

- Glossary of Accounting Terms—An alphabetical listing of important accounting terms, including all of the key terms plus additional terms, defines the terms and lists the page on which the term first appears.

Supplements for Use by the Instructor

Additional support for your efforts in the classroom is provided by our group of supplements.

Instructor's Resource Manual, 0-13-121813-1

This comprehensive resource includes *chapter overviews* that identify the chapter concepts, explains the chapter rationale and philosophy, and reviews the significant topics and points of the chapter. Also included are *chapter outlines* organized by objectives, *lecture suggestions, teaching tips,* various *chapter quizzes, transparency masters, group activities* derived from the textbook Discussion Questions (DQs) as well as the *Solutions to the DQs, communication exercises,* and *suggested readings.*

Solutions Manual and Transparencies

Solutions Manual, 0-13-121812-3

Transparencies, 0-13-121811-5

Solutions are provided for all the end-of-chapter assignments. The Solutions Manual is also available in acetate form and on disk to adopters.

Test Item File, 0-13-121809-3

The Test Item File includes test items that can be used as quiz and/or exam material. Each chapter contains multiple-choice questions (both conceptual and quantitative), problems, exercises, and critical thinking problems. Each question will identify the difficulty level, page reference, the corresponding learning objective(s), and the category classification according to Bloom's Taxonomy.

TestGen, 0-13-121810-7

This easy-to-use computerized testing program can create exams, evaluate, and track student results. The TestGen also provides on-line testing capabilities. Test items are drawn from the Test Item File. TestGen is made available as a component of the Instructor Resource CD.

PowerPoint Presentation, 0-13-121810-7

PowerPoint presentations are available for each chapter of the text. Each presentation allows instructors to offer a more interactive presentation using colourful graphics, outlines of chapter material, additional examples, and graphical explanations of difficult topics. Instructors have the flexibility to add slides and/or modify the existing slides to meet the course needs. The PowerPoint presentations are made available as a component of the Instructor Resource CD.

Acknowledgements

The authors for the Canadian adaptation of this textbook recognize that there are numerous people that contribute to the publication process. First, we would like to thank Samantha Scully, Executive Editor, and Paul Donnelly, Senior Developmental Editor, for their generous support, feedback, patience, and encouragement. Marisa D'Andrea played an essential role in the production on the book. Anita Smale, our copy editor, also deserves credit for her rigorous attention to detail and understanding of our time constraints.

We would also like to thank the faculty and staff of the Bissett School of Business, Mount Royal College for their friendship and help by creating an environment of collegiality and mutual support. In particular we would like to thank the Dean of the business school, Wendelin Fraser, for her indulgence in giving us the freedom to pursue projects of this nature. All of you contributed in some way to the success of this project.

Several other groups deserve special thanks and recognition for their valuable work:

Reviewers for the *Introduction to Financial Accounting: A User Perspective*:

Cecile Ashman	Algonquin College
Les Barnhouse	Athabasca University
Hilary Becker	Carleton University
Maria Belanger	Algonquin College
Michael Bozzo	Mohawk College
Peggy Coady	Memorial University
Leo Gallant	St. Francis Xavier
Dennis Huber	University of New Brunswick
Stephanie Ibach	Northern Alberta Institute of Technology
Stuart Jones	University of Calgary
Jean Pai	University of Manitoba
Penny Parker	Fanshawe College
Jeffrey Rudolph	Marianapolis College
Frank Sacucci	MacEwan College
Nancy Tait	Sir Sandford Fleming College
Jan Thatcher	Lakehead University
Dennis Wilson	Centennial College
Shu-Lun Wong	Memorial University
Elizabeth Zaleschuk	Douglas College

1

Introduction to Business in Canada

You have completed enough credit hours to graduate from college or university. While you are intelligent and creative, you spent enough time working through college to finish with a B− average; this semester the recruiters seem to prefer B+ and A− averages. In addition to your many talents of buying and selling logo products at sporting events, you dabble in pop music. You even managed to save a few dollars from the sporting goods sales. On the popular campus strip, an old pub is for sale. If you cannot find a job, maybe you should create one. Your best friend is in the same predicament, so you put your heads together.

What would it mean to own a business? How should you organize it—by yourself or with your friend? How will you know if you are making money? How much money will it take to get the business going and where will the money come from if it is more than you and your pal have right now? How much can you make and will that be enough to support one or both of you? Should you focus on music, food, and drink, or add logo products to the mix? Will the venture be a success or will it waste what little money you have saved? What to do? Your friend's father wants you both to visit his accountant for advice. What does accounting have to do with this decision?

Accounting touches each of us every day—in both our personal and professional lives. To be used properly, accounting information must be studied in context. Therefore, to better understand accounting for business enterprises and to help answer some of your questions, we must first explore business in its many different forms. ∎

The word *business* means different things to different people. For some, the word conjures up a dream of excitement and opportunity; for others, it represents a nightmare of greed and exploitation. Whether our view of business is positive or negative, each of us is touched every day by what goes on in the world of business.

The Canadian Oxford Dictionary gives several definitions of business:

> 1: One's regular occupation, profession, or trade. 2: A thing that is one's concern. 3: A task or duty... 6: A thing or series of things needing to be dealt with. 7: Volume of trade. 8a: A company or corporation; b: commercial enterprises collectively.[1]

As you can see, not only do people have different impressions of business, but the word itself has different meanings in different contexts. The last two definitions are particularly relevant for this book. It is important for you to understand that at times *business* is used to describe the entirety of commerce and trade, and at other times it is used to describe an individual company. In fact, in the economic world, and in books about the world of business (including this one), the words *company* and *business* are often used interchangeably. So whenever you see the word *business*, make sure you understand the context in which it is used.

The information in this chapter should provide you with the background necessary to put the accounting concepts presented throughout this text into the proper business context, and to seek information about an individual business entity. After all, accounting information is the key ingredient for making wise business decisions.

LEARNING OBJECTIVES

After completing your work on this chapter, you should be able to do the following:

1. Describe the four factors of production.
2. Explain the basic concepts of capitalism and how they relate to the profit motive.
3. Explain the basic issues in the debate over whether businesses have a social responsibility.
4. Distinguish among the three basic forms of business organization—the proprietorship, the partnership, and the corporation—and describe the advantages and disadvantages of each.
5. Distinguish among the three major types of business activities.
6. Explain the basic need for international business trade and the complications involved in this activity.
7. Describe the role that provincial regulatory bodies have in the development of reporting standards for Canadian corporations.
8. Describe the role that the Canadian Institute of Chartered Accountants (CICA) and other governing bodies have in the creation of accounting standards in Canada.
9. Explain the purpose of an independent financial audit.

WHAT IS BUSINESS?

business Depending on the context, the area of commerce or trade, an individual company, or the process of producing and distributing goods and services.

Essentially, **business** is the process of producing goods and services and then distributing them to those who desire or need them. This process sounds simple enough, but it is actually quite complex and few people ever gain a complete understanding of all its aspects.

[1]*The Canadian Oxford Dictionary* (Toronto: Oxford University Press, 1998), p. 191.

Although we cannot present an in-depth study of the many aspects of business, we must talk about a few basics at the outset to present accounting in its proper context. We begin with the factors of production.

Factors of Production

factors of production
The four major items needed to support economic activity: natural resources, labour, capital, and entrepreneurship.

natural resources Land and the materials that come from the land, such as timber, mineral deposits, oil deposits, and water. One of the factors of production.

labour The mental and physical efforts of all workers performing tasks required to produce and sell goods and services. This factor of production is also called the human resource factor.

capital A factor of production that includes the buildings, machinery, and tools used to produce goods and services. Also, sometimes used to refer to the money used to buy those items.

entrepreneurship
The factor of production that brings the other three factors—natural resources, labour, and capital—together to form a business.

The **factors of production** are the key ingredients needed to support economic activity (see Exhibit 1–1). Economists classify the factors of production into four categories:

1. **Natural resources**—land and the materials that come from the land, such as timber, mineral deposits, oil deposits, and water.
2. **Labour**—the mental and physical efforts of all workers, regardless of their skill or education, who perform the tasks required to produce and sell goods and services. Labour is sometimes called the human resource factor.
3. **Capital**—the buildings, machinery, and tools used to produce goods and services. The word *capital* has many meanings. Sometimes it refers to the money that buys the buildings, machinery, and tools used in production. Because this double usage can be confusing, be careful to note the context in which the word *capital* is being used.
4. **Entrepreneurship**—the activity that brings the first three factors together to form a business. *Entrepreneurs* accept the opportunities and risks of starting and running businesses. They acquire the capital, assemble the labour force, and utilize available natural resources to produce and sell goods and services.

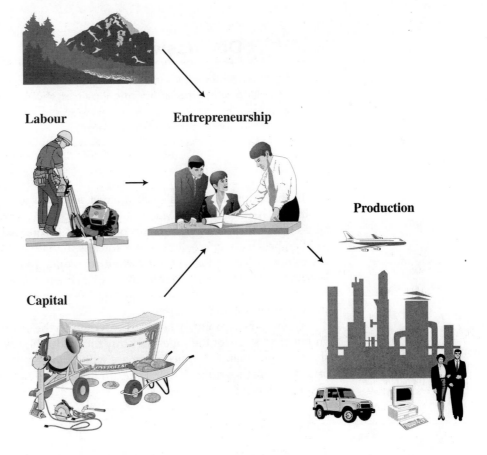

Natural Resources

Labour

Entrepreneurship

Production

Capital

Exhibit 1–1
Factors of Production

The way these four factors of production combine to produce goods and services depends on the type of economic system that organizes a society.

In a *planned economy*, a strong, centralized government controls all or most of the natural resources, labour, and capital used to produce goods and services, replacing the entrepreneur. In contrast, a **market economy** relies on competition in the marketplace to determine the most efficient way to allocate the economy's resources. Canada conducts business within the capitalistic economic system, also known as the free enterprise, free market, or private enterprise system.

market economy A type of economy in which all or most of the factors of production are privately owned and that relies on competition in the marketplace to determine the most efficient way to allocate the economy's resources.

The Profit Motive

The *profit motive* stimulates a person to do something when the benefit derived from doing it is greater than the sacrifice required to do it. A rational person desires to derive the greatest benefit with the least amount of sacrifice. When this natural desire in one person is pitted against the same desire in another person, competition results.

To illustrate the profit motive, assume that Martin needs a new pair of shoes. Because he is a rational person, Martin desires the best pair of shoes he can buy for the lowest possible price. Roy owns a shoe store. Being a rational person, Roy desires to sell his shoes for the highest price he can. Martin goes to Roy's shoe store and looks at a pair of shoes Roy has priced at $100. Assuming he likes the shoes and can afford to pay $100, Martin will buy them if he feels they provide him with the most benefit for the least sacrifice.

Now, add one other ingredient to the situation—competition. Enter Ellen, who also owns a shoe store. She sells shoes identical to the pair Martin is considering buying at Roy's. The difference is that she is selling them for $90.

 Discussion Questions

1-1. What do you think caused Roy and Ellen to establish different selling prices for an identical pair of shoes?

1-2. Assuming Martin decides to buy the shoes, what do you think will determine where he buys them?

In this example, Martin's self-interest pits the self-interests of Roy and Ellen against each other because Martin's desire to pay the lowest price possible for the shoes will make Roy and Ellen compete for his business. If Roy loses enough sales to Ellen because she is selling shoes for less than he is, he will be forced to lower his selling price. In fact, he may want to reduce his selling price for the shoes Martin liked to $85 to attract sales away from Ellen. She will then be forced to lower her selling price. No one makes Roy and Ellen lower their prices; the force comes from competition in the market.

There comes a point, of course, below which the selling price cannot go. If Roy and Ellen pay $55 for the shoes they buy for resale, they obviously cannot sell those shoes for less than $55, unless they are willing to accept a loss. **Profit** is the excess of benefit over sacrifice. Thus, if Martin buys the shoes from Roy for $100, Roy's gross profit can be calculated as:

profit The excess of benefit over sacrifice. A less formal name for net income or net profit.

Amount received from Martin (BENEFIT)	$100
Less what Roy paid for the shoes (SACRIFICE)	55
Equals GROSS PROFIT on the sale of shoes	$ 45

gross margin or gross profit
The excess of benefit received over the sacrifice made to complete a sale. Gross profit considers only the cost of the item sold; it does not consider the other costs of operations.

The $45 profit that Roy earned is called **gross margin** or **gross profit.** However, it does not represent his actual profit from operating the shoe store. In addition to the cost of the merchandise he buys to sell, he has other costs such as rent on the store, utilities, and wages paid to employees. All these items must be taken into account before he can calculate his *net earnings* or *net income.*

If Roy does not earn a sufficient profit on the shoe store business, he will close it and go into another line of work. The same, of course, holds true for Ellen. In a capitalistic economy, businesses that do not earn profits cease to exist.

Profits Versus Social Responsibility

Some people believe that profit connotes greed. These individuals believe that Canadian business should strike a balance between profit and social responsibility. On the other side of this issue are those who believe that business has no obligation beyond earning profits and no social responsibility.

We live in a society that seems to measure success by whether someone "beats" someone else. This situation is described as a zero-sum game, meaning that for every winner, there must be a loser. In recent years, however, society has renewed its concern over how the game of business is played. An increasing number of investors, creditors, and other economic decision makers have become interested not only in improving "the bottom line" (making money), but also in improving the way companies conduct themselves as citizens in the community. In other words, we can view business as a win-win situation.

Social Responsibility in Business Today

A growing number of Canadian consumers refuse to do business with companies they believe are insensitive to social and environmental concerns. In response to this concern, a great many Canadian companies make a concerted effort to communicate a commitment to responsible and ethical business practices.

stakeholder Anyone who is affected by the way a company conducts its business.

Each business affects its community with the decisions it makes and the manner in which it conducts its affairs. Any entity or individual affected by the way a company conducts its business becomes a **stakeholder** in that business and gains a vested interest in the way a company is run. A business must determine its responsibilities to each of its stakeholders. The first step in determining responsibility usually involves listing the identity of all the firm's stakeholders. Many companies include a section in the annual report about social responsibility to improve investor confidence in the company's good citizenship. The era when a company could conduct its business without regard to anything but making a profit is very likely gone forever. Many investors, both individuals and companies, will not invest in alcohol or tobacco companies, or in companies known to pollute the environment. So the marketplace eventually affects companies that are not socially responsible because certain investors will not invest their money in them.

Discussion Questions

1-3. Make a list of those to whom you think a chemical manufacturing company owes responsibility. What are the specific responsibilities it has to each of these stakeholders? How do you think the company could best go about fulfilling each of those responsibilities?

1-4. Make a list of those to whom you think a retail clothing company owes a responsibility. What are the stakes that each group has? How can the company fulfill its responsibility to each stakeholder?

1-5. Can you think of any companies that have fulfilled the responsibilities you outlined in your answers to question 1-3 or 1-4 and yet managed to remain profitable?

FORMS OF BUSINESS ORGANIZATION

There are three forms of business organization in Canada: sole proprietorships, partnerships, and corporations. Each has certain advantages and disadvantages for the firm's owners.

Sole Proprietorships

sole proprietorship An unincorporated business that is owned by one individual. Also called a proprietorship.

A **sole proprietorship,** or proprietorship, is an unincorporated business that is owned by a single individual. A common misconception about this form of business is that it is always small. While the majority of sole proprietorships are small, the classification suggests nothing about the size of the business, only that it has a single owner.

Advantages of Sole Proprietorships

1. **Easy and inexpensive to set up.** There are no special legal requirements associated with starting a sole proprietorship. All a person must do is decide what kind of business he or she wants to establish and obtain the necessary licenses and permits, and that person is in business.
2. **No sharing of profits.** A single owner shares profits only with the government in the form of taxes. Whatever the business earns after taxes belongs solely to the owner.
3. **Total control.** The desire for control probably inspires more people to start their own business than any other reason. The sole proprietor answers to no one when making decisions about how to run the business (as long as they are legal). A sole proprietor has the independence to determine the quantity and quality of business effort.
4. **Few government regulations.** As long as the owner pays his or her taxes and does not engage in illegal activities, a proprietorship is reasonably free of government regulation.
5. **No special income taxes.** From a legal standpoint, a sole proprietorship is simply an extension of its owner. Therefore, a proprietorship pays no separate income tax. The earnings of the company are considered the earnings of the owner and become a part of his or her personal taxable income.
6. **Easy and inexpensive to dissolve.** Sole proprietors can end their business as easily as they can start them. If the owner decides to shut the company down, all he or she must do is notify the appropriate licensing agents and pay off remaining debts.

1. **Unlimited liability.** From a legal standpoint, a sole proprietorship is simply an extension of its owner, so all business obligations become the owner's legal obligations. Therefore, if the company fails to pay its debts, the creditors can sue the owner for the owner's personal property, including his or her house, car, boat, or other holdings.
2. **Limited access to capital or money.** All businesses must have money and assets to operate, which are often referred to as capital. The amount of capital available to a sole proprietorship is limited to the amount of personal assets the owner can contribute to the business or the amount the owner can borrow on a personal loan. Remember that legally a proprietorship is not distinguished from its owner; therefore, when the business borrows money, the owner borrows money.
3. **Limited management expertise.** No one is an expert in everything. Many proprietorships fail because the owner lacks skills or expertise in areas critical to the survival of the company.
4. **Personal time commitment.** Running a business is hard work, and a sole proprietor works very long hours—probably longer hours than if he or she were employed. Most sole proprietors consider the time well spent because it benefits them personally. But without a doubt, it takes a tremendous amount of time to run your own business.
5. **Limited life.** The life of the business cannot exceed the life of the owner.

Notwithstanding the disadvantages of proprietorship, many people dream of owning their own business, and a large percentage of companies in Canada are sole proprietorships. Because most of them are small businesses, only a small percentage of all business revenues come from this form of business.

Partnerships

partnership A business form similar to a proprietorship, but having two or more owners.

Think of a **partnership** as a proprietorship with two or more owners who all share in the risks and profits of the business. A common misconception is that all partnerships are small businesses. In fact, some partnerships are quite large. Most large public accounting firms, for instance, are partnerships, and some of them have as many as 1,500 partners and 20,000 employees.

Advantages of Partnerships

1. **Easy to form.** From a legal standpoint, partners can form a partnership almost as easily as a proprietorship. Partners should commit the ownership and profit-sharing structure of the partnership into a formal partnership agreement, signed by each partner, to clarify their consensus about these issues. A well-written partnership agreement helps to resolve conflicts or problems in the future. Once the partners obtain the appropriate licences and permits, a partnership is in business.
2. **Increased management expertise.** Partners often form partnerships because each has skills in a critical area of business that complement those of the others. Combining those areas of expertise into a partnership enhances the business's chances of success.
3. **Access to more capital (money, property, or other assets).** Having more than one person involved in the ownership of the business usually increases access to capital. In fact, many partnerships form to combine one partner's special expertise with another's capital.
4. **Few government regulations.** Government subjects partnerships to relatively few regulations. As long as each partner pays his or her individual taxes and the partnership does not engage in illegal activities, government does not interfere.

5. **No special income taxes.** A partnership is not legally separate from its owners and therefore does not pay separate income taxes. Rather, a partnership information return allocates the partnership profits, according to the partnership profit-sharing agreement, among the partners. Each partner includes his or her share of the profits on the personal tax return as personal income.

6. **Greater business continuity.** Because more people are involved, partnerships tend to have longer lives than do sole proprietorships. When a partner dies or withdraws from the partnership, the legal life of the partnership ends. The heirs do not inherit the right to be partners in the firm. For all practical purposes, however, the business generally need not stop its operations. The partnership agreement may allow the remaining partner or partners to either continue with one less partner or admit another partner to the firm.

Disadvantages of Partnerships

1. **Unlimited liability.** Because partnerships are legally no different from their owners, the partners are personally liable for all obligations of the business. In fact, in most instances, each partner is personally liable for the total obligations of the partnership. Therefore, if any partner makes a decision that obligates the partnership, all the other partners become liable, even if they knew nothing about the decision.

2. **Sharing of profits.** When a partnership is formed, the partners prepare an agreement that outlines how to divide company profits. The profit-sharing arrangement usually considers the amount of capital each partner invests in the partnership, how much time each partner commits on a regular basis, and any special expertise a partner may contribute. Regardless of whether the agreement is fair and equitable, once a partnership has been formed, partners will share profits with each other.

3. **Potential conflicts between partners.** Suppose one partner wants the company to begin selling a new product and another partner disagrees. If the two partners have equal power, they have entered into gridlock. The bases for conflicts among partners range from personal habits to overall business philosophy, and there may be no other way to resolve them but to dissolve the partnership.

4. **Difficulty in dissolving.** Ending a partnership severs personal and professional ties and can be a devastating emotional experience. If individuals forming a partnership are wise, they will include specific provisions for dissolution in the original partnership agreement when all the partners have positive attitudes toward one another. You might think of this as the business version of a prenuptial agreement: The parties forming the business agree on how the business "marriage" will end.

While there are advantages to the partnership form of business, many people believe the disadvantages outweigh them. Only about 1 percent of all businesses in Canada are partnerships, and they account for just about 4 percent of all business revenues.

Separate Entity Assumption

separate entity assumption
The assumption that economic activity can be identified with a particular economic entity and that the results of activities for each entity will be recorded separately.

From a record-keeping and accounting standpoint, proprietorships, partnerships, and corporations are considered to be completely separate from their owners. This view reflects the **separate entity assumption** that economic activity can be identified with a particular economic entity whether it is an individual, proprietorship, corporation, or even a division of a business. However, from a legal standpoint, the corporation is the only form of business considered to be a separate legal entity from its owners.

Corporations

Chief Justice John Marshall of the United States Supreme Court made this statement in 1819:

> A corporation is an artificial being, invisible, intangible, and existing only in contemplation of law.

This ruling, which was subsequently upheld in Canadian courts, changed the course of business in Canada and the United States forever. As a separate legal entity, a **corporation** has many of the rights and obligations of a person, including the right to enter into contracts and the right to buy, own, and sell property. The law requires a corporation to discharge its obligations lawfully, and creditors can sue for recovery if it does not. A corporation can be taken to court if it breaks the law, and it is obligated to pay taxes like any other person. In addition to the legal obligations of corporations, the moral obligation of corporations to be socially responsible has been a topic of widespread discussion in recent years. The fact that corporations are separate legal entities leads to several distinct advantages and disadvantages.

corporation One of the three forms of business organization. The only form that is legally considered to be an entity separate from its owners.

shareholder A person who owns shares in a corporation.

Advantages of Corporations

1. **Limited liability.** Because a corporation is a separate legal entity from its shareholders, the owners are not personally liable for the corporation's obligations. With limited liability, a **shareholder** limits his or her losses to the amount of his or her investment and not everything else he or she owns.
2. **Greater access to capital.** By dividing the ownership of the firm into relatively low-cost shares, corporations can attract a great number of investors. Some corporations in Canada have more than a hundred thousand different shareholders.
3. **Easy transferability of ownership.** Because ownership shares in corporations usually cost less than $100, individual investors buy and sell shares much more easily than they could trade an ownership interest in a proprietorship or partnership. Freely traded shares require no approval or permission for trading, unlike the approval required to accept a partner into a business.
4. **Continuity of life.** Because a corporation is legally separate and distinct from its owner or owners, it continues to exist even when a complete change in ownership occurs. The transfer of shares has no effect on a corporation.
5. **Greater management expertise.** The shareholders (owners) of the corporation elect a *board of directors* who have the ultimate responsibility of managing the firm. The board of directors, in turn, hires professional managers to run the day-to-day operations.

Disadvantages of Corporations

1. **Potentially greater tax burden.** All businesses, regardless of form, must pay taxes. Corporations must pay a federal income tax and in many provinces also pay provincial and local income taxes. The board of directors distributes part of the firm's after-tax profit to the shareholders as dividends. The shareholders report dividends as personal income and pay personal income taxes on them. This practice is referred to as *double taxation*. Because of this, governments allow individuals to claim a dividend tax credit, which offsets the effect of the double taxation. Additionally, corporations are taxed at a lower rate than individuals, so if no dividends are declared, those profits can accumulate in the corporation at a lower tax rate.
2. **Greater government regulation.** Government subjects corporations to significantly more control than either sole proprietorships or partnerships.

Many corporations file reports with both federal and provincial regulatory bodies. Filing these reports costs time and money.

3. **Absentee ownership.** In almost all proprietorships and in most partnerships, the owners manage their business according to their wishes. In most corporations, few shareholders (owners) participate in the day-to-day operations of the business. The board of directors hires professional managers to operate the company on behalf of the owners. Professional managers sometimes operate the company in their own interests, rather than the owners' interest.

Although corporations represent a small percentage of the total number of businesses in Canada, corporations transact approximately six times as much business as all proprietorships and partnerships combined. Corporations also control the majority of business resources in Canada. Depite the potential for a greater tax burden faced by corporations, many small businesses choose to incorporate because of the many other advantages that corporations enjoy, such as limited liability and lower tax rates. Exhibit 1–2 summarizes the advantages and disadvantages of the three forms of business.

Exhibit 1–2
Advantages and Disadvantages of the Three Forms of Business Organization

Business Form	Advantages	Disadvantages
Proprietorship	1. Easy and inexpensive to set up. 2. No sharing of profits. 3. Owner has total control. 4. Few government regulations. 5. No special income taxes. 6. Easy and inexpensive to dissolve.	1. Unlimited liability. 2. Limited access to capital. 3. Limited management expertise. 4. Personal time commitment. 5. Limited life.
Partnership	1. Easy to form. 2. Increased management expertise. 3. Access to more capital. 4. Few government regulations. 5. No special income taxes. 6. Greater business continuity.	1. Unlimited liability. 2. Sharing of profits. 3. Potential conflicts between partners. 4. Difficulty in dissolving.
Corporation	1. Limited liability. 2. Greater access to capital. 3. Easy transferability of ownership. 4. Continuity of life. 5. Greater management expertise.	1. Potentially greater tax burden. 2. Greater government regulation. 3. Absentee ownership.

Other Business Forms

Evolutionary changes in business have prompted the creation of new forms of business organizations that combine characteristics of partnerships and corporations. A *limited partnership* consists of at least one general partner and one or more limited partners. The general partners have unlimited liability and operate the partnership. The limited partners enjoy limited liability (like corporate shareholders), but are precluded from a decision-making role in the organization. A *limited liability partnership (LLP)* limits the liability of a general partner to his or her own negligence or misconduct, or the conduct of persons he or she controls. In a regular partnership, each partner is liable for all partnership debts and the conduct of all partners and employees.

Discussion Question

1–6. Imagine that you have the opportunity to start a company. Would you prefer to be an owner (or part owner) of a proprietorship, partnership, or corporation? Cite specific reasons for your choice.

TYPES OF BUSINESSES

We can classify companies in Canada not only according to organizational form (proprietorship, partnership, or corporation), but also according to the type of business activity in which they engage. The three broad classifications are manufacturing, merchandising, and service. Although a single company can be involved in all three of these business activities, usually one of the three constitutes the company's major interest.

Manufacturing Companies

manufacturing The business activity that converts purchased raw materials into some tangible, physical product.

A **manufacturing** company purchases raw materials and converts them into some tangible, physical product. Raw materials consist of both unprocessed natural resources (one of the factors of production) and completely finished products manufactured by others. For example, a company that manufactures household appliances purchases many items, such as coils and generators used in the production of refrigerators. These coils and generators—raw materials to the refrigerator manufacturer—are manufactured finished products for another company.

Merchandising Companies

merchandising The business activity involving the selling of finished goods produced by other businesses.

Like a manufacturer, a **merchandising** company sells tangible, physical products, called merchandise, as its major business activity. Instead of manufacturing the product it sells, a merchandising company buys it in a finished form.

There are two kinds of merchandisers:

- *Wholesale merchandiser.* A wholesaler buys its product from the manufacturer (or another wholesaler) and then sells that product to another business that eventually sells it to the final consumer. An example of a wholesale merchandiser would be Scott National, a well-known grocery wholesaler. The name may be unfamiliar to you because, as a consumer, you most often deal directly with a retailer rather than with a wholesaler. Wholesalers provide a valuable service to retailers by making the retailers' purchasing convenient and cost-effective.
- *Retail merchandiser.* A retailer buys its product from a wholesaler or manufacturer and sells the product to the final consumer. Major national retailers are The Bay, Zellers, Sears, and Canadian Tire. Other retail chains, such as Saan and Loblaws, focus on specific regions of the country. Still other successful retailers, such as gift shops and specialty stores, have one location.

Service Companies

service A business activity that does not deal with tangible products, but rather provides some sort of service as its major operation.

A **service** company does not deal in tangible products, but performs a service as its major business activity. Doctors, lawyers, and accountants provide services instead of products (although they may provide a product, such as a report, as a result of their service). Service providers perform work for consumers and other businesses. Computer service centres, plumbers, auto mechanics, janitorial services, and copier technicians frequently provide services to businesses.

Multiple-Industry Companies

Some businesses participate in more than one type of industry. For example, General Motors Corporation manufactures automobiles and trucks and is therefore classified as a manufacturer. In recent years, however, GM has become involved in activities that are classified as services. GM created General Motors Acceptance Corporation (GMAC) to provide financing for customers purchasing GM cars and trucks.

In the near future, we can expect the distinction among manufacturing, merchandising, and service companies to become more blurred. As the struggle for survival in the global marketplace becomes even more intense, many companies find it beneficial to involve themselves in a wide variety of business activities.

 Discussion Question

1–7. In what type of business activity (manufacturing, merchandising, or service) would you like to be involved? Describe in detail the type of operation that most interests you. What characteristics of this type of business do you find appealing?

GLOBAL NATURE OF BUSINESS IN 2000 AND BEYOND

Canadian businesses cannot produce all the goods and services demanded in the Canadian marketplace. On the other hand, certain items produced in Canada either have no Canadian market or are produced in greater quantities than can be sold here. These situations are the forces that drive international business. Ford Motor Company sold an average of 5.8 million cars per year during the last five years. Of these cars, a large percentage were sold outside Canada. Clearly, international trade is important to the financial health of Ford, as it is to many other firms.

Foreign producers bring into Canada goods called *imports*. When Canadian producers sell goods outside Canada, they are called *exports*. Most countries' economic health depends upon the importing and exporting of goods; however, conducting business across national borders can cause economic and political complications.

Economic Complications

Complications can arise when a business located in one country does business with a firm located in another country with a different economic system. Another complication results from the use of different currencies by different countries: for example, Canada uses the dollar, Europe uses the euro, and Japan uses the yen. When companies in two different countries transact business, their contract establishes the currency they will use. One or both companies then must translate its funds into the specified currency. *Translation* means converting or exchanging the currency of one country (yen, for example) into its equivalent in another country's currency (dollars, for example).

Political Complications

Politics play an important role in international trade. Even countries with the same economic system experience difficulties in economic dealings with each other because each country seeks to protect its own self-interest by exporting a larger quantity of products than it imports. As an extreme example, assume that all of France's merchandisers decide to import all English products to sell in France, because English imports cost less than French-produced merchandise. Before long, all the French manufacturing companies close, all the French jobs disappear, and an essential part of France's economic base ceases to exist. To provide protection for their own economic bases and to prevent this kind of scenario, countries create trade agreements among themselves.

Trade agreements are formal treaties between two or more countries that are designed to control the relationship between imports and exports. These agreements generally establish quotas and/or tariffs on imported products. *Quotas* limit the quantities of particular items that can be imported. For example, a limit may be placed on the number of cars that Japan can bring into and sell in Canada. *Tariffs* are taxes that raise the price of imported products to about the same as that of similar domestic products.

Trade agreements can take years to negotiate due to their complexity. Shortly after World War II, 92 countries signed the General Agreement on Tariffs and Trade (GATT). This agreement was renegotiated in 1994. Other recent treaties are the Canada–United States Free Trade Agreement of 1989, which eliminated most trade barriers between those two countries, and the North American Free Trade Agreement (NAFTA) signed by Canada, the United States, and Mexico in 1993. Countries frequently break treaty terms, so compliance essentially depends on the good faith of the treaty members.

BUSINESS AND ACCOUNTING

Business is about making decisions—decisions about what business form to take (proprietorship, partnership, corporation), decisions about what type of business activity to engage in (manufacturing, merchandising, service), and decisions about whether to engage in international business. Accounting information, in one form or another, plays a significant role in all these decisions.

This is an accounting text. Its emphasis, however, is not so much on how accounting information is prepared as on how accounting information is used. To illustrate the relationship between accounting and business decisions, let us return to the example involving Roy, Martin, and Ellen.

Remember that Roy paid $55 for the pair of shoes he later sold to Martin for $100. We calculated the gross profit on the sale of these shoes as:

Amount received from Martin (BENEFIT)	$100
Less what Roy paid for the shoes (SACRIFICE)	55
Equals GROSS PROFIT on the sale of shoes	$ 45

We pointed out that the $45 does not represent Roy's real profit because he has other costs associated with his shoe store that must be considered before he can calculate his real profit. The function of accounting is to provide information to Roy, Ellen, and the shoe manufacturers so they can make sound business decisions.

 ## Discussion Questions

1-8. If rent and other costs associated with his shoe store amount to $3,000 a month, how many pairs of shoes must Roy sell at $100 a pair before he earns a profit?

1-9. What should Roy do if his competitor, Ellen, begins to take sales away by selling identical pairs of shoes for $90?

1-10. What should Roy do if he finds out he can buy the identical pair of shoes from a manufacturer in Mexico for only $40 instead of the $55 he is paying the Canadian manufacturer?

1-11. What should the Canadian shoe manufacturer do if it begins to lose sales to the Mexican shoe manufacturer that is selling these identical shoes at the cheaper price?

We live in the information age. Advances in computer and telecommunication technology give us access to a great deal of information about almost any interesting subject. Not only do we have access to more information, but we can also obtain it almost instantly. Every advance, however, has its price. We sometimes find ourselves in "information overload." Trying to find the optimal amount of information specific to your needs sometimes feels like standing on the beach trying to catch the incoming tide in your mouth. It is easy to drown in all the information available to you.

A Brief History of Accounting

The history of accounting can be traced back to early civilizations in Mesopotamia, and then later to the Egyptians, Romans, and Greeks. In those early days, accounting consisted of recording crop harvests, the collection of duties and taxes, and obligations resulting from these transactions. Therefore, the earliest records of accounting consisted of what we would now call the *balance sheet*. In other words, they were a reckoning of what was owned (the assets) by the "business" and what was owed (the liabilities). As time progressed, these early businesses found that their recording needs had changed and become more complex. Instead of simply recording their assets and liabilities, businesses needed to know *why* these things (the total "wealth" of the business) had changed over a particular period of time. This became important, because the owners of the business were increasingly no longer the *operators* of the business. In the case of landowners, they may have lived hundreds of kilometres from their landholdings. What they needed was a more comprehensive (and reliable) reporting of the operation of the business. They could not simply rely on the word of the person tending the land. Landowners needed an objective and accurate reporting on the performance of the business.

However, it was not until 1494 that an effective method of recording the change in wealth (and therefore the "performance") of a business was developed. Luca Pacioli of Italy described what became known as the "double-entry" system of bookkeeping. This was a major development in the history of accounting, because for the first time it allowed accountants to record the effect that a business transaction had on the wealth of that business. What we now regard as profit (or loss) is simply the change in wealth of a business over a particular period of time.

As businesses became even more complex, the resources of the business (assets) started to take on a less physical nature. When the assets of a business consist of grain, cloth, and gold, it is easy to measure its wealth. If it has more of these things at the end of the year than at the beginning, then its wealth has gone up, and it has made a "profit." However, what happens if the things that a business "owns" do not have any physical substance? What if its wealth consists of the gold that its customers *owe*, and it does not actually have any gold pieces in its possession? And to complicate matters even further, what if some of that gold that is owed to the business is, in turn, owed to somebody else? And to add another complication: what if it is not certain that the gold owed to the business will, in fact, be paid? Then how much is the business worth? Because of these complications, accountants were forced to address issues that, increasingly, had little to do with the actual physical assets of a business. This led to what is now known as "accrual" accounting (with all of its complicated rules). Accrual accounting rules are simply an attempt to take into account the fact that physical assets (such as gold) are not a very good measure of wealth, and therefore the change in those physical assets is not a very good measure of profit.

Authority over Accounting Reporting Standards

The purpose of this book is to provide you with the tools, knowledge, and skills you need to sift through and use the accounting information available to you. Members of the accounting profession have developed over time a set of standards to be used for financial reporting known as **generally accepted accounting principles (GAAP)**. GAAP provide assurance to outsiders that the information available in a given decision situation was prepared in accordance with a set of rules and guidelines.

The only companies required by law to follow GAAP are publicly traded companies—those whose shares or bonds are traded on an organized exchange. These companies must meet the requirements of the securities laws of the province in which the stock exchange is located. Companies that are not publicly traded may use whatever accounting principles they desire, unless external financial statement users demand that GAAP be followed. For instance, banks and other lending institutions prefer to see financial results prepared under GAAP rules and often require all borrowers to adhere to GAAP. Any nonregulated company that needs to be audited will likely follow GAAP reporting standards.

generally accepted accounting principles (GAAP) Guidelines for presentation of financial accounting information designed to serve external decision makers' need for consistent and comparable information.

 Discussion Question

1–12. Why do you think a company would be opposed to adopting GAAP?

The Ontario Securities Commission (OSC)

Ontario Securities Commission (OSC) The Ontario agency empowered to set reporting standards for all companies that trade their shares on the Toronto Stock Exchange

The leading provincial agency in Canada governing capital markets and the reporting of financial information is the **Ontario Securities Commission** (OSC: www.osc.gov.on.ca). All corporations in Canada whose shares are traded on the Toronto Stock Exchange must adhere to OSC regulations. Rules governing the calculation of revenues and expenses were begun in the early 1900s in response to the requirement to report taxable income. However, little progress was made in co-ordinating these reporting requirements with United States' laws until the stock market crash of 1929. With the beginning of the Great Depression of the 1930s, reforms took on greater urgency as regulators sensed the need for stricter regulations and the protection of shareholder rights and interests. Then, as now, the Canadian and United States' economies were significantly intertwined, and shareholders were demanding a greater integration of reporting requirements. Additionally, Canadian firms may also be listed on American stock exchanges and therefore also need to follow American regulations. In the United States, the major body responsible for regulating the reporting requirements of publicly traded companies is the Securities and Exchange Commission (SEC). To this day, the SEC exerts considerable influence over Canadian business practices. For the most part, the various regulatory agencies require that all financial and accounting information be presented in accordance with GAAP.

The Canadian Institute of Chartered Accountants (CICA)

Canadian Institute of Chartered Accountants (CICA) In Canada, the primary body responsible for setting generally accepted accounting principles (GAAP).

In Canada, the primary body responsible for the setting of generally accepted accounting principles (GAAP) is the **Canadian Institute of Chartered Accountants** (**CICA**: www.cica.ca). These principles and standards are published in the *CICA Handbook*, and provide considerable authority and guidance to the accounting profession in its conduct and approach to financial reporting. The *Canada Business Corporations Act* and provincial corporations legislation designated the *CICA Handbook* as GAAP. The *CICA Handbook* accounting standards are set by a committee of CICA members: the Accounting Standards Board (AcSB). The AcSB provides recommendations on the treatment of financial transactions and the reporting and presentation of accounting information. The *CICA Handbook* provides the basis for creating a conceptual framework from which accounting standards are set in Canada. This framework establishes the objectives of financial reporting and the qualitative characteristics of useful accounting information, and defines accounting objectives, principles, constraints, concepts, and assumptions (see Exhibit 1-3). We will present the basics of the conceptual framework throughout this text, beginning with Chapter 2.

It is important to remember that no set of guidelines or recommendations can possibly cover all the potential situations that an accountant may face in the day-to-day operation of a business. Therefore, accountants must exercise their *professional judgment* in determining the appropriate treatment of an accounting issue.

In Canada, there are three professional bodies responsible for setting professional standards of conduct for accountants and auditors. Chartered Accountants (CAs) are governed by the Canadian Institute of Chartered Accountants (discussed in the previous section). Certified Management Accountants (CMAs) are governed by the Society of Management Accountants of Canada (www.cma-canada.org). Certified General Accountants (CGAs) are governed by CGA-Canada (www.cga-canada.org).

Internationally, various governing bodies regulate the setting of accounting standards in other countries. In the United States, the Financial Accounting Standards Board (FASB: www.fasb.org) is responsible for setting accounting standards. The International Accounting Standards Committee (IASC: www.iasc.org.uk) is providing direction for the harmonization of international accounting practices.

Exhibit 1–3
Conceptual Framework
of Accounting

Objectives (from *CICA Handbook*)
The objective of financial statements is to communicate information that is useful to investors, members, contributors, creditors and other users in making their resource allocation decisions and/or assessing management stewardship.

Principles	Constraints	Qualitative Characteristics
1. Historical Cost	1. Benefit versus Cost	1. Understandability
2. Revenue Recognition	2. Materiality	2. Relevance
3. Matching	a. professional judgment	a. timeliness
4. Full Disclosure	b. particular circumstance	b. predictive value
		c. feedback value
		3. Reliability
		a. verifiability
		b. representational faithfulness
		c. neutrality
		d. conservatism
		4. Comparability
		5. Consistency

Assumptions
1. Accounting Entity
2. Monetary Unit
3. Time Period
4. Going-Concern

Discussion Questions

1–13. What are the pros and cons of having accounting rules established by government agencies?

1–14. What are the pros and cons of having accounting rules established by the accounting profession?

1–15. If the choice were yours, would you prefer to have accounting standards determined by a government agency or the accounting profession? Explain your decision.

OUTSIDE ASSURANCE ON FINANCIAL STATEMENTS

What Exactly Is an Audit?

audit Examination by an independent accountant of enough of a company's records to determine whether the financial statements have been prepared in accordance with GAAP and demonstrate a fair representation of the company's financial status.

Financial statement users rely on an audit report to assure them that they can rely on the information in the financial statements. During an **audit,** the auditor examines the client's financial statements, with the internal control structure and supporting documentation, to determine whether the financial statements present a fair picture of the client's financial condition and have been prepared in accordance with GAAP. To examine all the client's records would be cost prohibitive—

and the cost would outweigh the benefit derived. Statistical theory provides auditors with methods of sampling that allow the auditor to test the records and determine the probability that the records verify the fairness of the financial statement numbers. An auditor does not prepare the financial statements—the company's management prepares them and the auditor has no authority to make changes in the statements without the client's consent.

Generally accepted accounting principles were developed to establish *comparability* among the financial statements of different companies. These principles are also intended to maintain *consistency* in the way companies account for events and transactions from year to year. The audit was developed as a mechanism to provide assurance to external parties that the financial statements they use to make economic decisions have been prepared in accordance with established standards.

 Discussion Questions

1-16. Describe how you would decide which and how many records to examine to determine whether your social club's treasurer's report portrays a fair picture of the club's financial activity for the past year.

1-17. How might your answer to question 1-16 change if you were to look at your local Canadian Tire's records for one week?

Auditing standards require auditors to have an extensive knowledge of the economy, the relevant industry, and the client's business. Auditors make inquiries of company personnel and conduct numerous audit procedures, because they must achieve a reasonable assurance that there are no material misstatements in those financial statements. "Reasonable assurance" is what a rational person would consider sufficient. In an accounting context, something is *material* when it would influence the judgment of a reasonable person. A "material misstatement" would change a reasonable person's decision about a company's financial condition.

Who Performs Audits?

Each province has its own responsibility for the regulation and certification of accountants. Only professional accountants (CAs, CMAs, or CGAs) certified by a provincially authorized governing body can perform independent audits of Canadian businesses. However, not all accountants are auditors. Auditing is a highly specialized accounting function governed by a set of standards called *generally accepted auditing standards (GAAS)*. GAAS are guidelines developed by the CICA's Assurance Standards Board (ASB) and is the framework used by accounting professionals when conducting independent audits of Canadian companies.

Auditors walk a curious tightrope in our society. Lawyers have one responsibility: to represent their clients, who pay them to fulfill that responsibility. Doctors have one responsibility: to care for their patients, and doctors are paid to fulfill that responsibility. Auditors, on the other hand, have a dual responsibility: They are responsible to the clients who pay them, but they also have a responsibility to all the users of audited financial statements. Auditors must be independent of the entity they are auditing and objective in their assessment of the financial statements' fairness. It is a difficult balancing act, and auditors face a rising level of litigation from statement users who relied on financial statements and then suffered losses. If found guilty of professional negligence, auditors must pay damages to victims. Most auditors take their responsibility very seriously.

 Discussion Question

1–18. What potential problems do you think can arise from the auditor's dual responsibility?

The Audit Opinion

At the conclusion of an audit, the auditor issues an *opinion* as to the fairness of the financial statement presentation. GAAS allow the accountant to issue several different opinions, depending on the findings of the audit. Most firms receive an *unqualified opinion,* in which the accountant states that the financial statements "present fairly, in all material respects, the financial position . . . and the results of operations and its cash flows . . . in conformity with generally accepted accounting principles." A firm seeks to have this opinion, also called a *clean opinion,* given to its statements. A financial statement user should be concerned about financial statements that do not contain an unqualified opinion.

Auditors may issue several other opinions. If the auditor cannot render an opinion because the company did not provide enough evidence or allow enough performance of audit tests, he or she issues a *denial of opinion.* The financial statement user has no assurance from the auditor of fairness or conformity with GAAP with a denial of opinion. Auditors have the option to issue a *qualified opinion* in which they state an exception to general fairness of presentation or conformity with GAAP. Readers should carefully consider the exception(s) the auditor raises. The most devastating opinion an auditor renders is the *adverse opinion,* in which the auditor clearly states that the financial statements are not fairly presented or do not conform with GAAP. Readers should not rely on such financial statements. An informed financial statement user examines the audit opinion before reading the financial statements to determine the auditor's level of assurance.

 Discussion Question

1–19. Find the audit opinion in the annual report of Sobeys Inc. contained in the Appendix beginning on page A1. Who are the auditors? What type of opinion did the auditors issue?

Now that we have discussed generally accepted accounting principles and outside assurance, we can look more deeply into the financial accounting information available to external decision makers.

SUMMARY

Business has several different meanings, but in the context of this book, it means either commerce or trade as a whole, or a specific company involved in commerce or trade. All economic activity revolves around the four factors of production: natural resources, labour, capital, and entrepreneurship. In a market economy, most of the factors of production are privately owned.

Capitalism, the market economy within which Canadian business operates, depends on each participant's concern about his or her self-interests to create competition. This system relies on the profit motive and its resulting competition to allocate resources and force businesses to operate efficiently. Modern Canadian business practice balances the profit motive with a business's social responsibility to its stakeholders.

The three basic forms of business organization are the proprietorship (one owner), the partnership (two or more owners), and the corporation (a legal entity separate from its owners). Most business activity can be categorized as either manufacturing, merchandising, or service. Most Canadian companies see the world as a global economy, and many engage in international trade.

In response to the users' need for comparable and consistent financial information, accountants developed, over time, standards called generally accepted accounting principles (GAAP). The *Canada Business Corporations Act* has the legal authority to regulate accounting practice in Canada; however, this power is delegated to the various accounting professional associations. The Accounting Standards Board (AcSB) of the Canadian Institute of Chartered Accountants (CICA) establishes GAAP in Canada. The Financial Accounting Standards Board (FASB) establishes GAAP in the United States.

External users of financial statements require some form of outside assurance that the financial statements are fairly presented and are prepared according to GAAP. The most stringent form of outside assurance is the audit, in which independent auditors examine enough of a company's records to determine whether the company's financial statements fairly present the company's economic position and are prepared in accordance with GAAP. At the conclusion of the audit, the auditor issues an audit opinion.

APPENDIX

After completing your work on this appendix, you should be able to do the following:

10. Describe the information found in a typical annual report.

11. Gather information about a company and obtain an annual report.

CORPORATE REPORTING AND THE ANNUAL REPORT

financial reporting
Financial disclosures provided to economic decision makers that include both quantitative and qualitative information.

The two major consumers of corporate financial reports in Canada today are shareholders and regulators. Indeed, companies must regularly answer to these two groups. An important component of **financial reporting** is the *annual report,* which was developed to meet the demands of shareholders. The annual report, the most comprehensive presentation of financial reporting to shareholders, contains not only a company's financial statements but also other information designed to assist economic decision makers to predict the future and timing of cash flows.

How to Get an Annual Report

Firms prepare annual reports to communicate important information from the corporation to its owners, the shareholders. Thus, if you own shares in a corporation, you will automatically receive a copy of its annual report.

How should you go about getting an annual report if you are not a shareholder? You have three primary sources for information: the Internet (www.SEDAR.com), *The Financial Post*, and the library.

- Most companies maintain a web site on the Internet. Frequently, the web site includes the annual report, or the financial statement data from the annual report. Web site visitors can often download or print the annual report or complete a request in the investor relations section of the web site to receive a copy.
- Many libraries provide computers with CD-ROM capabilities. Among the most popular CD-ROM products offering company information are
  - Infotrac: contains company profiles, investment reports, and article citations.
  - Proquest: the CD-ROM version of ABI/Inform, the premier source of business articles. Contains citations and the full text of articles, including photos and graphical images.
- *The Financial Post* provides a comprehensive listing of Canadian publicly traded companies and financial information on those companies.

Do not hesitate to ask a company for its annual report. Corporations know that public image can be a crucial factor in a company's success or failure. Generally, corporations gladly honour requests for annual reports and will promptly send them. If you cannot order an annual report over the Internet, locate the corporate headquarters address, phone number, or fax number on the web site or other library reference source, and phone or fax your request to the public relations department.

Information Provided in Annual Reports

Many annual reports contain much the same information, mainly because in many jurisdictions in Canada, the OSC requires that most of it be included. The table of contents for Sobeys Inc.'s annual report for 2001, as follows, represents most of the information found in a modern annual report. An asterisk indicates that the OSC requires the information.

Financial and Operating Overview
At-a-Glance
Letters to Shareholders
Building Sustainable Worth
Feature Section
Investment Proposition
Fiscal 2002 Objectives
*Management's Discussion and Analysis
*Management's Responsibility for Financial Reporting
*Auditors' Report
*Consolidated Balance Sheet
*Consolidated Statement of Retained Earnings
*Consolidated Statement of Earnings

*Consolidated Statement of Cash Flows
*Notes to Consolidated Financial Statements
Building Better Communities
Leadership at Sobeys
*Board of Directors and Officers
Investor Information

 Discussion Question

1-20. What other information would you want to know about Sobeys? Would you feel comfortable calling, e-mailing, or writing to the company with a specific question? Where can you find the addresses and phone number for Sobeys in the annual report?

GATHERING ADDITIONAL INFORMATION ABOUT A COMPANY

Financial information and an annual report may not satisfy all your information needs for a particular company. If you are considering Sobeys as a share or bond investment, or as a prospective supplier, customer, or employer, you may need to learn when Sobeys was incorporated and in what province, how the business was started, how it grew into the company it is today, and what are its current projects. (If you apply for a job, you should go to the interview with some knowledge of the company's history, employment practices, and goals. You can ask more relevant questions and impress the interviewer with your industriousness.)

Detailed information about companies is easy to find in the information age. The same sources listed for you in the How to Get an Annual Report section can help you locate information. The Internet becomes a valuable source two ways:

1. The company's web site usually contains current press releases about company accomplishments, problems, financial results, and other important news.
2. You can conduct a search for news about the company with any of the search engines.

Remember to carefully consider the source of information on the Internet. Almost anyone can put information on the web, so the value of what you find there may be questionable. A reliable source of information for stock market reports and investor services is www.globeinvestor.com.

Libraries generally have a wide variety of resources available, including handbooks and periodicals.

Periodical indexes help you to find articles about the company. Usually available in hardback or CD-ROM, the *Business Periodicals Index* can be most helpful in locating information about a particular company. The most trustworthy sources for information in the press are *The Financial Post* and *The Globe and Mail*.

KEY TERMS

audit, p. 18
business, p. 2
Canadian Institute of
    Chartered Accountants, p. 16
capital, p. 3
corporation, p. 9
entrepreneurship, p. 3
factors of production, p. 3
financial reporting, p. 20
generally accepted accounting
    principles (GAAP), p. 15
gross margin or gross profit, p. 5
labour, p. 3

manufacturing, p. 11
market economy, p. 4
merchandising, p. 11
natural resources, p. 3
Ontario Securities
    Commission (OSC), p. 16
partnership, p. 7
profit, p. 4
separate entity assumption, p. 8
service, p. 12
shareholder, p. 9
sole proprietorship, p. 6
stakeholder, p. 5

REVIEW THE FACTS

1. What are the four factors of production? Define each.
2. Describe the primary difference between a planned economy and a market economy.
3. Explain what is meant by the profit motive.
4. Define gross profit (or gross margin) and net profit.
5. Explain the meaning of shareholder.
6. Name the three basic forms of business organization and describe several advantages and disadvantages of each.
7. Describe the separate entity concept.
8. Name and describe the three major classifications of business activity.
9. Define quotas and tariffs. Explain the purpose of each.
10. Describe the relationship between business and accounting.
11. Broadly define GAAP. Which companies must adhere to GAAP?
12. Explain the role of the OSC in the regulation of accounting practice.
13. What is the name and abbreviation for the current accounting standards-setting group?
14. Describe comparability and consistency and how they relate to corporate reporting.
15. What is the purpose of an audit and who can perform independent audits?
16. Explain "reasonable assurance" and "material misstatements."
17. Describe an auditor's dual responsibility and identify the standards by which auditors are governed.
18. Name and describe the four types of audit report an auditor can issue.
19. Distinguish between financial reporting and financial statements.
20. Why are corporations generally cooperative when individuals request their annual reports?
21. How can learning about a company before being interviewed for a job there be helpful?

APPLY WHAT YOU HAVE LEARNED

LO 1 & 2: Terminology

1. Presented below are items relating to some of the concepts presented in this chapter, followed by the definitions of those items in scrambled order.

a. Entrepreneurship
b. Labour
c. Planned economy
d. Capitalism

e. Factors of production
f. Natural resources
g. Capital
h. Profit motive

1. _____ The human resource factor.
2. _____ Land and materials that come from land.
3. _____ The factor of production that brings all the other factors of production together.
4. _____ The motivation to do something when the benefits exceed the sacrifice of doing it.
5. _____ A type of market economy.
6. _____ The four major items needed to support economic activity.
7. _____ Buildings, machinery, tools, and money used to produce goods and services.
8. _____ A type of economy in which a strong, centralized government controls all or most of the factors of production.

REQUIRED:

Match the letter next to each item on the list with the appropriate definition. Note that each letter will be used only once.

LO 2: Business Terminology

2. Presented below are items relating to some of the concepts presented in this chapter, followed by the definitions of those items in scrambled order.

a. Wholesaler
b. Imports
c. Exports
d. Tariffs
e. Manufacturing company

f. Merchandising company
g. Retailer
h. Translation
i. Quota

1. _____ Goods sold outside the country in which they were produced.
2. _____ A business that converts purchased raw materials into some tangible, physical product.
3. _____ A type of business operated by either a wholesaler or a retailer.
4. _____ A quantity limitation placed on imported goods.
5. _____ A business known as a middleman.
6. _____ The conversion of the currency of one country into its equivalent in another country's currency.
7. _____ Taxes that raise the price of imported products.
8. _____ A business that sells products to the final consumer.
9. _____ Goods brought into a country that were produced in another country.

REQUIRED:
Match the letter next to each item on the list with the appropriate definition. Note that each letter will be used only once.

LO 2:   Computation of Gross Profit and Net Profit

3. Larry Melman owns and operates a retail clothing store. Last month clothing sales totalled $5,200. Melman paid $2,800 for the clothing sold last month. He also paid rent of $300 and wages to employees totalling $900.

REQUIRED:
a. Calculate the gross profit on sales for last month.
b. Identify the expenses incurred during the month and explain whether they should be used to compute gross profit or net profit.
c. Calculate the net profit for last month.

LO 2:   Computation of Gross Profit and Net Profit

4. Zippo Marks sells fine imported cigars. During the month of December, Zippo sold 3,000 cigars at a total price of $15,000. Zippo paid $9,000 for the cigars that he sold in December.

REQUIRED:
a. Determine the gross margin for Zippo in December.
b. How would your answer differ if Zippo had paid $6,000 for the cigars?
c. List the expenses you would expect Zippo to have each month to run his store.

LO 2:   Computation of Gross Profit and Net Profit

5. Grouchy Marks owns and operates a retail hardware store. In June, sales were $18,000. The items sold cost $12,600. Mr. Marks spent $1,000 for store rent, $300 for utilities expense, and $1,500 for employee wages.

REQUIRED:
a. Calculate the gross profit on sales for June.
b. Identify the expenses incurred during the month and explain whether they should be used to compute gross profit or net profit.
c. Calculate the net profit for June.

LO 2:   Computation of Gross Profit and Net Profit

6. In August, Mary bought 24 quilts for $100 each.

REQUIRED:
a. If Mary sells the quilts for $150 each, what is her gross profit for each quilt?
b. If she sells all of the quilts in August, what is her total gross profit?
c. If Mary rents an office for $200 and pays utilities expense of $75, advertising expense of $150, and bank charges of $15, calculate her net income for August.

LO 2 & 4:   Computation of Gross Profit and Net Profit for Different Business Forms

7. The Computer Centre of Canada manufactures and sells computers. During the month of October, The Centre produced and sold 1,000 computers. The sale of the computers generated $1,000,000. The Centre

spent $300,000 for the parts to build the computers and paid $200,000 for the labour to assemble the computers. The Centre also paid $100,000 for all other costs (overhead) necessary to construct the computers. The Centre spent $50,000 on other operating expenses.

REQUIRED:

a. What type of business does The Centre operate (i.e., manufacturing, merchandising, or service)?
b. Calculate the gross profit for the month of October.
c. Calculate the net profit for the month of October.

LO 4 & 5: Shareholder vs. Stakeholder

8. Explain the concept behind the term *stakeholder,* and contrast it with the definition of the term *shareholder.*

LO 4: Forms of Business Organization

9. Presented below are the three basic forms of business in Canada, followed by some of the advantages relating to those forms of business:

   a. Sole proprietorship   b. Partnership   c. Corporation

   1. _____ Owner has total control
   2. _____ Greater business continuity
   3. _____ Easy transfer of ownership
   4. _____ Limited liability
   5. _____ Greater access to capital
   6. _____ Easy and inexpensive to establish
   7. _____ Few government regulations
   8. _____ Easy to dissolve
   9. _____ No special income taxes
   10. _____ No sharing of profits
   11. _____ Greater management expertise

REQUIRED:

Match the letter next to each form of business with the appropriate advantage. Note that each letter will be used more than once and it is possible that a particular advantage applies to more than one of the business forms.

LO 4: Forms of Business Organization

10. Presented below are the three basic forms of business in Canada, followed by some of the disadvantages relating to those forms of business:

    a. Sole proprietorship   b. Partnership   c. Corporation

    1. _____ Usually has less access to capital than the other two forms
    2. _____ Limited management expertise
    3. _____ Unlimited liability
    4. _____ Absentee ownership
    5. _____ Must share profits
    6. _____ Greater government regulation
    7. _____ Often difficult to dissolve
    8. _____ Potential ownership conflicts

REQUIRED:

Match the letter next to each form of business with the appropriate disadvantage. Note that each letter will be used more than once and it is possible that a particular disadvantage applies to more than one of the business forms.

LO 4: Forms of Businesses

11. Professor Sharyll Plato is opening a publishing company to publish and distribute accounting textbooks throughout Canada. She feels this will be a successful venture because the textbooks will be based upon a revolutionary new format of accounting education. Plato has extended an invitation to all her friends to invest in her new business. She is offering shares for a mere $10 each.

REQUIRED:
a. What form of business is Professor Plato proposing?
b. Briefly explain four advantages of doing business in this form.

LO 5: Distinguishing among Types of Businesses

12. Phil Jackson owns and operates a jewelry store. During the past month, he sold a necklace to a customer for $2,500. Phil paid $1,800 for the necklace.

REQUIRED:
a. What type of business does Phil own (manufacturer, wholesaler, retailer, etc.)? Explain how you determined your response.
b. Calculate Phil's gross margin on the sale of the necklace.
c. Identify four costs besides the $1,800 cost of the necklace that Phil might incur in the operation of his jewellery store.
d. If Phil's operating costs are $900 per month, what is his net income for the month?

LO 5: Types of Businesses

13. This chapter discusses four types of business in Canada, namely

1. Manufacturer
2. Wholesale merchandiser
3. Retail merchandiser
4. Service

REQUIRED:
a. Explain in your own words the characteristics of each type of business.
b. Discuss how each of these four types of business is different from the other three.
c. Give two examples of each type of business (do not use any examples given in the chapter) and explain how you determined your answers.

LO 7: Reporting Standards

14. Generally accepted accounting principles have been developed over time to aid in comparability among the financial statements of different companies. They are also intended to maintain consistency in the way a firm accounts for transactions and events from period to period.

An audit is intended to provide some assurance to external parties that the financial statements examined are reasonably presented.

REQUIRED:

a. What determines whether a company in Canada is required to prepare its financial statements according to GAAP?

b. Why are some companies forced to adhere to GAAP even though they are not required by law to do so?

LO 9: Financial Reporting

15. Presented below are some items related to the issue of outside assurance discussed in this chapter, followed by the definitions of those items in scrambled order.

a. Audit
b. Unqualified opinion
c. Adverse opinion

d. Qualified opinion
e. Denial of opinion

1. _____ Caused by placing a significant restriction on the auditor as to what records may be examined.

2. _____ The process of examining a company's records to determine whether the financial statements have been prepared in accordance with GAAP standards.

3. _____ Rendered when there are departures from GAAP so pervasive that a reasonable person cannot rely on the financial statements.

4. _____ Unofficially referred to as a "clean" opinion.

5. _____ An auditor states an exception in the audit report.

REQUIRED:

Match the letter next to each item with the appropriate definition. Each letter will be used only once.

LO 9: Financial Reporting

16. Your uncle who owns a small business knows that you are taking a course in accounting. He tells you that his banker is requiring him to provide an audited set of financial statements for the last fiscal year. He does not understand why the bank is making this request and he asks you why it would want an audit of his financial statements. How do you respond to his question?

LO 10: Annual Reports

17. Describe the basic information one would expect to find in an annual report of a publicly traded company.

LO 11: Annual Reports

18. Use the information contained in the annual report of Sobeys Inc., which is reproduced in the text starting on page A1, to answer the following:

REQUIRED:

a. What is the name of the CA firm that audited the financial statements?

b. What type of opinion was rendered by the firm?

c. Which paragraph of the audit report identifies the party responsible for the financial statements?

d. Which paragraph of the audit report identifies the party responsible for the audit of the financial statements?

e. Which paragraph of the audit report actually reports the expression of an opinion?

LO 11: Annual Reports

19. Use the information contained in the annual report of Sobeys Inc., which is reproduced in the text starting on page A1, to answer the following:

REQUIRED:

a. List the title of each financial statement included in the annual report.

b. The assets, liabilities, and shareholders' equity are listed in which of the financial statements?

c. The sales, cost of goods sold, and the operating expenses are reported in which financial statement?

LO 11: Annual Reports

20. Use the information contained in the annual report of Sobeys Inc., which is reproduced in the text starting on page A1, to answer the following:

REQUIRED:

a. Who wrote the letters to the shareholders? In your opinion, what were the three most important messages in the letter?

b. What are the divisions of Sobeys Inc.? For each division, list the following information:

(1) Name

(2) Major markets

(3) Distinction in the marketplace

(4) Goals for the current year

c. How does the information in parts a and b help a potential investor, creditor, or employee?

FINANCIAL REPORTING CASES

Comprehensive

21. The Buckle sells clothing to young people in upscale malls across the country. Known for its fashion sense, The Buckle has little debt, high profits, and a successful marketing strategy. In its 2004 annual report, The Buckle made no mention of community service work or social responsibility.

REQUIRED:

a. What conclusions might you draw about The Buckle's social responsibility if you read its annual report?

b. List three questions you would ask The Buckle's president about the company's social responsibility if he came to the store where you were shopping.

c. What advice would you give the president?

Comprehensive

22. The following is the opening section of the 1996 letter to shareholders from M. Anthony Burns, Chairman, President, and Chief Executive Officer of Ryder System, Inc.

Letter to Shareholders

The world in which our company operates has changed in many ways.

Our markets have changed. Some have grown, some have slowed, and all have become more competitive and demanding.

Our customers have changed. Many long-time customers now require new and different services, and the ways in which we relate to and serve our customers are not like they were only a few years ago. In many cases, the customers themselves are different or are in different parts of the world.

At the same time, in the face of all this change, we are eager to increase the value of the company to customers, employees and shareholders alike.

So, for Ryder, 1996 was a year of major decisions.

We launched the most sweeping restructuring of operations in the company's history, eliminated 2450 positions—including 2100 we announced in the fourth quarter, identified nearly 200 facilities and properties for disposal, sold our consumer truck rental business, put our automotive carrier business up for review and waged war on unnecessary costs and inefficiency.

We dramatically altered the shape of the company. We moved more than 80% of corporate staff positions into our business units, which are the engines of Ryder's future growth—Transportation Services, Integrated Logistics and Public Transportation Services. In addition, we combined management of Ryder International and Ryder Integrated Logistics in order to focus more sharply on high-margin, knowledge-based, global, integrated logistics opportunities.

Excluding Automotive Carriers, Ryder is now composed of three streamlined, contractually based, market-focused business units, responsible and accountable for the ambitious goals we have set for them. We have equipped and positioned them for success, and we will accept no less. We are single-minded in our campaign to reduce cost, increase margins and enhance shareholder value, and we are impatient in our dedication to deliver these results quickly. And, we reduced our capital spending $800 million to $1.3 billion, emphasizing investment in higher-return contractual business.

Our transformation was not without cost.

We took a pretax charge of $215 million in the fourth quarter of 1996 to cover the cost of the program, which should be completed by the end of 1997. As a result, full year pretax operating earnings of $204.2 million, before the gain on the sale of our consumer truck rental business, restructuring and other charges and the early extinguishment of debt at a premium, were reduced to a net loss of $41.3 million, or $0.51 a share.

REQUIRED:
  a. Summarize the main points of the CEO's message.
  b. How do you believe that a CEO should give bad news to shareholders? Why?

ANNUAL REPORT PROJECT

Comprehensive

During the term of this course, you will participate in an annual report project either as an individual or a group member. With this project, you will learn everything you can about one company using its annual report, the Internet, the press, stock market results, and contact with company officials. Each chapter contains a section of the project that correlates with the chapter material. You will accumulate these sections throughout the semester, and prepare a well-organized project folder for final submission. Your professors may require a short oral presentation of your findings at the end of the semester. By the end of the project, you will decide if this company is a good stock or bond investment, vendor, customer, or employment prospect.

To save yourself time and trouble, use word-processing software to generate this report so that you can update and rewrite with a minimum of effort. Be sure each group member has a hard copy *and* a disk copy of any group work at all times!

23. Select a publicly traded company that interests you as an investment or employment prospect.

REQUIRED:

  a. Determine how to obtain an annual report for this company, as explained in this chapter. Within 48 hours of this assignment, have a copy of the annual report either in your hand or in the mail from the company or *The Financial Post*. Each member of a group should secure his or her own copy of the report.

  b. From a second source, obtain a copy of the printed glossy annual report for your professor. (For group projects, the professor only needs one copy of the annual report.) Give the second copy to your professor as soon as you receive it.

  c. Individually, prepare a detailed listing of the annual report to become familiar with its contents. List each page, including the outside front cover, inside front cover, inside back cover, and outside back cover. For each page listed, write a brief list of the information contained on that page. For example:

Page 2	CEO's letter to the shareholders
Page 24	Consolidated Balance Sheet
Inside Back Cover	Corporate information including:
	Corporate address, web site, and phone number
	Ticker symbol
	Annual meeting date
	Dividend payment dates

  d. Hand in one copy of this assignment to the professor, keep one copy to use as a quick reference, and keep a clean copy for your final project folder.

2

Economic
Decision Making

*G*ood fortune has come your way. After several weeks of interviewing, you have received job offers from three firms. The offers differ greatly, which leaves you quite confused. You have made this list of the offers:

1. Large national firm, $12 per hour starting wage, life insurance and dental benefits paid by the company, a two-week paid vacation each year, and potential for rapid advancement.

2. Small local firm, $20 per hour starting wage, life insurance and dental benefits available but you must pay the premiums, a two-week paid vacation each year, share options and pension plan benefits, and potential for advancement.

3. Regional firm, $15 per hour starting wage, full life insurance and dental benefits, one-week paid vacation, good pension plan, and moderate advancement potential.

Will you consider the short run or the long run for this decision? Which offer provides you with the most today and which one the most over the next five years? What is the real economic value of the benefits? Aside from the monetary considerations, do you like the work you will perform in each position and the people with whom you will work? How do you organize your thoughts to make this decision?

Regardless of the form of organization or the business activity, success in the world of business—sometimes even survival—depends on making wise economic decisions. A key ingredient is an understanding of the decision-making process itself. Because economic decision making relies heavily on accounting information, it is crucial for that information to be useful to economic decision makers.

Life is a never-ending sequence of decisions, some very complex and others relatively simple. Because we cannot know the future, we strive to reduce uncertainty in any decision by collecting as much information as possible. We designed this chapter to help you learn a logical decision-making process. ■

LEARNING OBJECTIVES

After completing your work on this chapter, you should be able to do the following:

1. Explain the concepts of extrinsic and intrinsic rewards, sacrifices, and opportunity costs as they pertain to decision situations.
2. Describe the two types of economic decision makers and explain the basic differences between management accounting and financial accounting.
3. List the three questions all economic decision makers attempt to answer and explain why these questions are so important.
4. Describe the importance of cash as a measure of business success or failure.
5. Define accounting information and distinguish it from accounting data.
6. Describe the qualitative characteristics of useful accounting information and apply them in decision-making situations.
7. Explain the difference between reality and the measurement of reality.
8. Apply the criteria for revenue and expense recognition under the cash basis of accounting to determine periodic net income.
9. Apply the criteria for revenue and expense recognition under the accrual basis of accounting to determine periodic net income.

WHAT IS DECISION MAKING?

Decision making is the process of identifying alternative courses of action and selecting an appropriate alternative in a given decision situation. This definition presents two important parts:

1. *Identifying alternative courses of action* means that an ideal solution may not exist or might not be identifiable.
2. *Selecting an appropriate alternative* implies that there may be a number of appropriate alternatives and that inappropriate alternatives are to be evaluated and rejected. Thus, judgment is fundamental to decision making.

Choice is implicit in our definition of decision making. We may not like the alternatives available to us, but we are seldom left without choices.

Rewards and Sacrifices: The Trade-off

In general, the aim of all decisions is to obtain some type of reward, either economic or personal. Reward requires sacrifice. When you made the decision to attend college or university, for example, you certainly desired a reward. What was the sacrifice?

Discussion Questions

2–1. What reward or rewards do you hope to obtain by attending college or university?

2–2. What sacrifices are you personally making to attend college or university ?

opportunity cost The benefit or benefits forgone by not selecting a particular alternative. Once an alternative is selected in a decision situation, the benefits of all rejected alternatives become part of the opportunity cost of the alternative selected.

cost/benefit analysis Deals with the trade-off between the rewards of selecting a given alternative and the sacrifices required to obtain those rewards.

Think of some things you cannot do because you are attending college. Some sacrifices cannot be measured in dollars (such as loss of sleep, lack of home-cooked meals, and loss of leisure time). Some, however, can be measured. Suppose that instead of attending college you could work full time and earn $15,000 a year. Attending college, therefore, costs you that $15,000, in addition to what you pay for tuition and books. We call the $15,000 an opportunity cost of making the decision to attend college. An **opportunity cost** is the reward we forego because we choose a particular alternative instead of another. Most decisions include opportunity costs.

Decision makers want the reward or benefit from a decision to be greater than the sacrifice or cost required to attain it (see Exhibit 2–1). Examining the relationship between rewards and sacrifices is known as **cost/benefit analysis.** In a condition of absolute certainty, in which the outcome of a decision is known without doubt, cost/benefit analysis provides a certain outcome. Unfortunately, absolute certainty rarely, if ever, exists.

In examples that accountants use to describe the trade-off between rewards and sacrifices, money is usually the reward. Money is an *extrinsic reward,* meaning that it comes from outside ourselves and is a tangible object we can acquire. An *intrinsic reward* is one that comes from inside ourselves. When you accomplish a difficult task, the intrinsic reward comes from the sense of satisfaction you feel. An old adage says, "The best things in life are free." Not so! Anything worth having requires sacrifice.

Exhibit 2–1
Cost versus Benefit

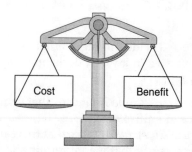

 Discussion Questions

2–3. What is the one thing you desire most from life? What sacrifices must you make to obtain it?

2–4. What sacrifice does a business owner make when purchasing machinery for the production plant?

2–5. What benefit does the owner derive from the sacrifice to purchase the machinery?

ECONOMIC DECISION MAKING

internal decision makers
Economic decision makers within a company who make decisions for the company. They have access to much or all of the accounting information generated within the company.

external decision makers
Economic decision makers outside a company who make decisions about the company. The accounting information they use to make those decisions is limited to what the company provides to them.

Economic decision making, in this book, refers to the process of making business decisions involving money. All economic decisions of any consequence require the use of some sort of accounting information, often in the form of financial reports. Anyone using accounting information to make economic decisions must understand the business and economic environment in which accounting information is generated, and they must also be willing to devote the necessary time and energy to make sense of the accounting reports.

Economic decision makers are either internal or external. **Internal decision makers** are individuals within a company who make decisions on behalf of the company, while **external decision makers** are individuals or organizations outside a company who make decisions that affect the company. Exhibit 2-2 illustrates some decisions made by internal and external decision makers.

Exhibit 2–2
External vs. Internal Decision Makers

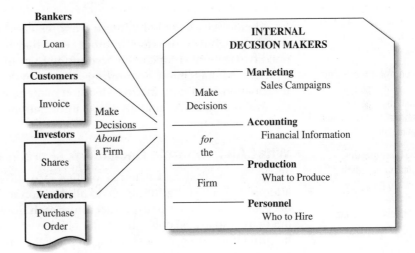

Internal Decision Makers

Internal decision makers decide whether the company should sell a particular product, whether it should enter a certain market, and whether it should hire or fire employees. Note that in all these matters, the responsible internal decision maker makes the decision not for himself or herself, but rather for *the company*.

Depending on their position within the company, internal decision makers may have access to much, or even all, of the company's financial information. They do not have complete information, however, because all decisions relate to the future and always involve unknowns.

External Decision Makers

External decision makers make decisions *about* a company. External decision makers decide whether to invest in the company, whether to sell to or buy from the company, and whether to lend money to the company.

Unlike internal decision makers, external decision makers have limited financial information on which to base their decisions about the company. In fact, they have only the information the company gives them—which in most cases is not all the information the company possesses.

Discussion Questions

2-6. Identify a particular company (large or small). Who do you think are considered internal and external economic decision makers of the company?

2-7. For what reasons do you think a company would withhold certain financial information from external parties?

2-8. Is it ethical for a company to limit the information available to internal decision makers? External decision makers?

The decisions made by internal and external decision makers are similar in some ways, but so different in other ways that the accounting profession developed two separate branches of accounting to meet the needs of the two categories of users. **Management accounting** is not constrained by GAAP and generates information for use by internal decision makers, whereas **financial accounting** is constrained by GAAP and generates information for use by external parties.

What All Economic Decision Makers Want to Know

Although internal and external parties face different decision situations, both attempt to predict the future, as do all decision makers. Specifically, all economic decision makers attempt to predict future **cash flow**—the movement of cash in and out of a company. So one of the major objectives of financial reporting is to provide helpful information to those trying to predict cash flows.

The difference between cash inflows and cash outflows is **net cash flow**. Positive net cash flow indicates that the amount of cash flowing into the company exceeds the amount flowing out of the company during a particular period. For example, a company that collects $1,000,000 during a period when it pays out $950,000 has a positive cash flow of $50,000. Negative net cash flow indicates that the amount of cash flowing out of the company exceeds the amount flowing into the company during a particular period (see Exhibit 2–3).

management accounting
The branch of accounting developed to meet the informational needs of internal decision makers.

financial accounting
The branch of accounting developed to meet the informational needs of external decision makers.

cash flow The movement of cash in and out of a company.

net cash flow The difference between cash inflows and cash outflows; it can be either positive or negative.

Exhibit 2–3
Cash Flow

Cash inflow	–	Cash outflow	=	Positive net cash flow
$1,000,000	–	$950,000	=	$50,000
Cash inflow	–	Cash outflow	=	Negative net cash flow
$ 500,000	–	$575,000	=	– $75,000

All economic decisions involve attempts to predict the future of cash flows by searching for the answers to the following three questions:

1. *Will I be paid?*
   This question refers to the *uncertainty* of cash flows.
2. *When will I be paid?*
   This question refers to the *timing* of cash flows.
3. *How much will I be paid?*
   This question refers to the *amounts* of cash flows.

The answer to each question contains two parts: return *on* investment and return *of* investment. Return on investment consists of the earnings and profits an investment returns to the investor. Return of investment is the ultimate return of the principal invested. Exhibit 2–4 shows the conceptual link between the three major questions posed by economic decision makers and the resulting cash flows using the following example. Assume you wish to invest in a $1,000 term deposit at your bank, which will earn 10 percent interest per year, payable every three months, over the course of two years. If you invest in this term deposit, you must hold it for two years, after which the bank will return your $1,000.

Exhibit 2–4
Three Big Questions for Economic Decision Makers

Questions	Concepts	Cash Outcome	
		Return *on* Investment	Return *of* Investment
1. Will I be paid?	Uncertainty	Interest	Term deposit maturity
2. When will I be paid?	Timing	Quarterly	2 years
3. How much will I be paid?	Amount	$25 per quarter	$1,000
		Total of $200	

Before you make this economic decision, you must attempt to answer the three questions:

1. *Will you be paid?* Because it is impossible to know the future, making an economic decision always involves risk. However, assuming the economy does not collapse and the bank stays in business, you will be paid both your return on investment and your return of investment.
2. *When will you be paid?* You will receive an interest payment every three months for two years (return on investment), and then you will receive your initial $1,000 investment back (return of investment).
3. *How much will you be paid?* The return on your investment is the interest you receive quarterly of $25 ($1,000 × 10 percent × 3/12), and the return of your investment is the $1,000 the bank gives you back. The total received in interest in two years is $200 (8 × $25).

Initial Investment		$1,000
Return on Investment	$ 200	
Return of Investment	1,000	
Total Return		1,200
Profit on Investment		$ 200

We can answer these questions easily for the insured term deposit. In the vast majority of economic decision situations, the answers to the three questions we asked are much less certain. We will show you how to use accounting information to answer them in various economic decision situations throughout this text.

Discussion Questions

2–9. Assume that you are a lender with three customers who wish to borrow $10,000. You can lend to only one of them. What information would you require each of them to present for you to answer the three questions? How would you make your decision?

Cash Is the "Ball" of Business

If business were any game such as baseball, football, or soccer, then cash would be the ball. To be successful, the players must keep their eye on the ball. Because the business game is so complex, businesspeople easily become distracted and lose sight of (the ball) cash. Various measures of performance such as gross profit, net income, net worth, and equity help those in business to make economic decisions. These are important measures of financial performance, but they are not cash! Never allow yourself to become so focused on any of them that you lose sight of cash, because when a company runs out of cash, it dies. Only cash pays the bills that keeps the company in business. The secret to becoming a street-smart user of accounting information is learning to balance the complexity of business with the simple rule of keeping your eye on cash flow.

ACCOUNTING INFORMATION

A company or a person generates accounting data with every business transaction. You generate a number of transactions each month when you pay your rent, buy groceries, make car payments, lend money to a friend, and so on. In fact, the volume of business accounting data can be staggering.

Data versus Information

accounting information
Raw data concerning transactions that have been transformed into financial numbers that can be used by economic decision makers.

information Data that have been transformed so that they are useful in the decision-making process.

Accounting data and **accounting information** are not interchangeable terms. Data are the raw results of transactions: data become **information** only when they are put into some useful form. Consider this example:

Carol Brown, vice president of sales for Balloo Industries, noticed that the recent gasoline expense for the sales staff's company cars was extremely high and she suspected that salespersons were using the company cars for personal trips. Knowing that sales personnel were required to keep detailed odometer records, she notified Jack Parsons, the sales supervisor, of her concerns. He agreed to prepare a report to provide her with the necessary information to determine if the expense was proper.

The report compiled by Mr. Parsons consisted of five columns of data:

1. salesperson's name;
2. make and model of that salesperson's company car;
3. date the car was issued to the salesperson;
4. odometer reading on the date of issue; and
5. odometer reading at time of most recent maintenance.

Ms. Brown quickly concluded that it contained little useful information. She told Parsons that she was trying to determine if any members of the sales force were using company cars for personal activities. Mr. Parsons retreated to his office to try again.

In his second attempt, Parsons included the previous five columns plus four additional columns:

6. sales region covered;
7. how long the salesperson had been with the company;
8. total sales generated by the salesperson this year; and
9. current odometer reading of the vehicle.

Was Ms. Brown pleased with the second version? No! Mr. Parsons had provided additional data, but no additional information.

 ## Discussion Question

2-10. Evaluate the usefulness to Ms. Brown of each column (1–9) of Parsons' data. What information could Parsons have provided Ms. Brown to help her make a determination?

Clearly, the correct data items must be gathered and converted into useful information before they are of any help to economic decision makers. Suppose you consider investing in shares of Dofasco Inc., the steel producer. You call your broker and she tells you the shares are currently selling at $30 per share. Do you want to invest? Although your broker has given you a datum (singular form of data), this datum provides insufficient information upon which to base a buying decision. You need to know something about the company's current and historic earnings, the share price behaviour over the past year, the steel industry's prospects, and so on. That is why brokerage firms such as RBC Dominion Securities, Scotia Capital, and TD Securities have research departments that extract such data and synthesize them into useful information for their clients.

Useful Accounting Information

The user of accounting information has the obligation to understand the business and be willing to study the information. The information provider has an obligation to present it in such a way that economic decision makers can make sense of it. As business and economic activities have become more complex, however, the accounting profession has responded with increasingly complex rules, many of which are difficult for nonaccountants to comprehend. There are certain characteristics that accounting information must possess to be considered useful for decision making. If the accounting profession does not provide what the information users need or does not prepare it in a way that makes sense, users must demand a change. Users and preparers must be mindful of the benefits provided by information, and the costs incurred to secure it (the cost/benefit analysis), and of its ultimate ability to make a difference in the decision (the **materiality** test).

materiality Something that will influence the judgment of a reasonable person.

Two parties decide what accounting information is useful and what is not. One is the users and the second is the accounting profession through the CICA. The CICA focuses on the *qualitative characteristics* of useful accounting information—

those qualities it must possess to be useful, whether it is financial or management accounting information.

QUALITATIVE CHARACTERISTICS OF ACCOUNTING INFORMATION

The two primary qualities that distinguish useful accounting information are **relevance** and **reliability.** If either of these qualities is missing, accounting information will not be useful.

Relevance

To be considered relevant, accounting information must have a bearing on the particular decision situation. In other words, does it make a difference to decision makers? The accuracy of the information is not important if the content does not matter to the decision being made.

Relevant accounting information possesses at least two characteristics:

- **Timeliness.** If information providers delay making information available until every number is perfectly accurate, it may be too late to be of any value. This does not mean that accuracy does not matter. But if accounting information is not timely, it has no value.

Timeliness alone, however, is not enough. To be relevant, accounting information must also possess at least one of the following characteristics:

- **Predictive Value.** Before economic decision makers commit resources to one alternative instead of another, they must satisfy themselves that a reasonable expectation of a return on investment and a return of investment exists. Accounting information that helps reduce the uncertainty of that expectation has predictive value.

or

- **Feedback Value.** After making an investment decision, the decision maker must have information to assess the progress of that investment. The decision maker might want to reevaluate the decision if new information becomes available and would certainly want to evaluate of the final outcome of the decision. If accounting information provides input for those evaluations, it has feedback value.

Reliability

To be considered reliable, accounting information must possess four qualities:

- **Verifiability.** We consider accounting information verifiable if several qualified persons, working independently of one another, would arrive at similar conclusions using the same data. For example, if we asked several people to determine the amount of Michael Simpson's wages this year, they should all come to the same conclusion: A simple review of payroll records should provide verifiable information for the amount.
- **Representational Faithfulness.** There must be agreement between what the accounting information says and what really happened. If a company's accounting information reports sales revenue of $1,000 and the company really

relevance One of the two primary qualitative characteristics of useful accounting information. It means the information must have a bearing on a particular decision situation.

reliability One of the two primary qualitative characteristics of useful accounting information. It means the information must be reasonably accurate.

timeliness A primary characteristic of relevance. To be useful, accounting information must be provided in time to influence a particular decision.

predictive value A primary characteristic of relevance. To be useful, accounting must provide information to decision makers that can be used to predict the future and timing of cash flows.

feedback value A primary characteristic of relevance. To be useful, accounting must provide decision makers with information that allows them to assess the progress of an investment.

verifiability A primary characteristic of reliability. Information is considered verifiable if several individuals, working independently, would arrive at similar conclusions using the same data.

representational faithfulness A primary characteristic of reliability. To be useful, accounting information must reasonably report what actually happened.

had sales revenue of $1,000, the accounting information is representationally faithful. However, if a company's accounting information reports sales revenue of $1,000 and the company really had sales revenue of only $800, then the accounting information lacks representational faithfulness.

- **Neutrality.** To be useful, accounting information must be free of bias, which means accountants should not omit details simply because the information is unpleasant. We have stressed how difficult it is to make good decisions. The problem becomes even worse when information is suppressed or slanted, either positively or negatively. The need to remain neutral is one of the most difficult challenges facing the accounting profession.

- **Conservatism.** There are times when the concept of neutrality needs to be altered. These times generally occur under conditions of uncertainty, when there can be no objective, verifiable method of determining the valuation of assets or revenues. In this case it is better to understate their value rather than risk overstating it. This applies conversely with liabilities and expenses. When in doubt, it is better to overstate the liability or expense. This does not mean you deliberately misrepresent the value of these items; rather, it is better to understate the wealth and net income of a business than overstate it.

Comparability and Consistency

Two secondary qualities of useful accounting information are comparability and consistency. Economic decision makers evaluate alternatives. Accounting information for one alternative must therefore be comparable to accounting information for the others. For example, assume you intend to make an investment in one of two companies. If each company uses different accounting methods, you would find it very difficult to make a useful comparison.

Now consider the concept of consistency. Imagine how difficult it would be to assess the progress of an investment if, through the years, different accounting treatments were applied to similar events. Consistency in the application of measurement methods over periods of time increases the usefulness of the accounting information provided about a company or an investment alternative.

Comparability is a quality of information from different entities or alternatives. Consistency describes information from the same source over time. Comparability and consistency often have similar effects on the decision-making process. Their presence increases the decision maker's confidence in his or her decision. The absence of these qualities decreases the decision maker's confidence or confounds the decision maker's ability to make a decision.

REALITY VERSUS THE MEASUREMENT OF REALITY

A firm performs the following four functions:

1. it operates to produce revenues,
2. it invests resources to enable it to operate,
3. it finances its operations and investments from internal and external sources, and
4. it makes decisions.

These activities constitute the reality of conducting business. Reality happens every moment of the business day. To keep records of business transactions, the firm's officers must measure the reality of each event. But remember this: *No matter how accurately the measurement of reality reflects that reality, it is not the reality.*

To illustrate this concept, think of a person giving testimony in court. A court reporter records the exact words uttered by the witness and the transcript accurately measures the reality of the words spoken. If Rob reads the trial transcript and Keri hears the testimony in court, could Rob and Keri draw different conclusions about the substance of the testimony?

 Discussion Questions

2-11. What is the difference between the transcript testimony and the actual testimony?

2-12. Is there any other measurement of the testimony that might better reflect the reality of the testimony?

Errors in measurement create more distortion between reality and the measurement of reality. Assume Laura's Business purchased some office supplies and wrote a cheque for $480. In recording the cheque in the cheque register, the accountant read the amount of the cheque incorrectly and entered $48. After the $48 was deducted, the cheque register indicated a balance of $1,127. However, the fact that the accountant entered the wrong amount for the cheque in no way changes the reality of how much money was spent and how much actually remains in the company's chequing account.

 Discussion Questions

2-13. Assuming the accountant made no other errors in the check register, what is the actual cash balance in Laura's Business's chequing account?

2-14. In what ways could this incorrect measurement of reality have an effect on reality? Explain.

We can easily grasp the concept that errors may cause differences between reality and the measurement of reality. Many people, however, find it difficult to understand that sometimes perfectly legitimate differences exist between reality and its measure. This discrepancy can best be demonstrated in the measurement of the revenues and expenses to be reported in the income statement of a company for a particular time period.

The Problems of Periodic Measurement

periodicity The assumption that the economic activities of an entity can be traced to some specific time period and results of those activities can be reported for any arbitrary time period chosen.

Most discrepancies between reality and its measurement occur when earnings activities are measured for a specific period of time (Exhibit 2–5). An accounting assumption of the conceptual framework, called **periodicity,** states that the economic activities of an entity can be traced to some specific time period and the results of those activities can be reported for any arbitrary time period. The assumption is often easier to understand than the practice of determining which revenues and which expenses should be included in the earnings (net income) of a particular period (month, quarter, or year). In fact, the only final measure of net income for a company is a comparison between revenues and expenses over the entire life of that company.

Exhibit 2–5
Periodic Measurement

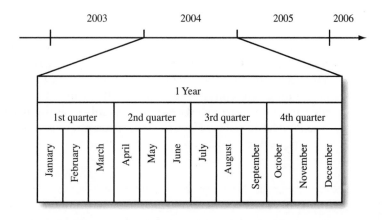

In some ways, determining net income in the fifteenth century was easier and more precise than it is today. In the era of Christopher Columbus, if an entrepreneur planned to sail to the New World and bring back goods to sell, the net income for that particular venture could be measured. The entrepreneur began with a sum of money. With those funds, he bought a ship and supplies and hired men to help with the expedition. The group would set sail, gather treasures and commodities from the New World, return, and sell the goods. Then the entrepreneur paid the workers, sold the ship, and counted the money. If the ending money exceeded the beginning funds, the difference was a net income. If the beginning money exceeded the ending funds, the entrepreneur suffered a loss on the venture.

In today's world, it is unrealistic to expect a company to stop operations and sell off all its assets to determine its "true" net income. So although lifetime net income is the only precise measurement of an operation's success or failure, users of accounting information demand current information every year, or quarter, or month. Only the need to artificially break the company's operations into various time periods requires us to make decisions about when revenues and expenses should be reported.

Revenue and Expense Recognition

In accounting, the term **recognition** has a very specific meaning. It refers to the process of (1) *recording* in the books and (2) *reporting* on the financial statements.

The problem of when to recognize an item applies to all the accounting elements that we will discuss. The greatest difficulties, however, occur in deciding when to recognize revenues and expenses.

What exactly *is* revenue? **Revenue** is an accounting element representing the inflows of assets as a result of an entity's ongoing major or central operations. In other words, it is the reward for doing business. Revenue may simply be described as the increase in wealth from engaging in a particular business transaction. Alternatively, **expense** is an accounting element representing the outflow of assets resulting from an entity's ongoing major or central operations (the sacrifice to generate revenue). Examples of expenses include salaries, rent, insurance, and advertising. An expense can therefore be thought of as a decrease in the wealth of a business. All businesses exist to generate revenues (and to avoid expenses).

recognition The process of recording an event in the accounting records and reporting it on the financial statements.

revenue An accounting element representing the inflows of assets as a result of an entity's ongoing major or central operations. This is the reward for doing business.

expense An accounting element representing the outflow of assets resulting from an entity's ongoing major or central operations. This is the sacrifice required to attain the rewards (revenues) of doing business.

The net income (or loss) of a business is the difference between the revenues generated and expenses incurred over a particular period of time. All revenues and their related expense activities must be recorded in the same fiscal period by the business to arrive at a reliable net income figure. Chapter 5 will describe the process of calculating net income in greater detail. But for now, remember the following equation:

Revenue − Expenses = Net Income (or Net Loss)

When should a revenue be recognized? When should an expense be recognized? These are two difficult questions, for which there are no perfect answers. The accounting establishment had to set criteria to determine when to recognize accounting elements, particularly revenues and expenses. Over time, the accounting profession developed several different recognition systems, each attempting to find some rational basis for the measurement of revenue and expense in a particular time period.

 ## Discussion Questions

2–15. Revenue is defined as the reward of doing business. At what point in the cycle of sales, from the customer's order point to the seller's delivery to the customer, do you think a sale should be recognized as revenue? Explain.

2–16. If an expense is defined as the sacrifice necessary to obtain a revenue, at what point in the sales cycle do you think an expense incurred to make a sale should be recognized? Explain.

Bases of Economic Measurement

There are two basic approaches to recording economic activity. Each presents a different measurement of reality. Each depicts a different, but important, version of the measurement of accounting elements, especially revenues and expenses.

We will use a single set of data to illustrate the two bases of measurement. Consider the following information concerning McCumber Enterprises (a proprietorship) for January 2004:

1. Gertie McCumber started the company on January 2 by investing $200,000.
2. McCumber Enterprises borrowed $100,000 from the Friendly Bank on January 2 by signing a one-year note payable (ignore the interest for now).
3. The company purchased a vehicle on January 2 for $14,000 cash. Gertie estimates that the vehicle will fill the company's needs for four years, after which she estimates she can sell it for $2,000.
4. The company paid cash for $75,000 of merchandise inventory on January 8.
5. On January 15, the company sold merchandise that cost $42,000 for a total selling price of $78,000 and collected the cash the same day.
6. On January 22, the company sold merchandise that cost $15,000 for a total selling price of $32,000 on account (a credit sale). The terms of the sale were 30 days, meaning McCumber Enterprises can expect to receive payment by February 21.
7. Cash payments for operating expenses in January totalled $22,500.

8. Besides the bank loan, the only amounts owed by the company at the end of the month were:
   a. $2,000 to company employees for work performed in January. They will be paid on February 3.
   b. A $700 utility bill that was received on January 26 and will be paid on February 15.

This information is the reality of what happened in McCumber Enterprises during January 2004. The measurement of that reality will be different, depending on the basis of accounting used to recognize the transactions. Remember, both treatments we will show are based on exactly the same reality—they are simply different methods of measuring that reality.

CASH BASIS OF ECONOMIC MEASUREMENT

cash basis accounting
A basis of accounting in which cash is the major criterion used in measuring revenue and expense for a given income statement period. Revenue is recognized when the associated cash is received, and expense is recognized when the associated cash is paid.

The first approach to measuring economic activity is **cash basis accounting**—the simpler of the two bases. Everyone understands what cash is and can readily grasp the measurement criterion of this method. Its greatest strength, however, lies in the fact that it keeps the user's eye on the ball. As its name implies, the cash basis has only one measurement criterion: CASH!

Under cash basis accounting, we recognize economic activity only when the associated cash is received or paid. Consequently, we recognize a revenue only when the company receives the associated cash as a result of the earnings process. But not all cash received by a firm is revenue. When cash is received from company owners, the inflow of assets is not due to ongoing operations but due to an owner's investment. When cash is received from lenders, the amount owed to an outside party increases. Again, the inflow of assets is not due to ongoing operations.

Similarly, we do not recognize all cash paid out as an expense in cash basis accounting. When a company pays a dividend to its owners, we recognize the expenditure not as a company expense, but as a distribution of profits or a return on the owners' original investment.

Cash Basis Revenue Recognition

The cash basis has two criteria for revenue recognition:

realization Actual receipt of cash or payment of cash. Once cash has been collected or a transaction is complete, it is considered to be realized.

1. Cash must be received, or *realized*, in the transaction. In accounting terminology, **realization** occurs.
2. The receipt of cash must relate to delivering or producing goods, rendering services, or other business activities.

If a transaction meets both these requirements, we recognize it as a revenue for cash basis accounting and report it on the income statement.

Cash Basis Expense Recognition

The cash basis has two criteria for expense recognition:

1. Cash must be paid in the transaction.
2. The disbursement, or payment, must relate to delivering or producing goods, rendering services, or conducting other business activities.

If a transaction meets both these requirements, we recognize it as an expense for cash basis accounting and report it on the income statement.

Cash Basis Accounting

As the previous two sections have illustrated, in order to complete the equation Revenue − Expenses = Net Income, we need to determine which of the cash receipts are revenues and which are additions to capital, and which are increases in the amounts owed to outside parties. Alternatively, not all cash outflows are expenses. Some may be reductions in the amounts owed to outside parties (paying off a debt), while others may be a distribution of the wealth of the business to the owners (dividends). Therefore in order to calculate the net income of McCumber Enterprises, we need to determine (recognize) which of the cash items are revenues and which are expenses. From our example of McCumber Enterprises, only the following activities meet the recognition criteria:

1. The company purchased a vehicle on January 2 for $14,000 cash. Gertie estimates that the vehicle will fill the company's needs for four years, after which she estimates she can sell it for $2,000. Under cash basis accounting, the $14,000 purchase is considered an expense in January.
2. The company paid cash for $75,000 of merchandise inventory on January 8. This is considered an expense in January.
3. On January 15, the company sold merchandise that cost $42,000 for a total selling price of $78,000 and collected cash the same day. The sale of $78,000 is considered revenue because the company received the cash. The cost of the merchandise *is not an expense at this point*, because it was already recorded as an expense when it was purchased on January 8 (item 2).
4. Cash payments for operating expenses in January totaled $22,500.

All the other activities that occurred during January were either contributions by the owner ($200,000), amounts owed to outside parties (borrowing $100,000 from the bank), or did not involve cash (the sale on account for $32,000). The money owed to employees and the utility bill *will only become expenses when they are paid* (as stated, in February).

We can record these activities according to whether they are revenues or expenses (see Exhibit 2-6).

Exhibit 2–6
Results of Cash Basis Accounting

Date	Revenue	(−)	Expenses	(=)	Net Income Loss
Jan. 2			$ 14,000		($14,000)
Jan. 8			$ 75,000		(89,000)
Jan. 15	$78,000				(11,000)
January			22,500		(33,500)
Totals	$78,000		$111,500		($33,500)

Consider the following items from Exhibit 2–6:

- *Revenue.* Because McCumber Enterprises received only $78,000 in cash from sales in the month of January, only that amount meets both cash basis revenue recognition criteria (cash received, and cash related to delivering goods or services).

- *Expenses.* The $111,500 is the total of the expenses for the month of January because it meets both of the expense recognition criteria (cash was paid, and cash related to delivering goods or service).

Therefore, when we calculate McCumber Enterprises' net income for the month of January, we find that the company experienced a loss of $33,500.

But let's not forget about the other two cash transactions. Gertie originally contributed $200,000 to the business, and the company borrowed an additional $100,000 from the bank. So the company started out with $300,000 cash in its bank account, and under the cash basis of accounting it lost $33,500, so the company's *net cash wealth* is $266,500 ($300,000 − $33,500). This would correspond to the cash balance in the company's bank account at the end of January. All the other events did not include a cash component, so therefore they have no effect on the company's net cash wealth. As we will see in Chapters 3 and 4, the net wealth (called owners' equity) of a business is reported on the *balance sheet* of the business. The balance sheet displays the total of everything a business owns (assets), minus what it owes (liabilities). In Chapter 5, we will cover the *income statement*, which is where the revenues and expenses of a business are recorded.

 ## Discussion Questions

2–17. Assume for a moment that you are McCumber Enterprises' loan officer at the bank. How would you evaluate the revenue and expense presented in Exhibit 2–6 in terms of the primary qualitative characteristic of relevance, including predictive value and feedback value?

2–18. If your response to Discussion Question 2–17 led you to the conclusion that there is a problem in terms of predictive value and feedback value, what item or items do you believe caused the problem? How do you think the company could account for the item or items to better relate costs to the revenues they generate?

Strengths and Weaknesses of Cash Basis Accounting

Besides its relative simplicity, the greatest strength of the cash basis of accounting is its objectivity. Cash basis accounting presents the *reality of cash,* an important reality in conducting a business. Cash basis accounting requires less subjective judgment than the other measurement basis. The cash basis has a weakness that prevents it from being the perfect measurement basis, however. Management can easily manipulate revenues and expenses reported in a particular income statement period simply by speeding up or delaying the receipt of revenues or the payment of amounts owed on expenses. The greatest weakness of the cash basis is that it makes no attempt to recognize expenses in the same period as the revenues they helped generate, offering a poor measurement of the *reality of performance.* This problem makes the cash basis income statement difficult to use either for predicting future profitability or for assessing past performance in cases where the company does not always receive cash at the point of sale or pay for expenses when it receives the goods and services.

2-19. Provide two examples of situations in which your chequebook balance did not provide relevant information.

ACCRUAL BASIS OF ECONOMIC MEASUREMENT

accrual basis accounting
A method of accounting in which revenues are recognized when they are earned, regardless of when the associated cash is collected. The expenses incurred in generating the revenue are recognized when the benefit is derived rather than when the associated cash is paid.

accrue As used in accounting, to come into being as a legally enforceable claim.

The second basis of economic measurement is **accrual basis accounting.** The accrual basis does not rely on the receipt or payment of cash to determine when revenues and expenses should be recognized. The key to understanding accrual basis accounting is to understand the word **accrue.** To accrue means

To come into being as a legally enforceable claim.

Essentially, in accrual basis accounting, sales, purchases, and all other business transactions are recognized whenever a legally enforceable claim to the associated cash is established. The main focus of accrual accounting is determining when a legally enforceable claim to cash has been established between the parties involved in the transaction.

Accrual Basis Revenue Recognition

Accrual accounting has two criteria for revenue recognition:

1. Revenue must be earned; that is, the earning process must be substantially complete.
2. There must be a legally enforceable claim to receive the asset traded for the revenue. When a legally enforceable claim exists, the cash or other asset becomes a realizable asset such as an account **receivable.** In the cash basis, the cash receipt had to be *realized.* In the accrual basis, it must only be *realizable.*

receivable Money due to an entity from an enforceable claim.

Both criteria must be met to recognize revenue.

Three possible relationships can exist between the timing of the cash movement and the recognition of the revenue.

1. *Cash is received at the time the revenue is earned.* When you pay cash for a pair of Gap jeans, the Gap recognizes revenue at the point of sale. Delivery of the jeans constitutes completion of the earning process and your payment of cash realizes receipt of cash. Both criteria are met because the revenue is earned and realized.
2. *Cash is received after the revenue has been earned.* When you go to Office Depot to buy supplies for your office and Office Depot allows you to pay next month on a 30-day charge, Office Depot will receive your cash after the revenue has been earned. Delivery of the supplies completes the earning process and your signing of the invoice gives the store an enforceable claim to your cash.
3. *Cash is received before the revenue has been earned.* If you subscribe to *Maclean's* magazine for one year, you pay the subscription at the beginning of the year. *Maclean's* realizes your cash but has not yet earned it. The earning process will not be complete until *Maclean's* delivers a whole year's worth of weekly issues to you.

Because revenue must be earned before it can be recognized, the timing of the cash receipt is irrelevant. When the earning process is substantially complete *and* an enforceable claim exists to receive the cash, then the revenue is recognized. In Examples 1 and 2, the revenue is recorded in the books and shown on the financial statements at the time the sale is made. The fact that in Example 2 the company did not receive cash at that time does not affect recognition of the revenue. In Example 3, the receipt of cash does not cause revenue to be recognized because, under accrual accounting, the revenue is not recognized until it is earned (when the publisher sends the magazines to the customer).

Identifying the point in time when a revenue is earned is not always a simple matter. Accountants try to answer three questions in determining when revenue has been earned and therefore should be recognized. To emphasize that these questions are in no way related to the three examples, we are using letters to list them.

a. *Has **title** (legal ownership) to whatever was sold been transferred to the customer?* If the answer to this question is yes, revenue should be recognized. This question can be applied more easily to the sale of tangible products than to the sale of services. Services must be substantially complete to recognize revenue.

b. *Has an exchange taken place?* Each party to the exchange gives the other party something of value—goods and services in exchange for cash or receivables. In other words, has the customer taken receipt of whatever he or she purchased? If the answer to this question is yes, the revenue will likely be recognized.

c. *Is the earnings process virtually complete?* This is the toughest of the three questions to answer and applies better to the sale of services than it does to the sale of tangible products. Suppose you have contracted with Bill Austin to remodel your kitchen. It is a two-week job, and at the end of the second week, Bill has completed everything but changing the lamp over the dinette area. He ordered the lamp two months ago, but the supplier back-ordered it. It should arrive within another week. Has Bill substantially completed the work? Probably yes. He can recognize the revenue because the job is "virtually" complete.

It is not necessary for all three questions to be answered "yes" for revenue to be recognized. In most cases, a positive answer to any one of them is persuasive evidence that revenue has been earned and should be recognized.

 Discussion Questions

2–20. On Saturday morning, you finally decide which model of computer to buy. The salesperson has agreed to have all the software you need installed and have the machine delivered to you by Tuesday afternoon. Because you purchased your last computer at Image Technologies, the store has agreed to extend credit to you as an established customer. You have 30 days to pay for your new computer. As of Monday,

   a. has title passed?

   b. has an exchange taken place?

   c. is the earnings process complete?

2–21. When should Image Technologies recognize revenue

   a. under the cash basis?

   b. under the accrual basis?

Accrual Basis Expense Recognition

Under accrual accounting, there is only one criterion for expense recognition: A firm recognizes an expense when it receives the benefit from the expense. Like revenue recognition, expense recognition under accrual accounting is unrelated to the movement of cash.

Again, there are three possible relationships between the timing of the cash movement and the recognition of an expense.

1. *Cash is paid **at the time** the expense is incurred.* If a company holds a Christmas party and pays for the food when the caterer delivers it, the company receives the benefit of the expense at the same time it transfers the cash to the vendor.
2. *Cash is paid **after** the expense has been incurred.* A public utility cannot immediately exchange electricity for cash and must bill its customers on a monthly basis. When a firm receives and pays an electric bill, it expends the cash after the receipt of the electric service.
3. *Cash is paid **before** the expense has been incurred.* All insurance contracts require cash in advance to issue the policy and keep it in force. The policy expires or the expense occurs for each day as time passes during the policy's time span.

 Discussion Question

2-22. Why would insurance companies require policies to be paid in advance?

If the one criterion for expense recognition is receiving the benefit from the expense, how do we know when the expense benefits the firm? For the most part, the key to expense recognition under accrual accounting is revenue recognition. Remember that to be useful for predicting future profitability and cash flow, an income statement should measure revenues for a specific period of time and the expenses required to obtain those revenues. Thus, accrual accounting attempts to capture the relationship between revenues and expenses. This relationship is referred to as matching.

If we re-examine the McCumber Enterprises transactions for January under the accrual basis of accounting (recognizing revenues and expenses), we will find that the company's net income is different than the $33,500 loss that was recorded the using the cash basis of accounting. First, it is largely irrelevant whether or not cash was actually received or paid out.

As with cash basis accounting, the $200,000 that Gertie started the company with on January 2 is not a revenue because it does not meet the criteria of being a revenue. The company is neither richer nor poorer (no change in its net wealth) as a result of this transaction. This is the same for the $100,000 borrowed from the bank on January 2 (still ignoring interest). The company may have $100,000 more in its bank account, but it now owes the bank $100,000; therefore there is no change in net wealth. The first difference between cash and accrual accounting is the vehicle purchased on January 2 for $14,000—it is *not* an expense under accrual accounting. The vehicle is only recognized as an expense when it is actually used to generate revenue. At this point, all the company has done is exchange one asset (cash) for another asset (the vehicle). There has been no change in net wealth. What the vehicle might be worth at the end of four years ($2,000) is irrelevant.

The merchandise purchased on January 8 for $75,000 is *not* an expense under accrual accounting. Just as with the vehicle, all the company has done is exchange one asset for another. When the company actually *sells* the merchandise, *then* it will record the cost of the merchandise sold as an expense. This occurs on January 15, when the company sold merchandise that cost $42,000 for $78,000 cash. The $42,000 is considered an expense of the business (called Cost of Goods Sold). The $78,000 is revenue, and the $42,000 is an expense. On January 22 the company sold merchandise that cost $15,000 for $32,000 (credit sale). It did not receive cash for this sale, but did receive something else of value. That thing of value is the *customer's promise to pay* cash at some future date (called an account receivable). This is considered revenue just as if the company had received cash (and the $15,000 is an expense). The cash payments ($22,000) for expenses incurred in January are expenses just like under cash basis accounting. The thing to remember is that those expenses must have been incurred in January for them to be considered an expense in January. It actually does not matter whether they were *paid* in January (but in this case they were). The $2,000 still owed to the company's employees is an expense for the month of January (since that is when the employees did the work), and, likewise, the $700 utility bill is also an expense in January. The fact that these expenses will not be paid until February is irrelevant.

Just as with cash basis accounting, we can record these activities according to whether they are revenues or expenses (see Exhibit 2.7).

Exhibit 2-7
Results of Accrual
Basis Accounting

Date	Revenue	(−)	Expenses	(=)	Net Income
Jan. 15	$78,000		$42,000		$36,000
Jan. 22	32,000		15,000		53,000
January			22,000		31,000
January			2,000		29,000
January			700		28,300
Totals	$110,000		$81,700		$28,300

Under accrual basis accounting, we can see that in January, McCumber Enterprises experienced a *profit* of $28,300. Under cash basis accounting the company recorded a *loss* of $33,500. Which is correct? Well, they both are correct because they are both recording the same events, but in different ways and at different times.

We can see that ultimately there is a considerable difference between cash basis and accrual basis accounting when we look at McCumber Enterprise's net wealth. Cash basis accounting never took into consideration the $100,000 the company owes the bank. Nor did it consider that the company owns a valuable asset (the vehicle worth $14,000). The company still has unsold merchandise that cost $18,000 and a customer that owes $32,000. Additionally, the company owes its employees $2,000, and has an unpaid utility bill for $700.

Therefore, in order to calculate McCumber Enterprises' net wealth, we need to take all these things into consideration. The company still has $266,500 in the bank (that doesn't change). Subtract from that the $100,000 owing to the bank, add the value of the vehicle ($14,000), add the remaining inventory ($18,000), add the money owed by the customer ($32,000), subtract the money owed to employees ($2,000) and subtract the utility bill ($700). This gives McCumber Enterprises a net wealth of $227,800.

At this point you should notice that under cash basis accounting, McCumber Enterprises *lost* $33,500 and ended up being worth *more* ($266,500) than under accrual basis accounting ($227,800). How is this possible? The answer lies in the timing of events and which ones get recognized. Eventually, the company will pay the money it owes and receive the money that is owed to it. Additionally, the company will eventually use up the vehicle (which was listed as an expense under cash basis accounting but not under accrual basis accounting) and sell all the remaining merchandise. When the company finally comes to the end of its business life and everything is liquidated (turned into cash), the company's change in wealth will be the same no matter which basis of accounting was used.

The important thing to remember is not which accounting system is "right," but which one provides the most useful and broadest method of measuring economic performance. Cash is a very narrow measure of economic performance because it only deals with one thing: cash. Accrual basis accounting expands how we view the performance of a business by recognizing all events leading to a legally enforceable claim to cash, no matter when cash is actually received or paid. Accrual accounting is much more useful to the decision maker because it includes more relevant information.

And finally, under GAAP, accrual basis accounting is the only acceptable basis for reporting economic performance to external parties. That is, all financial statements must be prepared using accrual accounting methods. Cash basis accounting may be used for internal reporting purposes, but not for external reporting.

 Discussion Question

2-23. Checker Business Systems sells computer equipment to small businesses. During 2004, the sales activity was as follows:

February: Sold $6,000 worth of equipment on account. The customers paid in full on March 15.

March: Sold $4,500 worth of equipment on account. Customers paid in full on April 15.

Describe the impact of different periodic measurements by determining how much should be included in each period if the business activity is measured

a. each month,

b. each quarter,

c. each year.

DECISION MAKERS AND UNDERSTANDABILITY

Now that you know the qualities required to make accounting information useful, you can appreciate the fact that, as a decision maker and user of accounting information, you must evaluate the qualities of available information to assess its usefulness. You must also recognize that the information you receive from accountants constitutes only a part of the information you need to make sound economic decisions. It is an important part, to be sure, but only a part. The reports generated from accounting information can be thought of as the tools of the accounting trade. As financial tools are introduced and discussed throughout the rest of this text, keep in mind that each has its limitations and imperfections. After working with the material provided here, however, you should be able to use each financial tool to its fullest potential.

SUMMARY

The aim of all decisions is to obtain some type of reward, either extrinsic or intrinsic, at a cost. Good decisions are made when a reasonable balance is found between the sacrifice and the reward in the context of uncertainty.

Economic decisions are those involving business transactions. Internal decision makers are individuals within a company who have access to most of the company's financial information and who make decisions on behalf of the organization. External decision makers are individuals or organizations outside a company who have access to the limited information provided to them by the company and who make decisions about the organization. Management accounting information is prepared for use by internal parties, and financial accounting information is prepared for use by external parties (but is also used by internal parties).

Both internal and external parties attempt to predict the future and timing of cash flows. Essentially, they are all trying to determine whether they will be paid, when they will be paid, and how much they will be paid. Cash flow becomes an important criterion to evaluate business success or failure, with other accounting measures of performance.

Accounting information is a key ingredient of good decision making. Business activity produces data. These data are of no value to decision makers until they are put into a useful form and become information. Accounting information must possess certain qualitative characteristics: (1) relevance, including timeliness and either predictive value or feedback value; and (2) reliability, including verifiability, representational faithfulness, and neutrality. Useful accounting information should also possess comparability and consistency, and be understandable to economic decision makers.

A firm performs four functions: It operates to produce revenues, invests in productive resources, finances those investments, and makes decisions. Such activities constitute the reality of business transactions and events. Accountants attempt to measure that reality in the accounting records and reports. The measurement of reality may not precisely reflect reality because of the basis selected to recognize revenues and expenses in a particular time period. This chapter presents two distinct bases: the cash basis and the accrual basis.

The cash basis of accounting recognizes revenues and expenses when realized—when the cash associated with revenue is received, and when the cash associated with an expense is paid. Periodic net income (or loss) under the cash basis is simply the difference between cash revenues received and cash expenses paid.

The accrual basis of accounting provides a broader measure of economic performance because it includes factors that a decision maker would be interested in knowing about. These factors include the future cash flows of a business (both inflows and outflows) as well as the obligations of the business and the business's other non-cash assets (vehicles, inventory, money owed to the business by customers). Because this provides a more useful measure of economic performance, future chapters will focus on the collection, summation, reporting, and presentation of accounting information under the accrual basis of accounting.

KEY TERMS

accounting information, p. 38
accrual basis accounting, p. 48
accrue, p. 48
cash basis accounting, p. 45
cash flow, p. 36
cost/benefit analysis, p. 34
expense, p. 43
external decision makers, p. 35
feedback value, p. 40
financial accounting, p. 36
information, p. 38
internal decision makers, p. 35
management accounting, p. 36
materiality, p. 39

net cash flow, p. 36
neutrality, p. 41
opportunity cost, p. 34
periodicity, p. 42
predictive value, p. 40
realization, p. 45
receivable, p. 48
recognition, p. 43
relevance, p. 40
reliability, p. 40
representational faithfulness, p. 40
revenue, p. 43
timeliness, p. 40
verifiability, p. 40

REVIEW THE FACTS

1. Provide two examples of rewards and sacrifices that may be involved when a decision is being made.
2. What is an opportunity cost?
3. Define *cost/benefit analysis.*
4. What is economic decision making?
5. Name the two broad categories of economic decision makers, and explain the differences between them.
6. What are the two major branches of accounting and how do they differ?
7. List the three major questions asked by economic decision makers.
8. What is accounting information?
9. Explain the difference between data and information.
10. Name the two primary qualitative characteristics of useful accounting information.
11. What characteristics are necessary for accounting information to be relevant?
12. List the characteristics necessary for accounting information to be reliable.
13. Explain the difference between the primary and secondary qualities of useful accounting information.
14. What are the secondary qualities of useful accounting information?
15. Explain the responsibility of both the accounting profession and the user for the understandability of accounting information.
16. Explain the difference between reality and the measurement of reality, and provide an example of each.
17. How does periodic measurement create complications?
18. In accounting, what does it mean for an item to be "recognized"?
19. In accounting, what does it mean for an item to be "realized"?
20. Under the cash basis of measurement, when does revenue recognition occur?
21. Under the cash basis, when are expenses recognized?
22. What is the greatest strength of the cash basis?
23. What is the greatest weakness of the cash basis?
24. Under the accrual basis of measurement, when does revenue recognition occur?
25. Explain the difference between the reality of cash and the reality of performance.

APPLY WHAT YOU HAVE LEARNED

LO 2 & 3:   Economic Decision Making

1. Tommy Hoag is a commercial artist who paints various types of signs for other businesses. He received a $15,000 order from Bill Bates Inc. for 1,500 signs to be displayed in Bates' retail outlets. This is a very large job for Tommy's new business. He has concerns because he estimates it will take him a month working full time to complete the signs and Bates proposes to pay him the full contract amount 30 days after he delivers the signs. These are Bates' standard payment terms. Tommy did a small job for Bates last year ($1,500) and received payment 50 days after completing the work.

    Tommy estimates the materials (sign board, paint, brushes, etc.) will cost $9,500, which he can buy on 30-day terms from Long's Art Supply Company (Tommy can pay for the materials 30 days after he buys them).

    Having taken the accounting course in which you are now enrolled, Tommy remembers that any economic decision entails attempting to answer the following three questions:

    - Will I be paid?
    - When will I be paid?
    - How much will I be paid?

REQUIRED:
a. If Tommy can satisfy himself as to the first question (Will I be paid?), what are the answers to the other two questions? Remember the last question (How much?) has two parts.
b. The problem states that Tommy has concerns. What do you think is troubling him about the order from Bill Bates Inc.?
c. Based on your answer to the previous requirement, identify three things Tommy could do to solve his dilemma.

LO 2 & 3:   Economic Decision Making

2. Jon Smythe is a trained automobile engine mechanic. He has received a $25,000 contract from David Watts Limited to repair 25 automobile engines for Watts' taxicabs. Jon has concerns about the terms of the contract. He estimates it will take him a month working full time to complete the engines and Watts will pay him 30 days after he completes the engines. These are Watts' standard payment terms, and in the past Watts has paid Jon on average after 40 days.

    Jon estimates the parts will cost $13,000, which he can buy on a 30-day charge from Sam's Auto Supply Company (meaning Jon can pay 30 days after the purchase). Jon has the normal questions of any economic decision:

    - Will I be paid?
    - When will I be paid?
    - How much will I be paid?

REQUIRED:

a. Jon believes that Watts will pay him based on their prior dealings. What are the answers to the other two questions? Remember the last question (How much?) has two parts.

b. The problem states that Jon is concerned about the contract terms. Why do you think he is concerned?

c. Based on your answer to the previous requirement, identify three things Jon could do to lessen his concerns.

LO 2 & 3: Economic Decision Making

3. Rob Schwinn is a manufacturer of quality furniture specializing in high-quality wooden tables and chairs. He received a $50,000 contract from Dillon Corporation to build 100 upholstered sofas, to be sold in Dillon's stores. Rob believes he needs two months to complete the sofas. He must purchase an industrial sewing machine for the fabric work on the sofas at a cost of $10,000 for the machine and training, which will equal the profit that he will make on this contract. Dillon has agreed to pay Rob Schwinn 30 days after delivery of the sofas.

   Rob knows that he can buy the sewing machine on a 90-day plan from Dan's Sewing Machine Company. Rob knows that any economic decision entails attempting to answer the following three questions:

   • Will I be paid?

   • When will I be paid?

   • How much will I be paid?

REQUIRED:

a. Assuming Rob can satisfy himself as to the first question (Will I be paid?), what are the answers to the other two questions? Remember the last question (How much?) has two parts.

b. List the pros and cons of Rob's accepting this contract.

LO 4: Cash Concepts

4. Interpret the following statement: "Cash is the 'ball' of business."

LO 5 & 6: Qualitative Characteristics of Accounting Information

5. Presented below are the qualitative characteristics of useful accounting information as discussed in the chapter, followed by definitions of those items in scrambled order.

a. Relevance		f. Verifiability
b. Timeliness		g. Representational faithfulness
c. Predictive value		h. Neutrality
d. Feedback value		i. Comparability
e. Reliability		j. Consistency

   1. _____ The same measurement application methods are used over time.

   2. _____ The accounting information is free of bias.

   3. _____ The information provides input to evaluate a previously made decision.

4. _____ The information allows the evaluation of one alternative against another alternative.
5. _____ In assessing the information, qualified persons working independently would arrive at similar conclusions.
6. _____ The information helps reduce the uncertainty of the future.
7. _____ The information has a bearing on a particular decision situation.
8. _____ The information is available soon enough to be of value.
9. _____ The information can be dependable.
10. _____ There must be agreement between what the information says and what really happened.

REQUIRED:
Match the letter next to each item with the appropriate definition. Each letter will be used only once.

LO 2, 3, 4, 5, & 6:   Chapter Concepts

6. Presented below are items relating to the concepts discussed in this chapter, followed by the definitions of those items in scrambled order:

a. Cash flow
b. Comparability
c. Data
d. Financial accounting

e. Information
f. Management accounting
g. Net cash flow
h. Economic decision making

1. _____ The raw results of transactions and events
2. _____ A branch of accounting developed to meet the information needs of internal decision makers
3. _____ Data transformed so they are useful in the decision-making process
4. _____ The movement of cash in and out of a company
5. _____ Any decision involving money
6. _____ Reports generated for one entity may be compared with reports generated for other entities
7. _____ The difference between the cash coming into a company and the cash going out of a company
8. _____ A branch of accounting developed to meet the information needs of external decision makers

REQUIRED:
Match the letter next to each item with the appropriate definition. Each letter will be used only once.

LO 2 & 6:   Qualitative Characteristics of Accounting Information

7. Emma Peel is the chief accountant of Venture Enterprises. She is trying to decide whether to extend credit to Freed Company, a new customer. Venture does most of its business on credit, but is very strict in granting credit terms. Frank Freed, the owner and president of Freed Company, has sent the following items for Emma to examine as she performs her evaluation.

1. All company bank statements for the past seven years (a total of 84 bank statements)
2. A detailed analysis showing the amount of sales the company expects to have in the coming year and its estimated profit

3. Another, less-detailed analysis outlining projected company growth over the next 20 years
4. A biographical sketch of each of the company's officers and a description of the function each performs in the company
5. Ten letters of reference from close friends and relatives of the company's officers
6. A report of the company's credit history prepared by company employees on Freed Company letterhead
7. A letter signed by all company officers expressing their willingness to personally guarantee the credit Venture extends to Freed. (You may assume this is a legally binding document.)

REQUIRED:

a. As she evaluates Freed Company's application for credit, is Emma Peel an internal decision maker or an external decision maker? Explain your reasoning.
b. Analyze each item Freed sent in light of the primary qualitative characteristics of relevance (including timeliness, predictive value, and feedback value) and reliability (including verifiability, representational faithfulness, and neutrality). Explain how each item either possesses or does not possess these characteristics.

LO 6: Qualitative Characteristics of Accounting Information

8. You are in the market for a used car. You notice a promising advertisement in the local newspaper and make an appointment to meet with the seller, whose name is Chet. During your meeting you obtain the following information:

1. The car is a 1999 model.
2. Chet said he has used the car only for commuting to and from work.
3. You notice the car has out-of-province licence tags.
4. The odometer reading is 105,118 km.
5. Chet reports that he has had the oil changed every 5,000 km since he bought the car new.
6. Chet says this is the greatest car he has ever owned.
7. The glove box contains a maintenance record prepared by a licensed mechanic.

REQUIRED:

a. Evaluate each item from the list above in terms of its relevance (specifically, predictive value and timeliness) to your decision about whether to buy Chet's car.
b. Evaluate each item from the list above in terms of its reliability (verifiability, representational faithfulness, and neutrality) for deciding whether to buy Chet's car.

LO 6: Qualitative Characteristics of Accounting Information

9. The chapter states that to be useful, accounting information must possess the primary qualitative characteristics of relevance (timeliness and predictive value or feedback value) and reliability (verifiability, representational faithfulness, and neutrality). These characteristics are also applicable to other types of information.

Suppose that prior to taking your midterm exam in this course, your instructor gives you two options:

Option 1: One week before the midterm exam you will be given a rough idea of what is going to be on the exam.

or

Option 2: On the day following the exam, you will be given a copy of the actual midterm exam with an answer key.

Assume further that you have two goals:

Goal 1: To prepare for the midterm exam.
Goal 2: To evaluate your performance on the midterm exam.

REQUIRED:
Within the context of each of your two goals, evaluate both options using the primary qualitative characteristics. Be sure to explain how the primary characteristics are present or absent, and how such presence or absence affects you as a rational decision maker.

LO 6: Qualitative Characteristics of Accounting Information

10. Suppose you are about to buy a new car. The car you want is a Nissan Maxima. You have $30,000 in the bank, ready to spend on the new car. You obtain the following items of information:

1. On your first visit to Quality Nissan, a salesperson casually tells you that the price of a new Nissan Maxima is $25,500.
2. A friend tells you he heard that someone was selling a three-year-old Maxima for $18,000.
3. Another friend just bought a new Chevy pickup truck for $22,000.
4. The sticker price of a Maxima with the options you want is $26,800.
5. A Nissan dealer in the area is advertising a new Maxima with the options you want for $26,200.
6. A friend tells you she heard that someone bought a new Maxima a couple of months ago for around $24,000.

Assume that you are about to visit a Nissan dealership and your goal is to buy a new Maxima for the best price. You intend to use the previous information to evaluate whether or not the price you get is a good deal.

REQUIRED:
a. Evaluate each item from the list above in terms of its relevance (feedback value, predictive value, and timeliness). Explain how the presence or absence of the characteristics affects your ability to use the information to determine if you are getting a good deal.
b. Evaluate each item from the list above in terms of its reliability (verifiability, representational faithfulness, and neutrality). Explain how the presence or absence of these characteristics affects your ability to use the information to determine if you are getting a good deal.

LO 6: Qualitative Characteristics of Accounting Information

11. Exactly two weeks from today you must take the midterm exam for this class. You feel you are in trouble because you cannot seem to grasp exactly how you should prepare for the exam. As you are walking across campus, you see the following notice pinned to a bulletin board:

I CAN HELP!!!

I GUARANTEE AN "A" OR "B"

WILL TUTOR FOR $15 PER HOUR

Qualifications:

1. Got an "A" in the course myself.
2. Have outlines of all chapters of the text.
3. Have over 120 satisfied customers from previous semesters.
4. Know the Professor personally.
5. Know the authors of the text personally.
6. Working on a graduate degree in History.

CALL BILL AUSTIN AT 555-5555

REQUIRED:
Evaluate each of Bill's claimed qualifications in relation to the primary characteristics of:
   a. Relevance (including timeliness and predictive value or feedback value).
   b. Reliability (including verifiability, representational faithfulness, and neutrality).

LO 7 & 8: Cash Basis Measurement

12. Katie Bales Enterprises began operation on January 2, 2004. During its first month of operation, the company had the following transactions:

- Purchased $35,000 worth of merchandise inventory on January 2. The amount due is payable on February 2.
- Paid January office rent of $3,000 on January 3.
- Purchased $10,000 worth of merchandise inventory on January 5. Paid cash at the time of purchase.
- Sold inventory that cost $18,000 for $30,000 to a customer on January 10 and received the cash on that date.
- Sold inventory that cost $5,000 for $9,000 to a customer on January 20. The sale was on account and the customer has until February 20 to pay.
- Paid cash expenses of $7,500 during January.
- Received bills for utilities, advertising, and phone service totalling $1,500. All these bills were for services received in January. They will all be paid the first week in February.

REQUIRED:
   a. Calculate the revenues, expenses, and net income or loss for Katie Bales Enterprises for the month of January 2004 using the cash basis of accounting.
   b. Do you think that the net income figure calculated in the previous requirement provides a good measure of the reality of the company's economic performance during the month of January? Explain your reasoning.

LO 9: Accrual Basis Measurement

13. Katie Bales Enterprises began operation on January 2, 2004. During its first month of operation, the company had the same seven transactions as noted in problem 12.

REQUIRED:
a. Calculate the revenues, expenses, and net income or loss for Katie Bales Enterprises for the month of January 2004 using the accrual basis of accounting.
b. Do you think that the net income figure calculated in the previous requirement provides a good measure of the reality of the company's economic performance during the month of January? Explain your reasoning.

LO 7 & 8: Cash Basis Measurement

14. Snow and Ice Enterprises began operation on June 1, 2004. During its first month of operation, the company had the following transactions:

- Purchased $40,000 worth of merchandise inventory on June 1. The amount due is payable on August 1.
- Paid June office rent of $2,000 on June 3.
- Purchased $20,000 worth of merchandise inventory on June 4. Paid cash at the time of purchase.
- Sold inventory that cost $30,000 for $42,000 to a customer on June 10 and received the cash on that date.
- Sold inventory that cost $10,000 for $14,000 to a customer on June 20. The sale was on account and the customer has until July 20 to pay.
- Paid cash expenses of $9,500 during June.
- Received bills for utilities, advertising, and phone service totalling $3,500. All these bills were for services received in June. They will all be paid the first week in July.

REQUIRED:
a. Calculate the revenues, expenses, and net income or loss for Snow and Ice Enterprises for the month of June 2004 using the cash basis of accounting.
b. Do you think that the net income figure calculated in the previous requirement provides a good measure of the reality of the company's economic performance during the month of June? Explain your reasoning.

LO 9: Accrual Basis Measurement

15. Snow and Ice Enterprises began operation on June 1, 2004. During its first month of operation, the company had the same seven transactions as noted in problem 14.

REQUIRED:
a. Calculate the revenues, expenses, and net income or loss for Snow and Ice Enterprises for the month of June 2004 using the accrual basis of accounting.
b. Do you think that the net income figure calculated in the previous requirement provides a good measure of the reality of the company's economic performance during the month of June? Explain your reasoning.

LO 8 & 9:   Cash versus Accrual

16. Roger Webb Enterprises began operation on January 2, 2004. During its first month of operation, the company had the following transactions:

- Paid January office rent of $2,000 on January 2.
- Purchased $25,000 worth of merchandise inventory on January 5. The amount due is payable on February 5.
- Purchased $15,000 worth of merchandise inventory on January 8. Paid cash at the time of purchase.
- Sold merchandise that cost $12,000 for $18,000 to a customer on January 16 and received the cash on that date.
- Sold merchandise that cost $9,000 for $13,500 to a customer on January 26. The sale was on account and the customer has until February 26 to pay.
- Paid February office rent of $2,000 on January 31.

REQUIRED:

a. Calculate the revenues, expenses, and net income or loss for Roger Webb Enterprises for the month of January 2004 using the cash basis of accounting.

b. Calculate the revenues, expenses, and net income or loss for Roger Webb Enterprises for the month of January 2004 using the accrual basis of accounting.

c. Explain in your own words what caused the differences between the net income reported under the cash basis of accounting and the one reported under the accrual basis.

d. Which of the two accounting approaches do you think:
- **(1)** provides better information as to cash flow for the month of January?
- **(2)** provides better information as to what Roger Webb Enterprises earned during the month of January?
- **(3)** better reflects the company's ability to generate future earnings and cash flow?

FINANCIAL REPORTING CASE

17. Look at Sobeys Inc.'s annual report to answer the following questions.

- **a.** List the divisions of Sobeys and the primary market of each division.
- **b.** What factors should Sobeys consider before adding a new division?
- **c.** For what reasons would Sobeys sell or close a division? What factors should management consider to make such a decision?

ANNUAL REPORT PROJECT

You now have your annual report and have prepared an index of its contents. Your annual report project eventually will contain the following sections.

- **I.** General Information
- **II.** SWOT Analysis
- **III.** Capital Structure
- **IV.** Assets
- **V.** Cash Flows

VI. Financial Ratio Analysis
VII. Internet and Library Research
VIII. Summary and Conclusions

17. Section I contains the following subsections.

    A. Record the Internet address of your company.

    B. Identify the company's industry.

    C. Identify the Standard Industrial Classification (SIC) code of your company. You can find SIC codes in several ways:

        1. Sometimes the annual report contains the SIC. Look in general information often at the end of the annual report.

        2. Try the Internet address of the firm. Look on the web site, or e-mail the company for the information.

        3. If all these fail, go to the library and consult a reference librarian to find a reference publication that will give you this information.

    D. Identify the stock exchange(s) where your company's shares trade.

    E. Record the ticker symbol of the company.

    F. Find the auditor's report and record the name of the auditing firm.

    G. Read the president's (or CEO's) message and prepare a brief summary of this message.

    H. Read any other promotional or informational material about the company. This information usually relates the firm's views on social responsibility, marketing strategy, direction for the future, environmental issues, and so on. Write a brief summary of this information provided in the annual report.

REQUIRED:

Complete section I of your project. Turn in one copy to your instructor and retain a clean copy for your final project folder. For group projects, divide the parts equitably among the group members.

3

The Balance Sheet: Initial Financing— Investment by Owners

*B*otany was your favorite nonmajor course in college. You were fortunate to have Dr. Bidlack, and he required a project to complete the course. Inspired by his unusual use of plant substances for practical home applications, you isolated a resin in petunia seeds that resists all dirt and moisture. You added this to paint, repainted a licence plate on the front of your car, and found that nothing stuck to it—not even road tar or mud. Could these be the seeds of your success?

Your best friend is a marketing major and would love to sell this idea to the paint industry for use in automotive vehicles and house paints. Dr. Bidlack could lend a lot of expertise. If you form a company for this endeavour, should it be a partnership or a corporation? How much money will it take to get started and where do you get it? Your banker asked you for a financial statement, and you have no earthly idea what he wants. Where do you start?

Financial statements should be thought of as tools for solving economic problems. Like all tools, the accounting profession developed these statements in response to specific needs. If these financial tools are adequate and properly used, they will produce satisfactory results. If they are inadequate or improperly used, they will not produce good results and disaster may result. In this chapter, we will cover only one financial statement—the balance sheet. There are several other kinds of financial statements, and we will cover them as we proceed through this text. ∎

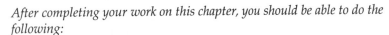

LEARNING OBJECTIVES

After completing your work on this chapter, you should be able to do the following:

1. Identify and explain the accounting elements contained in the balance sheet.
2. Demonstrate how the balance sheet provides information about the financial position of a business.
3. Compare and contrast the balance sheets of proprietorships, partnerships, and corporations.
4. Describe the basic organizational structure of a corporation.
5. Differentiate between common shares and preferred shares.
6. Describe the components of shareholders' equity.
7. Identify what information is available on a corporate balance sheet and what information is not available.
8. Explain the basic process operating in the primary and secondary stock markets.

THE FIRST TOOL: INTRODUCTION TO THE BALANCE SHEET

balance sheet A financial statement providing information about an entity's present condition. Reports what a company possesses (assets) and who has claim to those possessions (liabilities and owners' equity).

In Chapter 2, we defined the problems facing those who make economic decisions. As decision makers evaluate alternative investment opportunities, they try to determine whether they will be paid, and if so, when the payment will occur and how much it will be. This evaluation begins with an assessment of an investment's present condition and past performance. Remember that the present and the past are useful only if they have predictive value. Over time, accountants developed financial tools to convey information about the present condition and past performance of an entity. The financial tool that focuses on the present condition of a business is the **balance sheet.**

 ## Discussion Questions

3-1. Your uncle's will stipulates that you and your cousin Terry (with whom you have always competed) will inherit the two businesses he owned. You get first choice, and you may ask ten questions to determine the present condition of each company. Lawyers for the estate will provide the answers. List your ten questions.

3-2. You are locked in a room that has no windows and only one door. To get out of the room, you must request one tool and explain how you will use it to get through the door. You may not request a key or any lock-picking equipment. Choose the one tool you request and describe its features. Then explain in detail how you will use it to get out of the room.

The Accounting Elements

In this chapter, we will discuss three accounting elements that make up the balance sheet. We will present other accounting elements later in the text. As we discuss these elements, we will give both the actual CICA definition in italics and a less technical explanation in roman type.

The three accounting elements that are major components of a balance sheet are:

assets An accounting element that is one of the three components of a balance sheet. Assets are economic resources controlled by an entity as a result of past transactions or events—that is, what a company has.

liabilities An accounting element that is one of the three components of a balance sheet. Liabilities are obligations arising from past transactions or events that may be settled through the transfer or use of assets, provision of services, or other yielding of economic benefits in the future—that is, what a company owes.

equity An accounting element that is one of the three components of a balance sheet. Equity is the ownership interest in the assets of a profit-oriented enterprise after deducting its liabilities.

investments by owners That part of owners' equity generated by the receipt of cash (or other assets) from the owners.

earned equity The total amount a company has earned since its beginning, less any amounts distributed to the owner(s). In a corporation, this amount is called retained earnings.

1. **Assets.** *Economic resources controlled by an entity as a result of past transactions or events.* Assets are the things a company owns or controls (such as leased assets). Cash is the item most easily identified as an asset.
2. **Liabilities.** *Obligations arising from past transactions or events that may be settled through the transfer or use of assets, provision of services, or other yielding of economic benefits in the future.* Liabilities are the debts a company owes. A company may have an obligation to transfer assets to someone to pay off a debt or to provide services when the company received payment in advance. Liabilities arise from past transactions, not events that might occur in the future. An entity must, however, settle or pay liabilities some time in the future.
3. **Equity.** *The ownership interest in the assets of a profit-oriented enterprise after deducting its liabilities.* Equity is the ownership interest in a company. It is the difference between its assets and its liabilities on those assets. The result represents the portion of the assets that the owner(s) own free and clear. Consequently, some people refer to equity as net assets.

The present financial position of an entity can be captured in these three elements: assets, liabilities, and equity. Equity in a company comes from two sources:

a. **Investments by owners.** This accounting element represents the amount invested by the owner(s) of the company. It represents "seed money" put into the company to get it started or to finance its expansion.

b. **Earned equity.** This is the total amount a company has earned since it was first started, less any amounts that have been taken out by the owner(s). Earned equity comes from the profitable operation of the company over time.

Organization of the Balance Sheet

A constant relationship exists among the three main elements on the balance sheet (assets, liabilities, and equity). Logically, the assets of a company must be owned by someone. Therefore, the company's assets will be equal to the claims that are made on those assets—creditors' claims (liabilities) or the owners' claims (equity). In most cases, both creditors and owners share claims on the assets (see Exhibit 3–1). This relationship can be stated as an equation:

$$\text{ASSETS} = \text{LIABILITIES} + \text{EQUITY}$$

We call this equation the *accounting equation,* but we could easily call it the business equation because it sums up the reality of business. Accounting uses this equation to measure that reality. Because the equation has all the properties of a mathematical equation, we can rearrange it as:

$$\text{ASSETS} - \text{LIABILITIES} = \text{EQUITY}$$

This presentation of the equation shows equity for what it is: the owners' residual interest in the company. We usually use the phrase *owners' equity* instead of the word *equity*. Thus, the accounting equation is usually presented as:

$$\text{ASSETS} = \text{LIABILITIES} + \text{OWNERS' EQUITY}$$

Exhibit 3–1
Accounting Equation

If you buy an automobile by paying $3,000 in cash and borrowing $5,000 from the bank, both you and the bank have a claim against the car.

$$\text{Assets} = \text{Liabilities} + \text{Equity}$$
$$\text{Car} = \text{Bank Loan} + \text{Equity}$$
$$\$8,000 = \$5,000 + \$3,000$$

By rearranging the equation to

$$\text{Assets} - \text{Liabilities} = \text{Equity}$$
$$\$8,000 - \$5,000 = \$3,000$$

you can see that in this situation, you have a car worth $8,000, the bank has a $5,000 claim against the car, and you have a $3,000 equity in the automobile.

To understand the balance sheet, you must understand the meaning of the equation. The term *balance sheet* comes from the need to keep both sides of the equation in balance. Another name for a balance sheet is the *statement of financial position*, which describes the true purpose of the statement. Common usage in the business world, however, remains the *balance sheet*.

Balance sheets are presented in two different forms, the account form and the report form. The account form places assets on the left side of the page and the liabilities and equity on the right. As you can see in Exhibit 3–2, the story told by the balance sheet is

ASSETS = LIABILITIES + OWNERS' EQUITY

The same information can be placed on the page in a vertical format called the report form (Exhibit 3–3).

Note that the balance sheet is a "financial snapshot" of a company. Like any snapshot, it only shows what existed on the day it was taken. It is not a valid representation of the day before it was taken, nor the day after. What it shows is that on the day the financial snapshot was taken, these are the assets the company possessed and here is who had claim to those assets. Balance sheets are prepared by most businesses at the end of each month.

Exhibit 3–2
Account Form of the
Balance Sheet

BARTON ENTERPRISES
Balance Sheet
December 31, 2004

Assets:		Liabilities:		
	XXX		XXX	
	XXX		XX	XXXX
	XX			
	XX	Owners' Equity:		
	XX			XXX
Total Assets	XXXXX	Total Liabilities and Owners' Equity		XXXXX

THESE TWO AMOUNTS ARE EQUAL

Exhibit 3–3
Report Form of the
Balance Sheet

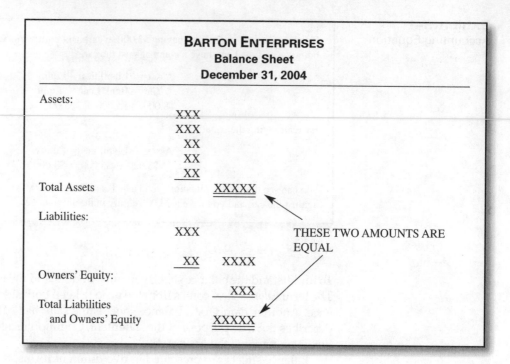

BARTON ENTERPRISES
Balance Sheet
December 31, 2004

Assets:

                                    XXX
                                    XXX
                                    XX
                                    XX
                                    XX

Total Assets   XXXXX

Liabilities:

                                    XXX   THESE TWO AMOUNTS ARE EQUAL

                                    XX   XXXX

Owners' Equity:

                                        XXX

Total Liabilities
  and Owners' Equity   XXXXX

STARTING A BUSINESS—INVESTMENTS BY OWNERS

Laura wants to begin the operation of her new company. What does she need to do? Starting out BIG may require many things—hiring a secretary and/or other employees, getting a company car, or renting office space. Even if she plans to begin as a one-person operation, she has many things to consider, such as having stationery and/or business cards printed, and insurance to protect the company in case of lawsuits.

Even the smallest company has start-up costs. Therefore, Laura's new operation needs cash! Normally, the entrepreneur's first task in starting a new company is obtaining the cash to get underway. The owner is the most logical source for this initial funding. As we develop the balance sheet in this chapter, we will assume that the new company will be initially financed with cash from owners.

Recall the three major forms of business organization in Chapter 1: proprietorships, partnerships, and corporations. Each form requires a slightly different presentation of the initial financing of a new company.

Balance Sheet for a Proprietorship

A proprietorship, a business entity with only one owner, keeps track of only one owner's equity. If Laura's proprietorship began operations on January 1, 2004, with an owner's investment of $10,000 cash, her company's first balance sheet would look like Exhibit 3–4.

Notice that the business (accounting) equation still holds true:

$$\text{ASSETS} = \text{LIABILITIES} + \text{OWNERS' EQUITY}$$
$$\$10,000 = \quad 0 \quad + \$10,000$$

We use a capital account to represent the owner's claim to the assets held by a sole proprietorship. In a proprietorship, there is only one owner; therefore, there will be only one capital account.

Exhibit 3–4
Balance Sheet for a
Proprietorship

LAURA'S BUSINESS
Balance Sheet
January 1, 2004

Assets:		Liabilities:	$ 0
Cash	$10,000		
		Owner's Equity:	
		Laura, Capital	10,000
		Total Liabilities and	
Total Assets	$10,000	Owners' Equity	$10,000

Balance Sheet for a Partnership

Partnerships, you recall, are organized like proprietorships, except that they have more than one owner. Assume that two partners, Laura and Stephanie, start the new company. If Laura invests $6,000 and Stephanie invests $4,000 to begin operations, the partnership's first balance sheet would look like Exhibit 3–5.

Compare the balance sheet for this partnership with that for the proprietorship (Exhibit 3–4). Notice that the total assets, $10,000 in cash, are the same. Total owners' equity ($10,000) is also the same. The only difference is that we must keep track of each partner's claim to the assets in a separate capital account.

In our example, one partner—Laura—provided 60 percent of the beginning capital ($6,000/$10,000 = 60 percent) and the other partner—Stephanie—provided 40 percent of the initial capital ($4,000/$10,000 = 40 percent). The proportional size of a partner's initial investment is generally reflected by the proportional size of the beginning balance in the partner's capital account.

Partners can construct partnership agreements that are simple or complex, but as long as the partners agree and understand clearly how their claims to the assets of the company (their capital balances) are being calculated, they can adopt any rules.

Balance Sheet for a Corporation

A corporation is a legal entity separate and apart from its owners. That characteristic sets it apart from proprietorships and partnerships. In Canada, companies can become incorporated under either federal or provincial laws. If a company is incorporating under federal law, the relevant legislation can be found in the *Canada*

Exhibit 3–5
Balance Sheet for a
Partnership

LAURA AND STEPHANIE'S BUSINESS
Balance Sheet
January 1, 2004

Assets:		Liabilities:		$ 0
Cash	$10,000			
		Owners' Equity:		
		Laura, Capital	$6,000	
		Stephanie, Capital	4,000	
		Total Owners' Equity		10,000
Total Assets	$10,000	Total Liabilities and		
		Owners' Equity		$10,000

Business Corporations Act. This Act requires companies to file articles of incorporation with the Corporations Directorate of Industry Canada.

The articles must include (1) basic information about the corporation and its purpose; (2) details concerning the types of shares of stock to be issued; and (3) the names of the individuals responsible for the corporation.

If the federal or provincial government agency approves the application, it issues a charter that entitles the corporation to begin operations. The incorporators then meet to formulate the corporate *bylaws.* These bylaws serve as basic rules for management to use in conducting the corporation's business. Next, the incorporators raise capital by issuing shares, thereby exchanging ownership interests in the corporation for cash. Once shares have been issued, the corporation has shareholders who elect a board of directors. The directors meet to appoint a president and such other officers as they deem necessary to manage the company.

CORPORATE ORGANIZATIONAL STRUCTURE

In the preceding section, we referred to several groups of people within the structure of the corporate form. Because these groups are critical to the successful operation of a corporation, we will now cover each of them in greater detail.

The Shareholders

The shareholders own the corporation. They provide cash or other assets to the corporation in exchange for ownership shares in the company. In most corporations, the shareholders are not involved in the daily management of the company, unless they have been elected to the board of directors or have been appointed as officers or managers.

When shareholders invest in the corporation they receive a *share certificate,* a legal document providing evidence of ownership and containing the provisions of the share ownership agreement. The shareholders usually meet once a year to elect members of the board of directors and conduct other business important to the corporation.

Board of Directors

The board of directors has ultimate responsibility for managing the corporation. In practice, however, most boards restrict themselves to formulating very broad corporate policy and appointing officers to conduct the corporation's daily operations. The board serves as a link between the shareholders and the officers of the company. If the officers are not managing the corporation in the best interests of the shareholders, the board of directors, acting on behalf of the shareholders, can replace the officers. The board of directors elects a chairperson, who can also serve as the corporate president.

Corporate Officers

A corporation's *chief executive officer (CEO)* normally is the corporate president (and sometimes concurrently the chairperson of the board of directors). The CEO is responsible for all activities of the company. In addition to the president, most corporations have one or more vice presidents who are responsible for specific functions of the company, such as marketing, finance, and production. Many corporations name a *chief financial officer (CFO)*, who directs the corporation's financial affairs, and a *chief operating officer (COO)*, who may work closely with the president to direct the daily operations of the company.

Other corporate officer positions include the *controller*, who is responsible for all accounting functions; the *treasurer*, who is responsible for managing the company's cash; and the *corporate secretary*, who maintains the minutes of the board of directors' and shareholders' meetings and may also represent the company in legal proceedings.

Exhibit 3–6 illustrates the relationship among the various groups in the corporate structure.

Very small corporations with only a few shareholders operate more like sole proprietorships and partnerships. The CEO may be the chairperson of the board of directors, president, and sole shareholder, and may empty the garbage cans at the end of the day. Any business may assume the corporate form providing it meets certain legal requirements of the province in which it operates. Although we may focus on larger, publicly held corporations in annual report projects, the concepts apply to corporations of any size.

 Discussion Questions

3–3. For many Canadian companies, the CEO is also the chairman of the board of directors. In light of our discussion of the functions of corporate officers and the board of directors, express your views concerning this information. Does this dual role present any conflict of interest? Support your view with specific reasons.

3–4. In many other countries there is less likelihood of a CEO also serving as the chairman of the board. Why do you think there is such a difference in this practice between Canada and other countries? Does this new information affect your response to Discussion Question 3–3?

Exhibit 3–6
An Example of
Corporate Structure

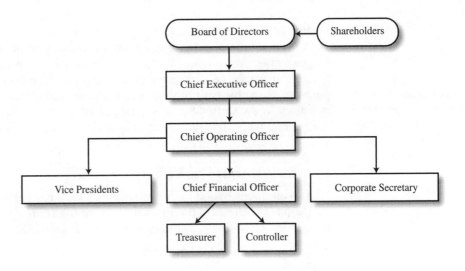

CORPORATE CAPITAL STRUCTURE

authorized shares The maximum number of shares a corporation has been given permission to issue under its corporate charter.

issued shares Shares that have been distributed to the owners of the corporation in exchange for cash or other assets.

outstanding shares Shares actually held by shareholders. The number may be different than that for issued shares because a corporation may reacquire its own shares.

contributed capital Total amount invested in a corporation by its shareholders.

retained earnings The sum of all earnings of a corporation since inception minus the amount of dividends declared.

dividends A distribution of earnings from a corporation to its owners. Dividends are most commonly distributed in the form of cash.

common share A share of ownership in a corporation. Each share represents one vote in the election of the board of directors and other pertinent corporate matters.

par value (for shares) An arbitrary amount assigned to each share by the incorporators at the time of incorporation.

As part of the formal application to create a corporation, the incorporators must include details of their plans to sell shares. They request the authority to issue (sell) a certain number of shares. **Authorized shares** are the maximum number of shares that can legally be issued under the corporate charter. In most jurisdictions, the maximum number of authorized shares can be unlimited. The shares do not exist until they are issued, however, and ownership in the corporation is based on outstanding, not authorized, shares. **Issued shares** refer to the number of shares already distributed to shareholders in exchange for cash or other assets. **Outstanding shares** refer to the number of shares currently being held by shareholders. In many instances, issued shares and outstanding shares will be the same number.

The equity of a corporation is called *shareholders' equity* (instead of owner's equity as in a proprietorship). In the corporate form, the equity of the shareholders is the excess of assets over liabilities, just as it is for proprietorships and partnerships. There are, however, some differences in the way equity items are classified on the balance sheet.

In the corporate form, the owners' capital accounts are replaced by common share accounts. Corporation laws require shareholders' equity to be divided into the portion invested by the owners and the portion earned by the company and retained in the corporation. Amounts received by the corporation in exchange for shares are called **contributed capital**. A classification called **retained earnings** is used to reflect earnings kept in the company and not distributed to the owners in the form of **dividends.** Total shareholders' equity is a combination of contributed capital and retained earnings.

Because most corporations have many shareholders, some into the thousands or millions, the individual ownership interests of each shareholder are not disclosed on the face of the balance sheet. Instead, only totals of the ownership interests represented by each class of share are shown. The two basic classes of shares are common shares and preferred shares.

Common Shares

Common shares are the voting shares of the corporation. Each share represents an equal share in the ownership of the corporation; therefore, the shareholders' equity portion of a corporate balance sheet will show information about common shares.

Common shares may or may not have a par value. Par value shares are no longer issued in Canada but they still exist for some companies in the United States. **Par value** is an arbitrary dollar amount placed on the shares by the incorporators. Par value has nothing to do with the market value of the shares. Most corporations in the United States set the par value of their shares considerably below their actual value. It is not unusual to see par values of $1 per share or even lower.

Shares Without Par Value

Almost all shares issued in Canada do not have a par value. Choosing to issue such shares has no effect on the market value of the shares. Shares without par value have at least two distinct advantages over par value shares:

- Accounting for share transactions is less complicated than it is for par value shares.

- There is no confusion as to the amount received from the sale of the shares. The relevant information is what shareholders were willing to pay for the shares; an arbitrary par value may mislead some investors.

To see what issuing common shares involves, assume that Laura selected the corporate form for her new company and the Laura Corporation Limited began operations on January 1, 2004, by issuing (selling) 2,000 shares for $5 per share. The business receives $10,000 in cash, so assets increase by that amount. The transaction also affects the other side of the accounting equation in shareholders' equity. The entire $10,000 proceeds from the sale of the shares would be classified as common shares and the balance sheet immediately after the sale would look like Exhibit 3–7.

Exhibit 3–7
Balance Sheet for a
Corporation That
Issued Common Shares
Without Par Value

LAURA CORPORATION LIMITED			
Balance Sheet			
January 1, 2004			
Assets:		Liabilities:	$ 0
Cash	$10,000		
		Shareholders' Equity:	
		Common Shares	$10,000
		Total Shareholders' Equity	10,000
		Total Liabilities and	
Total Assets	$10,000	Shareholders' Equity	$10,000

Understand what this balance sheet can and cannot tell you. The $10,000 shown as common shares is the par value of the common shares multiplied by the number of shares issued by the corporation. What is the value of those shares today? The answer to that question cannot be found on the balance sheet. Amounts shown on the corporate financial statements are intended to provide information about the results of past activities of the corporation—not the current market values of shares already issued to shareholders.

Shares With Par Value

Suppose Laura Corporation Limited began operations in the United States on January 1, 2004, by issuing (selling) 2,000 shares of its $1 par value shares for $5 per share. The business receives a total of $10,000 cash, so assets increase by that amount. Again, the transaction also affects the other side of the accounting equation in shareholders' equity. Only the par value of the share multiplied by the number of shares issued can be classified as common shares. In the case of Laura Corporation Limited, that would be $2,000 (2,000 shares × $1 par value). We classify the remaining $8,000 ($10,000 cash received less the $2,000 classified as common shares) on the balance sheet as **contributed surplus**. A balance sheet prepared immediately after the sale of the shares would look like Exhibit 3–8.

Like Exhibit 3–7, this balance sheet can tell us how much was received from the sale of the shares, but it does not tell us about the current market value of the shares.

contributed surplus The excess paid by shareholders for shares over the par value of the shares. Contributed surplus can also arise from increases in equity arising from the cancellation of shares.

LAURA CORPORATION LIMITED			
Balance Sheet			
January 1, 2004			

Assets:		Liabilities:		$ 0
Cash	$10,000			
		Shareholders' Equity:		
		Common Shares	$2,000	
		Contributed Surplus	8,000	
		Total Shareholders' Equity		10,000
		Total Liabilities and		
Total Assets	$10,000	Shareholders' Equity		$10,000

 Discussion Question

3–5. If the balance sheet of a corporation does not show the current market value of the shares, where do you think an investor could find this information?

Regardless of whether the shares have a par value, investors buy a lot of common shares. When they do so, they should accept the risk willingly in exchange for the rewards they may earn. The major risks of common share investments are:

1. risk of loss of investment; and
2. risk of no dividends, small dividends, or unstable dividends.

The rewards that investors seek with common shares are:

1. increase in market price of common shares (capital appreciation);
2. increase in or steady growth in the amount of dividends paid; and
3. a voice in the direction of the company.

Investors who buy common shares seek different opportunities and accept different risks from those who buy preferred shares.

Preferred Shares

preferred shares A share of ownership in a corporation that has preference over common shares as to dividends and as to assets upon liquidation of the corporation. Usually preferred shares do not have voting rights.

Preferred shares have certain preference features over common shares. Although it is extremely rare for preferred shareholders to have voting rights, they receive other types of benefits, outlined in the share agreement. Two benefits of ownership normally found in preferred share agreements are:

- Owners of preferred shares must receive a dividend before any dividend is paid to owners of common shares.
- In the event of a corporation's liquidation, preferred shareholders receive a distribution of assets before any assets can be distributed to common shareholders. Liquidation refers to the process of going out of business: The corporation is shut down, all assets are sold, and all liabilities are settled.

Preferred shares usually pay dividends. The dividend rate for a preferred share could be based on a percentage of the stated value of the share or it could be based on a fixed dollar amount per year for each share. For example, The Thomson

Corporation has issued preferred shares (called Series II preference shares) with a stated value of $25. The dividend rate on these shares is based on 70% of the prime lending rate of the Company's bank. This rate is then applied to the stated value to determine the amount of the dividend to be paid. Enbridge Corporation, on the other hand, has a fixed dividend rate of $1.375 for each Series A 5.5% preferred share. This fixed amount is exactly 5.5% of the stated value of each preferred share, which is $25.

Investors purchase preferred shares primarily to receive the dividend. Because, in most cases, the dividend amount will not change from year to year, the price of a preferred share will fluctuate little over time. If the price does change, it is usually in response to changes in interest rates. This type of an investment appeals to conservative investors who want to receive a stable inflow of dividend income.

To illustrate how preferred shares are issued, let's assume that Laura Corporation Limited, in addition to the common shares it issued as described in our previous discussion, issued (sold) 50 preferred shares for $105 per share on January 1, 2004. Then the amount the business received from the sale of preferred shares would be $5,250 (50 preferred shares × $105 = $5,250). The corporation's total contributed capital is $15,250 ($5,250 from the sale of preferred shares and $10,000 from the sale of common shares). A balance sheet prepared immediately after the sale of the two classes of shares would look like Exhibit 3–9.

Exhibit 3–9
Balance Sheet for a Corporation That Issued Preferred and Common Shares

LAURA CORPORATION LIMITED			
Balance Sheet			
January 1, 2004			
Assets:		Liabilities:	$ 0
Cash	$15,250	Shareholders' Equity:	
		Preferred Shares	$ 5,250
		Common Shares	10,000
		Total Shareholders' Equity	15,250
		Total Liabilities and	
Total Assets	$15,250	Shareholders' Equity	$15,250

Again, the balance sheet reveals the amounts received for issuing each class of shares ($10,000 for common and $5,250 for preferred), but the current market value of the shares is not shown.

The following information is a portion of the December 31, 2002, balance sheet of Earhart Supply Ltd. Look at it carefully, and then try to answer the following questions.

Common shares, 10,000 shares authorized,
5,000 shares issued $500,000

1. What was the total amount the corporation received for the sale of its shares?
2. What was the average selling price per share?
3. If the corporation wanted to sell all the shares it could possibly sell, how many more shares could it offer for sale?
4. If all the shares mentioned in question 3 were sold, how much money would the corporation receive?

Try to reason through each question, using what you have learned about shares from reading this chapter, before you look at the answers. Do not give up too easily! Here are the answers.

1. In total, the corporation received $500,000 for its shares.

2. If the corporation received a total of $500,000 from the sale of its shares, the average selling price was $100.

$$(\$500,000 / 5,000 \text{ shares} = \$100 \text{ per share})$$

3. The corporation has been authorized to sell up to 10,000 shares. If 5,000 shares have already been issued, an additional 5,000 shares could be sold.

4. Based solely on the information provided, there is no way to determine the current market value of the shares and, therefore, no way to determine how much money the corporation would receive. If the shares are traded on a public stock exchange, the current selling price is common knowledge. Business publications and the business sections of many daily newspapers publish share prices daily. We will provide more information about the trading of shares in the rest of this chapter.

 Discussion Question

3–6. If you were setting up a new corporation, would you issue common shares, or common shares and preferred shares? Why?

THE STOCK MARKET

In Chapter 1, we learned about the regulation of share sales on Canada's largest stock exchange, the Toronto Stock Exchange (TSX) by the Ontario Securities Commission (OSC). Regulation of share sales comes under provincial jurisdiction in Canada. For example, the second-largest stock exchange in Canada, called the TSX Venture Exchange, has its head office in Calgary, with other offices in Vancouver, Winnipeg, Toronto, and Montreal. If a company wants to sell shares in any province or territory in Canada, it must meet the regulations of that province's or territory's securities commission.

In the United States, the Securities and Exchange Commission (SEC), which is a federal agency, regulates share sales. The two largest stock exchanges in the United States are the New York Stock Exchange (NYSE) and the National Association of Securities Dealers' Automated Quotations (NASDAQ). The NYSE has been the major exchange in the United States for decades, but the NASDAQ has gained prominence in recent years because of the large number of technology companies that have listed their shares on that exchange. Many companies have listings on more than one exchange, and several Canadian companies are listed on both the TSX and the NYSE.

When a company lists its shares to be traded on public exchanges like those noted above, the corporation is considered to be a *public* corporation. The shares of a corporation, however, do not have to be traded in this manner. Shares can be sold privately between individual investors without the use of a stock exchange. Corporations whose shares trade in this way are known as *private* corporations.

Primary and Secondary Markets

When a corporation (such as Laura Corporation Limited) desires to raise additional capital (money) by selling shares, it makes what is referred to as a *share offer-*

ing. A share offering gives investors the opportunity to purchase ownership shares in the company. When a company offers shares to the general public for the first time, it is called an *initial public offering (IPO)*. The company announces the offering in various business publications, outlining the number of shares being offered and the anticipated selling price. If investors are interested in purchasing shares, the company can sell its shares and raise the money it needs.

Although a company can market its shares directly to the public, most offerings are made through investment bankers. **Investment bankers,** also called **underwriters,** act as intermediaries between the company issuing the shares and the investors who ultimately purchase those shares. An investment banker purchases all the shares being offered, then resells the shares to other investors (for a higher price). Some well-known Canadian underwriters include RBC Dominion Securities, TD Securities, CIBC World Markets, Scotia Capital, and BMO Nesbitt Burns. Some larger international underwriters, such as Merrill Lynch, Goldman Sachs, and Salomon Smith Barney, also operate in Canada.

What we have just described is known as the **primary stock market.** Primary means first or initial in this instance, not main or most important. Earlier in the chapter we illustrated the issuing (sale) of shares for Laura Corporation Limited and how the sale of those shares was reflected on the company's balance sheet. That illustration showed the primary or initial sale of the shares.

After a company has initially sold shares, all further sales of those shares take place in the **secondary stock market.** The company itself receives no money from the sale of its shares in the secondary market. It needs to be notified, of course, when shares are sold by one investor to another, because it must know to whom it should send dividend payments, important notices, and annual reports. But the company itself is not directly involved in the trading of its shares in the secondary market.

The daily reports we hear about fluctuations in the overall stock market refer to the trading of previously issued shares in the secondary stock market. Whether you someday own a corporation, work for one, or invest your money in one, you will find that a basic understanding of corporate structure and the operation of the stock market is quite valuable.

How Stock Prices Are Quoted

Stock market exchanges report the results of trading each day that the market is open. Reports differ depending upon the source, but often contain the following information:

- ticker symbol for each share (an abbreviation of the company name)
- dividends
- price earnings ratio
- number of shares traded during the day (volume)
- closing price for the day
- change from the closing price of the previous trading day

At the close of the week, share reports often indicate additional information such as the high and low price for the year.

The following depicts a typical daily stock market report:

Stock	Ticker	Dividend	PE	Volume	Close	Change
Manulife	MFC	0.72	12.6	25608	36.60	+0.49
Clarica	CLI	.76	17.3	1762	27.00	−0.14
Mitel pf	.....	2.00	—	2	25.75	−0.62
Molson A	MOL	.72	21.7	702	50.90	+0.21
Nortel	NT	.07	—	127574	8.77	−0.53

investment bankers
Intermediaries between the corporation issuing shares and the investors who ultimately purchase the shares. Also called *underwriters*.

underwriters Professionals in the field of investment banking. Also called *investment bankers*.

primary stock market
The business activity involved in the initial issue of shares from a corporation.

secondary stock market
The business activity focusing on trades of shares among investors subsequent to the initial issue.

Remember to identify the information contained in each column by referring to a legend in the report. For this report the columns (left to right) represent:

Ticker symbol
Latest dividend per share
PE = the price earnings ratio
Volume = the number of shares sold, expressed in hundreds
Close = the closing price sold
Change = the change in the closing price from the prior trading day

The report above lists share prices for Mitel preferred shares and common shares for the other companies. Notice that the preferred shares pay out a larger dividend and have a lower volume of trading. The price earnings ratio measures the relationship between the share price and the net income or earnings per common share (this is why the Mitel preferred share does not have a PE listed). For example, if a company has $1,000,000 of net income and 1,000,000 common shares outstanding, the earnings per share would be $1 per share. If the share trades at a price of $20 per share, the price earnings ratio is 20. The higher the ratio, the more expensive the share is relative to its earnings per share. If a company does not have any earnings (like Nortel), it cannot have a price earnings ratio value. Celestica has the highest price earnings ratio. One could conclude that this is because Celestica is expected to grow faster than the other companies listed and that the high price earnings ratio value is justified. On the other hand, some investors may believe that the Celestica share price is too high relative to its earnings and consider the shares too expensive. The larger well-known companies such as Nortel will typically have a higher volume of shares trading each day. For the day shown above, Celestica shares fell the most both in terms of the absolute price change and also in terms of the percentage of its share price.

Share indexes are used to understand how the stock market as a whole is performing. Share indexes track the daily price movement of a group of shares. The most famous index is the Dow Jones Industrial Average, which tracks the movement in the price of 30 major corporations in the United States. In Canada, the most used index is the Standard & Poors Toronto Stock Exchange Composite (S&P/TSX Composite), which tracks the movement of major Canadian corporations that meet specific criteria (currently, 227 corporations make up the index). In addition to these, there are other indexes that track the performance of major shares within a particular industry, and there are numerous indexes in use for all of the stock markets that operate throughout the world.

 Discussion Question

3–7. Because of the internet, investors are now able to receive information about a company's share performance more readily. They can also access information, such as press releases about a company, within minutes of this information becoming public. Investors are now able to buy and sell shares using the Internet and discount brokerage services, thus reducing the commissions paid for share purchases and sales. Because of these developments, the average holding period for a share has declined from several years to several months. Some experts believe we are no longer a nation of investors, but rather a nation of speculators. What do you think that statement means? What influence do you think this shorter-term ownership is having on the way companies are run?

SUMMARY

The balance sheet is a financial tool that provides information about the present financial position of an entity. This financial statement shows the relationship of three accounting elements: assets, liabilities, and owners' equity. This relationship is known as the accounting equation or business equation:

$$\text{ASSETS} = \text{LIABILITIES} + \text{OWNERS' EQUITY}$$

Basically, assets are what the company owns, liabilities are what the company owes to outsiders, and owners' equity is what is left when liabilities are subtracted from assets—the residual interest claims of the owners. Regardless of the type of business, the balance sheet shows the relationship among the company's assets, liabilities, and owners' equity.

Generally, the owner(s) of a new company must acquire first the cash needed to begin operations. Most often, this cash comes from the owner or owners of the company. The balance sheet for each type of business organization presents the results of this investment by owners in a slightly different way. Proprietorships have a single capital account, representing the ownership interest of the sole proprietor. Partnerships generally show a separate capital account for each partner, because their levels of ownership interest may vary. Corporations are legal entities owned by many shareholders; therefore, ownership interests are shown in share capital and contributed surplus accounts.

Because it is a separate legal entity, a corporation has a more complex organizational structure than either of the other two business forms. Corporate shareholders elect a board of directors to oversee the management of the corporation. The board, however, usually restricts itself to setting broad corporate policy; it appoints officers to conduct the daily affairs of the corporation. Corporate officers normally consist of a chief executive officer (usually the president), one or more vice presidents, a controller, a treasurer, and a corporate secretary.

Corporations may issue both common shares and preferred shares. Common shares have voting rights, and the common shareholders are the residual owners of the business. Common shares are almost always issued without a par value, although common shares of United States' corporations may have a par value. Preferred shares are usually nonvoting shares that enjoy two preferences over common shares: Dividends (which are usually based on a fixed amount per share or some percentage of the stated value) are paid first to preferred shareholders, and preferred shareholders have prior claim to net assets if the corporation is liquidated.

Corporate capital (shareholders' equity) is classified by source: contributed capital and earned capital (retained earnings). Contributed capital represents the cash or other assets acquired by the company from the owners, generally through the sale of shares. Retained earnings represents the amount of earnings held in the business rather than distributed to the owners in the form of dividends. For a number of reasons, a corporation might reacquire shares it previously issued. These shares may be cancelled or, for companies in the United States, held for resale in treasury. Treasury shares are still considered issued shares, but are no longer considered outstanding; they are shown on the balance sheet as a reduction of shareholders' equity. Treasury shares are not common in Canada.

The balance sheet is a representation of the financial position of the business on a particular date. The current market value of the corporation's shares cannot be determined from its balance sheet. Rather, the balance sheet provides information about how much was received by the corporation for the shares when they were originally issued.

Corporations initially issue shares in the primary stock market, either to individuals or to an investment banker (or underwriter), who resells the shares to individual investors. Secondary stock market activity includes all subsequent trading of the shares. Although the corporation does not receive money from trades in the secondary market, since these trades determine the market value of the shares, they are certainly important to the corporation. Activity in both the primary and secondary stock markets is regulated by provincial commissions such as the Ontario Securities Commission (OSC) or the Alberta Securities Commission (ASC).

KEY TERMS

assets, p. 66
authorized shares, p. 72
balance sheet, p. 65
common share, p. 72
contributed capital, p. 72
contributed surplus, p. 73
dividends, p. 72
earned equity, p. 66
equity, p. 66
investment bankers, p. 77

investments by owners, p. 66
issued shares, p. 72
liabilities, p. 66
outstanding shares, p. 72
par value (for shares), p. 72
preferred shares, p. 74
primary stock market, p. 77
retained earnings, p. 72
secondary stock market, p. 77
underwriters, p. 77

REVIEW THE FACTS

1. List and define the three accounting elements that are components of the balance sheet.
2. Describe the two sources from which a company builds equity.
3. State the business or accounting equation.
4. What is a more formal and descriptive name for the balance sheet?
5. Name and describe the two formats of the balance sheet.
6. How does the balance sheet for a proprietorship differ from that for a partnership?
7. In what ways does a shareholder of a corporation differ from a partner in a partnership?
8. Explain the differences among authorized, issued, and outstanding shares.
9. Name and describe the two major components of shareholders' equity.
10. What are the two major classes of shares and how do they differ?
11. What is meant by the par value of shares and what significance does it have?
12. Explain what a stock exchange and a share offering are.
13. What is the role of underwriters or investment bankers?
14. Distinguish between the primary stock market and the secondary stock market.
15. What type of organization is the Ontario Securities Commission (OSC) and what is its function?

Apply What You Have Learned

LO 1: Accounting Equation

1. a. Write the basic accounting equation.

   b. Define each element of the equation in your own words.

   c. Provide examples of each element of the basic accounting equation.

LO 1: Accounting Equation

2. Presented below is a list of three accounting elements, followed by partial definitions of those items in scrambled order:

  a. Assets   **b.** Liabilities   **c.** Equity

  1. _____ Debts of the company
  2. _____ Probable future economic benefits
  3. _____ "Things" of value a company has
  4. _____ The residual interest in the assets of an entity that remains after deducting its liabilities
  5. _____ Probable future sacrifices of economic benefits
  6. _____ What the company owes
  7. _____ What the company has less what it owes
  8. _____ The owner's interest in the company

REQUIRED:
For each partial definition, identify the element (a, b, or c) to which it refers.

LO 1: Accounting Equation

3. Presented below is a list of three accounting elements, followed by list of items in scrambled order:

  a. Assets   **b.** Liabilities   **c.** Equity

  1. _____ Cash
  2. _____ Automobile
  3. _____ Bonds payable
  4. _____ Land
  5. _____ Common shares
  6. _____ Retained earnings
  7. _____ Notes payable
  8. _____ Withdrawals
  9. _____ Partners' capital
  10. _____ Preferred shares

REQUIRED:
For each item in the list, identify the element (a, b, or c) to which it refers.

LO 1: Balance Sheet Terminology and Format

4. Examine the following balance sheet:

KAREN BEAN ENTERPRISES
Balance Sheet
For the Year Ended December 31, 2004

Assets		Liabilities and Owner's Equity	
Land	$120,000	Cash	$ 20,000
Less: Note Payable	40,000	Common Shares	90,000
		Retained Earnings	10,000
Total Assets	$ 80,000	Total Liabilities and Owner's Equity	$120,000

REQUIRED:

a. List the errors in the balance sheet.

b. Prepare a corrected balance sheet.

LO 1: Balance Sheet Terminology and Format

5. Examine the following balance sheet:

L. STALLWORTH, LTD.
Balance Sheet
November 31, 2004

Assets		Liabilities and Owner's Equity	
Equipment	$50,000	Note Payable	$20,000
Cash	20,000	Stallworth, Capital	40,000
		Retained Earnings	10,000
Total Assets	$70,000	Total Liabilities and Owner's Equity	$70,000

REQUIRED:

a. List the errors in the balance sheet.

b. Prepare a corrected balance sheet.

LO 1: Balance Sheet Terminology and Format

6. Examine the following balance sheet:

SWEET CORPORATION LTD.
Balance Sheet
For the Year Ended December 31, 2004

Assets		Liabilities and Owners' Equity	
Cash	$120,000	Note Payable	$30,000
Sweet Capital	20,000		
Barnes Capital	40,000	Retained Earnings	30,000
Total Assets	$180,000	Total Liabilities and Owner's Equity	$60,000

REQUIRED:

a. List the errors in the balance sheet.

b. Prepare a corrected balance sheet.

LO 2: Financial Position

7. The following balance sheet of Gerner Enterprises was compiled shortly after Gerner started his business:

GERNER ENTERPRISES
Balance Sheet
October 1, 2004

Assets		Liabilities and Owner's Equity	
Cash	$100,000	Note Payable—Metro Bank	$ 50,000
Land	50,000	Graham Gerner, Capital	100,000
Total Assets	$150,000	Total Liabilities and Equity	$150,000

REQUIRED:
a. Write a description of what Gerner did financially to start his business based on the information provided in the balance sheet.
b. What type of business organization is Gerner Enterprises?

LO 2: Financial Position

8. The following balance sheet of Susan Dick and Associates was compiled at the end of its first year of operations:

SUSAN DICK AND ASSOCIATES
Balance Sheet
December 31, 2004

Assets		Liabilities and Owners' Equity	
Cash	$40,000	Note Payable—Central Bank	$10,000
Land	20,000	Susan Dick, Capital	25,000
		Julie Pham, Capital	25,000
Total Assets	$60,000	Total Liabilities and Equity	$60,000

REQUIRED:
a. Write a description of what this balance sheet tells you about the financial position of the company.
b. What type of business organization is Susan Dick and Associates?
c. From the information provided, can you determine how much profit the company made in the first year?
d. From the information provided, can you determine how profits are split?

LO 2: Financial Position

9. The balance sheet below was compiled for Quynh Vu Limited at the end of its first year of operations:

QUYNH VU LIMITED
Balance Sheet
December 31, 2004

Assets		Liabilities and Shareholder's Equity	
Cash	$120,000	Note Payable—Sooner Bank	$ 20,000
		Common Shares	40,000
		Retained Earnings	60,000
		Total Liabilities and	
Total Assets	$120,000	Shareholder's Equity	$120,000

REQUIRED:

a. Write a description of what this balance sheet tells you about the financial position of the company.

b. What type of business organization is Quynh Vu Limited?

c. From the information provided, can you determine how much profit the company made in its first year?

d. How many shareholders does Quynh Vu Limited have?

e. How many shares did Quynh Vu Limited sell and what was the selling price?

LO 3: Balance Sheets for Different Types of Business Organizations

10. On January 2, 2004, Randy Peoples started an appliance repair business.

REQUIRED:

a. Prepare a balance sheet as of January 2, 2004, assuming Randy's company is a sole proprietorship named Randy Peoples Enterprises and that he invested $5,000 cash in the operation.

b. Now assume that the business organized on January 2, 2004, was a partnership started by Randy and his brother, Sandy, which they have named R&S Enterprises. Randy invested $2,000 and Sandy invested $3,000. Prepare a balance sheet as of January 2, 2004, for the partnership to reflect the partners' investment.

c. Now assume that the business organized on January 2, 2004, was a corporation started by Randy and his brother Sandy, which they have named R&S Enterprises, Ltd. Randy invested $2,000 and received 200 common shares. Sandy invested $3,000 and received 300 common shares. Prepare a balance sheet as of January 2, 2004, for the company to reflect the shareholders' investment.

d. Explain why Randy might want to form a partnership rather than a sole proprietorship.

LO 3: Types of Business Organizations

11. On June 2, 2004, Arthur Johnson started a manufacturing business.

REQUIRED:

a. Prepare a balance sheet as of June 2, 2004, assuming Arthur's company is a sole proprietorship named Arthur Johnson Enterprises and that he invested $50,000 cash in the operation.

b. Now assume that the business organized on June 2, 2004, was a partnership started by Arthur and his friend Charles Smith, which they have named A&C Enterprises. Arthur invested $50,000 and Charles invested $30,000. Prepare a balance sheet as of June 2, 2004, for the partnership to reflect the partners' investment.

c. Now assume that the business organized on June 2, 2004, was a corporation started by Arthur and his friend Charles, which they have named A&C Enterprises, Ltd. Arthur invested $50,000 and received 5,000 common shares. Charles invested $30,000 and received 3,000 common shares. Prepare a balance sheet as of June 2, 2004, for the company to reflect the shareholders' investment.

d. Explain how the balance sheet describes the financial position of the business entity.

LO 3: Types of Business Organizations

12. On July 2, 2004, Fred Berfel started a retail business.

REQUIRED:
a. Prepare a balance sheet as of July 2, 2004, assuming Fred's company is a sole proprietorship named Fred Berfel Enterprises and that he invested $90,000 cash in the operation.
b. Now assume that the business organized on July 2, 2004, was a partnership started by Fred and his father Dan, which they have named F&D Enterprises. Fred invested $40,000 and Dan invested $50,000. Prepare a balance sheet as of July 2, 2004, for the partnership to reflect the partners' investment.
c. Now assume that the business organized on July 2, 2004, was a corporation started by Fred and his father Dan, which they have named F&D Enterprises, Ltd. Fred invested $40,000 and received 4,000 common shares. Dan invested $50,000 and received 5,000 common shares. Prepare a balance sheet as of July 2, 2004, for the company to reflect the shareholders' investment.
d. Describe the advantages of forming a corporation over a partnership.

LO 3: Types of Business Organizations

13. On March 1, 2004, Sandy Sanders started a business.

REQUIRED:
a. Prepare a balance sheet as of March 1, 2004, assuming Sandy's company is a sole proprietorship named Sandy Sanders Enterprises and that he invested $40,000 cash in the operation and a piece of land valued at $5,000.
b. Now assume that the business organized on March 1, 2004, was a partnership started by Sandy and his brother Darryl, which they have named S&D Enterprises. Sandy invested $40,000 cash and a piece of land valued at $10,000, and Darryl invested $30,000 cash. Prepare a balance sheet as of March 1, 2004, for the partnership to reflect the partners' investment.
c. Now assume that the business organized on March 1, 2004, was a corporation started by Sandy and his other brother Darryl, which they have named S&D Enterprises, Inc. Sandy invested $40,000 cash and the piece of land valued at $10,000 and received 5,000 common shares. Darryl invested $30,000 cash and received 3,000 common shares. Prepare a balance sheet as of March 1, 2004, for the company to reflect the shareholders' investment.
d. Describe the advantages of forming a corporation rather than a partnership.

LO 3: Types of Business Organizations

14. The chapter discusses the balance sheet presentations for each of the three forms of business organization. Discuss the similarities and differences in the balance sheets of proprietorships, partnerships, and corporations.

LO 4: Terminology of the Corporate Business Form

15. Presented below is a list of items relating to the corporate form of business, followed by definitions of those items in scrambled order:

a. Incorporators	e. Share certificate
b. Articles of incorporation	f. Board of directors
c. Bylaws	g. Corporate officers
d. Shareholders	h. Market value

1. ___ The group of men and women who have the ultimate responsibility for managing a corporation
2. ___ The owners of a corporation
3. ___ The formal document that is filed with authorities when incorporating
4. ___ The group of men and women who manage the day-to-day operations of a corporation
5. ___ The person or persons who submit a formal application with the appropriate government agencies to form a corporation
6. ___ A legal document providing evidence of ownership in a corporation
7. ___ Rules established to conduct the business of a corporation
8. ___ The amount at which a common share sells

REQUIRED:

Match the letter next to each item on the list with the appropriate definition. Each letter will be used only once.

LO 4:   Terminology of the Corporate Form of Organization

16. a. Identify the various officers of a corporation and describe their individual duties.

   b. Explain the difference between authorized shares, issued shares, and outstanding shares.

LO 4:   Terminology of the Corporate Form of Organization

17. The balance sheet of Ramona Rahill, Inc. (a U.S. corporation) contains the following information in its equity section:

Shareholders' Equity:

Common Shares, 1,000,000 shares authorized, 800,000 shares issued and outstanding	$ 8,800,000
Retained Earnings	2,000,000
Total Shareholders' Equity	$10,800,000

REQUIRED:

 a. How many shares could Ramona Rahill Inc. issue if the board of directors desired to do so?
 b. What is the average price per share at which the corporation sold its shares?
 c. If the board of directors declared a $1.25 per share dividend, how much cash would be required to issue the dividend?
 d. If Ramona Rahill Inc. has distributed $3,500,000 to shareholders since its formation, how much profit has the corporation earned since its formation?

LO 4:   Terminology of the Corporate Form of Organization

18. The following is an excerpt from the equity section of the balance sheet of Richard Corporation:

Shareholders' Equity:

Common Shares, 1,000,000 shares authorized, 800,000 shares issued and 750,000 shares outstanding	$16,000,000
Retained Earnings	9,500,000
Total Shareholders' Equity	$25,500,000

REQUIRED:

a. How many shares could Richard Corporation sell if the board of directors desired to do so?

b. What is the average price per share at which Richard Corporation sold its shares?

c. If the board of directors declared a $2 per share dividend, how much cash would be required to issue the dividend?

d. If Richard has distributed $5,500,000 to shareholders since its formation, how much profit has the corporation earned since its formation?

e. If the board of directors wished to raise $5,000,000, for how much would it have to sell each share if all available shares were sold?

LO 4:   Terminology of the Corporate Form of Organization

19. The following is an excerpt from the equity section of the balance sheet of Luza Corporation:

Shareholders' Equity:

Common Shares, 1,000,000 shares authorized,	
950,000 shares issued and outstanding	$18,000,000
Retained Earnings	9,500,000
Total Shareholders' Equity	$27,500,000

REQUIRED:

a. How many shares could the corporation sell if the board of directors desired to do so?

b. What is the average price per share at which the corporation sold its shares?

c. If the board of directors declared a $1.50 per share dividend, how much cash would be required to issue the dividend?

d. If Luza Corporation has earned $9,500,000 since its formation, how much profit has the corporation distributed to shareholders in the form of dividends since its formation?

e. If the current market price of the shares is $60 per share, how much cash could the board of directors raise if it sold all available shares?

LO 5:   Differences between Common and Preferred Shares

20. A corporation with both preferred shareholders and common shareholders is in the process of liquidating its assets. Identify the group of shareholders who will receive a distribution and explain why.

LO 5:   Differences between Common and Preferred Shares

21. Assume you have $20,000 to invest and you are trying to decide between investing in the preferred shares of Alpha Limited and the common shares of Alpha Limited.

REQUIRED:

a. List and briefly explain at least two reasons why you would invest in the preferred shares rather than the common shares of Alpha Limited.

b. List and briefly explain at least two reasons why you would invest in the common shares rather than the preferred shares of Alpha Limited.

LO 5: Differences between Common and Preferred Shares

22. For each characteristic listed below, determine if the characteristic applies to common share (C), preferred share (P), both (B), or neither (N).

1. _____ Can legally pay a dividend.
2. _____ Pays a pre-established dividend amount.
3. _____ Usually has voting rights.
4. _____ Usually does not have voting rights.
5. _____ Has preference in dividends.
6. _____ Has preference in liquidation.
7. _____ Is preferred by all investors.
8. _____ Represents the residual ownership in the corporation.

LO 5: Differences between Common and Preferred Shares

23. Discuss the characteristics of investors who invest in

a. Common shares
b. Preferred shares

Include in your discussion willingness to take risk, desire for current income, and desire for capital appreciation in addition to other factors.

LO 5, 6, & 8: Share Issuances

24. Klauss Limited began operations in 1972 by issuing 20,000 common shares for $5 per share. The following details provide information about the company's common shares in the years since that time.

1. In 1992, the company issued an additional 50,000 common shares for $15 per share.
2. Klauss Limited shares are traded on the Toronto Stock Exchange (TSX). During an average year, about 25,000 of its common shares are sold by one set of investors to another.
3. On December 31, 2003, Klauss Limited common shares were quoted on the TSX at $38 per share.
4. On December 31, 2004, Klauss Limited common shares were quoted on the TSX at $55 per share.

REQUIRED:

a. Which of the share transactions described above involved the primary stock market and which ones involved the secondary stock market?
b. How much money has Klauss Limited received in total from the sales of its common shares since it was incorporated in 1972?
c. When Klauss Limited prepares its balance sheet as of December 31, 2004, what dollar amount will it show in the shareholders' equity section for common shares?
d. What, if anything, can you infer about Klauss Limited's performance during 2004 from the price of its common shares on December 31, 2003, and December 31, 2004?

LO 5, 6, & 8: Share Issuances

25. Shiner Limited began operations in 1988 by issuing 35,000 common shares for $10 per share. The following details provide information about the company's common shares in the years since that time.

1. In 1992, the company issued an additional 80,000 common shares for $15 per share.
2. Shiner Limited shares are traded on the Toronto Stock Exchange (TSX). During an average year, about 40,000 of its common shares are sold by one set of investors to another.
3. On December 31, 2003, Shiner Limited common shares were quoted on the TSX at $79 per share.
4. On December 31, 2004, Shiner Limited common shares were quoted on the TSX at $45 per share.

REQUIRED:

a. Which of the share transactions described above involved the primary stock market and which ones involved the secondary stock market?
b. How much money has Shiner Limited received in total from the sales of its common shares since it was incorporated in 1988?
c. When Shiner Limited prepares its balance sheet as of December 31, 2004, what dollar amount will it show in the shareholders' equity section for common shares?
d. What, if anything, can you infer about Shiner Limited's performance during 2004 from the price of its common shares on December 31, 2003, and December 31, 2004?

LO 5, 6, & 8: Share Issuances

26. Kooteney Limited began operations in January 1992 by issuing 90,000 common shares for $25 per share and 10,000 shares of its $100 stated value 6% preferred shares. The following details provide information about the company's shares in the years since that time.

1. In January, 1993, the company issued an additional 50,000 common shares for $35 per share and 5,000 preferred shares for $150 per share.
2. Kooteney Limited shares are traded on the Toronto Stock Exchange (TSX). During an average year, about 100,000 shares of its common shares and 6,000 of its preferred shares are sold by one set of investors to another.
3. On December 31, 2003, Kooteney Limited common shares were quoted on the TSX at $55 per share. The preferred shares were quoted at $135 per share.
4. On December 31, 2004, Kooteney Limited common shares were quoted on the TSX at $65 per share. The preferred shares were quoted at $150 per share.

REQUIRED:

a. Which of the share transactions described above involved the primary stock market and which ones involved the secondary stock market?
b. How much money has Kooteney Limited received in total from the sales of its shares since it was incorporated in 1992?
c. When the company prepares its balance sheet as of December 31, 2004, what dollar amount will it show in the shareholders' equity section for common shares and for preferred shares?

d. What is the market value of the company's shares on December 31, 2003, and December 31, 2004?
   e. How much has the company earned in profits since incorporation?
   f. How much has the company paid in dividends to common shareholders and preferred shareholders since incorporation?

LO 5, 6, & 8:   Share Issuances

27. Bennett Limited began operations in 1979 by issuing 40,000 common shares for $10 per share. The following details provide information about the company's shares in the years since that time.

    1. In 1992, the company issued an additional 70,000 common shares for $15 per share.
    2. The company's shares are traded on the Toronto Stock Exchange (TSX). During an average year, about 50,000 of its common shares are sold by one set of investors to another.
    3. On December 31, 2003, Bennett Limited common shares were quoted on the TSX at $56 per share.
    4. On December 31, 2004, Bennett Limited common shares were quoted on the TSX at $35 per share.

REQUIRED:
   a. Which of the share transactions described above involved the primary stock market and which ones involved the secondary stock market?
   b. How much money has Bennett Limited received in total from the sales of its common shares since it was incorporated in 1979?
   c. When Bennett Limited prepares its balance sheet as of December 31, 2004, what dollar amount will it show in the shareholders' equity section for common shares?
   d. What, if anything, can you infer about Bennett Limited's performance during 2004 from the price of its common shares on December 31, 2003, and December 31, 2004?

LO 5 & 6:   Share Issuances

28. Lake Huron Limited began operations on July 10, 2004, by issuing 10,000 common shares and 2,000 preferred shares with a stated value of $100 per share. The common shares sold for $10 per share and the preferred shares sold for $130 per share.

REQUIRED:
Prepare a balance sheet for Lake Huron Limited at July 10, 2004, immediately after the shares were issued.

LO 5 & 6:   Share Issuances

29. Sudbury Sheets Limited began operations on May 5, 2004, by issuing 150,000 common shares and 25,000 preferred shares with a stated value of $100 per share. The common shares sold for $10 per share and the preferred shares sold for $150 per share.

REQUIRED:
Prepare a balance sheet for Sudbury Sheets Limited at May 5, 2004, immediately after the shares were issued.

LO 5 & 6:   Share Issuance

30. Mayes Limited began operations on April 15, 2004, by issuing 200,000 common shares and 20,000 preferred shares with a stated value of $50 per share. The common shares sold for $25 per share and the preferred shares sold for $125 per share.

REQUIRED:

Prepare a balance sheet for Mayes Limited at April 15, 2004, immediately after the shares were issued.

LO 7:   Balance Sheet Information

31. The questions below are based on this selected information from the balance sheet of G. Garretson, Ltd., a company based in Canada.

(Dollars in millions)

	December 31	
	2004	**2003**
Common Shares, 900,000,000 shares authorized; issued at Dec. 31: 2004—671,242,137; 2003—669,847,961	$4,821	$4,744

REQUIRED:

a. What was the average selling price of a common share that had been issued as of December 31, 2003?
b. How many common shares were issued during 2004?
c. What is the maximum number of shares that Garretson could issue during 2005?

FINANCIAL REPORTING CASES

Comprehensive

32. Using the sedar.com web site, obtain the August 2002 financial statements for Shaw Communications Inc.

REQUIRED:

a. What types of shares are reported in the notes to the financial statements?
b. For each type of stock listed, identify the number of shares authorized, the number issued, and the number outstanding for each year presented on the balance sheet.
c. Why might Shaw Communications Inc. issue preferred shares?
d. Write the accounting equation for Shaw Communications Inc. for both years presented in the balance sheet.

ANNUAL REPORT PROJECT

You are now ready to complete Section III (Capital Structure) of the Annual Report Project. Section II (SWOT Analysis) of the Annual Report Project will be completed after Chapters 5 and 6.

33. Section III contains the following information:

   A. List of the total liabilities (be sure you have included all the liabilities, both current and long-term) and the total shareholders' equity for each year presented in your balance sheet.

   B. Comment on how the mix of liabilities and equity relates to or impacts your company. (Hint: Look at the text of the management's discussion and analysis or read the footnotes for information on how the debt may be used.)

   C. List the number of outstanding shares (common and preferred) for each year shown in the report.

   D. List the stock market prices quoted in the annual report.

REQUIRED:

Complete Section III of your project. Turn in one copy to your instructor and retain a clean copy for your final project folder. For group projects, divide the parts equitably among the group members.

4

The Balance Sheet (Continued): Additional Financing

*Y*our small business has done very well. It has generated enough income for you and your spouse to finally have your dream home—with an appropriate mortgage. Yesterday, an employee brought you an idea that may revolutionize your product and give you at least a five-year lead on the competition. That is the good news. The bad news is that it will require at least $5,000,000. After checking with the controller, you discover that you have a $210,000 cash reserve. What are the risks involved in this venture? How should you raise the money? Should you borrow from one bank, issue bonds, or issue more common shares? Which costs the least? What should you do?

Businesses often need more funding than is available through investments by their owners. Additional cash to support day-to-day operations or expansion of the business is often acquired through borrowing. Results of borrowing are reflected on a company's balance sheet.

No matter what organizational form companies take (proprietorship, partnership, corporation), or the type of business (service, merchandise, manufacturing), all companies have one thing in common: Each must obtain capital (money) to support operations. In the long run, a company must finance its activities with the profits from its operations. We call this **internal financing.** However, either when starting out or in a time of expansion, almost all companies find it necessary to obtain capital from sources other than the profits. This is **external financing.** ■

internal financing
Providing funds for the operation of a company through the earnings process of that company.

external financing
Acquiring funds from outside the company. Equity and debt financing are the two major types of external financing.

equity financing
Acquiring funds for business operations by giving up ownership interest in the company. For a corporation, this means issuing capital stock. Equity financing is one type of external financing.

debt financing
Acquiring funds for business operations by borrowing. Debt financing is one type of external financing.

The two external sources of capital are equity financing and debt financing. **Equity financing** offers ownership interest in the company in exchange for the needed cash. Most businesses begin their operations using cash invested by the owners. Chapter 3 illustrated the impact of this initial financing on the balance sheets of proprietorships, partnerships, and corporations. In many cases, however, the owners need more cash than they can raise to get the operation started. Almost all companies, at one time or another, need additional funds from outsiders. To obtain these funds, companies can sell more ownership shares or they can borrow funds. Borrowing funds for business operations is **debt financing.**

Neither a borrower nor a lender be!

—WILLIAM SHAKESPEARE

Although Shakespeare's advice may serve you well in your personal life, many companies could not survive without borrowing. Borrowing and lending have become an integral part of today's business world. In this chapter, you will learn about several different approaches to debt financing. As you will see, financial institutions function as primary lenders. The bond market also serves as a source of debt financing. Companies borrow funds for various reasons. The need for external funding does not indicate a weakness. On the contrary, a company often needs funds because it is growing even faster than expected.

LEARNING OBJECTIVES

After completing your work on this chapter, you should be able to do the following:

1. Describe how banks earn profits.
2. Explain the effects on a company's balance sheet when funds are borrowed from a bank.
3. Distinguish among notes, mortgages, and bonds.
4. Calculate interest payments for notes and bonds.
5. Explain the functions of underwriters in the process of issuing bonds.
6. Describe the effect of market interest rates on bond selling prices.
7. Contrast the operations of the primary and secondary bond markets.
8. Compare and contrast two investment alternatives—equity investment and debt investment.

short-term financing
Financing secured to support an operation's day-to-day activities. Repayment is usually required within three years.

long-term financing
Any financing in which repayment extends beyond three years. This type of financing supports the long-range goals of the company.

The financing requirements of companies fall into two general categories. A company needs short-term financing to run its day-to-day operations and long-term financing to achieve its long-range goals. From a financial market perspective, **short-term financing** is any financing that must be repaid within three years. **Long-term financing** has a repayment period that extends past three years. These definitions do not correspond to the accounting definition of short-term and long-term liabilities, which we will consider in Chapter 9. Several sources provide these two types of financing to businesses.

BORROWING FROM FINANCIAL INSTITUTIONS

consumer borrowing
Loans obtained by individuals to buy homes, cars, or other personal property.

commercial borrowing
The process that businesses go through to obtain financing.

The commercial banking industry has changed dramatically in the past two decades. Banks and credit unions used to provide a narrow range of services to limited customer groups. Today, the banking industry includes all types of financial institutions, which serve a broad range of customers. Financial institutions meet the needs of individuals and companies, creating both consumer and commercial borrowing.

Banks base the classification of a loan on its purpose, not its amount. If the purpose of the loan is personal, to pay for such items as homes, cars, vacations, school tuition, and other personal needs, the loan is classified as **consumer borrowing.** When a company negotiates a loan to finance day-to-day operations or achieve long-term goals, the loan is classified as **commercial borrowing.**

Several distinct types of financial institutions serve consumer and commercial borrowing needs. Some originated to satisfy the need for consumer loans, while others began to meet the financing needs of businesses, though the distinction between consumer lenders and commercial lenders has become somewhat blurred over the past several years.

There are several major types of financial institutions operating in Canada. The most significant of these are the chartered banks. When given a charter, a bank must abide by special federal regulations. In the past, these banks provided traditional banking services, such as accepting deposits, providing chequing services, and making loans. Now, however, banks are performing a vast array of services for their clients because of their involvement with the other types of financial institutions discussed below. Exhibit 4-1 is a list of the five largest Canadian chartered banks.

Credit unions (caisses populaires in Quebec) provide services similar to those of the chartered banks, but unlike banks, they are owned by their members rather than by shareholders.

Another type of financial institution is the trust company. Trust companies were originally established to undertake fiduciary responsibilities involving the administration of assets held in trusts, pension funds, and estates. In recent years, the chartered banks have acquired most of the larger trust companies.

Investment dealers represent another type of financial institution. Known to many as brokerage firms, these are non-depository institutions that assist clients in buying and selling financial securities. The chartered banks have also acquired a number of investment dealers.

Insurance companies provide casualty, property, life, and health insurance to customers. When you buy certain policies, such as whole-life policies, a portion of the insurance premium represents an investment. Consequently, these companies have large pools of such funds.

Exhibit 4–1
The Five Largest Banks in Canada

	2002 Revenues (in $ millions)	2002 Net Earnings (in $ millions)
Royal Bank of Canada	$14,672	$2,762
The Bank of Nova Scotia	14,368	1,797
The Toronto-Dominion Bank	11,751	(76)
Canadian Imperial Bank of Commerce	11,524	653
Bank of Montreal	9,135	1,417

Source: Annual Reports of the Banks Listed

Mutual fund companies sell units in their investment funds to customers. A mutual fund is a large pool of capital that is professionally managed. Managers of these funds will take the monies received from clients and invest them in a range of securities. The growth of money held within these mutual funds has exploded over the past decade. Many banks and trust companies also manage their own mutual funds.

Recent deregulation has now allowed chartered banks and any of the other institutions to perform almost all of the services offered above. The one exception is that chartered banks are not allowed to sell insurance.

This book deals primarily with business and how accounting information is used in making business decisions. Therefore, when we refer to "the bank," we mean a commercial bank.

How Banks Earn Profits

Think back to our discussion of Roy and his shoe store in Chapter 1. To stay in business, Roy must be profitable. He must sell shoes for enough money to recover what the shoes cost him, plus pay all other expenses associated with running his store. Whatever is left after all those costs have been covered is his profit. A bank is a business also, and to stay in business, a bank must be profitable. The majority of a bank's income comes from the interest paid on loans by borrowers.

interest The cost to the borrower of using someone else's money. Also, what can be earned by lending money to someone else.

Interest represents rent paid to use borrowed money. The bank rents money from its depositors and then in turn rents it out to borrowers. Logic dictates that the rent the bank pays (interest expense) must be less than the rent it receives (interest revenue) if it is to be profitable. For example, you open a savings account at the bank by depositing $100. The bank agrees to pay you 5 percent annual interest on the amount you have deposited. If you leave the $100 in the bank for a full year, you will earn $5 interest.

Assume that nine other people did exactly as you did and opened savings accounts at the bank by depositing $100 each. The bank agreed to pay each depositor 5 percent annual interest on the deposits. The bank now has $1,000 ($100 × 10 depositors), and the interest the bank must pay on this $1,000 is $50 ($5 to each of the ten depositors).

The bank can now lend the $1,000 to a borrower. Obviously, it must charge something greater than 5 percent interest on the loan(s) it makes with the $1,000, or it will lose on the exchange. Assume that the bank lends the $1,000 to someone for one year and that person agrees to pay the bank 9 percent annual interest on the loan.

At the end of the year, the person who borrowed the $1,000 repays the loan, plus $90 interest ($1,000 × 9%). After the bank adds $5 to the account of each of the ten depositors, it has earned a gross profit of $40, calculated as follows:

Interest the bank received on the loan	$90
Less the interest paid to the 10 depositors	50
Equals gross profit on the loan	$40

Although this process seems simple enough, there are a number of possible complications. Two complications immediately come to mind.

default A failure to repay a loan as agreed.

1. The person who borrowed the $1,000 may fail to repay the loan. Failure to repay is known as a **default** on the loan.
2. One or more of the ten depositors may decide to not leave their $100 deposit in the bank for the full year.

Discussion Questions

4-1. In addition to the two complications described in the text, what other factors may complicate the process whereby banks earn their profits by making loans?

4-2. What steps would you suggest to the bank to overcome the two complications listed in the text plus the ones you thought of in your response to Discussion Question 4-1?

By the way, the $40 profit we calculated for the bank on the loan does not constitute the bank's real profit. As was the case with Roy selling a pair of shoes to Martin in Chapter 1, the profit we just calculated represents gross profit (see Exhibit 4–2). All other costs involved in running the bank must be deducted before the net profit (real profit) can be calculated.

Exhibit 4–2
How Banks Earn Profits

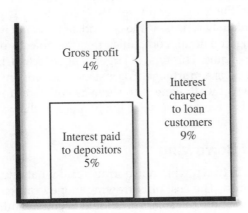

Notes Payable

When a company purchases assets from suppliers, the suppliers will usually issue an invoice that is to be paid within 30 days. Sometimes however, the company may not be able to pay the amount owed within this time period. Sometimes the amount purchased is significant and the supplier wants to receive from the company something that is more secure than simply a promise to pay the invoice when due. In these cases, the supplier will ask the company to sign a promissory note, which will appear in the company's balance sheet as a liability called **note payable**. A note payable differs from an accounts payable because it bears interest, is usually due at a later date, and provides the holder of the note with greater security of collection.

note payable An agreement between a lender and a borrower that creates a liability for the borrower.

A note payable can also be issued in exchange for cash borrowings.

Building upon the Laura Corporation Limited example introduced in Chapter 3, we illustrate the effects of borrowing funds in Exhibit 4-3. The balance sheet information indicates that the company borrowed $1,000 by signing a note payable. This transaction provided the company with $1,000 additional cash, so total assets rose to $11,000. Because the additional asset amount is claimed by someone external to the business, it counts as a liability. Notice that the business equation still holds true:

$$\text{ASSETS} = \text{LIABILITIES} + \text{OWNERS' EQUITY}$$
$$\$11,000 = \$1,000 + \$10,000$$

LAURA CORPORATION LIMITED
Balance Sheet
January 1, 2004

Assets:		Liabilities:		
		Notes Payable	$ 1,000	
Cash	$11,000	Total Liabilities		$1,000
		Shareholders' Equity:		
		Common Shares	$10,000	
		Total Shareholders' Equity		10,000
		Total Liabilities and		
Total Assets	$11,000	Shareholders' Equity		$11,000

promissory note A legal promise to repay a loan.

collateral Something of value that will be forfeited if a borrower fails to make payments as agreed.

mortgage A document that states the agreement between a lender and a borrower who has secured the loan by offering something of value as collateral, usually buildings and property.

A note payable requires the signing of a **promissory note**, a legal "promise to repay." In addition, the lender requires the use of collateral to secure the loan. **Collateral** is something of value that is forfeited to the lender if the borrower fails to make payments as agreed. For example, if you borrow money from a bank to buy a new car, the car generally serves as collateral. If you fail to make the payments, the bank may repossess the car and sell it to get its money back.

By offering collateral, companies may be able to borrow more funds for a greater length of time. This type of larger, longer-term debt that identifies a specific item as collateral is a **mortgage.** For instance, a company can mortgage a piece of property it owns by allowing it to serve as collateral for a loan. In this case, the lender (bank) has the right to seize the property if the borrower defaults.

The Cost of Borrowing

The difference between what one borrows and what one repays is the cost of borrowing or interest. The cost of borrowing money can be determined using information about the note payable. You should become familiar with the terminology used when funds are borrowed. Here's an example:

> Ontario Enterprise Limited borrowed $5,000 on January 2, 2004, by signing an 8 percent, three-year note. The lender requires annual interest payments to be made on the anniversary of the note.

principal In the case of notes and mortgages, the amount of funds actually borrowed.

The rate of interest is always stated as an annual percentage. Therefore, 8 percent refers to the amount of interest the lender requires for a full year, regardless of the loan terms. Interest is based on the amount borrowed, the **principal.** The formula to determine the annual interest amount is:

$$\text{Principal} \times \text{Rate} = \text{Annual Interest}$$

In our example of the Ontario Enterprise Limited note, the amount of interest due each year is calculated as:

$$\text{Principal} \times \text{Rate} = \text{Annual Interest}$$
$$\$5,000 \times 0.08 = \$400$$

Notice that for purposes of calculations, the percentage rates can be converted to decimals. The note terms require the following schedule of payments:

Date	Interest Payments	Principal Payments	Total Payments
January 1, 2005	$ 400		$ 400
January 1, 2006	400		400
January 1, 2007	400	$5,000	5,400
Totals	$1,200	$5,000	$6,200

Remember that the difference between what is borrowed and what is paid back represents the cost of borrowing:

Amount received from the loan	$5,000
Amount repaid	6,200
Cost of borrowing (interest)	$1,200 for the three-year period

The term (length of time between borrowing and repaying) of notes payable varies. If Ontario Enterprise Limited needed to borrow the funds from the bank for only a short time, the note may have been described as a

$5,000, 8%, 3-month note

This terminology suggests that the $5,000 must be repaid three months from the day the funds were borrowed. On that day, Ontario Enterprise Limited would pay the lender the principal ($5,000) and the interest due. Recall that interest rates are stated in annual terms, so 8 percent indicates the amount of interest that would be due if the funds were held for one year. If the funds are held for three months, only a portion of the year's interest would be due.

Now we can use a formula that considers the length of time the funds are held:

$$\text{Principal} \times \text{Rate} \times \text{Time} = \text{Interest}$$
$$P \quad \times \quad R \quad \times \quad T \quad = \quad I$$

The calculation to determine the interest owed by Ontario Enterprise Limited is:

$$P \quad \times \quad R \quad \times \quad T \quad = \quad I$$
$$\$5{,}000 \times 0.08 \times 3/12 = \$100$$

Because the interest rate is annual, the time factor in the calculation is a fraction of the year. If the funds are borrowed for three months, time is represented by 3/12, indicating three of the 12 months in a year. If, however, the note read:

$5,000, 8%, 90-day note

the time factor represents the number of days involved as a proportion of the number of days in a year. When this method is used, the previous calculation could be presented as:

$$\$5{,}000 \times 0.08 \times 90/365 = \$98.63$$

With the advent of personal computers and financial calculators, banks typically use 365 days. When the note specifies months, use the monthly calculation approach. When the note specifies days, use the actual number of days. For example, how many days span the time from December 4 to March 4 in a non–leap year? (Do not count the first day because interest begins on that day.)

December (31 days minus 4 days)	27
January	31
February (non–leap year)	28
March	4
Total days	90

In this case the three-month period equals 90 days. What if we measure March 4 to June 4?

March (31 days minus 4 days)	27
April	30
May	31
June	4
Total days	92

Remember that not all three-month intervals contain the same number of days.

Discussion Questions

4-3. In the example given in the text of the Ontario Enterprise LImited three-month loan, what is the lender's return of investment and return on investment?

Note: The next two Discussion Questions require that you go to the business section of your local newspaper or the web site of a bank and look up current interest rates.

4-4. List the different rates a major bank is paying on various guaranteed investment certificates (GICs). Explain why the bank is offering these various rates.

4-5. What are the current rates banks are charging for mortgages in your area? What are the current credit card rates? Why are there differences between these two rates?

Effective Interest Rate

Lenders write loan terms to conform to the specific needs of the lender or the borrower. Therefore, not all terms are the same for each customer or for all loans made to one customer. Look at the following loan information:

Ontario Enterprise Limited deposited $9,000 as the proceeds (cash received) of a $10,000 discounted loan due one year from today.

discounted or **non-interest-bearing note**   A loan arrangement in which the bank deducts the interest from the proceeds of the loan.

The lender deducted the 10 percent interest on the loan in advance. We call this arrangement whereby a bank deducts the full interest in advance a **discounted note.** Such a note is often referred to as a **non-interesting-bearing note**. This term is a bit misleading, however, because, although the note does not bear explicit interest with a rate stated on the face of the note, it bears implicit interest that, as we see, was deducted in advance. What are the implications of such an action? Return to our analysis model for the cost of borrowing:

Amount received from the loan	$ 9,000
Amount repaid	10,000
Cost of borrowing (interest)	$ 1,000

We used the following formula to calculate the interest for an annual loan:

$$P \times R = I$$

By rearranging the equation, we can solve for the interest rate (R). The principal of the loan should be considered the amount received in the loan process.

$$R = \frac{I}{P} = \frac{\$1,000}{\$9,000} = 11.11\%$$

effective interest rate   The rate of interest actually earned by a lender. This amount will be different from the nominal interest rate if a bond is bought at a discount or premium, or a note is discounted. Also called yield rate or market interest rate.

As you can see, the **effective interest rate** is not the 10 percent quoted by the bank, but 11.11 percent. The act of discounting the note—deducting the interest from the proceeds—effectively increases the true interest paid on the borrowing. Is the bank lying about the interest? No, because each lender must indicate clearly the true cost of borrowing, the annual percentage rate (APR), on the face of the note. The bank will disclose the true (effective) interest rate of 11.11 percent. The business community understands the implications of a discounted note and the fact that it increases the effective interest rate of the loan.

Interest costs are an important factor in the decision whether or not to borrow funds. Businesspersons in various capacities (CEOs, regional managers, store managers) frequently face financing decisions. We began our discussion of how companies are financed by saying that companies require both short-term financing to run day-to-day operations and long-term financing to achieve long-range goals. The coordination of short-term activities with short-term financing and long-term activities with long-term financing is called *matching maturities*. Good cash management relies on matching maturities to effectively manage the cash inflows and outflows. While the use of collateral may allow a company to secure financing for a longer term, a bank is ideally suited to provide short-term financing.

Although no law prevents banks from lending money to companies for long periods of time, a couple of factors may make this type of lending arrangement unattractive for most banks. First, many companies are looking for financing for as long as 40 years, and most banks are not interested in making loans of that duration because the depositors will not commit to leave their deposits for such a long time. Second, and perhaps more importantly, the amount of money required for long-term financing in many large companies is more than a single bank can accommodate. Even very large banks are unwilling or unable to address the borrowing needs of these large companies. For this reason, another source of financing is available for corporations.

Discussion Questions

4-6. Banks frequently require a borrower to maintain a compensating balance. If the bank agrees to loan a business $100,000 but requires the borrower to keep no less than $30,000 (the compensating balance) in its bank account at all times, how much of the loan can the business utilize? On how much of the loan does the business pay interest? How might this affect the effective interest rate of the loan?

4-7. A credit card company offers to grant you $1,000 of credit at 21% in a special offer for first-time credit card holders. It also requires that you deposit $500 in a savings account paying 5%, from which you may not make withdrawals as long as there is a balance on the credit card. Comment on the effective interest rate on the credit card assuming that your balance is the full $1,000.

BORROWING BY ISSUING BONDS

bond An interest-bearing debt instrument that allows corporations to borrow large amounts of funds for long periods of time and creates a liability for the borrower.

debenture An unsecured bond payable.

A **bond** is a type of note payable, usually a $1,000 interest-bearing debt instrument. The main differences between a bond and a note payable to a bank are the length of time the debt will be outstanding and the amount of money borrowed. Notes payable are usually up to five years in duration and are limited to the amount of money a single lender can lend to one customer. Bonds payable can have a term of 40 years. One type of bond is a **debenture** bond, a bond with no collateral pledged for it. Corporations sell bonds to (borrow money from) many different parties so the total amount borrowed can exceed what one bank could lend.

Businesses use bonds as a major source of external financing and typically have millions or billions of dollars in long-term debt on their balance sheets. For example, TELUS Corporation had over $1.0 billion in bonds outstanding as of December 31, 2002.

par value (for bonds) The amount that must be paid back upon maturity of a bond. Also called *face value* or *maturity value*.

nominal interest rate The interest rate set by the issuers of bonds, stated as a percentage of the par value of the bonds. Also called the *contract rate, coupon rate*, or *stated rate*.

indenture The legal agreement made between a bond issuer and a bondholder that states repayment terms and other details.

selling price The amount received when bonds are issued or sold. This amount is affected by the difference between the nominal interest rate and the market rate. Selling price is usually stated as a percentage of the bond's par value. Also called the *market price*.

Bonds are issued in a set denomination, generally $1,000 for each bond. **Par value** represents the principal of the loan and is also called the *face value* or the *maturity value*. The par value of such bonds is $1,000, indicating that when the borrower pays back the debt, $1,000 will be repaid.

The **nominal interest rate** governs the amount of annual interest paid on a bond and is always a percentage of the par value of the bond. In other words, it is the rate of interest that the issuing company (borrower) has agreed to pay on the face value of the bond. The nominal rate is also called the *contract rate, coupon rate,* or *stated rate,* and these terms are used interchangeably.

Each bond issue provides information such as the par value and the nominal interest rate in its bond **indenture.** This legal document details the agreement between the company issuing the bonds (the borrower) and the buyers of the bonds (the lenders), including the timing of the interest payments and repayment (retirement) of the bonds.

In contrast to the nominal interest rate, which is set at the time bonds are issued and remains constant, the effective interest rate fluctuates with market conditions. The effective interest rate denotes the actual interest rate that the bondholder will earn over the life of the bond. Unlike the nominal rate, which is determined by the issuing company, the effective rate is determined by the financial markets and may cause a bond to sell for more or less than its par value. The effective rate is also called the *yield rate* or *market interest rate;* these terms are used interchangeably.

The **selling price** is the amount for which a bond actually sells and is also called the *market price.* As we stated, it is determined by the effective or market interest rate. If the effective interest rate and the nominal interest rate are the same, a bond is said to be selling at par or 100, meaning at 100 percent of its face or par value. Bonds may sell for less than par value. For instance, a selling price of 95 means the bond is selling at 95 percent of its par value. This situation occurs when the stated rate is less than the market rate. If you think about it, you will realize why, if you are trying to sell a bond that pays a rate lower than the market rate, you will be forced to lower the price. Only by lowering the price will you attract the investors (buyers) you need.

If Manitoba Industries Limited issues one thousand $1,000, 12 percent, 10-year bonds at 95 (to yield 12.92 percent), the bonds sell below par because the market wants a 12.92 percent rate of return on investment and the bonds pay only a 12 percent return on investment.

Bond proceeds (1,000 bonds × $1,000 × 0.95)		$ 950,000
Amount repaid:		
Maturity value ($1,000 × 1,000)	$1,000,000	
Interest paid ($1,000,000 × 12% × 10 years)	1,200,000	2,200,000
Total cost of borrowing for 10 years		$1,250,000

As you can see, the total cost of borrowing for ten years ($1,250,000) exceeds the cash payments for interest ($1,200,000). Therefore, the yield rate of interest is higher than the 12 percent nominal rate. Because bonds exceed more than one year of life, the effective rate of interest must be computed using present value techniques, which you will study in future courses.

Bonds may also sell for more than their par value. This happens when a bond's stated rate of interest is more than the market interest rate. A bond with a sale price of 106 is selling for 106 percent of its par value. If Manitoba Industries Limited issues one thousand $1,000, 12 percent, 10-year bonds at 104 (to yield 11.31 percent), the bonds sell above par because the market requires only an 11.31 percent rate of return on investment and the bonds will pay a 12 percent cash return on investment.

Bond proceeds (1,000 bonds × $1,000 × 1.04)		$1,040,000
Amount repaid:		
Maturity value ($1,000 × 1,000)	$1,000,000	
Interest paid ($1,000,000 × 12% × 10 years)	1,200,000	2,200,000
Total cost of borrowing for 10 years		$1,160,000

The total cost of borrowing for ten years ($1,160,000) is less than the cash interest paid ($1,200,000) indicating that the bonds yield less than the cash interest paid. The market interest rate required is less than the nominal rate.

 ## Discussion Questions

4–8. If Keri Manufacturing Ltd. sells 1,000, 10-year, 9% $1,000 bonds at 98, what are the proceeds of the bond issue?

4–9. Refer to Discussion Question 4-8. Describe the total cost of borrowing over the life of the bonds. What is the annual cash payment for interest? Is the effective interest rate more than 9% or less than 9%? How can you determine this?

4–10. How would your answers to Discussion Question 4-9 change if the bonds sold at 103?

Issuing Bonds Sold at Par

To illustrate the impact of issuing bonds at par value, assume Laura Corporation Limited issued $300,000 worth of 10-year, 8 percent bonds on January 1, 2004. From Exhibit 4–3, we know that Laura Corporation Limited sold $10,000 worth of common shares and borrowed $1,000 from the bank. Exhibit 4–4 shows results of all three of these activities.

On January 1, 2004 (the day the bonds were sold), Laura Corporation Limited records the sale of the bonds. Assets (cash) increase by $300,000, and liabilities (bonds payable) increase by the same amount. The business equation remains in balance:

$$\text{ASSETS} = \text{LIABILITIES} + \text{OWNERS' EQUITY}$$
$$\$311,000 = \$301,000 + \$10,000$$

As stated earlier, most bonds are issued in denominations of $1,000; Laura Corporation Limited sold 300 of these $1,000 bonds, agreeing to pay 8 percent of the par value per year in interest. Therefore, the nominal rate on the bonds is 8 percent. If other opportunities for investors offer 8 percent per year for using their money, the market interest rate is said to be 8 percent. When the market interest rate and the nominal interest rate are the same, investors are generally indifferent between buying the bonds and choosing other investment opportunities. This indifference results in these bonds being sold at par or 100, meaning 100 percent of their par value.

Interest payments on corporate bonds are generally paid semiannually (twice each year). In the case of Laura Corporation Limited, interest will be paid each June 30 and December 31. As we did for the examples of notes payable, we can calculate the annual interest due on the corporate bonds issued by Laura Corporation Limited:

$$\$300,000 × 0.08 = \$24,000$$

LAURA CORPORATION LIMITED
Balance Sheet
January 1, 2004

Assets:		Liabilities:		
Cash	$311,000	Notes Payable	$ 1,000	
		Bonds Payable	300,000	
		Total Liabilities		$301,000
		Shareholders' Equity:		
		Common Shares	$ 10,000	
		Total Shareholders' Equity		10,000
		Total Liabilities and		
Total Assets	$311,000	Shareholders' Equity		$311,000

This indicates that $24,000 is the annual interest the corporation owes to its bond-holders. If interest payments are made every six months, Laura Corporation Limited will send a total of $12,000 to its bondholders on each interest payment date. The semi-annual interest payments are to be made throughout the ten-year life of the bonds. At the end of ten years, Laura Corporation Limited must pay back the principal amount borrowed, $300,000. For Laura Corporation Limited, the cost of borrowing is calculated as follows:

Bond proceeds (300 bonds × $1,000 × 1.00)		$300,000
Amount repaid:		
Maturity value ($1,000 × 300)	$300,000	
Interest paid ($300,000 × 8% × 10 years)	240,000	540,000
Total cost of borrowing for 10 years		$240,000

In this case, the cost of borrowing equals the interest paid because the bonds sold at par.

Corporate bonds, as we noted earlier, were developed to accommodate companies' long-term financing needs. Bonds also facilitate borrowing larger sums of money than any single lender is either willing or able to handle. If businesses are to have access to large sums of money, there must be some mechanism for bringing together companies that want to issue bonds and investors who are interested in buying them. That mechanism is the bond market, and it is similar to the stock market.

Initial Offerings—The Primary Bond Market

As with shares, there is both a primary and a secondary market for bonds. The initial sale of bonds by the issuing corporation occurs in the primary bond market. Most corporations do not attempt to handle the details of the actual sale of their bonds to individual investors. For this reason, most corporations with large bond offerings hire an intermediary investment banker, or a group of such bankers called a **syndicate,** to sell large bond offerings to the public. The bankers, serving as underwriters, buy all the bonds available in the offering and then resell them to interested investors at a higher price. The underwriters' basic fee is known as the spread—the difference between the price paid to the issuer and the price at which securities are

syndicate A group of underwriters working together to get a large bond issue sold to the public.

sold to the public. Underwriters typically charge a fee of 1 percent of the total amount of bonds issued.

The underwriter assists the corporation in completing all the necessary steps for a successful bond issue. One of the most important steps in the process is preparing the prospectus. The **prospectus** provides important information to prospective buyers of the bonds, including information about the issuing corporation and about the bond issue itself. The preliminary prospectus is just one of the documents that must be filed with the securities commissions. It contains no selling price information and no offering date. While the securities commissions are reviewing the documents filed by the corporation, no sale of the bonds may take place.

The final selling price results from the negotiations between the underwriter and the corporation and is determined at the very last minute, often just one day prior to offering the bonds for sale. After the securities commissions grant approval to the corporation to issue the bonds, a crucial meeting takes place at which the corporate officials and the underwriter settle the selling price of the bonds to the underwriter. Investors in the open market determine how much they are willing to pay for the bonds based upon their calculations of the present value of the bonds at their desired rate of return. Bond selling prices are stated in relation to their par value. That is, if a bond sells below its par value, it is said to be selling at a **discount.** Bonds with prices above par value are said to be selling at a **premium.** Most underwriters hope to be able to sell bonds for par value or at only a slight discount. Psychologically, it is easier to sell a bond that is priced at or below par value than it is to sell one at a premium. For this reason, new issues are rarely sold at a premium.

When the bonds are ready to be sold to the public, the underwriter makes a bond offering, which is similar to the share offering discussed in Chapter 3. The offering is announced in business publications and in major newspapers across the country. The announcement includes information about the number of bonds being offered, the denomination of each bond, the interest rate being offered, the term of the bonds, and other features of the bonds. If the underwriter has negotiated well, investors will buy all the bonds within a few days, and the risk originally taken by the underwriter will be quickly eliminated. At that point, the agreement is between the issuing corporation and the investors. Any subsequent trades are part of the secondary bond market.

Interest Rates and the Secondary Bond Market

Once the bonds have been issued, those who purchased them are free to sell the bonds to other investors. After a company initially sells its bonds, it receives no money when those bonds are resold. It needs to be notified, of course, when the bonds pass from one investor to another, because it must know to whom it should send the interest payments and who should receive the repayment amount when the bonds are retired (repaid).

During the life of a bond, the investment may be traded many times. Remember that the corporation fixed the coupon rate or stated interest rate prior to the original sale of the bonds. However, the market rate of interest—what investors expect as a return on their investments—fluctuates considerably. For this reason, during the life of a bond, its price on the secondary market may fluctuate considerably as well.

Market pressure and competing opportunities for investors affect the price of a bond selling in the secondary bond market. Remember that the interest payment made by the corporation is the coupon rate, and is unaffected by the current selling price of the bond.

Examples and an explanation of bond information that appear in financial newspapers are shown in the box below.

---

prospectus A description of an upcoming bond issue that is provided as information for potential investors.

discount If a bond's selling price is below its par value, the bond is being sold at a discount. This will occur if the market or effective interest rate is higher than the stated rate on the bond.

premium If a bond's selling price is above its par value, the bond is being sold at a premium. This will occur if the market or effective interest rate is lower than the stated rate on the bond.

Business publications offer daily information about bonds traded in the secondary market. In the first column, we find the name of the borrower that issued the bonds. Bond issuers are typically governments or corporations. The second column lists the coupon rate of the bond. This is the rate of interest that the bond issuer pays to the owners of the bonds each year. The third column lists the maturity date, the day on which the issuer will repay the amount borrowed. The fourth column lists the bid price, which is the price that the bonds are selling at on that day. The bid price is a percentage of the face value of the bond. For example, if you were to purchase the Government of Canada bond shown below, you would pay $138.93 to buy a $100 bond. On the maturity date, the government would give you back $100, but between now and then, you would be earning interest on your bond at 9%. At the time, this was considered to be a high rate of interest, so you were willing to pay a premium of $38.93 when you bought the bond in order to receive a higher rate of interest. Taking into consideration the effect of the premium, you are actually earning not 9% but 5.92% on the bond. This is known as the yield, which is listed in the fifth column. The yield is higher for corporate bonds because these organizations have lower credit ratings than governments.

Bonds	Coupon	Maturity Date	Bid	Yield
Government of Canada	9.00	Jun 01/25	138.93	5.92
Government of Quebec	6.25	Jun 01/32	96.12	6.54
Loblaw Companies Limited	6.65	Nov 08/27	94.46	7.12
Government of Germany	5.00	July 04/08	100.72	4.90

 ## Discussion Question

4–11. If you wish to earn 10% on a bond investment, does it matter whether you buy a bond at a discount price or a bond at a premium price if the yield is 10%? Explain your answer.

The bond market receives much less attention from the media than the stock market. Nevertheless, it plays a significant role in the way corporations finance their long-term capital needs. As Exhibit 4–5 shows, businesses use both internal and external financing to support their operations. The two types of external financing provide investment opportunities for those with excess funds. From an investor's point of view, the stock market and the bond market offer two distinctly different types of investment that we can compare.

EQUITY AND DEBT INVESTMENTS COMPARED

We presented equity and debt financing in this and the preceding chapter from the standpoint of the company receiving the proceeds from the sale of shares and bonds. We will now look at the same subject from the standpoint of the investor. Consider the following:

Charlene's Aunt Tillie recently passed away and left Charlene $1,000,000. After all the income taxes were paid, Charlene received $750,000. Upon

Exhibit 4–5
Financing a Business

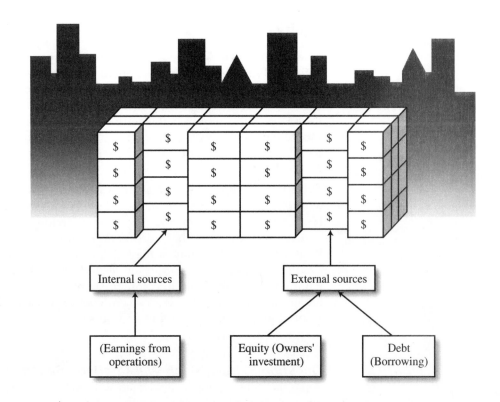

mature reflection, she decides to blow $250,000 on cars, world cruises, and other such extravagant items. She plans to invest the remaining $500,000 on January 2, 2004, and has narrowed the list of possible investments to the following two. Both alternatives involve Weatherman Limited, a large company with an impressive track record over the past 35 years.

- Charlene can purchase shares of Weatherman's common shares. On January 2, 2004, the shares will be selling for about $50 each, so Charlene would be able to purchase 10,000 shares. Weatherman has a million shares outstanding, so Charlene would own only 1 percent of the company.
- Charlene can purchase 500 of Weatherman's $1,000, five-year, 8 percent bonds. Weatherman pays interest semiannually on June 30 and December 31. The bonds will be issued on January 2, 2004, and will mature on December 31, 2008. The first interest payment will be made on June 30, 2004.

Does it make more sense for Charlene to buy shares in Weatherman Limited (equity investment) or to buy the company's corporate bonds (debt investment)? Before we can decide that question, we need to ask how the two investment alternatives answer the three questions that should be posed by all economic decision makers:

1. Will I be paid?
2. When will I be paid?
3. How much will I be paid?

Remember that inherent in these three questions is a consideration of return on the investment and return of the investment.

Equity Investments

Question 1: Will Charlene Be Paid?   There is no way to answer this question with absolute certainty; it is dependent on how Weatherman Limited performs in the future. If it is a solid company with a good market for its products and/or services, if the economy is (and stays) strong, and if the industry is (and stays) healthy, she will probably receive both a return on and a return of her investment. Charlene should be aware, however, that with only a 1 percent ownership interest, she will be able to exert little influence on how the company is run.

Question 2: When Will Charlene Be Paid?   We cannot answer this question with absolute certainty either. Payment on a share investment is of two types. First, Charlene may receive a periodic dividend on each share she owns. Remember, however, that corporations are not required to pay dividends. Weatherman Limited may or may not pay dividends to its shareholders. Second, Charlene can sell her shares in the secondary stock market if other investors are willing to buy Weatherman common shares. In any event, the company itself is under no obligation to return Charlene's $500,000. She has contributed that amount to the company and must find some third party to buy her shares if she desires to sell them.

Question 3: How Much Will Charlene Be Paid?   Like the first two questions, this one cannot be answered with absolute certainty. To answer it at all, we need to explain the two components of return on investment for an equity investment.

   a. *Dividends.* The dividend component is easy to understand. Charlene pays $50 for each of the 10,000 shares she buys. If Weatherman Limited currently pays an annual dividend of $1.50 per share, and has a stable earnings record, Charlene anticipates receiving $15,000 (10,000 shares × $1.50) per year. This constitutes a part of the return on her $500,000 investment.
   b. *Share Appreciation.* In most instances, share appreciation represents the greater part of return on investment. If Weatherman Limited performs well in the future, the price of each share will go up in the secondary stock market. The shares appreciate in value because as the company posts profits, more and more investors will want to own shares. They will, in effect, bid up the price. For example, suppose Weatherman posts record profits and the share price rises to $125. If Charlene sells her 10,000 shares, she will have earned a return on investment of $75 per share, or a total of $750,000, calculated as follows:

	Per Share	Total
What Charlene sold the shares for	$125	$1,250,000
What Charlene paid for the shares	50	500,000
Charlene's return on investment	$ 75	$ 750,000

Note that when Charlene sold the shares, she received not only a return on her investment, but also a return of her investment. Also note that we talked about "share appreciation" and "sale" as if they had already happened. But as Charlene ponders whether or not to buy Weatherman's common shares, she has no way of knowing for sure whether the corporation will perform well enough to drive the share price to the level we used (or even whether the company will be profitable at all). Charlene also faces the risk that the share price could fall below the current $50 per share.

In the final analysis, the equity investment alternative yields rather vague answers to the three questions. Now let's see how the debt investment alternative answers the same three questions.

Debt Investments

Question 1: Will Charlene Be Paid?   The answer to this first question is essentially the same for the debt investment alternative as it was for the equity investment alternative. That is, it is dependent on how Weatherman Limited performs in the future. Again, if it is a solid company with a good market for its products and/or services, if the economy is (and stays) strong, and if the industry is (and stays) healthy, Charlene will probably receive both a return on and a return of her investment.

As a creditor of the company rather than a shareholder, Charlene will have absolutely no voice in how Weatherman conducts its business, as long as it makes the periodic interest payments on the bonds and accumulates a sufficient amount of cash to retire the bonds when they mature.

Charlene must also consider that by law the investors who purchase the bonds will be paid the periodic interest *before* any dividends are paid to the investors who purchase common shares.

Question 2: When Will Charlene Be Paid?   Assuming Weatherman Limited performs well enough to make the interest payments on the bonds and retire them upon maturity, the answer to this question of when Charlene will be paid is absolutely certain. Charlene will be paid interest every June 30 and December 31 throughout the life of the bonds. On December 31, 2008, in addition to the final interest payment, Charlene will receive her initial investment back.

Question 3: How Much Will Charlene Be Paid?   The answer to this question, too, is absolutely certain assuming Weatherman Limited performs well enough to meet the financial obligations created by issuing the bonds. Over the life of the bonds, Charlene will earn a return on her investment of $200,000 ($20,000 $\times$ 10 semiannual interest payments). On December 31, 2008, she will receive $500,000, which represents the return of her investment.

In the final analysis, if Charlene satisfies herself as to Question 1, the answers to the last two questions are very certain for the debt investment alternative.

Which Is Better, Equity Investment or Debt Investment?

Take a few minutes to ponder the way the two investment alternatives answered the three questions. If you were advising Charlene, which investment would you suggest she make? If you were the one with the $500,000 to invest, which alternative would you choose?

On the surface, it appears to be no contest. Although the answer to Question 1 was essentially the same for both alternatives, the debt investment alternative is much more certain in its answers to Questions 2 and 3 than is the equity investment alternative. So why would Charlene (or anyone, for that matter) even consider the equity investment as an alternative? The one-word answer to that question is POTENTIAL!

Although risk is associated with any investment, equity investments are inherently riskier than debt investments. With the additional risk, however, comes the potential for greater reward.

Assume that the following events happen during the five-year period of Charlene's two investment alternatives in Weatherman Limited. The company earns net income each year of $10 million for the next five years. If Charlene chooses the bond alternative, she will receive $20,000 interest every six months for five years and then will receive her $500,000 back. But what if Weatherman's net income turns out to be $100 million each year for the next five years, or even $1 billion each year? How will that affect Charlene's return if she purchases the bonds? The answer is that it does not matter how profitable Weatherman is, Charlene will receive only $20,000 every six months, plus the return of her $500,000 when the bonds mature after five years.

If Charlene chooses to buy the 10,000 common shares, however, the return on her $500,000 investment will be very different if Weatherman earns $1 billion profit each year than if the company earns $10 million or $100 million each year. For one thing, the more profitable the company is, the higher its dividends are likely to be. For another, the market price of Weatherman's shares in the stock market will almost certainly increase as the company's profits increase, thereby increasing Charlene's return. In other words, the potential associated with the equity investment alternative is theoretically unlimited.

Whether a person chooses an equity investment or a debt investment depends on how that person feels about the trade-off between the amount of risk involved and the potential reward. The real key to evaluating any investment alternative is reducing the uncertainty surrounding the question: Will I be paid? In attempting to predict an alternative's future cash flow potential, economic decision makers must consider the past performance and present condition of that alternative. Most big-name public companies have issued both debt and equity—they need both sources of funds to grow and prosper. But a few are so successful that they can grow rapidly without any debt financing. One example is Microsoft, the big software developer. Between 1992 and 1998, the company's sales rose from $2.8 billion to $14.5 billion. Its long-term debt is $0.

In Chapters 3 and 4 we introduced you to the balance sheet, a financial tool that provides information about the present condition of a company. Chapter 5 will introduce you to two additional financial tools—the income statement and the statement of owners' equity.

SUMMARY

Companies often need more funds than they can get from their owners. The other major source of external financing is debt financing, or borrowing. Banks earn their profits by charging borrowers interest. Therefore, at agreed-upon intervals or when the loan is repaid, the company will pay interest in addition to the original amount borrowed.

If a company makes a bank loan, it incurs a liability—commonly called notes payable—and it receives cash. Loans from commercial banks usually meet companies' needs for short-term financing (three years or less).

A company may be required to provide collateral for its loan. If a particular asset is identified as collateral in the loan agreement, the note is generally referred to as a mortgage. Bank loans are generally suitable only for short-term financing; if a company needs long-term financing (up to 40 years or more), the alternative is to issue bonds. Bonds are similar to notes payable in that (1) both are liabilities and (2) both require repayment of the borrowed amount plus interest. Bonds are issued in set denominations, generally $1,000, and are sold to many different investors. Corporations can issue bonds for very large amounts.

Regardless of the type of borrowing involved, the amount of interest being charged can be calculated using the formula Principal × Rate × Time = Interest. In this calculation, *principal* refers to the amount owed, *rate* refers to the annual interest rate, and *time* reflects how much of the year is being considered in this particular borrowing situation.

Most corporations do not have the expertise necessary to tend to all the details involved in issuing bonds. Documents must be filed with regulatory agencies, and the actual transactions of issuing bonds to a large number of investors may be quite involved. For this reason, corporations usually use underwriters, or investment bankers, who for a fee assist the corporation in preparing the bond issue. The underwriters assume all the risk of the debt issuance by buying the entire bond issue. They then immediately resell the bonds to individual investors.

The face value or par value of a bond is the principal amount that must be repaid (generally in denominations of $1,000). If a bond is said to be selling at par, it is sold for $1,000. To entice investors, bond issuers usually have to sell their bonds at a discount (below par value) when the market rate of interest is higher than the rate paid on the bond.

The buying and selling of bonds is the focus of the bond market. Like the stock market, the bond market consists of activity in both a primary and secondary market. The activity of the primary bond market is centred on the initial issuance of corporate bonds. In the secondary bond market, the debt investments are traded. If the market rate of interest is lower than the nominal rate, investors will pay a premium (a sale price above par value) for the bonds. Conversely, if the market rate of interest (the return available to investors through other investments) is higher than the rate paid by a bond, that bond will sell below its par value (at a discount).

Activity in the bond market is similar to activity in the stock market, even though these two markets represent the activity of investors with regard to two different investment alternatives. Investors may purchase bonds (make a debt investment) or purchase shares (make an equity investment). Each type of investment has its own advantages and disadvantages. Debt investments and equity investments were compared in light of the three questions asked by economic decision makers:

1. Will I be paid?
2. When will I be paid?
3. How much will I be paid?

KEY TERMS

bond, p. 101
collateral, p. 98
commercial borrowing, p. 95
consumer borrowing, p. 95
debt financing, p. 94
debenture, p. 101
default, p. 96
discount, p. 105
discounted note, p. 100
effective interest rate, p. 100
equity financing, p. 94
external financing, p. 94
indenture, p. 102
interest, p. 96

internal financing, p. 94
long-term financing, p. 94
mortgage, p. 98
nominal interest rate, p. 102
non-interest-bearing note, p. 100
note payable, p. 97
par value (for bonds), p. 102
premium, p. 105
principal, p. 98
promissory note, p. 98
prospectus, p. 105
selling price, p. 102
short-term financing, p. 94
syndicate, p. 104

REVIEW THE FACTS

1. Explain the difference between internal and external financing.
2. What are the two major sources of external financing?
3. Contrast consumer borrowing and commercial borrowing.
4. What types of services do the chartered banks provide to Canadians?
5. What is interest?
6. Describe the effects of borrowing on the balance sheet of a business.
7. Explain the formula used to determine the amount of interest owed for a particular time period.
8. What is collateral? How can it help a borrower?
9. What is a mortgage, and how is it different from a note payable?
10. Why are bonds sometimes necessary to meet the borrowing needs of businesses?
11. Explain the terms *par value* and *stated rate* as they pertain to bonds.
12. How do the nominal rate and the market rate of bonds differ?
13. What is the relationship between the selling price of a bond and its face value?
14. What is the primary function of underwriters?
15. Explain what causes a bond to sell for either a premium or a discount.
16. How do the primary and secondary bond markets differ?
17. Explain the calculation used to determine the annual effective interest rate earned by an investor.
18. On what basis do investors choose between equity investments and debt investments?

APPLY WHAT YOU HAVE LEARNED

LO 1:   Effect of Interest on Banks

1. a. Explain in your own words how banks make a profit when you borrow money to buy a new car.

   b. Distinguish between consumer lending and borrowing, and commercial lending and borrowing.

LO 1:   Comparison of Financial Institutions

2. Compare and contrast credit unions and commercial banks.

LO 1:   Effect of Interest on Banks

3. Bill Walters decided to buy a new boat. The boat will cost $15,000 and Bill plans to borrow 80% of the purchase price from his bank.

   a. If the bank charges Bill 9% interest, how much interest will the bank earn in the first year of the loan?

   b. If Bill makes a $2,000 principal payment at the end of year one and the bank continues to charge 9% interest, how much interest will the bank earn for the second year of the loan?

LO 1: Effect of Interest On Banks

4. Ted Bandy decided to buy a new car to be used in his business. The car will cost $20,000 and Ted plans to borrow 70% of the purchase price from his bank.

   a. If the bank charges Ted 10% interest, how much interest will the bank earn in the first year of the loan?

   b. If Ted makes a $3,000 principal payment at the end of year one and the bank continues to charge 10% interest, how much interest will the bank earn for the second year of the loan?

LO 1: Effect of Interest on Banks and the Borrower

5. Susan Ryan decided to buy a new computer to be used in her business. The computer will cost $10,000 and Susan plans to borrow 75% of the purchase price from her bank.

   a. If the bank charges Susan 12% interest, how much interest will the bank earn in the first year of the loan?

   b. If Susan makes a $2,000 principal payment at the end of year one and the bank continues to charge 12% interest, how much interest will the bank earn for the second year of the loan?

   c. If Susan makes a $4,000 principal payment at the end of year one, how much interest will she save in year two compared to making no principal payment?

LO 2: Effect of Borrowing on the Balance Sheet

6. Fred and Ethel formed F&E Enterprises Limited on January 2, 2004. Fred invested $20,000 and received 2,000 common shares. Ethel invested $10,000 and received 1,000 common shares. A balance sheet prepared immediately after the corporation was formed was as follows:

F&E ENTERPRISES LIMITED
Balance Sheet
January 2, 2004

Assets:		Liabilities:	$ 0
Cash	$30,000	Shareholders' Equity:	
		Common Shares	$30,000
		Total Liabilities and	
Total Assets	$30,000	Shareholders' Equity	$30,000

On January 3, 2004, F&E Enterprises Limited borrowed $20,000 from the Alberta Bank by signing a one-year, 8% note. The principal and interest on the note must be paid to the bank on January 2, 2005.

REQUIRED:

   a. Prepare a balance sheet for F&E Enterprises Limited at January 3, 2004, to reflect the $20,000 note payable.

   b. Calculate the amount of interest the company must pay on January 2, 2005.

   c. Think about the three questions all economic decision makers are trying to answer (Will I be paid? When? How much?). Assuming Alberta Bank has satisfied itself as to the first question, how would the bank answer the second and third questions regarding the loan to F&E Enterprises Limited?

LO 2:   Effect of Borrowing on the Balance Sheet

7. Assume the same facts as in the preceding application question, except that the note is for three months rather than one year, so it must be repaid on April 2, 2004.

REQUIRED:

a. Prepare a balance sheet for F&E Enterprises Limited at January 3, 2004, to reflect the $20,000 note payable.

b. Calculate the amount of interest F&E Enterprises Limited must pay on April 2, 2004.

c. If the note were for 90 days instead of three months, what would be the due date? How much interest would be due the bank on the due date?

d. Think about the three questions all economic decision makers are trying to answer (Will I be paid? When? How much?). Assuming Alberta Bank has satisfied itself as to the first question, how would the bank answer the second and third questions regarding the loan to F&E Enterprises Limited?

LO 2:   Effect of Borrowing on the Balance Sheet

8. Refer to the opening balance sheet of F&E Enterprises Limited in application problem 6.

On January 3, 2004, F&E Enterprises Limited sold 100 of its $1,000, five-year, 10% bonds. Interest is to be paid semiannually on July 2 and January 2. The bonds mature (must be repaid) on January 2, 2009.

REQUIRED:

a. Prepare a balance sheet for F&E Enterprises Limited at January 3, 2004, to reflect the sale of the bonds, assuming they sold at their par value.

b. Calculate the amount of interest the company must pay each July 2 and January 2.

c. How much would the company have received from the sale of the bonds on January 3, 2004, assuming they sold at 98 (a discount)?

d. How much would the company have received from the sale of the bonds on January 3, 2004, assuming they sold at 103 (a premium)?

LO 3:   Terminology

9. Presented below are some items related to notes payable and bonds payable, followed by definitions of those items in scrambled order.

a. Interest	f. Premium
b. Nominal interest rate	g. Principal
c. Effective interest rate	h. Defaulting
d. Maturity value	i. Note payable
e. Discount	j. Bonds payable

1. _____ The amount above par value for which a bond is sold
2. _____ The amount of funds actually borrowed
3. _____ The rate of interest actually earned by a bondholder
4. _____ Failing to repay a loan as agreed
5. _____ Liabilities that allow corporations to borrow large amounts of money for long periods of time
6. _____ The cost of using someone else's money
7. _____ The amount below par value for which a bond is sold

8. _____ An agreement between a lender (usually a bank) and borrower that creates a liability for the borrower

9. _____ The interest rate set by the issuers of bonds, stated as a percentage of the par value of the bonds

10. _____ The amount that is payable at the end of a borrowing arrangement

REQUIRED:

Match the letter next to each item on the list with the appropriate definition. Each letter will be used only once.

LO 3: Bonds versus Notes

10. The two main instruments of debt financing are bonds and notes. Explain under what circumstances each instrument is generally used.

LO 3: Terminology

11. Presented below are two definitions of items related to interest on bonds payable, followed by a list of terms used to describe bond interest.

   a. The rate of interest actually earned by the bondholder
   b. The interest rate set by the issuer of the bond, stated as a percentage of the par value of the bond

   1. _____ Nominal interest rate
   2. _____ Effective interest rate
   3. _____ Stated interest rate
   4. _____ Coupon rate
   5. _____ The interest rate printed on the actual bond
   6. _____ Market interest rate
   7. _____ Contract rate
   8. _____ Yield rate

REQUIRED:

For each of the eight items above, indicate to which definition (a or b) it refers.

LO 3: Notes versus Bonds

12. Miller Limited needs to borrow funds to modernize its factory. Miller Limited decided to issue $50 million worth of 30-year bonds in the primary bond market. Explain why Miller Limited would rather issue bonds than borrow money at the bank.

LO 3 & 4: Due Dates

13. Weaver Company Limited borrowed $20,000 at the bank. The note was a 90-day, 8% note. Calculate the due date of the note assuming the note was signed on the following dates:

   a. March 3   c. July 19
   b. April 20   d. October 5

LO 3 & 4: Due Dates

14. Regina Construction Limited borrowed $8,000 at the bank. The note was a 120-day, 7% note. Calculate the due date of the note assuming the note was signed on the following dates:

a. March 7
b. April 19

c. May 5
d. August 10

LO 3 & 4: Due Dates

15. Niagra Development Ltd. borrowed $5,000 at the bank. The note was a 60-day, 7% note. Calculate the due date of the note assuming the note was signed on the following dates:

a. April 3
b. May 19

c. June 5
d. July 10

LO 3 & 4: Computation of Effective Interest Rates

16. The Commerce Bank discounted a $20,000, 8% loan to Eastern Townships Limited for a period of 120 days. The loan was signed on April 25. Answer the following questions.

a. What is the due date of the loan?
b. What is the total of the loan proceeds the bank should receive as repayment?
c. Compute the effective interest rate for the bank.

LO 3 & 4: Computation of Effective Interest Rates

17. The Commerce Bank discounted a $20,000, 10% loan to Eastern Townships Limited for a period of 120 days. The loan was signed on April 25. Answer the following questions.

a. What is the due date of the loan?
b. What is the net amount of loan proceeds that the company will deposit to its account?
c. What is the total amount the bank should receive as repayment?
d. Compute the effective interest rate for the bank.

LO 3 & 4: Computation of Effective Interest Rates

18. The Bank of New Brunswick discounted a $50,000, 8% loan to East Coast Oil Ltd. for a period of 90 days. The loan was signed on May 5. Answer the following questions.

a. What is the due date of the loan?
b. What is the net amount of loan proceeds that East Coast Oil Ltd. will deposit to its account?
c. What is the total amount the bank should receive as repayment?
d. Compute the effective interest rate for the bank.

LO 3 & 4: Computation of Effective Interest Rates

19. The Bank of Manitoba discounted a $10,000, 12% loan to Lake Winnipeg Boats Ltd. for a period of 180 days. The loan was signed on March 19. Answer the following questions.

    a. What is the due date of the loan?
    b. What is the net amount of loan proceeds that the company will deposit to its account?
    c. What is the total amount the bank should receive as repayment?
    d. Compute the effective interest rate for the bank.

LO 4:   Return on Investment

20. Assume that a company sells 6,500 five-year, $1,000 bonds paying 8% interest at 96.

REQUIRED:

    a. How much cash will the company selling the bonds receive from the sale?
    b. How much total cash will the bond buyers receive each year as interest?
    c. Determine the return on investment and the return of investment for each $1,000 bond over its life.
    d. Is the effective (market) interest rate less than, equal to, or greater than 8%? How can you determine this?

LO 4:   Return on Investment

21. Assume a company sells 2,500 five-year, $1,000 bonds paying 12% interest at 103.

REQUIRED:

    a. How much cash will the company selling the bonds receive from the sale?
    b. How much total cash will the bond buyers receive each year as interest?
    c. Determine the return on investment and the return of investment for each $1,000 bond over its life.
    d. Is the effective (market) interest rate less than, equal to, or greater than 12%? How can you determine this?

LO 4:   Calculation of Interest (Return on Investment)

22. Assume that an investor pays $950 for a five-year, $1,000 bond paying 9% interest.

REQUIRED:

    a. How much cash will the investor receive each year as interest?
    b. Calculate the return on investment and the return of investment for the $1,000 bond.
    c. Is the effective (market) interest rate less than, equal to, or greater than 9%? How can you determine this?

LO 4:   Calculation of Interest (Return on Investment)

23. Assume an investor pays $1,040 for a five-year, $1,000 bond paying 8% interest.

REQUIRED:

    a. How much cash will the person buying the bond receive each year as interest?
    b. Calculate the return on investment and the return of investment over the life of the bond.
    c. Is the effective (market) interest rate less than, equal to, or greater than 8%? How can you determine this?

LO 4: Computation of Interest

24. Alto Limited borrowed $10,000 on July 1, 2004, by signing a 10% note at ABC Bank due December 31, 2004.

REQUIRED:

a. Determine the total amount Alto Limited will have to pay (principal and interest) on December 31, 2004.

b. How much interest will ABC Bank earn on this note?

c. How will the answer to part b differ if the note was signed on October 1, 2004, and is due December 31, 2004?

LO 4: Computation of Interest and Principal

25. Laval Limited borrows $20,000 in the year 2004, to finance a piece of equipment. Calculate the interest and principal the company would pay to the bank for the year 2004 if the loan is due December 31, 2004, and:

a. the loan is at 12%, signed on January 2, 2004.

b. the loan is at 10%, signed on January 2, 2004.

c. the loan is at 12%, signed on April 1, 2004.

d. the loan is at 9%, signed on September 1, 2004.

LO 4: Computation of Interest and Principal

26. Bluenose Limited borrows $100,000 to purchase a building. Calculate the interest the company would pay to the bank for the year 2004 if the loan is due December 31, 2004, and:

a. the loan is at 6%, signed on February 1, 2004.

b. the loan is at 8%, signed on February 1, 2004.

c. the loan is at 6%, signed on July 2, 2004.

d. the loan is at 8%, signed on October 1, 2004.

LO 5: Underwriters

27. Describe the function of underwriters and explain why they are important to the financial markets.

LO 5: Matching

28. Presented below are some items related to underwriters and bonds payable, followed by definitions of those items in scrambled order.

a. syndicate
b. prospectus
c. discount
d. premium
e. spread
f. RBC Dominion Securities

1. _____ Difference between price paid to the issuer and the price at which securities are sold to the public

2. _____ A group of underwriters working together to get a large bond issue sold to the public

3. _____ A description of a bond issue that provides information to potential investors

4. _____ Bond selling price is below its par value

5. _____ Bond selling price is above par value

6. _____ A major Canadian underwriter

LO 6:   Effect of Market Interest Rate on Bond Selling Prices

29. Explain how an increase in the market rate of interest will impact a new issuance of bonds in terms of the selling price of the bonds.

LO 6:   Effect of Market Interest Rate on Bond Selling Prices

30. Explain how a decrease in the market rate of interest will impact a new issuance of bonds in terms of the selling price of the bonds.

LO 6 & 7:   Effect of Market Interest Rate on Bond Selling Prices

31. King Limited has decided to sell bonds. King Limited is prepared to issue 5,000 bonds with a par value of $1,000 paying interest of 6%. If the market rate of interest is currently 8%, answer the following questions:

    a. Would you expect the bonds to sell for par value, a premium, or a discount? Explain.

    b. Will these bonds sell in the primary or secondary bond market?

LO 6 & 7:   Effect of Market Interest Rate on Bond Selling Prices

32. Tamara Limited has decided to sell bonds. Tamara Limited is prepared to issue 9,000 bonds with a par value of $1,000 paying interest of 8%. If the market rate of interest is currently 7%, answer the following questions:

    a. Would you expect the bonds to sell for par value, a premium, or a discount? Explain.

    b. Will these bonds sell in the primary or secondary bond market?

LO 6 & 7:   Effect of Market Interest Rate on Bond Selling Prices

33. St. John Limited has decided to sell bonds. St. John Limited is prepared to issue 7,000 bonds with a par value of $1,000 paying interest of 5%. If the market rate of interest is currently 5%, answer the following questions:

    a. Would you expect the bonds to sell for par value, a premium, or a discount? Explain.

    b. Will these bonds sell in the primary or secondary bond market?

LO 8:   Equity versus Debt

34. Edie Bennett formed Bennett Engines, Ltd. on January 2, 2004. Edie invested $24,000 and received 1,200 common shares. On January 3, 2004, Bennett Engines, Ltd. borrowed $12,000 from the Royal Bank by signing a one-year, 9% note. The principal and interest on the note must be paid to the bank on January 2, 2005.

REQUIRED:

    a. Prepare a balance sheet as of January 2, 2004, immediately following Edie's investment of $24,000.

    b. Prepare a balance sheet as of January 3, 2004, that reflects both Edie's investment of $24,000 and the $12,000 borrowed from the bank.

    c. Calculate the amount of interest Bennett Engines, Ltd. must pay on January 3, 2005.

d. Assume that the note was for six months rather than one year, so it must be repaid on July 3, 2004. Calculate the amount of interest Bennett Engines, Ltd. must pay on July 3, 2004.

LO 8:   Equity versus Debt

35. Teddy Stowers formed Stowers Public Relations Ltd. on January 2, 2004. Teddy invested $30,000 cash and received 3,000 common shares. On January 3, 2004, Stowers Public Relations Ltd. sold 100 of its $1,000, five-year, 9% bonds at par. Interest is to be paid semiannually on June 2 and January 2. The bonds mature (must be repaid) on January 2, 2009.

    a. Prepare a balance sheet for Stowers Public Relations Ltd. at January 2, 2004, to reflect Stowers' investment of $30,000.

    b. Prepare a balance sheet for Stowers Public Relations Ltd. at January 3, 2004, to reflect both Stowers' investment of $30,000 and the sale of the bonds, assuming they sold at their par value.

    c. Calculate the amount of interest Stowers Public Relations Ltd. must pay each June 2 and January 2.

    d. How much would Stowers Public Relations Ltd. have received from the sale of the bonds on January 3, 2004, if they had sold at 99 (a discount)?

    e. How much would Stowers Public Relations Ltd. have received from the sale of the bonds on January 3, 2004, if they had sold at 105 (a premium)?

LO 8:   Equity versus Debt

36. Gloria's Limited had the following balance sheet at December 31, 2004:

GLORIA'S LIMITED
Balance Sheet
December 31, 2004

Assets:		Liabilities and Shareholders' Equity:	
		Liabilities	$ 0
Cash	$200,000	Shareholders' Equity:	
		Common Shares	$200,000
		Total Liabilities and	
Total Assets	$200,000	Shareholders' Equity	$200,000

On January 2, 2005, Gloria's Limited issued $300,000 worth of 10-year, 10% bonds at their par value.

REQUIRED:
Prepare a new balance sheet for Gloria's Limited reflecting the sale of the bonds on January 2, 2005.

LO 8:   Equity versus Debt

37. Chapters 3 and 4 of the text discuss two very different forms of financing available to corporations: debt and equity.

REQUIRED:
  a. Explain why a corporation would prefer to issue bonds rather than common shares.

  b. Explain why an investor would prefer to purchase common shares rather than a company's corporate bonds.

LO 7 & 8: Equity versus Debt

38. Define nominal interest rates and market interest rates for a bond, and briefly explain how these rates affect a bond's selling price.

LO 7 & 8: Equity versus Debt

39. Ed Furgol has $20,000 to invest. His options are as follows:

Option 1: Big Corporation's five-year, $1,000 par value, 8% bonds, which are selling for 98 on the secondary bond market.

Option 2: Little Corporation's initial offering of common shares, which is selling for $20 per share. Although there is no formal requirement to pay dividends, it is anticipated that Little Company will pay an annual dividend of $0.80 per share on its common shares.

REQUIRED:

a. How many of the Big Corporation bonds can Ed buy with his money?

b. How much cash will Ed receive from Big Corporation each year if he buys the bonds?

c. What will Ed's return on investment and return of investment be for the bonds if he holds them until maturity?

d. How many shares of Little Corporation's common shares can Ed purchase with his $20,000?

e. Assuming Little Corporation does pay the anticipated annual dividend on its common shares, how much will Ed receive each year if he invests his $20,000 in the shares?

f. Based on your answer to part e, what is the effective rate of return Ed would earn on his investment in Little Corporation's shares?

LO 7 & 8: Equity versus Debt

40. Julia Pak has $50,000 to invest. Her options are as follows:

Option 1: Grand Oil Limited's five-year, $1,000 par value, 12% bonds, which are selling for 103 on the secondary bond market.

Option 2: Little Giant Oil Limited's initial offering of common shares, which is selling for $75 per share. Although there is no formal requirement to pay dividends, it is anticipated that Little Giant Oil Limited will pay an annual dividend of $2 per share on its common shares.

REQUIRED:

a. How many of the Grand Oil Limited bonds can Julia buy with her money?

b. How much cash will Julia receive from Grand Oil Limited each year if she buys the bonds?

c. What will Julia's return on investment and return of investment be for the bonds if he holds them until maturity?

d. How many shares of Little Giant Oil Limited's common shares can Julia purchase with her $50,000?

e. Assuming Little Giant Oil Limited does pay the anticipated annual dividend on its common shares, how much will Julia receive each year if she invests her $50,000 in the shares?

f. Based on your answer to part e, what is the effective rate of return Julia would earn on her investment in Little Giant Oil Limited's shares?

FINANCIAL REPORTING CASES

Comprehensive

41. Using the sedar.com web site, find the most recent annual report for Rogers Communications Inc.

REQUIRED:

a. The company has a convertible debenture outstanding. What is it convertible into? What are the maturity date and value of the debenture?

b. Do you think there is any significant difference between long-term notes and debentures?

c. What do you think the terms "second priority" and "subordinated" mean when they are used to describe long-term notes and debentures?

d. Why do you think the company has so many different types of notes and debentures?

ANNUAL REPORT PROJECT

42. You can now complete Section VI of the project. The information you develop in this part of the report may be helpful in preparing other sections of the project. In this section of the project report, you will obtain (a) financial and operating information about the company during a period subsequent to the date of the annual report, (b) industry information, and (c) secondary stock market data. In this section of the project (VI), you should obtain the following:

a. Current press releases. Using the Internet, locate the company's web page. Select and print three press releases that pertain to your company that were issued after the annual report date. In addition to the web page, you may use other financial news services available on the Internet, such as CNN financial news (cnnfn.com), yahoo.com, globeinvestor.com, and newswire.ca.

b. Secondary stock activity. Using *The Globe and Mail* or *The National Post* or the Internet, record the following weekly market activity for the company's shares for each week included in your term:
   (1) Weekly trading volume
   (2) Closing price on each Friday
   (3) Net change for the week

REQUIRED:
Complete Section VI of your report. Make a copy for your instructor and keep a copy for your final report.

5

The Income Statement and Statement of Owners' Equity

Your father comes to you for some help with a problem. He learned recently that he will retire early in a few months. Being an active person who wants to keep working, he investigated several businesses that are for sale. He narrowed his list to a few that he finds interesting, but needs help making his final decision. The sellers were to give him balance sheets and income statements from each business, but when you examine them, you find that one seller gave him three sets of year-end statements, one seller gave him only last year's tax return, and another seller gave him a balance sheet and income statement that is two years old. You now understand the balance sheet, but wonder exactly what the income statements can tell you. What does an income statement predict and how well does it predict the future? You wish to give your father sound advice, so you need to understand these income statements.

Accounting information, in the form of financial statements, provides a major source of information to economic decision makers. In Chapters 3 and 4, you encountered the first financial tool—the balance sheet. This financial statement provides information that helps economic decision makers evaluate the present condition of a company. The balance sheet tells what the company owns (assets), what it owes (liabilities), and what claim the owners have to the remaining resources (owners' equity). This picture of the financial position of a company is an important item of information. It is not, however, enough information to support the decision-making process. ■

To make wise decisions, economic decision makers must gather all the information they need to assess the future timing and amounts of cash flows. Accurate prediction of the future performance of a company depends on high-quality assessment of both the present condition *and* the past performance of the firm.

To assess the past performance of a company, decision makers rely on another financial tool—the income statement. The income statement provides information about the business activities of a company during a particular period.

In addition to the income statement, in this chapter we introduce you to one other financial tool—the statement of owners' equity. This third financial statement provides a bridge between the information provided by the income statement and that provided by the balance sheet.

By the time you finish this chapter, you will have explored three financial statements. Remember that these are tools for economic decision makers. Their importance lies in their usefulness and contribution to the decision-making process.

LEARNING OBJECTIVES

After completing your work on this chapter, you should be able to do the following:

1. Describe how the income statement provides information about the past performance of a business.
2. Distinguish between single-step and multistep income statements.
3. Explain the impact of net income or net loss on owners' equity.
4. Construct statements of owners' equity for proprietorships and partnerships.
5. Compare and contrast the impact of drawings on statements of owner's equity and the impact of dividends on statements of retained earnings.
6. Explain why dividends are paid and under what circumstances they can be paid.
7. Describe in your own words the linking of income statements, balance sheets, and statements of owners' equity or statement of retained earnings.
8. Explain the concept of matching and describe how it relates to amortization.
9. Describe the difference between accruals and deferrals, and provide examples of each.

INTRODUCTION TO THE INCOME STATEMENT

income statement   A financial statement providing information about an entity's past performance. Its purpose is to measure the results of the entity's operations for some specific time period. Also called the *statement of earnings* or the *statement of results of operations*.

The **income statement** is a financial tool that provides information about a company's past performance. Recall that the balance sheet, the financial tool we studied in detail, lists assets, liabilities, and owners' equity. The income statement includes the following elements:

1. **Revenues.** *Inflows of assets to an entity from delivering or producing goods, rendering services, or carrying out other activities.* Recall from Chapter 2 that revenue represents what a company's customers pay for its goods or services. Revenues are the reward of doing business. Revenues can also be described as the increase in wealth of a business.
2. **Expenses.** *Outflows or other using up of assets from delivering or producing goods, rendering services, or carrying out other activities.* Expenses are the sacrifices required to attain revenues. Again, recall from Chapter 2 that expenses are decreases in wealth.

net income The amount of profit that remains after all costs have been considered. The net reward of doing business for a specific time period. Also called *earnings* or *net earnings*.

net loss The difference between revenues and expenses of a period in which expenses are greater than revenues.

The difference between the rewards (revenues) and the sacrifices (expenses) for a given period of activity is the net reward of doing business, which we call **net income.** Accountants also call net income *earnings,* or *net earnings*. If the expenses for the period are greater than the revenues for the period, the result is a **net loss.** The relationship between revenues, expenses, and either net income or net loss can be represented by the following equation:

REVENUES − EXPENSES = NET INCOME (OR NET LOSS)

You should memorize the income statement equation and fix its meaning in your mind because we will deal with it over and over again.

 Discussion Questions

5–1. Identify the transactions in your personal finances during the last month. Which transactions resulted in revenues and which resulted in expenses?

5–2. Use the equation given in the text and your responses to Discussion Question 5–1 to determine whether you had a net income or a net loss for the month.

Construction of the Income Statement

period Length of time (usually a month, quarter, or year) for which activity is being reported on an income statement.

The basic format of an income statement is shown in Exhibit 5–1. The heading must include the name of the business, the name of the statement, and the **period** for which activity is being reported. You may know that economists use the terms *stock* to describe a quantity at a given point in time and *flow* to describe a quantity over a period of time. A balance sheet provides stock information, and its heading includes the precise date for which the information is presented. If the balance sheet is a "snapshot" of a business at a particular point in time, then the income

Exhibit 5–1
Basic Format of the
Income Statement

LAURA'S BUSINESS
Income Statement
For the Year Ended December 31, 2004

Revenues:		
	XXX	
	XX	
	XX	
Total Revenues		XXXX
Expenses:		
	XX	
	XX	
	XX	
	X	
	X	
Total Expenses		XXX
Net Income		XX

statement, which provides flow information, is something of a "home video" of a company for a period of time (usually a month, quarter, or year). For that reason, the income statement heading identifies the period of time described. The income statement indicates that during this specific time period, the company earned so much revenue, incurred so much expense, and produced either a net income or a net loss. Accountants produce income statements annually, quarterly, monthly, or for some other interval that provides useful accounting information.

The income statement's formal name is the *statement of results of operations*, which is a far better description of its function than income statement. It is also sometimes called the *statement of earnings*. However, most companies use the informal title, "Income Statement."

Notice that the basic format of the income statement illustrated in Exhibit 5–1 suggests that a company may have more than one type of revenue. Revenues comprise earned inflows of the company arising from primary operations or incidental company activities. A business may be a service organization that produces service revenues or professional fees such as a law firm, lawn service company, or accounting firm. If a business is involved in merchandising or manufacturing, its major revenue will be sales of tangible products.

 Discussion Question

> **5–3.** Which of the following companies earn revenues primarily from manufacturing products, reselling products, or providing services?
> **a.** Bombardier Inc.
> **b.** Imperial Oil Limited
> **c.** The Bay
> **d.** Tim Hortons
> **e.** Canadian General Insurance
> **f.** Indigo Books & Music Inc.

In addition to the revenues from its major operations, a company may produce revenues through other activities. For example, it may rent out portions of the office building it owns to produce rent revenue. If the company has invested some of its cash in guaranteed investment certificates (GICs), it earns interest revenue.

The income statement format in Exhibit 5–1 also allows for several different types of expenses. Expenses are the outflows of the company that allow the firm to produce revenue. Expenses take many different forms, such as salary or wage expense for employees, or rent expense for the sales office. If a company maintains vehicles, the income statement may show fuel expense and/or maintenance expense. These are just a few examples of the numerous expenses a company faces.

Merchandisers and manufacturers sell goods to generate primary revenues. Costs associated with these goods make up the expense called the **cost of goods sold,** or *cost of sales*, or *cost of products sold*. For many companies, cost of goods sold comprises the major expense of doing business.

cost of goods sold The cost of the product sold as the primary business activity of a company. Also called *cost of products sold* or *cost of sales*.

Discussion Questions

5–4. Some items could be in either the revenue or the expense category (e.g., interest, rent). If you were in charge of keeping track of a company's revenues and expenses, describe how you would know whether "rent" or "interest" was a revenue or an expense.

5–5. Think of a fast-food restaurant, such as Taco Time. List the costs you think the restaurant incurs in its day-to-day operations. Which of these costs do you think should be included in the cost of goods sold and which ones are other expenses? Explain.

Single-Step Format of the Income Statement

single-step income statement A format of the income statement that gathers all revenues into "total revenues" and all expenses into "total expenses." Net income is calculated as a subtraction of total expenses from total revenues.

In the basic form of the income statement, all revenues are added to provide "total revenues," and all expenses are added to create "total expenses." This format is called the **single-step income statement,** because in one step, total expenses are subtracted from total revenues to determine net income (or net loss).

We can use Laura's Business to illustrate the single-step format of the income statement. Assume that Laura's Business had $2,690 in sales revenue and $990 in rent revenue during 2004. Also assume that, during the period, the company spent $955 for cost of goods sold, $675 for wages, $310 for utilities, and $120 for interest payments. Based on that information, the company's 2004 income statement, prepared in a single-step format, would be as shown in Exhibit 5–2.

Unlike the balance sheet, the income statement is not directly affected by the type of business organization involved. Income statements for proprietorships, partnerships, and corporations all take the same general form. The only difference is in the name of the company included in the heading of the statement. Companies do, however, have the option of using either of the basic formats—the single-step format we have been discussing or the multistep format.

Exhibit 5–2
Single-Step Format of the Income Statement

LAURA'S BUSINESS
Income Statement
For the Year Ended December 31, 2004

Revenues:		
Sales	$2,690	
Rent Revenue	990	
Total Revenues		$3,680
Expenses:		
Cost of Goods Sold	$ 955	
Wages Expense	675	
Utilities Expense	310	
Interest Expense	120	
Total Expenses		2,060
Net Income		$1,620

Multistep Format of the Income Statement

multistep income statement
An income statement format that highlights gross margin and operating income.

The **multistep income statement** provides two items of information not presented in income statements using the single-step format: (1) **gross margin** or *gross profit* and (2) **operating income** or *income from operations*.

Choice of format does not change the bottom line or net income. However, the information provided within the income statement differs from one format to another. The single-step income statement format sums all revenues to form "total revenues" and all expenses to form "total expenses." No special treatment is given to any specific revenue or expense. In contrast, the multistep format highlights the relationships among various items of accounting information.

gross margin   An item shown on a multistep income statement, calculated as: Sales—Cost of Goods Sold. Also called *gross profit*.

operating income   Income produced by the major business activity of the company. An item shown on the multistep income statement. Also called *income from operations*.

Gross margin is one piece of information not shown on a single-step income statement. This item highlights the relationship between sales revenue and cost of goods sold. Recall that **sales revenue** is the revenue produced by the primary activity of the firm, which for a merchandiser or manufacturer comes from selling tangible units of product. Cost of goods sold is the cost of the tangible units of product sold and is very often the largest expense relating to sales. The difference between sales revenue and cost of goods sold is the gross margin or gross profit. For example, sales of running shoes is the revenue produced by Nike, Inc. Cost of goods sold is the cost of the shoes to Nike. The difference between these amounts represents Nike's gross margin.

sales revenue   The revenue generated from the sale of a tangible product as a major business activity. Also called *sales*.

 Discussion Questions

> **5–6.** For Nike, Inc., what specific costs do you think are included in the cost of goods sold related to running shoes?
>
> **5–7.** Identify two additional manufacturing or merchandising companies. For each company, describe the source of its sales revenues and the components of its costs of goods sold.

A merchandiser or manufacturer cannot possibly be profitable unless it sells its product for more than what it paid for that product. Gross margin represents how much more a company received from the sale of its products than what the products cost the company. It also represents the amount available from sales to cover all other expenses the company incurs. For example, assume Kearns Company (a merchandiser) sells its product for $30 per unit. Each unit of product costs Kearns Company $24. If the company sold 5,000 units of product in January, it would have a gross margin of $30,000, calculated as follows:

Sales (5,000 × $30)	$150,000
LESS: Cost of goods sold (5,000 × $24)	120,000
Gross margin	$ 30,000

This $30,000 represents the amount Kearns Company has to cover all its other January expenses. Assuming the company had no revenues other than sales, if those other expenses were less than $30,000, the company had a net income for the month; if they were greater than $30,000, the company experienced a net loss.

Economic decision makers frequently use gross margin as one measure to evaluate the performance of a manufacturing or merchandising company. Examining gross margin allows financial statement readers to quickly see the relationship among revenue produced by selling product, the cost of the product, and all the other expenses the company incurs. Gross margins tend to be similar among firms in the same industry but vary widely from one industry to another.

 Discussion Question

5–8. Consider the following simplified multistep income statement for Kanaly Company:

Sales (1,000 units)	$ 375,000
LESS: Cost of Goods Sold	380,000
Gross Margin	$(5,000)
LESS: Other Expenses	32,000
Net Income (Loss)	$(37,000)

a. What can you learn about Kanaly Company from its gross margin?

b. How many units must the company sell to earn a net income?

c. At what unit selling price would Kanaly Company earn a $5,000 net income?

In addition to highlighting the relationship between sales and cost of goods sold, the multistep income statement separates income generated by the ongoing major activity of the firm from the revenues and expenses produced by other business activities. Operating income or income from operations denotes the results of the merchandising or manufacturing activity that is the company's primary business activity. This income can be expected to continue, but some of the revenues and expenses associated with secondary activities of the company may not be repeated. When economic decision makers are attempting to use the past performance of a company as presented on the income statement to predict the future, operating income may be more useful than final net income as an indicator of performance. Therefore, multistep income statements, which show both net income and operating income, may prove more useful to users of accounting information than single-step income statements, which show only net income.

Exhibit 5–3 depicts Laura's Business's income statement for 2004 in the multistep format. As you can see, the net income reported is the same as that shown in Exhibit 5–2, using the single-step format. Notice, though, that the multistep format makes two important stops before arriving at the bottom line: gross margin and operating income (thus the term *multistep*).

Net Income as an Increase in Owners' Equity

Owners' equity has four components:

1. Contributions by owners
2. Revenues
3. Expenses
4. Distributions to owners

Contributions by owners and revenues increase owners' equity, while expenses and distributions to owners decrease owners' equity. Positive net income increases the owners' interest in the business because the revenue increase exceeds the expense

Exhibit 5–3
Multistep Format of the
Income Statement

LAURA'S BUSINESS
Income Statement
For the Year Ended December 31, 2004

Sales	$2,690	
LESS: Cost of Goods Sold	955	
Gross Margin		$1,735
Wages Expense	$ 675	
Utilities Expense	310	
Total Operating Expenses		985
Operating Income		$ 750
Other Revenues:		
Rent Revenue		990
Other Expenses:		
Interest Expense		120
Net Income		$1,620

decrease. Net losses (negative net income) decrease owners' equity. Revenues and expenses make up earned equity, one of two sources of owners' equity. Earned equity is directly affected by net income because each revenue is an asset received (increasing earned equity), and each expense is an asset sacrificed (decreasing earned equity). A net income, therefore, increases earned equity, whereas a net loss decreases earned equity.

If a company's earned equity increases, it follows that its owners' equity also increases. Net income is thus a particular period's addition to the owners' equity in the company and links the information on the income statement with the information on the balance sheet. This link is logical when you realize that the past performance of a company is at least partially responsible for the present condition of that company.

INTRODUCTION TO THE STATEMENT OF OWNERS' EQUITY

statement of owners' equity
The financial statement that reports activity in the capital accounts of proprietorships and partnerships and in the retained earnings account of corporations. The statement of owners' equity serves as a bridge between the income statement and the balance sheet. Also called *statement of partners' equity* for a partnership.

A third financial statement connects the income statement with the balance sheet. The **statement of owners' equity** shows how the owners' equity, as reported on the balance sheet, moved from its balance at the beginning of the period to its balance at the end of the period. Although the specifics of the statement vary according to the organizational form of the company, the basic format of this financial statement is shown in Exhibit 5–4. Notice that the format contains the four components of equity.

Proprietorships—Statement of Owner's Equity

Earned equity goes by various names, depending on the form of the business. Proprietorships and partnerships usually make no distinction between the equity from owners' investment and earned equity. Because both forms of business legally are considered to be extensions of the owner or owners, the two types of equity are added together under the title "owner's equity." Exhibit 5–4 shows the format of a proprietor's statement of owners' equity that indicates the changes in capital arising from the four components of capital.

You will notice from the heading that the statement of owner's equity represents a flow, the changes in equity during a particular time period. The beginning balance used in Exhibit 5–4 is actually the ending balance from the previous period. The net income amount is drawn directly from the income statement. The amount of distributions to owners reduces the equity, and the ending balance is calculated as shown. This ending balance appears not only on the statement of owner's equity but also in the owner's equity section of the balance sheet. Earlier we referred to the statement of owner's equity as a bridge statement because it uses the net income figure from the income statement for the period and shows the calculation of the ending owner's equity amount that appears on the balance sheet.

Examine the statement of owner's equity for Laura's Business in Exhibit 5–4. Laura had no previous balance for equity because her business began during the current year and she made no withdrawals.

Exhibit 5–4
Statement of Owner's
Equity for a
Proprietorship

LAURA'S BUSINESS		
Statement of Owner's Equity		
For the Year Ended December 31, 2004		
Laura, Capital, January 1, 2004		$ 0
ADD: Contributions by Owner	$10,000	
Net Income	1,620	11,620
DEDUCT: Distributions to Owner		0
Laura, Capital, December 31, 2004		$11,620

Partnerships—Statement of Partners' Equity

statement of partners' equity
A statement of owners' equity
for a partnership.

A similar statement produced for a partnership would follow the same general outline but might be designated a **statement of partners' equity.** Of course, there would be a capital balance for each partner, and the net income for the period ($1,620) would be shared by the partners according to the rules stated in their partnership agreement. Using Laura and Stephanie's Business for our example, Exhibit 5–5 shows a statement of owners' equity for this type of business form.

Exhibit 5–5 assumes that the partners, Laura and Stephanie, have agreed to share the net income in the same proportion as their initial investments. Thus, Laura's capital balance is increased by 60 percent of the total net income for the period, and Stephanie's capital balance is increased by 40 percent of the net income.

Exhibit 5–5
Statement of Owners'
Equity for a Partnership

LAURA AND STEPHANIE'S BUSINESS		
Statement of Partners' Equity		
For the Year Ended December 31, 2004		
Laura, Capital, January 1, 2004	$ 0	
ADD: Laura's Contribution	6,000	
Net Income	972	
Laura, Capital, December 31, 2004		$ 6,972
Stephanie, Capital, January 1, 2004	$ 0	
ADD: Stephanie's Contribution	4,000	
Net Income	648	
Stephanie, Capital, December 31, 2004		4,648
Total Partners' Capital, December 31, 2004		$11,620

Corporations—Statement of Retained Earnings

statement of retained earnings A corporate financial statement that shows the changes in retained earnings during a particular period.

Because a corporation is a legal entity separate from its owner or owners, keeping the equity from owners' investment and the earned equity separate is a legal requirement. In corporations, you will recall, the investment by owners is called *contributed capital* and earned equity is called *retained earnings*. A **statement of retained earnings** is a corporate financial statement that shows the changes in retained earnings during a particular period and uses a format similar to that shown in Exhibit 5–6.

Exhibit 5–6
Statement of Retained Earnings for a Corporation

LAURA CORPORATION LIMITED

Statement of Retained Earnings
For the Year Ended December 31, 2004

Retained Earnings, January 1, 2004	$0
ADD: Net Income	1,620
	$1,620
DEDUCT: Dividends Declared	0
Retained Earnings, December 31, 2004	$1,620

Exhibit 5-6 presents Laura Corporation Limited's statement of retained earnings for 2004. Note that the beginning balance for retained earnings is zero, because this is the company's first year of operation. The net income figure comes directly from the income statement, and the ending balance for retained earnings is calculated as shown. Also notice that the statement of retained earnings does not contain any information about the contributions by the owners of the corporation. This is because changes in contributed capital (common shares and preferred shares) are shown directly on the balance sheet, with an explanation in the notes to the financial statements. Therefore, in addition to showing an account for retained earnings with a balance of $1,620, Laura Corporation Limited's balance sheet for December 31, 2004, would show a common share balance of $10,000. This would be accompanied by an explanation in the notes to the financial statements that common shares were issued totaling $10,000.

Exhibit 5–7 outlines the differences among owners' equity for the three business forms as we examined them for Laura's business activities.

Exhibit 5–7
Owners' Equity by Business Organizational Form

	Proprietorship	Partnership	Corporation
Name of Statement	Statement of Owner's Equity	Statement of Partners' Equity	Statement of Retained Earnings
Statement Section	Capital	Partners' Capital	Retained Earnings
Equity Account Titles	Laura, Capital	Laura, Capital Stephanie, Capital	Common Shares Retained Earnings

Discussion Question

5-9. How would it be possible for Laura Corporation Limited to have a zero balance in retained earnings on January 1, 2004, if 2004 were not the company's first year of business? Is there any other financial statement information that might confirm that this was the first year of operations?

DISTRIBUTIONS TO OWNERS

With time, if the operations of a company are successful, owners' equity will increase. Eventually, the owner, or owners, will expect some type of distribution of this equity. Just as net income increases owners' equity, distributions to owners decrease owners' equity.

Do not interpret these distributions as some sort of salary paid to the owners. Distributions are not considered expenses of the company and thus are not shown on the income statement. Rather, distributions to owners represent a return on the investment they made. We handle distributions to owners in different ways, depending on the organizational form of the company. However, in each case, these distributions reduce total owners' equity.

Drawings—Proprietorships and Partnerships

drawings Distributions to the owners of proprietorships and partnerships. Also called *withdrawals*.

In the case of a proprietorship, little beyond common sense restricts the owner from taking funds out of the company. If the cash is available and is not needed to cover future business expenses, the owner may take it for his or her personal use. In this case, the distributions to the owner are called **drawings** or *withdrawals*. If Laura chose to take $500 in cash from her proprietorship, the drawing would be reflected on the statement of owner's equity as shown in Exhibit 5–8.

Partnership agreements may state explicitly when and in what amounts partners may take withdrawals, or they may leave it to the discretion of the partners. Clearly, the partnership must have sufficient cash to support the actions of its owners. When thinking of making a withdrawal of cash from the company, a partner must consider the impact of this action on his or her capital account. Partners may take withdrawals that are disproportionate to the profit-sharing arrangement.

Exhibit 5–8
Distributions to Owners in a Proprietorship: Drawings

LAURA'S BUSINESS	
Statement of Owner's Equity	
For the Year Ended December 31, 2004	
Laura, Capital, January 1, 2004	$ 0
ADD: Contributions by Owner	10,000
Net Income	1,620
	$11,620
DEDUCT: Drawings	500
Laura, Capital, December 31, 2004	$11,120

Frequently, partners agree to allow one partner to take larger withdrawals because of an unusual personal need. Another partner may decide to not take normal withdrawals but to leave the capital in the business. The timing and amount of partners' withdrawals can become a common source of partnership conflict, however, and can lead to the dissolution of a partnership.

Using the partnership of Laura and Stephanie, we can examine the impact of a withdrawal made by only one of the partners. Assume that Stephanie finds herself in a personal cash bind. Since the partnership agreement does not restrict withdrawals and sufficient cash is on hand, she decides to withdraw $500. This action reduces Stephanie's capital account and the total amount of owners' equity, but it has no impact on Laura's capital balance. Exhibit 5–9 shows the resulting statement of partners' equity for the partnership.

Exhibit 5–9
Distributions to Owners in a Partnership: Drawings

LAURA AND STEPHANIE'S BUSINESS		
Statement of Partners' Equity		
For the Year Ended December 31, 2004		
Laura, Capital, January 1, 2004	$ 0	
ADD: Laura's Contribution	6,000	
Net Income	972	
Laura, Capital, December 31, 2004		$ 6,972
Stephanie, Capital, January 1, 2004	$ 0	
ADD: Stephanie's Contribution	4,000	
Net Income	648	
	$4,648	
DEDUCT: Drawings	500	
Stephanie, Capital, December 31, 2004		4,148
Total Partners' Equity, December 31, 2004		$11,120

Distributions to Owners—Corporate Form

Owners of corporations (shareholders) have much less control over when and in what amount they receive a distribution than do owners of a proprietorship or partnership. This is particularly true in large corporations. Distributions to owners of a corporation are called *dividends*. By law, dividend distributions to shareholders must be proportionate to the number of shares they own. Although not legally required to do so, virtually all corporations pay dividends at some point in their existence.

Why do corporations pay dividends if they are not legally required to do so? In the long run, investors (those who buy the corporation's shares) demand this distribution. A number of factors cause a company's shares to either go up or go down in value, but probably the most important factor is whether or not the company is profitable. Profitability becomes most meaningful to shareholders when demonstrated by the payment of dividends. A profitable corporation periodically pays a dividend to shareholders (usually every three months) as a demonstration of its ability and willingness to reward the shareholders for investing in the company.

If a corporation sustains losses or lacks the free cash flow to pay dividends, investors and potential investors may become dissatisfied with the return on their investment. This dissatisfaction may translate into a decline in demand for the company's shares and a fall in the share's price. When this situation occurs, the corporation may find it difficult to obtain funds necessary to support its operations. Opportunities for both major types of external funding—issuing shares and borrowing funds—may disappear. Eventually, if enough people lose faith in the company, it will run out of cash and cease to exist.

Communication is a powerful tool. Some successful companies resist the pressure to pay dividends in order to reinvest profits in research and development, and they clearly communicate this strategy to the shareholders. Microsoft is one such company. Investors have accepted Microsoft's reinvestment policy as a wise business strategy, and the company's share price has not suffered. Ben and Jerry's is another successful company that does not pay dividends on its shares. By publicizing the corporate philosophy of using profits to keep the company healthy and growing, Ben and Jerry's has avoided any misinterpretation of its actions. Shareholders are well aware of the company's business strategy and have demonstrated their confidence in it by holding the shares.

The board of directors makes all decisions associated with the corporation's dividend policy. The policy includes whether or not to pay a dividend, the type of dividend to be paid, and when the dividend will be paid. The board of directors can also choose to distribute additional shares of the firm's shares as a dividend, called a **share dividend.** It is, however, much more common for companies to distribute cash dividends.

share dividend A dividend paid in the corporation's own shares.

Cash Dividends on Common Shares
A cash payment is what comes to mind when we hear the word *dividend*. To be able to pay a cash dividend, a corporation must possess two things: sufficient retained earnings and sufficient cash.

1. *Sufficient Retained Earnings.* Dividends are distributions of earnings; however, corporations are not restricted to the current year's earnings to cover the distribution. Although it may be desirable for a company to declare dividends from the current year's earnings, dividends are actually declared from retained earnings. Remember, net income is only this period's addition to retained earnings; thus, it is not necessary that current net income be greater than the dividend amount. The legal requirement is that the retained earnings balance exceed the amount of the dividend.

Exhibit 5–10 shows how retained earnings increase over time and how they are affected by net income, losses, and dividends.

Exhibit 5–10
How Retained Earnings Are Created

	2000	2001	2002	2003	2004
Beginning Balance	$ 0	$ 800	$1,300	$ 700	$1,150
Net Income (Loss)	800	1,000	(100)	950	400
Dividends	0	(500)	(500)	(500)	(500)
Ending Balance	$800	$1,300	$ 700	$1,150	$1,050

Note two things as you look at Exhibit 5–10. First, the ending balance of one period (in this case, a year) becomes the beginning balance of the next period. Second, the payment of dividends is not directly related to profits in a given period. In 2002, this company paid dividends even though it experienced a net loss for the year, and in 2004, it paid out more in dividends than it earned for the year. This company appears to have adopted a policy of paying $500 per year in total dividends, regardless of its net income or loss for a particular year. This policy is perfectly acceptable, as long as the company has both sufficient retained earnings and sufficient cash each year to cover the dividend amount.

2. *Sufficient Cash.* Retained earnings are not cash. The only item on the balance sheet that represents cash is the cash account. Retained earnings are the sum of all profits earned by the corporation since its inception minus all dividends declared. Except by extraordinary coincidence, the amount of retained earnings and the amount of cash on hand at a given time differ. In fact, the amount of cash and the amount of retained earnings are unrelated amounts. A corporation must make certain it has sufficient cash to pay the dividend. A company may feel it so important to pay a regular cash dividend that it will borrow short-term cash if it has insufficient cash to cover its regular dividend amount.

Laura Corporation Limited has sufficient retained earnings and sufficient cash to pay a dividend to its shareholders. Recall that the corporation has 2,000 common shares outstanding. If the corporation declared a $0.25 per share dividend, the total dividend amount would be $500. Dividends reduce retained earnings and total shareholders' equity. Laura Corporation Limited's statement of retained earnings after the payment of a $500 dividend is shown in Exhibit 5–11.

Exhibit 5–11
Distribution to Owners in a Corporation: Dividends

LAURA CORPORATION LIMITED	
Statement of Retained Earnings	
For the Year Ended December 31, 2004	
Retained Earnings, January 1, 2004	$0
ADD: Net Income	1,620
	$1,620
DEDUCT: Dividends Declared	500
Retained Earnings, December 31, 2004	$1,120

Again, notice that there is no mention of common or preferred shares. Any changes to shares would be reported directly on the owners' equity portion of the balance sheet. Both net income and declared dividends change the balance in retained earnings, but neither affects any portion of the issued common or preferred shares.

Dividend Dates The ownership shares of most large corporations are held by many different people, and these shares change hands constantly. Because their shares are widely traded, most corporations do not know exactly who their shareholders are on any given day. For this reason, most corporations do not declare and pay a dividend on the same day.

Three important dates are associated with the payment of a cash dividend:

date of declaration The date upon which a corporation announces plans to distribute a dividend. At this point, the corporation becomes legally obligated to make the distribution: A liability is created.

date of record Owners of the shares on this day are the ones who will receive the dividend announced on the date of declaration.

1. **Date of Declaration.** As stated earlier, the board of directors decides whether and when a cash dividend is to be paid. The day the board votes to pay a dividend is the date of declaration. The date of declaration marks the creation of a legal liability for the corporation.
2. **Date of Record.** The date of record may follow the date of declaration by several weeks. Whoever owns shares on the date of record will receive the dividend. Every time a company's shares change hands, the company is notified, though that notification may take several days or even weeks, especially in large corporations.

3. **Date of Payment.** The date the dividend is actually paid is the date of payment. The corporation pays the dividend to whoever owned shares on the date of record, even though some of those people may have sold their shares between the date of record and the date of payment. The payment of the cash dividend removes the liability for the dividend from the company's records.

Generally, on the date the board of directors declares a dividend, the date of record and the date of payment are announced as shown in Exhibit 5–12.

Exhibit 5–12
Example of Dividends Reported in the Business Press

Dividends Reported in 2000 by Canadian Companies				
Company	**Type of Equity**	**Amount**	**Record Date**	**Payable Date**
Enbridge Inc.	common	$0.3025	Feb. 9	Mar. 1
Multibanc NT Financial	common	0.11	Feb. 9	Mar. 5
Nfld Power Inc.	pfd ser D 7.25%	0.18125	Feb. 9	Mar. 1
Nortel Networks Corp.	pfd A ser 5	0.31875	Feb. 11	Mar. 1
Sears Canada Inc.	common	0.06	Feb. 11	Mar. 31
Shell Canada Ltd.	class A (common)	0.18	Feb. 11	Mar. 15
Hollinger Inc.	common	0.15	Feb. 23	Mar. 10
Algoma Central Corp.	common	0.25	Feb. 14	Mar. 1
Groupe Videotron	common	0.015	Feb. 28	Mar. 21
Petro-Canada	common	0.10	Mar. 1	Apr. 1
Canadian National Railway	common	0.175	Mar. 2	Mar. 27
Suncor Energy Inc.	common	0.17	Mar. 13	Mar. 24
Trimark Financial Corp.	common	0.05	Mar. 21	Apr. 6
Great Eastern Corp.	pfd 4.5% 1st	0.1125	Mar. 30	May 1
TransCanada Pipelines	pfd 1st ser S	0.64375	Apr. 26	May 15

Source: *The Financial Post*

Discussion Questions

Use the information in Exhibit 5–12 to answer Discussion Questions 5–10 through 5–13.

5–10. If you had owned 500 shares of Petro-Canada, how much of a dividend would you have received, and when would you have expected payment?

5–11. If you were considering selling your shares in Nortel Networks Corp., what data should you consider?

5–12. Shell Canada Ltd., Petro-Canada, and Suncor Energy Inc. are all large oil and gas companies. If you were planning to invest in one of these companies in the oil and gas industry, what information would you consider?

5–13. Both Enbridge Inc. and TransCanada Pipelines are energy transportation companies. The Enbridge common shares pay a dividend roughly one-half of the TransCanada preferred shares. Why do you suppose the Enbridge dividends on common shares would be less than the TransCanada preferred shares?

Discussion Questions (continued)

5–14. As you listen to a broadcast of investor news on the radio, you hear an angry investor advocate accuse large corporations of taking advantage of the small shareholder. As part of the attack, the investor advocate cites the following example:

Mega-Millions Ltd. pays only $0.10 per share dividend each year on its common shares, even though its retained earnings balance is now in excess of $6 billion.

The investor advocate then goes on the accuse Mega-Millions Ltd. of hoarding profits. How would you respond to the advocate's accusation if you were the spokesperson for Mega-Millions Ltd.?

Cash Dividends on Preferred Shares   The procedures associated with the payment of dividends on preferred shares are exactly the same as those for common shares. The distinctions between these two classes of shares are based on the preference features of preferred shares. If a corporation has preferred shares and elects to pay dividends, the preferred shareholders receive their dividend before the common shareholders can be paid.

ARTICULATION

articulation   The links among the financial statements.

Earlier in this chapter, we referred to the link between income and owners' equity. We call this link the **articulation** (or connection) of the financial statements. The three financial statements discussed thus far are definitely linked. Articulation is an important concept to understand. The income statement tells the story of the company's earnings activity for this period, and the balance sheet presents a picture of the company's current financial position. The third statement we introduced, the statement of owners' equity, provides a bridge between the other two. Let's look closer at how these three tools fit together.

Financial Statements of a Proprietorship

For a proprietorship, the set of these statements would look like that shown in Exhibit 5–13, which presents articulation visually. The arrows connecting items from the three financial statements show the relationships that should always exist. Net income is calculated on the income statement and used on the statement of owner's equity. The ending balance shown on the statement of owner's equity is used on the balance sheet. The following accounting equation shows that this important relationship still holds true.

$$A = L + OE$$
$$\$12,120 = \$1,000 + \$11,120$$

Exhibit 5–13 illustrates each of the three statements in a very simplistic form. Notice that Laura's Business has only one asset—cash—the assumption being that all activities recorded in these three statements involved cash. If only accounting statements really were so simple! Make sure you know how to use the information

Exhibit 5–13
Income Statement,
Statement of Owner's
Equity, and Balance
Sheet for a
Proprietorship

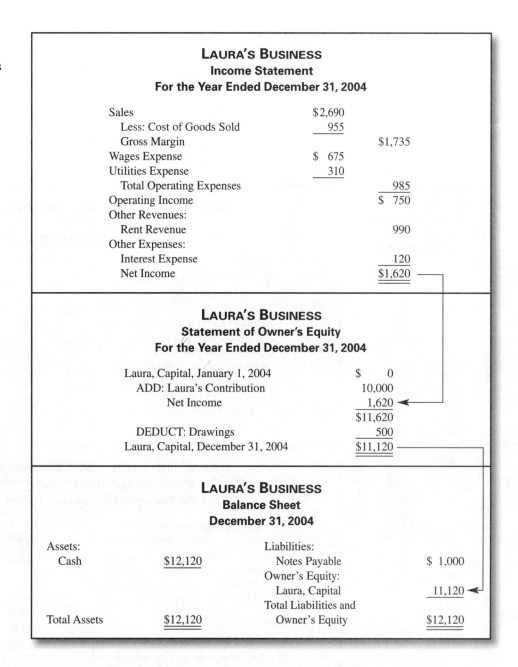

LAURA'S BUSINESS
Income Statement
For the Year Ended December 31, 2004

Sales	$2,690	
Less: Cost of Goods Sold	955	
Gross Margin		$1,735
Wages Expense	$ 675	
Utilities Expense	310	
Total Operating Expenses		985
Operating Income		$ 750
Other Revenues:		
Rent Revenue		990
Other Expenses:		
Interest Expense		120
Net Income		$1,620

LAURA'S BUSINESS
Statement of Owner's Equity
For the Year Ended December 31, 2004

Laura, Capital, January 1, 2004	$ 0
ADD: Laura's Contribution	10,000
Net Income	1,620
	$11,620
DEDUCT: Drawings	500
Laura, Capital, December 31, 2004	$11,120

LAURA'S BUSINESS
Balance Sheet
December 31, 2004

Assets:		Liabilities:	
Cash	$12,120	Notes Payable	$ 1,000
		Owner's Equity:	
		Laura, Capital	11,120
		Total Liabilities and	
Total Assets	$12,120	Owner's Equity	$12,120

provided on this simple set of statements before we move on to investigate more complex sets of statements. Also, be sure you can explain in your own words how the information provided on each statement is affected by the information shown on the others.

 Discussion Question

5–15. If a clerk in Laura's Business decided to slip the cash from a sale into his pocket and not record the sale, how would each of the statements in Exhibit 5–13 be affected?

Financial Statements of a Partnership

By now it should be clear that the formats of the financial statements of partnerships are only slightly different from those for proprietorships. To provide a complete set of examples, however, we present the articulated statements of Laura and Stephanie's partnership in Exhibit 5–14.

Again, the arrows show the articulation between statements. The major difference between this set of statements and the set prepared for a proprietorship

Exhibit 5–14
Income Statement,
Statement of Partners'
Equity, and Balance
Sheet for a Partnership

LAURA AND STEPHANIE'S BUSINESS
Income Statement
For the Year Ended December 31, 2004

Sales	$2,690	
LESS: Cost of Goods Sold	955	
Gross Margin		$1,735
Wages Expense	$ 675	
Utilities Expense	310	
Total Operating Expenses		985
Operating Income		$ 750
Other Revenues:		
Rent Revenue		990
Other Expenses:		
Interest Expense		120
Net Income		$1,620

LAURA AND STEPHANIE'S BUSINESS
Statement of Partners' Equity
For the Year Ended December 31, 2004

Laura, Capital, January 1, 2004	$ 0	
ADD: Laura's Contribution	6,000	
Net Income	972	
Laura, Capital, December 31, 2004		$ 6,972
Stephanie, Capital, January 1, 2004	$ 0	
ADD: Stephanie's Contribution	4,000	
Net Income	648	
	$4,648	
DEDUCT: Drawings	500	
Stephanie, Capital, December 31, 2004		4,148
Total Partners' Capital, December 31, 2004		$11,120

LAURA AND STEPHANIE'S BUSINESS
Balance Sheet
December 31, 2004

Assets:		Liabilities:		
Cash	$12,120	Notes Payable		$ 1,000
		Partners' Capital:		
		Laura, Capital	$6,972	
		Stephanie, Capital	4,148	
		Total Partners' Capital		11,120
		Total Liabilities and		
Total Assets	$12,120	Partners' Capital		$12,120

(Exhibit 5–13) is that these provide information about the activity in each partner's capital account and the statement of partners' equity.

As we explained in Chapter 1, not all partnerships are small organizations. KPMG, for example, is one of the largest accounting firms in Canada and the United States; it has more than 1,600 partners. With an organizational structure of that size, the financial statements of KPMG could not possibly offer details of each partner's holdings. Instead, figures are presented in terms of average amounts "per partner."

Financial Statements of a Corporation

Financial statements providing information about corporate activities differ from those based on the activities of proprietorships or partnerships. Income statements for the three business forms generally use the same format. The differences occur in the other two financial statements. To illustrate these differences, examine Exhibit 5–15, which shows the full set of three financial statements for Laura Corporation Limited.

Exhibit 5–15
Income Statement, Statement of Retained Earnings, and Balance Sheet for a Corporation

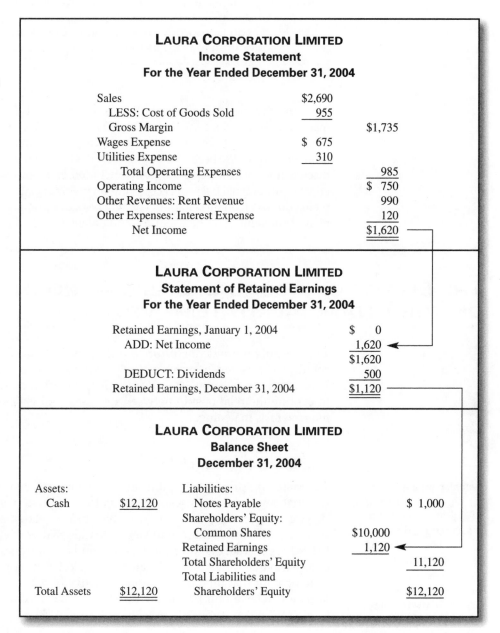

LAURA CORPORATION LIMITED
Income Statement
For the Year Ended December 31, 2004

Sales	$2,690	
LESS: Cost of Goods Sold	955	
Gross Margin		$1,735
Wages Expense	$ 675	
Utilities Expense	310	
Total Operating Expenses		985
Operating Income		$ 750
Other Revenues: Rent Revenue		990
Other Expenses: Interest Expense		120
Net Income		$1,620

LAURA CORPORATION LIMITED
Statement of Retained Earnings
For the Year Ended December 31, 2004

Retained Earnings, January 1, 2004	$ 0
ADD: Net Income	1,620
	$1,620
DEDUCT: Dividends	500
Retained Earnings, December 31, 2004	$1,120

LAURA CORPORATION LIMITED
Balance Sheet
December 31, 2004

Assets:		Liabilities:		
Cash	$12,120	Notes Payable		$ 1,000
		Shareholders' Equity:		
		Common Shares	$10,000	
		Retained Earnings	1,120	
		Total Shareholders' Equity		11,120
		Total Liabilities and		
Total Assets	$12,120	Shareholders' Equity		$12,120

Once again, the arrows demonstrate the articulation of these corporate statements. As you can see, the income statement is exactly like that in Exhibits 5–13 and 5–14, because the form of business organization does not affect that statement. The information from the income statement is used on the statement of retained earnings in Exhibit 5–15. Note that the balance sheet, although different from that for a proprietorship or partnership, still reflects the same ending balance in the shareholders' equity section as it does in the proprietorship and partnership.

Exhibit 5–15 completes our demonstration of articulation. Here Laura Corporation Limited uses a statement of retained earnings. Note that the same relationships among the statements hold true.

 ## Discussion Question

5–16. The balance sheet for the corporate form of business is a bit more detailed than that for the proprietorship. Comparing the two, what can you learn from the corporate balance sheet that you would not know from looking at the proprietorship's balance sheet?

Now that you have been introduced to the first three major financial statements and have seen how they fit together, you may be wondering when you can begin using them to make economic decisions and predict future cash flows. The more you know, the better you can utilize the financial statements, so we must first discuss how we measure the items included in them. Next, we will discuss the effect of the accrual basis of accounting on the financial statements. After you complete your work on this chapter, you will be better prepared to use the income statement, statement of owners' equity, and balance sheet to predict future cash flows.

THE EFFECT OF ACCRUAL BASIS ACCOUNTING ON THE FINANCIAL STATEMENTS

To be useful for predicting future profitability and cash flow, an income statement should measure revenues for a specific period of time and the expenses required to obtain those revenues. Recall from Chapter 2 that accrual accounting attempts to capture the relationship between revenues and expenses. This relationship is referred to as matching.

The Matching Principle

matching principle
Accounting principle that relates the expenses to the revenues of a particular income statement period. Once it is determined in which period a revenue should be recognized, the expenses that helped to generate the revenue are matched to that same period.

The **matching principle** requires that we match revenue with the cost of producing that revenue (expenses). Therefore, the first step in the accrual matching process requires us to determine in which income statement period to recognize a particular revenue. The second step demands that we determine which expenses helped to generate that revenue. Consequently, we recognize both the revenue and expense in that same financial statement period. This approach makes the income statement for that time period more reflective of true earnings results, and therefore more relevant for predicting future potential. Accrual accounting attempts to portray the *reality of performance.* Do not be misled. It can be very difficult to determine which expenses are responsible for generating which revenue, so we exercise a significant amount of judgment in recognizing expenses under the accrual basis of accounting.

Two possible relationships exist between revenues and expenses that determine when to recognize expenses:

1. *Direct cause and effect.* When a direct link can be found between an expense and the revenue it helps generate, we can easily apply the matching principle. If Canadian General Insurance Company (CGI) pays a 10 percent sales commission to its salespersons, and a salesperson makes a sale of $1,000, the company incurs a $100 expense. Once CGI determines in which income statement period to recognize the $1,000 revenue, it recognizes the $100 in that same period.

2. *No direct cause and effect.* When no direct cause and effect exists, a firm has two possible expense recognition treatments:

   a. ALLOCATION TO THE PERIODS BENEFITED. If a purchased item provides a discernible benefit to future income statement periods and the periods can be reasonably estimated, the item is recorded as an asset when purchased. (Remember that an asset has a probable future benefit to the entity.) The cost of that item is then systematically converted to expense in the periods benefited. For example, when we pay a two-year premium for insurance coverage, a benefit to future periods exists. Further, we can clearly estimate which of those future periods benefit from the policy—the next 24 months. As time passes during the two years, we allocate the cost of the insurance coverage to expense.

   b. IMMEDIATE RECOGNITION. Two situations make immediately recording the expense the most appropriate course of action.

   1. If a purchased item has no discernible future benefit, or the periods benefited cannot be reasonably estimated, we immediately recognize the cost of the item as an expense. Honda's television advertising, intended to increase sales of the Civic, provides Honda with immediate benefits and some lasting benefits such as name recognition. Television ads purchased and presented to the public in one period probably benefit future periods, but we cannot reasonably estimate how many periods and how much benefit in each of those periods. Thus, we usually recognize the cost of television advertising as an expense in the periods when the ads are presented to consumers.

   2. When the amount of an expenditure that provides future benefits is not material, we immediately recognize it as an expense because allocation of the cost over several periods provides us with no additional useful information. As an example, if IBM purchases a $10 stapler that can last five years, the recognition of $2 per year for five years versus $10 in the year of purchase is immaterial to IBM's income statement in any of those years. In addition, the record-keeping cost of recording the stapler as an asset on the balance sheet and then allocating $2 per year as an expense on the income statement for five years far outweighs the benefit of doing so. Therefore, we use the cost/benefit assumption to recognize the $10 cost as an immediate expense.

amortization The systematic and rational conversion of a long-lived asset's cost from asset to expense in the income statement periods benefited.

When a firm acquires assets that will benefit the company for more than one accounting period, the cost is recorded as an asset (unexpired cost) on the balance sheet. As time passes, the cost is transferred to expense on the income statement. We call this form of "allocation to the periods benefited" **amortization.** Amortization is applied to a variety of long-lived assets such as machinery, buildings, and equipment. One asset that has a long life but is not amortized is land.

Accounting Amortization

Accounting amortization is a systematic and rational allocation of the cost of a long-lived item from asset to expense. Recall the McCumber Enterprises transactions from Chapter 2. Under cash basis accounting, McCumber Enterprises' purchase of a $14,000 vehicle resulted in a $14,000 expense because that amount of cash was spent. Did the company use all the benefits of that vehicle in that year, or does the asset still have a future benefit? Clearly the vehicle has not been used up all in a single year, nor has the company received all the benefit from it. The accrual basis of measurement takes the position that the $14,000 cash payment represents an asset because it has probable future benefit to McCumber Enterprises. Over time, McCumber Enterprises will convert the cost of the vehicle from asset to expense as it derives the benefit from the use of the vehicle. The resulting expense is called **amortization expense.**

amortization expense The amount of cost associated with a long-lived asset converted to expense in a given income statement period.

Do not confuse the accounting term *amortization* with the common usage of depreciation. Common usage of *depreciation* involves the loss of market value. Accounting amortization is the systematic allocation of cost to expense for long-lived assets. This allocation requires two highly subjective estimates: (1) the useful life of the asset and (2) the residual value of the asset.

The useful life of an asset is the length of time the asset will be of use to the company (not the length of time the asset will exist). Notice that in the case of the McCumber Enterprises, Gertie McCumber feels that the vehicle will fill the company's needs for four years, which is not the same as saying the vehicle will last four years. There is an important distinction.

If the estimated useful life of an asset is less than the physical life of that asset, it follows that the asset will probably be sold at the end of its useful life. The estimated amount for which the asset can be sold at the end of its useful life is known as its **residual value,** *salvage value,* or *scrap value.*

residual value The estimated value of an asset when it has reached the end of its useful life. Also called *salvage* or *scrap value.*

In calculating amortization, we subtract the estimated residual value from the asset cost to arrive at the **amortizable base.** McCumber Enterprises recorded the $14,000 cost of the vehicle and estimated that at the end of its four-year useful life, the vehicle could be sold for $2,000. The amortizable amount is $12,000 ($14,000 − $2,000). In one sense, McCumber Enterprises' true vehicle cost is $12,000, because the company expects to recoup $2,000 of the purchase price when the vehicle is sold.

amortizable base The total amount of amortization expense that is allowed to be claimed for an asset during its useful life. The amortizable base is the cost of the asset less its residual value.

Once the useful life and residual value of the asset have been estimated, a company must select an amortization method. Members of the accounting profession have developed several over the years. The simplest method is **straight-line amortization,** and we will use it to demonstrate how to calculate amortization.

straight-line amortization A method of calculating periodic amortization. The amortizable base of an asset is divided by its estimated useful life. The result is the amount of amortization expense to be recognized in each year of the item's estimated useful life: (Cost − Residual Value)/N = Annual Amortization Expense.

The straight-line approach allocates an equal amount of amortization expense to each period of the asset's estimated useful life. The amount of expense is calculated by dividing the estimated useful life of the asset into the amortizable amount of the asset. In the case of McCumber Enterprises' vehicle, the expense amount equals $3,000 per year ($12,000/4). Each year of the four-year estimated useful life, the company will transfer $3,000 of the asset "vehicle" on the balance sheet into the expense "amortization" on the income statement, until the entire amortizable base has been recognized as expense.

The amortization process is one example of the matching principal at work. Because the timing of cash receipts and payments does not always coincide with the proper recognition of revenues and expenses, we have to explore other needed adjustments.

Discussion Question

5–17. Recall the scenario, introduced in Discussion Question 2–20, involving your purchase of a computer from Image Technologies. If the computer is to be used in the business you operate from your home, how should the purchase be treated

    a. under the cash basis?

    b. under the accrual basis?

Accruals and Deferrals

Because accrual accounting attempts to recognize revenues in the income statement period they are earned, and to match the expenses that generated the revenue to the same income statement period, adjustments must be made each period to ensure that these guidelines have been followed. The adjustment process takes place at the end of the financial statement period, but before the financial statements can be prepared. This process involves reviewing the financial records to be sure that all items that should be recognized in the current period have been recorded, and that no items that should be recognized in future periods appear in the current period's records.

The two basic types of **adjustments** that are necessary are accruals and deferrals.

1. **Accruals** are adjustments made to recognize items that should be included in the income statement period but have not yet been recorded. Accrual adjustments recognize revenue or expense *before* the associated cash is received or paid. There are two types of accruals:

   a. Accrued revenues are revenues that are considered to be earned during the financial statement period, because they met the revenue recognition criteria, but that have not yet been recognized. Consider Warner Management Consulting Services, Inc. For regular clients, the company sends bills on the second day of each month for work done during the previous month. Warner has a legal claim at the end of December to services it provided in that month. Revenues recognized (recorded) should include the amount earned in December, even though the clients will not be billed until January 2 of the next year.

   b. Accrued expenses are expenses that are deemed to have been incurred during the financial statement period but that have not yet been recognized. Assume Pellum Company pays its employees every two weeks for work performed in the previous two weeks. If part of the two-week pay period is in 2004 and part is in 2005, Pellum must make an adjustment at the end of 2004 to recognize the portion of wages expense incurred during that period.

2. **Deferrals** are postponements of the recognition of revenue or expense even though the cash has been received or paid. Deferrals are adjustments of revenues for which the cash has been collected but not yet earned, and of expenses for which cash has been paid but no benefit has yet been received.

   a. Unearned revenues are created when cash is received before it is earned. For example, Chad's Lawn Service provides lawn care to many local families. On June 1, the Bidlack family sends the company $450 for the cost of three months' lawn service. As of June 1, Chad's Lawn Service has not earned any revenue, even though it has received cash. In fact, receipt

---

adjustments Changes made in recorded amounts of revenues and expenses in order to follow the guidelines of accrual accounting.

accruals Adjustments made to record items that should be included on the income statement, but have not yet been recorded.

accrued revenues Revenues appropriately recognized under accrual accounting in one income statement period although the associated cash will be received in a later income statement period.

accrued expenses Expenses appropriately recognized under accrual accounting in one income statement period although the associated cash will be paid in a later income statement period.

deferrals Situations in which cash is either received or paid, but the income statement effect is delayed until some later period. Deferred revenues are recorded as liabilities, and deferred expenses are recorded as assets.

unearned revenues
Revenues created when cash is received before the revenue is earned. Because the cash received has not yet been earned, an obligation is created and a liability is recorded. Later, when the cash is deemed to have been earned, it will be recognized as a revenue.

prepaid expenses Expenses created when cash is paid before any benefit is received. Because the benefit to be derived is in the future, the item is recorded as an asset. Later, when the benefit is received from the item, it will be recognized as an expense.

of unearned cash creates a liability. The company owes the Bidlack family either three months of lawn service or a cash refund. The key here is who has legal claim to the cash. Because Chad's Lawn Service has no legal claim to the cash, it cannot account for it as earned revenue. By the time the month ends in June, however, the company earns one month's fees and recognizes $150 as revenue. The remaining $300, representing two month's fees, remains an unearned revenue. This amount represents a liability for Chad's Lawn Service and will remain so until the company either performs the services required to attain a legal claim to the cash, or returns the cash to the Bidlack family.

b. **Prepaid expenses** are created when cash is paid before an expense has been incurred. On January 2, 2004, Crockett Cookie Company purchased a three-year insurance policy for $2,400. By December 31, 2004, one-third of the insurance coverage has expired (one-third of the benefit has been received). Financial statements prepared for 2004 should reflect the fact that one-third of the cost of the policy ($800) is an expense for that year. The remaining portion of the policy, two years' worth of coverage, is an asset providing future benefits to the company. Even though the entire $2,400 was spent in 2004, two-thirds of the cost is prepaid expense, an asset that will be recognized as an expense in future periods.

The adjusting process preserves the integrity of accrual basis accounting. Keep in mind the following:

1. Accruals occur in situations when the cash flow has not yet taken place, but the revenue or expense should be recognized.
2. Deferrals are necessary in cases when the cash flow has already taken place, but the associated revenue or expense should not yet be recognized. The type of adjustments necessary to reflect the guidelines of accrual accounting depends on the way the item is originally recorded. Understand, too, that the original transaction (the receipt or payment of cash) is not an adjustment, but rather it creates a situation in which an adjustment will be necessary later.

Whether they reflect expenses or revenues, accruals and deferrals will always possess the following three characteristics:

1. *A revenue item or an expense item will always be affected.* The whole purpose of the adjustment process is to make certain that revenues and expenses associated with a given financial statement period are recognized in that period. Clearly, adjustments will always affect the income statement.
2. *An asset item or a liability item will always be affected.* Accruals and deferrals require the adjustment or recognition of an asset or liability. Thus, the balance sheet will also be affected by the adjustment process.
3. *Cash is never affected by accruals or deferrals.* Remember, adjustments are made to properly recognize accounting elements. It is assumed that inflows and outflows of cash were properly recorded at the time they occurred.

Accrual Basis Financial Statements

Let's revisit the transactions of McCumber Enterprises (a proprietorship) for the month of January 2004, which were first seen in Chapter 2. For your convenience, the descriptions of the company's transactions are restated here and a few additional details are provided.

1. Gertie McCumber started the company on January 2 by investing $200,000.

2. McCumber Enterprises borrowed $100,000 from the Friendly Bank on January 2 by signing a one-year, 12 percent note payable. Although the $100,000 does not have to be repaid until January 2, 2005, the interest charge must be paid each month, beginning on February 2, 2004. (Note the addition of interest.)

3. The company purchased a vehicle on January 2 for $14,000 cash. Gertie estimates that the vehicle will fill the company's needs for four years, after which she estimates she can sell it for $2,000.

4. The company paid cash for $75,000 of merchandise inventory on January 8.

5. On January 15, the company sold merchandise that cost $42,000 for a total selling price of $78,000 and collected the cash the same day.

6. On January 22, the company sold merchandise that cost $15,000 for a total selling price of $32,000 on account (a credit sale). The terms of the sale were 30 days, meaning McCumber Enterprises can expect to receive payment by February 21.

7. Cash payments for operating expenses in January totaled $22,500.

8. Besides the bank loan, the only amounts owed by the company at the end of the month were:

   a. $2,000 to company employees for work performed in January. They will be paid on February 3.

   b. A $700 utility bill that was received on January 26 and will be paid on February 15.

All eight transactions will affect the income statement and/or the balance sheet and statement of owner's equity under the accrual basis of accounting. The income statement for January 2004 looks like Exhibit 5–16.

Exhibit 5–16
Accrual Basis Income
Statement

McCUMBER ENTERPRISES		
Income Statement		
For the Month Ended January 31, 2004		
Sales Revenue	$110,000	
Cost of Goods Sold	57,000	
Gross Margin		$53,000
Expenses:		
Cash Operating Expenses	$ 22,500	
Wages Expense	2,000	
Utilities Expense	700	
Interest Expense	1,000	
Amortization Expense	250	
Total Operating Expenses		26,450
Net Income		$26,550

Most of the items on this income statement differ from those items prepared under the cash basis (Exhibit 2–6 on page 46). Look closely at each item:

- *Sales Revenue.* Under the accrual basis, we recognize revenue when it is earned and either is realized or the company has an enforceable claim to receive the cash. McCumber Enterprises made two sales during January; one was received in cash and the other created an enforceable account receivable. We recognize both as sales revenue for January of $110,000 ($78,000 cash sale + $32,000 credit sale).

- *Cost of Goods Sold.* Accrual accounting attempts to match all expenses to the same income statement period as the revenues they help generate. Cost of goods sold directly relates to the sales made in January because it is the cost of those items sold in January. The inventory sold cost $57,000 ($42,000 + $15,000). McCumber Enterprises purchased $75,000 of inventory and sold $57,000, leaving $18,000 of merchandise inventory on hand. We will discuss this remaining inventory when we talk about the balance sheet.
- *Cash Operating Expenses.* Under the accrual basis measurement, expenses paid in cash this period to support operations during this period (with no future benefits) are considered to be expenses for this period.
- *Wages Expense of $2,000.* Because employees earned wages during January, McCumber Enterprises has a legal liability at January 31 for this amount. Because McCumber Enterprises derived the benefit from the employees' work in January, we recognize the expense in January, regardless of when McCumber Enterprises pays the employees.
- *Utilities Expense of $700.* Because McCumber Enterprises received the bill in January, it represents utilities purchased and used during January. In that case, the expense should be recognized in January.
- *Interest Expense of $1,000.* When McCumber Enterprises borrows money from the bank, interest accrues from the first day of the loan. Because the company had the $100,000 throughout the month of January, the interest cost for the month should be recognized as a January expense. The amount is calculated using the formula explained in Chapter 4:

$$\text{Principal} \times \text{Rate} \times \text{Time} = \text{Interest}$$
$$\$100{,}000 \times 12\% \times 1/12 = \$1{,}000$$

- *Amortization Expense of $250.* Accrual accounting amortizes the cost of long-lived assets over the period useful to the entity. Using straight-line amortization, amortization equals $3,000 per year ($14,000 − $2,000)/4. Because McCumber Enterprises' financial statements depict only the month of January 2004, the amount of amortization expense would be only $250 ($3,000/12) for the month.

Discussion Questions

5-18. Reexamine each item on McCumber Enterprises' accrual basis income statement. Identify the items that result from the adjustment process.

5-19. Consider the following statement as it relates to the accrual basis of economic measurement: "Net income is an opinion, cash is a fact." What do you think this means?

Now that we have discussed the effect of accrual accounting on the income statement, we can see how this system affects the statement of owner's equity. The $200,000 investment by the owner is treated just as it was under the cash basis (see Exhibit 5-17).

Exhibit 5–17
Accrual Basis
Statement of Owner's
Equity

McCUMBER ENTERPRISES
Statement of Owner's Equity
For the Month Ended January 31, 2004

G. McCumber, Capital, January 1, 2004	$ 0
Investment by Owner	200,000
Net Income	26,550
G. McCumber, Capital, January 31, 2004	$226,550

Exhibit 5–18 illustrates the accrual basis balance sheet for McCumber Enterprises at January 31, 2004. Note that the items we discussed for the income statement also have an effect on the balance sheet.

Exhibit 5–18
Accrual Basis
Balance Sheet

McCUMBER ENTERPRISES
Balance Sheet
January 31, 2004

Assets:			Liabilities:	
Cash		$266,500	Accounts Payable	$ 700
Accounts Receivable		32,000	Wages Payable	2,000
Inventory		18,000	Interest Payable	1,000
Vehicle	$14,000		Note Payable	100,000
Less: Accumulated			Total Liabilities	$103,700
Amortization	(250)		Owner's Equity:	
Vehicle, Net		13,750	G. McCumber, Capital	226,550
			Total Liabilities	
Total Assets		$330,250	and Owner's Equity	$330,250

- *Cash of $266,500.* The cash amount results from the cash transactions. The method of measurement does not change cash.
- *Accounts Receivable of $32,000.* Transaction 6 created the account receivable. McCumber Enterprises recognized the sale because an exchange took place and title to the merchandise inventory passed to the customer, creating an enforceable claim to $32,000 in February. The claim provides McCumber Enterprises with a probable future benefit or an asset. It will remain classified as an asset until the customer pays McCumber Enterprises the cash.
- *Inventory of $18,000.* The remaining amount of merchandise inventory not sold has probable future benefit to McCumber Enterprises. It will remain classified as an asset until it is sold.
- *Vehicle of $14,000.* The original cost of the vehicle remains on the balance sheet until McCumber Enterprises sells or disposes of the asset.
- *Accumulated Amortization of $250.* To alert users that a portion of the original vehicle cost was converted to expense, we deduct an amount called **accumulated amortization** from the asset cost to derive a **net book value** of $13,750. The accumulated amortization amount grows until it reaches the amortizable base; likewise, the net book value declines until it reaches the residual value.
- *Accounts Payable of $700.* As McCumber Enterprises uses utilities during the month, it accrues a legal liability to pay the utility company. When McCumber Enterprises receives the bill, it can measure the amount of the liability. McCumber Enterprises recognizes the utilities expense, and the corresponding

accumulated amortization
The total amount of cost that has been systematically converted to expense since a long-lived asset was first purchased.

net book value The original cost of a long-lived asset less its accumulated amortization.

liability that requires the future sacrifice of assets (cash) in the future. It will remain classified as a liability until McCumber Enterprises pays the bill.

- *Wages Payable of $2,000.* McCumber Enterprises owes its employees for wages at the balance sheet date. We recognize the expense and the liability during the adjustment process.
- *Interest Payable of $1,000.* McCumber Enterprises owes the bank at the balance sheet date for the interest accrued during January. We recognize the expense and the liability during the adjustment process.
- *Note Payable of $100,000.* McCumber Enterprises owes Friendly Bank for the loan borrowed in January.
- *Capital of $226,550.* The ending capital balance shown on the accrual basis statement of owner's equity articulates to the accrual basis balance sheet. The complete set of financial statements for McCumber Enterprises is shown in Exhibit 5–19.

Exhibit 5–19
Set of Financial
Statements

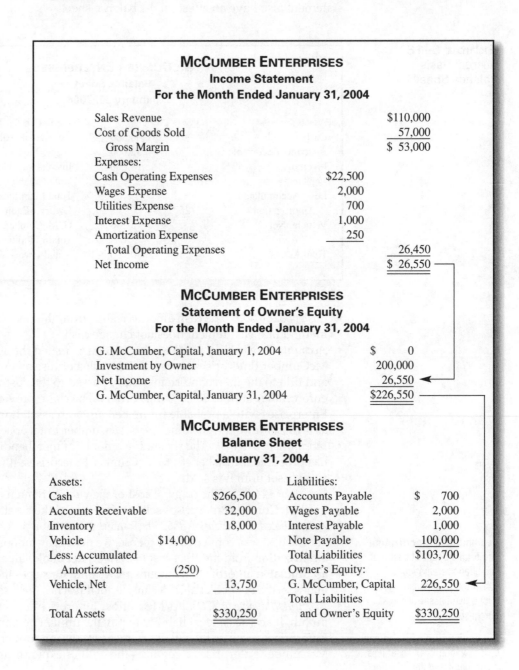

McCUMBER ENTERPRISES
Income Statement
For the Month Ended January 31, 2004

Sales Revenue		$110,000
Cost of Goods Sold		57,000
Gross Margin		$ 53,000
Expenses:		
Cash Operating Expenses	$22,500	
Wages Expense	2,000	
Utilities Expense	700	
Interest Expense	1,000	
Amortization Expense	250	
Total Operating Expenses		26,450
Net Income		$ 26,550

McCUMBER ENTERPRISES
Statement of Owner's Equity
For the Month Ended January 31, 2004

G. McCumber, Capital, January 1, 2004	$ 0
Investment by Owner	200,000
Net Income	26,550
G. McCumber, Capital, January 31, 2004	$226,550

McCUMBER ENTERPRISES
Balance Sheet
January 31, 2004

Assets:			Liabilities:	
Cash		$266,500	Accounts Payable	$ 700
Accounts Receivable		32,000	Wages Payable	2,000
Inventory		18,000	Interest Payable	1,000
Vehicle	$14,000		Note Payable	100,000
Less: Accumulated			Total Liabilities	$103,700
Amortization	(250)		Owner's Equity:	
Vehicle, Net		13,750	G. McCumber, Capital	226,550
			Total Liabilities	
Total Assets		$330,250	and Owner's Equity	$330,250

You may have found that accumulation of the information to prepare the financial statements was complicated. This process becomes much easier with an accounting system to properly capture the data. Chapter 6 introduces the basics of the accounting cycle to help us accumulate and organize transactions into meaningful information.

SUMMARY

The income statement is a financial statement providing information about the past performance of a company during a particular period of time. It consists of information about the rewards (revenues) and sacrifices (expenses) of doing business. The income statement shows the result of subtracting expenses from revenues. If revenues are greater than expenses, the result is net income; if expenses are greater than revenues for the period, the result is net loss.

Income statements may be prepared following either the single-step or multistep format. In the single-step income statement format, all revenues are gathered to form "total revenues." Then all expenses are listed and totaled to form "total expenses." In one step, expenses are subtracted from revenues, and the resulting net income or net loss is presented. The multistep format begins with one special revenue—sales. From that revenue, cost of goods sold is subtracted to determine gross margin. All remaining operating expenses are then subtracted to determine income from operations. Any other revenues or expenses are then presented to arrive at the final "net income" or "net loss." The bottom line (net income or net loss) of the two formats of income statements is the same, but the presentation of the revenues and expenses for the period is different.

Regardless of the income statement format chosen, net income results in an increase in owners' equity, and net losses result in a decrease in owners' equity. The effect of net income or net loss on owners' equity is shown on the statement of owners' equity. This financial statement shows the beginning balance in owners' equity at a particular point in time and how that balance was affected during the period to arrive at the ending balance.

The statement of owners' equity will take one of several forms, depending on the organizational form of the company. The owners' equity sections of proprietorships and partnerships consist of capital accounts for each owner. Therefore, we call a proprietorship statement a statement of owner's equity and a partnership statement a statement of partners' equity.

Corporations prepare statements of retained earnings.

In addition to net income or net loss, another item that affects the balance of owners' equity is distributions to owners. For proprietorships and partnerships, these distributions are called drawings or withdrawals. In a corporate setting, distributions to owners are called dividends, and cause a reduction of retained earnings. Both dividends and drawings reduce total owners' equity.

Dividends are paid to provide investors with a return on their investment and also to indicate the corporation's financial well-being. Two criteria must be met before a corporation can pay a dividend: (1) sufficient cash must be available to actually make the payment; and (2) the corporation's balance in retained earnings must exceed the dividend amount.

The income statement, statement of owners' equity or retained earnings, and balance sheet are all connected. The way in which these three financial statements fit together is known as articulation. The net income (or net loss) reported on the income statement is shown as an increase (or decrease) to owners' equity on the statement of owners' equity, or statement of retained earnings. The ending balance shown on this bridge statement is reported on the balance sheet. Articulation exists among the financial statements of a company, regardless of its form of business organization.

Under accrual accounting, revenue is recognized when it is both earned and realizable (when the company has a legal claim to the associated cash). Expenses are recognized when their benefit is deemed to have been received, regardless of when the associated cash is paid. Further, accrual accounting utilizes the matching principle to recognize expenses in the same income statement period as the revenues they helped generate.

The matching principle provides the foundation for accrual accounting's treatment of long-lived assets. The cost of a long-lived asset represents an asset because it provides the company with future benefits. The asset cost is systematically converted from asset to expense in the income statement periods benefited by the conversion process called amortization.

In addition to amortization, we record accrual and deferral adjustments in the accounting records to ensure that accrual accounting's revenue and expense recognition guidelines have been met before we prepare the financial statements. Accruals are adjustments made prior to any cash inflow or outflow to record earned-but-unreceived revenues and incurred-but-unpaid expenses. Deferrals are adjustments made for situations when the cash flow has already occurred to record unearned revenues and unexpired expenses.

KEY TERMS

accruals, p. 145	matching principle, p. 142
accrued expenses, p. 145	multistep income statement, p. 128
accrued revenues, p. 145	net book value, p. 149
accumulated amortization, p. 149	net income, p. 125
adjustments, p. 145	net loss, p. 125
amortizable base, p. 144	operating income, p. 128
amortization, p. 143	period, p. 125
amortization expense, p. 144	prepaid expenses, p. 146
articulation, p. 138	residual value, p. 144
cost of goods sold, p. 126	sales revenue, p. 128
date of declaration, p. 136	single-step income statement, p. 127
date of payment, p. 137	statement of owners' equity, p. 130
date of record, p. 136	statement of partners' equity, p. 131
deferrals, p. 145	statement of retained earnings, p. 132
drawings, p. 133	share dividend, p. 135
gross margin, p. 128	straight-line amortization, p. 144
income statement, p. 124	unearned revenues, p. 146

REVIEW THE FACTS

1. Name and define in your own words the accounting elements used to determine net income.
2. What is the primary expense associated with the products sold by merchandisers and manufacturers?

3. Name the two formats of the income statement and describe the differences between them.
4. What item is responsible for the primary increase in shareholders' equity?
5. What is the difference between a statement of owners' equity and a statement of retained earnings?
6. What is the effect of owners' drawings, and on what financial statement is this information reported?
7. Under what circumstances is a corporation able to pay a dividend?
8. How is a corporation's financial position affected by the payment of a dividend?
9. Explain the following terms: date of declaration, date of record, and date of payment.
10. Describe the meaning of articulation as it is used in accounting.
11. Under the accrual basis of accounting, when are expenses recognized?
12. Explain the concept of matching.
13. What is amortization and why is it necessary in accrual accounting?
14. Compare and contrast accruals and deferrals.

APPLY WHAT YOU HAVE LEARNED

LO 1:   Income Statement Terminology

1. Define the following terms in your own words:

   a. Revenue
   b. Expense
   c. Net income

   d. Net loss
   e. Gross margin
   f. Earnings

LO 1 & 2:   Terminology

2. Presented below is a list of items relating to the concepts discussed in this chapter, followed by definitions of those items in scrambled order:

   a. Revenues
   b. Expenses
   c. Income statement
   d. Statement of owners' equity
   e. Dividends

   f. Drawings
   g. Date of declaration
   h. Date of record
   i. Date of payment
   j. Articulation

   1. _____ The date distributions of earnings to owners of a corporation are actually paid
   2. _____ Inflows of assets from delivering or producing goods, rendering services, or other activities
   3. _____ Distribution of earnings to the owners of a corporation
   4. _____ The link between the income statement and the balance sheet
   5. _____ A bridge statement showing how the income statement and balance sheet are related
   6. _____ Distribution of earnings to the owners of proprietorships and partnerships
   7. _____ Outflows or other using up of assets from delivering or producing goods, rendering services, or carrying out other activities

8. _____ The date a corporation announces it will make a distribution of earnings to its owners

9. _____ A financial tool providing information about an entity's past performance

10. _____ Whoever owns shares on this date will receive the distribution of earnings previously declared

REQUIRED:

Match the letter next to each item on the list with the appropriate definition. Each letter will be used only once.

LO 2:   Income Statement Preparation

3. Phil Brock and Company had $75,985 in sales revenue during 2004. In addition to the regular sales revenue, the company rented out a small building it owned and received $4,800 for the year. Cost of goods sold for the year totaled $31,812. Other expenses for the year were as follows:

Rent	$10,500
Utilities	2,195
Advertising	4,265
Wages	$12,619
Interest	996

REQUIRED:

a. Prepare a 2004 income statement for Phil Brock and Company using a single-step format.

b. Prepare a 2004 income statement for Phil Brock and Company using a multistep format.

LO 2:   Income Statement Preparation

4. Sam Sosa and Company had $245,000 in sales revenue during 2004. In addition, Sosa had interest revenue of $7,600 for the year. Cost of goods sold for the year totaled $102,000. Other expenses for the year were:

Rent	$24,000
Wages	13,500
Advertising	2,200
Utilities	2,900

REQUIRED:

a. Prepare a 2004 income statement for Sam Sosa and Company using a single-step format.

b. Prepare a 2004 income statement for Sam Sosa and Company using a multistep format.

LO 2:   Income Statement Preparation

5. Pipkin's Camera and Video Ltd. had sales revenue of $770,000 during 2004. Expenses for the year were:

Wages	$ 72,000
Rent	64,000
Advertising	16,400
Cost of goods sold	550,000
Utilities	13,600

REQUIRED:

a. Prepare a 2004 income statement for Pipkin's Camera and Video Ltd. using a single-step format.

b. Prepare a 2004 income statement for Pipkin's Camera and Video Ltd. using a multistep format.

LO 2: Income Statement Preparation

6. The following information is taken from the accounting records of Albert's Baseball Card Shop for 2004:

Sales	$650,000
Wages	220,000
Store rent	39,000
Interest expense	42,000
Advertising	28,200
Electricity	6,800
Telephone	1,400
Cost of goods sold	$420,000
Rent revenue	18,000

REQUIRED:

a. Prepare a 2004 income statement for Albert's Baseball Card Shop using a single-step format.

b. Prepare a 2004 income statement for Albert's Baseball Card Shop using a multistep format.

c. If you were the owner of the company, which format of income statement would you prefer to use? Why?

LO 2: Income Statement Preparation

7. The following information is taken from the accounting records of Bea's Pet Shop for 2004:

Sales	$830,000
Cost of goods sold	440,000
Wages	280,000
Utilities	34,000
Rent	28,000
Advertising	22,000
Interest revenue	5,000

REQUIRED:

a. Prepare a 2004 income statement for Bea's Pet Shop using a single-step format.

b. Prepare a 2004 income statement for Bea's Pet Shop using a multistep format.

LO 3: Impact of Net Income on Owners' Equity

8. Refer to Bea's Pet Shop in the previous question.

REQUIRED:

a. Prepare the statement of owner's equity for Bea's Pet Shop for 2004 assuming that it operates as the sole proprietorship of Beatrice Wilson, who had a beginning capital balance of $10,000 and withdrew $20,000 during 2004.

b. Prepare the statement of retained earnings for Bea's Pet Shop Limited for 2004 assuming that Bea is the sole shareholder, the beginning retained earnings balance is $21,000, and Bea paid a cash dividend of $12,000.

LO 3: Impact of Net Income on Owner's Equity

9. Alvin Smith Enterprises reported the following information in the accounting records for 2004:

Sales	$250,000
Cost of goods sold	120,000
Salaries	70,000
Utilities	4,000
Rent	3,000
Advertising	1,000
Interest expense	2,000

REQUIRED:
a. Prepare the income statement for Alvin Smith Enterprises for 2004 using the multistep format.
b. Explain how the result determined in part (a) will affect the owner's equity for the year assuming that the company is a sole proprietorship.

LO 3: Impact of Net Income on Owners' Equity

10. Refer to Alvin Smith Enterprises in the previous question.

REQUIRED:
a. Prepare the statement of owners' equity for Alvin Smith Enterprises assuming it operates as the sole proprietorship of Alvin Smith, Sr., who had a beginning capital balance of $50,000.
b. Prepare the statement of partners' equity for Alvin Smith Enterprises assuming it operates as a partnership between Alvin Smith, Sr., and Al Smith, Jr.

	Alvin Smith, Sr.	Al Smith, Jr.
Partners share of profits	60%	40%
Beginning equity balance	$50,000	$5,000
Withdrawals	$20,000	$20,000

LO 3: Impact of Net Income on Owner's Equity

11. Jones Company reported the following information in the accounting records for 2004:

Sales	$530,000
Cost of goods sold	220,000
Wages	160,000
Utilities	74,000
Rent	8,000
Advertising	11,000
Interest revenue	3,000

REQUIRED:
a. Prepare the income statement for Jones Company for 2004 using the single-step format.
b. Explain how the result determined in part (a) will affect the owner's equity for the year assuming that the company is a sole proprietorship.

c. Explain how the result determined in part (a) will affect the equity if the company is Jones Company Inc., a corporation. (What account will be affected?)

LO 3: Impact of Net Income on Owners' Equity

12. Refer to Jones Company in the previous question.

REQUIRED:
a. Prepare the statement of owners' equity for Jones Company assuming it operates as the sole proprietorship of Ben Jones, who had a beginning capital balance of $50,000.
b. Prepare the statement of partners' equity for Ben Jones Company assuming it operates as a partnership between Ben Stiller and Kathy Jones.

	Ben Stiller	Kathy Jones
Partners' share of income	35%	65%
Beginning equity balance	$15,000	$45,000
Withdrawals	$12,000	$25,000
Additional capital contributions	$ 5,000	$ 0

LO 3: Impact of Net Income on Retained Earnings

13. Smythe Corporation reported the following information in its accounting records for 2004:

Net loss	$ 5,000
Sales	85,000
Beginning balance—Retained Earnings	26,000
Cost of sales	55,000
Expenses	35,000
Dividends	2,000

REQUIRED:
a. What is the balance of retained earnings at the end of 2004?
b. Prepare a single-step income statement for 2004.
c. Prepare the statement of retained earnings for 2004.

LO 4 & 5: Preparation of a Statement of Owners' Equity

14. Pfister Enterprises was organized on January 3, 2004. Although many companies are not profitable in their first year, Pfister experienced a modest net income of $9,500 in 2004.

REQUIRED:
a. Prepare a statement of owner's equity for Pfister Enterprises for the year ended December 31, 2004, assuming Ken Pfister began the company as a sole proprietorship by investing $20,000 of his own money.
b. Prepare a statement of partners' equity for Pfister Enterprises for the year ended December 31, 2004, assuming Kendra Pfister, Stephanie Winters, and Harriet Higgins began the company as a partnership. The three partners have agreed to share any income or loss in the same proportion as their initial investments, which were as follows:

Pfister	$ 6,000
Winters	4,000
Higgins	2,000
Total	$12,000

LO 4 & 5: Preparation of Statement of Equity

15. This problem is a continuation of problem 14. It is now December 31, 2005, and it is time to prepare the statement of owners' equity for Pfister Enterprises. Net income for the year ending December 31, 2005, was $18,000, and there were no additional owner investments during the year.

REQUIRED:

a. Prepare a statement of owner's equity for Pfister Enterprises for the year ended December 31, 2005, assuming the business was a proprietorship and that Ken Pfister took drawings totaling $8,000 during 2005.

b. Prepare a statement of partners' equity for Pfister Enterprises for the year ended December 31, 2005, assuming the partnership form. Recall from the previous problem that the partners share income in the same proportion as their initial investment. Drawings by the three partners during 2005 were as follows:

Pfister	$4,000
Winters	2,500
Higgins	1,500
Total	$8,000

LO 4, 5, & 6: Preparation of a Statement of Equity

16. Modell Company was organized on January 3, 2004. Many companies are not profitable in their first year, and Modell experienced a modest net loss of $4,500 in 2004.

REQUIRED:

a. Prepare a statement of owner's equity for Modell Company for the year ending December 31, 2004, assuming Art Modell began the company as a sole proprietorship by investing $50,000 of his own money. During 2004, Modell withdrew $5,000.

b. Prepare a statement of partners' equity for Modell Company for the year ended December 31, 2004, assuming Art Modell, Sally Weber, and Hillary Hager began the company as a partnership. The three partners have agreed to share any income or loss in the same proportion as their initial investments, which were as follows:

Modell	$ 5,000
Weber	4,000
Hager	1,000
Total	$10,000

LO 4 & 5: Preparation of a Statement of Equity

17. This problem is a continuation of problem 16. It is now December 31, 2005, and it is time to prepare the statement of owners' equity for Modell Company. Net income for the year ended December 31, 2005, was $54,000, and there were no additional owner investments during the year.

REQUIRED:

a. Prepare a statement of owner's equity for Modell Company for the year ended December 31, 2005, assuming the business was a proprietorship and that Art Modell took drawings totaling $18,000 during 2005.

b. Prepare a statement of partners' equity for Modell Company for the year ended December 31, 2005, assuming the partnership form. Recall from the previous problem that the partners share income in the same proportion as their initial investment. Drawings by the three partners during 2005 were as follows:

Modell	$ 8,000
Weber	5,000
Hager	5,000
Total	$18,000

LO 2, 4, & 7:   Identification of Business Type

18. Use the following set of financial statements to meet the requirements.

BONITA HERNANDEZ COMPANY
Income Statement
For the Year Ended December 31, 2004

Sales		$88,722
LESS: Cost of Goods Sold		41,912
Gross Margin		$46,810
Rent	$17,500	
Wages	14,408	
Advertising	7,345	
Utilities	1,640	
Total Operating Expenses		40,893
Operating Income		$ 5,917
Other Revenues: Rent Revenue		2,700
Other Expenses: Interest Expense		1,166
Net Income		$ 7,451

BONITA HERNANDEZ COMPANY
Statement of Owner's Equity
For the Year Ended December 31, 2004

B. Hernandez, Capital, January 1, 2004	$33,806
ADD: Net Income	7,451
	$41,257
DEDUCT: Drawings	9,000
B. Hernandez, Capital, December 31, 2004	$32,257

BONITA HERNANDEZ COMPANY
Balance Sheet
December 31, 2004

Assets:		Liabilities:	
Cash	$57,257	Notes Payable	$25,000
		Owner's Equity:	
		B. Hernandez, Capital	32,257
		Total Liabilities and	
Total Assets	$57,257	Owner's Equity	$57,257

REQUIRED:

a. Is Bonita Hernandez Company a sole proprietorship, a partnership, or a corporation? Explain how you arrived at your answer.

b. Is Bonita Hernandez Company's income statement in the single-step or multistep format? Explain how you determined your answer.

c. Explain the term *articulation,* and describe how the financial statements of Bonita Hernandez Company articulate.

LO 2, 4, & 7: Identification of Business Type

19. Use the set of financial statements that follow to meet the requirements.

REQUIRED:

a. Is The Christopher Wyont Company a sole proprietorship, a partnership, or a corporation? Explain how you arrived at your answer.

b. Prepare a single-step income statement for The Christopher Wyont Company.

c. Explain the term *articulation,* and describe how the financial statements of The Christopher Wyont Company articulate.

THE CHRISTOPHER WYONT COMPANY
Income Statement
For the Year Ended December 31, 2004

Sales		$688,250
LESS: Cost of Goods Sold		422,745
Gross Margin		$265,505
Rent	$ 38,456	
Wages	112,144	
Advertising	7,345	
Utilities	24,000	
Total Operating Expenses		181,945
Operating Income		$ 83,560
Other Revenues: Rent Revenue		24,600
Other Expenses: Interest Expense		3,246
Net Income		$104,914

THE CHRISTOPHER WYONT COMPANY
Statement of Owner's Equity
For the Year Ending December 31, 2004

C. Wyont, Capital, January 1, 2004	$388,560
ADD: Net Income	104,914
	$493,474
DEDUCT: Drawings	38,000
C. Wyont, Capital, December 31, 2004	$455,474

THE CHRISTOPHER WYONT COMPANY
Balance Sheet
December 31, 2004

Assets:		Liabilities:	
Cash	$705,474	Notes Payable	$250,000
		Owner's Equity:	
		Wyont, Capital	455,474
		Total Liabilities and	
Total Assets	$705,474	Owner's Equity	$705,474

LO 5: Statement of Retained Earnings

20. Wynn Corporation had the following information available for 2004:

Common shares (100,000 shares issued and outstanding)	$100,000
Net income for 2004	10,000
Dividends for 2004	5,000
Retained earnings at January 1, 2004	250,000

REQUIRED:

Prepare a statement of retained earnings for 2004 for Wynn Corporation.

LO 5: Statement of Retained Earnings

21. Bishop Corporation had the following information available at the end of 2004:

Common shares, January 1, 2004 (50,000 shares authorized and issued)	$125,000
Net income for 2004	20,000
Dividends for 2004	10,000
Retained earnings at January 1, 2004	70,000

REQUIRED:

Prepare a statement of retained earnings for 2004 for Bishop Corporation.

LO 5: Statement of Retained Earnings

22. Rook Corporation had the following information available for 2004:

Common shares, January 1, 2004 (50,000 shares authorized, 25,000 shares issued and outstanding)	$175,000
Net loss for 2004	35,000
Dividends for 2004	10,000
Retained earnings at January 1, 2004	197,000
Sale of 10,000 shares during 2004	100,000

REQUIRED:

Prepare a statement of retained earnings for 2004 for Rook Corporation.

LO 5: Statement of Retained Earnings

23. Einstein Corporation had the following information available for 2004:

Common shares, January 1, 2004 (150,000 shares authorized, 25,000 shares issued and outstanding)	$250,000
Net income for 2004	55,000
Dividends for 2004	25,000
Retained earnings at January 1, 2004	160,000
Sale of 10,000 shares on March 10	150,000

REQUIRED:

Prepare a statement of retained earnings for 2004 for Einstein Corporation.

LO 6: Dividend Terminology

24. Sampson Corporation will pay a cash dividend to its shareholders. This dividend is the first that has ever been paid, and the board of directors has questions about the proper procedure.

REQUIRED:

Explain the procedure for the payment of cash dividends by explaining what happens on the three important dates that control the payment of dividends.

LO 6: Dividends

25. The board of directors of McCormick Corporation is trying to decide whether or not to issue a cash dividend for the current year.

REQUIRED:

Identify and discuss the various business and legal issues that the board of directors must consider when setting the corporate dividend policy.

LO 6: Dividends

26. Cronin Corporation has paid a quarterly divided for each of the past 45 quarters. The current quarter posted a $150,000 loss, which is not unusual for the second quarter each year. Cronin Corporation is in an unfortunate position of having only $25,000 more in cash reserves than required to operate during the next 45 days.

REQUIRED:

a. List at least three alternatives that Cronin Corporation has in this situation.

b. Select the best of your alternatives and indicate how this will help the company in this dilemma.

LO 2 & 4: Comprehensive

27. The Michelle Miller Enterprises began on January 15, 2004, when Michelle Miller contributed $10,000 to a business account. During 2004, she contributed another $10,000 on June 1 and $15,000 on September 30. Ms. Miller withdrew $5,000 on December 20. The following is a summary of the remaining receipts and expenditures for the year of 2004:

Receipts:	
Sales	$235,000
Inventory loan from bank	50,000
Expenditures:	
Inventory	140,000
Repayment of loan	40,000
Selling expenses	37,000
Operating expenses	39,000
Interest expense	2,000

REQUIRED:

a. Prepare a multistep income statement for the year of 2004 for Michelle Miller Enterprises.

b. Prepare a statement of owner's equity for Michelle Miller Enterprises for the year of 2004.

LO 4: Comprehensive

28. Gan Manufacturing Company began on March 10, 2004, when LiLi Gan contributed $16,000 and MiMi Gan contributed $8,000. During the year, LiLi contributed an additional $5,000 and MiMi contributed an additional $2,000. The partnership agreement requires that income be divided two-thirds to LiLi and one-third to MiMi and that losses be divided equally. Because the partnership agreement also requires that any withdrawals be equal, each partner withdrew $4,000 in December.

REQUIRED:
a. Prepare a statement of partners' equity assuming that the net income for the year was $6,000.
b. Prepare a statement of partners' equity assuming that the net loss for the year was $8,000.

LO 8: The Matching Principle

29. Chrisco Inc. purchased $100,000 worth of merchandise inventory on December 15, 2004, on a 30-day account. It sold merchandise that cost $35,000 in December and the remainder in January 2005.

REQUIRED:
a. On what date should Chrisco Inc. pay for the merchandise?
b. Calculate how much of the $100,000 of merchandise appears in Cost of Goods Sold in December 2004 and how much appears on the balance sheet in Merchandise Inventory on December 31, 2004.

LO 8: The Matching Principle

30. Karen Price Inc. purchased $150,000 worth of merchandise inventory on December 5, 2003, on a special 90-day account. It sold merchandise that cost $55,000 in December and $70,000 in January 2004.

REQUIRED:
a. On what date should Karen Price Inc. pay for the merchandise?
b. Calculate how much of the $150,000 worth of merchandise appears in Cost of Goods Sold in December 2003 and how much appears on the balance sheet in Merchandise Inventory on December 31, 2003.
c. Calculate how much of the $150,000 worth of merchandise appears in Cost of Goods Sold in January 2004 and how much appears on the balance sheet in Merchandise Inventory on January 31, 2004.

LO 8: The Matching Principle

31. Geoffrey Corporation purchased a two-year insurance policy on May 1, 2004, by paying $4,800 on that date.

REQUIRED:
a. Indicate how Geoffrey Corporation will list information concerning this policy on its December 31, 2004, income statement and balance sheet under the accrual basis of accounting.
b. Indicate how Geoffrey Corporation will list information concerning this policy on its December 31, 2005, income statement and balance sheet under the accrual basis.

LO 8: The Matching Principle

32. Kazu & Liu paid its landlord $10,000 for five months' rent on November 1, 2004. The partnership has a calendar year end.

REQUIRED:

a. Indicate how Kazu & Liu will list information concerning this rental on its December 31, 2004, income statement and balance sheet under the accrual basis of accounting.

b. Indicate how Kazu & Liu will list information concerning this rental on its December 31, 2005, income statement and balance sheet under the accrual basis.

LO 8: The Matching Principle

33. Regina's Closet paid its landlord $1,600 for the first and last months' rent on March 1, 2004, when the business opened. The lease on the shop is for one year.

REQUIRED:

Indicate how Regina's Closet will list information concerning this rental on the March 31, 2004, income statement and balance sheet under the accrual basis of accounting.

LO 8: The Matching Principle

34. Lechleiter Real Estate Company collected $10,000 from Kazu & Liu for five months' rent on November 1, 2004. Lechleiter operates on a February 28 year end.

REQUIRED:

a. How much rental income will Lechleiter recognize in its February 28, 2005, income statement under the accrual basis of accounting? How will this affect the February 28, 2005, balance sheet?

b. How much rental income will Lechleiter recognize in its February 28, 2006, income statement under the accrual basis of accounting? How will this affect the February 28, 2006, balance sheet?

LO 8: The Matching Principle

35. Gaylon Garretson paid her accountant, Shannon Davis, $675 for three months' services in advance on December 16, 2004. By the end of December, Davis had completed the December services.

REQUIRED:

a. How much should Davis report as income for 2005 under the accrual basis of accounting? How will this affect Davis' January 31, 2005, balance sheet?

b. How should Garretson report this payment on her income statement and balance sheet for December 31, 2004, under the accrual basis?

LO 8: The Matching Principle

36. Dylan Hillhouse borrowed $10,000 for three months from First Fidelity Bank on November 1, 2004. Because Dylan was a recent graduate, the bank deducted the interest from the proceeds and deposited $9,700 to Dylan's bank account.

REQUIRED:

a. How much interest income should the bank report for 2004 for this loan if it uses the accrual basis of accounting?

b. How much interest expense should Dylan report for 2004 for this loan if he uses the accrual basis of accounting?

LO 8: The Matching Principle

37. Dolf Imports Company purchased with cash $200,000 worth of merchandise inventory in 2004, its first year of operations. In addition, the company paid $10,000 to package and label the entire inventory with its private label. It cost $12,000 to ship the items sold to customers. The company sold 75% of the inventory by year end.

REQUIRED:

List the expenses Dolf Imports Company would show on his income statement for 2004 under the accrual basis of accounting. How would this information affect the December 31, 2004, balance sheet?

LO 8: The Matching Principle

38. Perry Dennis borrowed $15,000 for his business at 9% interest from the Nations Bank on June 1, 2003, due on May 31, 2004. Interest is payable on the due date of the note.

REQUIRED:

a. How much interest will the business owe the bank when it pays the note on May 31, 2004?

b. How will Dennis report this event on his business's income statement and balance sheet for calendar year 2003 if it uses the accrual basis of accounting?

LO 8: The Matching Principle and Amortization

39. Tiffany's Toppers bought a commercial stitching machine on July 1, 2004, for $25,000. The owner estimates this machine will be useful for five years and will have no residual value because there is little market for used stitching machines.

REQUIRED:

a. Assuming the company uses the accrual basis of accounting, how much will it recognize as expense for the stitching machine in 2004, 2005, and 2006?

b. Assuming the company uses the accrual basis of accounting, how will it report this machine on its ending balance sheets for 2004, 2005, and 2006?

LO 8: The Matching Principle and Amortization

40. Christine's Delivery Service purchased a van on October 1, 2004, to deliver parcels for local merchants. The manager estimates that the van will last four years and can be sold for $2,000 at the end of the fourth year.

REQUIRED:

a. For accrual basis accounting, what will be the amortization expense for the calendar years of 2004, 2007, and 2009 if the cost of the van was
  (1) $26,000?
  (2) $34,000?

b. What will be the balance of Accumulated Amortization on December 31, 2004, 2007, and 2009 if the cost of the van was
  (1) $26,000?
  (2) $34,000?

LO 8: The Matching Principle and Amortization

41. Pitman Photo purchased a racing boat for $300,000 on March 31, 2004, to enter sporting events as a method of advertising. The owner believes that the boat can last ten years (unless it is wrecked). He knows, however, that to remain competitive, he will need to replace the boat after five years. If he keeps the boat five years, the residual value will be 50% of cost; and if he keeps it ten years, the residual value will be 15% of cost.

REQUIRED:

a. For accrual basis accounting, how much will Pitman Photo recognize as amortization expense for the calendar years of 2004, 2006, and 2008 if the owner plans to keep the boat
  (1) 5 years?
  (2) 10 years?

b. What will be the balance of Accumulated Amortization on December 31, 2004, 2006, and 2008 if the owner plans to keep the boat
  (1) 5 years?
  (2) 10 years?

LO 9: Accruals and Deferrals

42. Explain the difference between a prepaid expense and an accrued expense. A simple definition of these items will not suffice. You should concentrate on what these items really mean. Include in your answer at least one example of a prepaid expense and one example of an accrued expense.

LO 9: Accruals and Deferrals

43. Explain why accruals and deferrals are necessary under accrual basis accounting but not under cash basis accounting. Your answer should include a discussion of accruals and deferrals as they apply to both revenues and expenses.

LO 9: Accruals and Deferrals

44. Pratt Company reported sales of $200,000 for the year ended December 31, 2004. Sales were reported on the accrual basis. The accounts receivable at December 31, 2004, were $25,000 and at December 31, 2003, the receivables were $12,000.

REQUIRED:
Calculate the amount Pratt Company collected from customers during 2004.

LO 9: Accruals and Deferrals

45. The Foskin Company reported accounts receivable of $35,000 at December 31, 2003, and $48,000 at December 31, 2004. Cash collections from customers were $196,000 for the year.

REQUIRED:
Calculate the amount of sales reported on the accrual basis for the calendar year 2004.

LO 9: Accruals and Deferrals

46. The Frazier Corporation purchases all merchandise for resale on account. The balance of Accounts Payable at December 31, 2004, was $34,000 and the balance at December 31, 2005, was $29,000. The company paid $245,000 for merchandise purchases during the year. The company uses the accrual basis of accounting.

REQUIRED:
Determine the amount of merchandise purchases for the year of 2005.

LO 9: Accruals and Deferrals

47. The Tyson Corporation purchases all merchandise for resale on account. The balance of Accounts Payable at December 31, 2004, is $96,000 and the balance at December 31, 2005, is $120,000. Tyson Corporation paid $365,000 for merchandise purchases during the year.

REQUIRED:
Determine the amount of merchandise purchases on the accrual basis for the year 2005.

LO 9: Errors

48. Academy Inc. sold some merchandise inventory for cash during the current month. Unfortunately, the company's accounting clerk simply slipped the cash from the sale into his pocket and did not record the sale. Academy Inc. uses accrual accounting.

REQUIRED:
Explain how each of the following financial statements would be affected by the accounting clerk's behaviour. Avoid using one-word responses such as *understated* and *overstated*. You should approach this requirement as if you were explaining the effects to someone with no knowledge of accounting or financial statements.
  (1) Income statement
  (2) Statement of retained earnings
  (3) Balance sheet

LO 9:   Errors

49. The bookkeeper for Ajax Corporation mistakenly recorded a disbursement for equipment as if the payment had been for repairs and maintenance expense.

REQUIRED:

Explain how each of the following financial statements would be affected by the bookkeeper's error. Avoid using one-word responses such as *understated* and *overstated*. You should approach this requirement as if you were explaining the effects to someone with no knowledge of accounting or financial statements.

   (1) Income statement

   (2) Statement of retained earnings

   (3) Balance sheet

LO 9:   Errors

50. The bookkeeper for Miller Corporation mistakenly recorded a disbursement for advertising expense as if the payment had been for a parcel of land.

REQUIRED:

Explain how each of the following financial statements would be affected by the bookkeeper's error. Avoid using one-word responses such as *understated* and *overstated*. You should approach this requirement as if you were explaining the effects to someone with no knowledge of accounting or financial statements.

   (1) Income statement

   (2) Statement of retained earnings

   (3) Balance sheet

LO 9:   Errors

51. The bookkeeper for Elmendorf Corporation mistakenly recorded a disbursement for rent expense as if the payment had been for an insurance expense.

REQUIRED:

Explain how each of the following financial statements would be affected by the bookkeeper's error. Avoid using one-word responses such as *understated* and *overstated*. You should approach this requirement as if you were explaining the effects to someone with no knowledge of accounting or financial statements.

   (1) Income statement

   (2) Statement of retained earnings

   (3) Balance sheet

FINANCIAL REPORTING CASE

Comprehensive

52. Following are the comparative income statements for WestJet Airlines Ltd. for the fiscal years ended 2001 and 2000:

WESTJET AIRLINES LTD.
Consolidated Statements of Earnings & Retained Earnings (adapted)
For the Fiscal Years Ended December 31, 2001 and 2000
(amounts in thousands)

	2001	2000
Revenues:		
Passenger revenues	$452,910	$315,931
Charter & other	25,483	16,588
	$478,393	$332,519
Expenses:		
Passenger services	95,613	64,090
Aircraft fuel	84,629	55,875
Maintenance	72,317	49,512
Amortization	34,332	17,959
Sales & marketing	30,862	21,763
Flight operations	20,916	13,923
General & administration	20,893	12,147
Reservations	17,777	12,497
Aircraft leasing	15,284	6,770
Inflight	16,104	10,972
Employee profit share	10,311	13,549
	$419,038	$279,057
Earnings from operations	$ 59,355	$ 53,462
Non-operating income (expense)		
Interest income	2,837	2,463
Interest expense	(5,086)	(2,937)
Gain (loss) on disposal of capital assets	187	(282)
Gain on foreign exchange	986	—
	$ (1,076)	$ (756)
Earnings before income taxes	$ 58,279	$ 52,706
Income taxes:		
Current	15,974	18,102
Future	5,105	4,350
	$ 21,079	$ 22,452
Net earnings	$ 37,200	$ 30,254
Retained earnings, beginning of year	55,702	25,448
Retained earnings, end of year	$ 92,902	$ 55,702

Source: Westjet Airlines Ltd. 2001 Annual Report

a. Are the income statements presented in single-step or multistep format?

b. What is the total dollar increase in earnings from operations from fiscal year 2000 to fiscal year 2001?

c. What is the percentage of net earnings in relationship to total revenues for each of fiscal year 2000 and fiscal year 2001?

d. Based on these statements, how much of a dividend did Westjet declare in each of fiscal year 2000 and fiscal year 2001? What do you suppose would be the reason for this?

e. Summarize your opinion of Westjet's earnings performance for these two years and its potential as an investment. What information would you need to compare Westjet's performance to the performance of other Canadian airlines?

ANNUAL REPORT PROJECT

53. You can now begin your work on Section II of the annual report project. Section II involves the preparation of a SWOT analysis for your selected company. The acronym SWOT stands for strengths, weaknesses, opportunities, and threats. This section of the report should include an analysis of each of these four elements. The strengths and weaknesses of the company should be viewed from an internal perspective, and the opportunities and threats are viewed from an external perspective. You will focus on the external opportunities and threats in Chapter 6 and the internal strengths and weaknesses in this chapter. This part of your project is very interesting and informative. It should improve your ability to come to an overall conclusion about your company at the end of the project.

For this assignment, analyze the internal strengths and weaknesses of your company using the following outline:

I. List the specific strengths and weaknesses in your company in the areas of:
   A. Corporate Structure
      1. Does the structure improve decision making?
      2. Does the structure fit the current business environment?
   B. Corporate Culture
      1. What are the beliefs, values, and expectations of the personnel?
      2. Is the corporate mission clear to employees, customers, and the community?
      3. Is the corporate mission consistent with the corporate beliefs and values?
      4. Is the mission carried out well?
   C. Corporate Resources—How strong or weak are the following resources?
      1. Human resources
      2. Financial resources
      3. Management information system
      4. Manufacturing
      5. Research and development
      6. Marketing
      7. Distinctive competencies (Something this company is known for doing very well.)

Information gathered for the Section I may provide you with some good insight into your findings for the SWOT analysis. The press releases and articles published about your company and its industry will be helpful in finding the necessary information. A major source of information for this part of the project may be found in the Management's Discussion and Analysis of your company's annual report.

II. After listing the attributes of your company, write at least a two-paragraph summary of your analysis of the internal environment of the company.

Turn this assignment in to your professor and keep a copy for your final report.

6 Accumulating Accounting Data

*Y*our mother recently retired, or tried to retire. The only problem was that her former clients continued to call her with small jobs. Because she could not say no, her retirement has turned into a new job as a consultant. Mom always worked for someone else and never kept records beyond weekly expense reports. At the end of the year she realized that she would soon need to prepare her tax return. She is not sure what to report. You try to explain to her about expenses and net income but she is confused. When you ask to see her books, her response is, "What books?" Sounds like she could use your help.

Although financial statement users often do not care how the numbers got to the financial statements, the better a user understands the accounting process, the more he or she can understand the implications of those numbers. When we understand how the accounting system interprets the revenue recognition and the expense recognition principles, we understand the meaning of the income and expense numbers on the income statement. When we comprehend the checks and balances inherent in the accounting system, we can appreciate the need for internal control to protect those checks and balances. When we grasp the concept of financial statement articulation, we notice when something is not right with a set of financial statements. ■

So where do we begin? We will walk through each step of the accounting process, learning how to apply the accounting equation in each decision-making situation. We will apply the concepts discussed in Chapter 5 about revenue and expense recognition, accruals, and deferrals. We will exercise the financial statement concepts from Chapters 3, 4, and 5. In essence, we will apply accounting principles within an accounting system that transforms events and data into valuable accounting information.

LEARNING OBJECTIVES

After completing your work on this chapter, you should be able to do the following:

1. Identify the eight steps of the accounting cycle.
2. Distinguish between debits and credits and apply them to the accounting equation.
3. Describe accounts, journals, ledgers, and worksheets.
4. Record transactions in journals and post them to the general ledger.
5. Prepare trial balances and worksheets.
6. Prepare adjusting journal entries and reconcile a bank account.
7. Prepare financial statements from a worksheet.
8. Prepare closing journal entries.
9. Prepare a post-closing trial balance.

THE ACCOUNTING CYCLE

You may have found it frustrating to prepare financial statements from the transactions in Chapter 5 because you had no way of easily accumulating the number you needed for each item on the financial statements. Humans figured this out as early as ancient Roman times and developed a system to ease the frustration. We call this system the accounting cycle.

accounting cycle The sequence of steps repeated in each accounting period to enable the firm to analyze, record, classify, and summarize the transactions into financial statements.

The **accounting cycle** is the sequence of steps repeated in each accounting period to enable the firm to analyze, record, classify, and summarize the transactions into financial statements. The steps are:

Step 1: Analyzing Transactions

Step 2: Journalizing Transactions

Step 3: Posting Transactions to the General Ledger

Step 4: Preparing the Trial Balance (or Worksheet)

Step 5: Adjusting the Accounts and Reconciling the Bank Statement

Step 6: Preparing Financial Statements

Step 7: Preparing and Posting Closing Entries

Step 8: Preparing the Post-Closing Trial Balance

Exhibit 6–1
The Accounting Cycle:
A Dynamic System

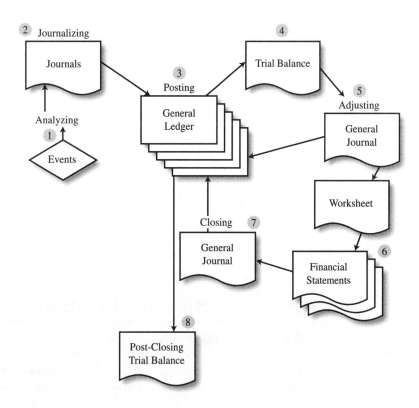

The accounting process is a cycle because some events occur daily, some monthly, and some annually (see Exhibit 6–1). At the end of the annual cycle, the process begins anew.

We will look at what happens in each step of the cycle and then learn how to apply each step of the cycle to the McCumber Enterprises transactions we viewed in Chapter 5.

Step 1: Analyzing Transactions

Analyzing transactions, the most important step in the accounting cycle, consists of two parts (see Exhibit 6–2). The first is deciding when a transaction occurs. The simple answer is that a transaction occurs when an accounting element changes. For example, if a customer pays the company, cash increases and accounts receivable decrease. Assets both increase and decrease, and a transaction occurs. What if a company orders merchandise that the vendor will deliver in three weeks? Has a transaction occurred? No. Neither assets, nor liabilities, nor equity has changed. When will this transaction occur? The transaction will occur when title to the merchandise passes from the vendor to the buyer during the shipping process. At that moment, the company will have new assets and a new liability.

The second part of analyzing transactions is identifying the nature of the transaction. If we correctly determine that a transaction occurs but misinterpret the transaction, we introduce an error into the accounting system. If we classify the merchandise purchase on credit as a long-term asset and reduce cash by the amount, we have created errors in four accounts—inventory, long-term assets, accounts payable, and cash are either overstated or understated. As you can see, knowing when to record a transaction and how to record the transaction are critical to maintaining the integrity of the accounting records. We make the decision about transactions as frequently as we journalize transactions.

Exhibit 6–2
Analyzing Transactions

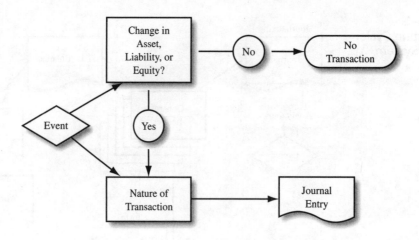

 Discussion Questions

6–1. With the many "accounting for dummies" software packages on the market, why do we need accountants?

6–2. What is the difference between a bookkeeper and an accountant?

Step 2: Journalizing Transactions

journal A book of original entry in which is kept a chronological record of an entity's transactions.

Journalizing transactions is the act of recording accounting transactions into a journal. A **journal** is a book of original entry where we record a chronology of the business entity's transactions. In the days of pen and ink, the accountant or bookkeeper kept the journal in a book. Today, with computerization, a journal may be a listing of transactions on a computer printout or a file in the computer. Regardless of form, the journal lists transactions in order of occurrence. Employees, management, and auditors frequently use the journal's chronological listing of transactions to trace transactions and answer inquiries. For this reason, we record transactions formally into journals daily, weekly, or sometimes monthly for small businesses. Large companies use on-line, real-time processing techniques that create the journals as the transactions occur. Sophisticated cash register systems often create journals simultaneously as the cashier scans the items sold.

special journal A book of original entry designed to record a specific type of transaction.

general journal A book of original entry in which is recorded all transactions not otherwise recorded in a special journal.

Businesses use a number of journals to capture details. The most common forms are sales journals, cash receipt journals, cash payment journals, purchases journals, and the general journal. All except the general journal are called **special journals,** which record a specific type of transaction such as sales. The sales journal, for instance, contains a record of the firm's sales to its customers but no other type of transaction. We use the **general journal** to record all transactions that cannot be recorded in a special journal. If a firm has no special journals, it records all transactions in the general journal (see Exhibit 6–3). Why do we have special journals? Special journals save a great deal of time when a firm experiences many similar transactions during a period. The reason for this will become obvious when we discuss posting to the general ledger, the next step in the accounting cycle.

Journals have many uses in the business operation, but the long lists of data contained in them lack the quality of information. The next step in the cycle helps us to produce usable information.

Exhibit 6–3
Journalizing
Transactions

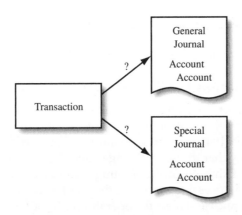

Step 3: Posting Transactions to the General Ledger

With the journals full of difficult-to-use data, we need a method of sorting or classifying the data into usable information. The information we desire is the amount of sales we made, the amount of cash or inventory we have, how much we owe for purchases, and so on. Each of the accounting elements provides us with information about the financial statements, so the elements become the classification system for accounting records.

account A record that contains the history of all increases and decreases of an accounting element.

chart of accounts A list of all the accounts used by a business entity. The list usually contains the name of the account and the account number.

general ledger A book of final entry that includes a record for each account in the chart of accounts.

We sort transactions into the increases and decreases for each accounting element. Each accounting element has an **account,** which contains the history of all increases and decreases in the accounting element. A **chart of accounts** is a list of all the accounts used by a business entity. The chart of accounts lists each account with its account number (particularly important in computerized systems) in the order of assets, liabilities, equity, revenue, and expense accounts. To be systematic, charts of account normally appear in balance sheet and income statement order. The chart of accounts becomes a reference tool to accountants and expands as needed to record new types of transactions. Each business entity should tailor its chart of accounts to its business activities.

The entire group of accounts makes up the **general ledger.** Each account is a page or a file in the general ledger. At the end of a month or a week, the accounting system posts the journal transactions to the general ledger (see Exhibit 6–4). In a computerized system, the software actually re-sorts the transactions from a date order to an account number order and accumulates like account numbers in each account. Then we have a record of what happened to each account as a result of these transactions. We add all increases and subtract all decreases to the previous balance of the account to arrive at a new account balance. We use the general ledger

Exhibit 6–4
Posting to the
General Ledger

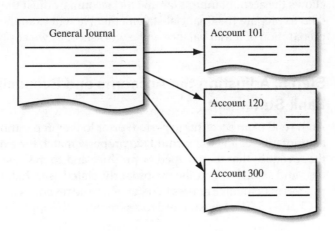

account balances to prepare financial statements after two additional steps in the accounting cycle.

Step 4: Preparing the Trial Balance (or Worksheet)

trial balance   The listing of the general ledger account balances that proves that the general ledger and, therefore, the accounting equation are in balance.

Each time we post a month's or a week's transactions from the journals, we need to make sure that the accounting equation remains in balance. To accomplish this, we prepare a trial balance. A **trial balance** is a listing of each general ledger account balance to verify that the general ledger, and therefore the accounting equation, is in balance (see Exhibit 6–5). Accounting software packages often print a trial balance after each processing session. Others automatically check to be sure that the system is in balance and alert the operator if it is out of balance.

Exhibit 6–5
Preparing the Trial Balance

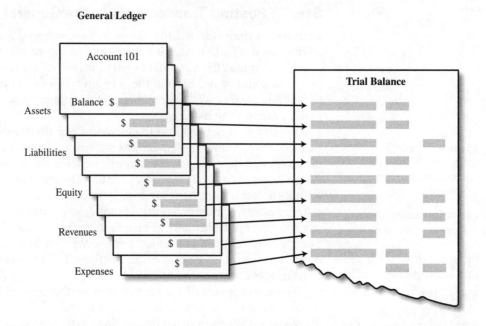

worksheet   A tool used by the accountant to accumulate the necessary information used to prepare the financial statements.

Frequently, accountants use a **worksheet** to aid in the preparation of the financial statements. Most firms prepare monthly financial statements and follow this step each time financial statements are prepared. (Some firms prepare financial statements weekly, quarterly, or semiannually.) The first two columns of the ten-column worksheet are the trial balance as of the balance sheet date. The worksheet allows the accountant to examine the accounts, adjust the accounts, and gather the data to prepare the financial statements. We will examine the details of worksheet preparation of a trial balance and a worksheet as we apply these concepts.

Step 5: Adjusting the Accounts and Reconciling the Bank Statement

At the end of an accounting period, prior to the preparation of financial statements, accountants review the accounts to properly match the expenses of the period with the revenues that they helped to produce and to make sure that the assets, liabilities, and equity accounts are properly stated (see Exhibit 6–6). The adjustment process may involve entries to defer or accrue revenues or expenses as we discussed in Chapter 5. The adjustment process requires the application of the following steps:

Exhibit 6–6
Adjusting the Accounts
and Reconciling the
Bank Statement

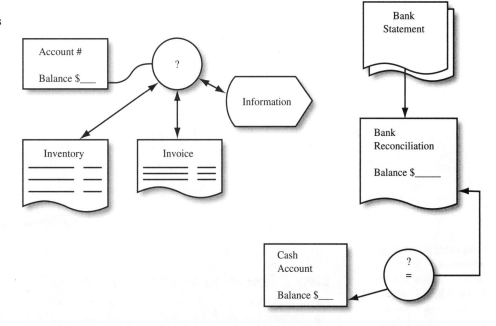

1. Identification of any accounts requiring adjustment
2. Determination of the correct balance in each account requiring adjustment
3. Preparation of the necessary adjusting entry or entries to bring the accounts into agreement with the balances determined in the previous step

Another major step in the adjusting process is reconciling the bank statement. Because most transactions ultimately result in the receipt or the payment of cash, it is important to reconcile the bank statement as part of the firm's internal control structure. Since cash represents the most liquid and easily transported of the firm's assets, the use of a chequing account by a business entity requires the implementation of some important internal controls. For example, only designated persons should have the authority to sign cheques, and the person designated to reconcile the bank account should have no other duties involving the receipt or disbursement of funds. We will prepare a bank reconciliation as we apply these concepts later in the chapter.

Step 6: Preparing Financial Statements

When the accountant is satisfied that the bank accounts are reconciled and the accounts listed on the worksheet represent fair amounts, he or she will prepare the financial statements (see Exhibit 6–7). The accountant should verify that the financial statements articulate. Specifically, the net income or net loss figure for the period must agree with the net income or net loss on the statement of owners' equity or the statement of retained earnings.

Discussion Question

6–3. How often should a company prepare its financial statements?

Exhibit 6–7
Preparation of the
Financial Statements

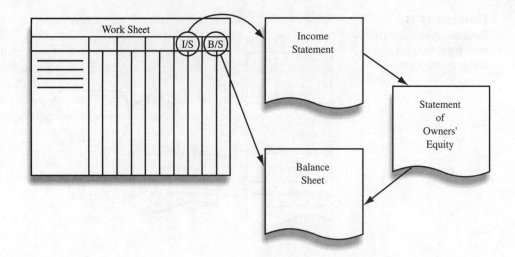

temporary (or nominal) accounts The general ledger accounts that are closed to a zero balance at the end of the fiscal year in the closing process. Temporary accounts include revenues, expenses, gains, losses, owner withdrawals, and dividend accounts.

Step 7: Preparing and Posting Closing Entries

At the end of each fiscal year, after the accounting staff adjusts all the accounts and the auditors have finished the audit, we close the books. The closing process resets the temporary accounts to zero and moves the net income to the appropriate equity accounts (see Exhibit 6–8). **Temporary** (or **nominal**) **accounts** are all revenue, expense, gain, and loss accounts that are part of net income plus the owner with-

Exhibit 6–8
Closing the
Temporary Accounts

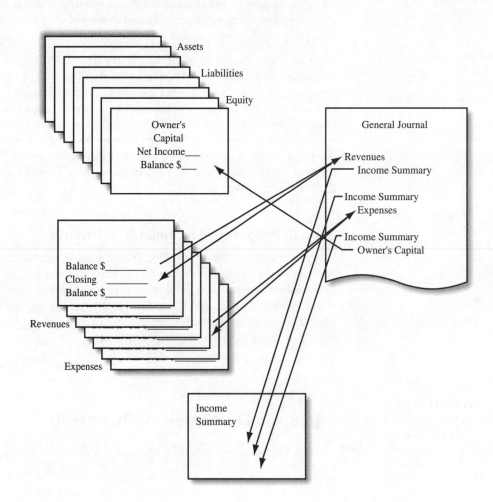

drawals (if unincorporated) and dividend accounts (if incorporated). We do not close permanent accounts in this process. **Permanent** (or **real**) **accounts** include asset, liability, and equity accounts, except for owner withdrawals and dividend accounts. The closing entries zero the temporary accounts much like a trip switch on an automobile odometer. The odometer (like permanent accounts) continues to record miles, but we reset the trip switch (like temporary accounts) to zero before each event (the new fiscal year). Each year we reset the temporary accounts to zero to accumulate the current year's net income. In essence, temporary accounts are temporary equity accounts that help us to explain in more detail the changes in retained earnings or capital accounts over the year. Once the year is over, their job is done. At the end of the year, we close the net income into the equity accounts and start over again. We make four closing entries:

1. Close the revenue accounts to Income Summary.
2. Close the expense accounts to Income Summary.
3. Close the Withdrawals accounts to Owner's or Partners' Capital accounts or Dividend accounts to Retained Earnings.
4. Close Income Summary to Owner's or Partners' Capital accounts or Retained Earnings.

Step 8: Preparing the Post-Closing Trial Balance

After we prepare the closing entries and post them to the general ledger, only the balance sheet accounts should have a balance remaining. In addition, any owner withdrawal or dividend accounts should have a zero balance. We prepare a **post-closing trial balance** after the closing entries to prove that the closing entries zeroed the temporary accounts (see Exhibit 6–9). In a computerized system, this step is crucial to verify the integrity of the closing process and that the accounting equation remains in balance.

Before we apply the steps of the accounting cycle to McCumber Enterprises, we need to discuss several topics necessary to begin the data accumulation.

Exhibit 6–9
Post-Closing
Trial Balance

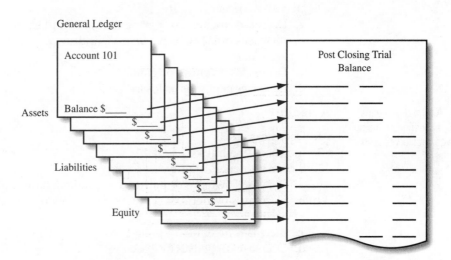

Debits and Credits

An **accounting system** gathers data from source transactions to create the books and records that transform the data into a manageable format that will eventually produce useful information in the form of financial statements. The accounting system bases its process on the basic accounting equation:

$$\text{Assets} = \text{Liabilities} + \text{Equity}$$

As we know from mathematics, a change in one side of the equation requires a change in the other side to keep the equation in balance. This concept is the origin of the term *double-entry bookkeeping*.

When Friar Luca Pacioli published his accounting text in 1494 in Venice, he stressed the importance of a balanced accounting equation. His *Summa de Arithmetica, Geometria, Proportioni et Proportionalita* was written in Latin. In Latin, *debere* means "to owe" and *credere* means "to lend." Debits appear on the left side of the equation and credits appear on the right side. Thus,

$$\text{Assets} = \text{Liabilities} + \text{Equity}$$
$$\text{Left} = \text{Right}$$
$$\text{Debit} (\textit{Debere}) = \text{Credit} (\textit{Credere})$$

When our accounting system is in balance, the debits equal the credits; left equals right.

We assign the term debit or credit to each account depending upon which side of the equation it normally resides. Therefore, assets have normal debit balances and liabilities and equity accounts have normal credit balances. An account's **normal balance** defines the type of entry that increases the account; debits increase debit balance accounts, and credits decrease debit balance accounts.

normal balance The balance of the account derived from the type of entry (debit or credit) that increases the account.

$$\text{Assets} = \text{Liabilities} + \text{Equity}$$
$$\text{Normal Balance: Debit} = \text{Credit} + \text{Credit}$$

We also learned in Chapter 5 about the four components of equity. We can expand the accounting equation to include these components of equity as follows:

Assets = Liabilities + Owners' Contributions − Owners' Withdrawals + Revenues − Expenses
Debit   = Credit   +   Credit   −   Debit   + Credit − Debit

With the expanded equation we can identify the normal balances of revenues, expenses, and owners' withdrawals. Therefore, a **debit:**

debit A term that means "to owe," appearing on the left side of a general ledger account.

1. Increases assets
2. Decreases liabilities
3. Decreases owners' equity
   a. Decreases owner's or partners' capital and share capital accounts
   b. Increases owner's or partners' withdrawal accounts or the dividend account
   c. Decreases revenues or gains
   d. Increases expenses or losses

A **credit:**

credit A term that means "to lend," appearing on the right side of a general ledger account.

1. Decreases assets
2. Increases liabilities
3. Increases owners' equity
   a. Increases owner's or partners' capital or share capital accounts
   b. Decreases owner's or partners' withdrawal accounts or the dividend account
   c. Increases revenues or gains
   d. Decreases expenses or losses

The Account

Each account contains a summary of its activity during the year. It includes the following important information:

1. Account name and number
2. Date of each transaction
3. Beginning balance
4. Each posting from journals, including the date, reference, and amount
5. Ending balance

A typical account might look like that shown in Exhibit 6–10.

Exhibit 6–10
The Account Form

Account Name	Cash in Bank				Account Number		101
2004		Post			Balance		
Date	Description	Ref.	Debit	Credit	Debit	Credit	
Dec 1	Beginning Balance				34,589.26		
31		CR34	54,197.75		88,787.01		
31		CD57		56,110.68	32,676.33		

When you read the account, you learn that on December 1, 2004, this company began with $34,589.26 in the bank. It collected $54,197.75, recorded on page 34 of the Cash Receipts Journal, and paid out $56,110.68, recorded on page 57 of the Cash Payments Journal. At month's end, the company had $32,676.33 in the bank. Notice that there are no dollar signs in the general ledger. Dollar signs appear in financial statements and reports, such as a trial balance, but not on journals, ledgers, or worksheets.

For discussion purposes, we often use an abbreviated account form called the T-account. The **T-account** represents the general ledger account with only two columns. The balance appears after a horizontal line. We use this form to save time when analyzing an account. Exhibit 6–11 contains the T-account version of the cash account illustrated in Exhibit 6–10.

T-account An account form that represents the general ledger account with only two columns.

Exhibit 6–11
T-Account

Cash in Bank 101

2004			
Dec. 1	34,589.26		
Dec. 31	54,197.75	56,110.68	Dec. 31
	32,676.33		

The Journal Entry

For simplicity, we will utilize only the General Journal in this chapter. Proper general journal entries contain the pertinent details of the transaction in an easy-to-read format. Exhibit 6–12 illustrates a general journal page that contains a journal entry.

Exhibit 6–12
The General Journal

General Journal			Page 423	
Date 2004	**Description**	**Post Ref.**	**Debit**	**Credit**
Jan 24	Account Receivable	110	23,425.00	
	Sales	401		23,425.00
	To record the sale of 1500 units to			
	John George, Inc. Terms 2/10, n 30			

Discussion Questions

6–4. From the entry made into the General Journal in Exhibit 6-12, describe what happened with this transaction.

6–5. Where will the entry in Exhibit 6-12 be posted in the General Ledger?

6–6. Can each journal entry have only one debit and one credit?

The journal entry provides us with the following information:

1. The date of the transaction
2. The accounts affected by the transaction
3. A description of the transaction with any important details
4. The amounts of the debit or credit to each account

compound journal entry
Any entry recorded in the general journal that contains more than two accounts.

Notice that the debit equals the credit. Journal entries with more than two accounts are called **compound journal entries**. Regardless of the number of accounts involved, the total debits must equal the total credits for each transaction or the system will be out of balance. Now that we know what to do and how to do it, we can apply the accounting cycle to actual transactions.

ACCOUNTING CYCLE APPLICATION

To illustrate the accounting cycle, we will use the McCumber Enterprises proprietorship accrual-basis transactions for January 2004 that you examined in Chapter 5. We have reproduced those here for your convenience.

1. Gertie McCumber started the company on January 2 by investing $200,000.
2. McCumber Enterprises borrowed $100,000 from the Friendly Bank on January 2 by signing a one-year, 12 percent note payable. Although the $100,000 does not have to be repaid until January 2, 2005, the interest charge must be paid each month, beginning on February 2, 2004.

3. The company purchased a vehicle on January 2 for $14,000 cash. Gertie estimates that the vehicle will fill the company's needs for four years, after which she estimates she can sell it for $2,000.
4. The company paid cash for $75,000 worth of merchandise inventory on January 8.
5. On January 15, the company sold merchandise that cost $42,000 for a total selling price of $78,000 and collected the cash the same day.
6. On January 22, the company sold merchandise that cost $15,000 for a total selling price of $32,000 on account (a credit sale). The terms of the sale were 30 days, meaning McCumber Enterprises can expect to receive payment by February 21.
7. Cash payments for operating expenses in January totaled $22,500.
8. Besides the bank loan, the only amounts owed by the company at the end of the month were:
   a. $2,000 to company employees for work performed in January. They will be paid on February 3.
   b. A $700 utility bill that was received on January 26 and will be paid on February 15.

The first seven transactions should be recorded in the first two steps of the accounting cycle: analyzing and journalizing transactions. We analyzed these entries in Chapter 5 and now know how to record them properly in the general journal.

Steps 1 & 2—Analyzing and Journalizing Transactions

We would normally begin by examining the chart of accounts. McCumber Enterprises' chart of accounts is as follows:

101	Cash in Bank
110	Accounts Receivable
120	Inventory
150	Automotive Equipment
155	Accumulated Amortization
200	Accounts Payable
210	Wages Payable
220	Interest Payable
250	Notes Payable
300	Gertie McCumber, Capital
310	Gertie McCumber, Withdrawals
400	Sales
500	Cost of Goods Sold
600	Operating Expenses
620	Wages Expense
640	Utilities Expense
660	Interest Expense
680	Amortization Expense
800	Income Summary

We have recorded each of transactions 1 through 7 on the general journal beginning with page 1.

After examining the general journal on the following page you might notice the following items:

1. Dates—We write the name of the month only at the top of each page, unless it changes in the middle of the page. All entries are in chronological order.
2. Account titles—We write all debits first in one journal entry and then the credits. Write debits on the margin and indent the credits five spaces.

General Journal   Page 1

Date 2004		Description	Post Ref.	Debit	Credit
Jan	1	Cash in Bank		200,000	
		Gertie McCumber, Capital			200,000
		To record the owner's capital			
		contribution.			
	2	Cash in Bank		100,000	
		Notes Payable			100,000
		To record loan from Friendly Bank			
		due January 2, 2005, with 12%			
		interest payable monthly.			
	2	Automotive Equipment		14,000	
		Cash in Bank			14,000
		To record the purchase of a vehicle,			
		4-year useful life, $2,000 residual			
		value.			

General Journal   Page 2

Date 2004		Description	Post Ref.	Debit	Credit
Jan	8	Inventory		75,000	
		Cash in Bank			75,000
		To record the purchase of inventory.			
	15	Cash in Bank		78,000	
		Sales			78,000
		To record sales that cost $42,000.			
	15	Cost of Goods Sold		42,000	
		Inventory			42,000
		To record the cost of the previous sale.			
	22	Accounts Receivable		32,000	
		Cost of Goods Sold		15,000	
		Sales			32,000
		Inventory			15,000
		To record a sale terms net 30 that cost			
		$15,000.			
	31	Operating Expenses		22,500	
		Cash in Bank			22,500
		To record the payment of cash			
		operating expenses.			

3. Posting references—Nothing is written in this column. We write the account number in this column as we post to the general ledger in Step 3. This tells the bookkeeper whether the item is posted.
4. Debit and credit amounts—Since this problem is in whole dollars, we omitted the cents. There are no dollar signs because this is a journal.
5. Explanations—A complete explanation follows each journal entry so that the reader can understand the analysis of the transaction.
6. Compound entry—The January 22 journal entry is similar to the two entries on January 15. To save time writing two explanations, the January 22 entry combined the separate entries of January 15. Either way is acceptable in a general journal because the sale of merchandise involves all four accounts, but it may be thought of as two separate transactions or one complex transaction. A compound journal entry has more than one debit or credit.

Assuming that these transactions represent all transactions for the month of January, we can now post these to the general ledger in Step 3.

Step 3—Posting to the General Ledger

Although time-consuming, the posting process presents no serious challenge since it simply involves recording the transactions a second time. When transactions are recorded a second time, or posted, they are recorded in the general ledger. Unlike journals, where the entire transaction is recorded in one place chronologically, the transactions recorded in the general ledger are done so on an account-by-account basis. This means that, when viewing an account in the general ledger, you may see only one side of the journal entry, namely the side that affects that account. Posting requires attention to detail in the following procedures:

1. Post to the general ledger each entry in the order that it appears in the general journal.
2. Record the date as the same date as the entry in the general journal.
3. There is no need to write any description unless you wish to indicate a special notation.
4. For the posting reference on the general ledger, use the page number of the journal page, such as GJ1 or GJ2.
5. Record the amount of the entry in the correct debit or credit column.
6. Place the general ledger account number in the posting reference column of the general journal.

Exhibit 6–13 shows the postings of the first two general journal entries. Then Exhibit 6–14 presents the final appearance of the general journal pages 1 and 2 and the general ledger accounts for each account that has a balance after the monthly transactions.

Now that we have posted the general ledger, we can prepare the trial balance.

Step 4—Preparing the Trial Balance

To prepare the trial balance, simply list in order each general ledger account and its account balance. Put each debit balance in the debit column and each credit balance in the credit column. Total each column and verify that the debits equal the credits. The trial balance appears in Exhibit 6–15 on page 189.

Because the debits equal the credits in the trial balance, our general ledger balances.

Exhibit 6–13
The Posting Process

General Journal			Page	1	

Date 2004		Description	Post Ref.	Debit	Credit
Jan	1	Cash in Bank	101	200,000	
		Gertie McCumber, Capital	300		200,000
		To record the owner's capital			
		contribution.			
	2	Cash in Bank	101	100,000	
		Notes Payable	250		100,000
		To record loan from Friendly Bank			
		due January 2, 2005, with 12%			
		interest payable monthly.			

Account Name Cash in Bank   **Account Number** 101

2004			Post			Balance	
Date	Description		Ref.	Debit	Credit	Debit	Credit
Jan 1			GJ1	200,000		200,000	
2			GJ1	100,000		300,000	

Account Name Notes Payable   **Account Number** 250

2004			Post			Balance	
Date	Description		Ref.	Debit	Credit	Debit	Credit
Jan 2			GJ1		100,000		100,000

Account Name Gertie McCumber, Capital   **Account Number** 300

2004			Post			Balance	
Date	Description		Ref.	Debit	Credit	Debit	Credit
Jan 1			GJ1		200,000		200,000

Exhibit 6–14
After the Posting Process

General Journal			Page 1		
Date 2004		**Description**	**Post Ref.**	**Debit**	**Credit**
Jan	1	Cash in Bank	101	200,000	
		Gertie McCumber, Capital	300		200,000
		To record the owner's capital			
		contribution.			
	2	Cash in Bank	101	100,000	
		Notes Payable	250		100,000
		To record loan from Friendly Bank			
		due January 2, 2005, with 12%			
		interest payable monthly.			
	2	Automotive Equipment	150	14,000	
		Cash in Bank	101		14,000
		To record the purchase of a vehicle,			
		4-year useful life, $2,000 residual			
		value.			

General Journal			Page 2		
Date 2004		**Description**	**Post Ref.**	**Debit**	**Credit**
Jan	8	Inventory	120	75,000	
		Cash in Bank	101		75,000
		To record the purchase of inventory.			
	15	Cash in Bank	101	78,000	
		Sales	400		78,000
		To record sales that cost $42,000.			
	15	Cost of Goods Sold	500	42,000	
		Inventory	120		42,000
		To record the cost of the previous sale.			
	22	Accounts Receivable	110	32,000	
		Cost of Goods Sold	500	15,000	
		Sales	400		32,000
		Inventory	120		15,000
		To record a sale terms net 30 that cost			
		$15,000.			
	31	Operating Expenses	600	22,500	
		Cash in Bank	101		22,500
		To record the payment of cash			
		operating expenses.			

Exhibit 6-14
Continued

Account Name *Cash in Bank*   **Account Number** *101*

2004		Post			Balance	
Date	Description	Ref.	Debit	Credit	Debit	Credit
Jan 1		GJ1	200,000		200,000	
2		GJ1	100,000		300,000	
2		GJ1		14,000	286,000	
8		GJ2		75,000	211,000	
15		GJ2	78,000		289,000	
31		GJ2		22,500	266,500	

Account Name *Accounts Receivable*   **Account Number** *110*

2004		Post			Balance	
Date	Description	Ref.	Debit	Credit	Debit	Credit
Jan 22		GJ2	32,000		32,000	

Account Name *Inventory*   **Account Number** *120*

2004		Post			Balance	
Date	Description	Ref.	Debit	Credit	Debit	Credit
Jan 8		GJ2	75,000		75,000	
15		GJ2		42,000	33,000	
22		GJ2		15,000	18,000	

Account Name *Automotive Equipment*   **Account Number** *150*

2004		Post			Balance	
Date	Description	Ref.	Debit	Credit	Debit	Credit
Jan 2		GJ1	14,000		14,000	

Account Name *Notes Payable*   **Account Number** *250*

2004		Post			Balance	
Date	Description	Ref.	Debit	Credit	Debit	Credit
Jan 2		GJ1		100,000		100,000

Exhibit 6-14
Continued

Account Name Gertie McCumber, Capital   **Account Number** 300

2004		Post			Balance	
Date	Description	Ref.	Debit	Credit	Debit	Credit
Jan 1		GJ1		200,000		200,000

Account Name Sales   **Account Number** 400

2004		Post			Balance	
Date	Description	Ref.	Debit	Credit	Debit	Credit
Jan 15		GJ2		78,000		78,000
22		GJ2		32,000		110,000

Account Name Cost of Goods Sold   **Account Number** 500

2004		Post			Balance	
Date	Description	Ref.	Debit	Credit	Debit	Credit
Jan 15		GJ2	42,000		42,000	
22		GJ2	15,000		57,000	

Account Name Operating Expenses   **Account Number** 600

2004		Post			Balance	
Date	Description	Ref.	Debit	Credit	Debit	Credit
Jan 31		GJ2	22,500		22,500	

Exhibit 6-15
The Trial Balance

McCumber Enterprises
Trial Balance
January 31, 2004

	Account	Debit	Credit
101	Cash in Bank	$266,500	
110	Accounts Receivable	32,000	
120	Inventory	18,000	
150	Automotive Equipment	14,000	
250	Notes Payable		$100,000
300	Gertie McCumber, Capital		200,000
400	Sales		110,000
500	Cost of Goods Sold	57,000	
600	Operating Expenses	22,500	
	Totals	$410,000	$410,000

Discussion Questions

6–7. If the debits equal the credits, does this mean that the general ledger is correct? If not, what can be wrong?

6–8. If the debits do not equal the credits, what are the most likely causes of the imbalance?

When we want to prepare financial statements, we prepare a worksheet. The worksheet has five pairs of columns; each pair contains a debit and a credit column. To complete the worksheet, we use the following steps.

1. Place a heading on the worksheet that includes the company name, the title "Worksheet," and the period covered by the worksheet.
2. Head the columns with the titles:
   a. Account
   b. Trial Balance (followed by the date of the trial balance)
   c. Adjustments
   d. Adjusted Trial Balance
   e. Income Statement
   f. Balance Sheet
3. Place the trial balance amounts in the trial balance columns after the account name. It is easiest to list the accounts in the general ledger order and include accounts without balances that might be used in the worksheet. Verify that the trial balance balances.
4. Examine each account, using additional information you have available, to determine if any adjusting journal entries should be made (see Step 5). Write the adjustments in their columns, then add the two columns down to verify that the debits equal the credits.
5. After completing all adjustments, add the first four columns across to create an adjusted trial balance. Verify that the adjusted trial balance balances.
6. Place each amount listed on the adjusted trial balance in the appropriate income statement or balance sheet columns. Total the four columns. The amounts will not balance, but what you should find is that each set of columns is off by the same amount. That amount is net income. See Exhibit 6–16 for the completed worksheet.

Step 5—Adjusting the Accounts and Reconciling the Bank Statement

We examine each account to see whether the balance is reasonable and to determine whether any accrual, deferral, or correcting entry is needed. Cash normally appears first in the chart of accounts. The best way to examine the cash account is to reconcile the bank statement. Each month the bank sends a statement that lists the beginning and ending account balance according to the bank's records. It also lists each cheque that cleared and each deposit the bank received. Remember that the bank refers to debits and credits from the bank's perspective. The bank's debits and credits are the opposite of the company's debits and credits. How is this possible? Because our bank account has a debit balance, but our bank account is a liability to the bank and a liability has a credit balance. On February 5, 2004, McCumber Enterprises received the bank statement on page 192 from Friendly Bank.

Exhibit 6–17 contains a standard bank reconciliation format. We will use it to reconcile McCumber Enterprises' bank account and verify the cash balance.

Exhibit 7-16
The Worksheet

McCumber Enterprises
Worksheet
For the Month Ended January 31, 2004

#	Account Name	Trial Balance Debit	Trial Balance Credit	Adjustments Debit	Adjustments Credit	Adjusted Trial Balance Debit	Adjusted Trial Balance Credit	Income Statement Debit	Income Statement Credit	Balance Sheet Debit	Balance Sheet Credit
101	Cash in Bank	266,500				266,500				266,500	
110	Accounts Receivable	32,000				32,000				32,000	
120	Inventory	18,000				18,000				18,000	
150	Automotive Equipment	14,000				14,000				14,000	
155	Accumulated Amortization				250		250				250
200	Accounts Payable				700		700				700
210	Wages Payable				2,000		2,000				2,000
220	Interest Payable				1,000		1,000				1,000
250	Notes Payable		100,000				100,000				100,000
300	Gertie McCumber, Capital		200,000				200,000				200,000
400	Sales		110,000				110,000		110,000		
500	Cost of goods Sold	57,000				57,000		57,000			
600	Operating Expense	22,500				22,500		22,500			
620	Wages Expense			2,000		2,000		2,000			
640	Utilities Expense			700		700		700			
660	Interest Expense			1,000		1,000		1,000			
680	Amortization Expense			250		250		250			
	Totals	410,000	410,000	3,950	3,950	413,950	413,950	83,450	110,000	330,500	303,950
	Net Income							26,550			26,550
								110,000	110,000	330,500	330,500

Friendly Bank

Account Name:	McCumber Enterprises 125 McKenzie Rd. Yellowknife, NWT	Account Number: 3489432 Date: January 31, 2004

Previous statement balance 12–31–03	$ 0.00
3 Deposits or other credits totaling	378,000.00
2 Checks or other debits totaling	89,000.00
Current balance as of statement date 01–31–04	$ 289,000.00

Account Transactions

Date	Debits	Credits	Description
Jan02		200,000.00	Deposit
Jan02		100,000.00	Deposit Loan Proceeds
Jan17		78,000.00	Deposit

Checks

Date	Cheque	Amount	Date	Cheque	Amount
Jan05	1001	14,000.00	Jan19	1002	75,000.00

Exhibit 6–17
Standard Bank
Reconciliation Format

COMPANY NAME
Bank Reconciliation
Date

Balance per Bank Statement $ _____
Add: Deposits in Transit

   _____   _____
   _____   _____
   _____   _____   _____

Deduct: Cheques Outstanding
#____ _____   #____ _____
#____ _____   #____ _____
#____ _____   #____ _____   _____

Corrected Bank Balance $ _____

Balance per Books $ _____
Add: _____

   _____
   _____   _____

Deduct: Service Charges $ _____

   _____
   _____   _____

Corrected Book Balance $ _____

Reconciling a bank statement uses the following process:

1. Record the bank statement's ending balance on the appropriate line.
2. Record any deposits recorded in the books that have not been included in the bank statement. These deposits should be at the end of the month. If you find other deposits missing, notify the bank at once. Most banks require that you notify them within ten days of the bank statement date of any errors. Beyond that time, the bank assumes that the statement is correct.
3. Look at the list of cheques that cleared the bank on the bank statement. List any cheques that were written through the end of the month but did not appear on the bank statement. Those are outstanding cheques.
4. Compute the corrected bank balance. Write the balance per the general ledger on the appropriate line. If that balance agrees with the book balance, the reconciliation is complete.
5. If the corrected bank balance and the book balance do not agree, you must look for the difference. This process can be simple or aggravating. Following are the most likely errors that occur and help with how to spot them:
    a. Bank service charges—Banks charge for many services and do not notify the firm of the charges except with the bank statement. These include cheque printing charges, monthly service fees, overdraft charges, and special service fees.
    b. Cheques or deposits recorded incorrectly in the journals—Transposed cheque amounts, such as recording $275 as $257, will cause an error in the cash account. Transposition errors are always evenly divisible by nine. For example, if the cheque was recorded as $257 instead of $275 the difference is $18, evenly divisible by nine. When the difference between the corrected bank balance and the book balance is divisible by nine, look for a transposition error.
    c. Other deductions by the bank—Banks deduct cheques returned from the firm's deposits and other items that may not be included in the bookkeeping records. These would usually include non-sufficient funds (NSF) cheques received. If an NSF cheque is received from a customer, the company will increase the balance in its cash account when the cheque is received and deposited initially. However, notification from the bank that the cheque was NSF may not be received until the bank statement arrives. Consequently, the bank balance will be lower than the accounting records. The account balance for cash is overstated and should be reduced by the amount of the NSF cheque received.
    d. If the balances still do not agree, the next step is to check the bank's encoding of the cheque or deposit amount against the amount of the deposit or cheque. The bank's encoding is in the bottom, right-hand corner of the cheque or deposit slip. Banks seldom make errors but can on occasion.

McCumber Enterprises' bank reconciliation has only one reconciling item. The bank statement includes all deposits for the month but omits the final cheque written on January 31. Because the balance in the account is so high, the bank did not deduct a service charge for the month.

MCCUMBER ENTERPRISES
Bank Reconciliation
January 31, 2004

Balance per Bank Statement		$289,000
Add: Deposits in Transit		0
Deduct: Cheques Outstanding		
#1003	$22,500	22,500
Corrected Bank Balance		$266,500
Balance per Books		$266,500
Deduct: Service Charges $0		0
Corrected Book Balance		$266,500

Now that the Cash in Bank balance is verified, we can proceed down the list of accounts looking for possible adjustments.

1. Accounts Receivable traces to the last sale of the month and appears to be correct. With complicated activity, we would compare the accounts receivable balance to a listing prepared by an accounts receivable clerk to verify accuracy.

2. Inventory consists of the unsold items that were purchased on January 8. Normally, we could compare this to a computer-generated inventory list or to a physical count of the inventory.

3. The company still owns the vehicle listed in the Automotive Equipment account. However, since it was used this month, amortization should be recorded in an adjusting journal entry. The amortization expense equals $250 for the month computed as

Cost $14,000 − Residual Value $2,000 = Amortizable Base $12,000
$12,000 / 48 months = $250 per month

4. Item 8 in McCumber Enterprises' information tells us that the company owes employees $2,000 and a utility provider $700 at month end in addition to the bank loan. This information requires three adjusting journal entries for the wages, the utilities, and the loan interest. To compute the loan interest

Interest = Principal $100,000 × Rate 12% × Time 1/12 = $1,000

5. Notes Payable and Gertie McCumber's capital are correctly stated, as are Sales, Cost of Sales, and Operating Expenses. Sales can normally be verified from a sales journal or listing. We usually check the cost of goods sold percentage to determine whether the cost of sales amount seems reasonable.

We can prepare the four required journal entries in Exhibit 6–18.

The final step is to post these to the general ledger accounts. After we have posted the adjusting entries, the general ledger will agree with the worksheet in Exhibit 6–16.

Exhibit 6–18
Adjusting Journal
Entries

General Journal			Page 3		
Date 2004		Description	Post Ref.	Debit	Credit
Jan	31	Amortization Expense	680	250	
		Accumulated Amortization	155		250
		To record amortization on vehicle			
		($12,000 / 48 = $250)			
	31	Wages Expense	620	2,000	
		Wages Payable	210		2,000
		To accrue wages owed on 31-01-04.			
	31	Utilities Expense	640	700	
		Accounts Payable	200		700
		To accrue utility bill due 15-02-04.			
	31	Interest Expense	660	1,000	
		Interest Payable	220		1,000
		To accrue one month's interest.			
		($100,000 × 12% × 1/12 = $1,000)			

Step 6—Preparing Financial Statements

We have all the information we need from the worksheet to prepare the income statement, statement of owner's equity, and balance sheet. Exhibit 6–19 contains the completed financial statements.

Compare the financial statements in Exhibit 6–19 to the accrual-basis statements in Chapter 5, and you will see that they are identical.

Step 7—Closing the Accounts

For the sake of simplicity, assume that McCumber Enterprises decided to have a January 31 year end. Many companies choose a fiscal year that differs from the calendar year but coincides with the end of the normal business cycle for the industry. This simplifies inventory taking and year-end accounting procedures. To close McCumber Enterprises' books, we will attempt to zero the temporary or nominal accounts and close them to income summary. We can review the four normal closing entries for a sole proprietorship:

1. Close the revenue and gain accounts to Income Summary.
2. Close the expense and loss accounts to Income Summary.
3. Close the Withdrawals account to the owner's capital account.
4. Close the Income Summary account to the owner's capital account.

Exhibit 6–19
McCumber Enterprises
Financial Statements
January 31, 2004

McCUMBER ENTERPRISES
Income Statement
For the Month Ended January 31, 2004

Sales Revenue		$110,000
Cost of Goods Sold		57,000
Gross Margin		$ 53,000
Expenses:		
Cash Operating Expenses	$22,500	
Wages Expense	2,000	
Utilities Expense	700	
Interest Expense	1,000	
Amortization Expense	250	
Total Operating Expenses		26,450
Net Income		$ 26,550

McCUMBER ENTERPRISES
Statement of Owner's Equity
For the Month Ended January 31, 2004

G. McCumber, Capital, January 1, 2004	$ 0
Investment by Owner	200,000
Net Income	26,550
G. McCumber, Capital, January 31, 2004	$226,550

McCUMBER ENTERPRISES
Balance Sheet
January 31, 2004

Assets:			Liabilities:		
Cash		$266,500	Accounts Payable		$ 700
Accounts Receivable		32,000	Wages Payable		2,000
Inventory		18,000	Interest Payable		1,000
Vehicle	$14,000		Note Payable		100,000
Less: Accumulated			Total Liabilities		$103,700
Amortization	(250)				
Vehicle, Net		13,750	Owner's Equity:		
			G. McCumber, Capital		226,550
			Total Liabilities		
Total Assets		$330,250	and Owner's Equity		$330,250

From the worksheet we can tell that there is one revenue account and seven expense accounts to close. The owner made no withdrawals during this period. Therefore, we must make only three closing entries as follows:

\multicolumn{7}{c}{General Journal — Page 4}
Date 2004		Description	Post Ref.	Debit	Credit
Jan	31	Sales	400	110,00	
		Income Summary	800		110,000
		To close the revenue account.			
	31	Income Summary	800	83,450	
		Cost of Goods Sold	500		57,000
		Operating Expenses	600		22,500
		Wages Expense	620		2,000
		Utilities Expense	640		700
		Interest Expense	660		1,000
		Amortization Expense	680		250
		To close the expense accounts.			
	31	Income Summary	800	26,550	
		Gertie McCumber, Capital	300		26,550
		To close the Income Summary account.			

The posting process is the same as in Step 3. After posting the closing entries, the general ledger appears as follows:

Account Name Cash in Bank					Account Number 101	
2004		Post			\multicolumn{2}{c}{Balance}
Date	Description	Ref.	Debit	Credit	Debit	Credit
Jan 1		GJ1	200,000		200,000	
2		GJ1	100,000		300,000	
2		GJ1		14,000	286,000	
8		GJ2		75,000	211,000	
15		GJ2	78,000		289,000	
31		GJ2		22,500	266,500	

Account Name *Accounts Receivable*   **Account Number** *110*

2004		Post			Balance	
Date	Description	Ref.	Debit	Credit	Debit	Credit
Jan 22		GJ2	32,000		32,000	

Account Name *Inventory*   **Account Number** *120*

2004		Post			Balance	
Date	Description	Ref.	Debit	Credit	Debit	Credit
Jan 8		GJ2	75,000		75,000	
15		GJ2		42,000	33,000	
22		GJ2		15,000	18,000	

Account Name *Automotive Equipment*   **Account Number** *150*

2004		Post			Balance	
Date	Description	Ref.	Debit	Credit	Debit	Credit
Jan 2		GJ1	14,000		14,000	

Account Name *Accumulated Amortization*   **Account Number** *155*

2004		Post			Balance	
Date	Description	Ref.	Debit	Credit	Debit	Credit
Jan 31		GJ3		250		250

Account Name *Accounts Payable*   **Account Number** *200*

2004		Post			Balance	
Date	Description	Ref.	Debit	Credit	Debit	Credit
Jan 31		GJ3		700		700

Account Name *Wages Payable*   **Account Number** *210*

2004		Post			Balance	
Date	Description	Ref.	Debit	Credit	Debit	Credit
Jan 31		GJ3		2,000		2,000

Account Name *Interest Payable*   **Account Number** *220*

2004 Date	Description	Post Ref.	Debit	Credit	Balance Debit	Balance Credit
Jan 31		GJ3		1,000		1,000

Account Name *Notes Payable*   **Account Number** *250*

2004 Date	Description	Post Ref.	Debit	Credit	Balance Debit	Balance Credit
Jan 2		GJ1		100,000		100,000

Account Name *Gertie McCumber, Capital*   **Account Number** *300*

2004 Date	Description	Post Ref.	Debit	Credit	Balance Debit	Balance Credit
Jan 1		GJ1		200,000		200,000
31	To close income summary	GJ4		26,550		226,550

Account Name *Sales*   **Account Number** *400*

2004 Date	Description	Post Ref.	Debit	Credit	Balance Debit	Balance Credit
Jan 15		GJ2		78,000		78,000
22		GJ2		32,000		110,000
31	To close	GJ4	110,000			0

Account Name *Cost of Goods Sold*   **Account Number** *500*

2004 Date	Description	Post Ref.	Debit	Credit	Balance Debit	Balance Credit
Jan 15		GJ2	42,000		42,000	
22		GJ2	15,000		57,000	
31	To close	GJ4		57,000	0	

Account Name *Operating Expenses*   **Account Number** *600*

2004 Date	Description	Post Ref.	Debit	Credit	Balance Debit	Balance Credit
Jan 31		GJ2	22,500		22,500	
31	To close	GJ4		22,500	0	

| Account Name | Wages Expense | | | | Account Number | 620 |

2004		Post			Balance	
Date	Description	Ref.	Debit	Credit	Debit	Credit
Jan 31		GJ3	2,000		2,000	
31	To close	GJ4		2,000	0	

| Account Name | Utilities Expense | | | | Account Number | 640 |

2004		Post			Balance	
Date	Description	Ref.	Debit	Credit	Debit	Credit
Jan 31		GJ3	700		700	
31	To close	GJ4		700	0	

| Account Name | Interest Expense | | | | Account Number | 660 |

2004		Post			Balance	
Date	Description	Ref.	Debit	Credit	Debit	Credit
Jan 31		GJ3	1,000		1,000	
31	To close	GJ4		1,000	0	

| Account Name | Amortization Expense | | | | Account Number | 680 |

2004		Post			Balance	
Date	Description	Ref.	Debit	Credit	Debit	Credit
Jan 31		GJ3	250		250	
31	To close	GJ4		250	0	

| Account Name | Income Summary | | | | Account Number | 800 |

2004		Post			Balance	
Date	Description	Ref.	Debit	Credit	Debit	Credit
Jan 31	To close revenues	GJ4		110,000		110,000
31	To close expenses	GJ4	83,450			26,550
31	To close account	GJ4	26,550			0

Step 8—Preparing the Post-Closing Trial Balance

We have reached the final step in the process. By preparing the post-closing trial balance, we verify that each temporary account is closed and the general ledger remains in balance. The post-closing trial balance becomes the opening balances for the new fiscal year. Exhibit 6–20 contains McCumber Enterprises' post-closing trial balance at January 31, 2004.

Exhibit 6–20
Post-Closing Trial
Balance

McCumber Enterprises
Post-Closing Trial Balance
January 31, 2004

	Account	Debit	Credit
101	Cash in Bank	$266,500	
110	Accounts Receivable	32,000	
120	Inventory	18,000	
150	Automotive Equipment	14,000	
155	Accumulated Amortization		$ 250
200	Accounts Payable		700
210	Wages Payable		2,000
220	Interest Payable		1,000
250	Notes Payable		100,000
300	Gertie McCumber, Capital		226,550
	Total	$330,500	$330,500

So far we have examined how accountants measure reality and accumulate data to provide meaningful information to financial decision makers. Later, we will explore areas in which we allow flexibility in the recognition of revenues and expenses. These variations reduce the comparability of financial statement information between companies. Therefore, to be an informed user, you should understand the variations and their influence on the financial statements.

EFFECTS OF COMPUTERS AND THE INTERNET ON THE ACCOUNTING CYCLE

Before computers were used for accounting purposes, one group of accounting clerks would make entries into the general and special journals while another group would post these entries into the general ledger. Posting is now done automatically by accounting software, so the second group of accounting clerks is no longer needed. Closing entries are now done automatically by the same software at year end, so the use of a step-by-step closing process using income summary accounts is becoming rare.

With the increasing use of the Internet, some transactions, such as sales, may actually be recorded by customers as they click on various items on a company's web site. Transactions affecting bank accounts may be recorded first by the bank and then simply downloaded into a company's accounting records. Because of these developments, there are fewer transactions for the first group of accounting clerks to record.

Does this mean that there are fewer accounting jobs? No. It means that accounting jobs now involve fewer clerical functions and require a higher level of skills, including analysis of the data that are automatically processed and the establishment of safe, reliable accounting systems that utilize the lastest technological developments to produce useful accounting information.

SUMMARY

The accounting cycle is an eight-step process of accumulating accounting data and transforming them into useful accounting information.

1. Analyzing transactions requires deciding when a transaction occurs and determining which accounts it affects. Analysis occurs at least daily.
2. Journalizing transactions records the transaction chronologically in a journal, a book of original entry. The proper journal for each entry depends on the unique accounting system the company employs. Some systems have only a general journal and others have special journals to record similar transactions. Journalizing occurs at least monthly.
3. Posting transactions transfers the journal information to the general ledger, sorted by account. Each account indicates the beginning and ending balance and all transactions recorded during the period for that account. Posting occurs at least monthly in most systems.
4. Preparing a trial balance proves that the general ledger (and the accounting equation) is in balance. We prepare a worksheet to aid in the preparation of financial statements. A trial balance should be prepared each time we post journals to the general ledger, and worksheets are prepared as often as the firm prepares financial statements.
5. Adjusting the accounts records all accruals, deferrals, and corrections necessary to provide quality accounting information. We adjust accounts as often as we prepare financial statements.
6. Preparing the financial statements represents the final step in the transformation of data into information. Most firms prepare financial statements at least monthly for internal users and quarterly for external users.
7. Closing the temporary (nominal) accounts occurs one time each year after the final adjustments are made to the accounts. We close the temporary accounts to owner's equity, partners' equity, or retained earnings.
8. Preparing the post-closing trial balance ensures that all temporary accounts were properly closed and that the permanent (real) accounts left in the general ledger are in balance. This occurs annually after the closing entries. The post-closing trial balance amounts become the opening balances for the new fiscal year.

The accounting system records transactions as either debits or credits. Debit means to owe and credit means to lend, with debits appearing on the left side of the accounting equation and credits appearing on the right side. Debits must always equal credits in each transaction, each journal, and the general ledger to keep the equation in balance. Debits increase assets and expenses, and decrease liabilities, equity, and revenues. Credits increase liabilities, equity, and revenues, and decrease assets and expenses.

KEY TERMS

REVIEW THE FACTS

1. List the eight steps in the accounting cycle.
2. Distinguish between debits and credits, and explain how they relate to the accounting equation.
3. Describe the differences between an account, a journal, a ledger, and a worksheet.
4. Explain the purposes of the general journal and special journals.
5. List the important elements of a general journal entry.
6. Describe how to post general journal entries to the general ledger.
7. Describe the purpose of the trial balance and the worksheet.
8. Describe at least four causes of a trial balance failing to balance.
9. Explain how a worksheet aids in the preparation of the financial statements. Include as part of your answer a description of the worksheet's five pairs of columns.
10. What is the purpose of the closing entries?
11. Describe the contents of the post-closing trial balance and explain its purpose.

APPLY WHAT YOU HAVE LEARNED

LO 1:   Terminology

1. Presented below is a list of items relating to the concepts discussed in this chapter, followed by definitions of those items in scrambled order.

a. Accounting cycle	**f.** Credit
b. General Journal	**g.** Account
c. General Ledger	**h.** Chart of Accounts
d. Trial Balance	**i.** Posting
e. Debit	**j.** Journalizing

1. _____ A collection of all the accounts of a business entity
2. _____ The left side of an account
3. _____ The series of steps repeated each accounting period to enable a business entity to record, classify, and summarize financial information
4. _____ A book of original entry
5. _____ A device used to sort accounting data into similar groupings
6. _____ The process of recording into the general ledger from a journal
7. _____ The process of recording transactions into the book of original entry
8. _____ A listing to prove the equality of debits and credits
9. _____ The complete list of the account titles used by an entity
10. _____ The right side of an account

REQUIRED:
Match the letter next to each item on the list with the appropriate definition. Each letter will be used only once.

LO 1: The Accounting Cycle

2. Identify and list in order of occurrence the steps of the accounting cycle.

LO 1: The Accounting Cycle

3. Define the following terms.

    a. Journal
    b. Ledger
    c. Posting
    d. Trial balance
    e. Adjusting entries
    f. Closing entries

LO 2: Normal Account Balances

4. Examine the following accounts.

    1. _____ Cash
    2. _____ Accounts Payable
    3. _____ J. Smith, Capital
    4. _____ Revenues
    5. _____ Prepaid Insurance
    6. _____ Merchandise Inventory
    7. _____ Rent Expense
    8. _____ Income Tax Expense
    9. _____ Income Taxes Payable
    10. _____ Common Shares

REQUIRED:

Indicate whether the normal balance of each account is a debit (DR) or credit (CR) in the space provided.

LO 2: Permanent or Temporary Accounts

5. Examine the following accounts.

    1. _____ Cash
    2. _____ Accounts Payable
    3. _____ J. Smith, Capital
    4. _____ Revenues
    5. _____ Prepaid Insurance
    6. _____ Merchandise Inventory
    7. _____ Rent Expense
    8. _____ Income Tax Expense
    9. _____ Income Taxes Payable
    10. _____ Common Shares

REQUIRED:

Indicate whether the type of account is permanent (P) or temporary (T) in the space provided.

LO 2: Normal Account Balances

6. Examine the following accounts.

1. _____ Accounts Receivable
2. _____ Notes Payable
3. _____ S. Jones, Drawings
4. _____ Sales
5. _____ Prepaid Rent
6. _____ Supplies Inventory
7. _____ Insurance Expense
8. _____ Interest Expense
9. _____ Wages Payable
10. _____ Retained Earnings

REQUIRED:

Indicate whether the normal balance of each account is a debit (DR) or credit (CR) in the space provided.

LO 2: Permanent or Temporary Accounts

7. Examine the following accounts.

1. _____ Accounts Receivable
2. _____ Notes Payable
3. _____ S. Jones, Drawings
4. _____ Sales
5. _____ Prepaid Rent
6. _____ Supplies Inventory
7. _____ Insurance Expense
8. _____ Interest Expense
9. _____ Wages Payable
10. _____ Retained Earnings

REQUIRED:

Indicate whether the type of account is permanent (P) or temporary (T) in the space provided.

LO 2: Account Classification

8. Examine the following accounts.

1. _____ Prepaid Taxes
2. _____ Advertising Expense
3. _____ Retained Earnings
4. _____ Amortization Expense
5. _____ Rent Revenue
6. _____ Automotive Equipment
7. _____ Supplies Inventory
8. _____ Truck Expense
9. _____ Gasoline Expense
10. _____ Common Shares

REQUIRED:

Indicate the classification of each of the accounts listed above.

a. Asset
b. Liability
c. Revenue
d. Expense
e. Equity

LO 2: Account Classification

9. Examine the following accounts.

1. _____ Cash
2. _____ Accounts Payable
3. _____ C. Smith, Capital
4. _____ Service Revenues
5. _____ Prepaid Insurance
6. _____ Merchandise Inventory
7. _____ Rent Expense
8. _____ Income Tax Expense
9. _____ Income Taxes Payable
10. _____ Preferred Shares

REQUIRED:

Indicate the classification of each of the accounts listed above.

a. Asset	**d.** Expense
b. Liability	**e.** Equity
c. Revenue	

LO 2: Account Classification

10. You are presented with the following accounts.

1. _____ Accounts Receivable
2. _____ Notes Payable
3. _____ N. Jones, Drawings
4. _____ Sales
5. _____ Prepaid Rent
6. _____ Office Supplies Inventory
7. _____ Insurance Expense
8. _____ Income Tax Expense
9. _____ Wages Payable
10. _____ Unearned Subscription Revenue

REQUIRED:

Indicate the classification of each of the accounts listed above.

a. Asset	**d.** Expense
b. Liability	**e.** Equity
c. Revenue	

LO 2 & 3: Normal Account Balances

11. Examine the following accounts.

1. _____ Prepaid Taxes
2. _____ Advertising Expense
3. _____ Retained Earnings
4. _____ Amortization Expense
5. _____ Rent Revenue
6. _____ Automotive Equipment
7. _____ Unearned Subscription Revenue
8. _____ Truck Expense
9. _____ Gasoline Expense
10. _____ Common Stock

REQUIRED:

Indicate whether the normal balance of each account is a debit (DR) or credit (CR) in the space provided.

LO 2 & 3: Transaction Analysis

12. On May 1, Bill Simon started a computer repair business. Simon opened a bank account for the business by depositing $7,000. He paid two months' rent in advance totaling $400. On May 3, Simon purchased computer repair supplies for $700 and three computers at a total cost of $4,500. Simon hired a student helper, agreeing to pay the helper $1,000 per month, of which he paid $500 on May 15 and May 31. On May 25, Simon paid $200 for a newspaper advertisement to announce the opening of the business. Bill earned $3,500 in July, of which he collected $2,800 in cash.

REQUIRED:

Prepare journal entries to record these transactions.

LO 2 & 3: Transaction Analysis

13. On July 1, Katy Tener began KT Travel Agency (KT) and deposited $10,000 in a company bank account. KT paid $500 for one month's rent. On July 5 the company purchased office supplies for $700 and three desks at a total cost of $1,500. KT hired a travel consultant, agreeing to pay her $20 per hour. The consultant worked 100 hours in July, for which KT will pay her on August 1. KT paid $100 on July 29 for a newspaper advertisement to announce the opening of the business. KT booked a cruise for its first customer and received a cheque from the cruise line for $800 on July 22. On July 31, the company borrowed $12,000 from the bank for two years at 9%.

REQUIRED:

Prepare journal entries to record these transactions.

LO 4: Transaction Analysis

14. On December 1, 2004, Jogina Sisemore, CA, opened a practice. She contributed $5,000 to a company bank account and paid office rent for three months in advance, totaling $900. On December 2, the company purchased a desk for cash of $500 and bought $1,200 worth of office supplies on account. The company also borrowed $1,500 from the bank for three years at 6% to purchase computer equipment from a local dealer.

REQUIRED:

Prepare journal entries to record these transactions.

LO 4: Recording Transactions

15. The transactions for September 2004 for Tom Miller's Two Mile High Flight School are as follows:

Sept. 1   Deposited $125,000 in a business bank account from personal funds.
   1   Purchased an airplane for $80,000.
   2   Purchased fuel for the airplane costing $1,500.
   2   Paid $260 for a newspaper advertisement.

<table>
<tr><td>2</td><td>Paid rent on an airplane hangar for six months in advance totaling $3,000.</td></tr>
<tr><td>5</td><td>Collected $100 for a new student's first lesson.</td></tr>
<tr><td>5</td><td>Purchased a desk for $200.</td></tr>
<tr><td>5</td><td>Borrowed $10,000 from the bank for two years at 8%.</td></tr>
<tr><td>6</td><td>Purchased office supplies for $450.</td></tr>
<tr><td>8</td><td>Collected $100 for the student's second lesson.</td></tr>
<tr><td>12</td><td>Withdrew $1,000 for personal living expenses.</td></tr>
<tr><td>15</td><td>Paid the telephone directory's advertising bill of $800.</td></tr>
<tr><td>20</td><td>Ordered $1,000 worth of repair parts for the airplane.</td></tr>
<tr><td>23</td><td>Received the parts ordered on September 20, paying cash.</td></tr>
<tr><td>29</td><td>Paid the $150 utility bill received today.</td></tr>
</table>

REQUIRED:

Record each of the above transactions in a general journal.

LO 4: Recording Transactions

16. The Ace Termite proprietorship transactions for October 2004 are as follows:

<table>
<tr><td>Oct. 1</td><td>Proprietor Helen Laws deposited $35,000 in a business bank account from her personal savings account.</td></tr>
<tr><td>1</td><td>Purchased a truck for $18,000.</td></tr>
<tr><td>1</td><td>Borrowed $8,000 from the bank using the truck as collateral. Interest of 9% will be paid monthly on the first day of each month.</td></tr>
<tr><td>2</td><td>Purchased spraying equipment for the truck costing $3,500, including $400 worth of chemicals.</td></tr>
<tr><td>2</td><td>Paid $600 for a newspaper advertisement to run each week in October.</td></tr>
<tr><td>2</td><td>Paid rent on an office for six months in advance totaling $6,000.</td></tr>
<tr><td>5</td><td>Collected $75 for spraying a new residence.</td></tr>
<tr><td>5</td><td>Purchased a desk for $100 at a garage sale.</td></tr>
<tr><td>5</td><td>Billed a customer $150 for spraying the lawn.</td></tr>
<tr><td>6</td><td>Purchased office supplies for $200.</td></tr>
<tr><td>8</td><td>Collected $100 for a termite inspection.</td></tr>
<tr><td>9</td><td>Collected the $150 from the October 5 customer.</td></tr>
<tr><td>12</td><td>Withdrew $500 for personal living expenses.</td></tr>
<tr><td>15</td><td>Paid the telephone directory advertising bill of $300.</td></tr>
<tr><td>20</td><td>Ordered $1,000 worth of chemicals.</td></tr>
<tr><td>23</td><td>Received the chemicals ordered on October 20 with payment due in ten days.</td></tr>
<tr><td>28</td><td>Collected $2,300 for termite inspections for a loan company and billed an apartment complex $1,200 for spraying 40 units.</td></tr>
<tr><td>29</td><td>Paid the office utility bill for $135.</td></tr>
</table>

REQUIRED:

Record each of the above transactions in a general journal.

LO 4: Recording Transactions

17. The transactions for December 2004 for Brad Sanders Auto Repair Shop are as follows:

Dec. 1 Deposited $45,000 in a business bank account from Brad's personal chequing account.

1 Purchased a wrecker for $30,000.

1 Borrowed $25,000 at 8% interest from the bank to pay for the wrecker, using it as collateral. Interest is payable monthly on the first day of the month, and a semiannual principal payment of $5,000 is due the first day of June and December each year.

2 Purchased shop equipment costing $12,500.

2 Paid $360 for a newspaper advertisement to announce the opening of the business.

2 Paid rent totalling $8,100 on garage and office for six months in advance.

5 Signed a contract to perform maintenance service on all auto equipment for a car rental shop.

5 Purchased a desk and chair for $250.

5 Billed a customer $250 for auto repairs.

6 Purchased office supplies for $250.

8 Billed the rental agency $2,500 for work performed.

10 Collected $250 from the December 5 customer.

12 Withdrew $500 for personal living expenses.

15 Paid the telephone bill of $300.

21 Paid the local parts distributor $600 for parts used on jobs and ordered $1,300 worth of parts for inventory.

25 Received the parts ordered on December 21 and paid cash on delivery.

29 Paid the office and shop electric bill of $320.

31 Billed the rental agency $3,600 for services that used $680 worth of parts.

REQUIRED:

Record each of the above transactions in a general journal.

LO 4: Posting Transactions

18. Refer to problem 13.

REQUIRED:

a. Prepare a chart of accounts for KT Travel Agency.
b. Post the transactions in the general ledger.
c. Prepare a trial balance after completion of the posting process.

LO 4: Posting Transactions

19. Refer to problem 14.

REQUIRED:

a. Prepare a chart of accounts for Jogina Sisemore, CA.
b. Post the transactions to the general ledger.
c. Prepare a trial balance after completion of the posting process.

LO 4: Posting Transactions

20. Refer to problem 15.

REQUIRED:
a. Prepare a chart of accounts for Tom Miller's Two Mile High Flight School.
b. Post the transactions to the general ledger.
c. Prepare a trial balance after completion of the posting process.

LO 6: Adjusting Entries

21. Arnold Zinfandel, a proprietorship, had the following accrual information available at the end of the year 2004.

a. Unpaid wages to employees were $2,500.
b. Interest due on a loan to the bank was $1,000.
c. Sales taxes collected during December and unpaid to the province were $3,000.
d. A customer owed one year's interest on a note to Arnold Zinfandel for $4,000.
e. One of Arnold Zinfandel's renters failed to pay the December rent of $5,000 because she was out of the country. She will pay this amount when she returns on January 10, 2005.

REQUIRED:
Prepare the appropriate general journal entries with explanations to record the above adjustments.

LO 6: Adjusting Entries

22. Pat Haney Corporation Ltd. had the following information available at the end of the year 2004.

a. The accountant completed the 2004 amortization schedule, which showed the amortization expense as $10,520. The Amortization Expense account has a balance of $8,500.
b. Commissions for December of $22,000 will be paid to the company's sales staff on January 5. The Commissions Payable account has a zero balance.
c. The company's Accounts Receivable account shows $64,500. After the accountant completed an analysis, he discovered that it should be $68,400. The difference is a sale made on December 31 that was not recorded.
d. A good customer borrowed $20,000 on July 1 for one year at 12% interest. The principal and interest will be paid on June 30, 2005.
e. On July 1, the company paid $14,000 in rent for one year on a temporary warehouse. The accountant recorded this payment as rent expense.

REQUIRED:
Prepare the appropriate general journal entries with explanations to record the above adjustments.

LO 6: Adjusting Entries

23. Buttram Enterprises has the following information available at year end on December 31.

    a. Wages earned by employee but not paid at year end is $4,000.
    b. A two-year insurance policy was paid for on October 1 for $2,000. The Insurance Expense account's balance is $2,000.
    c. Service Fee Income earned but not collected at year end is $14,000. Accounts Receivable has a zero balance.
    d. Property taxes unpaid at year end are $3,900.
    e. Interest owed to the bank but not paid at year end is $2,200.

REQUIRED:

Prepare the appropriate general journal entries with explanations to record the above adjustments.

LO 6: Adjusting Entries—Prepaid Items

24. The trial balance for Koch Company Ltd. at June 30, its year end, has the following balances before adjustments.

Unearned Rental Income	$7,200
Prepaid Rent Expense	3,600
Prepaid Insurance	4,800
Supplies Inventory	1,200

    a. On May 1, the company paid the rent expense for one year in the amount of $3,600.
    b. On April 1, the company collected rental income in advance for the following 24 months in the amount of $14,400.
    c. On June 1, the company paid for its business insurance policy for the next two years in the amount of $4,200.
    d. At year end, the physical count of the supplies inventory indicated that $295 worth of supplies were on hand.

REQUIRED:

Prepare the appropriate adjusting entries with explanations to record the above information.

LO 6: Adjusting Entries—Prepaid Items

25. The trial balance for Earhart Company Ltd. at June 30, its year end, has the following balances before adjustments.

Unearned Rental Income	$7,200
Prepaid Rent	3,600
Insurance Expense	4,800
Supplies Inventory	200

    a. On October 1, the company paid the rent expense of $3,600 for one year's rent in advance.
    b. On March 1, the company collected rental income of $600 per month in advance for the following 24 months.
    c. On May 1, the company paid for a catastrophe insurance policy for the next two years at a rate of $2,400 per year. This was the only policy in force.

d. On June 30, the physical count of the supplies inventory on hand was $400.

REQUIRED:

Prepare the appropriate adjusting entries with explanations to record the above adjustments.

LO 6: Adjusting Entries—Prepaid Items

26. In 2004, the *Fare of the Hearty Cooking* monthly magazine sold 1,000 annual monthly subscriptions for $16 each. It also sold 500 two-year subscriptions for $25 each and 250 two-year subscriptions for $32 each.

REQUIRED:

a. Prepare the appropriate adjusting entries with explanations to record the adjustments necessary at the end of years 1 and 2 if the subscriptions were all sold at the beginning of 2004 and were originally recorded as income.

b. Prepare the appropriate adjusting entries with explanations to record the adjustments necessary at the end of years 1 and 2 if the subscriptions were all sold at the beginning of 2004 and were originally recorded as a liability.

LO 6: Adjusting Entries—Amortization

27. At the beginning of the year, Smeltzer Limited purchased a copy machine for $2,000. The firm believed the machine would have an estimated useful life of six years and a salvage value of $200. The firm also purchased a delivery van costing $28,000 with an estimated useful life of four years and a salvage value of $4,000. The company decided to use straight-line amortization for both assets.

REQUIRED:

a. Prepare the appropriate adjusting entries with explanations to record the amortization expense at the end of year 1.

b. Prepare the appropriate adjusting entries with explanations to record the amortization adjustment at the end of year 1 if the Accumulated Amortization account had a balance of $4,500 at the end of year 1 and these were the only amortizable assets the company owned.

LO 6: Adjusting Entries—Amortization

28. At the beginning of the year, Walsh Enterprises purchased a copy machine for $3,000. The firm believed the machine would have an estimated useful life of four years and a salvage value of $200. The firm also purchased a tractor costing $56,000 with an estimated useful life of six years and a salvage value of $2,000. The company decided to use straight-line amortization for both assets.

REQUIRED:

a. Prepare the appropriate adjusting entries with explanations to record the amortization adjustment at the end of year 1 assuming that the company recorded no amortization in the first year.

b. Prepare the appropriate adjusting entries with explanations to record the amortization adjustment at the end of year 1 if the Accumulated Amortization account has a balance of $10,800 and these are the only amortizable assets the company owns.

LO 6:   Adjusting Entries—Amortization

29. At the start of the year, Marshall Corporation Ltd. purchased a piece of equipment for $36,000. The firm believed the machine would have an estimated useful life of five years and a salvage value of $6,000. The firm also purchased a building costing $200,000 with an estimated useful life of 40 years and no residual value. The company uses straight-line amortization.

REQUIRED:

a. Prepare the appropriate adjusting entries with explanations to record the amortization adjustment at the end of year 1 if the company did not record any amortization.

b. Prepare the appropriate adjusting entries with explanations to record the amortization adjustment at the end of year 1 assuming that the Accumulated Amortization account had a balance of $30,000 and these are the only amortizable assets the company owns.

LO 6:   Adjusting Entries

30. At the beginning of the year, Lynn Hughes Company Ltd. purchased a computer for $3,000. The firm believed the computer would last three years with a residual value of $200. The firm also purchased a truck costing $56,000 with an estimated useful life of four years and a salvage value of $6,000. The company uses straight-line amortization for both assets. At year end, the general ledger contains the following accounts and balances:

Office Equipment	$ 2,800 Debit
Accumulated Amortization—O.E.	200 Debit
Automotive Equipment—A.E.	56,000 Debit
Accumulated Amortization	14,000 Credit
Amortization Expense	14,000 Debit

REQUIRED:

Prepare the appropriate adjusting entries with explanations to record the amortization adjustment at the end of year 1.

LO 6:   Adjustments from Trial Balance Accounts with Supplemental Information

31. The following is a partial trial balance for Denton Limited as of December 31, 2004.

DENTON LIMITED
Partial Trial Balance
December 31, 2004

	Debit	Credit
Prepaid Insurance	$12,000	
Prepaid Rent Expense	18,000	
Interest Receivable	0	
Wages Payable		$10,000
Unearned Fee Income		36,000
Interest Income		12,000

Additional information includes the following:

a. The insurance policy indicates that on December 31, 2004, seven months remain on the 24-month policy that originally cost $18,000.

b. Denton Limited has a note receivable with $2,500 of interest due and payable on January 1, 2005.

c. The books show that two-thirds of the fees paid in advance by a customer on June 30 have now been earned.

d. The company prepaid rent for nine months on July 1.

e. The wages payable on December 31 were $7,000. The amount in the Wages Payable account is from December 31, 2003.

REQUIRED:

Record in proper general journal form the adjustments required by the above information.

LO 6: Adjustments from Trial Balance Accounts with Supplemental Information

32. The following is a partial trial balance for Reese Limited as of December 31, 2004.

REESE LIMITED
Partial Trial Balance
December 31, 2004

	Debit	Credit
Prepaid Insurance	$ 6,000	
Prepaid Rent Expense	10,000	
Wages Expense	25,000	
Subscription Income		$72,000
Interest Expense	38,000	

Additional information includes the following:

a. The company paid a $7,200 premium on a three-year business insurance policy on July 1, 2003.

b. Reese Limited borrowed $200,000 on January 2 and must pay 12% interest on January 2, 2005, for the entire year of 2004.

c. The books show that $60,000 in subscriptions has now been earned and the balance is a liability.

d. The company prepaid ten months' rent in advance on November 1, 2004, to take advantage of a special discount that reduced the rent to $1,000 per month.

e. Wages for December 31 of $3,000 will be paid to employees on January 6, 2005.

REQUIRED:

Record in proper general journal form the adjustments required by the above information.

LO 6: Adjustments from Trial Balance Accounts with Supplemental Information

33. The following is a partial trial balance for Marr Limited as of December 31, 2004.

MARR LIMITED
Partial Trial Balance
December 31, 2004

	Debit	Credit
Office Supplies Expense	$ 36,000	
Cost of Goods Sold	122,000	
Merchandise Inventory	63,000	
Office Supplies Inventory	400	
Wages Payable	41,500	
Wages Expense	4,000	

Additional information includes the following:

a. Office supplies on hand at year end were $1,230.
b. The ending merchandise inventory was $61,350. The cost of the goods sold during the year was $122,000.
c. The total payroll cost for the year 2004 was $50,000. At the end of last year, the company owed employees $4,000 for December wages and at December 31, 2004, the company owes employees $4,500 for December wages.

REQUIRED:

Record in proper general journal form the adjustments required by the above information.

LO 6: Bank Reconciliation

34. Kelowna Katerers Limited showed a cash balance of $2,517 on November 30, 2004. The company received the bank statement for November 2004 that showed a balance of $2,750. The other differences that appear between the company's book balance of cash and the bank statement include the following:

a. A deposit of $500 that was made on November 30 was not included in the bank statement.
b. Outstanding cheques on November 30 were $1,280.
c. Bank service charges imposed by the bank were $35.
d. The bank included a debit memo for an NSF (nonsufficient funds) cheque totaling $512.

REQUIRED:

a. Prepare a bank reconciliation for Kelowna Katerers Limited as of November 30, 2004.
b. Prepare the general journal entries necessary to adjust the accounts.

LO 6:   Bank Reconciliation

35. Saskatoon Supplies Limited received the bank statement for October 2004. The following information is available for the bank reconciliation of October 31, 2004:

Balance per general ledger	$7,500
Balance per bank statement	8,250
NSF cheque from customer returned by the bank	1,000
Outstanding cheques total	2,365
Deposits in transit	1,800
Bank charges	60
Credit memo for collection from customer of amount owed on a note	1,245

REQUIRED:

a. Prepare a bank reconciliation for Saskatoon Supplies Limited as of October 31, 2004.

b. Prepare the general journal entries necessary to adjust the accounts.

LO 6:   Bank Reconciliation

36. Manitoba Movers Inc. received the bank statement for December 2004. The company showed a cash balance of $1,838 on December 31, 2004, but the bank statement showed a balance of $3,500. The other differences that appear between the company's book balance of cash and the bank statement include the following:

1. A deposit of $300 that was made on December 31 was not included in the bank statement.
2. Outstanding cheques on December 31 were $1,280.
3. Bank service charges imposed by the bank were $28.
4. The bank included a debit memo for credit card discounts totaling $690.
5. Included in the bank statement was a credit memo for $1,400 for the collection of an outstanding account owed by a customer.

REQUIRED:

a. Prepare a bank reconciliation for Manitoba Movers Inc. of as December 31, 2004.

b. Prepare the general journal entries necessary to adjust the accounts.

LO 6 & 7:   Adjustments and the Impact on Financial Statements

37. Conception Bay Clothiers Limited has the following account balances at the end of the year:

Prepaid Insurance	$6,000
Rental Income	4,800
Wages Expense	7,660
Taxes Payable	4,398
Interest Income	2,325

The company also has the following information available at the end of the year:

1. $4,000 of the prepaid insurance has now expired.
2. $2,200 of the rental income has not yet been earned.

3. The company must accrue an additional $1,500 of wages expense.
4. The Taxes Payable account and the Taxes Expense account are both overstated by $398.
5. The company has earned an additional $500 of interest income.

REQUIRED:
a. Prepare the journal entries necessary to adjust the accounts.
b. Use T-accounts to compute and present both the income statement and balance sheet account balances after the adjustments have been prepared.

LO 6 & 7: Adjustments and the Impact on Financial Statements

38. Kenora Engineering Inc. has the following account balances at the end of the year:

Insurance Expense	$4,000
Unearned Rental Income	3,800
Wages Payable	5,550
Taxes Expense	4,398
Amortization Expense	7,625

The company also has the following information available at the end of the year:

1. $1,000 of the Insurance Expense has not yet expired.
2. $1,600 of the Unearned Rental Income has now been earned.
3. The company currently owes employees $1,200 in wages.
4. The company owes an additional $4,900 in property taxes.
5. Amortization expense for the year is a total of $8,743.

REQUIRED:
a. Prepare the journal entries necessary to adjust the accounts.
b. Use T-accounts to compute and present both the income statement and balance sheet account balances after the adjustments have been prepared.

LO 6 & 7: Adjustments and the Impact on Financial Statements

39. The Quebec Consulting Group Limited has the following account balances at the end of the year:

Insurance Expense	$5,400
Unearned Fee Income	3,525
Wages Payable	3,000
Advertising Expense	9,500
Amortization Expense	3,850

The company also has the following information available at the end of the year:

1. $3,200 of the Insurance Expense has not yet expired.
2. $1,200 of the Unearned Fee Income was earned in the last month of the year.
3. The company must accrue an additional $1,800 of wages expense.
4. The company paid $1,900 for advertisements that will be shown next month.
5. Amortization expense for the year is a total of $8,625.

REQUIRED:

a. Prepare the journal entries necessary to adjust the accounts.

b. Use T-accounts to compute and present both the income statement and balance sheet account balances after the adjustments have been prepared.

LO 6 & 7: Adjustments and the Impact on Financial Statements

40. Charlottetown Transportation Limited has the following account balances at the end of the year:

Supplies Expense	$2,000
Supplies Inventory	230
Unearned Subscription Income	3,758
Prepaid Rent Expense	4,950
Taxes Expense	1,259
Accumulated Amortization	8,964

The company also has the following information available at the end of the year.

1. $500 of the supplies are still on hand.
2. $1,785 of the Unearned Subscription Income has now been earned.
3. Two months of rent at $850 per month is still prepaid.
4. The Taxes Expense account and the Income Taxes Payable account are both overstated by $189.
5. Amortization expense for the year is a total of $12,326.

REQUIRED:

a. Prepare the general journal entries necessary to adjust the accounts.

b. Use T-accounts to compute and present both the income statement and balance sheet account balances after the adjustments have been prepared.

Comprehensive

41. Alco Home Improvement Centre began operations on November 1, 2004. Transactions for the month of November are as follows:

Nov. 1 Herb Alco invested $45,000 in his new venture.

5 The company signed a lease on a store and paid six months' rent in advance of $9,450.

6 Purchased $500 worth of office supplies from Mott's Office Supply on account.

8 Purchased $25,000 worth of merchandise for resale from Associated Supply on account.

10 Paid $100 for the freight bill on the November 8 purchase.

11 Paid $175 for a radio ad to announce the store opening.

12 Borrowed $5,000 from The Commercial Bank. Signed a 9%, 90-day note with interest payable on the last day of each month.

14 Sold merchandise costing $2,400 for $4,000 cash.

15 Sold merchandise that cost $1,750 for $2,500 on a 30-day account to J. Adams.

16 Paid freight on sale to Adams of $75.

17 Sold merchandise that cost $1,950 for $3,000 on a 30-day account to A. Bear.

19 Purchased merchandise costing $10,000 from Rider Company Ltd. on account.

Nov. 20 Sold merchandise costing $13,200 for $20,000 cash.
21 Paid Mott's Office Supply for November 6 purchase.
23 Paid Associated Supply for the purchase on November 8.
24 Collected payment in full from A. Bear for the November 17 purchase.
25 Paid Rider Company Ltd. for the purchase on November 19.
25 Received payment in full from J. Adams for the November 15 purchase.
26 Purchased a forklift to move merchandise for $5,000 cash.
28 Paid $800 for utilities for the month of November.
29 Paid wages of $4,000 for the month.
30 Herb Alco withdrew $1,000 for personal living expenses.

REQUIRED:

a. Journalize the transactions for the month of November in the general journal.
b. Open the necessary accounts in the general ledger and post the November transactions to the appropriate accounts in the general ledger.
c. Prepare a trial balance on November 30, 2004.
d. Prepare adjusting entries and complete a worksheet using the following information in addition to that listed in the transactions:

1. The company amortized the forklift for the entire month of November, assuming straight-line amortization with no residual value and a five-year estimated life.
2. The company accrued the interest on the bank loan for 18 days.
3. The company incurred property tax expense of $900 for the month.

e. Prepare a balance sheet as of November 30, 2004, and an income statement and a statement of owner's equity for the month ended November 30, 2004.

Comprehensive

42. Baer Distributing proprietorship began operations on December 1, 2004. Transactions for the month of December are as follows:

Dec. 1 Max Baer invested $75,000 in his new venture.
2 The company signed a lease on a warehouse and paid six months' rent in advance of $6,000.
5 Purchased $1,500 worth of office supplies from Mardel Office Supply on account.
7 Purchased $15,000 worth of merchandise for resale from Agape Supply on account.
9 Paid $200 to the carrier for the freight bill on the December 7 purchase.
11 Paid the *Time Express* newspaper $350 for an ad to announce the grand opening of the distribution centre.
11 Borrowed $10,000 from The Commercial Bank. Signed a 10%, 180-day note.
13 Sold merchandise costing $6,300 for $8,200 cash.
14 Sold merchandise that cost $3,725 for $5,000 on account to J. Adair.
15 Paid freight of $175 on sale to Adair.
16 Sold merchandise that cost $3,050 for $4,000 on account to J. Bronson.
17 Purchased merchandise costing $20,000 from Lowe Company Ltd. on account.

Dec.	19	Sold merchandise that cost $7,950 for $10,000 cash.
	21	Paid Mardel Office Supply for the December 5 purchase.
	22	Paid Agape Supply for the purchase on December 7.
	24	Collected payment in full from J. Adair for the December 14 purchase.
	26	Paid Lowe Company Ltd. for the purchase on December 17.
	27	Received payment in full from J. Bronson for the December 16 purchase.
	30	Purchased a used truck to deliver merchandise for $14,000 cash.
	30	Paid $1,800 for utilities for the month.
	31	Paid wages of $7,000 for the month.
	31	Max Baer withdrew $1,800 for personal living expenses.

REQUIRED:

a. Journalize the transactions for the month of December in the general journal.

b. Open the necessary accounts in the general ledger and post the December transactions to the appropriate accounts in the general ledger.

c. Prepare a trial balance at December 31, 2004.

d. Prepare adjusting entries and complete a worksheet using the following information in addition to that included in the transactions:

1. The company amortized the truck for the entire month of December, assuming straight-line amortization with no residual value and a three-year estimated life.
2. The company accrued the interest on the bank loan for 20 days.
3. The company incurred property tax expense of $1,900 for the month.

e. Prepare a balance sheet as of December 31, 2004, and an income statement and a statement of owner's equity for the month ended December 31, 2004.

ACCOUNTING CYCLE CASES

Sole Proprietorship

43. John Robles began his retail clothing business, Fineries, on November 1, 2004, as a sole proprietor. The post-closing trial balance at November 30, 2004, appeared as follows:

FINERIES
Post-Closing Trial Balance
November 30, 2004

	Debits	Credits
Cash	$40,000	
Prepaid Rent	200	
Merchandise Inventory	24,000	
Fixtures	6,000	
Accumulated Amortization		$ 1,000
Wages Payable		1,500
J. Robles, Capital		67,700
Totals	$70,200	$70,200

The following transactions occurred in the month of December, 2004.

Dec. 1 Robles invested an additional $100,000 cash in his venture.

1 Bought store fixtures on account from the Acme Company Ltd. for $13,600, terms n/30.

1 Paid six months' rent in advance, $12,000.

5 Purchased $8,000 worth of merchandise on account from Triad Company Ltd.

7 Paid for a 36-month contents insurance policy for fire damage at a cost of $1,440.

8 Purchased merchandise for resale for $25,000 cash.

9 Returned damaged merchandise to Triad Company Ltd. and received credit for $1,600.

10 Sold merchandise to Jean Peoples on account for $12,600. The cost of the goods sold was $3,600.

12 Paid the balance due to Triad Company Ltd.

15 Cash sales for the first half of the month totaled $27,500. The cost of the goods sold relating to these cash sales was $8,000.

16 Sold merchandise to Janeal Foster on account for $10,000. The cost of these goods was $3,000.

16 Paid wages for the first half of the month totaling $5,500, including the balance due from November.

18 Purchased merchandise on account from Kerr Company Ltd. for $9,500.

20 Purchased office supplies totaling $250.

22 Received merchandise returned by Janeal Foster. Issued a credit memo for $1,500. The cost of the goods returned was $450.

22 Received a cheque from Jean Peoples for her invoice.

25 Received a cheque from Janeal Foster for payment of invoice.

28 Sold merchandise on account to Paul Larsen, $8,600. The cost of the goods sold was $2,500.

28 Paid utility bill of $300 for December.

28 Received telephone bill for $100 for the month of December.

28 Paid Kerr Company Ltd. for the invoice of December 18.

31 Recorded cash sales for the second half of December totaling $44,900. The cost of these goods was $22,900.

31 Paid wages for the second half of December, $4,500.

31 Received a bill for delivery services for December, $250.

REQUIRED:

a. Journalize the transactions for the month of December in the general journal.

b. Open the necessary accounts in the general ledger and post the December transactions to the general ledger.

c. Prepare a trial balance at December 31, 2004.

d. Prepare adjusting entries and complete a worksheet using the following information and the information found in the transactions:

1. The company accrued payroll expense of $1,200 for the month.
2. Store fixtures had a six-year life and no salvage value.
3. Ending inventory balance was $14,000.

e. Prepare a balance sheet as of December 31, 2004, and an income statement and a statement of owner's equity for the month ended December 31, 2004.

Corporation

44. Jay Chambless started a retail hardware store, Chambless Home Haven Ltd., on December 1, 2004. The following transactions occurred in the month of December:

Dec. 1 Chambless invested $200,000 cash to purchase 100,000 common shares of Chambless Home Haven Ltd. There were 200,000 shares authorized.

1 Bought store fixtures on account from Ace Company for $22,000, terms n/30.

1 Paid three months' rent in advance, $9,000.

5 Purchased merchandise on account from Taylor Company Ltd. for $50,000.

7 Paid for a 12-month contents insurance policy for fire damage at a cost of $1,200.

8 Purchased merchandise for resale for $30,000 cash.

9 Returned damaged merchandise to Taylor Company Ltd. and received credit for $16,000.

10 Sold merchandise to A.V. Hill on account, $24,000. The cost of the goods sold was $18,000.

12 Paid the balance due to Taylor Company Ltd.

15 Cash sales for the first half of the month totaled $30,000. The cost of the goods sold relating to these cash sales was $22,000.

16 Sold merchandise to Mel Hays on account $5,000. The cost of the goods sold was $3,000.

16 Paid wages totalling $7,000 for the first half of the month.

18 Purchased merchandise on account from McGee Company Limited for $18,000.

20 Purchased office supplies for $400 cash.

22 Received merchandise returned by Mel Hays. Issued a credit memo for $700. The cost of the goods returned was $400.

22 Received a cheque from A.V. Hill for her invoice.

25 Received a cheque from Mel Hays for payment of his invoice.

28 Sold merchandise on account to Dennis Rhodes for $12,600. The cost of the goods sold was $8,600.

28 Paid utility bill of $600 for December.

28 Received telephone bill for $200 for the month of December due on January 12.

28 Paid McGee Company Limited for the invoice of December 18.

31 Recorded cash sales totalling $35,200 for the second half of December. The cost of these goods was $26,200.

31 Paid wages for the second half of December, $7,500.

31 Received a bill for delivery services for December for $400 due January 10.

31 The company declared and paid a $0.10 per share cash dividend.

REQUIRED:

a. Journalize the transactions for the month of December in the general journal.

b. Open the necessary accounts in the general ledger and post the December transactions to the appropriate accounts.

c. Prepare a trial balance at December 31, 2004.

d. Prepare adjusting entries and complete a worksheet using the following information:

1. The company accrued payroll expense of $2,000 for the month.
2. Fixtures are amortized using the straight-line method over four years and have no salvage value.
3. Ending inventory balance is $15,000.
4. The combined corporate tax rate is 40%.

e. Prepare a balance sheet as of December 31, 2004, and an income statement and a statement of retained earnings for the month ended December 31, 2004.

f. Assume that the company has a December 31 year end. Prepare the closing entries to close the year.

g. Prepare a post-closing trial balance at December 31, 2004.

Partnership

45. The Blues brothers began a management consulting business on October 1, 2004, called Blues Brothers Consulting. The following transactions occurred in the month of October.

Oct. 1	John Blue invested $6,000 in the partnership for a 60% interest in the business, and his brother Art invested $4,000 for a 40% interest in the business.
1	Purchased a computer for $3,000 and a copy machine for $2,000. Each piece of equipment had an expected life of five years with no residual value. The computer was financed with a three-year, 10% interest bank loan that calls for monthly interest payments and annual principal payments of $1,000 on September 30 each year.
1	Paid three months' rent in advance, $3,000.
5	Purchased office supplies on account from Spring Company Ltd. for $700. The invoice date was October 5, terms 2/10, n/30.
6	Paid for a one-year contents insurance policy for fire damage at a cost of $600.
7	Returned damaged merchandise to Spring Company Ltd. and received credit for $100.
10	Performed consulting services and billed Sam Hall on account, $14,000. The terms were 1/10, n/30.
11	Received $4,000 cash for consulting services performed.
15	Paid for the office supplies purchased from Spring Company Ltd. on October 5.
15	Received $2,000 cash for consulting services performed.
15	Billed Gary Suter $5,000 for consulting fees, terms 2/10, n/30.
16	Paid assistant's wages totalling $1,000 for the first half of the month.
19	Purchased computer supplies on account from Dale Company Ltd., $400. The invoice date was October 19, terms 2/10, n/30.
20	Purchased office supplies for $400 cash.
20	Received payment from Sam Hall for the October 10 purchase.
25	Received a cheque from Gary Suter for payment of his invoice less the discount.
28	Provided services on account to Dan Lee for $1,600. The terms were 1/10, n/30.
28	Paid utility bill of $300 for October.
28	Received telephone bill for $250 for the month of October.
28	Paid Dale Company Ltd. for the invoice of October 19, less the discount.
31	Paid wages for the second half of October, $1,500.

31 Received a bill for fax services for October, $100.
31 John Blue withdrew $1,500 for personal expenses, and Art Blue withdrew $1,200.

REQUIRED:

a. Journalize the transactions for the month of October in the general journal.
b. Open the necessary accounts in the general ledger and post the October transactions to the appropriate accounts.
c. Prepare a trial balance at October 31, 2004.
d. Prepare adjusting entries and complete a worksheet using the following information and the information listed in the transactions:

1. Accrued payroll expense is $300 for the month.
2. Office supplies worth $100 were on hand at October 31.
3. There were no computer supplies left at October 31.
4. The partnership agreement indicates that the partners share profits and losses equally.

e. Prepare a balance sheet as of October 31, 2004, and an income statement and a statement of partners' equity for the month ended October 31, 2004.
f. Assume that Blues Brothers Consulting selected October 31 as the year end. Prepare and post the closing entries to close the year.
g. Prepare a post-closing trial balance at October 31, 2004.

7

Long-Lived Amortizable Assets: A Closer Look

While working your way through college, you spent over two years in a campus copy shop. After learning the business from every angle, you have the opportunity to purchase the shop from Connie, the retiring owner. She recently replaced all the equipment and has maintained it well. Your accountant suggests that you use as rapid an amortization method as possible. Not wanting to sound ignorant, you let the comment pass. Later, your friend Jon, an accounting major, explained some of the concepts to you but asks you to consider some additional issues. He wants to know how rapidly the technology changes in copiers, how many copies each machine can run economically before it begins to break down, and how many copies the shop runs each year. You vow to find the answers to these questions, but still do not understand all the implications of his issues. What do these issues have to do with the profitability of the copy shop?

Because accrual accounting recognizes revenues in the periods in which they were earned and it tries to record expenses in the same periods as the revenues they helped earn, it requires more judgment and estimation than cash accounting. One of the best examples of the effects of estimates in accrual accounting is the amortization of long-lived assets.

In this chapter, we extend our discussion of amortization by considering several issues that further complicate the amortization process. First, we consider the impacts of management's estimates of an asset's useful life and its residual value. Second, we examine the effects of management's selection of different amortization methods. Third, we look at the effects of disposing of assets and how such transactions create a gain or loss. ■

LEARNING OBJECTIVES

After completing your work on this chapter, you should be able to do the following:

1. Explain the process of amortizing long-lived assets as it pertains to accrual accounting.
2. Determine amortization expense amounts using both straight-line and double-declining-balance amortization methods.
3. Describe in your own words the effects on the income statement and balance sheet of using different methods of amortization.
4. Compare gains and losses to revenues and expenses.
5. Calculate a gain or loss on the disposal of a long-lived amortizable asset.
6. Explain the effects on a company's financial statements when management disposes of an amortizable asset.
7. Draw appropriate conclusions when presented with gains or losses on an income statement.
*8. Complete the recording process for long-lived assets and amortization.

AMORTIZATION

historical cost Total of all costs required to bring an asset to a productive state.

As you recall from our discussion in Chapter 5, amortization is defined as a systematic and reasoned allocation of the cost of a long-lived asset. Over time, the amortization process transfers the historical cost of the asset from the balance sheet to amortization expense on the income statement, to match the expenses more closely with the revenues they help produce. We measure **historical cost** as the total costs to bring an asset to a usable state. This includes the invoice price, applicable sales tax, installation costs, cost of insurance while in transit, shipping costs, and cost of training personnel to use the machine. It does not include repairs and maintenance or insurance once the asset becomes productive.

tangible property Property used in a business, such as buildings, equipment, machinery, furniture, and fixtures.

When a firm purchases **tangible property** to be used to produce revenues in more than one income statement period, it recognizes the item as a balance sheet asset that will produce future benefits to the company. Under the matching principle, the company allocates part of the cost of that asset to the period in which it produces revenues through amortization expense on the income statement. Just how much it recognizes as expense in a given year depends on several factors, including the estimates of useful life and residual value made and the amortization method used.

The Effect of Estimates

Estimates of the length of the asset's useful life and the amount of its residual value directly affect the amount of amortization expense recognized each year. For example, assume McMillan & Cox, a consulting firm, purchases a new computer network for $40,000. If management estimates that the computer system has a residual value of $4,000, the asset has an amortizable base of $36,000 (cost less residual value). The amount of amortization expense recognized each year will be different if the useful life is estimated to be four years rather than three or five years. By the same token, the amortizable base will be different if the residual value is estimated to be $2,000 rather than $4,000. Exhibit 7–1 shows how different amortizable bases result in different amounts of amortization expense being recognized each year of the useful life of the machine.

Exhibit 7–1
McMillan & Cox's New $40,000 Computer Network

Option	Details	Amortizable Base	Annual Expense
Decision 1	Residual value: $4,000 Useful life: 4 years	$36,000	$9,000
Decision 2	Residual value: $4,000 Useful life: 5 years	$36,000	$7,200
Decision 3	Residual value: $2,000 Useful life: 4 years	$38,000	$9,500
Decision 4	Residual value: $2,000 Useful life: 5 years	$38,000	$7,600

 Discussion Questions

7–1. What factors do you think a company should consider in determining the estimated useful life of a long-lived asset?

7–2. How do you think a company would go about determining the estimated residual value of a long-lived asset?

7–3. Consider a long-lived asset with a cost of $30,000. How would net income be affected by using an estimated useful life of six years and an estimated residual value of $6,000 rather than a four-year estimated useful life and a residual value of $5,000? Explain.

The Effect of Different Amortization Methods

Most companies have more than one amortizable asset, and many firms use more than one amortization method. As users of the financial accounting information provided by these companies, you should understand the impact of amortization method choice on financial statements. To illustrate these effects, we will explore in detail the two most commonly used amortization methods—straight-line amortization and **double-declining-balance amortization.**

Most companies use straight-line amortization as a method of allocating the cost of an asset over its useful economic life. Straight-line amortization assumes that an asset's economic usefulness (revenue-producing potential) is constant throughout its life, so therefore the cost should be equal for every accounting period. However, this does not always hold true, so therefore other methods may also be employed. Those other methods fall under the general category of **accelerated amortization.** Many companies use both straight-line and accelerated methods to amortize their long-lived assets. Do not confuse these methods with **capital cost allowance (CCA).** CCA is the method that the Canada Customs and Revenue Agency employs to amortize assets. The application of CCA is slightly different from the GAAP methods (straight-line and accelerated). CCA is used exclusively for tax calculation purposes and does not conform to GAAP. Therefore, most companies are required to use two methods of calculating amortization—one for tax purposes and the other for financial statement purposes. However, the calculation for capital cost allowance is very similar to accelerated amortization.

double-declining-balance method An accelerated amortization method in which amortization expense is twice the straight-line percentage multiplied by the book value of the asset.

accelerated amortization methods Those methods that record more amortization expense in the early years of an asset's life and less in the later years.

capital cost allowance (CCA) Amortization method taxpayers use to calculate amortization expense for tax purposes.

How do companies make the choice between using straight-line amortization and an accelerated amortization method? Recall that the matching principle requires us to match expenses with the revenues they help produce. Theoretically, we should use straight-line amortization for an asset that produces the same amount of revenue in each period of its useful life, and, conversely, an accelerated amortization method for an asset that produces more revenue in the early years and less as time goes by. However, the choice of amortization method is more likely to be made on more practical grounds.

When considering the cost/benefit constraint, firms often select straight-line amortization because it is easy to implement. Another reason is the anticipated effect on the financial statements during the asset's useful life. Exhibit 7–2 contrasts amortization expense recorded under the straight-line method to the amount recorded if an accelerated method is used. As we explore the consequences of amortization method choice, you can see the significant impact this decision can have on the accounting information offered to economic decision makers.

Exhibit 7–2
Straight-Line Amortization versus Accelerated Amortization

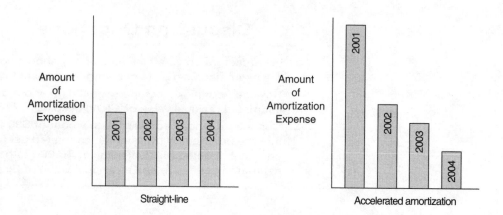

To illustrate that impact, we will contrast the results of straight-line amortization with those of an accelerated amortization method—the double-declining-balance method, which is the most widely used of the accelerated methods. We will explore the application of this method, not simply so you can learn how to use it, but, more importantly, to demonstrate the impact of the choice of amortization method on amortization expense (and therefore on reported net income).

Straight-Line Amortization

In Chapter 5, we introduced the concept of amortization with an example of the straight-line method. To review how straight-line amortization is calculated, assume Beavers Corporation purchased a milling machine on January 2, 2004, for a total price of $300,000. The company's management estimates the useful life of this machine to be five years, at the end of which the machine can be sold for an estimated $25,000. For simplicity, we will assume that the company owns only this machine.

We compute Beaver Corporation's yearly amortization expense as $55,000:

Cost	$300,000
Less: Residual Value	25,000
Amortizable Base	$275,000
Divided by Useful Life	5
Annual Amortization	$ 55,000

We could also decide that the life of this milling machine might be better measured by the number of units it could produce over its useful life. Instead of time as the straight-line measure, we could use units of production. If the milling machine can produce 100,000 units of hardware, we might measure its amortization in units of product. This type of straight-line amortization is called the **units of production amortization method**. The units of production amortization method is appropriate for many types of assets when the useful life is based, not on time passing, but on the amount of usage. For these assets, the quantity used has more to do with length of life and residual value than the passage of time. In our example of the milling machine, if we measured amortization in terms of units produced, we would calculate it in this manner:

units of production amortization method
A straight-line amortization method that uses production activity as the base to assign amortization expense.

Estimated units of production   100,000 units
Per unit amortization   = Amortizable base/Units
                                   = $275,000/100,000 units
                                   = $2.75 per unit

If Beavers Corporation produces 25,000 units the first year, we recognize $68,750 in amortization expense. See Exhibit 7–3 for a breakdown of the amortization over the life of the asset. Notice that the difference in amortization expense in each year is based upon the difference in production from one year to the next.

Exhibit 7–3
Book Value Using Units of Production Method Straight-Line Amortization

	Book Value Beginning of Year	Current Year's Production	Per Unit Amortization	Current Year's Amortization	Book Value End of Year
2004	$300,000	25,000	$2.75	$ 68,750	$231,250
2005	231,250	25,000	2.75	68,750	162,500
2006	162,500	20,000	2.75	55,000	107,500
2007	107,500	20,000	2.75	55,000	52,500
2008	52,500	10,000	2.75	27,500	25,000
Total		100,000		$275,000	

 Discussion Questions

7–4. How would you set the units of production for the following types of assets?

    a. Long-distance truck

    b. Commercial airliner

    c. Milling machine

    d. Cruise ship

7–5. Name five assets that would best be amortized by the passage of time.

Return to our regular straight-line example based on time. In each of the five years of the asset's useful life, we will transfer $55,000 of the original asset cost from the asset balance on the balance sheet to amortization expense on the income statement. To see this point, locate Beavers Corporation's income statements and balance sheets for the years 2004 through 2008 in Exhibit 7–4. For ease of interpre-

Exhibit 7–4
Beavers Corporation's Financial Statements Using Straight-Line Amortization

Income Statements

	2004	2005	2006	2007	2008
Sales	$755,000	$755,000	$755,000	$755,000	$755,000
Cost of Goods Sold	422,000	422,000	422,000	422,000	422,000
Gross Margin	$333,000	$333,000	$333,000	$333,000	$333,000
Operating Expenses Other than Amortization	(236,000)	(236,000)	(236,000)	(236,000)	(236,000)
Amortization Expense	(55,000)	(55,000)	(55,000)	(55,000)	(55,000)
Net Income	$ 42,000	$ 42,000	$ 42,000	$ 42,000	$ 42,000

Balance Sheets

	2004	2005	2006	2007	2008
ASSETS:					
Cash	$ 50,000	$ 96,000	$157,000	$213,000	$289,000
Accounts Receivable	206,000	257,000	293,000	334,000	355,000
Inventory	77,000	77,000	77,000	77,000	77,000
Machine	300,000	300,000	300,000	300,000	300,000
LESS: Accumulated Amortization	(55,000)	(110,000)	(165,000)	(220,000)	(275,000)
Total Assets	$578,000	$620,000	$662,000	$704,000	$746,000
LIABILITIES AND SHAREHOLDERS' EQUITY:					
Accounts Payable	$206,000	$206,000	$206,000	$206,000	$206,000
Notes Payable	170,000	170,000	170,000	170,000	170,000
Common Shares	110,000	110,000	110,000	110,000	110,000
Retained Earnings	92,000	134,000	176,000	218,000	260,000
Total Liabilities and Shareholders' Equity	$578,000	$620,000	$662,000	$704,000	$746,000

tation, we held constant most of the items not affected by the amortization process applied to the machine.

Note that regardless of what else happened in Beaver Corporation's operations for the years 2004 through 2008, the amount of amortization expense each year did not change. This constant amortization expense is one of the main characteristics of straight-line amortization. You should also note the direct correlation between the yearly amortization expense shown on the income statements and the book value of the machine on the balance sheets. Recall from Chapter 5 that book value is the cost of a long-lived asset less all the amortization expense recognized since the asset was placed in service (Exhibit 7–5). The total amortization expense recognized since the asset was put in service is reflected in the balance of accumulated amortization. Therefore,

Book Value = Cost − Accumulated Amortization

Each year, as $55,000 of amortization expense is recognized, the balance in accumulated amortization increases by that amount, reducing the book value of the machine by that same $55,000. This example illustrates that straight-line amor-

Exhibit 7–5
Book Value Using
Straight-Line
Amortization

	Book Value Beginning of Year	Current Year's Amortization	Book Value End of Year
2004	$300,000	$ 55,000	$245,000
2005	245,000	55,000	190,000
2006	190,000	55,000	135,000
2007	135,000	55,000	80,000
2008	80,000	55,000	25,000
Total Amortization		$275,000	

tization causes the book value of assets to decline by the same amount each year. The book value at the end of 2008 is $25,000 ($300,000 – $275,000), which is equal to the estimated residual value. A total of $275,000 amortization expense has been recorded, which is the amount of the amortizable base, and is therefore the maximum amount of allowable amortization expense. At this point, the asset is considered to be fully amortized.

 Discussion Question

7–6. Refer back to Exhibit 7–1, which illustrates McMillan & Cox's four possible sets of estimates relating to its new copy machine. For each decision setting, determine the book value of the asset after three years of amortization have been recorded.

Obviously, a different estimated useful life or a different estimated residual value would change the amount of yearly amortization expense. So, too, would the selection of a different method of calculating yearly amortization expense. To demonstrate how the choice of amortization method can affect amortization expense, we explore the most widely used accelerated amortization method.

Double-Declining-Balance Amortization

The double-declining-balance method received its name because it calculates amortization expense at twice the straight-line rate, and it applies the doubled rate to its book value at the beginning of each period.

These are the simple steps to calculating double-declining-balance method each year:

1. Calculate the straight-line rate as a percentage.
   (100%/N, where N = number of years in the asset's useful life)
2. Double the straight-line percentage.
3. Multiply the doubled percentage by the asset's book value.

As an example, apply this method to Beaver Corporation's milling machine for the first year. These steps follow the previous directions:

1. Calculate the straight-line percentage. **100%/5 = 20% (per year)**
2. Double the straight-line percentage. **20% × 2 = 40% (per year)**
3. Multiply the doubled percentage by the asset's book value.
   40% × $300,000 = $120,000

For 2004, Beavers Corporation would record $120,000 amortization expense. Step 3 of this process uses the book value of the asset. Note that in the first year of the asset's useful life, before any amortization has been recorded, the book value of the asset equals the cost of the asset. Though it may seem that the double-declining-balance method ignores the residual value, the maximum we can amortize using the double-declining-balance method is the same amortizable base used in straight-line amortization.

Exhibit 7–6 shows how we calculate the yearly amortization expense for Beavers Corporation's $300,000 machine using double-declining-balance amortization, a $25,000 residual value, and a five-year estimated useful life.

Exhibit 7–6
Book Value Using Double-Declining-Balance Amortization

	Book Value Beginning of Year		Double Rate	Current Year's Amortization	Book Value End of Year
2004	$300,000	×	40%	$120,000	$180,000
2005	180,000	×	40%	72,000	108,000
2006	108,000	×	40%	43,200	64,800
2007	64,800	×	40%	25,920	38,880
2008	38,880			13,880	25,000
Total Amortization				$275,000	

As you examine the calculations in the exhibit, you should note several points. First, the book value of the machine declines each year by the amount of amortization expense recognized that year, just as with straight-line amortization.

Second, the final year's amortization does not equal 40 percent of the book value at the beginning of the year ($38,820 × 40% = $15,552). Because the asset cannot amortize below its residual value, the amount of amortization expense in 2008 has been limited to $13,880 ($38,880 – $25,000 = $13,880.) As shown in Exhibit 7–5, total amortization over the five-year life of the asset is $275,000 for both straight-line and double-declining-balance methods.

Third, amortization expenses start out high but quickly decrease. This rapid decrease is characteristic of all accelerated amortization methods and has a profound effect on the financial statements of companies using accelerated amortization methods. Beavers Corporation's income statements for the years 2004 through 2008 and its balance sheets at the end of each of those years using the double-declining-balance method of calculating amortization illustrate this point in Exhibit 7–7. Again, many items not affected by the company's choice of amortization method have been held constant from year to year.

 Discussion Questions

7-7. Based on the financial statements of Beavers Corporation presented in Exhibit 7–7, and assuming no dividends were declared during 2004, what was the balance in retained earnings at the beginning of 2004?

7-8. Construct the 2004 statement of retained earnings if Beavers Corporation had not recorded any amortization on its milling machine.

Exhibit 7–7
Beavers Corporation's Financial Statements Using Double-Declining-Balance Amortization

Income Statements

	2004	2005	2006	2007	2008
Sales	$755,000	$755,000	$755,000	$755,000	$755,000
Cost of Goods Sold	422,000	422,000	422,000	422,000	422,000
Gross Margin	$333,000	$333,000	$333,000	$333,000	$333,000
Operating Expenses Other than Amortization	(236,000)	(236,000)	(236,000)	(236,000)	(236,000)
Amortization Expense	(120,000)	(72,000)	(43,200)	(25,920)	(13,880)
Net Income (Loss)	$(23,000)	$ 25,000	$ 53,800	$ 71,080	$ 83,120

Balance Sheets

	2004	2005	2006	2007	2008
ASSETS:					
Cash	$ 50,000	$ 96,000	$157,000	$213,000	$289,000
Accounts Receivable	206,000	257,000	293,000	334,000	355,000
Inventory	77,000	77,000	77,000	77,000	77,000
Machine	300,000	300,000	300,000	300,000	300,000
LESS: Accumulated Amortization	(120,000)	(192,000)	(235,200)	(261,120)	(275,000)
Total Assets	$513,000	$538,000	$591,800	$662,880	$746,000
LIABILITIES AND SHAREHOLDERS' EQUITY:					
Accounts Payable	$206,000	$206,000	$206,000	$206,000	$206,000
Notes Payable	170,000	170,000	170,000	170,000	170,000
Common Shares	110,000	110,000	110,000	110,000	110,000
Retained Earnings	27,000	52,000	105,800	176,880	260,000
Total Liabilities and Shareholders' Equity	$513,000	$538,000	$591,800	$662,880	$746,000

Understanding the Impact of Amortization Method Choice

When you compare Beavers Corporation's income statements and balance sheets prepared using straight-line amortization (Exhibit 7–4) with those same statements prepared using double-declining-balance amortization (Exhibit 7–7), you should notice several differences and similarities:

- There are significant differences in the reported amortization expense in each of the five years.
- There are significant differences in the reported net income in each of the five years.
- *Total* amortization expense and *total* net income over the five-year period are exactly the same regardless of which amortization method is used. The differences occur in individual years, not over the total five-year period.
- There are significant differences in the amounts of accumulated amortization on the balance sheets for years 2004 through 2007. The 2008 balance sheet, however, shows exactly the same amount of accumulated amortization in both presentations. In fact, the 2008 balance sheets in the two presentations are identical.

Exhibit 7–8

Comparison of Amortization Expense, Net Income, and Book Value of Beavers Corporation's Machine under the Two Amortization Methods

	Straight-Line			Double-Declining-Balance		
Year	Amortization Expense	Net Income	Book Value of Machine	Amortization Expense	Net Income	Book Value of Machine
2004	$ 55,000	$ 42,000	$245,000	$120,000	($ 23,000)	$180,000
2005	$ 55,000	$ 42,000	$190,000	$ 72,000	$ 25,000	$108,000
2006	$ 55,000	$ 42,000	$135,000	$ 43,200	$ 53,800	$ 64,800
2007	$ 55,000	$ 42,000	$ 80,000	$ 25,920	$ 71,080	$ 38,880
2008	$ 55,000	$ 42,000	$ 25,000	$ 13,880	$ 83,120	$ 25,000
Total	$275,000	$210,000		$275,000	$210,000	

Neither the straight-line method nor the double-declining-balance method is better than the other. Exhibit 7–8 depicts how the amortization method can have a substantial effect on reported net income and on portions of the balance sheet from year to year, but over the life of the asset, the method of amortization is irrelevant.

Discussion Questions

7-9. Explain why the 2008 balance sheets for Beavers Corporation, using the two different amortization methods, are identical, while all five income statements and the first four years' balance sheets are different.

7-10. Compare the amount of cash shown on the Beavers Corporation balance sheets using straight-line amortization and double-declining-balance amortization for each given year. Explain your findings.

7-11. Assume that Exhibit 7–8 depicts information from two different companies, and you are making an investment decision in 2005 with only the 2004 accounting information. How would you make a decision based on the given information?

DISPOSAL OF AMORTIZABLE ASSETS

Ideally, a firm would use a long-lived asset for exactly the time originally estimated, after which it would sell the asset for exactly the residual value originally estimated. In reality, this situation rarely occurs. The actual useful life of an asset normally differs from its estimated useful life, because a company may dispose of an asset at any time. A company holds an asset as long as it is productive, regardless of how long the company estimated it would hold it at the time of its purchase. Technological advances, competition, market changes, changes in business strategy, and many other factors affect the length of time an asset remains productive. A firm might sell an asset shortly after acquisition because it fails to be useful, or it may use an asset long after it is fully amortized.

technological obsolescence
Occurs when an asset is no longer compatible with current technology.

functional obsolescence
Occurs when an asset can no longer perform the function for which it was purchased.

When a firm determines the estimated useful life of an asset, it needs to consider the possibility of both the technological obsolescence and the functional obsolescence of the asset. **Technological obsolescence** occurs when technology exceeds the asset's current version. **Functional obsolescence** occurs when the firm can no longer use the asset to create revenue. Consider the case of computers. If you have a computer with workable software that fulfills all your needs, it does not matter to you whether it is the most current version of technology. It does not even matter that it may be technologically obsolete; it still is functional. If, however, your professor assigns an Internet assignment, and your computer cannot be connected to the Internet because it lacks the proper capacity to install and run the appropriate software, it has now become functionally obsolete. Functional obsolescence affects the asset's useful life. Both functional and technological obsolescence should be considered in determining the useful life of the asset.

A company has no guarantee that it will receive the estimated residual amount when it sells the asset. Technological obsolescence dramatically reduces the asset's residual value. Functional obsolescence may not reduce the asset's residual value if the asset has current technology. What is no longer functional to one company may still be functional to another company. The decision to keep or dispose of an asset should be based on the needs of the business, not on accounting considerations about amortization.

As a general rule, disposing of amortizable assets is not an ongoing central activity in a company; it is incidental or peripheral to the major operation of the business. For this reason, we do not consider any increase or decrease in equity from the disposal of amortizable assets as a revenue or expense. Rather, equity changes from the disposition of assets represent the accounting elements reported on the income statement as gains (increases) and losses (decreases).

Gains and Losses—Important Accounting Elements

Gains and losses can be described as follows:

gains Net inflows resulting from peripheral activities of a company. An example is the sale of an asset for more than its book value.

losses Net outflows resulting from peripheral activities of a company. An example is the sale of an asset for less than its book value.

1. **Gains.** Increases in equity from peripheral or incidental transactions of an entity and from all other transactions and other events and circumstances affecting the entity except those that result from revenues or investments by owners.
2. **Losses.** Decreases in equity from peripheral or incidental transactions of an entity and from all other transactions and other events and circumstances affecting the entity except those that result from expenses or distributions to owners.

With this knowledge of gains and losses, we can now expand the four components of capital from Chapter 5 to include them. The four components of capital are

1. Contributions by owners
2. Revenues and gains
3. Expenses and losses
4. Distributions to owners

Why do we distinguish between revenues and gains or between expenses and losses? Remember that an income statement provides information about the past performance of a company so that decision makers can better predict the company's future performance. Because gains and losses are incidental to a company's central operations and are usually one-time events, we cannot depend on them to predict the future success of a company's operations. Therefore, the income statement presents revenues and expenses as components of operating income and presents gains and losses separately. Decision makers can assign different predictive values to operating income (revenue minus expenses) and gains and losses. Gains and losses expand the net income equation from Chapter 5 as follows:

REVENUES + GAINS − EXPENSES − LOSSES = NET INCOME

Calculating Gains and Losses

We calculate gains and losses on the disposal of assets by comparing the value received and the value given. The value given consists of the net book value of the asset on the date of disposal. Amortization should always be calculated and recorded up to the date of disposal before we attempt to calculate any gain or loss.

Asset received − net book value of asset given = gain (loss)

Return to the Beavers Corporation and its $300,000 milling machine. Assume the company amortized this machine using the straight-line method over a five-year estimated useful life, with an estimated residual value of $25,000 (Exhibit 7–4).

On January 2, 2009, Beavers Corporation decides to sell the machine because it no longer benefits the company's operations. The machine has a $25,000 book value at the end of 2008 ($300,000 cost − $275,000 accumulated amortization). Although the accounting records indicate a $25,000 net book value, that seldom represents the market value. The net book value is based on an estimate made five years ago and is irrelevant in the marketplace because buyers pay market value. Market value depends on the condition of the machine, the state of technology, and the selling price of comparable used machines. However, we use the net book value to calculate accounting gains and losses.

Gain on Disposal Assume Beavers Corporation sells the machine for a cash price of $32,000. Because the company has received more than the net book value of the machine, it recognizes a gain.

Asset received − net book value of asset given = gain (loss)
$32,000 − $25,000 = $7,000

The $7,000 appears as a gain on the income statement for 2009. Exhibit 7–09 shows Beavers Corporation's income statements for the years 2008 and 2009 and its balance sheets at the end of each of those years, reflecting a $7,000 gain on the disposal of its machine.

As you examine these financial statements, consider the following points:

- On the income statement for the year 2009, the $7,000 gain is shown in a different place than revenues from Beavers Corporation's ongoing major operations.
- The $7,000 gain has exactly the same effect on net income as the revenues from the company's ongoing major operations on the income statement for the year 2009.
- Both the cost of the machine ($300,000) and the accumulated amortization ($275,000) have been removed from the balance sheet at the end of the year 2009.

 Discussion Question

7-12. Note that Beavers Corporation's income statements are presented in a multistep format in Exhibit 7–9. What specific items on the income statements are unique to this format and would not appear on a single-step statement?

BEAVERS CORPORATION

Income Statements

	2008	2009
Sales	$755,000	$941,000
Cost of Goods Sold	422,000	525,000
Gross Margin	$333,000	$416,000
Operating Expenses		
Other than Amortization	(236,000)	(319,000)
Amortization Expense	(55,000)	0
Operating Income	$ 42,000	$ 97,000
Gain on Sale of Machine	0	7,000
Net Income	$ 42,000	$104,000

Balance Sheets

	2008	2009
ASSETS:		
Cash	$289,000	$225,000
Accounts Receivable	355,000	313,000
Inventory	77,000	172,000
Machine	300,000	0
LESS: Accumulated Amortization	(275,000)	0
Total Assets	$746,000	$710,000
LIABILITIES AND		
SHAREHOLDERS' EQUITY:		
Accounts Payable	$206,000	$216,000
Notes Payable	170,000	20,000
Common Shares	110,000	110,000
Retained Earnings	260,000	364,000
Total Liabilities and Shareholders' Equity	$746,000	$710,000

Loss on Disposal   Assume Beavers sells the machine for a cash price of only $19,000. Because the company received less than the net book value of the machine, it recognizes a loss.

$$\text{Asset received} - \text{net book value of asset given} = \text{gain (loss)}$$
$$\$19,000 - \$25,000 = \$(6,000)$$

The $6,000 will be reported as a loss on the income statement for the year 2009. Exhibit 7–10 shows Beavers Corporations' income statements for the years 2008 and 2009 and its balance sheets at the end of each of those years, reflecting a $6,000 loss on the disposal of its machine.

As you study these financial statements, consider the following points:

- On the income statement for the year 2009, the $6,000 loss is shown in a different place than expenses required to support the company's ongoing major operations.
- The $6,000 loss has exactly the same effect on net income as the expenses required to support the company's ongoing major operations on the income statement for the year 2009.
- Both the cost of the machine ($300,000) and the accumulated amortization ($275,000) have been removed from the balance sheet at the end of the year 2009.

Exhibit 7–10
Beavers Corporation's
Financial Statements
for 2008 and 2009
Reflecting a Loss on the
Sale of Its Machine

BEAVERS CORPORATION

Income Statements

	2008	2009
Sales	$755,000	$941,000
Cost of Goods Sold	422,000	525,000
Gross Margin	$333,000	$416,000
Operating Expenses		
Other than Amortization	(236,000)	(319,000)
Amortization Expense	(55,000)	0
Operating Income	$ 42,000	$ 97,000
Loss on Sale of Machine	0	(6,000)
Net Income	$ 42,000	$ 91,000

Balance Sheets

	2008	2009
ASSETS:		
Cash	$289,000	$212,000
Accounts Receivable	355,000	313,000
Inventory	77,000	172,000
Machine	300,000	0
LESS: Accumulated Amortization	(275,000)	0
Total Assets	$746,000	$697,000
LIABILITIES AND		
SHAREHOLDERS' EQUITY:		
Accounts Payable	$206,000	$216,000
Notes Payable	170,000	20,000
Common Shares	110,000	110,000
Retained Earnings	260,000	351,000
Total Liabilities and Shareholders' Equity	$746,000	$697,000

In our examples of both a gain and a loss, we have assumed that Beavers Corporation was able to sell its machine for some amount of cash. However, there are times when an asset has no market value and must simply be abandoned. If this were the case with the Beavers Corporation machine, it would result in a loss of $25,000 ($0 cash received − $25,000 book value = a $25,000 loss).

 Discussion Question

7-13. Look again at Beavers Corporation's income statements and balance sheets in Exhibit 7–10. What items on the financial statements for the year 2009 would be different (and by how much) if Beavers Corporation had simply abandoned the machine?

Disposal with No Gain or Loss Assume now that Beavers Corporation sells the machine for a cash price of $25,000. Because the company received exactly the net book value of the machine, there is neither a gain nor a loss.

Asset received − net book value of asset given = gain (loss)

$25,000 − $25,000 = $0

As Exhibit 7–11 shows, the sale of the machine will not directly affect the income statement for the year 2009, but it will affect the balance sheet.

As you examine these statements, there are two points you should note:

- There is no gain or loss from the disposal of the machine on the income statement for the year 2009.
- Both the cost of the machine ($300,000) and the accumulated amortization ($275,000) have been removed from the balance sheet at the end of the year 2009.

Thus far you have seen how to calculate gains and losses, and how these elements affect a company's financial statements. We now are ready to see how to properly interpret gains and losses when they are a part of the accounting information made available during the decision-making process.

Exhibit 7–11

Beavers Corporation's Financial Statements for 2008 and 2009 Reflecting the Sale of Its Machine for Book Value

BEAVERS CORPORATION

Income Statements

	2008	2009
Sales	$755,000	$941,000
Cost of Goods Sold	422,000	525,000
Gross Margin	$333,000	$416,000
Operating Expenses		
Other than Amortization	(236,000)	(319,000)
Amortization Expense	(55,000)	0
Operating Income	$ 42,000	$ 97,000
Gain (Loss) on Sale of Machine	0	0
Net Income	$ 42,000	$ 97,000

Balance Sheets

	2008	2009
ASSETS:		
Cash	$289,000	$218,000
Accounts Receivable	355,000	313,000
Inventory	77,000	172,000
Machine	300,000	0
LESS: Accumulated Amortization	(275,000)	0
Total Assets	$746,000	$703,000
LIABILITIES AND SHAREHOLDERS' EQUITY:		
Accounts Payable	$206,000	$216,000
Notes Payable	170,000	20,000
Common Shares	110,000	110,000
Retained Earnings	260,000	357,000
Total Liabilities and Shareholders' Equity	$746,000	$703,000

Understanding the True Meaning of Gains and Losses

Assume that two companies have business activities that are identical in almost all respects. The companies have exactly the same sales for the year, and all their operating expenses (except amortization) are the same.

The two companies in this example are Straight Arrow Automotive and Accelerated Automotive. Both companies purchased a fleet of trucks for $228,000 on January 2, 2004. In addition, both companies estimated a useful life of four years and a residual value of $92,000 for the trucks. Because Straight Arrow Automotive uses straight-line amortization and Accelerated Automotive uses the double-declining-balance method, we expect to see differences in their financial statements. Exhibit 7–12 contains the 2004 income statement and balance sheet for each company.

 ## Discussion Questions

Refer to Exhibit 7–12 to answer the following questions.

7-14. The amount of amortization expense recorded by each company is given. Provide computations to explain how these amounts were determined.

7-15. The financial statements indicate four items on the income statements that differ between the companies. Six items on the balance sheets differ between the companies. Identify each item and explain the cause of the difference.

7-16. Assuming that no dividends were paid by either company, what was the balance in retained earnings on January 1, 2004, for each company?

7-17. What are the amortization expense and accumulated amortization for each company? Are these two items always the same?

7-18. What are the accumulated amortization and book value of the trucks for each company? Why are Accelerated Automotive's figures the same, but Straight Arrow Automotive's figures different?

The impact of the choice of amortization method becomes even more evident over time. Exhibit 7–13 shows the income statements and balance sheets of Straight Arrow Automotive and Accelerated Automotive at the end of 2005. Again, we have held constant the items that are not affected by the use of different amortization methods.

 ## Discussion Question

7-19. Provide computations and an explanation to show how Accelerated Automotive's amortization expense amount of $22,000 was determined (Exhibit 7–13).

Income Statements
For the Year Ended December 31, 2004

	Straight Arrow Automotive		Accelerated Automotive	
Sales	$769,000		$769,000	
LESS: Cost of Goods Sold	295,500		295,500	
Gross Margin		$473,500		$473,500
Wages Expense	$ 67,500		$ 67,500	
Utilities Expense	31,000		31,000	
Amortization Expense	34,000		114,000	
Total Operating Expenses		132,500		212,500
Operating Income		$341,000		$261,000
Other Revenues and Expenses:				
Interest Expense		(120,000)		(120,000)
Net Income		$221,000		$141,000

Balance Sheets
December 31, 2004

	Straight Arrow Automotive		Accelerated Automotive	
ASSETS:				
Cash		$226,000		$226,000
Accounts Receivable		198,000		198,000
Inventory		223,000		223,000
Trucks	$228,000		$228,000	
Accumulated Amortization	(34,000)		(114,000)	
Trucks, Net		194,000		114,000
Total Assets		$841,000		$761,000
LIABILITIES:				
Accounts Payable	$ 22,000		$ 22,000	
Notes Payable	61,000		61,000	
Total Liabilities		$ 83,000		$ 83,000
Shareholders' Equity:				
Common Shares	$394,000		$394,000	
Retained Earnings	364,000		284,000	
Total Shareholders' Equity		758,000		678,000
Total Liabilities				
and Shareholders' Equity		$841,000		$761,000

Even more profound than the differences occurring on the financial statements as the companies record amortization, is the effect of an early disposal. Suppose that Straight Arrow Automotive and Accelerated Automotive both decide to sell their trucks on December 31, 2005. All trucks have the identical age, condition, and market value. In exchange for its truck fleet, each company receives $150,000 cash—the market value of the truck fleet on the day of the sale. Because the sale occurs on the last day of the year, both companies must record amortization for the full year, as reflected in the previous statements.

Exhibit 7–13
2005 Financial Statements of Straight Arrow Automotive and Accelerated Automotive

Income Statements
For the Year Ended December 31, 2005

	Straight Arrow Automotive		Accelerated Automotive	
Sales	$769,000		$769,000	
LESS: Cost of Goods Sold	295,500		295,500	
Gross Margin		$473,500		$473,500
Wages Expense	$ 67,500		$ 67,500	
Utilities Expense	31,000		31,000	
Amortization Expense	34,000		22,000	
Total Operating Expenses		132,500		120,500
Operating Income		$341,000		$353,000
Other Revenues and Expenses:				
Interest Expense		(120,000)		(120,000)
Net Income		$221,000		$233,000

Balance Sheets
December 31, 2005

	Straight Arrow Automotive		Accelerated Automotive	
ASSETS:				
Cash		$ 426,000		$426,000
Accounts Receivable		253,000		253,000
Inventory		223,000		223,000
Trucks	$228,000		$228,000	
Accumulated Amortization	(68,000)		(136,000)	
Trucks, Net		160,000		92,000
Total Assets		$1,062,000		$994,000
LIABILITIES:				
Accounts Payable	$ 22,000		$ 22,000	
Notes Payable	61,000		61,000	
Total Liabilities		$ 83,000		$ 83,000
Shareholders' Equity:				
Common Shares	$394,000		$394,000	
Retained Earnings	585,000		517,000	
Total Shareholders' Equity		979,000		911,000
Total Liabilities				
and Shareholders' Equity		$1,062,000		$994,000

 Discussion Question

7–20. Were the companies wise to sell the fleet? Did they get "a good deal"? What information would help you decide whether the companies made a smart move?

Even though Straight Arrow Automotive and Accelerated Automotive incurred the identical transactions, the financial statement presentation of the results of the sale appears quite different, as shown in Exhibit 7–14.

Exhibit 7-14
Impact of the Sale of Trucks at the End of 2005 on the Financial Statements of Straight Arrow Automotive and Accelerated Automotive

Income Statements

For the Year Ending December 31, 2005

	Straight Arrow Automotive		Accelerated Automotive	
Sales	$769,000		$769,000	
LESS: Cost of Goods Sold	295,500		295,500	
Gross Margin		$473,500		$473,500
Wages Expense	$ 67,500		$ 67,500	
Utilities Expense	31,000		31,000	
Amortization Expense	34,000		22,000	
Total Operating Expenses		132,500		120,500
Operating Income		$341,000		$353,000
Other Revenues and Expenses:				
Gain on Sale of Trucks				58,000
Loss on Sale of Trucks		(10,000)		
Interest Expense		(120,000)		(120,000)
Net Income		$211,000		$291,000

Balance Sheets

December 31, 2005

	Straight Arrow Automotive		Accelerated Automotive	
ASSETS:				
Cash	$576,000		$576,000	
Accounts Receivable	253,000		253,000	
Inventory	223,000		223,000	
Totals Assets		$1,052,000		$1,052,000
LIABILITIES:				
Accounts Payable	$ 22,000		$ 22,000	
Notes Payable	61,000		61,000	
Total Liabilities		$ 83,000		$ 83,000
Shareholders' Equity:				
Common Shares	$394,000		$394,000	
Retained Earnings	575,000		575,000	
Total Shareholders' Equity		969,000		969,000
Total Liabilities				
and Shareholders' Equity		$1,052,000		$1,052,000

When both companies made exactly the same transaction, why do the financial statements show different results of the sale? Straight Arrow Automotive recorded a $10,000 loss, but the same activity resulted in a $58,000 gain for Accelerated Automotive. However, both companies paid cash of $228,000 for the trucks and sold them for $150,000 after using the fleet for two years. The moral of the story? Smart financial statement users understand the true meaning of gains or losses on productive, amortizable assets. Remember, gains and losses on amortizable assets represent only the difference between the book value and the market value of assets sold. Do not assume that a gain indicates the sale was "good for business," or that a loss signifies that management made a bad move. In our example, we do not have enough information to determine whether the sale of the trucks for $150,000 was a wise business decision or a poor one. Clearly, though, the sale was no wiser for one company than for the other.

Also note that the retained earnings balance shown by Straight Arrow Automotive and Accelerated Automotive in Exhibit 7–14 is the same—$575,000. If Straight Arrow shows a loss on the sale and Accelerated shows a gain on the sale, how can both show the same retained earnings balance? The answer lies in the fact that both companies transferred the same amount of cost to the income statement over the life of the assets. See Exhibit 7–15 to verify that the same cost of $78,000 was transferred to each income statement—the same amount as the difference between the purchase price of $228,000 and the sale price of $150,000.

Exhibit 7–15
Total Costs Transferred to Expense by Straight Arrow Automotive and Accelerated Automotive

		Straight Arrow Automotive	Accelerated Automotive
2004	Amortization Expense	$34,000	$114,000
2005	Amortization Expense	34,000	22,000
2006	Result of Sale [(Gain) or Loss]	10,000	(58,000)
	TOTAL COST TRANSFERRED	$78,000	$ 78,000

Because accelerated amortization methods transfer costs more rapidly than straight-line methods, firms that employ accelerated amortization methods have a greater chance of showing gains on the disposal of an asset before the end of its useful life. The earlier the disposition, the more likely the firm is to record a gain.

As you can see from our discussion of the items presented in this chapter, the amortization and disposal of long-lived amortizable assets can have a significant impact on a company's reported net income for a given year during the useful life of an asset. The issues surrounding amortization are complex, and users of financial statements must have some understanding of them if they hope to be able to use financial statements for predicting a company's future or assessing its past performance.

Many issues besides amortization have complicating effects under the accrual basis of accounting. We will continue our discussion of these complications in Chapter 8, where we consider issues surrounding the sale of merchandise inventory.

SUMMARY

Amortization is the process of allocating the cost of long-lived assets to the periods in which they help to earn revenues. When a firm purchases an asset, its historical cost is recorded on the balance sheet. As time passes, the company transfers the cost from an asset on the balance sheet to an expense on the income statement. The recording of amortization expense accomplishes this transfer. The amount of accumulated amortization for an asset represents all the amortization expense related to that asset that has been recognized thus far. We report accumulated amortization on the balance sheet as a reduction of the asset cost.

GAAP allow several amortization methods. Straight-line methods allocate cost, measured either in time or productivity, evenly over the asset life. Accelerated amortization methods, such as the double-declining-balance method, recognize a greater amount of amortization expense in the early years of an asset's life and a smaller amount in the later years.

The choice of amortization methods affects companies' financial statements. In total, over the useful life of an asset, straight-line and double-declining-balance amortization methods record the same amount of amortization expense. In any particular period, however, different amortization methods usually result in different amounts of amortization expense, which causes a difference in reported net income. Because the amount of amortization expense affects accumulated amortization, the balance sheets of companies using different amortization methods will also be different during most of the asset's life.

Eventually, a company disposes of its amortizable assets, and these transactions usually result in a gain or a loss. Gains increase and losses decrease net income in a manner similar to that of revenues and expenses, but gains and losses do not appear in operating income. Gains and losses result from activities peripheral to the major activity of the company; revenues and expenses are direct results of the company's primary business activity.

An asset's net book value is its original cost less the amount of its accumulated amortization. If an asset sells for more than its net book value, the transaction results in a gain. Conversely, selling an asset for less than its net book value results in a loss.

If the disposal of an asset results in a gain or loss, that outcome is reported on the income statement. If, however, an asset is sold for exactly its net book value, the transaction results in no gain or loss. In any case, when a company disposes of an asset, both the asset and its corresponding accumulated amortization account are removed from the balance sheet.

Gains and losses on the sale of productive amortizable assets do not indicate that the company has won or lost anything. The cost of using an asset over its life is the difference between its original cost and its final sale price. Gains and losses simply adjust the total amortization charged to the income statement to total cost of using the asset. Accelerated amortization methods tend to show more gains if an asset is sold in the early years of its life.

APPENDIX—RECORDING LONG-LIVED ASSETS AND AMORTIZATION

After completing Chapter 6, you can look at the journal entries for long-lived assets and amortization. The recording process for long-lived assets involves three types of entries:

1. Purchase of an asset
2. Annual amortization
3. Disposal of an asset

To record these types of entries, we need to have four accounts available for use:

1. Long-lived asset
2. Accumulated amortization (a contra asset account)
3. Amortization expense
4. Gain (loss) on the disposal of assets

Remember that debits increase assets, expenses, and losses, and credits increase liabilities, equity, revenues, and gains. All journal entries must contain equal dollar amounts of debits and of credits.

We can examine the journal entries that Beavers Corporation made to record the transactions for its milling machine. The following illustrates the straight-line example when Beavers Corporation sells the asset for $32,000.

Straight-Line Amortization

1. Purchase of an asset:

2004		Debit	Credit
January 2	Milling Machine	300,000	
	Cash		300,000
	To record the purchase of a milling machine.		

2. Annual Amortization:

2004		Debit	Credit
December 31	Amortization Expense	55,000	
	Accumulated Amortization		55,000
	To record annual amortization expense.		

This same entry is made each year on December 31 for the years 2005, 2006, 2007, and 2008.

3. Disposal of an asset:

2009		Debit	Credit
January 2	Cash	32,000	
	Accumulated Amortization	275,000	
	Milling Machine		300,000
	Gain on Sale of Asset		7,000
	To record the sale of the milling machine.		

Before we make the final entry to record the disposal, we must record any expired and unrecorded amortization. Because the milling machine was last amortized on December 31, 2008, and is now fully amortized, no entry is required. The final entry removes the asset and accumulated amortization accounts from the asset accounts. Because a gain increases equity, a gain creates a credit to balance the journal entry. Look at the following T-accounts to see how the entries affect each account.

	Milling Machine		Accumulated Amortization	
02-01-04	300,000			
31-12-04			55,000	31-12-04
31-12-05			55,000	31-12-05
31-12-06			55,000	31-12-06
31-12-07			55,000	31-12-07
31-12-08			55,000	31-12-08
	300,000			275,000
02-01-09		300,000	275,000	02-01-09
	0			0

Notice that the accounts show the history of what happened to this asset. See now how the entries change when Beavers Corporation selects the double-declining-balance method of amortization.

Double-Declining-Balance Amortization

1. Purchase of an asset:

2004		Debit	Credit
January 2	Milling Machine	300,000	
	Cash		300,000
	To record the purchase of a milling machine.		

2. Annual Amortization:

2004		Debit	Credit
December 31	Amortization Expense	120,000	
	Accumulated Amortization		120,000
	To record annual amortization expense for 2004.		

2005		Debit	Credit
December 31	Amortization Expense	72,000	
	Accumulated Amortization		72,000
	To record annual amortization expense for 2005.		

2006		Debit	Credit
December 31	Amortization Expense	43,200	
	Accumulated Amortization		43,200
	To record annual amortization expense for 2006.		

2007		Debit	Credit
December 31	Amortization Expense	25,920	
	Accumulated Amortization		25,920
	To record annual amortization expense for 2007.		

2008		Debit	Credit
December 31	Amortization Expense	13,880	
	Accumulated Amortization		13,880
	To record annual amortization expense for 2008.		

A different entry is made each year on December 31 for the years 2005, 2006, 2007, and 2008.

3. Disposal of an asset:

2009		Debit	Credit
January 2	Cash	32,000	
	Accumulated Amortization	275,000	
	Milling Machine		300,000
	Gain on Sale of Asset		7,000
	To record the sale of the milling machine.		

Notice that the purchase entry is the same regardless of the amortization method. When the asset has been fully amortized, the sale entry is also the same. See how these entries affect the individual accounts.

	Milling Machine		Accumulated Amortization	
02-01-04	300,000			
31-12-04			120,000	31-12-04
31-12-05			72,000	31-12-05
31-12-06			43,200	31-12-06
31-12-07			25,920	31-12-07
31-12-08			13,880	31-12-08
	300,000		275,000	
02-01-09		300,000	275,000	02-01-09
	0			0

Recording a Loss

When the asset is fully amortized, the method of amortization makes no difference when the asset is sold. How would the final entry change if Beavers Corporation received only $19,000 for the machine on January 2, 2009?

2009		Debit	Credit
January 2	Cash	19,000	
	Accumulated Amortization	275,000	
	Loss on Sale of Asset	6,000	
	Milling Machine		300,000
	To record the sale of the milling machine.		

Because a loss reduces equity, the loss creates a debit entry to the loss account to balance the journal entry.

Sale at Book Value

When a sale occurs for book value, no gain or loss is recognized. Look at the journal entry to record the sale for $25,000.

2009		Debit	Credit
January 2	Cash	25,000	
	Accumulated Amortization	275,000	
	Milling Machine		300,000
	To record the sale of the milling machine.		

Sale before the End of Asset Life

If we look at the sale of Accelerated Automotive's fleet in the second year of life, we see how the journal entries unfold for an asset that has not been fully amortized. The entries are the same as for a fully amortized asset, except that we must be careful to record any unrecognized amortization from the last time amortization was recorded to the date of disposal.

1. Purchase of an asset:

2004		Debit	Credit
January 2	Truck Fleet	228,000	
	Cash		228,000
	To record the purchase of a truck fleet.		

2. Annual Amortization:

2004		Debit	Credit
December 31	Amortization Expense	120,000	
	Accumulated Amortization		120,000
	To record the first year's amortization expense.		

3. Disposal of an asset:
   a. First, bring the asset's amortization up to date. The fleet was last amortized on December 31, 2004, one year ago. A full year's amortization expired since that time, but has not been recorded.

2005		Debit	Credit
December 31	Amortization Expense	72,000	
	Accumulated Amortization		72,000
	To record the second year's amortization expense.		

   b. Second, record the asset disposal in accordance with the terms of the sale.

2005		Debit	Credit
December 31	Cash	150,000	
	Accumulated Amortization	192,000	
	Truck Fleet		228,000
	Gain on Sale of Asset		114,000
	To record the sale of the truck fleet.		

SUMMARY TO APPENDIX

Recording transactions for long-lived assets involves four accounts: a long-lived asset, accumulated amortization, amortization expense, and a gain or loss on the disposal of the asset. We record the original purchase of the asset as a debit to the asset account. Annual amortization results in a debit to amortization expense and a credit to the accumulated amortization, a contra asset account. When the owner sells an asset, we must first recognize all amortization up to the date of disposal. When amortization is current, we debit the asset received (usually cash), debit the accumulated amortization, credit the asset, and credit gain on sale or debit loss on sale as the balancing item in the journal entry.

KEY TERMS

accelerated amortization methods, p. 227
double-declining-balance method, p. 227
functional obsolescence, p. 235
Capital Cost Allowance (CCA), p. 227
gains, p. 235
historical cost, p. 226

losses, p. 235
tangible property, p. 226
technological obsolescence, p. 235
units of production amortization method, p. 229

REVIEW THE FACTS

1. Provide three examples of long-lived amortizable assets.
2. In your own words, describe the units of production amortization process.
3. What two estimates made by management will affect the amount of amortization recorded each period?
4. What is the amortizable base of an asset?
5. Explain the two bases we can use for straight-line allocation of the cost of long-lived amortizable assets.
6. Explain what is meant by an accelerated amortization method. Theoretically, in what situation is an accelerated amortization method the appropriate choice?
7. Explain how the amount of amortization expense is calculated using straight-line amortization.
8. What is meant by an asset's net book value?
9. What does the amount of accumulated amortization represent?
10. In your own words, describe the process of determining amortization expense using the double-declining-balance method.
11. Compared to straight-line amortization, what is the effect of an accelerated amortization method on the balance sheet? On the income statement?
12. Regardless of what amortization method is used, at what point is an asset considered "fully amortized"?
13. On what financial statement do gains and losses appear?
14. What is the difference between a revenue and a gain? A loss and an expense?
15. How is a gain or loss calculated?
16. What effect does the disposal of an asset that results in no gain or loss have on the income statement? On the balance sheet?

APPLY WHAT YOU HAVE LEARNED

LO 1: Terminology

1. Presented below is a list of items relating to the concepts discussed in this chapter, followed by definitions of those items in scrambled order.

a. Accelerated amortization	f. Straight-line amortization
b. Net book value	g. Gains
c. Gain on sale of asset	h. Loss on sale of asset
d. Losses	i. Amortizable base
e. Estimated useful life	j. Units of production method

1. __e.__ A factor determining how much of an asset's cost will be allocated to the periods supposedly benefited.
2. __j.__ An amortization method that uses activity instead of time as the basis of allocation.
3. __a.__ More of the cost of a long-lived asset is converted to expense in the early years of its life than in later years.
4. __b(i)__ The cost of a long-lived asset less the estimated residual value.
5. __c.__ Results when an amortizable asset is sold for more than its book value.
6. __f.__ An equal amount of a long-lived asset's cost is converted to expense in each year of its useful life.

7. __g__ Net inflows resulting from peripheral activities.
8. __b,j,i__ The cost of a long-lived amortizable asset less its accumulated amortization.
9. __h__ Results when an amortizable asset is sold for less than its book value.
10. __d__ Net outflows resulting from peripheral activities.

REQUIRED:
Match the letter next to each item on the list with the appropriate definition. Each letter will be used only once.

LO 1: Amortization Process

2. Evaluate the following: "The amortization process is a process designed to value long-lived assets on the balance sheet."

LO 2: Computation of Amortization Expense—Straight-Line Method

3. Jerry Garcia and Company purchased a lathe for use in its manufacturing operation. The machine cost $150,000, has a five-year estimated useful life, and will be amortized using the straight-line method. The only thing remaining to be determined before yearly amortization expense can be calculated is the estimated residual value. The alternatives are

   1. $10,000 estimated residual value
   2. $20,000 estimated residual value
   3. $30,000 estimated residual value

REQUIRED:
a. Calculate the yearly amortization expense for the new lathe under each of the alternatives given.
b. Which of the three alternatives will result in the highest net income?
c. How long will the new lathe be useful to Jerry Garcia and Company?

LO 2: Computation of Amortization Expense—Straight-Line Method

4. Jones and Werner Ltd. has just purchased a minicomputer for use in its manufacturing operation. The machine cost $75,000, has a four-year estimated useful life, and will be amortized using the straight-line method. The only thing remaining to be determined before yearly amortization expense can be calculated is the estimated residual value. The alternatives are

   1. $7,500 estimated residual value
   2. $12,500 estimated residual value
   3. $17,500 estimated residual value

REQUIRED:
a. Calculate the yearly amortization expense for the new minicomputer under each of the alternatives given.
b. Which of the three alternatives will result in the highest net income? Which of the three alternatives will result in the lowest net income?
c. How long will the new minicomputer be useful to Jones and Werner Ltd.?

LO 2: Computation of Amortization Expense— Straight-Line Method

5. Nathan Verner Publishing Corporation purchased a new printing press for a total installed cost of $700,000. The printing press will be amortized using the straight-line method, in accordance with corporate policy. Robert Sloan, the corporate controller, is trying to decide on an estimated useful life and an estimated residual value for the asset. The alternatives are

   1. A six-year estimated useful life with a $40,000 estimated residual value
   2. A five-year estimated useful life with a $100,000 estimated residual value
   3. A four-year estimated useful life with a $140,000 estimated residual value

REQUIRED:

a. Calculate the yearly amortization expense for the new printing press under each of the alternatives given.
b. Which of the three alternatives will result in the lowest yearly net income? Which of the three alternatives will result in the highest yearly net income?
c. What should be the deciding factor in selecting among the three alternatives?

LO 2: Computation of Amortization Expense— Straight-Line Method

6. Pizzeria Restaurant Inc. purchased a new walk-in freezer for a total installed cost of $250,000. The walk-in freezer will be amortized using the straight-line method, in accordance with corporate policy. Jan Noel, the corporate controller, is trying to determine an estimated useful life and residual value for the asset. Her alternatives are

   1. A five-year estimated useful life with a $10,000 estimated residual value
   2. A four-year estimated useful life with a $25,000 estimated residual value
   3. A three-year estimated useful life with a $50,000 estimated residual value

REQUIRED:

a. Calculate the yearly amortization expense for the new walk-in freezer under each of the alternatives given.
b. Which of the three alternatives will result in the lowest yearly net income? Which of the three alternatives will result in the highest yearly net income?
c. What should be the deciding factor in selecting among the three alternatives?

LO 2: Computation of Double-Declining-Balance Amortization Expense and Net Book Value

7. Wedtech Company purchased a high-tech assembler on January 2, 2004, for a total cost of $600,000. The assembler has an estimated useful life to the company of five years. Wedtech Company thinks it can sell the used assembler for $40,000 after five years. The company chose to amortize the new assembler using the double-declining-balance method.

REQUIRED:

a. Prepare a schedule showing the amount of amortization expense for each of the five years of the estimated useful life.
b. What will be the net book value of the assembler at the end of the five-year estimated useful life?
c. What does net book value represent?

LO 2: Computation of Double-Declining-Balance Amortization Expense and Net Book Value

8. Mothball Company purchased an earthmoving machine on January 2, 2004, for a total cost of $900,000. The earthmover has an estimated useful life to the company of four years. Mothball Company believes it can sell the used earthmover for $80,000 after four years. The company selected the double-declining-balance method of amortization.

REQUIRED:

a. Prepare a schedule showing the amount of amortization expense for each of the four years of the estimated useful life.
b. What will be the net book value of the earthmover at the end of the four-year estimated useful life?
c. What does net book value represent?

LO 2: Computation of Amortization Expense— Straight-Line and Double-Declining-Balance

9. Wanda Company purchased a sophisticated stamping machine on January 2, 2004, for $480,000. The estimated useful life of the stamping machine is six years. Wanda Company estimates the machine's residual value is $40,000.

REQUIRED:

a. Calculate the yearly amortization expense for the stamping machine assuming the company uses the straight-line amortization method.
b. Prepare a schedule showing the amount of amortization expense for each of the six years of the estimated useful life assuming the company uses the double-declining-balance amortization method.

LO 2: Computation of Amortization Expense— Straight-Line and Double-Declining Balance

10. WebCo Ltd. purchased a pasteurizing machine on January 2, 2004, for $375,000. The estimated useful life of the machine is four years with a residual value of $45,000.

REQUIRED:

a. Calculate the yearly amortization expense for the machine assuming the company uses the straight-line amortization method.
b. Prepare a schedule showing the amount of amortization expense for each of the four years of the estimated useful life assuming the company uses the double-declining-balance amortization method.

LO 2 & 5: Computation of Amortization Expense and Gains or Losses—Units of Production Method

11. Knoorfleet Ltd. purchased a delivery truck on January 2, 2004, for $70,000. Knoorfleet Ltd. estimates the estimated useful life of the vehicle is 1,000,000 kilometres, and the residual value is $10,000. The truck is driven 200,000 kilometres in 2004; 225,000 kilometres in 2005; 300,000 kilometres in 2006; and 275,000 kilometres in 2007.

REQUIRED:

a. Calculate the yearly amortization expense for the vehicle assuming the company uses the units of production amortization method.

b. Calculate the gain or loss on the sale if Knoorfleet Ltd. sells the truck at the end of 2007 for $15,000.

c. Calculate the gain or loss on the sale if Knoorfleet Ltd. sells the truck at the end of 2007 for $5,000.

d. Calculate the gain or loss on the sale if Knoorfleet Ltd. sells the truck at the end of 2007 for $1,000.

LO 2 & 5: Computation of Amortization Expense and Gains or Losses—Units of Production Method

12. Janek Ltd. purchased a printing press on January 2, 2004, for $95,000. Janek Ltd. estimates the useful life of the press is 2,000,000 pages or five years, after which it can be sold for $5,000. The press produced 500,000 pages in 2004; 400,000 pages in 2005; 430,000 pages in 2006; 600,000 pages in 2007; and 350,000 pages in 2008.

REQUIRED:

a. Calculate the yearly amortization expense for the press assuming the company uses the units of production amortization method.

b. Calculate the gain or loss on the sale if Janek Ltd. sells the press at the end of 2008 for $15,000.

c. Calculate the gain or loss on the sale if Janek Ltd. sells the press at the end of 2008 for $5,000.

d. Calculate the gain or loss on the sale if Janek Ltd. sells the press at the end of 2008 for $2,000.

LO 2 & 5: Computation of Amortization Expense and Gains or Losses—Units of Production Method

13. Rufus Ltd. purchased a lathe on January 2, 2004, for $200,000. Rufus Ltd. estimates its useful life as 1,600,000 hours or four years, and its residual value at $4,000. The lathe was used for 500,000 hours in 2004; 430,000 hours in 2005; 300,000 hours in 2006; and 300,000 hours in 2007.

REQUIRED:

a. Calculate the yearly amortization expense for the machine assuming the company uses the units of production amortization method.

b. Calculate the gain or loss on the sale if Rufus Ltd. sells the lathe after four years for $12,000.

c. Calculate the gain or loss on the sale if Rufus Ltd. sells the lathe after four years for $3,000.

d. Calculate the gain or loss on the sale if Rufus Ltd. sells the lathe after four years for $10,000.

LO 2 & 3: Computation of Amortization Expense—
Straight-Line and Double-Declining-Balance Method

14. Pepco Ltd. purchased a fleet of delivery trucks on January 2, 2004, for $700,000. The estimated useful life of the fleet is four years, after which Pepco Ltd. estimates it can sell the entire fleet for $50,000.

REQUIRED:

a. Calculate the yearly amortization expense for the fleet of vehicles assuming the company uses the straight-line amortization method.

b. Prepare a schedule showing the amount of amortization expense for each of the four years of the estimated useful life assuming the company uses the double-declining-balance amortization method.

c. Address the following questions:

(1) Double-declining-balance calculates amortization at twice the straight-line rate. Why is the amount of amortization expense in 2004 under double-declining-balance not exactly twice the amount under straight-line for 2004?

(2) Over the four-year estimated useful life of the vehicles, how much amortization expense will be charged against income using the straight-line method? How much will be charged against income using the double-declining-balance method?

(3) Discuss the impact on the net income of each method of amortization in the first two years of life of the asset.

LO 2 & 3: Computation of Amortization Expense—
Straight-Line and Double-Declining-Balance Methods

15. Ozzie and Harriet Ltd. purchased a fleet of taxis on January 2, 2004, for $600,000. The corporation estimates the useful life of the vehicles is three years, after which it can sell the entire fleet for $50,000.

REQUIRED:

a. Calculate the yearly amortization expense for the fleet of vehicles assuming the company uses the straight-line amortization method.

b. Prepare a schedule showing the amount of amortization expense for each of the three years of the estimated useful life assuming the company uses the double-declining-balance amortization method.

c. Address the following questions:

(1) Double-declining-balance calculates amortization at twice the straight-line rate. Why is the amount of amortization expense in 2004 under double-declining-balance not exactly twice the amount under straight-line for 2004?

(2) Over the three-year estimated useful life of the vehicles, how much amortization expense will be charged against income using the straight-line method? How much will be charged against income using the double-declining-balance method?

(3) Discuss the impact on the net income of each method of amortization in the first two years of life of the asset.

LO 4 & 5: Computation of Gain or Loss

16. Cruse Company purchased a machine in January 2004 for $200,000. When originally purchased, the machine had an estimated useful life of five years and an estimated residual value of $25,000. The company uses straight-line amortization. It is now June 30, 2007, and the company has decided to dispose of the machine.

REQUIRED:
a. Calculate the net book value of the machine as of June 30, 2007.
b. Calculate the gain or loss on the sale of the machine assuming Cruse Company sells it for $102,000.
c. Calculate the gain or loss on the sale of the machine assuming Cruse Company sells it for $25,000.

LO 4 & 5: Computation of Gain or Loss

17. Farr Company purchased a machine in January 2004 and paid $150,000 for it. When originally purchased, the machine had an estimated useful life of four years and an estimated residual value of $10,000. The company uses straight-line amortization. It is now September 30, 2006, and the company has decided to dispose of the machine.

REQUIRED:
a. Calculate the net book value of the machine as of September 30, 2006.
b. Calculate the gain or loss on the sale of the machine assuming Farr Company sells it for $172,000.
c. Calculate the gain or loss on the sale of the machine assuming Farr Company sells it for $25,000.

LO 4 & 5: Computation of Gain or Loss

18. Simpson Company purchased a machine in January 2004 for $450,000. When originally purchased, the machine had an estimated useful life of ten years and an estimated residual value of $50,000. The company uses straight-line amortization. It is now January 2, 2011, and the company has decided to dispose of the machine.

REQUIRED:
a. Calculate the net book value of the machine as of December 31, 2010.
b. Calculate the gain or loss on the sale of the machine assuming Simpson Company sells it for $130,000.
c. Calculate the gain or loss on the sale of the machine assuming Simpson Company sells it for $30,000.

LO 4, 5, & 6: Impact of Amortization Methods on Gains and Losses

19. Millie and Maude are twins. Each of them has her own company. Three years ago, on the same day, they each purchased copiers for use by their companies. The machines were identical in every way and cost exactly the same amount ($28,000). The machines had the same estimated useful life (five years) and the same estimated residual value ($3,000). The only difference was the amortization method chosen. Millie chose to amortize her copier using straight-line based on time, while Maude selected an accelerated amortization method.

Owing to rapid technological developments in the machines, Millie decided at the end of two years to sell her old machine and buy a new one. Maude decided to do the same thing. In fact, they each received exactly the same amount when they sold their machines ($16,500). Later, while they were having lunch together, Maude mentioned that when she sold her copier, she had a gain of more than $6,000 on the sale. Millie kept quiet, but was confused because she knew she had sold her copier for exactly the same amount as Maude, yet the sale of her copier had resulted in a loss of $1,500.

REQUIRED:
Explain how Millie could have had a loss of $1,500 on the sale of her copier, while Maude had a $6,000 gain.

LO 4, 5, & 6: Impact of Amortization Methods on Gains and Losses

20. Red and Green each ran their own automotive repair shop. Each bought a new piece of equipment costing $10,000 on January 2. The equipment is expected to have a five-year life and no salvage value. Red used straight-line amortization, and Green used double-declining-balance amortization. At the end of three years, each of them sold their machines for $5,500.

REQUIRED:
a. Compute the amortization for both Red and Green through the third year.
b. Compute the gain or loss that each would recognize on the sale of the machine.
c. If the gain or loss is different for each of them, explain why.

LO 4, 5, & 6: Impact of Amortization Methods on Gains and Losses

21. Ethel and Lucy each run their own cooking school. Each bought a new piece of equipment costing $20,000 on January 2. The equipment is expected to have a five-year life and no salvage value. Ethel uses straight-line amortization, and Lucy uses double-declining-balance amortization. At the end of three years, each of them sold their machines for $11,000.

REQUIRED:
a. Compute the amortization for both Ethel and Lucy through the third year.
b. Compute the gain or loss that each would recognize on the sale of the machine.
c. If the gain or loss is different for each of them, explain why.

LO 4, 5, & 6: Impact of Amortization Methods on Gains and Losses

22. Ricky and Fred each ran their own construction business. Each bought a new piece of equipment costing $40,000 on January 2. The equipment is expected to have a five-year life and no salvage value. Ricky used straight-line amortization and Fred used double-declining-balance amortization. At the end of three years, each of them sold their machines for $22,000.

REQUIRED:

a. Compute the amortization for both Ricky and Fred through the third year.

b. Compute the gain or loss that each would recognize on the sale of the machine.

c. If the gain or loss is different for each of them, explain why.

LO 7: Meaning of Gains and Losses

23. Explain in your own words what a gain or loss on the sale of a piece of equipment means, and how the gain or loss relates to amortization expense.

LO 7: Comprehensive

24. Exhibit 7–7 in the text illustrates Beavers Corporation's financial statements, based on double-declining-balance amortization. Use the income statements and balance sheets presented in the exhibit as a basis for completing the following requirements.

REQUIRED:

a. Prepare statements of retained earnings for Beavers Corporation as of the end of 2004, 2005, 2006, 2007, and 2008.

b. What can you conclude about the dividend policy of Beaver Corporation from the information provided and your response to Requirement a?

c. If no amortization had been recorded, how would the statements of retained earnings have been different?

LO 7: Comprehensive

25. Barker Company Ltd. opened for business on January 2, 2004. During its first month of operation, the company had the following transactions.

Jan. 2   Purchased a truck for $10,000 and paid cash. The truck has an estimated useful life of three years. The company estimates the truck's residual value to be $1,000, and uses straight-line amortization.

Jan. 2   Purchased $40,000 worth of merchandise inventory on account. Payment in full is due February 2.

Jan. 3   Paid January office rent of $2,500.

Jan. 5   Purchased $15,000 worth of merchandise inventory and paid cash on that date.

Jan. 10 Sold merchandise inventory that cost $12,000 for $25,000 to a customer and received the cash on that date.

Jan. 20 Sold merchandise inventory that cost $7,000 for $11,000. The sale was on account and the customer has until February 20 to pay.

Jan. 24 Paid miscellaneous January operating expenses totaling $8,000.

Jan. 31 Received bills for utilities, advertising, and phone service totaling $1,200. All these bills were for services provided in January. They will all be paid the first week in February.

Use the January 2004 income statements for Barker Company Ltd. prepared under the cash and accrual bases of accounting to complete the following requirements.

REQUIRED:

a. Explain why the Cost of Goods Sold amounts on the two income statements differ.

b. Barker Company Ltd. purchased $55,000 worth of merchandise inventory during January 2004. However, under the accrual basis of accounting, the company properly expensed $19,000 as cost of goods sold for the month. Explain where (if anywhere) the company shows the remaining $36,000 of merchandise inventory.

c. Barker Company Ltd. purchased $55,000 worth of merchandise inventory during January 2004. Under the cash basis of accounting, the company properly expensed $15,000 as cost of goods sold for the month. Explain where (if anywhere) the company shows the remaining $40,000 of merchandise inventory.

d. Both income statements show an expense related to the truck purchased on January 2, 2004. How were the amounts on each income statement determined? Include in your answer what the amounts represent and why the cost of the truck is treated as it is.

e. What will be the net book value of the truck on the December 31, 2004, balance sheet under
   (1) cash basis accounting?
   (2) accrual basis accounting?

f. What will be the net book value of the truck on the December 31, 2006, balance sheet under
   (1) cash basis accounting?
   (2) accrual basis accounting?

g. Comment generally on why the net income (loss) amounts on the two income statements are so different.

BARKER COMPANY LTD.

Income Statement

For the Month Ended January 31, 2004

Cash Basis

Sales	$25,000	
LESS: Cost of Goods Sold	15,000	
Gross Margin		$ 10,000
Operating Expenses:		
Truck	$10,000	
Rent	2,500	
Miscellaneous Expenses	8,000	
Total Operating Expenses		20,500
Net Income (Loss)		$(10,500)

BARKER COMPANY LTD.

Income Statement

For the Month Ended January 31, 2004

Accrual Basis

Sales	$36,000	
LESS: Cost of Goods Sold	19,000	
Gross Margin		$17,000
Operating Expenses:		
Rent	$2,500	
Amortization—Truck	250	
Miscellaneous Expenses	8,000	
Accrued Expenses	1,200	
Total Operating Expenses		11,950
Net Income (Loss)		$ 5,050

LO 8: Recording Assets and Amortization

*26. Cunningham Corporation purchased a new piece of equipment for $60,000 cash. It estimates the useful life of the equipment at five years with a salvage value of $10,000.

REQUIRED:
a. Prepare the journal entry to record the purchase of the asset.
b. Prepare the journal entries to record the amortization for the first year of life of the asset assuming
   (1) straight-line amortization.
   (2) double-declining-balance amortization.

LO 8: Recording Assets and Amortization

*27. Buffington Ltd. purchased a new piece of equipment for $560,000. The company paid $125,000 in cash and borrowed the remainder from the bank. Buffington Ltd. estimates the useful life of the equipment at six years with a salvage value of $60,000.

REQUIRED:
a. Prepare the journal entry to record the purchase of the asset.
b. Prepare the journal entry to record the amortization for the first year of life of the asset assuming
   (1) straight-line amortization.
   (2) double-declining-balance amortization.

LO 8: Recording Assets and Amortization

*28. Buffington Ltd. purchased a new piece of equipment for $560,000. The company paid $125,000 in cash and borrowed the remainder from the bank. Buffington Ltd. estimates the useful life of the equipment at six years with a salvage value of $60,000.

REQUIRED:
a. Compute the gain or loss if the company sells the equipment for $86,000 at the end of the fourth year using straight-line amortization.
b. Prepare the journal entry to record the sale of the equipment.

LO 8: Recording Assets and Amortization

*29. Malph Corporation purchased a new piece of equipment for $75,000 cash. The company estimates the useful life of the equipment at seven years with a salvage value of $5,000.

REQUIRED:
a. Prepare the journal entry to record the purchase of the asset.
b. Prepare the journal entry to record the amortization for the first year of life of the asset assuming
   (1) straight-line amortization.
   (2) double-declining-balance amortization.

---

*Refers to material in this chapter's appendix.

LO 8: Recording Assets and Amortization

*30. Dustin Corporation purchased a new piece of equipment for $75,000. The company paid $5,000 in cash and borrowed the remainder from the bank. Dustin Corporation estimates the useful life of the equipment at seven years with a salvage value of $12,000.

REQUIRED:
a. Prepare the journal entry to record the purchase of the asset.
b. Prepare the journal entry to record the amortization for the first year of life of the asset assuming
   (1) straight-line amortization.
   (2) double-declining-balance amortization.

LO 8: Recording Assets and Amortization

*31. Dustin Corporation purchased a new piece of equipment for $75,000. The company paid $5,000 in cash and borrowed the remainder from the bank. Dustin Corporation estimates the useful life of the equipment at seven years with a salvage value of $12,000.

REQUIRED:
a. Compute the gain or loss if the company sells the equipment for $8,000 at the end of the fourth year using double-declining-balance amortization.
b. Prepare the journal entry to record the sale of the equipment.

LO 8: Recording Assets and Amortization

*32. Randall Company purchased a stamping machine on January 2, 2004, for $480,000. The estimated useful life of the stamping machine is five years. The machine has an estimated residual value of $40,000.

REQUIRED:
a. Calculate the yearly amortization expense for the stamping machine assuming the company uses the straight-line amortization method.
b. Record the journal entries for the amortization that would be required each year.
c. Prepare the required journal entries to record the sale of the machine at the end of two years for $200,000.

LO 8: Recording Assets and Amortization

*33. Wooten Company purchased a pasteurizing machine on January 2, 2004, for $375,000. The estimated useful life of the machine is five years. The machine has an estimated residual value of $40,000.

REQUIRED:
a. Calculate the yearly amortization expense for the machine assuming the company uses the double-declining-balance amortization method, and prepare the journal entries to record amortization each year.
b. Assuming the machine is sold at the end of 2006 for $50,000, prepare the required entries to record the sale.
c. Assuming the machine is sold at the end of April 2008 for $50,000, prepare the required entries to record the sale.

LO 8:   Recording Assets and Amortization

*34. Chesley Ltd. purchased a fleet of delivery trucks on January 2, 2004, for $700,000. The estimated useful life of the vehicles is four years, after which the company thinks it will be able to sell the entire fleet for $50,000.

REQUIRED:

a. Calculate the yearly amortization expense for the fleet of vehicles assuming the company uses the straight-line amortization method, and prepare the journal entries to record the amortization.

b. Assume the fleet is sold at the end of its useful life for $70,000. Prepare the journal entries to record the transaction.

c. Assume the fleet is sold on March 31, 2007, for $30,000. Prepare the journal entries to record the transaction.

LO 8:   Recording Assets and Amortization

*35. Ricky and Fred each run their own construction business. Each bought a new piece of equipment costing $40,000 on January 2, 2004. The equipment is expected to have a five-year life and no salvage value. Ricky uses straight-line amortization and Fred uses double-declining-balance amortization. On June 30, 2007, each of them sold their machine for $22,000.

REQUIRED:

a. Compute the amortization for both Ricky and Fred through the date of sale.

b. Compute the gain or loss that each would recognize on the sale of the equipment.

c. Prepare the journal entries necessary to record the purchase, annual amortization, and sale of Ricky's and Fred's equipment.

ANNUAL REPORT PROJECT

36. You will complete a portion of Section IV of the project. For Property, Plant, and Equipment you should do the following:

a. List the total of Property, Plant, and Equipment for the three years listed in your company's report.

b. List the total of Accumulated Amortization associated with Property, Plant, and Equipment for the three years listed in your company's report.

c. Identify the method or methods of amortization used by your company.

d. List the total of all assets for the three years listed in your company's report.

e. List the total of the current assets for the three years listed in your company's report.

f. Is your company capital-intensive; that is, does it have many more long-lived assets than other assets?

g. Does your company appear to be growing in terms of long-lived assets?

    h. In the period presented in the balance sheet, has your company had significant changes in asset structure, such as major purchases of other companies, investments, or discontinued operation?

    i. If your company has acquired long-lived assets, how were they financed?

    j. Does your company have major resources it does not report on the balance sheet, such as brand names or significant human resources?

REQUIRED:

Complete this part of Section IV of your report. Make a copy for your instructor and keep a copy for your final report.

8

Merchandise Inventory and Cost of Goods Sold

*Y*our boss has offered you a promotion to manage the inventory in a new division the company is opening in Calgary. You want this opportunity because you love to ski, and you enjoy working with inventory. You will be part of the team that selects the inventory software package and designs the inventory protection system. Part of your compensation package includes a bonus at the end of the year based upon both the gross profit percentage and the net income. How does inventory management relate to gross profit and net income? Your assistant reminds you to be careful about LIFO and FIFO. What is she talking about, and how does that tie into profits? Time to find an accounting textbook.

In Chapter 7, we explored one source of variation across companies' financial statements—choice of amortization method. Remember that GAAP allow companies a choice, among generally accepted accounting principles, because different industries have different operating characteristics. Accounting principles do not specify just one practice that fits all.

To gauge the cost of goods a firm sells, GAAP allow several alternative methods that measure the cost flow of inventory. The way a company accounts for its merchandise inventory purchases and sales can have a direct and significant impact on the firm's reported net income. ■

After completing your work on this chapter, you should be able to do the following:

1. Explain goods available for sale (GAFS) and name its components.
2. Describe the relationship between ending inventory and cost of goods sold.
3. Differentiate between the physical flow of merchandise and the cost flow of merchandise.
4. Explain the differences between periodic and perpetual inventory systems.
5. List different inventory cost flow assumptions and contrast how the use of each affects reported net income on the income statement.
6. Calculate cost of goods sold and ending inventory using FIFO, LIFO, and average cost inventory cost flow assumptions.
*7. Calculate cash discounts and invoice due dates, and determine who bears the freight expense from the freight terms.
*8. Complete the recording process for inventory purchases and sales.

TRACKING INVENTORY COSTS

Merchandising Companies

merchandise inventory
The physical units (goods) a company buys to resell as part of its business operation. Also called *inventory.*

beginning inventory The amount of merchandise inventory (in units or dollars) on hand at the beginning of the income statement period.

purchases The amount of merchandise inventory bought during the income statement period.

goods available for sale (GAFS) The total amount of merchandise inventory a company has available to sell in a given income statement period.

cost of goods sold (COGS) The cost of the merchandise inventory no longer on hand and assumed sold during the period. Also called *cost of sales.*

ending inventory The amount of inventory (in units or dollars) still on hand at the end of an accounting period.

The tangible products that merchandisers sell are called **merchandise inventory,** or **inventory.** For example, Office Depot sells office equipment, Lay-Z-Boy sells desks and chairs, and Chrysler sells cars and trucks. The product each firm sells is called inventory. However, to customers, these products may be long-lived assets.

When we discuss inventory, we must consider two aspects: the number of units of inventory and the cost of each of those units. To apply the matching principle, we must determine the quantity of units sold and how much expense matches the sales of the period. A mathematical relationship exists between the beginning inventory, the purchases during the period, the cost of goods sold, and the ending inventory.

At the beginning of an income statement period, a firm has an amount of merchandise inventory on hand called **beginning inventory.** During the period, the firm buys additional inventory we call **purchases.** The cost of purchases includes all the costs to bring the item to a saleable state, including freight, packaging, and make-ready costs. A firm can sell only the goods it has on hand during a period, represented by the total of the beginning inventory plus the amount it bought (purchases). We call this total the **goods available for sale (GAFS).** Whether we are referring to the physical count of inventory units or its cost, the following relationship between beginning inventory (BI), purchases (Purch), and goods available for sale (GAFS) holds true:

$$\text{Beginning Inventory} + \text{Purchases} = \text{Goods Available for Sale}$$
$$\text{BI} + \text{Purch} = \text{GAFS}$$

Once a firm has goods to sell, reality dictates that at the end of the period, the merchandise is either gone or still on hand. We recognize the inventory that is gone as an income statement expense of the period called **cost of goods sold (COGS)** or **cost of sales.** The inventory still on hand is the **ending inventory,** a balance sheet asset, because it has probable future economic benefit since it can generate future sales. We can calculate the cost of goods sold (COGS) by subtracting the ending inventory from goods available for sale. Thus, the total amount that we could have sold (GAFS) minus the amount we still had at the end of the period (EI) equals the amount that we sold (COGS):

$$GAFS - EI = COGS$$

Conversely, if we know cost of goods sold, we can determine a company's ending merchandise inventory for a given period. The total amount we could have sold (GAFS) less the amount we did sell (COGS) is the amount we should have left at the end of the period (EI):

$$GAFS - COGS = EI$$

These relationships hold true whether we are considering the quantity of inventory (physical units) or the cost of that inventory.

 ## Discussion Question

8-1. If inventory is gone at the end of a period but was not sold, what could have happened to it?

Exhibit 8–1 shows examples of these relationships in terms of both units and dollar amounts for Strawn Book Company for one month's operations. The month starts with 200 books on hand; Strawn buys 600 new books, sells 650 books, and has 150 books on hand at the end of the month. This information contains four different data items. We need only three of these items to compute any fourth item. In the first table in the exhibit, we use ending inventory to calculate cost of goods sold, and in the second table, we use cost of goods sold to calculate ending inventory. It is important to learn from these two calculations that the total of ending inventory and cost of goods sold will always equal goods available for sale (in units and in dollars).

Exhibit 8–1
Relationships among BI, Purch, GAFS, EI, and COGS for Strawn Book Company

	Units	Cost	
Beginning Inventory	200	$2,000	BI
+ Purchases	600	6,000	+ Purch
= Goods Available for Sale	800	$8,000	= GAFS
− Ending Inventory	150	1,500	− EI
= Cost of Goods Sold	650	$6,500	= COGS

OR

	Units	Cost	
Beginning Inventory	200	$2,000	BI
+ Purchases	600	6,000	+ Purch
= Goods Available for Sale	800	$8,000	= GAFS
− Cost of Goods Sold	650	6,500	− COGS
= Ending Inventory	150	$1,500	= EI

Discussion Question

8–2. You invite your friends to a party. You check your supplies and find hot dogs, dip, and pretzels. You go to the store to buy soft drinks, chips, hot dog buns, peanuts, and ice cream. Following an enjoyable party, you survey the aftermath and find the pantry and refrigerator bare. The freezer is full of ice cream because everyone forgot to eat it. To figure out how much the party cost you, describe the following:

    a. beginning inventory

    b. purchases

    c. goods available

    d. ending inventory

    e. "cost" of the party

raw materials inventory
The inventory of raw materials to be transferred into production in a manufacturing company.

work-in-process inventory
The cost of raw materials, labour, and other expenses associated with unfinished units during the process of converting raw materials into finished goods for a manufacturing company.

finished goods inventory
The inventory ready to sell in a manufacturing company. Also called *finished goods*.

cost of goods manufactured
The cost of converting raw materials into finished goods in a manufacturing firm. The cost is equivalent to purchases in a merchandising firm.

Manufacturing Companies

The inventory that manufacturing companies sell can have different forms—goods ready for retail sale or component parts for other manufacturers. Manufacturers convert raw materials to another form for customers. In the manufacturing process, a manufacturer has three inventories. A manufacturer buys raw materials and keeps these costs in its **raw materials inventory.** While the workers convert the raw materials into the finished product, the material costs and other costs accumulate in the **work-in-process inventory.** The manufacturer calls its final products *finished goods* and records the cost in the **finished goods inventory.** When the manufacturer sells the inventory, the cost of goods sold formula is exactly the same for a manufacturer and a merchandiser except the manufacturer has **cost of goods manufactured** instead of purchases. As you can see, although the same concepts for tracking costs presented for merchandising firms apply to manufacturing firms, manufacturing accounting is complicated and is, therefore, covered in management accounting texts.

INVENTORY SYSTEMS

A firm selects the type of inventory system it uses to determine the reality of the inventory quantity it has and the measurement of that reality. Over time, businesses have developed two major inventory systems—the periodic and the perpetual methods. Each has advantages and disadvantages in comparison.

periodic inventory system
An inventory system in which all inventory and cost of goods sold calculations are done at the end of the income statement period.

Periodic Inventory System

Under a **periodic inventory system,** the purchases of new inventory are treated as an expense until the end of the period. Unsold goods (ending inventory) become an asset on the balance sheet. At the end of the income statement period, we make the cost of goods sold calculations similar to the calculations in Exhibit 8–1. Detailed inventory records are not updated during the period. A company using this system does not track which products have been sold until the end of period, when it prepares its financial statements.

The strength of the periodic inventory system is that it involves relatively little additional record keeping. This fact may be important to a firm with 10,000 different inventory items. Its greatest weakness is that it does not provide the company with any day-to-day information about the status of its inventory.

Prior to the computer age, most companies with a moderate volume of inventory employed the periodic inventory system, because keeping detailed inventory records manually was too time-consuming. The costs of keeping timely inventory information far outweighed the benefits of the knowledge. However, current computer technology has made the task of keeping daily records of inventory transactions a low-cost and reasonably efficient process. Today's software includes features that automatically reorder inventory when it reaches a preselected level. Scanning devices even automate the record-keeping process. Consequently, the perpetual inventory system has grown in popularity.

Inventory data consist of two components: units and dollar costs. Although many companies now keep detailed information about the quantity of the inventory units, it is not certain that all companies keep perpetual cost information. Keeping cost information requires much more time, expense, and computer storage space. Some companies may keep both the units and dollar costs on the periodic system, and others may keep only the dollar costs on the periodic basis. Therefore, we will consider the accounting treatment of the periodic system to determine cost of goods sold and ending inventory.

Perpetual Inventory System

perpetual inventory system
An inventory system in which both the physical count of inventory units and the cost classification (asset or expense) are updated when a transaction involves inventory.

Under a complete **perpetual inventory system,** both the physical count of inventory units and the cost classification (asset or expense) are updated whenever the transaction involves inventory. A perpetual inventory system considers inventory an asset until it is sold, when it is transferred to the expense cost of goods sold. Each inventory item has its own control report that the system updates daily, weekly, or monthly depending upon the needs of the business. So a business that sells 1,000 different items will have 1,000 control reports, one for each item. If all the units in Exhibit 8–1 were the same inventory item, the control report for the month of June might look like Exhibit 8–2.

This report shows four important facts for this inventory:

1. the beginning balance of 200 units that cost $2,000
2. the total purchases during the month of 600 units that cost $6,000
3. the total sales during the month of 650 units that cost $6,500
4. the ending balance of inventory of 150 units that cost $1,500

Exhibit 8–2
Inventory Control Report under Perpetual Inventory System

Date	Explanation	Purchases			Cost of Goods Sold			Inventory Balance		
		Units	Unit Cost	Total Cost	Units	Unit Cost	Total Cost	Units	Unit Cost	Total Cost
June 01	Beg. Balance							200	$10	$2,000
June 10	Purchase	400	$10	$4,000				600	$10	$6,000
June 15	Sale				300	$10	$3,000	300	$10	$3,000
June 20	Purchase	200	$10	$2,000				500	$10	$5,000
June 30	Sale				350	$10	$3,500	150	$10	$1,500
	Total	600		$6,000	650		$6,500			

We expect to find the cost of goods sold of $6,500 on the income statement for the period and the ending balance of inventory of $1,500 on the balance sheet for the last day of the period. In addition, we see the history of the purchases and sales for the inventory item. This detail provides marketing managers, purchasing agents, and other company employees with valuable information. In this way, accounting data contribute to the efficient operation of the entire business.

Strawn Book Company uses a computerized accounting system to generate its inventory control reports automatically. Computerized systems capture purchases and sales data either by keyboard entries or by a scanning device. Retailers use scanners to read bar codes—formally known as Universal Product Codes (UPCs)—printed on the inventory labels. The computer can be programmed to assign a given cost to a given inventory item and thus can perform the necessary calculations to update inventory records. In addition to ringing up the sales price of a book, the computer software simultaneously updates the inventory records by changing the number of physical units on hand and transferring the cost of the book sold from merchandise inventory to cost of goods sold. This technology gives Strawn Book Company's employees a timely report to help them determine the number of books sold and the number of books remaining on the shelf without physically counting them.

 Discussion Questions

8-3. Assume that a book's inventory control report shows 25 books remaining on the shelf. Just to make sure, the bookstore manager goes over to the shelf, counts the remaining books, and finds there are only 22. What might explain the discrepancy?

8-4. If you were the manager responsible for inventory, how often would you count the items to verify the inventory control records? Are there any events that might encourage you to perform a physical count?

The Necessity of a Physical Inventory Count

Regardless of whether a firm chooses a periodic or perpetual inventory system, it must conduct physical counts of its inventory at least annually to satisfy Canada Customs and Revenue Agency regulations and auditors' requirements. The nature of the inventory determines the most cost-effective frequency for physical inventory counts. Normally, the higher the number of different items and the lower the cost per unit, the less frequently the company physically counts. Consider the case of a grocery store or variety store that contains thousands of different items with relatively low cost per item. Contrast this with a car dealership. A cost-benefit analysis would tell you that one person could count the cars on the lot in an hour, and if there were a discrepancy of one vehicle, the dollar value would be substantial. A whole team of employees would have to work eight or ten hours to count the items in a grocery store, and the dollar value of missing items might be less than the dollar cost of the employees' wages to count.

Beyond the need to satisfy external parties' requirements, why would a company conduct a physical count? If the company maintains a periodic inventory system, the physical count is mandatory to determine the amount of both the ending inventory and, consequently, the cost of goods sold. Does this mean that a firm with a perpetual inventory system can omit the physical count? The accounting

book inventory The amount of ending inventory (units and dollars) resulting from transactions recorded by a perpetual inventory system.

system generates the amount of ending inventory, called **book inventory.** Book inventory may or may not coincide with the merchandise inventory actually on hand at the end of the period. Errors in the recording process, shoplifting, and employee theft can cause the book inventory to differ from the actual inventory. In addition, inventory can be intentionally or accidentally damaged, discarded, or spoiled. Some inventory actually evaporates over time. The results of a physical inventory help management to pinpoint possible problems and to improve the internal control procedures and physical control of the inventory. Remember that for most merchandising firms, inventory may represent the largest investment in assets. Safeguarding assets is critical to the success of the firm, not only because shoplifting is a problem, but because, in many companies, the employees are the major source of losses from thefts.

Results of the physical inventory count take precedence over the book inventory generated by the inventory records. We adjust both the inventory asset and the cost of goods sold for the period for any differences between the physical count and the book inventory so that the periodic count is reflected in the financial statements. To illustrate, assume that Strawn Book Company takes a physical count of books and finds only 130 books on hand instead of 150 that the inventory record shows. Exhibit 8–3 shows the calculation of cost of goods sold and ending inventory based on the physical records and the amounts adjusted for the ending physical count.

Exhibit 8–3
Adjusted Record of Ending Inventory after Physical Count

	Per Books		Per Physical Count	
	Units	Cost	Units	Cost
Beginning Inventory, January 1	200	$2,000	200	$2,000
+ Purchases	600	6,000	600	6,000
= Goods Available for Sale	800	$8,000	800	$8,000
− Ending Inventory, January 31	150	1,500	130	1,300
= Cost of Goods Sold	650	$6,500	670	$6,700

In this case, an adjustment of the records is necessary to reflect reality: The amount shown on the balance sheet as ending inventory must be the amount actually on hand. Because we know that cost of goods available for sale ($8,000) will end up as either cost of goods sold or ending inventory, a change in the amount shown as ending inventory will cause a change in the amount shown as cost of goods sold. The cost of goods sold reported as an expense on the income statement for the period is $6,700. The merchandise inventory reported as an asset on the balance sheet is $1,300, which reflects the reality of the number of units actually on hand at the end of the period. With this adjustment of the records, Strawn Book Company's financial statement amounts will more accurately reflect reality.

 Discussion Questions

8-5. If careless employees break inventory items and discard them, or dishonest employees steal inventory items, how is a company's income statement affected?

8-6. How can companies guard against shoplifting and employee theft?

The Physical Movement of Inventory (Reality)

A merchandising company purchases goods from a manufacturer or wholesale distributor that delivers the goods to the company's warehouse. A firm's warehouse may not always be a building with four walls and a roof. The natural differences among products causes the warehousing function to differ. Consider the following examples:

1. Corn delivered to a silo
2. Gravel stored in a pit
3. Oil placed in an underground storage tank
4. Cars, trucks, and vans parked on a lot

first in, first out (FIFO) The inventory flow concept based on the assumption that the first units of inventory purchased are the first ones sold.

When a farmer delivers corn to a silo, he deposits the corn in the top of the silo and receives payment from the grain dealer. When the grain dealer sells the corn to a customer, the customer extracts the corn from the bottom of the silo. Silos function because of the law of gravity, so the oldest corn is in the bottom of the silo and the newest corn is in the top of the silo. Therefore, the physical movement of the corn is on a **first-in, first-out (FIFO)** basis. The first corn deposited into the silo is the first corn removed from the silo.

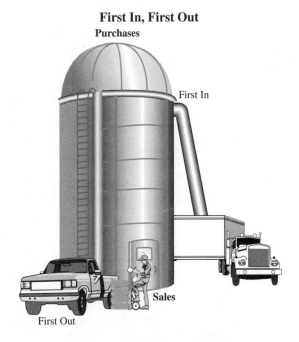

First In, First Out
Purchases

First In

Sales

First Out

last in, first out (LIFO) The inventory flow concept based on the assumption that the last units of inventory purchased are the first ones sold.

Gravel dealers frequently keep the gravel inventory in a pit. When new gravel arrives at the dealer's location, the truck driver dumps the gravel into the pit. When the gravel dealer makes a sale, she removes the gravel from the top of the pit because she cannot access the bottom. The physical movement of the gravel is on a **last-in, first-out (LIFO)** basis. The last gravel deposited into the pit is the first gravel to be removed.

Last In, First Out

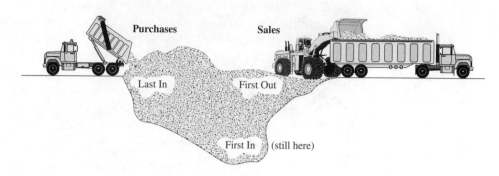

When an oil producer delivers oil to a customer, it frequently delivers the oil to an above-ground storage tank. Because of the physical properties of oil, it blends with other oil when added into a container. So when oil enters a storage tank, it mixes with other oil and loses its unit identity. Therefore, any oil extracted from the tank is a mixture of all oil added to the tank. We might say that extracted oil represents an **average** of the oil inventory.

Average Cost

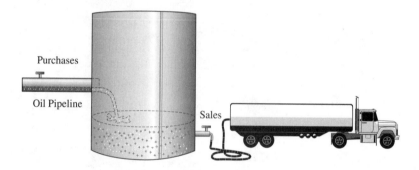

Finally, look at a dealer's lot of cars, trucks, and vans. Each vehicle has unique characteristics and a serial number. The dealer places the vehicles wherever there is room and frequently moves the vehicles around the lot. Customers purchase their choice of vehicle, based not on its location, but on its ability to suit their needs. Each customer specifically identifies the vehicle he or she wants. The physical movement of the vehicles is based upon the specific identification of the desired unit.

Discussion Questions

8-7. For what products would it be important that the first units purchased be the first ones sold? Explain.

8-8. Describe five different categories of products for sale in a grocery store. How do stock personnel typically restock the shelves for each of these products? Why?

8-9. If you owned a retail computer store, what reasons would you have for insisting that your employees sell the first computer received before the ones that arrived at the store later?

The Flow of Inventory Cost (Measurement of Reality)

We have discussed the physical flow of units in and out of inventory. But what about the cost of these units? As a firm purchases inventory, we add its cost to inventory in the accounting records. Likewise, as the firm sells the merchandise, we remove its cost from inventory and transfer it to cost of goods sold. You might suppose that accounting rules require the flow of costs through a company's accounting records to reflect the reality of the way the physical units flow through the company's inventory. However, accounting rules do not require that the cost flow for inventory mirror the flow of physical units. Regardless of how physical units flow through inventory, a company may select any cost flow assumption it chooses. Thus we see another example of how reality and the measurement of reality may differ.

COST FLOW ASSUMPTIONS

When a company purchases one product and sells it before it buys another product, the physical flow of product equals the cost flow of the product. However, when a firm buys many products at different times for different amounts, the physical inventory flow (reality) and the cost flow (measurement of reality) seldom coincide. As you might guess from our discussion of the physical flow of goods, accounting has four basic cost flow assumptions:

1. First in, first out (FIFO)
2. Last in, first out (LIFO)
3. Average cost
4. Specific identification

The most common flow of goods is first in, first out (FIFO); however, GAAP do not require that the inventory cost method match the physical flow of inventory. Many firms use more than one cost flow assumption by using different assumptions for different types of inventory. Many Canadian firms use FIFO because that method is the one approved by the Canada Customs and Revenue Agency for tax reporting purposes (along with weighted average and specific identification). LIFO is a method that is used quite extensively in the United States because United States tax laws allow for LIFO. The advantage of using LIFO is that in a period of inflation, it results in a higher cost of goods sold, resulting in a lower net income, and therefore a lower tax expense. While LIFO is not allowed in Canada for tax purposes, GAAP do allow it, and many Canadian firms use that method for financial reporting purposes (but not tax reporting purposes). One of the reasons for using LIFO in Canada is that many "Canadian" firms are subsidiaries of larger American firms. By using LIFO, they are reporting their cost of goods sold and ending inventory using the same method as their parent company, and therefore maintaining consistency across the entire firm.

Financial statement users should understand the way in which companies track inventory costs and arrive at the amount presented on their financial statements, because as you will see, the inventory costing method selected changes the net income and balance sheet assets. To understand these differences, we will explore different cost flow assumptions that take different approaches to measuring the flow of inventory costs through both a periodic and a perpetual inventory system. Because the specific identification method is unique and results in the same valuation regardless of periodic or perpetual system, we will look at this method first.

Specific Identification Cost Flow Assumption

specific identification The method of inventory cost flow that identifies each item sold by a company.

Dobbs Motor Company sells antique cars to an exclusive clientele and appropriately uses the **specific identification** method to cost its vehicles. Exhibit 8–4 details the cars in the inventory at the beginning of March, those purchased during the month, and those sold during March.

Exhibit 8–4
Dobbs Motor Company Inventory Transactions for March 2004

Date of Purchase	Description	Cost	Date Sold	Selling Price
15-10-2003	1926 Bentley	$35,000	05-03-2004	$45,000
25-12-2003	1935 Mercedes	42,000		
25-01-2004	1955 Thunderbird	25,000	09-03-2004	38,000
10-02-2004	1935 Model T Ford	24,000	18-03-2004	36,000
10-03-2004	1940 Cadillac	38,000		
25-03-2004	1932 Silver Cloud	80,000		

We can analyze this information to determine Dobbs Motor Company's sales, cost of goods sold, and gross profit for the month of March as follows:

1. Sales total $119,000 ($45,000 + $38,000 + $36,000).
2. The beginning inventory consisted of the first four cars listed:

1926 Bentley	$ 35,000
1935 Mercedes	42,000
1955 Thunderbird	25,000
1935 Model T Ford	24,000
Total Cost	$126,000

3. Dobbs Motor Company purchased two cars during March:

1940 Cadillac	$ 38,000
1932 Silver Cloud	80,000
Total Cost	$118,000

4. The cost of goods sold included three cars:

1926 Bentley	$35,000
1955 Thunderbird	25,000
1935 Model T Ford	24,000
Total Cost	$84,000

5. The ending inventory includes three cars:

1935 Mercedes	$ 42,000
1940 Cadillac	38,000
1932 Silver Cloud	80,000
Total Cost	$160,000

6. Summary of information in the format of the income statement:

Sales		$119,000
Cost of Goods Sold:		
Beginning Inventory	$126,000	
Purchases	118,000	
Goods Available for Sale	$244,000	
Ending Inventory	160,000	
Cost of Goods Sold		84,000
Gross Profit		$ 35,000

Because each inventory item is unique, there is no cost determination difference between a periodic system and a perpetual system with a specific identification method. The same is true if each product included in beginning inventory and each item purchased (or made) during the period cost exactly the same amount per unit. LIFO, FIFO, and average cost methods would result in identical measurements of reality. However, the cost of products rarely remains constant because of technological advances, economic conditions, and competition. Using the periodic and perpetual inventory systems, we will look at the effect of changing prices on inventory and cost of goods sold.

COST FLOW ASSUMPTIONS UNDER A PERIODIC INVENTORY SYSTEM

Changes in the cost of inventory items over time cause different cost flow assumptions to result in different amounts for cost of goods sold and ending inventory. To illustrate this in a periodic system, we examine the effect of three different cost flow assumptions on one product sold by Harwood Equipment Company Ltd. Exhibit 8–5 contains the inventory activity for the company during September 2004.

Exhibit 8–5
Harwood Equipment Company Ltd. Inventory Transactions

Date	Transaction	Units	Unit Cost	Unit Selling Price
Sept. 01	Beginning Inventory	1	$ 800	
Sept. 03	Purchase	2	1,025	
Sept. 17	Sale	1		$1,500
Sept. 22	Purchase	1	1,100	
Sept. 26	Purchase	1	1,200	
Sept. 29	Purchase	1	1,450	
Sept. 30	Sale	2		1,500

We can analyze the information based on our knowledge of inventory cost, cost of goods sold, and gross profit.

1. Harwood Equipment Company Ltd. sold three units at $1,500 for a total of $4,500.
2. The company had a beginning inventory of one unit that cost $800.
3. Harwood Equipment Company Ltd. purchased the following items:

Sept. 03	2 @ $1,025	$2,050
Sept. 22	1 @ $1,100	1,100
Sept. 26	1 @ $1,200	1,200
Sept. 29	1 @ $1,450	1,450
Total purchases		$5,800

4. The goods available for sale is $6,600: Beginning inventory of $800 plus purchases of $5,800.

The goods available for sale will be $6,600 no matter which method we use to determine the cost of goods sold and the ending inventory. In the periodic system, we determine the cost of the units sold and the cost of the ending inventory for the whole period of time.

First-In, First-Out Method (FIFO)

Using the first-in, first-out (FIFO) cost method under a periodic system, we assume that the first units owned were sold, and the last units purchased make up the ending inventory. Harwood had six units to sell during September, sold three, and had three remaining at the end of the month. Using FIFO, we assume that the first three units owned were sold:

Beginning inventory	1 @ $800	$ 800
September 3 purchase	2 @ $1,025	2,050
Cost of units sold		$2,850

Likewise, the ending inventory comes from the last purchases:

September 29	1 @ $1,450	$1,450
September 26	1 @ $1,200	1,200
September 22	1 @ $1,100	1,100
Cost of ending inventory		$3,750

By using the cost of sales calculation, we can determine from an accounting viewpoint which units were sold and which units remain.

	Units	Cost
Beginning inventory	1	$ 800
Purchases	5	5,800
Goods available for sale	6	$6,600
Ending inventory	3	3,750
Cost of goods sold	3	$2,850

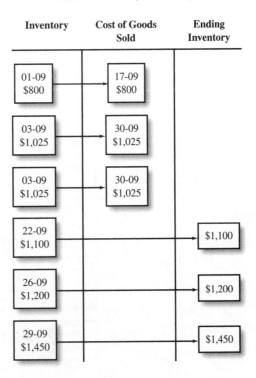

Last-In, First-Out Method (LIFO)

Using the last-in, first-out (LIFO) cost method under a periodic system, we assume that the last units owned were sold, and the first units purchased comprise the ending inventory—exactly the opposite of the FIFO method. Harwood Equipment Company Ltd. had six units to sell during September, sold three, and had three remaining at the end of the month. Under LIFO, we assume that the last three units purchased were sold:

September 29	1 @ $1,450	$1,450
September 26	1 @ $1,200	1,200
September 22	1 @ $1,100	1,100
Cost of units sold		$3,750

Likewise, the ending inventory comes from the first units owned:

Beginning inventory	1 @ $800	$ 800
September 3 purchase	2 @ $1,025	2,050
Cost of ending inventory		$2,850

By using the cost of sales calculation, we can determine from an accounting viewpoint which units were sold and which units remain.

	Units	Cost
Beginning inventory	1	$ 800
Purchases	5	5,800
Goods available for sale	6	$6,600
Ending inventory	3	2,850
Cost of goods sold	3	$3,750

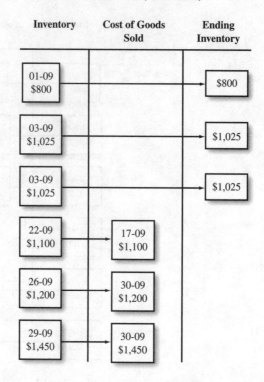

Inventory	Cost of Goods Sold	Ending Inventory
01-09 $800		$800
03-09 $1,025		$1,025
03-09 $1,025		$1,025
22-09 $1,100	17-09 $1,100	
26-09 $1,200	30-09 $1,200	
29-09 $1,450	30-09 $1,450	

Average Cost Method

average cost method The inventory cost flow method that assigns an average cost to the units of inventory on hand at the time of each sale.

Instead of separating the inventory cost into two groups, the **average cost method** assigns the same cost to each inventory unit. Harwood Equipment Company Ltd. owned six units of inventory that cost $6,600. The average cost method is simple to apply. Divide the cost of goods available for sale by the number of units available to determine the average unit cost.

$$\text{Average cost} = \frac{\text{Total cost of goods available for sale}}{\text{Number of units available for sale}} = \frac{\$6,600}{6} = \$1,100 \text{ per unit}$$

Use the cost of sales calculation to measure the cost of the units sold and the cost of the units remaining from an accounting viewpoint.

	Units	Cost
Beginning inventory	1	$ 800
Purchases	5	5,800
Goods available for sale	6	$6,600
Ending inventory	3	3,300
Cost of goods sold	3	$3,300

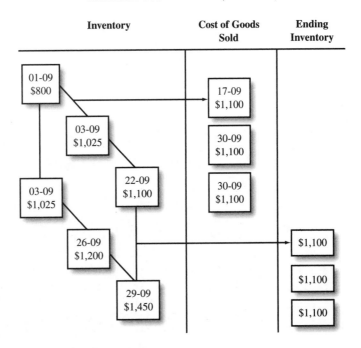

Comparison of Methods

We stated earlier that the three assumptions produced different results. Exhibit 8–6 indicates these differences in cost of goods sold, ending inventory, and gross profit.

Exhibit 8–6
Comparison of
Inventory Cost
Assumptions
under a Periodic
Inventory System

HARWOOD EQUIPMENT COMPANY LTD.
Schedule of Gross Profit
For the Month of September 2004

	FIFO	LIFO	Average Cost
Sales	$4,500	$4,500	$4,500
Cost of Goods Sold:			
Beginning Inventory	$ 800	$ 800	$ 800
Purchases	5,800	5,800	5,800
Goods Available for Sale	$6,600	$6,600	$6,600
Ending Inventory	3,750	2,850	3,300
Cost of Goods Sold	$2,850	$3,750	$3,300
Gross Profit	$1,650	$ 750	$1,200

Discussion Questions

8–10. What accounts for the difference in cost of goods sold, ending inventory, and gross profit among the three methods?

8–11. Which units actually were sold in each scenario?

8–12. What would happen to gross profit for each method if the costs were decreasing with each purchase instead of increasing?

As you may have concluded, the differences among methods occur because of the changing prices. As prices rise, LIFO produces the highest cost of sales and the lowest ending inventory. As prices fall, the opposite occurs and FIFO produces the highest cost of sales and the lowest ending inventory. Normally, the average cost method will produce costs in between LIFO and FIFO. Now consider what results when we apply the perpetual method to these three cost methods.

COST FLOW ASSUMPTIONS UNDER A PERPETUAL INVENTORY SYSTEM

Under the periodic system, we applied the cost methods to the entire period. When we utilize a perpetual inventory system, we determine the cost of inventory items sold at the time of each sale. This complicates the decision-making process and produces different results for LIFO and average cost methods. We will use the same information for Harwood Equipment Company Ltd. for our study of the perpetual system. As we analyzed the information under the periodic system, we were not concerned about the dates of the sales. Under the perpetual system, the date controls the application of the cost flow method.

Consider the Harwood Equipment Company Ltd. transactions. Which items were sold on September 17 and 30? In reality, the items sold were probably the ones conveniently located in the warehouse. About the only thing you can determine, however, is that the unit sold on September 22 was purchased before September 22. Because the purchase prices of the units varied, we cannot determine the cost of goods sold unless we know which units were sold. The cost allocation methods define the accounting measurement of which items were sold, regardless of which specific products left the warehouse. Our goal remains to separate the $6,600 into the cost of goods sold and the ending inventory.

First-In, First-Out Method

The first-in, first-out (FIFO) method in a perpetual inventory system assumes that the first items purchased are the first to be sold, exactly as in the periodic system. The first sale took place on September 17. At that time, Harwood Equipment Company Ltd. held three units, and the earliest of those was from the beginning inventory, which cost $800. The second sale took place on September 30 when the company held five units. The first units acquired were purchased on September 3 for $1,025 each. Therefore, we can separate the cost of sales and ending inventory as follows:

Units sold:

Beginning inventory	1 @ $800	$ 800
September 3 purchase	2 @ $1,025	2,050
Cost of units sold		$2,850

Ending inventory:

September 29	1 @ $1,450	$1,450
September 26	1 @ $1,200	1,200
September 22	1 @ $1,100	1,100
Cost of ending inventory		$3,750

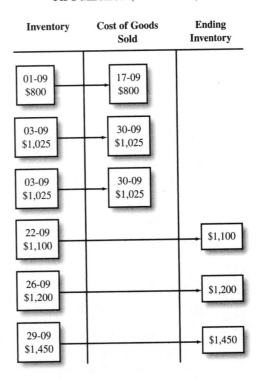

Inventory	Cost of Goods Sold	Ending Inventory
01-09 $800	17-09 $800	
03-09 $1,025	30-09 $1,025	
03-09 $1,025	30-09 $1,025	
22-09 $1,100		$1,100
26-09 $1,200		$1,200
29-09 $1,450		$1,450

The cost of goods sold calculation will appear as follows:

	Units	Cost
Beginning inventory	1	$ 800
Purchases	5	5,800
Goods available for sale	6	$6,600
Ending inventory	3	3,750
Cost of goods sold	3	$2,850

Notice that, under both FIFO perpetual and FIFO periodic systems, the cost of goods sold and ending inventory are the same ($2,850 and $3,750 respectively). The only difference is *when* these amounts are recorded *during* the accounting period. Under the perpetual system, these amounts are tracked on an on-going basis, whereas under periodic system they are recorded only at the end of the period. By the end of the period, using either the periodic or perpetual systems, the total amounts will be the same.

 Discussion Questions

8-13. Compare the cost of goods sold and ending inventory amounts with the FIFO example under the periodic system on page 277. Is the result of your comparison a coincidence?

8-14. When Harwood Equipment Company Ltd. makes its next sale of two items, which two will the FIFO method in a perpetual system assume are sold?

We will now turn our attention to the LIFO method in a perpetual inventory system.

Last-In, First-Out Method

The last-in, first-out (LIFO) method under the perpetual inventory system assumes that the last units placed in inventory are the first units sold. In applying this assumption, we assume that the very last item purchased is the one sold. On September 17, Harwood Equipment Company Ltd. held three units, the most recently purchased on September 3 for $1,025. Under LIFO, we designate the $1,025 unit as sold on September 17. On September 30, the company held five units, the last two of which were purchased on September 29 and 26, at a cost of $1,450 and $1,200 respectively. We can separate the cost of goods sold and the ending inventory as follows:

Units sold:

September 29	1 @ $1,450	$1,450
September 26	1 @ $1,200	1,200
September 3	1 @ $1,025	1,025
Cost of units sold		$3,675

Likewise, the ending inventory comes from the first units owned:

Beginning inventory	1 @ $800	$ 800
September 3 purchase	1 @ $1,025	1,025
September 22 purchase	1 @ $1,100	1,100
Cost of ending inventory		$2,925

By using the cost of sales calculation, we can determine from an accounting viewpoint which costs transfer to cost of goods sold on the income statement and which costs remain on the balance sheet in ending inventory.

	Units	Cost
Beginning inventory	1	$ 800
Purchases	5	5,800
Goods available for sale	6	$6,600
Ending inventory	3	2,925
Cost of goods sold	3	$3,675

Discussion Questions

8–15. Compare the cost of goods sold and ending inventory amounts with the LIFO example under the periodic system on page 278. Can you draw a conclusion about LIFO costs under the different inventory systems?

8–16. If Harwood Equipment Company Ltd. sells two more units before purchasing any more of the item, which two will be assumed sold under LIFO in a perpetual system?

Although the results for LIFO differ for the periodic and the perpetual systems, the methods of determining the costs are relatively simple. This is not as true when we look at the moving average method of costing inventory under the perpetual system.

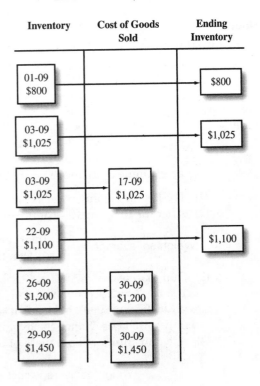

Moving Average Cost Method

moving average cost method The inventory cost flow method that assigns an average cost to the units of inventory on hand at the time of each sale in a perpetual inventory system.

The **moving average cost method** derives its name from the process that computes a new weighted average cost of all units of inventory on hand each time a new purchase is made. We will carefully build a table in which we can make the calculations for the moving average. Applying average cost logic, we assign all units on hand an average cost and assume that one of the units at that cost was sold. Remember that each time Harwood Equipment Company Ltd. purchases new units, the average cost changes. The formula to determine the average at any time is:

$$\text{Weighted average cost} = \frac{\text{Total cost of inventory on hand}}{\text{Number of units on hand}}$$

We construct the weighted average table with the following columns:

(A) Number of units for the current transaction
(B) Unit cost for the current transaction
(C) Total cost of the transaction (A × B)
(D) Cumulative cost, which equals column D from the prior transaction plus C from the current transaction
(E) Cumulative units, which equal column E from the prior transaction plus A from the current transaction
(F) Average cost, which equals D divided by E

	Date	Description	(A) # of Units	(B) Unit Cost	(C) Total Cost	(D) Cumulative Cost	(E) Cumulative Units	(F) Average Cost
(1)	01-09	Beginning Inventory	1	$800	$800	$800	1	$800
(2)	03-09	Purchase	2	1,025	2,050	2,850	3	950
(3)	17-09	Sale	<1>	<950>	<950>	1,900	2	950
(4)	22-09	Purchase	1	1,100	1,100	3,000	3	1,000
(5)	26-09	Purchase	1	1,200	1,200	4,200	4	1,050
(6)	29-09	Purchase	1	1,450	1,450	5,650	5	1,130
(7)	30-09	Sale	<2>	<1,130>	<2,260>	3,390	3	1,130

We can examine each line to verify the calculations:

(1) The beginning inventory is one unit at a cost of $800.

(2) After the first purchase of two units for $2,050, apply the formula:

$$\text{Weighted average cost} = \frac{\text{Total cost of inventory on hand}}{\text{Number of units on hand}} \text{ or } \frac{D}{E} = \frac{\$2,850}{3} = \$950$$

(3) Cumulative cost is $800 + $2,050 − $950 = $1,900. Cumulative units are 1 + 2 − 1 = 2. Apply the formula and the average remains $950 ($1,900 / 2 = $950). Notice that sales do not change the average cost; only purchases change the average cost.

(4) After an additional purchase of one unit for $1,100, apply the formula:

$$\text{Weighted average cost} = \frac{D}{E} = \frac{\$1,900 + \$1,100}{3} = \$1,000$$

(5) After an additional purchase of one unit for $1,200, apply the formula:

$$\text{Weighted average cost} = \frac{D}{E} = \frac{\$3,000 + \$1,200}{4} = \$1,050$$

(6) After an additional purchase of one unit for $1,450, apply the formula:

$$\text{Weighted average cost} = \frac{D}{E} = \frac{\$4,200 + \$1,450}{5} = \$1,130$$

(7) After the sale of two units, the ending inventory results in three units at a total cost of $3,390.

The cost of goods sold calculation will appear as follows:

	Units	Cost
Beginning inventory	1	$ 800
Purchases	5	5,800
Goods available for sale	6	$6,600
Ending inventory	3	3,390
Cost of goods sold	3	$3,210

Comparison of Methods

Just as with the periodic system, the three assumptions produced different results with the perpetual inventory system. Exhibit 8–7 indicates the differences in cost of goods sold, ending inventory, and gross profit under the latter system.

Exhibit 8–7
Comparison of Inventory Cost Assumptions under a Perpetual Inventory System

HARWOOD EQUIPMENT COMPANY LTD.
Schedule of Gross Profit
For the Month of September 2004

	FIFO	LIFO	Average Cost
Sales	$4,500	$4,500	$4,500
Cost of Goods Sold:			
Beginning Inventory	$ 800	$ 800	$ 800
Purchases	5,800	5,800	5,800
Goods Available for Sale	$6,600	$6,600	$6,600
Ending Inventory	3,750	2,925	3,390
Cost of Goods Sold	$2,850	$3,675	$3,210
Gross Profit	$1,650	$825	$1,290

Discussion Questions

8–17. What accounts for the difference in the cost of goods sold, ending inventory, and gross profit among the three methods?

8–18. Which units actually were sold in each scenario?

8–19. What would happen to gross profit for each method if the costs decreased with each purchase instead of increased?

The comparison of the three methods in a perpetual inventory system produces similar results to the periodic method because FIFO produces the highest gross profit, LIFO produces the lowest, and the moving average is in between FIFO and LIFO. The opposite is generally true when prices decrease during a period, depending on the timing of the purchases and sales during the period. Remember that FIFO produces the same results in a periodic or perpetual system, something that seldom happens with LIFO or average cost methods.

We examined the effects of each method for both periodic and perpetual systems. Now we will look at the effect that inventory assumptions and the inventory system have on financial statements.

The Effects of Inventory Cost Flow Assumption Choice

Assume that Harwood Equipment Company Ltd. had no other transactions during September except those related to this product and the payment of $200 in warehouse rent. Exhibit 8–8 portrays the August 31, 2004, balance sheet representing the beginning balances, the September income statement, and the resulting balance sheet for September 30, 2004, under all three cost flow assumptions for a periodic inventory system.

Exhibit 8–9 portrays the August 31, 2004, balance sheet representing the beginning balances, the September income statement, and the resulting balance sheet for September 30, 2004, under all three cost flow assumptions for a perpetual inventory system. As you examine Exhibit 8–9, compare it with the results in Exhibit 8–8 for a periodic inventory system.

HARWOOD EQUIPMENT COMPANY LTD.
Income Statement
For the Month Ended September 30, 2004

	FIFO	LIFO	Average Cost
Sales	$4,500	$4,500	$4,500
Cost of Goods Sold	2,850	3,750	3,300
Gross Margin	$1,650	$ 750	$1,200
Operating Expenses:			
Warehouse Rent	200	200	200
Net Income	$1,450	$ 550	$1,000

HARWOOD EQUIPMENT COMPANY LTD.
Balance Sheet
August 31, 2004, and September 30, 2004

	August 31	FIFO	LIFO	Average Cost
ASSETS:		September 30		
Cash	$21,000	$22,300	$22,300	$22,300
Accounts Receivable	1,500	4,500	4,500	4,500
Merchandise Inventory	800	3,750	2,850	3,300
Total Assets	$23,300	$30,550	$29,650	$30,100
LIABILITIES AND SHAREHOLDERS' EQUITY:				
Accounts Payable	$ 0	$ 5,800	$ 5,800	$ 5,800
Common Shares	23,000	23,000	23,000	23,000
Retained Earnings	300	1,750	850	1,300
Total Liabilities and Shareholders' Equity	$23,300	$30,550	$29,650	$30,100

 ## Discussion Questions

8–20. The financial statements prepared using FIFO in Exhibits 8–8 and 8–9 show Harwood Equipment Company Ltd. to be more profitable than the financial statements for LIFO or average cost regardless of the inventory system used. Would the company be more profitable if it used FIFO instead of LIFO or average cost?

8–21. Did Harwood Harwood Equipment Company Ltd. pay for the purchases of inventory during September? How can you determine this?

8–22. Did Harwood Harwood Equipment Company Ltd.'s customers pay for their purchases during September? How can you determine this?

8–23. How do you explain the increase in cash from $21,000 to $22,300 from August to September?

HARWOOD EQUIPMENT COMPANY LTD.
Income Statement
For the Month Ended September 30, 2004

	FIFO	LIFO	Average Cost
Sales	$4,500	$4,500	$4,500
Cost of Goods Sold	2,850	3,675	3,210
Gross Margin	$1,650	$ 825	$1,290
Operating Expenses:			
Warehouse Rent	200	200	200
Net Income	$1,450	$ 625	$1,090

HARWOOD EQUIPMENT COMPANY LTD.
Balance Sheet
August 31, 2004, and September 30, 2004

		FIFO	LIFO	Average Cost
ASSETS:	**August 31**		**September 30**	
Cash	$21,000	$22,300	$22,300	$22,300
Accounts Receivable	1,500	4,500	4,500	4,500
Merchandise Inventory	800	3,750	2,925	3,390
Total Assets	$23,300	$30,550	$29,725	$30,190
LIABILITIES AND SHAREHOLDERS' EQUITY:				
Accounts Payable	$ 0	$ 5,800	$ 5,800	$ 5,800
Common Shares	23,000	23,000	23,000	23,000
Retained Earnings	300	1,750	925	1,390
Total Liabilities and Shareholders' Equity	$23,300	$30,550	$29,725	$30,190

Companies may choose from a variety of inventory cost flow assumptions. We have explored three approaches most commonly used in periodic and perpetual inventory systems and have seen how these different cost flow assumptions result in different net profits on the income statements and inventory amounts on the balance sheets. The reality of the sales and delivery of inventory to the customer is the same. What differs is the measurement of that reality. However, the choice of inventory method does not change the ultimate profitability of a company. To illustrate, we will extend our example to October.

Assume that Harwood Equipment Company Ltd. purchased no additional units in October but sold the remaining three units in October. Further assume that the only expense in October was the warehouse rent of $200.

The cost of goods sold calculation for the *periodic* system is as follows:

	Units	FIFO	LIFO	Average Cost
Beginning inventory	3	$3,750	$2,850	$3,300
Purchases	0	0	0	0
Goods available for sale	3	$3,750	$2,850	$3,300
Ending inventory	0	0	0	0
Cost of goods sold	3	$3,750	$2,850	$3,300

The cost of goods sold calculation for the *perpetual* system is as follows:

	Units	FIFO	LIFO	Average Cost
Beginning inventory	3	$3,750	$2,925	$3,390
Purchases	0	0	0	0
Goods available for sale	3	$3,750	$2,925	$3,390
Ending inventory	0	0	0	0
Cost of goods sold	3	$3,750	$2,925	$3,390

Now we can see the effect that October's activity has on the balance sheet and income statement. Exhibit 8–10 contains the October balance sheets and income statements for all three cost methods under a periodic inventory system.

Exhibit 8–11 contains the October 31, 2004, balance sheets and income statements under all three cost assumptions in a perpetual system. Note the similarities and differences between the October 31, 2004, financial statements for the periodic and perpetual inventory systems and each of the cost flow assumptions.

Exhibit 8–10
Comparative Financial Statements Using a Periodic Inventory System for FIFO, LIFO, and Average Cost Methods

HARWOOD EQUIPMENT COMPANY LTD.
Income Statement
For the Month Ended October 31, 2004

	FIFO	LIFO	Average Cost
Sales	$4,500	$4,500	$4,500
Cost of Goods Sold	3,750	2,850	3,300
Gross Margin	$ 750	$1,650	$1,200
Operating Expenses:			
Warehouse Rent	200	200	200
Net Income	$ 550	$1,450	$1,000

HARWOOD EQUIPMENT COMPANY LTD.
Balance Sheet
October 31, 2004

	FIFO	LIFO	Average Cost
ASSETS:		October 31	
Cash	$20,800	$20,800	$20,800
Accounts Receivable	4,500	4,500	4,500
Merchandise Inventory	0	0	0
Total Assets	$25,300	$25,300	$25,300
LIABILITIES AND SHAREHOLDERS' EQUITY:			
Accounts Payable	$ 0	$ 0	$ 0
Common Shares	23,000	23,000	23,000
Retained Earnings	2,300	2,300	2,300
Total Liabilities and Shareholders' Equity	$25,300	$25,300	$25,300

Exhibit 8–11
Comparative Financial
Statements Using a
Perpetual Inventory
System for FIFO,
LIFO, and Average
Cost Methods

HARWOOD EQUIPMENT COMPANY LTD.
Income Statement
For the Month Ended October 31, 2004

	FIFO	LIFO	Average Cost
Sales	$4,500	$4,500	$4,500
Cost of Goods Sold	3,750	2,925	3,390
Gross Margin	$ 750	$1,575	$1,110
Operating Expenses:			
Warehouse Rent	200	200	200
Net Income	$ 550	$1,375	$ 910

HARWOOD EQUIPMENT COMPANY LTD.
Balance Sheet
October 31, 2004

	FIFO	LIFO	Average Cost
ASSETS:			
Cash	$20,800	$20,800	$20,800
Accounts Receivable	4,500	4,500	4,500
Merchandise Inventory	0	0	0
Total Assets	$25,300	$25,300	$25,300
LIABILITIES AND SHAREHOLDERS' EQUITY:			
Accounts Payable	$ 0	$ 0	$ 0
Common Shares	23,000	23,000	23,000
Retained Earnings	2,300	2,300	2,300
Total Liabilities and			
Shareholders' Equity	$25,300	$25,300	$25,300

 ## Discussion Questions

8-24. Because the balance sheet is affected by the income statement, how can the ending balance sheets at the end of October be identical under all three inventory cost flow methods for both periodic and perpetual systems when the income statements for October were different?

8-25. Compute the total gross profit for September and October for each inventory cost method for both the periodic and perpetual systems. How do they compare?

8-26. Which method (FIFO, LIFO, or average cost) matches the most recent cost to current revenues?

8-27. Which inventory cost method is the best to use? Which inventory system is the best to use?

After examining Harwood Equipment Company Ltd.'s financial statements for two months, you might rightly come to the conclusion that no one method of determining inventory cost flow is better than another. Likewise, the type of inventory system does not change the profit reality over time. From the time a firm buys its first item of inventory to the time it sells its last item of inventory, its total gross profit over time will be equal, regardless of inventory method or system. For one firm, we may conclude that the choice of inventory costing method is relevant in the short term and irrelevant in the long term. It becomes important, however, when comparing the profitability of two firms that use different costing methods.

As was the case with accounting for amortization of long-lived assets, accounting for the cost of merchandise inventory has a significant impact on a company's reported net income for a given income statement period and for the reported inventory on the balance sheet. Informed financial statement users must have an understanding of the impact of inventory cost flow method choice to utilize the information to the fullest extent possible.

Now that you have an understanding of some of the issues and situations that impact financial statements, we will explore in more detail the construction of the balance sheet and income statement in Chapter 9.

SUMMARY

Merchandise inventory represents the physical units of goods that a company plans to sell. Inventory on hand at the beginning of a given income statement period (beginning inventory) and the inventory bought during the period (purchases) constitute the total amount of goods the company could sell (goods available for sale). Goods available for sale will either remain on hand at the end of the period or be assumed sold.

Accountants developed two types of systems to track inventory costs. The periodic system counts inventory and traces costs only at the end of each income statement period, whereas the perpetual system updates inventory counts and costs each time a sale or purchase is made. Perpetual inventory systems usually make use of computer technology and scanners that read UPC. Even though inventory records are updated often when a perpetual system is in place, physical inventory counts are still necessary. Determining the actual amount of inventory on hand may uncover theft, damage, or spoilage of inventory. Some businesses use a perpetual system to track the number of units in inventory and integrate the counts into automatic purchasing reorder systems, but they may cost the inventory under a periodic system.

In a periodic system using accrual-basis accounting, we use the computation of cost of goods sold to determine the amount of expense on the income statement. The ending inventory is reported on the balance sheet as an asset. Under accrual accounting in a perpetual inventory system, when a company purchases inventory, its cost is considered an asset to the company and is listed as such on the balance sheet. As inventory is sold, its cost is converted from an asset to an expense, which is listed on the income statement as cost of goods sold. It follows, then, that the total cost of goods available for sale will end up either as ending inventory (an asset on the balance sheet) or as cost of goods sold (an expense on the income statement).

The physical flow of inventory may differ from the flow of inventory costs. Several methods have been developed to trace inventory costs as they move from the balance sheet to the income statement. All these methods are cost flow assumptions that prescribe which inventory items are assumed to be the ones sold.

Specific identification relates the exact cost of each unit of inventory to cost of goods sold when the item is sold. Firms that deal in expensive and unique items (such as cars, boats, and luxury items) utilize the specific identification method. The first-in, first-out (FIFO) method assumes that the first units of inventory purchased are the first ones sold. Conversely, the last-in, first-out (LIFO) method assumes that the last units of inventory purchased are the first sold. The average cost method assigns a weighted average cost to the units of inventory.

In a periodic system, we apply the cost assumptions for the entire period. In a perpetual system, we apply FIFO, LIFO, and moving average cost assumptions at the time of each sale, which produces different results than when we apply the assumptions for the entire period. Average cost method under a periodic system calculates one inventory cost for all goods sold and remaining in inventory, while the moving average method under a perpetual system recalculates the average each time a new purchase is made.

Companies may choose to use any of these cost flow assumptions. If the price they pay for inventory items varies during the period, the choice will impact both net income and asset values reported on the company's financial statements each year. In the long run, however, choice of inventory cost method makes no difference to one firm. Financial statement users must be aware of the differences that inventory methods make when comparing companies that use different inventory cost methods.

APPENDIX—INVENTORY PURCHASING ISSUES

Two issues arise for firms that purchase merchandise inventory—freight costs and cash discounts. When negotiating purchase terms, buying agents pay particular attention to the freight and payment terms. Careful negotiations can decrease the cost of purchasing merchandise.

Cash Discounts

A firm frequently encourages its customer to pay invoices quickly by offering a cash discount, which improves the firm's cash flow. A company may devise its own credit terms that appeal to its customers; the following represent frequently used payment terms and their meaning.

1. *2/10, net 30 days*—A 2 percent discount is allowed if paid within 10 days from the invoice date; otherwise payment is due 30 days after the invoice date.
2. *net 30 days*—The net amount is due 30 days after the invoice date with no cash discount.
3. *1/10, EOM, net 60 days*—A 1 percent discount is allowed if paid within 10 days after the end of the month; otherwise payment is due 60 days from the invoice date.

Return to our example of Harwood Equipment Company Ltd. If the purchase on September 3 had terms of 2/10, net 30, the company would pay the invoice by September 13 to receive a 2 percent discount. Payment required by September 13 would be 98 percent of $2,050, or $2,009. The discount of $41 (2% × $2,050) reduces the cost of the purchase to Harwood Equipment Company Ltd. Good cash managers take advantage of cash discounts.

Discussion Questions

8-28. When would payment be due by Harwood Equipment Company Ltd. if the terms were net 30 days? 1/10 EOM, net 60 days?

8-29. What is the annual percentage rate of a 2 percent discount for payment in 10 days instead of 30 days? One percent discount for 15 days instead of 30 days?

Freight Terms

Freight terms define the point at which title passes between the seller and the purchaser. *FOB (free on board) shipping point* indicates that the title passes when the merchandise leaves the seller's shipping dock. *FOB destination* indicates that the title passes when the merchandise arrives at the purchaser's loading dock. Transportation costs transfer to the buyer at the FOB point when the title passes. Therefore, if the terms are FOB shipping point, title passes at the seller's dock and the buyer bears the freight expense. If the terms are FOB destination, the seller owns the goods until delivery and bears the freight expense.

Payment of the freight adds another complication. When the seller arranges for transportation, it contracts either for freight prepaid or freight collect. Shippers such as Loomis Courier contract mostly for prepaid freight, while other common carriers can accommodate either payment method. When the terms are FOB destination and the seller pays the shipper directly, or when the terms are FOB shipping point and the seller sends the goods freight collect, the correct entity pays the expense. However, when the seller ships freight prepaid for FOB shipping point, the seller must bill the buyer for the freight cost. If the seller ships freight collect for FOB destination, the buyer must deduct the freight costs from its accounts payable when it pays the seller.

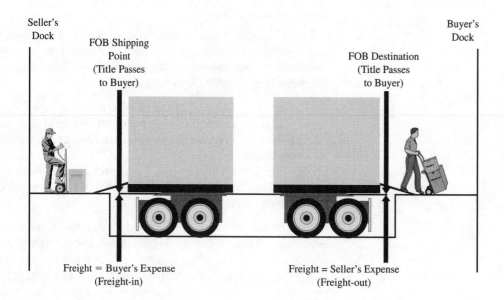

If Harwood Equipment Company Ltd. buys two units from Taylor Equipment Ltd. on September 3, terms FOB shipping point, freight collect, Harwood will pay the $125 shipping costs directly to the common carrier. If Harwood Equipment

Company Ltd. buys the goods freight collect with terms FOB destination, Harwood will pay the carrier direct and pay its vendor only $1,925 in full payment of the $2,050 invoice amount.

 Discussion Question

8–30. If Harwood Equipment Company Ltd. buys two units from Taylor Equipment Ltd. on September 3 with terms of 2/10, net 30, FOB shipping point, freight prepaid, and the shipping charges are $210, how much will Harwood pay Taylor if it pays on September 3? On October 3?

APPENDIX—RECORDING INVENTORY

After completing Chapter 8, you can look at the journal entries required to account for inventory. The recording process differs for periodic and perpetual inventory systems. We will look at the periodic system first.

Periodic Inventory Systems

The recording process for periodic inventory systems involves eight types of entries:

1. Purchase of the inventory
2. Return of defective merchandise
3. Payment of freight charges on purchases
4. Payment of the vendor
5. Recording ending inventory in closing entries
6. Sale of inventory
7. Payment of freight charges on sales
8. Receipt of cash from customer

To record these entries, we will use several new accounts:

Asset account:	Inventory, or Merchandise Inventory
Expense accounts:	Purchases
	Purchase Discounts
	Purchase Returns and Allowances
	Freight-in (a cost of goods sold expense)
	Freight-out (a selling expense)
Revenue accounts:	Sales
	Sales Returns and Allowances
	Sales Discounts

To apply these concepts, we use the transactions during September 2004 for Harwood Equipment Company Ltd. with the addition of a few items. In a periodic system, the costs of purchasing merchandise are charged to the previously listed expense accounts for Purchases, Purchase Returns and Allowances, Freight-in, and Purchase Discounts. We ignore the asset account for Inventory until the closing entries for the year.

To record the purchase of two units totaling $2,050 from Taylor Equipment Ltd. on September 3, terms 2/10, net 30, FOB destination, freight collect:

2004		Debit	Credit
September 3	Purchases	2,050	
	Accounts Payable—Taylor		2,050
	To record purchase of two units,		
	terms 2/10, net 30, FOB destination.		

To record the receipt and payment of a freight bill to Mistletoe Express for $125: Because this freight is not the expense of Harwood, it will reduce the amount that Harwood must pay to Taylor for the invoice.

		Debit	Credit
September 4	Accounts Payable—Taylor	125	
	Cash		125
	To record the payment of freight		
	collect on FOB destination.		

To record payment of the invoice within the discount period:

		Debit	Credit
September 12	Accounts Payable—Taylor	1,925	
	Purchase Discounts		41
	Cash		1,884
	To record the payment of Taylor's		
	03-09-2004 invoice.		

The payment to Taylor was for a $2,050 invoice less a 2 percent discount and less freight charges of $125, leaving an amount due of $1,884 ($2,050 − $41 − $125).

To record the sale on September 17 of one unit to Earhart Industries for $1,500, terms 2/10, net 30, FOB shipping point, freight collect:

		Debit	Credit
September 17	Accounts Receivable—Earhart	1,500	
	Sales		1,500
	To record sale to Earhart, 2/10, net 30,		
	FOB shipping point.		

Because Harwood shipped the goods freight collect, the buyer will pay its freight costs. In the periodic system, no recognition occurs for the cost of each sale because the purchases are being recorded as an expense and the income statement computes the cost of goods sold with the cost of sales calculation.

To record the purchase of one unit from Allen Corp., terms 1/15, net 30, FOB shipping point, freight collect (shipping charges were $93):

		Debit	Credit
September 22	Purchases	1,100	
	Accounts Payable—Allen		1,100
	To record purchase from Allen, 1/15,		
	net 30, FOB shipping point.		

To record the payment of the freight to Mistletoe Express:

		Debit	Credit
September 24	Freight-in	93	
	Cash		93
	To record the freight charges on the		
	Allen purchase.		

Because the terms of the purchase were FOB shipping point, Harwood records the freight bill as an expense.

To record the purchase of one unit from Bostwick Exchange, terms 2/10, net 30, FOB destination, freight prepaid (shipping charges $85):

		Debit	Credit
September 26	Purchases	1,200	
	Accounts Payable—Bostwick		1,200
	To record purchase from Bostwick 2/10, net 30, FOB destination.		

After Harwood received the Bostwick purchase, the inventory control specialist realized that the equipment item was defective. Harwood notified Bostwick and on September 28, Bostwick issued a credit memorandum to Harwood. Harwood returned the merchandise to Bostwick freight collect.

To record the return of the Bostwick purchase:

		Debit	Credit
September 28	Accounts Payable—Bostwick	1,200	
	Purchases returns and allowances		1,200
	To record the return of defective merchandise to Bostwick.		

To record the purchase of one unit from Allen Corp., terms 1/15, net 30, FOB shipping point, freight collect (shipping costs $115):

		Debit	Credit
September 29	Purchases	1,450	
	Accounts Payable—Allen		1,450
	To record the purchase from Allen, 1/15, net 30, FOB shipping point.		

To record the freight expense on the Allen purchase:

		Debit	Credit
September 30	Freight-in	115	
	Cash		115
	To record payment of freight expense on Allen purchase.		

To record the sale of two units to Kiamichi Inc., terms 1/10, net 30, FOB destination, freight prepaid:

		Debit	Credit
September 30	Accounts Receivable—Kiamichi	3,000	
	Sales		3,000
	To record the sale to Kiamichi, 1/10, net 30, FOB destination.		

To record payment of freight on Kiamichi sale for $146 on September 30:

		Debit	Credit
September 30	Freight-out	146	
	Cash		146
	To record payment of freight on Kiamichi sale.		

Periodic Inventory Closing Entries

We close all revenue and expense accounts (temporary accounts) at the close of each year. Assume that the following revenue and expense accounts appeared on the adjusted trial balance of Harwood Equipment Company Ltd. at its year end of December 31, 2004:

	Debit	Credit
Sales		75,000
Sales Returns and Allowances	1,500	
Sales Discounts	940	
Purchases	48,000	
Purchase Returns and Allowances		2,400
Purchase Discounts		800
Freight-in	2,300	
Warehouse Rent	2,400	
Freight-out	1,950	

In addition, the Inventory account shows a balance of $2,300, which represents the beginning balance on January 1, 2004. In a periodic inventory system, only two closing entries are made to the Inventory account each year. Therefore, the Inventory asset account always carries the beginning inventory amount except for the last day of the fiscal year. The physical count of the inventory on December 31 indicated a $4,550 inventory using the FIFO costing assumption.

The following are the closing entries for Harwood Equipment Company Ltd. for 2004:

		Debit	Credit
December 31	Sales	75,000	
	Purchase Returns and Allowances	2,400	
	Purchase Discounts	800	
	Income Summary		78,200
	To close the accounts with credit balances.		
December 31	Income Summary	57,090	
	Sales Returns and Allowances		1,500
	Sales Discounts		940
	Purchases		48,000
	Freight-in		2,300
	Warehouse Rent		2,400
	Freight-out		1,950
	To close accounts with debit balances.		
December 31	Income Summary	2,300	
	Inventory		2,300
	To close the beginning inventory amount.		
December 31	Inventory	4,550	
	Income Summary		4,550
	To record the ending inventory amount.		

The periodic system income statement for Harwood Equipment Company Ltd. for the year 2004 is as follows:

HARWOOD EQUIPMENT COMPANY LTD.
Income Statement
For the Year Ended December 31, 2004

Sales			$75,000
Less: Sales Returns and Allowances		$ 1,500	
Sales Discounts		940	2,440
Net Sales			$72,560
Cost of Goods Sold:			
Beginning Inventory		$ 2,300	
Purchases	$48,000		
Less: Returns and Allowances	$2,400		
Discounts	800	(3,200)	
Add: Freight-in		2,300	
Net Purchases		47,100	
Goods Available for Sale		$49,400	
Less: Ending Inventory		4,550	
Cost of Goods Sold			44,850
Gross Profit			$27,710
Operating Expenses:			
Warehouse Rent		$ 2,400	
Freight-out Expense		1,950	4,350
Net Income			$23,360

We now turn our attention to the recording process for the perpetual inventory system.

Perpetual Inventory Systems

The recording process for perpetual inventory systems involves nine types of entries:

1. Purchase of the inventory
2. Return of defective merchandise
3. Payment of freight charges on purchases
4. Payment of the vendor
5. Recording ending inventory in closing entries
6. Sale of inventory
7. Recording of cost of goods sold
8. Payment of freight charges on sales
9. Receipt of cash from customer

To record the entries, we will use the following accounts:

Asset account:	Inventory, or Merchandise Inventory
Expense accounts:	Cost of Goods Sold
	Freight-out (a selling expense)
Revenue accounts:	Sales
	Sales Returns and Allowances
	Sales Discounts

To introduce these procedures for the perpetual system, we will use the same transactions as we used for the periodic system. In a perpetual system, all inventory costs are debited directly to the asset account, and reductions for returns or discounts are likewise credited directly to the asset account. Each time a unit is sold, we credit the Inventory account for its cost and debit the Cost of Goods Sold expense account.

To record the purchase of two units totaling $2,050 from Taylor Equipment Ltd. on September 3, terms 2/10, net 30, FOB destination, freight collect:

2004		Debit	Credit
September 3	Inventory	2,050	
	Accounts Payable—Taylor		2,050
	To record purchase of two units,		
	terms 2/10, net 30, FOB destination.		

To record the receipt and payment of a freight bill to Mistletoe Express for $125:
Because this freight is not the expense of Harwood, it will reduce the amount that Harwood must pay to Taylor for the invoice.

		Debit	Credit
September 4	Accounts Payable—Taylor	125	
	Cash		125
	To record the payment of freight		
	collect on FOB destination.		

To record payment of the invoice within the discount period:

		Debit	Credit
September 12	Accounts Payable—Taylor	1,925	
	Inventory		41
	Cash		1,884
	To record the payment of Taylor's		
	03-09-2004 invoice.		

The payment to Taylor was for a $2,050 invoice less a 2 percent discount and less freight charges of $125, leaving an amount due of $1,884 ($2,050 − $41 − $125). Because we debited the Inventory account for the whole amount before the discount on the invoice date, we reduce the Inventory account for the discount to lower the cost of the purchase to $2,009.

To record the sale on September 17 of one unit to Earhart Industries for $1,500, terms 2/10, net 30, FOB shipping point, freight collect:

		Debit	Credit
September 17	Accounts Receivable—Earhart	1,500	
	Sales		1,500
	To record sale to Earhart, 2/10,		
	net 30, FOB shipping point.		

Because Harwood shipped the goods freight collect, the buyer will pay its freight costs. In the perpetual system, we must recognize the cost of each sale. We also make the following entry:

		Debit	Credit
September 17	Cost of Goods Sold	800	
	Inventory		800
	To record the cost of the sale under		
	the FIFO cost assumption.		

To record the purchase of one unit from Allen Corp., terms 1/15, net 30, FOB shipping point, freight collect (shipping charges were $93):

		Debit	Credit
September 22	Inventory	1,100	
	Accounts Payable—Allen		1,100
	To record purchase from Allen, 1/15,		
	net 30, FOB shipping point.		

To record the payment of the freight to Mistletoe Express:

		Debit	Credit
September 24	Inventory	93	
	Cash		93
	To record the freight charges on the		
	Allen purchase.		

Because the terms of the purchase were FOB shipping point, Harwood records the freight bill as a cost of the inventory.

To record the purchase of one unit from Bostwick Exchange, terms 2/10, net 30, FOB destination, freight prepaid (shipping charges $85):

		Debit	Credit
September 26	Inventory	1,200	
	Accounts Payable—Bostwick		1,200
	To record purchase from Bostwick		
	2/10, net 30, FOB destination.		

After Harwood received the Bostwick purchase, the inventory control specialist realized that the equipment item was defective. Harwood notified Bostwick, and on September 28 Bostwick issued a credit memorandum to Harwood. Harwood returned the merchandise to Bostwick freight collect.

To record the return of the Bostwick purchase:

		Debit	Credit
September 28	Accounts Payable—Bostwick	1,200	
	Inventory		1,200
	To record the return of defective		
	merchandise to Bostwick.		

To record the purchase of one unit from Allen Corp., terms 1/15, net 30, FOB shipping point, freight collect (shipping costs $115):

		Debit	Credit
September 29	Inventory	1,450	
	Accounts Payable—Allen		1,450
	To record the purchase from Allen,		
	1/15, net 30, FOB shipping point.		

To record the freight expense on the Allen purchase:

		Debit	Credit
September 30	Inventory	115	
	Cash		115
	To record payment of freight expense		
	on Allen purchase.		

To record the sale of two units to Kiamichi Inc., terms 1/10, net 30, FOB destination, freight prepaid:

		Debit	Credit
September 30	Accounts Receivable—Kiamichi	3,000	
	Sales		3,000
	To record the sale to Kiamichi, 1/10,		
	net 30, FOB destination.		

		Debit	Credit
September 30	Cost of Goods Sold	2,009	
	Inventory		2,009
	To record the cost of the sale made		
	to Kiamichi at $2,009.		

To record payment of freight on Kiamichi sale for $146 on September 30:

		Debit	Credit
September 30	Freight-out	146	
	Cash		146
	To record payment of freight on Kiamichi sale.		

Perpetual Inventory Closing Entries

We close all revenue and expense accounts (temporary accounts) at the close of each year. Assume that the following revenue and expense accounts appeared on the adjusted trial balance of Harwood Equipment Company Ltd. at its year end of December 31, 2004:

	Debit	**Credit**
Sales		75,000
Sales Returns and Allowances	1,500	
Sales Discounts	940	
Cost of Goods Sold	44,440	
Warehouse Rent	2,400	
Freight-out	1,950	

In addition, the Inventory account shows a balance of $4,960, which represents the ending balance on December 31, 2004. The physical count of the inventory on December 31 indicated a $4,550 inventory using the FIFO costing assumption.

The following are the closing entries for Harwood Equipment Company Ltd. for 2004:

		Debit	Credit
December 31	Sales	75,000	
	Income Summary		75,000
	To close the accounts with credit balances.		

		Debit	Credit
December 31	Income Summary	48,790	
	Cost of Goods Sold		44,440
	Warehouse Rent		2,400
	Freight-out		1,950
	To close accounts with debit balances.		

		Debit	Credit
December 31	Income Summary	410	
	Inventory		410
	To adjust the ending inventory amount to the physical count.		

The perpetual system income statement for Harwood Equipment Company Ltd. for the year 2004 is as follows:

HARWOOD EQUIPMENT COMPANY LTD.
Income Statement
For the Year Ended December 31, 2004

Sales		$75,000
Less: Sales Returns and Allowances	$1,500	
Sales Discounts	940	2,440
Net Sales		$72,560
Cost of Goods Sold		44,850
Gross Profit		$27,710
Operating Expenses:		
Warehouse Rent	$2,400	
Freight-out Expense	1,950	4,350
Net Income		$23,360

Remember that the FIFO method produces the same results in a periodic or perpetual system. Therefore, both income statements show the same final results in net income—only the presentation of the cost of goods sold section differs.

SUMMARY OF THE APPENDICES

Cash discounts encourage customers to pay invoices ahead of normal credit terms by reducing the amount paid for the invoice. The terms quoted on the invoice indicate the discount period length and the percentage of the discount.

Freight terms define the point that title passes from seller to buyer. When terms are FOB shipping point, title passes when goods leave the seller's shipping dock and the buyer bears the freight expense. When terms are FOB destination, title passes when the goods arrive at the buyer's loading dock and the seller bears the freight expense.

Periodic inventory systems record purchases in detailed expense accounts. The Inventory asset account carries the beginning inventory all year, and closing entries adjust the balance to the ending inventory balance at year end. The Cost of Goods Sold section of the income statement computes the cost of goods sold using the balances of the Purchases, Purchase Returns and Allowances, Purchase Discounts, and Freight-in accounts. The Freight-out account accumulates freight paid for customers and is considered a selling expense.

Perpetual inventory systems accumulate all inventory costs, including Freight-in and reduced by cash discounts and returns or allowances, in the Inventory asset account. As each sale is made, the cost of the sale is transferred to the Cost of Goods Sold account by debiting it and crediting the Inventory account. The only year-end adjustment to Inventory reconciles the balance to the physical inventory count.

KEY TERMS

average cost method, p. 278
beginning inventory, p. 265
book inventory, p. 270
cost of goods manufactured, p. 267
cost of goods sold (COGS), p. 265
ending inventory, p. 265
finished goods inventory, p. 267
first in, first out (FIFO), p. 271
goods available for sale (GAFS), p. 265

last in, first out (LIFO), p. 271
merchandise inventory, p. 265
moving average cost method, p. 283
periodic inventory system, p. 267
perpetual inventory system, p. 268
purchases, p. 265
raw materials inventory, p. 267
specific identification, p. 274
work-in-process inventory, p. 267

REVIEW THE FACTS

1. Define the terms *inventory* and *merchandise inventory*.
2. What two amounts are added to determine goods available for sale (GAFS)?
3. GAFS is allocated to two places in financial statements. Name them.
4. Under accrual accounting, which financial statement shows the cost of inventory still on hand at the end of the period?
5. Under accrual accounting, which financial statement shows the cost of inventory no longer on hand at the end of the period?
6. Explain the difference between the physical flow of merchandise and the cost flow of merchandise.
7. What are the two types of inventory systems? Explain the differences between them.
8. List three causes of differences between book inventory and the results of a physical inventory count.
9. Why are FIFO, LIFO, and average cost referred to as "assumptions"?
10. Describe in your own words the differences among the FIFO, LIFO, and average cost inventory methods.

APPLY WHAT YOU HAVE LEARNED

LO 1: Terminology

1. Presented below is a list of items relating to the concepts presented in this chapter, followed by definitions of those items in scrambled order:

   a. Periodic inventory system
   b. Perpetual inventory system
   c. Goods available for sale
   d. Cost of goods sold

   e. Merchandise inventory
   f. First-in, first-out method
   g. Last-in, first-out method
   h. Average cost method

   1. __c__ The total amount of merchandise inventory a company can sell during a particular income statement period.
   2. __a__ A system in which all inventory and cost of goods sold calculations are done at the end of the period.
   3. __f__ A method in which the cost of goods sold is determined on the assumption that the first units acquired are the first ones sold.
   4. __b__ A system that updates both the physical count of inventory units and the cost classification of those units when a transaction involves inventory.
   5. __d__ The physical units of product a company buys and then resells as part of its business operation.
   6. __g__ A method in which the cost of goods sold is based on the assumption that the last units acquired are the first ones sold.
   7. __h__ A method in which the cost of goods sold is calculated from the total cost of inventory units divided by the number of units.
   8. __e__ The cost of merchandise inventory that has been converted from an asset on the balance sheet to an expense on the income statement.

REQUIRED:

Match the letter next to each item on the list with the appropriate definition. Each letter will be used only once.

LO 1: Elements of Cost of Goods Sold

2. Ned Flanders Company began the month of March 2004 with 304 units of product on hand at a total cost of $3,648. During the month, the company purchased an additional 818 units at $30 per unit. Sales for March were 732 units at a total cost of $10,068.

REQUIRED:

From the information provided, complete the following schedule:

		Units	Cost
	Beginning Inventory	___	$___
+	Purchases	___	___
=	Goods Available for Sale	___	___
−	Cost of Goods Sold	___	___
=	Ending Inventory	___	___

LO 1: Elements of Goods Available for Sale

3. Identify the various components of goods available for sale and define each component.

LO 1: Elements of Cost of Goods Sold

4. Kenny H. Company began the month of June 2004 with 150 units of product on hand at a total cost of $3,000. During the month, the company purchased an additional 460 units at $40 per unit. Sales for June were 510 units at a total cost of $17,400.

REQUIRED:

From the information provided, complete the following schedule:

		Units	Cost
	Beginning Inventory	150	$3000
+	Purchases	460	18400
=	Goods Available for Sale	610	21400
−	Ending Inventory	100	4000
=	Cost of Goods Sold	510	17400

LO 1: Elements of Cost of Goods Sold

5. Edward Murdoch Company began the month of April 2004 with 452 units of product on hand at a cost of $54 per unit. During the month, the company purchased an additional 1,500 units at a total cost of $40,500. At the end of April, 616 units were still on hand at a cost of $16,632.

REQUIRED:

From the information provided, complete the following schedule:

		Units	Cost
	Beginning Inventory	452	$24,408
+	Purchases	1500	40,500
=	Goods Available for Sale	1952	64,908
−	Ending Inventory	616	16632
=	Cost of Goods Sold	1336	48,276

LO 1: Elements of Cost of Goods Sold

6. Vaughan and Miles Company began the month of July 2004 with 412 units of product on hand at a cost of $34 per unit. During the month, the company purchased an additional 1,300 units at a total cost of $22,100. At the end of July, 712 units were still on hand at a cost of $12,104.

REQUIRED:

From the information provided, complete the following schedule:

		Units	Cost
	Beginning Inventory	____	$____
+	Purchases	____	____
=	Goods Available for Sale	____	____
−	Ending Inventory	____	____
=	Cost of Goods Sold	____	____

LO 1: Elements of Cost of Goods Sold

7. Celine Corporation began the month of February 2004 with 650 units of product on hand at a total cost of $11,050. During the month, the company purchased an additional 1,884 units at $36 per unit. Sales for February were 1,734 units at $64 per unit. The total cost of the units sold was $30,812, and operating expenses totaled $18,900.

REQUIRED:

a. From the information provided, complete the following schedule:

		Units	Cost
	Beginning Inventory	____	$____
+	Purchases	____	____
=	Goods Available for Sale	____	____
−	Ending Inventory	____	____
=	Cost of Goods Sold	____	____

b. Prepare Corporation's income statement for the month ended February 29, 2004.

LO 1: Elements of Cost of Goods Sold

8. Burton Incorporated began the month of October 2004 with 470 units of product on hand at a total cost of $7,520. During the month, the company purchased an additional 1,244 units at $34 per unit. Sales for October were 1,280 units at $60 per unit. The total cost of the units sold was $21,290, and operating expenses totaled $11,300.

REQUIRED:

a. From the information provided, complete the following schedule:

		Units	Cost
	Beginning Inventory	____	$____
+	Purchases	____	____
=	Goods Available for Sale	____	____
−	Ending Inventory	____	____
=	Cost of Goods Sold	____	____

b. Prepare Burton Incorporated's income statement for the month ended October 31, 2004.

LO 2: Relationship between Cost of Goods Sold and Ending Inventory

9. How do changes in the ending inventory affect the cost of goods sold?

LO 3 & 4: Cost Flow versus Physical Flow of Goods

10. Joan Stone TV Sales and Service began the month of March with two identical TV sets in inventory. During the month, six additional TV sets (identical to the two in beginning inventory) were purchased as follows:

2 on March 9
1 on March 13
3 on March 24

The company sold two of the TV sets on March 12, another one on March 17, and two more on March 28.

REQUIRED:

a. Assuming the company uses a perpetual inventory system and the first-in, first-out cost flow method:
   (1) Which two TV sets were sold on March 12?
   (2) Which one was sold on March 17?
   (3) Which two TV sets were sold on March 28?
   (4) The cost of which three TV sets will be included in the company's inventory at the end of March?
b. If the company uses a perpetual inventory system and the last-in, first-out cost flow method, the cost of which three TV sets will be included in the company's inventory at the end of March?

LO 3 & 4: Cost Flow versus Physical Flow of Goods

11. Pfeiffer's Piano Sales & Service began the month of February with two identical pianos in inventory. During the month, six additional pianos (identical to the two in the beginning inventory) were purchased as follows:

2 on February 10
1 on February 20
3 on February 26

The company sold two of the pianos on February 12, another one on February 17, and two more on February 28.

REQUIRED:

a. Assuming the company uses a perpetual inventory system and the first-in, first-out cost flow method:
   (1) Which two pianos were sold on February 12?
   (2) Which one was sold on February 17?
   (3) Which two pianos were sold on February 28?
   (4) The cost of which three pianos will be included in the company's inventory at the end of February?
b. If the company uses a perpetual inventory system and the last-in, first-out cost flow method, the cost of which three pianos will be included in the company's inventory at the end of February?

LO 4: Inventory Cost

12. Springer Company Ltd. purchased 500 drill presses from Falcon Machinery Company. Each drill press cost $350. The presses are to be sold for $700 each. Springer Company Ltd. paid $1,850 for freight and $260 for insurance while the presses were in transit. Springer Company Ltd. hired two more salespeople for a cost of $4,000 per month.

REQUIRED:

Calculate the cost of the inventory of drill presses to be recorded in the books and records.

LO 4: Inventory Cost

13. Baker Company Ltd. acquired 4,000 hand saws from Snaggletooth Saw Company. Each saw cost $10. The saws are to be sold for $25 each. Baker Company Ltd. paid $750 for freight and $250 for insurance while the saws were in transit. Baker Company Ltd. ran a special newspaper ad costing $800 to advertise the saws.

REQUIRED:

Calculate the cost of the inventory of saws to be recorded in the books and records.

LO 4: Inventory Cost

14. Winter Company Ltd. acquired 10,000 cases of wine from the Sonoma Wine Company. Each case of wine cost $130 and contains 12 bottles. The wine will sell for $20 per bottle. Sonoma Wine Company paid $1,200 for freight and $550 for insurance while the cases were in transit. Winter Company Ltd. ran a special newspaper ad costing $1,800 to advertise the wine.

REQUIRED:

Calculate the cost of the inventory of wine to be recorded in the books and records.

LO 4: Inventory Cost

15. Zeus Grocery Store began operations on July 1. The following transactions took place in the month of July.

  a. Cash purchases of merchandise during July were $500,000.
  b. Purchases of merchandise on account during July were $400,000.
  c. The cost of freight to deliver the merchandise was $25,000.
  d. Warehouse costs including taxes, amortization, and utilities totaled $19,000 for the month.
  e. Zeus Grocery Store returned $22,000 of merchandise purchased in part b to the supplier.
  f. The grocery store manager's salary is $3,000 for the month.

REQUIRED:

Calculate the amount that Zeus Grocery Store should include in the valuation of its merchandise inventory.

LO 4: Inventory Cost

16. Michaelangelo Gift Shop began operations on September 1. The following transactions took place in the month of September.

a. Cash purchases of merchandise during September were $175,000.
b. Purchases of merchandise on account during September were $225,000.
c. The cost of freight to deliver the merchandise was $5,000.
d. Rental expenses including utilities totaled $6,000 for the month.
e. Michaelangelo Gift Shop returned $13,000 worth of merchandise purchased in part b to the supplier.
f. The store manager's salary is $3,000 for the month.
g. Advertising for the month of September totaled $4,000.

REQUIRED:
Calculate the amount that Michaelangelo Gift Shop should include in the valuation of its merchandise inventory.

LO 4, 5, & 6: Periodic Inventory Systems

17. The College Bookstore reported the following information for the year 2004 for sweatshirts with the school logo.

Date	Units	Unit Cost	Total Cost
Inventory on January 2, 2004	1,000	$10	$10,000
Purchases:			
January 15	1,500	11	16,500
March 23	1,200	12	14,400
June 10	1,000	13	13,000
August 18	1,100	10	11,000
December 1	1,400	11	15,400
Total Goods Available for Sale	7,200		$80,300

At the end of the year, a physical count is taken and there are 1,800 sweatshirts left on December 31, 2004.

REQUIRED:
Use the periodic inventory system and determine the ending inventory and the cost of goods sold using:

a. LIFO cost flow method
b. FIFO cost flow method
c. Weighted average cost flow method

LO 4, 5, & 6: Periodic Inventory Systems

18. The College Bookstore reported the following information for the year 2004 for ball caps with the school logo.

Date	Units	Unit Cost	Total Cost
Inventory on January 2, 2004	500	$10	$ 5,000
Purchases:			
January 23	800	11	8,800
March 14	600	12	7,200
July 5	500	12	6,000
August 10	1,100	10	11,000
December 15	1,200	9	10,800
Total Goods Available for Sale	4,700		$48,800

At the end of the year, a physical count is taken and there are 600 ball caps left on December 31, 2004.

REQUIRED:

Use the periodic inventory system and determine the ending inventory and the cost of goods sold using:

a. LIFO cost flow method
b. FIFO cost flow method
c. Weighted average cost flow method

LO 4, 5, & 6: Periodic Inventory Systems

19. Widget Manufacturing Company reported the following information for the year 2004 for widgets :

Date	Units	Unit Cost	Total Cost
Inventory on January 2, 2004	5,000	$10	$ 50,000
Purchases:			
January 23	8,000	12	96,000
March 14	7,000	13	91,000
July 5	6,000	12	72,000
August 10	11,000	10	110,000
December 15	12,000	9	108,000
Total Goods Available for Sale	49,000		$527,000

At the end of the year, a physical count is taken and there are 8,350 widgets left on December 31, 2004.

REQUIRED:

Use the periodic inventory system and determine the ending inventory and the cost of goods sold using:

a. LIFO cost flow method
b. FIFO cost flow method
c. Weighted average cost flow method

LO 4, 5, & 6: Periodic Inventory Systems

20. Powell Jewellery Manufacturing Company purchases silver by the ounce to manufacture fine jewellery. During the month of August, its first month of operations, the company acquired the following:

	Quantity	Cost per Ounce	Total Cost
August 1	50 ounces	$35.00	$1,750
August 8	25 ounces	40.00	1,000
August 19	30 ounces	42.00	1,260
August 22	10 ounces	43.00	430
August 30	20 ounces	45.00	900
Total Goods Available for Sale	135 ounces		$5,340

The company's inventory at the end of August is 27 ounces of silver. Assume a periodic system of inventory.

REQUIRED:

Compute the cost of the inventory at August 31 and the cost of goods sold for the month of August under each of the following cost flow assumptions:

a. FIFO
b. LIFO
c. Weighted average

LO 4, 5, & 6: Periodic Inventory Systems

21. The Reo Rock Company purchases rock by the tonne to sell to homebuilders. During the month of June, its first month of operations, The Reo Rock Company purchased the following:

	Quantity (tonnes)	Cost per Tonne	Total Cost
June 1	700	$100	$ 70,000
June 6	250	140	35,000
June 17	300	125	37,500
June 24	150	130	19,500
June 30	200	145	29,000
Total Goods Available for Sale	1,600		$191,000

The Reo Rock Company's inventory at the end of June is 230 tonnes of rock. Assume a periodic system of inventory.

REQUIRED:

Compute the cost of the inventory at June 30 and the cost of goods sold for the month of June under each of the following cost flow assumptions:

a. FIFO
b. LIFO
c. Weighted average

LO 4, 5, & 6: Perpetual Inventory Systems

22. Widget Manufacturing Company reported the following information for the year 2004 for widgets:

Date	Units	Unit Cost	Total Cost
Inventory on January 2, 2004	5,000	$10	$ 50,000
Purchases:			
January 23	8,000	12	96,000
March 14	7,000	13	91,000
July 5	6,000	12	72,000
August 10	11,000	10	110,000
December 15	12,000	9	108,000
Total Goods Available for Sale	49,000		$527,000

Sales of widgets occurred in the following manner:

January 28	6,000 units
February 15	3,000 units
July 6	15,000 units
August 12	10,000 units
December 24	6,650 units

At the end of the year a physical count is taken and there are 8,350 widgets left on December 31, 2004.

REQUIRED:

Use the perpetual inventory system and determine the ending inventory and the cost of goods sold using:

a. LIFO cost flow method
b. FIFO cost flow method
c. Average cost flow method

LO 4, 5, & 6: Perpetual Inventory Systems

23. Powell Silver Distribution distributes silver by the ounce, selling to manufacturers of fine jewellery. During the month of August, its first month of operations, the company had the following transactions:

		Purchases (ounces)	Cost per Ounce	Total Costs
August 1		50	$35	$1,750
August 3	Sold 40 ounces			
August 8		25	40	1,000
August 11	Sold 20 ounces			
August 19		30	42	1,260
August 20	Sold 18 ounces			
August 22		10	43	430
August 29	Sold 30 ounces			
August 30		20	45	900
Total Goods Available for Sale		135		$5,340

The company's inventory at the end of August is 27 ounces of silver. Assume a perpetual system of inventory.

REQUIRED:

Compute the cost of the inventory at August 31 and the cost of goods sold for the month of August under each of the following cost flow assumptions:

a. FIFO
b. LIFO
c. Moving average

LO 4, 5, & 6: Perpetual Inventory Systems

24. The Reo Rock Company purchases rock by the tonne to sell to homebuilders. During the month of June, its first month of operations, The Reo Rock Company engaged in the following transactions:

		Purchases (tonnes)	Cost per Tonne	Total Costs
June 1		700	$100	$70,000
June 3	Sold 400 tonnes			
June 6		250	140	35,000
June 17		300	125	37,500
June 20	Sold 400 tonnes			
June 24		150	130	19,500
June 26	Sold 570 tonnes			
June 30		200	145	29,000
Total Goods Available for Sale		1,600		$191,000

The company's inventory at the end of June is 230 tonnes of rock. Assume a perpetual system of inventory.

REQUIRED:

Compute the cost of the inventory at June 30 and the cost of goods sold for the month of June under each of the following cost flow assumptions:

a. FIFO
b. LIFO
c. Moving average

LO 5 & 6:   Comparison of Cost Flow Assumptions

25. Cox Company buys and then resells a single product as its primary business activity. This product is called the Whatzit and is subject to rather severe cost fluctuations. Following is information concerning Cox Company's inventory activity for the Whatzit product during the month of July 2004:

July 1:	431 units on hand, $3,017
July 2:	Sold 220 units
July 9:	Purchased 500 units for $11 per unit
July 12:	Purchased 200 units for $9 per unit
July 16:	Sold 300 units
July 21:	Purchased 150 units for $6 per unit
July 24:	Purchased 50 units for $8 per unit
July 29:	Sold 500 units

REQUIRED:

Assuming Cox Company employs a perpetual inventory system, calculate cost of goods sold (units and cost) for the month of July 2004 and ending inventory (units and cost) at July 31, 2004, using the following:

a. FIFO cost flow assumption
b. LIFO cost flow assumption
c. Moving average cost flow assumption (round all unit cost calculations to the nearest cent)
d. Which of the three methods resulted in the highest cost of goods sold for July? Which one will provide the highest ending inventory value for Cox Company's balance sheet?
e. How would the differences among the three methods affect Cox Company's income statement and balance sheet for the month?

LO 5 & 6:   Comparison of Cost Flow Assumptions

26. Naifeh Company buys and then resells a single product as its primary business activity. Following is information concerning Naifeh Company's inventory activity for the product during October 2004:

October 1:	216 units on hand at $4 per unit
October 5:	Sold 80 units
October 7:	Purchased 150 units for $7 per unit
October 11:	Purchased 100 units for $11 per unit
October 15:	Sold 200 units
October 21:	Purchased 300 units for $13 per unit
October 25:	Purchased 50 units for $18 per unit
October 29:	Sold 350 units

REQUIRED:

a. Assuming Naifeh Company employs a perpetual inventory system, calculate cost of goods sold (units and cost) for the month of October using the following:
   (1) FIFO cost flow assumption
   (2) LIFO cost flow assumption
   (3) Moving average cost flow assumption (round all unit cost calculations to the nearest cent)

b. Which of the three methods resulted in the highest cost of goods sold for October? Which one will provide the highest ending inventory value for Naifeh Company's balance sheet?

c. How would the differences among the three methods affect Naifeh Company's income statement and balance sheet for the month?

LO 5 & 6:   Comparison of Cost Flow Assumptions

27. Harris Company buys and then resells a single product as its primary business activity. Following is information concerning Harris Company's inventory activity for the product during August 2004:

August 1:	216 units on hand at $18 per unit
August 5:	Sold 80 units
August 7:	Purchased 150 units for $13 per unit
August 11:	Purchased 100 units for $11 per unit
August 15:	Sold 200 units
August 21:	Purchased 300 units for $7 per unit
August 25:	Purchased 50 units for $4 per unit
August 29:	Sold 350 units

REQUIRED:

a. Assuming Harris Company employs a perpetual inventory system, calculate cost of goods sold (units and cost) for the month of August using the following:
   (1) FIFO cost flow assumption
   (2) LIFO cost flow assumption
   (3) Moving average cost flow assumption (round all unit cost calculations to the nearest cent)

b. Which of the three methods resulted in the highest inventory amount for Harris Company's August 31 balance sheet?

c. How would the differences among the three methods affect Harris Company's income statement and balance sheet for the month?

LO 5 & 6:   Comparison of Cost Flow Assumptions

28. Lee Company buys and then resells a single product as its primary business activity. Following is information concerning Lee Company's inventory activity for the product during the month of July 2004:

July 1:	216 units on hand at $4 per unit
July 5:	Sold 80 units
July 7:	Purchased 150 units for $4 per unit
July 11:	Purchased 100 units for $4 per unit
July 15:	Sold 200 units
July 21:	Purchased 300 units for $4 per unit
July 25:	Purchased 50 units for $4 per unit
July 29:	Sold 350 units

REQUIRED:

a. Assuming Lee Company employs a perpetual inventory system, calculate cost of goods sold (units and cost) for the month of July, using the following:
  (1) First-in, first-out method
  (2) Last-in, first-out method
  (3) Moving average cost flow assumption (round all unit cost calculations to the nearest cent)
b. Which of the three methods resulted in the highest cost of goods sold for July?
c. Describe the differences among income statements and balance sheets prepared under the three cost flow assumptions.

LO 5 & 6: Impact of Errors on Financial Statements

29. Rugby Company's records reported the following at the end of the fiscal year:

Beginning Inventory	$ 25,000
Ending Inventory	35,000
Cost of Goods Sold	128,000

The staff completed a physical inventory count and found that the inventory was actually $39,500.

REQUIRED:
Determine the impact of the inventory error on each of the financial statements.

LO 5 & 6: Impact of Errors on Financial Statements

30. Owens Company's records reported the following at the end of the fiscal year:

Beginning Inventory	$ 80,000
Ending Inventory	75,000
Cost of Goods Sold	280,000

The staff completed a physical inventory count and found that the inventory was actually $68,000.

REQUIRED:
Determine the impact of the inventory error on each of the financial statements.

LO 5 & 6: Impact of Errors on Financial Statements

31. Corning Company's records reported the following at the end of the fiscal year:

Beginning Inventory	$190,000
Ending Inventory	160,000
Cost of Goods Sold	495,000

The staff completed a physical inventory count and found that the inventory was actually $168,000.

REQUIRED:
Determine the impact of the inventory error on each of the financial statements.

Comprehensive

32. Blades Company and Behar Company both began their operations on January 2, 2004. Both companies experienced exactly the same reality during 2004: They purchased exactly the same number of units of merchandise inventory during the year at exactly the same cost, and they sold exactly the same number of inventory units at exactly the same selling price during the year. They also purchased exactly the same type and amount of long-lived assets and paid exactly the same amount for those purchases.

At the end of 2004, the two companies prepared income statements for the year. Blades Company reported net income of $92,000, and Behar Company reported net income of $55,000.

REQUIRED:

List and discuss all items you can think of that might have caused the reported net income for the two companies to be different. (Note: Do not restrict yourself to items covered in Chapter 8.)

Comprehensive

33. Rush Corporation is a merchandiser. The company uses a perpetual inventory system, so both the physical count of inventory units and the cost classification (asset or expense) are updated when a transaction involves inventory. The company's accounting records yielded the following schedule for October 2004:

		Units	Cost
	Beginning Inventory, October 1	200	$ 600
+	Purchases during October	1,700	5,100
=	Goods Available for Sale	1,900	$5,700
−	Cost of Goods Sold	1,500	4,500
=	Ending Inventory, October 31	400	$1,200

On October 31, 2004, Rush Corporation conducted a physical count of its inventory and discovered there were only 375 units of inventory actually on hand.

REQUIRED:

a. Show Rush Corporation's schedule of cost of goods sold and ending inventory as it should be to reflect the results of the physical inventory count on October 31.

b. Explain in your own words how the company's income statement and balance sheet will be affected by the results of the physical inventory count on October 31.

c. What are some possible causes of the difference between the inventory amounts in Rush Corporation's accounting records and the inventory amounts from the physical count?

LO 7: Freight Terms and Cash Discounts

*34. Fallwell Company made the following purchases from Grode Company in August of the current year:

Aug. 2   Purchased $5,000 of merchandise, terms 1/10, n/30, FOB shipping point. The goods were received on August 8.

Aug. 5   Purchased $2,000 of merchandise, terms 2/10, n/45, FOB shipping point. The goods were received on August 15.

Aug. 10   Purchased $4,000 of merchandise, terms 3/10, n/15, FOB destination. The goods were received on August 18.

_____

*Refers to material in this chapter's appendix.

REQUIRED:

For each of the purchases listed, answer the following questions.

a. When is the payment due assuming the company takes advantage of the discount?

b. When is the payment due if the company does not take advantage of the discount?

c. What is the amount of the cash discount allowed?

d. Assume the freight charges are $250 on each purchase. Which company is responsible for the freight charges?

e. What is the total amount of inventory costs for the month of August assuming that all discounts were taken?

LO 7: Freight Terms and Cash Discounts

*35. Gruber Company made the following purchases from Belte Company in May of the current year:

May 2   Purchased $3,000 worth of merchandise, terms 2/10, n/30, FOB destination point. The goods were received on May 10.

May 10   Purchased $2,800 worth of merchandise, terms 2/10, n/60, FOB shipping point. The goods were received on May 19.

May 20   Purchased $6,000 worth of merchandise, terms 3/10, n/20, FOB destination. The goods were received on May 23.

REQUIRED:

For each of the purchases listed, answer the following questions.

a. When is the payment due assuming the company takes advantage of the discount?

b. When is the payment due if the company does not take advantage of the discount?

c. What is the amount of the cash discount allowed?

d. Assume the freight charges are $400 on each purchase. Which company is responsible for the freight charges?

e. What is the total amount of inventory costs for the month of May assuming that all discounts were taken?

LO 7: Freight Terms and Cash Discounts

*36. Payne Company made the following purchases from Ritz Company in July of the current year:

July 3   Purchased $7,000 worth of merchandise, terms 2/10, n/15, FOB shipping point. The goods were received on July 9.

July 7   Purchased $1,700 worth of merchandise, terms 1/10, n/60, FOB shipping point. The goods were received on July 17.

July 20   Purchased $9,000 worth of merchandise, terms 4/10, n/10, FOB destination. The goods were received on July 23.

REQUIRED:

For each of the purchases listed, answer the following questions.

a. When is the payment due assuming the company takes advantage of the discount?

b. When is the payment due if the company does not take advantage of the discount?

c. What is the amount of the cash discount allowed?

d. Assume the freight charges are $400 on each purchase. Which company is responsible for the freight charges?

e. What is the total amount of inventory costs for the month of July assuming that all discounts were taken?

LO 7: Recording Purchase, Purchase Discounts, and Freight Costs

*37. Fallwell Company made the following purchases from Grode Company in August of the current year:

Aug. 2   Purchased $5,000 worth of merchandise, terms 1/10, n/30, FOB shipping point. The goods were received on August 8.

Aug. 5   Purchased $2,000 worth of merchandise, terms 2/10, n/45, FOB shipping point. The goods were received on August 15.

Aug. 10   Purchased $4,000 worth of merchandise, terms 3/10, n/15, FOB destination. The goods were received on August 18.

REQUIRED:

a. For each of the purchases listed, prepare the journal entries to record the purchase assuming the discount is taken.

b. For each of the purchases listed, prepare the journal entries to record the purchase and the freight charge assuming the discount is not taken. Assume the freight charges are $250 on each purchase.

LO 7: Recording Purchase, Purchase Discounts, and Freight Costs

*38. Gruber Company made the following purchases from Belte Company in May of the current year:

May 2   Purchased $3,000 worth of merchandise, terms 2/10, n/30, FOB destination point. The goods were received on May 10. Paid freight charges of $200 when the goods were received.

May 10   Purchased $2,800 worth of merchandise, terms 2/10, n/60, FOB shipping point. The goods were received on May 19.

May 20   Purchased $6,000 worth of merchandise, terms 3/10, n/20, FOB destination. The goods were received on May 23. Paid freight charges of $100 upon receipt of the goods.

REQUIRED:

a. For each of the purchases listed, prepare the journal entries to record the purchase and the freight charge assuming the discount is taken.

b. For each of the purchases listed, prepare the journal entries to record the purchase and the freight charge assuming the discount is not taken.

LO 7: Recording Purchase, Purchase Discounts, and Freight Costs

*39. Payne Company made the following purchases from Ritz Company in July of the current year:

July 3   Purchased $7,000 worth of merchandise, terms 2/10, n/15, FOB shipping point. The goods were received on July 9.

July 7   Purchased $1,700 worth of merchandise, terms 1/10, n/60, FOB shipping point. The goods were received on July 17.

July 20   Purchased $9,000 worth of merchandise, terms 4/10, n/10, FOB destination. The goods were received on July 23. Paid freight charges of $50 upon receipt of the goods.

REQUIRED:
a. For each of the purchases listed, prepare the journal entries to record the purchase and the freight charge assuming the discount is taken.
b. For each of the purchases listed, prepare the journal entries to record the purchase and the freight charge assuming the discount is not taken.

LO 8: Preparation of Journal Entries for a Perpetual Inventory System

*40. Edwards Company has a beginning inventory of $50,000 and completes the following transactions during the month.

2004

June 1   Purchased 1,000 radios for cash from Barrow Company at a cost of $20 per unit, terms 2/10, n/30.

June 3   Purchased 2,500 clocks on account from Adams Company at a cost of $10 per unit, terms 1/10, n/30.

June 6   Purchased 3,000 clocks on account from Adams Company at a cost of $10 per unit, terms 1/10, n/30.

June 12   Paid for the units purchased in the June 3 transaction.

June 17   Paid for the units purchased in the June 6 transaction.

June 25   Paid cash for office supplies costing $2,000.

June 26   Purchased on account a piece of office furniture costing $800.

REQUIRED:
Prepare the general journal entries to record the transactions using the perpetual inventory method.

LO 8: Preparation of Journal Entries for a Periodic Inventory System

*41. Edwards Company has a beginning inventory of $50,000 and completes the following transactions during the month.

2004

June 1   Purchased 1,000 radios for cash from Barrow Company at a cost of $20 per unit, terms 2/10, n/30.

June 3   Purchased 2,500 clocks on account from Adams Company at a cost of $10 per unit, terms 1/10, n/30.

June 6   Purchased 3,000 clocks on account from Adams Company at a cost of $10 per unit, terms 1/10, n/30.

June 12   Paid for the units purchased in the June 3 transaction.

June 17   Paid for the units purchased in the June 6 transaction.

June 25   Paid cash for office supplies costing $2,000.

June 26   Purchased on account a piece of office furniture costing $800.

REQUIRED:
Prepare the general journal entries to record the transactions using the periodic inventory method.

LO 8: Entries to Record Ending Inventory—Perpetual Method

*42. Refer to Problem 29. Assume that at the end of the period the inventory is $45,000.

REQUIRED:

Prepare the entry necessary to adjust the ending inventory to the proper balance.

LO 8: Entries to Record Ending Inventory—Periodic Method

*43. Refer to Problem 30. Assume that at the end of the period the inventory is $45,000.

REQUIRED:

Prepare the entries necessary to close the beginning inventory and to create the ending inventory.

LO 8: Entries for a Perpetual Inventory System

*44. Sosa Company maintains a perpetual inventory system. It accepts all purchases FOB destination and returns merchandise at the supplier's expense. The following items represent a summary of the data from the records for April 2004, the first month of operation.

Purchases on account	$490,000
Purchases for cash	160,000
Purchase returns of merchandise for credit	50,000
Cash operating expenses	100,000
Sales on account	850,000
Cash sales	200,000
Cost of goods sold per inventory records	525,000

REQUIRED:

a. Prepare journal entries dated April 30, 2004, to record the purchases, purchase returns, sales, and operating expenses.
b. Prepare the appropriate closing entries.

LO 8: Entries for a Periodic Inventory System

*45. Sosa Company maintains a periodic inventory system. It accepts all purchases FOB destination and returns merchandise at the supplier's expense. The following items represent a summary of the data from the records for April 2004, the first month of operation.

Purchases on account	$490,000
Purchases for cash	160,000
Purchase returns of merchandise for credit	50,000
Cash operating expenses	100,000
Sales on account	850,000
Cash sales	200,000
Inventory per physical count on April 30	75,000

REQUIRED:

a. Prepare journal entries dated April 30, 2004, to record the purchases, purchase returns, sales, and operating expenses.
b. Prepare the appropriate closing entries.

LO 8: Entries for a Perpetual Inventory System

*46. Alou Company maintains a perpetual inventory system. It accepts all purchases FOB destination and returns merchandise at the supplier's expense. The following items represent a summary of the data from the records for July 2004.

Beginning inventory	$ 85,000
Purchases on account	355,000
Purchases for cash	280,000
Purchase returns of merchandise for credit	80,000
Cash operating expenses	125,000
Sales on account	642,000
Cash sales	258,000
Cost of goods sold per inventory records	475,000

REQUIRED:

a. Prepare journal entries dated July 31, 2004, to record the purchases, purchase returns, sales, and operating expenses.

b. Prepare the appropriate closing entries.

LO 8: Entries for a Periodic Inventory System

*47. Alou Company maintains a periodic inventory system. It accepts all purchases FOB destination and returns merchandise at the supplier's expense. The following items represent a summary of the data from the records for July 2004.

Beginning inventory	$ 85,000
Purchases on account	355,000
Purchases for cash	280,000
Purchase returns of merchandise for credit	80,000
Cash operating expenses	125,000
Sales on account	642,000
Cash sales	258,000
Inventory per physical count on July 31	165,000

REQUIRED:

a. Prepare journal entries dated July 31, 2004, to record the purchase, purchase returns, sales, and operating expenses.

b. Prepare the appropriate closing entries.

LO 8: Entries for a Perpetual Inventory System

*48. Rose Company maintains a perpetual inventory system. It accepts all purchases FOB destination and returns merchandise at the supplier's expense. The following items represent a summary of the data from the records for August 2004.

Beginning inventory	$ 37,000
Purchases on account	126,000
Purchases for cash	138,000
Purchase returns of merchandise for credit	30,000
Cash operating expenses	103,000
Sales on account	321,000
Cash sales	258,000
Cost of goods sold per inventory records	129,000

REQUIRED:

a. Prepare journal entries dated August 31, 2004, to record the purchases, purchase returns, sales, and operating expenses.
b. Prepare the appropriate closing entries.

LO 8: Entries for a Periodic Inventory System

*49. The Morgan Company maintains a periodic inventory system. It accepts all purchases FOB destination and returns merchandise at the supplier's expense. The following items represent a summary of the data from the records for September 2004.

Beginning inventory	$ 25,000
Purchases on account	133,000
Purchases for cash	120,000
Purchase returns of merchandise for credit	20,000
Cash operating expenses	195,000
Cash sales	236,000
Inventory per physical count on September 30	75,000

REQUIRED:

a. Prepare journal entries dated September 30, 2004, to record the purchases, purchase returns, sales, and operating expenses.
b. Prepare the appropriate closing entries.

LO 8: Adjusting Entries for Errors in Inventory Systems

*50. The Sweiss Company manufactures a product for the computer industry. At the end of the first year of operations, the company reported the following information under the perpetual inventory method.

Beginning Inventory	$ 0
Cost of Goods Sold	295,000
Ending Inventory	88,000

The company determined that the ending inventory was in error and was actually $95,000.

REQUIRED:

a. Prepare the journal entry or entries necessary to correct this discovery.
b. Assume the company uses a periodic system of inventory, and prepare the necessary journal entry or entries to correct this discovery.

LO 8: Adjusting Entries for Errors in Inventory Systems

*51. The Pippen Company manufactures a product for the automotive industry. At the end of the first year of operations, the company reported the following information under the perpetual inventory method.

Beginning Inventory	$ 0
Cost of Goods Sold	880,000
Ending Inventory	165,000

The company determined that the ending inventory was in error and was actually $148,000.

REQUIRED:

a. Prepare the journal entry or entries necessary to correct this discovery.

b. Assume the company uses a periodic system of inventory, and prepare the necessary journal entry or entries to correct this discovery.

LO 8: Adjusting Entries for Errors in Inventory Systems

*52. The Dowers Company manufactures seats for the aircraft industry. At the end of the first year of operations, the company reported the following information under the perpetual inventory method.

Beginning Inventory	$ 0
Cost of Goods Sold	996,000
Ending Inventory	287,000

The company determined that the ending inventory was in error and was actually $298,000.

REQUIRED:

a. Prepare the journal entry or entries necessary to correct this discovery.

b. Assume the company uses a periodic system of inventory, and prepare the necessary journal entry or entries to correct this discovery.

ANNUAL REPORT PROJECT

*53. You may now complete Section IV of the project. For inventories you should do the following:

a. List the different inventories of your firm, assuming that your firm has inventories.

b. Identify the method or methods used by your company to value the inventories.

c. List the total dollar value of inventory for each balance sheet presented in your company's annual report.

d. Compute the percentage of inventories to total assets for each year of your annual report's balance sheets.

e. Does your company's inventories appear to be growing as a percentage of total assets?

f. List the Cost of Goods Sold and the Gross Margin or Gross Profit for your company for each income statement appearing in the annual report.

g. Calculate the percentage of Cost of Goods Sold to Net Sales and the percentage of Gross Margin or Gross Profit to Net Sales for each period presented.

h. Does it appear that the Cost of Goods Sold and Gross Margin or Gross Profit percentages have remained relatively stable for the income statements appearing in the report? If not, describe the changes.

REQUIRED:

Complete Section IV of your report. Make a copy for your instructor and keep a copy for your final report.

9

The Balance Sheet and Income Statement: A Closer Look

*Y*our brother-in-law, the one you like, just sent you an annual report of a company that he believes will be the next Microsoft in terms of growth and market domination. He wants you to consider getting in on the ground floor and knows that you have a little money set aside that you might want to invest. Although you have only seen a few annual reports, none seemed this complex. The balance sheet contains a lot of "intangible" assets. If these assets are not tangible, what are they, thin air? The income statement has numerous items after operating income. Should you really care about those figures? To top it off, the earnings per share are calculated two ways. Which one of them is the right one to use to compute a basic market price? The highest is only $0.45 a share, and your brother-in-law wants you to pay $12 per share! That is almost 27 times the annual income per share, if you are looking at the right one. Maybe this brother-in-law is a real turkey, just like the other three.

Balance sheets and income statements are generally more complex than the ones we have explored so far. An understanding of the organization of these two financial statements is crucial, particularly when very detailed information is included. Even complex balance sheets and income statements are organized in a manner that serves to clarify rather than complicate the information provided.

In this chapter, to help you to better comprehend the information provided by them, we will explore in further detail the organization of the balance sheet and income statement. After all, the primary purpose of these and other financial statements is to provide information useful to economic decision makers. In addition, understanding the construction of the income statement and balance sheet is necessary to do financial statement analysis, which we will discuss in Chapter 11. ■

After completing your work on this chapter, you should be able to do the following:

1. Describe how the balance sheet and income statement were developed as financial statements.
2. Explain the organization and purpose of the classified balance sheet.
3. Explain why recurring and nonrecurring items are presented separately on the income statement.
4. Interpret the net of tax disclosure of extraordinary items and discontinued business operations.
5. Calculate earnings per share and properly disclose it on the income statement.
6. Describe the additional information provided by comparative financial statements.
*7. Complete the recording process for income taxes.

HISTORY AND DEVELOPMENT OF THE BALANCE SHEET AND INCOME STATEMENT

Ever since human beings began living in organized societies, they have kept track of their business affairs by accounting for economic events and transactions, recording them on stone or clay tablets, papyrus, paper, or whatever writing material was available.

Originally, accounting records were kept to assist in conducting a company's operation rather than to report on the operation of a company. Amounts owed to suppliers, for example, were recorded primarily so a company could keep track of what had and had not been paid, without regard for balance sheet presentation. Eventually, however, record keeping began for the specific purpose of preparing financial statements. In *A History of Accounting Thought*, Michael Chatfield describes this transition as follows:

> More than most accounting tools, financial statements are the result of cumulative historical influences. Before the Industrial Revolution they were usually prepared as arithmetic checks of ledger balances. Afterward the roles were reversed and it was account books which were reorganized to facilitate statement preparation. As statements became communication devices rather than simple bookkeeping summaries, the journal and ledger evolved from narratives to tabulations of figures from which balances could easily be taken.[1]

Financial statements as we know them are a relatively recent phenomenon. While accounting has been with us since about 5000 B.C., the balance sheet's function as a financial statement only emerged during the Renaissance, around A.D. 1600. For the next several hundred years, the balance sheet was the primary output of the accounting process. Accountants developed the income statement in the late 1800s, but did not consider the information nearly as important as the balance sheet figures. In his landmark work, *Accounting Evolution to 1900*, A. C. Littleton makes the following observation:

---

[1] Michael Chatfield, *A History of Accounting Thought* (Huntington, NY: R. E. Kriger Publishing Co., 1974), 164.

... it seems that the primary motive for separate financial statements was to obtain information regarding capital; this was the center of the interest of partners, shareholders, lenders, and the basis of the calculation of early property taxes. Thus balance-sheet data were stressed and refined in various ways, while expense and income data were incidental—in fact, the latter in the seventeenth century were presented merely as a "proof of estate"—to demonstrate by another route the correctness of the balance sheet.[2]

At the beginning of the 20th century, banks served as the chief form of external financing to Canadian companies. For this reason, creditors were the primary audience for whom financial statements were prepared. Creditors looked at a company's ability to repay its debts and at the balance sheet—which focuses on the relationships among assets, liabilities, and owners' equity—to assure themselves.

During the first two decades of the 20th century, Canadian companies changed the methods of financing expansion. Relying less on debt financing and more on equity financing, companies began to borrow less from banks and issue more shares in order to raise capital. When selling shares became the major source of external financing, shareholders became the primary users of financial statements. Shareholders were interested in the performance of the company and its impact on dividend payments and the value of the company's shares. Shareholders focused on net income, so the income statement came to be considered more important than the balance sheet. Over time even long-term creditors realized that earning power was crucial to debt repayment, so they also began to rely more on the income statement than on the balance sheet.

By the 1930s, it became apparent that the balance sheet and the income statement are best used together. Neither is more important than the other because each provides valuable information for economic decision makers. By learning more about the detailed structure of the balance sheet and income statement, you can make the best use of the information provided by each statement.

ORGANIZATION OF THE BALANCE SHEET

In introducing the balance sheet in Chapter 3, we used this simple equation:

$$\text{Assets} = \text{Liabilities} + \text{Owners' Equity}$$

The equation does not distinguish one asset from another or one liability from another. A balance sheet prepared for Eliason and Company Ltd. at December 31, 2003, using the basic format, would look like Exhibit 9–1.

This balance sheet gives economic decision makers little useful information about the financial position of Eliason and Company Ltd. at December 31, 2004. Even if the company uses the cash basis of accounting (meaning the $1,516,800 of assets is cash), we see no indication of how soon the $851,000 of liabilities must be paid or how much of the $665,800 of shareholders' equity represents contributed capital and how much represents retained earnings.

Why does any of this matter and what difference does it make to those who use the balance sheet? The answer is obvious if you remember that economic decision makers are attempting to predict the future and timing of cash flows by looking at the balance sheet. Accountants developed a more detailed balance sheet in response to users' need for additional information.

---

[2]A. C. Littleton, *Accounting Evolution to 1900* (New York: Russell & Russell, 1966), 153.

Exhibit 9–1
Basic Format
Balance Sheet

ELIASON AND COMPANY LTD.
Balance Sheet
December 31, 2004

Total Assets	$1,516,800
Liabilities	$851,000
Shareholders' Equity	665,800
Total Liabilities and Shareholders' Equity	$1,516,800

The Classified Balance Sheet

classified balance sheet
A balance sheet showing assets and liabilities categorized into current and long-term items.

A **classified balance sheet** prepared from the same accounting data as Exhibit 9–1 for Eliason and Company Ltd. at December 31, 2004, would look like Exhibit 9–2. Notice that the assets still total $1,516,800; total liabilities are still $851,000; and shareholders' equity is still $665,800. The only difference in the two balance sheet presentations is the amount of detail disclosed.

As we explain why the classified balance sheet is organized as it is, we will refer to the Eliason and Company Ltd. classified balance sheet in Exhibit 9–2.

 Discussion Question

9–1. Which of the two balance sheet presentations for Eliason and Company Ltd. do you think would be more useful in predicting the future and timing of the company's cash flow? Provide three specific examples to support your position.

---

current assets Assets that are either cash or will become cash within one year.

operating cycle The length of time it takes for an entity to complete one revenue-producing cycle from purchase of goods to collection of cash.

The accrual accounting basis of measurement creates a need to segregate, or classify, assets on the balance sheet because, under this basis, items besides cash are considered assets. Two classifications of assets are identified on Eliason and Company Ltd.'s balance sheet: current and long-term. **Current assets** are defined as assets that either are cash already or are expected to become cash within one year or one operating cycle, whichever is longer. An **operating cycle** is the length of time it takes for an entity to complete one revenue-producing cycle. For a manufacturer, a revenue cycle is the length of time from receiving raw materials, including producing and selling the final product, to collecting cash from its customers. For a merchandiser, the operating cycle is the time it takes from receiving merchandise to collecting the cash from its customers. Most businesses have several operating cycles in one year. Some businesses, such as wineries, timber operations, or long-term construction companies, have operating cycles that last as long as five years or more. As you can see from Exhibit 9–2, accounts receivable and inventory are examples of current assets.

long-term assets Assets that are expected to benefit the company for longer than one year.

Long-term assets are defined as those assets that are expected to benefit the organization more than one year or that are not anticipated to become cash within one year. Amortizable assets such as buildings, equipment, and vehicles are examples of long-term assets. Because of the way the classified balance sheet is organized, users can tell at a quick glance just which assets (and their dollar amount) the company thinks will be turned into cash within the next year (current assets) and which ones are not expected to be converted into cash (long-term assets). The major types of long term assets are property, plant, and equipment (long-lived assets).

Exhibit 9–2
Classified Balance
Sheet

ELIASON AND COMPANY LTD.
Balance Sheet
December 31, 2004

ASSETS:

Current Assets:

Cash			$ 100
Accounts Receivable			251,000
Inventory			298,900
Prepaid Expenses			50,000
Total Current Assets			$ 600,000
Property, Plant, and Equipment			
Land		$125,000	
Plant and Equipment	$1,075,000		
Less: Accumulated Amortization	(283,200)		
Plant and Equipment, Net		791,800	
Total Property, Plant, and Equipment			916,800
Total Assets			$1,516,800

LIABILITIES:

Current Liabilities:		
Accounts Payable		$ 501,000
Short-Term Note Payable		50,000
Total Current Liabilities		$ 551,000
Long-Term Liabilities:		
Bonds Payable		300,000
Total Liabilities		$ 851,000

SHAREHOLDERS' EQUITY:

Common Shares, Authorized Unlimited	
10,000 Shares Issued and Outstanding	$400,000
Retained Earnings	265,800
Total Shareholders' Equity	665,800
Total Liabilities and Shareholders' Equity	$1,516,800

liquidity An item's nearness
to cash.

Assets are listed on a classified balance sheet in order of decreasing liquidity. **Liquidity** means nearness to cash. Notice that we always list cash first on the balance sheet because by definition it is the most liquid asset. The farther down you read the asset section of a classified balance sheet, the less likelihood there is that an item will be converted to cash in the near future. In the case of Eliason and Company Ltd., current assets total $600,000 and long-term assets consisting of property, plant, and equipment total $916,800.

 Discussion Questions

9–2. Are there any items listed as current assets on Eliason and Company Ltd.'s December 31, 2004, classified balance sheet (Exhibit 9–2) that you think will never be converted into cash? If there are, why do you think they are classified as current assets?

9–3. Eliason and Company Ltd. has classified plant and equipment as long-term assets in 2004. Does this mean the company cannot sell one of its buildings in 2005? Explain your reasoning.

There are various types of long-term assets: property, plant, and equipment, natural resources, intangibles, goodwill, and investments. As plant and equipment are used, we amortize the cost over the useful life of these assets. Natural resources are typically depleted (amortized) on the basis of production as a proportion of the total amount of the natural resource.

Intangible assets are assets with no physical substance; they consist of contractual rights such as patents, copyrights, trademarks, and purchased goodwill. Goodwill is the "extra" amount paid for a company above the market value of its underlying assets less liabilities. Commencing January 2002, if intangible assets do not have a defined economic life, their cost is not amortized. For example, suppose a television station has obtained a broadcast licence that expires in five years. If the station can renew the licence easily and has every intention of renewing the licence indefinitely, the licence is considered to have an indefinite life and would not be amortized. The carrying value, or value on the balance sheet, of the licence would be reviewed annually to determine if there was a need to write it down. As of January 2002, goodwill is not amortized. Instead, its market value is reviewed each year. If the market value falls below the carrying value, the goodwill is written down to market value.

Investments represent the cost paid to acquire shares or bonds issued by other companies. These would be shown as long-term if the intent of management was to hold the investments for more than one year.

intangible assets Assets consisting of contractual rights such as patents, copyrights, and trademarks.

investments Assets that represent long-term ownership in subsidiaries, or the shares or bonds of other companies.

Discussion Questions

9-4. Do intangibles such as copyrights, patents, and trademarks have value? Do companies try to protect the value of such intangibles?

9-5. How would you determine the economic life of an intangible?

When we classify liabilities in liquidity order, we look at how quickly they must be settled. If settlement involves cash, liquidity represents the order of payment. If settlement requires performance, such as delivery of goods or services, liquidity refers to how soon performance is required. Liquidity and priority of claims require that liabilities be listed on the balance sheet before shareholders' equity: If a company goes out of business, obligations to creditors must be paid before funds can be distributed to the owners.

Current liabilities require settlement within one year. Certainly, the suppliers to whom Eliason and Company Ltd. owes a total of $501,000 (accounts payable) expect repayment within the year, usually within 30 to 60 days. Eliason and Company Ltd. classifies debts not requiring settlement within the next year as **long-term liabilities.** Because of the way the balance sheet is organized, users know at a glance which liabilities are expected to be retired within the next year (current liabilities) and which ones are not (long-term liabilities). This enables them to assess future cash flows. Eliason and Company Ltd.'s current liabilities total $551,000 and long-term liabilities total $300,000.

Exhibit 9–3 illustrates the current and long-term classifications of assets and liabilities.

current liabilities
Liabilities that must be settled within one year.

long-term liabilities
Amounts that are not due for settlement until at least one year from now.

Exhibit 9–3
Examples of Current
and Long-Term Assets
and Liabilities

Assets		**Liabilities**	
Current	**Long-Term**	**Current**	**Long-Term**
• Cash	• Property, Plant, and	• Accounts	• Notes Payable
• Marketable	Equipment	Payable	• Bonds Payable
Securities	• Intangibles	• Short-Term	• Mortgages
• Inventory	• Investments	Notes Payable	Payable
• Accounts			• Bank Loans
Receivable			
• Prepaids			

Discussion Questions

9–6. Provide three examples of current liabilities and three examples of long-term liabilities not shown on the Eliason and Company Ltd. balance sheet in Exhibit 9–2.

9–7. Eliason and Company Ltd. shows $600,000 of current assets and $551,000 of current liabilities. Who might be interested in these amounts, and why?

The shareholders' equity section of a classified balance sheet is also separated into two classifications. Because all equity is either contributed by owners or earned, we classify equity into contributed and earned. Contributed capital consists of the share capital issued by the company. Earned capital consists of retained earnings. Preferred shareholders have first priority in paying out dividends and in liquidation. Therefore, the contributed capital section of equity begins with preferred shares, followed by common shares. In the case of Eliason and Company Ltd., we first list the $400,000 common shares. Because there are no other types of share capital, we list retained earnings next. At December 31, 2004, Eliason and Company Ltd. had a retained earnings balance of $265,800.

Discussion Questions

9–8. Explain the exact meaning of the $265,800 of retained earnings on Eliason and Company Ltd.'s balance sheet.

9–9. On average, how much did Eliason and Company Ltd. receive for each common share?

9–10. What is the total current market value of the Eliason and Company shares?

ORGANIZATION OF THE INCOME STATEMENT

When we introduced the income statement in Chapter 5, we used the following simple equation:

$$Revenues - Expenses = Net\ Income$$

An income statement prepared for Eliason and Company Ltd. for the year ended December 31, 2004, using this simple format, would look like Exhibit 9–4.

Exhibit 9–4
Basic Format
Income Statement

ELIASON AND COMPANY LTD.
Income Statement
For the Year Ended December 31, 2004

Revenue	$752,500
Less: Expenses	840,400
Net Loss	$ (87,900)

Net income or net loss discloses whether or not a company has been profitable for a given period. Although net income or net loss is very important, the net loss for 2004 does not tell Eliason and Company Ltd.'s performance story very well.

Accountants have developed income statement presentation guidelines to furnish a more complete picture of what happened to a business during a particular income statement period. Income statements prepared following these guidelines provide more detail than that given in the basic format shown in Exhibit 9–4, as well as important information about the characteristics of the revenues and expenses. Exhibit 9–5 presents an income statement for Eliason and Company Ltd. for the year ended December 31, 2004, prepared using the expanded format.

Exhibit 9–5
Expanded Format
Income Statement

ELIASON AND COMPANY LTD.
Income Statement
For the Year Ended December 31, 2004

Sales Revenue		$752,500
Less: Cost of Goods Sold		352,800
Gross Profit on Sales		$399,700
Less: Operating Expenses:		
Selling	$60,250	
General and Administrative	96,250	
Total Operating Expenses		156,500
Operating Income		$243,200
Less: Interest Expense		30,650
Income Before Taxes		$212,550
Less: Income Taxes		64,660
Income Before Extraordinary Item		$147,890
Extraordinary Loss (Less: Income Taxes of $87,420)		(235,790)
Net Loss		$ (87,900)

Although this income statement bears little resemblance to the one presented earlier in our discussion, revenues still total $752,500; total deductions from revenues still total $840,400; and the net loss is still $87,900. You should be familiar with the beginning of the format because only the last few lines are new.

 Discussion Questions

9–11. Is Exhibit 9–5 a single-step or multistep income statement? How can you tell?

9–12. If you were considering some kind of economic involvement with Eliason and Company Ltd., which number on the expanded income statement would you consider most reliable in predicting the company's future profitability? Explain.

Recurring and Nonrecurring Items

Besides presenting more detail concerning Eliason and Company Ltd.'s regular revenues and expenses for 2004, the income statement in Exhibit 9–5 shows an extraordinary loss of $235,790, which is separated from the company's regular, recurring revenues and expenses. An extraordinary loss (or gain) is one of the items the accounting profession has determined should be shown separately as a nonrecurring item on the income statement.

nonrecurring item Results of activities that cannot be expected to occur again, and therefore should not be used to predict future performance.

A **nonrecurring item** can be broadly defined as any item (either positive or negative) that should not be considered a normal part of continuing operations because it is not expected to recur. We will explore the logic of separating recurring and nonrecurring items on the income statement.

Suppose an event happened to a company during the income statement period that was not expected to recur. Whether the event was good or bad, the company must report its occurrence, even though it is not likely to happen again. If you were attempting to predict the company's ability to generate future profits and cash flows, and the company included this one-time event with revenues and expenses that happen each year, your prediction would not be realistic. Therefore, if nonrecurring items do not represent the ongoing results of a company's operations, we should report them separately from recurring items to protect the integrity of reported earnings.

If the extraordinary loss is truly a nonrecurring item for Eliason and Company Ltd., then the net loss of $87,900 for 2004 is not a good predictor of future profitability and cash flow. In fact, the best predictive number on this income statement is probably the $147,890 listed as the income before extraordinary item.

In this section, we will more fully explain the presentation and interpretation of information about nonrecurring items on the income statement. Throughout our discussion, we will use the Pursifull Ltd. income statement for the year ended December 31, 2004, presented in Exhibit 9–6.

The first half of Pursifull Ltd.'s income statement reflects results of activities that will probably continue in the future. The income tax amount shown ($64,260) relates only to the ongoing activities of the company and is calculated as:

Income Tax Expense = Income from Continuing Operations Before Tax × Tax Rate
$64,260 = $160,650 × 40%

PURSIFULL LTD.
Income Statement
For the Year Ended December 31, 2004

Sales		$858,600
Less: Cost of Goods Sold		456,800
Gross Profit on Sales		$401,800
Less: Operating Expenses:		
Selling	$ 94,450	
General and Administrative	116,050	
Total Operating Expenses		210,500
Operating Income		$191,300
Less: Interest Expense		30,650
Income from Continuing Operations Before Taxes		$160,650
Less: Income Taxes		64,260
Income from Continuing Operations		$ 96,390
Discontinued Operations:		
Income from Discontinued Operations		
(Less: Income Taxes of $47,520)	$ 71,280	
Loss on Disposal of Discontinued Operation		
(Less: Income Taxes of $36,000)	(54,000)	17,280
Income Before Extraordinary Item		$113,670
Extraordinary Gain (Less: Income Taxes of $63,400)		95,100
Net Income		$208,770

Notice the item identified as Income from Continuing Operations. The $96,390 represents the net results of Pursifull Ltd.'s ongoing operations, which we assume have a predictive value for future earnings. Information provided on the income statement below this point relates to nonrecurring items. The Income from Continuing Operations separates the recurring from nonrecurring activities. Some income statements show the title as Income Before Extraordinary Items. Regardless of the title, nonrecurring items always come after the income tax expense.

There are two general types of nonrecurring items, listed in their order of presentation on the income statement:

1. Discontinued operations
2. Extraordinary items

Proper classification of items as recurring or nonrecurring is critical to the usefulness of the accounting information. A company might be tempted to treat an item as nonrecurring because it reduces net income or to include an item with recurring revenues when it increases net income. To prevent companies from confusing the users of financial statements this way, the accounting profession restricts the items that may be considered nonrecurring. We will consider the criteria for each of these items after we discuss the income tax effects of these nonrecurring items.

Income Tax Disclosure

Did you know that income taxes were recorded in four places on Pursifull Ltd.'s income statement? The first two items included the income tax expense of $64,260 related to income from continuing operations and the income tax expense of $47,520 related to income from discontinued operations. The third and fourth items included the income tax *savings* of $36,000 related to the loss on disposal of discontinued operations and finally, the income tax expense of $63,400 related to the extraordinary gain. The total of these four tax amounts is $139,180 ($64,260 + $47,520 − $36,000 + $63,400).

Notice that we do not show the total tax expense in one place on the income statement. If we did, it would appear in the normal location for income tax expense, which would be just below the income from continuing operations. It would appear as follows:

Income from Continuing Operations Before Taxes	$160,650
Less: Income Taxes	139,180
Income from Continuing Operations	$ 21,470

This example makes it appear that Pursifull Ltd. pays tax at a rate of 86.6% ($139,180 ÷ $160,650).

To eliminate the distortion and confusion, members of the accounting profession decided that the only tax expense shown on the income statement as a separate line item will be the amount associated with continuing operations. Therefore, the two major types of nonrecurring items included on the income statement are shown "less income tax," or "net of tax."

Net of tax means that the amount shown for an item has been adjusted for any income tax effect. To calculate the tax expense, simply multiply the effective tax rate by the amount of the nonrecurring gain or loss. In Pursifull Ltd.'s example, we calculate the amounts as:

net of tax The proper presentation format for nonrecurring items shown below income from continuing operations on the income statement.

Income from Discontinued Operations	$118,800 × 40% = $47,520
Disposal of Discontinued Operation	$ 90,000 × 40% = $36,000
Extraordinary Gain	$158,500 × 40% = $63,400

How did we determine the full amount of each nonrecurring item? There are two accurate ways. The first is simply to add the tax to the gain or loss amount. The second is to divide the net-of-tax amount of gain or loss by the reciprocal of the tax amount or (1 − Tax Rate), in this case 60 percent.

$$\text{Income from Discontinued Operations} = \$71,280 + \$47,520 = \$118,800$$
$$\text{or} = \$71,280/0.60 = \$118,800$$

When a business experiences a gain, the total income of the business increases and more income taxes are paid. The gain increases the amount of taxes owed, which in turn reduces the amount of the gain (see Exhibit 9–7). When a business experiences a loss, the total income of the business decreases and less taxes are paid. The loss decreases the amount of taxes owed, which in turn reduces the amount of the loss.

Current accounting rules require that on the face of the income statement the tax effect on each of these nonrecurring items and the amount of that item after the tax effect be shown. With this information, financial statement users can determine the actual amount of the item before any tax effect.

Now look again at the income statement for Pursifull Ltd. (Exhibit 9–6 on page 331). Notice that the statement includes examples of the two major types of nonrecurring items, and both receive the same general presentation: Each is shown below the Income from Continuing Operations line, and each is shown "net of tax."

We now explore the criteria for and specific presentation of each of these types of nonrecurring items.

Discontinued Operations

If a company disposes of a major segment of its business, the results of operations for the segment of the company sold and any gain or loss from the actual disposal of the business segment are reported as nonrecurring items on the income state-

Exhibit 9–7
Effect of Tax on
Gains and Losses

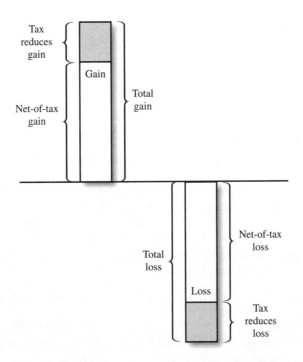

business segment A
portion of the business for
which assets, results of
operations, and activities can
be identified separately.

discontinued operations
The disposal of a business
segment. One of the non-
recurring items shown net of
tax on the income statement.

ment. A **business segment** may be a portion of an entity representing either a separate major line of business or class of customer. If the actual disposal has not yet occurred, management must have approved a formal plan to dispose of the business segment in order for it to be treated as **discontinued operations**.

Examples of a discontinued business segment would include a disposal by a diversified company of an entire business, such as a car manufacturer selling its car-loan business, or an oil and gas company selling its chain of service stations while retaining its refineries and oil-producing properties.

Once a judgment has been made that the discontinued operations should be considered the disposal of a business segment, GAAP require specific disclosures on the income statement. To illustrate, recall Exhibit 9–6 on page 331, the income statement for Pursifull Ltd. for the year ended December 31, 2004.

Pursifull Ltd. buys and resells toys. Many years ago, Pursifull Ltd. purchased a company that manufactured hats. Although this portion of the business has always been profitable, current management did not believe that the hat business fitted into the corporation's strategic plans and sold it during 2004. Two items presented on Pursifull Ltd.'s 2004 income statement reflect the disposal of the hat operation.

Pursifull Ltd. reported income from discontinued operations of $71,280. In 2004, prior to being sold, the hat operation had revenues of $220,100 and expenses of $101,300. So its pretax income for the time Pursifull Ltd. owned it during the year was $118,800 ($220,100 revenues − $101,300 expenses). Income taxes on the results of discontinued operations totaled $47,520, so the amount shown for income from discontinued operations on the income statement is $71,280 ($118,800 − $47,520). Because the hat operation is gone by the end of the year and can no longer be expected to generate income, the results for that part of the business are reported separately, net of tax.

Pursifull Ltd. also shows a $54,000 loss on the disposal of discontinued operations. When the company sold the hat operation, it incurred a $90,000 pretax loss on the sale. This loss resulted in a reduction of $36,000 in income taxes for the year. The after-tax loss was $54,000 ($90,000 − $36,000).

After we report each component of the results of discontinued operations, we combine the two amounts. We then net the $71,280 income from discontinued operations and the $54,000 loss on disposal of the discontinued operations, which results in a total of $17,280 under discontinued operations, properly reported on Pursifull Ltd.'s income statement for 2004.

Extraordinary Items

extraordinary item A gain or loss that is both unusual in nature and infrequent in occurrence. One of the nonrecurring items shown net of tax on the income statement.

For an event to result in an **extraordinary item** under GAAP, the event must have three characteristics. It cannot be expected to recur for several years, it cannot relate to normal business operations of the company, and it could not have arisen because of a decision made by management. The statement preparer must exercise judgment in deciding whether to classify the result of an event as an extraordinary item or a special item in continuing operations.

The following events or transactions should be presented as extraordinary items on the income statement.

1. A hailstorm destroys a large portion of a tobacco manufacturer's crops in an area where hailstorms are rare.
2. A steel fabricating company is forced to sell land because it was expropriated by local authorities so that a highway expansion could occur. The company acquired the land ten years ago for future expansion but shortly thereafter abandoned all plans for expansion and held the land for appreciation in value instead.
3. A tornado in Alberta destroys one of the oil refineries owned by a large multinational oil company.

 Discussion Question

9–13. The following examples do not qualify as extraordinary items. For each one, explain specifically what criterion or criteria have not been met.

a. A business located near the Red River in Winnipeg is flooded for the third time in ten years.

b. The city was planning to expropriate land owned by a company in order to build a new recreation centre for the town. Prior to the decision being made, the company sold the land to another party.

c. A company signs an order to sell products for the "end of the millennium" New Year's Eve party. The order doubles the company's sales.

Because extraordinary items enter the income statement after income from continuing operations, we present them net of tax. Return to the income statement for Pursifull Ltd. (Exhibit 9–6). Pursifull Ltd. reported an extraordinary gain of $95,100 ($158,500 less income taxes of $63,400). This gain resulted from the city government's purchase of Pursifull Ltd.'s land adjacent to the municipal airport. The government expropriated the land to complete an airport expansion, and Pursifull Ltd. had no choice but to sell the property to the government and pay income tax on the gain.

EARNINGS PER SHARE

earnings per share (EPS)
A calculation indicating how much of a company's total earnings is attributable to each common share.

Many investors and other financial statement users rely on one statistic more than any other to measure a company's performance—earnings per share. To comply with GAAP, income statements must disclose the firm's **earnings per share (EPS),** which reveals how much of a company's total earnings is attributable to each common share. We calculate basic earnings per share with the following formula:

$$\text{Earnings per share} = \frac{\text{Net income} - \text{Preferred dividends}}{\text{Weighted average number of common shares outstanding}}$$

basic earnings per share
A simple calculation of earnings per common share based on shares outstanding on the balance sheet date.

convertible securities
Debt or equity securities that can be converted into the company's common shares.

diluted earnings per share
A calculation of earnings per common share including all potentially dilutive securities.

GAAP require that two measures of EPS be calculated—basic and diluted. **Basic earnings per share** computes EPS based on the reality of the status of the company on the balance sheet date. If a company has convertible securities on its balance sheet, the current status of the company may change in the future. **Convertible securities** are debt or equity securities that owners may, at their option, convert to common shares. Examples are convertible bonds and convertible preferred shares. Because these pose a possible dilutive threat to the current and future common shareholders, we must disclose the consequences of having such securities. The dilutive threat arises because the owners of the bonds or preferred shares may convert these to common shares. The earnings must then be shared among more shareholders and the earnings per share will decrease. **Diluted earnings per share** includes the potential impact of any issued dilutive securities. When we calculate the diluted earnings per share, we modify the formula as if the conversion took place at the beginning of the year. We can illustrate the appropriate changes in an example.

Calculating Earnings per Share

Pursifull Ltd.'s shareholders' equity section of the balance sheet appears in Exhibit 9-8. Assume that each preferred share is convertible into six common shares and that Pursifull Ltd. sold the 5,000 shares of new common shares on April 1, 2004. Also assume that the company paid $45,000 in dividends to the preferred shareholders in 2004. We must first compute the weighted average number of common shares outstanding for the year, just as we computed the weighted average cost of inventory. Look at the following computational chart:

Exhibit 9–8
Pursifull Ltd.'s Shareholders' Equity Section of the Balance Sheet for December 31, 2004 and 2003

PURSIFULL LTD.
Shareholders' Equity Section
December 31

	2004	2003
Share Capital:		
9% Preferred Shares,		
5,000 authorized, issued, and outstanding	$ 500,000	$ 500,000
Common Shares, 100,000 authorized,		
90,000 issued and outstanding in 2004		
(85,000 in 2003)	900,000	850,000
Retained Earnings	1,244,050	1,065,580
Total Shareholders' Equity	$2,644,050	$2,415,580

Date	(A) Number of Shares Outstanding	(B) Period of Time	(A) × (B)
January 1	85,000	3/12	21,250
April 1	90,000	9/12	67,500
	Weighted average shares		88,750

Now we can calculate basic and diluted earnings per share for Pursifull Ltd.:

Basic Earnings per Share:

$$\text{EPS} = \frac{\text{Net income} - \text{Preferred dividend}}{\text{Weighted average number of common shares outstanding}}$$

$$= \frac{\$208,770 - \$45,000}{88,750}$$

$$= \$1.85 \text{ per share (rounded)}$$

Diluted Earnings per Share:

$$\text{EPS} = \frac{\text{Net income} - \text{Preferred dividend}}{\text{Weighted average number of common shares outstanding}}$$

$$= \frac{\$208,770 - 0}{88,750 + (6 \times 5,000)} = \frac{\$208,770}{118,750} = \$1.76 \text{ per share (rounded)}$$

To understand the calculation of diluted EPS, look first to the numerator of the equation. If the preferred shares were converted at the beginning of the year, there is no requirement to pay dividends for the year. The denominator changes because, if the preferred shares were converted, there would be an additional 30,000 shares outstanding all year. The result lowers the EPS by $0.09 per share and warns prospective investors that this is the worst-case scenario for the current earnings attributed to one common share.

Income Statement Presentation

GAAP require that basic and diluted earnings per share be prominently displayed on the income statement for each item on the income statement below income tax expense. Exhibit 9–9 illustrates the proper income statement presentation for Pursifull Ltd.

We can look at the calculations of (a) through (e):

Basic EPS	Diluted EPS
(a) $\dfrac{\$96,390 - \$45,000}{88,750} = \$0.58$	$\dfrac{\$96,390}{118,750} = \$0.81$
(b) $\dfrac{\$71,280}{88,750} = \$0.80$	$\dfrac{\$71,280}{118,750} = \$0.60$
(c) $\dfrac{\$(54,000)}{88,750} = \$(0.61)$	$\dfrac{\$(54,000)}{118,750} = \$(0.45)$
(d) $\dfrac{\$113,670 - \$45,000}{88,750} = \$0.77$	$\dfrac{\$113,670}{118,750} = \$0.96$
(e) $\dfrac{\$95,100}{88,750} = \$1.07$	$\dfrac{\$95,100}{118,750} = \$0.80$

We have applied the EPS formula to each income item, treating that item as the numerator in place of net income. Notice that only the net income from continuing operations, net income before extraordinary items, and net income subtract

PURSIFULL LTD.
Income Statement
For the Year Ended December 31, 2004

Sales		$858,600			
Less: Cost of Goods Sold		456,800			
Gross Profit on Sales		$401,800			
Less: Operating Expenses:					
Selling	$ 94,450				
General and Administrative	116,050				
Total Operating Expenses		210,500			
Operating Income		$191,300			
Less: Interest Expense		30,650			
Income from Continuing Operations Before Taxes		$160,650	Basic	Diluted	
Less: Income Taxes		64,260	EPS	EPS	
Income from Continuing Operations		$96,390	$0.58	$0.81	(a)
Discontinued Operations:					
Income from Discontinued Operations					
(Less: Income Taxes of $47,520)	$71,280		0.80	0.60	(b)
Loss on Disposal of Discontinued Operation					
(Less: Income Taxes of $36,000)	(54,000)	17,280	(0.61)	(0.45)	(c)
Income Before Extraordinary Item		$113,670	$0.77	$0.96	(d)
Extraordinary Gain (Less: Income Taxes of $63,400)		95,100	1.07	0.80	(e)
Net Income		$208,770	$1.84	$1.76	

the preferred dividends from the numerator in computing basic earnings per share. Mathematically, you should ignore the preferred dividends in all other EPS calculations.

The income statement provides users with a great deal of information with which to predict the future amount and timing of a company's cash flows. Understanding the details of the information provided in an income statement will make you a wiser financial statement user. But one year's information is for a relatively short period of time—too short to be used in making many long-term economic decisions. For this reason, serious analysis of income statement and balance sheet information requires financial statements for more than one accounting period.

COMPARATIVE FINANCIAL STATEMENTS

comparative financial statements Financial statements showing results from two or more consecutive periods.

Comparative financial statements show results for two or more consecutive periods—usually years or quarters. Financial statement analysts use comparative statements to develop a sense of the big picture of the company's performance over time. Comparative statements help the statement user to find trends in the information that improve future income and cash flow predictions.

To illustrate the presentation of comparative financial statements, we provide the 2003 and 2004 income statements and balance sheets for Norton Ltd. in Exhibit 9–10.

Exhibit 9-10
2004 and 2003 Financial Statements for Norton Ltd.

NORTON LTD.
Income Statements
For the Years Ended December 31, 2004 and 2003
(in thousands)

		2004		2003
Sales		$14,745		$12,908
Less: Cost of Goods Sold		10,213		8,761
Gross Profit on Sales		$ 4,532		$ 4,147
Less: Operating Expenses				
Selling	$1,022		$ 546	
General and Administrative	2,721		2,451	
Total Operating Expenses		3,743		2,997
Operating Income		$ 789		$ 1,150
Less: Interest Expense		172		137
Income Before Taxes		$ 617		$ 1,013
Less: Income Taxes		123		355
Net Income		$ 494		$ 658

NORTON LTD.
Balance Sheets
December 31, 2004, and December 31, 2003
(in thousands)

Assets:		2004		2003
Current Assets:				
Cash		$ 2,240		$1,936
Accounts Receivable		2,340		2,490
Merchandise Inventory		776		693
Prepaid Expenses		200		160
Total Current Assets		$ 5,556		$5,279
Property, Plant, and Equipment:				
Land		$ 1,000		$1,000
Buildings	$6,723		$5,423	
Less: Accumulated Amortization	3,677		3,534	
Buildings, Net		3,046		1,889
Equipment	$2,687		$2,387	
Less: Accumulated Amortization	1,564		1,523	
Equipment, Net		1,123		864
Total Property, Plant, and Equipment		$ 5,169		$3,753
Total Assets		$10,725		$9,032
Liabilities:				
Current Liabilities:				
Accounts Payable		$ 1,616		$1,080
Notes Payable		2,720		2,920
Total Current Liabilities		$ 4,336		$4,000
Long-Term Liabilities		2,000		1,600
Total Liabilities		$ 6,336		$5,600
Shareholders' Equity:				
Common Shares		$ 3,000		$2,400
Retained Earnings		1,389		1,032
Total Shareholders' Equity		$ 4,389		$3,432
Total Liabilities and Shareholders' Equity		$10,725		$9,032

Discussion Questions

9–14. Using the comparative income statements and balance sheets of Norton Ltd. presented in Exhibit 9–10, prepare the company's 2004 statement of retained earnings.

9–15. What specific information that was not apparent from Norton Ltd.'s income statements or balance sheets did the statement of retained earnings you developed for Discussion Question 9–15 provide?

Comparative financial statements enhance the user's ability to analyze a company's past performance and present condition. They also make it possible to perform several analytical techniques, which we will explore in later chapters. Financial statement analysis, in fact, begins with the use of the statement of cash flows—the fourth financial statement, which we introduce in the next chapter.

SUMMARY

Both the balance sheet and income statement are useful tools. By learning more about the construction and organization of these statements, users of balance sheet and income statement information are able to use the information contained in the statements more effectively.

The classified balance sheet separates assets and liabilities into current and long-term categories. These classifications provide additional information to users of the information.

Income statements often include items that are not part of the company's normal operations and are not expected to recur. These nonrecurring items must be separated from results of activities that are expected to recur as part of the company's normal, ongoing operations. Reporting recurring items and nonrecurring items separately offers financial statement users additional useful information. Two major types of nonrecurring items (discontinued operations and extraordinary items) are presented below income from continuing operations and are shown net of tax. The other most common type of nonrecurring item, one that meets some but not all of the criteria for treatment as an extraordinary item, is shown within the section of the income statement related to continuing operations, but is identified as a separate item.

GAAP also require that basic and diluted earnings per share be disclosed on the income statement for each item of income from *income from continuing operations* through *net income*. Comparative financial statements, providing information for two or more consecutive periods, offer a clearer view of a company's performance and financial position.

APPENDIX—
RECORDING INCOME TAX EXPENSE

In previous chapters we ignored the effect of income taxes on income statements. Because proprietorships and partnerships have no income taxes, this treatment is proper for them. However, a corporation pays corporate income taxes because it has the legal status of a person. Accounting for income taxes requires two basic entries and three new accounts. We will make entries to:

1. Accrue the income tax expense as computed for the income statement.
2. Record the payment of accrued taxes.
3. Record the payment of prepaid or estimated taxes.

To make these entries we will need the following accounts:

1. Expense account—Income Tax Expense
2. Current liability account—Income Taxes Payable
3. Prepaid asset account—Prepaid Income Taxes

We can look at the Pursifull Ltd. example in Exhibit 9–6 on page 331 and prepare the journal entries to record the expense and the liability. We make the entries to record the expense and liability for the income taxes without regard to the character of the income tax. Remember that the aim of recording and reporting differ. Recording accumulates the reality of measurement of transactions and events (data) while reporting provides information (organized data) to users. In the recording process, we record Pursifull Ltd.'s total income tax expense and liability.

To record income tax expense and liability:

2004		Debit	Credit
December 31	Income Tax Expense	139,180	
	Income Taxes Payable		139,180
	To record the 2004 expense		
	per the income statement.		

$$(\$64{,}260 + \$47{,}520 - \$36{,}000 + \$63{,}400)$$

Assume that Pursifull Ltd. paid the resulting liability on February 28, 2005, when the CFO filed the corporate tax return.

To record payment of tax liability:

2005		Debit	Credit
February 28	Income Taxes Payable	139,180	
	Cash		139,180
	To record payment of 2004		
	income taxes.		

The above entries assume that income taxes are paid once each year. This only happens in the first year of operations. After that, the Canada Customs and Revenue Agency has requirements for corporations to pay estimated income taxes 12 times each year, a concept similar to individuals allowing income taxes to be withheld from each paycheque. This transfers money to the government during the year and prevents the corporations from using the cash for other purposes and being unable to pay the taxes at year end. Assume that on the 10th day of each month Pursifull Ltd. paid estimated taxes of $11,000 in anticipation of the 2004 expense. Look how the entries would be made:

To record estimated tax payments:

2004		Debit	Credit
January 10	Prepaid Income Taxes	11,000	
	Cash		11,000
	To record estimated income tax payments for 2004.		

The entries for each month would be exactly the same. By the end of 2004, the company has paid 12 tax instalments of $11,000 each for a total of $132,000.

To record accrual of income tax expense:

December 31	Income Tax Expense	139,180	
2004	Prepaid Income Taxes		132,000
	Income Taxes Payable		7,180
	To record income tax expense for 2004.		

To record final payment of taxes:

2005			
February 28	Income Taxes Payable	7,180	
	Cash		7,180
	To record payment of the final tax liability for 2004.		

SUMMARY OF APPENDIX

We record income tax expense in the same manner as other expenses. The cash outflow may precede the expense accrual and be recorded as a prepaid expense. The cash outflow may follow the accrual and extinguish the liability. In the recording process, we ignore income statement separation of the income tax expense into recurring and nonrecurring activities and add all the amounts together into one amount.

KEY TERMS

basic earnings per share, p. 335
business segment, p. 333
classified balance sheet, p. 325
comparative financial statements, p. 337
convertible securities, p. 335
current assets, p. 325
current liabilities, p. 327
diluted earnings per share, p. 335
discontinued operations, p. 333
earnings per share (EPS), p. 335

extraordinary item, p. 334
intangible assets, p. 327
investments, p. 327
liquidity, p. 326
long-term assets, p. 325
long-term liabilities, p. 327
net of tax, p. 332
nonrecurring item, p. 330
operating cycle, p. 325

REVIEW THE FACTS

1. What was the original purpose of accounting records?
2. What caused the shift in attention from the balance sheet to the income statement?
3. Explain why a decision maker may prefer a classified balance sheet to one using the simplest possible format.
4. What is the difference between current and long-term assets? Offer two examples of each.
5. In what order are assets presented on a classified balance sheet?
6. Describe investments and intangible assets, and provide two examples of each that are not listed in the chapter.
7. Describe the difference between current and long-term liabilities, and provide two examples of each.
8. Explain the difference between recurring and nonrecurring items on an income statement. Why are these items reported separately?
9. Identify the two major types of nonrecurring items that are shown net of tax on the income statement.
10. Explain the effect of taxes on both gains and losses.
11. What is a business segment?
12. What criteria must be met for an item to be considered extraordinary?
13. Define earnings per share, and distinguish between basic and diluted earnings per share.
14. Describe comparative financial statements and explain their benefits to economic decision makers.

APPLY WHAT YOU HAVE LEARNED

LO 2: Balance Sheet Terminology

1. Presented below are items related to the organization of the classified balance sheet, followed by the definitions of those items in scrambled order.

   a. Liquidity
   b. Current assets
   c. Long-term assets
   d. Current liabilities
   e. Intangible asset
   f. Long-term liabilities
   g. Shareholders' equity
   h. Total liabilities and shareholders' equity
   i. Plant and equipment, net
   j. Investment

   1. _f._ Obligations not requiring payment within the next year
   2. _c._ Items controlled by a company that are not expected to become cash within the next year
   3. _a._ An item's nearness to cash
   4. _g._ The owners' residual interest in a corporation
   5. _i._ Long-lived tangible assets less all the amortization expense ever recognized on those assets
   6. _d._ Obligations that must be retired within the next year
   7. _h._ Equal to total assets
   8. _b._ Items controlled by a company that are expected to become cash within the next year
   9. _e._ An investment in a contractual arrangement such as a patent
   10. _j._ A long-term commitment to ownership of other entities

REQUIRED:

Match the letter next to each item with the appropriate definition. Each letter will be used only once.

LO 2:   Balance Sheet Accounts

2. a. What are investments on a balance sheet and how are they classified?
   b. Provide three examples of investments and discuss how they would be classified on the balance sheet.

LO 2:   Balance Sheet Accounts

3. a. Define intangible assets in your own words.
   b. Provide three examples of intangible assets and discuss how they would be classified on the balance sheet.
   c. What is the term applied to the process of matching the cost of an intangible with the periods of time benefited or with the revenues they help to create?

LO 2:   Balance Sheet Accounts

4. Presented below are the major sections of the classified balance sheet, followed by a list of items normally shown on the balance sheet.

a.	Current assets	**e.**	Long-term liabilities
b.	Property, plant, and equipment	**f.**	Share capital
c.	Current liabilities	**g.**	Retained earnings
d.	Intangible assets	**h.**	Investments

1. _____ Accounts payable
2. _____ Common shares
3. _____ Franchise
4. _____ Accounts receivable
5. _____ Note payable due within one year
6. _____ Prepaid expenses
7. _____ Preferred shares
8. _____ Note payable due in two years
9. _____ Amounts earned by the company but not yet distributed to the owners of the business
10. _____ Goodwill
11. _____ Bonds held for the interest to be earned
12. _____ Land
13. _____ Shares of a subsidiary
14. _____ Wages payable
15. _____ Vehicles
16. _____ Copyright
17. _____ Cash
18. _____ Buildings
19. _____ Bonds payable
20. _____ Trademark

REQUIRED:

Indicate where each item on the list should be shown on the classified balance sheet by placing the letter of the appropriate balance sheet section in the space provided. The letters may be used more than once.

LO 2: Preparation of Balance Sheet

5. The following items relate to Dana Corporation at December 31, 2004:

Land	$210,000
Cash	14,600
Accounts Receivable	92,300
Accounts Payable	74,000
Common Shares (75,000 Shares Outstanding)	300,000
Bonds Payable	100,000
Preferred Shares (10,000 Shares Outstanding)	10,000
Inventory	118,000
Prepaid Expenses	11,200
Taxes Payable	17,000
Short-Term Note Payable	50,000
Buildings and Equipment	400,000
Retained Earnings	?
Wages Payable	35,800

Accumulated Amortization (which is not reflected in the previous totals) is $142,000 on the Buildings and Equipment.

REQUIRED:

a. At what average price did Dana Corporation issue its common shares? Explain how you determined your answer.

b. Prepare a classified balance sheet for Dana Corporation at December 31, 2004.

LO 2: Preparation of Balance Sheet

6. The following items relate to Wesnidge and Company Ltd. at December 31, 2004:

Accounts Payable	$172,000
Common Shares (200,000 Shares Outstanding)	400,000
Bonds Payable	307,700
Prepaid Expenses	9,800
Taxes Payable	47,000
Short-Term Note Payable	70,000
Buildings and Equipment	875,000
Preferred Shares (24,000 Shares Outstanding)	240,000
Land	490,000
Cash	124,200
Accounts Receivable	212,000
Inventory	338,000
Retained Earnings	?
Wages Payable	77,600

Accumulated Amortization (which is not reflected in the previous totals) is $271,000 on the Buildings and Equipment.

REQUIRED:

a. What is Wesnidge and Company Ltd.'s retained earnings balance on December 31, 2004?

b. Prepare a classified balance sheet for Wesnidge and Company Ltd. at December 31, 2004.

LO 2:   Preparation of Balance Sheet

7. The following items relate to Marple Limited at December 31, 2004:

Accounts Payable	$516,000
Common Shares (400,000 Shares Outstanding)	800,000
Bonds Payable	923,100
Prepaid Expenses	29,400
Taxes Payable	141,000
Short-Term Note Payable	210,000
Buildings and Equipment	985,000
Preferred Shares (24,000 Shares Outstanding)	240,000
Land	690,000
Cash	124,200
Accounts Receivable	212,000
Inventory	338,000
Retained Earnings	?
Wages Payable	132,800

Accumulated Amortization (which is not reflected in the previous totals) is $385,000 on the Buildings and Equipment.

REQUIRED:

a. What is Marple Limited's retained earnings balance on December 31, 2004?

b. Prepare a classified balance sheet for Marple Limited at December 31, 2004.

LO 2:   Classified Balance Sheet

8. Assets on the classified balance sheet are identified as either current or long-term. Liabilities on the classified balance sheet are also identified as either current or long-term.

REQUIRED:

a. What criterion is used to determine whether an asset or liability is classified as current or long-term?

b. Explain in your own words why the following parties would be interested in the separation of current and long-term assets and liabilities on a company's balance sheet:

(1) Short-term creditors (other businesses from whom the company buys inventory, supplies, etc.)

(2) Long-term creditors (banks and others from whom the company borrows money on a long-term basis)

(3) The company's shareholders

(4) The company's management

LO 2:   Classified Balance Sheet

9. Shareholders' equity on the classified balance sheet of a corporation is divided into two major categories: contributed capital and retained earnings.

REQUIRED:

a. Explain in your own words what each of the two major categories under shareholders' equity represents.

b. Explain in your own words why the following parties would be interested in the relative amounts of contributed capital and retained earnings in the shareholders' equity section of a company's balance sheet:

(1) Short-term creditors (other businesses from which the company buys inventory, supplies, etc.)

(2) Long-term creditors (banks and others from which the company borrows money on a long-term basis)

(3) The company's shareholders

(4) The company's management

LO 3: Income Statement Terminology

10. Presented below are several sections of the multistep income statement, followed by several independent situations or transactions.

a. Sales

b. Cost of goods sold

c. Income from continuing operations

d. Discontinued operation

e. Extraordinary item

1. _____ A manufacturing company sells a warehouse with a book value of $20,000 for $20,000.

2. _____ A company sells units of inventory in the normal course of its business operation.

3. _____ A company located in Whitehorse, Yukon, experiences a loss from earthquake damage. This loss is determined to be a "special" item.

4. _____ A company disposes of a major segment of its business.

5. _____ A company pays wages, rent, utilities, and so forth.

6. _____ A company located in Vancouver, B.C., experiences a loss from an ice storm. This loss is determined to be infrequent in occurrence.

REQUIRED:

Indicate where the result of each situation or transaction should be shown on the multistep income statement by placing the letter of the appropriate income statement section in the space provided. The letters may be used more than once. Note: The results of some situations or transactions may not be shown on the income statement. If so, place the letter *n* in the space provided.

LO 3: Income Statement Terminology

11. Presented below are items related to the multistep income statement as discussed in this chapter, followed by the definitions of those items in scrambled order.

a. Gross profit on sales

b. Operating expenses

c. Income from continuing operations

d. Discontinued operation

e. Extraordinary item

f. Recurring item

g. Nonrecurring item

1. _e._ A material gain or loss that does not relate to normal operations, is not expected to recur, and did not arise as a result of management's decisions

2. _c._ Generally, the difference between normal ongoing revenues and normal ongoing expenses

3. _d._ The difference between sales and cost of goods sold

4. _g._ Any item that should not be considered a normal part of continuing operations because it is not expected to happen again

5. __b.__ Sacrifices incurred in the normal day-to-day running of a business
6. __f.__ Any item considered a normal part of continuing operations because it is expected to happen on an ongoing basis
7. __d.__ The disposal of a business segment

REQUIRED:

Match the letter next to each item with the appropriate definition. Each letter will be used only once.

LO 3: Income Tax Disclosure

12. a. What is the purpose of reporting discontinued items and extraordinary gains and losses net of income taxes?
     b. Discuss the meaning of the phrase "net of tax" and how this is reported on the income statement.

LO 3: Discontinued Operations

13. On March 1, 2004, the board of directors of Tabitha Company Ltd. approved the disposal of a segment of its business. For the period of January 1 through February 28, 2004, the segment had revenues of $200,000 and expenses of $350,000. The company sold the assets of the segment at a loss of $100,000.

REQUIRED:

Describe how the corporation should report this information on the financial statements. Be as specific as possible.

LO 3: Discontinued Operations

14. On July 1, 2004, the board of directors of Elwood Limited approved the sale of a segment of its business. For the period of January 1 through June 30, 2004, the segment had revenues of $1,100,000 and expenses of $1,500,000. The company sold the assets of the segment at a gain of $200,000.

REQUIRED:

Describe how the corporation should report this information on the financial statements. Be as specific as possible.

LO 3: Discontinued Operations

15. On October 1, 2004, the board of directors of Grande Prairie Resources Ltd. approved the disposal of a segment of its business. For the period of January 1 through September 30, 2004, the segment had revenues of $1,500,000 and expenses of $2,500,000. The company sold the assets of the segment at a gain of $300,000.

REQUIRED:

Describe how the corporation should report this information on the financial statements. Be as specific as possible.

LO 4: Multistep Income Statement

16. The following items relate to Cape Breton Enterprises for the year ended December 31, 2004:

    - Sales for the year totaled $665,000.
    - Cost of goods sold for the year totaled $271,000.
    - Regular operating expenses for the year were $145,000.
    - Interest expense for the year was $27,000.
    - On February 18, 2004, one of the company's warehouses burned to the ground. The company's loss (after the insurance settlement) was $106,000 before any tax effect. This loss was determined to be both unusual in nature and infrequent in occurrence.
    - The income tax rate is 40% on all items.

REQUIRED:

Prepare Cape Breton Enterprises' income statement for the year ended December 31, 2004, using the expanded multistep format presented in this chapter.

LO 4: Multistep Income Statement

17. The following items relate to Prince Albert Supplies Ltd. for the year ended December 31, 2004:

    - Sales for the year totaled $575,000.
    - Cost of goods sold for the year totaled $372,500.
    - Regular operating expenses for the year were $121,500.
    - Interest expense for the year was $16,000.
    - On September 5, 2004, the company sold the only land it owned at a pretax gain of $50,000. The land was acquired in 1996 for future expansion, but shortly thereafter the company abandoned all plans for expansion and held the land for appreciation.
    - The company's income tax rate is 30% on all items.

REQUIRED:

Prepare the company's income statement for the year ended December 31, 2004, using the expanded multistep format presented in this chapter.

LO 4: Multistep Income Statement

18. The following items relate to Annapolis Valley Groceries Ltd. for the year ended December 31, 2004:

    - Sales for the year totaled $1,075,000.
    - Cost of goods sold for the year totaled $667,000.
    - Operating expenses for the year were $102,500.
    - Interest expense for the year was $43,000.
    - On June 30, 2004, the company sold a major segment of its business at a loss of $95,000 before any tax effects. This segment of the company represented a major line of business that was totally separate from the rest of the company's operation.
    - Prior to being sold, the business segment had sales during 2004 of $150,000, cost of goods sold of $90,000, and operating expenses of $45,000. These amounts are not included in the previous information provided.
    - The company's income tax rate is 40% on all items.

REQUIRED:

Prepare the company's income statement for the year ended December 31, 2004, using the expanded multistep format presented in this chapter.

LO 4: Multistep Income Statement

19. The following items relate to Ojibway Products Ltd. for the year ended December 31, 2004:

    - Sales for the year totaled $465,000.
    - Cost of goods sold for the year totaled $239,000.
    - Operating expenses for the year were $113,200.
    - Interest expense for the year was $11,000.
    - On July 16, 2004, the company sold a major segment of its business at a gain of $50,000 before any tax effects. This segment of the company represented a major line of business that was totally separate from the rest of the company's operation.
    - Prior to being sold, the business segment had sales during 2004 of $60,000, cost of goods sold of $40,000, and operating expenses of $35,000. These amounts are not included in the previous information provided.
    - The company's income tax rate is 30% on all items.

REQUIRED:

Prepare the company's income statement for the year ended December 31, 2004, using the expanded multistep format presented in this chapter.

LO 5: Earnings Per Share—Simple Capital Structure

20. Jacobs Company Ltd. reported income after taxes for the year ended December 31, 2004, of $337,600. At the end of the year 2004, Jacobs Company Ltd. had the following shares outstanding:

    Preferred Shares, nonconvertible, 10,000 issued and outstanding. Dividends of $10 per preferred share were declared.

    Common Shares, 40,000 shares issued and outstanding.

REQUIRED:

Calculate basic earnings per share for 2004.

LO 5: Earnings Per Share—Simple Capital Structure

21. Schweizer Limited reported income after taxes for the year ended December 31, 2004, of $337,600. During the year 2004, Schweizer Limited had the following shares outstanding:

    Preferred Shares, nonconvertible, 10,000 issued and outstanding. Dividends amounting to $100,000 were declared in 2004.

    Common Shares, 40,000 shares issued and outstanding on January 1, 2004.

    Additional 5,000 common shares issued April 1, 2004.

REQUIRED:

Calculate basic earnings per share for 2004.

$$40,000 + 5000 \times \frac{9}{12}$$

$$43750$$

LO 5: Earnings Per Share—Simple Capital Structure

22. Ward Limited reported income after taxes for the year ended December 31, 2004, of $775,200. During the year 2004, Ward Limited had the following shares outstanding:

Preferred Shares, nonconvertible, 20,000 issued and outstanding. Preferred share dividends of $5 per share were declared in 2004.

Common Shares, 80,000 shares issued and outstanding on January 1, 2004.

Additional 10,000 common shares issued July 1, 2004.

REQUIRED:

Calculate basic earnings per share for 2004.

LO 5: Earnings per Share—Complex Capital Structure

23. Schweizer Limited reported income after taxes for the year ended December 31, 2004, of $337,600. During the year 2004, Schweizer Limited had the following shares outstanding:

Preferred Shares, 10,000 issued and outstanding, each share convertible into three common shares. Preferred dividends of $10 per share were declared in 2004.

Common Shares, 40,000 shares issued and outstanding on January 1, 2004.

Additional 5,000 common shares issued October 1, 2004.

REQUIRED:

a. Calculate basic earnings per share.
b. Calculate diluted earnings per share.

LO 5: Earnings per Share—Complex Capital Structure

24. Ward Limited reported income after taxes for the year ended December 31, 2004, of $775,200. During the year 2004, Ward Limited had the following shares outstanding:

Preferred Shares, convertible, 20,000 issued and outstanding. Each preferred share is convertible into five common shares.

Common Shares, 80,000 shares issued and outstanding on January 1, 2004.

Additional 10,000 common shares issued July 1, 2004.

REQUIRED:

a. Calculate basic earnings per share.
b. Calculate diluted earnings per share.

LO 5: Earnings per Share—Complex Capital Structure

25. Ward Limited reported income after taxes for the year ended December 31, 2004, of $775,200. During the year 2004, Ward Limited had the following shares outstanding:

Preferred Shares, convertible, 20,000 issued and outstanding. Each preferred share is convertible into five common shares.

Common Shares, 80,000 shares issued and outstanding on January 1, 2004.

Additional 10,000 common shares issued April 1, 2004.

Additional 5,000 common shares issued October 1, 2004.

REQUIRED:

a. Calculate basic earnings per share.

b. Calculate diluted earnings per share.

LO 7: Income Tax Entries

*26. Hassenfuss Limited reports $385,000 of net income subject to a 40% tax rate. The company has paid timely estimated tax payments of $87,000.

REQUIRED:

Prepare the journal entry to record the income tax expense and the remaining liability for the year.

LO 7: Income Tax Entries

*27. Okanagan Limited reports $160,000 of net income before taxes and an extraordinary gain of $10,000. The company is subject to a 30% tax rate. The company has paid timely estimated tax payments of $25,000.

REQUIRED:

Prepare the journal entry or entries to record the income tax expense and the remaining liability for the year.

LO 7: Income Tax Entries

*28. Brandon Limited reports $200,000 of net operating income before taxes and an extraordinary loss of $25,000. The company is also reporting a loss from discontinued operations of $70,000. The company is subject to a 35% tax rate. The company has paid timely estimated tax payments of $10,000.

REQUIRED:

Prepare the journal entry or entries to record the income tax expense and the remaining liability for the year.

ANNUAL REPORT PROJECT

29. At this point in your preparation of the annual report project, you will locate information that will help you in the final phase of the report. In this segment, you only need to fill in the blanks with the requested information. This information will be used to prepare the required ratios at the end of Chapter 11. By preparing the information at this point, the computations will require minimal time and effort.

    From the financial statements in your annual report, locate or determine the following items. Remember that you may have to review footnotes if you do not find a particular piece of information.

---

*Refers to material in this chapter's appendix.

Current Assets _____

Current Liabilities _____

Working Capital (CA-CL) _____

Quick Assets _____

Total Assets _____

Total Liabilities _____

Net Worth _____

Sales _____

Accounts Receivable _____

Cost of Sales _____

Inventory _____

Net Income Before Taxes _____

Net Income After Taxes _____

Total Equity _____

Interest Expense _____

After you have completed this worksheet, you need only retain it to complete the ratios at the end of Chapter 11.

10

The Statement of Cash Flows: Bringing the Focus Back to Cash

*Y*our business has been growing by leaps and bounds. It seems that your customers cannot get enough of the product, and the order department continues to add new employees. Your accountant moans constantly about trying to reduce the taxes on your climbing net income. You added two new inventory warehouses and still have only a week's supply of inventory on hand. At the same time, the controller continually complains about being short of cash. How can such a thriving business be short of cash? You do not know whether the accountant cannot count or someone is stealing cash. Your accountant guarantees that if you read the statement of cash flows, it might answer all of your questions. What is a statement of cash flows?

We have explored three major financial statements: the income statement, the statement of owners' equity (or retained earnings), and the balance sheet. We focused on information produced under the accrual basis of measurement. Recall that accrual accounting is affected by a number of items, which we have also discussed:

- Determining when revenue should be recognized under accrual accounting
- Matching expenses to the same income statement period as the revenues they helped generate
- Estimating the useful life and residual value required for amortization
- Choosing the inventory cost flow assumption (e.g., FIFO, LIFO) and amortization method (e.g., straight-line or double-declining-balance method). ■

These are just a few of the items that cause net income under accrual accounting to be different from the change in cash.

Net income is an opinion; cash is a fact.

—Anonymous

Considering the number of estimates and assumptions necessary to measure accrual accounting, this statement rings true. However, the accounting profession put the eye back on cash by requiring a fourth financial statement tool: the statement of cash flows. When information from this additional source is combined with the information contained in the other three financial statements, decision makers have a more complete picture of a company's financial health.

LEARNING OBJECTIVES

After completing your work on this chapter, you should be able to do the following:

1. Explain the purpose of the statement of cash flows.
2. Describe the three types of activities that can either generate or use cash in any business.
3. Reconcile accrual net income to the change in cash.
4. Determine where a company obtains its financing by examining its statement of cash flows.

BASIC ORGANIZATION OF THE STATEMENT OF CASH FLOWS

statement of cash flows
A financial statement that provides information about the causes of a change in a company's cash balance from the beginning to the end of a specific period.

working capital The difference between current assets and current liabilities.

In its present format, the **statement of cash flows** has existed only since 1988. However, other forms of the statement have been in existence for a very long time. These earlier forms were known by such names as the "statement of source and application of funds" and the "statement of changes in financial position." The earlier versions had similar objectives as today's statement of cash flows but focused on working capital rather than on cash in the analysis. **Working capital** consists of current assets and current liabilities. So although they helped users interpret the impact of accrual accounting procedures, they did not bring the financial statement user's focus firmly back to cash.

 Discussion Question

10–1. How do revenue recognition and expense recognition criteria under accrual accounting take the focus off cash?

In addition to providing information about a company's cash receipts and cash payments during a specific period, the statement of cash flows helps investors, creditors, and other external parties to:

1. Assess a company's ability to generate positive future net cash flows
2. Assess a company's need for external financing and its ability to pay its debts and pay dividends
3. Assess a company's overall financial health
4. Reconcile the differences between net income and the change in cash

As you recall from Chapter 5, a firm performs four functions—it operates to generate revenues, invests earnings to support operations, finances operating and investing activities, and makes decisions. To accomplish the disclosure objectives previously listed, we separate the cash inflows and outflows into three categories that conform to the first three functions of a firm:

> Operating
> Investing
> Financing

Exhibit 10–1 contains the basic format of the statement of cash flows.

Exhibit 10–1
Basic Form of the Statement of Cash Flows

Statement of Cash Flows		
For the Year Ended December 31, 2004		
Cash Flows from Operating Activities:		
	$ XXX	
	XX	
Net Cash Provided (Used) by Operating Activities		$XXX
Cash Flows from Investing Activities:		
	$ XX	
	XX	
Net Cash Provided (Used) by Investing Activities		XXX
Cash Flows from Financing Activities:		
	$XXXX	
	XX	
Net Cash Provided (Used) by Financing Activities		XXX
Net Increase (Decrease) in Cash during 2004		$XXX
Beginning Cash Balance, January 1, 2004		XXX
Ending Cash Balance, December 31, 2004		$XXX

Discussion Question

10–2. If you owned a small bookstore, what do you think would be your

   a. operating activities?

   b. investing activities?

   c. financing activities?

Explain your reasons for the classifications you made.

To develop a statement of cash flows, we must identify the business activities that took place during the period and to categorize them as operating, investing, or financing activities. We now describe each type of activity in turn.

Operating Activities

operating activities
Activities that result in cash inflows and outflows generated from the normal course of business.

Operating activities are those centred on the company's primary business activities. These activities generate the company's operating revenues and expenses and utilize the company's current assets and current liabilities. Operating cash inflows come from the firm's customers or from interest or dividends the company receives. Some customers pay for sales at the time of sale and others charge their purchases and pay for them later. Operating cash outflows come from the myriad of expenses a company incurs, whether paid for in cash as incurred or paid for later by paying accounts payable or other payables. How do the cash inflows and outflows differ from income measurement? For cash flow purposes, we measure only the cash inflow or outflows, not the revenues and expenses. Thus, we have come full circle back to the cash basis income.

Discussion Question

10–3. Where would you look for the information to determine net cash flow from operations if your business used the cash basis of accounting?

If you think about the items listed in the previous paragraph, you will see they are all items that are reported on the income statement. Therefore, when attempting to determine the cash inflow and cash outflow from operating activities, we start with the income statement for the period. If a company uses the cash basis of accounting, net income for the period will equal the net cash inflow (or outflow) for the period from operating activities. If, however, a company uses the accrual basis of accounting, the net income figure must be adjusted for any revenue item that did not provide cash during this income statement period and any expense item that did not use cash during this income statement period. You will discover that to determine the operating activities for the cash flow statement, you will analyze the income statement and the current assets and liabilities for items that represent accruals and deferrals of revenues and expenses. We will illustrate how this works later in the chapter.

Discussion Questions

10–4. Recall the situation in which you owned a small bookstore. If one of your customers placed a large book order on account and had 30 days after she received the books to pay for them, how would the revenue from this credit sale be reported for your company
  a. on a cash basis?
  b. on an accrual basis?

10–5. Continuing this scenario, for your company's statement of cash flows, how would you determine the net cash flow from operations in an accrual basis accounting system?

Investing Activities

investing activities
Business activities related to long-term assets. Examples are the purchase and sale of property, plant, and equipment.

Investing activities provide the resources that support operations. This support may take the form of either investments in assets necessary to operate the business or investments outside the company that make wise use of any excess funds. When a company invests in long-term assets, it uses cash. When it sells these assets, it receives cash inflow.

Companies normally sell these types of assets when they are no longer useful to the firm. However, a company cannot logically sell assets it needs to run its operations because the cash generated through operating activities would eventually cease. An airline could generate cash by selling all its airplanes, but if it did so, it would no longer be able to transport passengers and would go out of business. Instead of selling its property, plant, and equipment to generate cash, a growing and healthy company will likely use cash to acquire additional assets that can generate additional revenues. For this reason, healthy, growing companies will usually experience negative net cash flow from investing activities. In such an instance, negative investing cash flow represents economic health.

A company can use cash to purchase the shares of other companies or lend other companies money. Cash is generated when a company sells equity or debt investments (shares or bonds of other companies). If you think about the examples of investing activities mentioned in the previous two paragraphs, you will see they all involve items that are reported in the long-term asset sections of the balance sheet. The only exceptions are current investments and cash loans made to other entities or individuals. All investments and cash loans, whether current or long term, are considered to be investing activities. Current assets, other than cash, that represent accruals of revenue or deferrals of expenses are classified as operating activities. Therefore, when attempting to determine the cash inflow and cash outflow from investing activities, you must analyze the current and long-term asset section of the balance sheets at both the start and the end of the period. We will demonstrate the process a little later in the chapter.

Financing Activities

financing activities
Business activities, such as the issuance of debt or equity and the payment of dividends, that focus on the external financing of the company.

Because internal financing is accomplished through operating activities, **financing activities** reported on the statement of cash flows deal only with external financing. A company obtains cash financing from two external sources: (1) selling common or preferred shares (equity financing) or (2) borrowing from lenders in the form of loans or issuing corporate bonds (debt financing). A company uses cash for financing activities when it repays loan or bond principal, pays dividends to shareholders, and buys back common or preferred shares. Notice that we included only the principal on borrowed money. Cash paid for interest expense is an operating cash outflow.

To determine the items that are reported in the financing activities of the cash flow statement, we analyze the right side of the balance sheet, primarily the long-term liability or owners' equity section. Most of the current liabilities are involved with the operating activities, except for any liabilities representing cash borrowed from banks or other lenders. Any current liabilities that involve cash borrowed instead of expenses accrued are financing activities. Current liabilities that represent expense accruals or revenue deferrals are part of operating activities. We will demonstrate this analysis process a little later in the chapter.

Exhibit 10–2 summarizes the three types of business activities as they are reported in the statement of cash flows. You should refer to this exhibit often as we discuss the construction and uses of the statement, because every inflow and outflow of cash can be classified as a result of operating, investing, or financing activities.

Exhibit 10–2
Summary of the Three
Types of Business
Activities Reported on
the Statement of Cash
Flows

Operating Activities (Income Statement Items)

Cash inflows:

From customers as a result of the sale of goods or services.

From interest earned on loans to others.

From dividends received from investment in the shares of other companies.

Cash outflows:

To suppliers for the purchase of inventory.

To employees for salaries and wages.

To governments for taxes.

To creditors for interest on loans.

To others for operating expenses.

Investing Activities (Long-Term Asset Items)

Cash inflows:

From the sale of property, plant, and equipment.

From the sale of investments in debt or equity securities of other companies.

From the collection of monies loaned to others.

Cash outflows:

To purchase property, plant, and equipment.

To purchase debt and equity investments in other companies or loan money to others.

Financing Activities (Long-Term Liability and Owners' Equity Items)

Cash inflows:

From selling common shares or preferred shares.

From loan proceeds or the sale of corporate bonds.

Cash outflows:

To pay dividends to shareholders.

To reacquire shares from shareholders.

To repay principal of loans or redeem corporate bonds.

Before we begin to construct the statement of cash flows, we must recognize that GAAP, as presented in the *CICA Handbook*, allow us to use two different methods to present the operating cash flows.

Direct Method versus Indirect Method

direct method The format of a statement of cash flows that provides detail about the individual sources and uses of cash associated with operating activities.

indirect method The format of the statement of cash flows that begins with a reconciliation of accrual net income to the cash provided by or used by operating activities.

The *CICA Handbook* allows two methods of preparing the operating section of the statement of cash flows: the direct method and the indirect method. Both arrive at exactly the same amount of cash flow from operations. The difference lies in how the information is presented. Please note that both methods present investing and financing activities in identical formats.

The **direct method** uses a series of calculations to determine the amount of cash inflow (from customers, interest earned on loans, dividends received, etc.) and cash outflow (to suppliers, employees, creditors, for taxes and interest, etc.) by each source. The **indirect method** is more closely tied to accrual accounting. Unlike the direct method, it does not attempt to provide any detail about the individual sources and uses of cash associated with the operating activities of a company. When the indirect method is used, the operating section begins with the accrual net income for the period. Then adjustments are made for all items included in the calculation of net income that did not either generate or use cash.

Recent changes to the *CICA Handbook* include comments encouraging companies to use the direct method, although in practice the indirect method is still the prevalent approach because it is easier to prepare.

CONSTRUCTION OF THE STATEMENT OF CASH FLOWS

We need three financial statements to prepare a statement of cash flows: two consecutive balance sheets and the income statement that bridges them. We will analyze and account for each change in the balance sheet accounts by utilizing the information contained in the income statement and balance sheets. If you think about it, the sum of all items on the left side of the balance sheet equals the sum of all items on the right side of the balance sheet. If we explain the difference in each account other than cash from the beginning to the end of the year, we have successfully explained the difference in cash from the beginning to the end of the year.

To understand this better, consider the following formulas that take the balance sheet equation and convert it into an equation for the statement of cash flows (the symbol Δ means "the change in"):

$$\text{Assets} = \text{Liabilities} + \text{Equity}$$
$$\Delta \text{ Assets} = \Delta \text{ Liabilities} + \Delta \text{ Equity}$$
$$\Delta \text{ Cash} + \Delta \text{ Other Assets} = \Delta \text{ Liabilities} + \Delta \text{ Equity}$$
$$\Delta \text{ Cash} = \Delta \text{ Liabilities} + \Delta \text{ Equity} - \Delta \text{ Other Assets}$$
$$\text{Cash Flow} = \Delta \text{ Liabilities} + \Delta \text{ Equity} - \Delta \text{ Other Assets}$$

As you can see, cash flow can be measured by explaining the change in the balance sheet accounts that are not cash.

For our example, we will use the information provided by the comparative balance sheets of Pipkin Limited for 2004 and 2003 in Exhibit 10–3, and assume Pipkin Limited uses accrual accounting for its income statement in Exhibit 10–4. Be sure you understand that the balances in the asset, liability, and shareholders' equity accounts at the end of one period become the beginning balances in the next period. Thus, Exhibit 10–3 provides beginning and ending balances for all Pipkin Company's balance sheet accounts for the year 2004—necessary information for the preparation of the company's statement of cash flows for 2004.

There are six logical steps to prepare the cash flow statement:

1. Gather the information needed to prepare the statement:
   a. Comparative, consecutive balance sheets
   b. The income statement for the period between the two balance sheets
   c. Any other information needed about noncash transactions
2. Determine the net change in each account of the balance sheets.
3. Determine the method to use for the operating activities section and complete it.
4. Complete the investing activities section.
5. Complete the financing activities section.
6. Add the operating, investing, and financing activities to derive the net change in cash. Check to see whether it agrees with the balance sheet. If it does not, retrace steps one through five.

PIPKIN LIMITED

Balance Sheets

December 31, 2004, and December 31, 2003

(in thousands)

Assets:		2004		2003
Current Assets:				
Cash		$ 2,800		$ 2,420
Accounts Receivable		2,925		3,112
Merchandise Inventory		970		866
Prepaid Expenses		250		200
Total Current Assets		$ 6,945		$ 6,598
Plant and Equipment:				
Land		$ 100		$ 100
Buildings	$9,554		$7,929	
LESS: Accumulated Amortization	4,597		4,417	
Buildings, Net		4,957		3,512
Equipment	$3,359		$2,984	
LESS: Accumulated Amortization	1,955		1,904	
Equipment, Net		1,404		1,080
Total Plant and Equipment		$ 6,461		$ 4,692
Total Assets		$13,406		$11,290
Liabilities:				
Current Liabilities:				
Accounts Payable		$ 2,020		$ 1,816
Notes Payable		3,400		2,700
Total Current Liabilities		$ 5,420		$ 4,516
Long-Term Liabilities		2,500		2,000
Total Liabilities		$ 7,920		$ 6,516
Shareholders' Equity:				
Common Shares		$ 3,400		$ 3,000
Retained Earnings		2,086		1,774
Total Shareholders' Equity		$ 5,486		4,774
Total Liabilities and Shareholders' Equity		$13,406		$11,290

Step 1 Gather information:

    a. Balance sheets are in Exhibit 10–3.

    b. Income statement is in Exhibit 10–4.

    c. Additional information was gathered from Pipkin Limited employees:

        (1) During 2004, Pipkin Limited paid cash for a building for a total cost of $1,625,000 and equipment for a total cost of $375,000.

        (2) During 2004, Pipkin Limited paid $137,000 in cash dividends to its shareholders.

Exhibit 10–4
Income Statement for
Pipkin Limited for 2004

PIPKIN LIMITED

Income Statement

For the Year Ended December 31, 2004

(in thousands)

Sales		$15,158
LESS: Cost of Goods Sold		11,151
Gross Profit		$ 4,007
LESS: Operating Expenses:		
Amortization—Buildings	$ 180	
Amortization—Equipment	51	
Other Selling and Administration	3,047	
Total Operating Expenses		3,278
Operating Income		$ 729
LESS: Interest Expense		160
Income Before Taxes		$ 569
Income Taxes		120
Net Income		$ 449

Discussion Questions

Refer to Exhibit 10–3 to answer the following questions:

10–6. What was Pipkin Limited's balance in accounts receivable on January 1, 2004? Did accounts receivable increase or decrease during 2004?

10–7. What was Pipkin Limited's balance in retained earnings on January 1, 2004? What do you think caused the increase from the beginning of 2004 to the end of the year?

Before we tackle the preparation of the statement of cash flows, we should take a few minutes to review Pipkin Limited's balance sheets and income statement. There are a few items you should note about the financial statements. First, if you look at the cash balances on the two balance sheets in Exhibit 10–3, you will see that cash increased from the start of 2004 to the end of 2004 ($2,800 − $2,420 = $380). Note that the Pipkin Limited's financial statements are presented "in thousands" of dollars so that the $380 increase in cash is really $380,000. What caused the increase? As we discussed before, the increase was caused by all the cash transactions that caused all other balance sheet accounts to change, including the net income. Remember that net income causes the retained earnings account to change. The statement of cash flows, if properly prepared and analyzed, will disclose exactly what caused cash to change by the amount it did and will reconcile the net income figure with that change in cash.

Discussion Question

10–8. Back to the scenario in which you own a small bookstore. . . What cash flows could you receive or pay out in your book business that would not show up in cash basis net income?

Now we have all the necessary information to prepare Pipkin Limited's statement of cash flows. This detailed explanation of the construction of this statement is not intended to make you an expert preparer, but rather to help you become a wiser user of this financial tool. Knowing how the amounts on a statement of cash flows were determined will help you to assess their usefulness and impact on your decision-making process.

We begin by creating a format for Pipkin Limited's statement of cash flows in Exhibit 10–5.

Exhibit 10–5
Basic Format of the Statement of Cash Flows for Pipkin Limited

PIPKIN LIMITED	
Statement of Cash Flows	
For the Year Ended December 31, 2004	
(in thousands)	
Cash Flows from Operating Activities:	
Net Cash Provided (Used) by Operating Activities	$?
Cash Flows from Investing Activities:	
Net Cash Provided (Used) by Investing Activities	?
Cash Flows from Financing Activities:	
Net Cash Provided (Used) by Financing Activities	?
Net Increase (Decrease) in Cash during 2004	$ 380
Beginning Cash Balance, January 1, 2004	2,420
Ending Cash Balance, December 31, 2004	$2,800

Note two items about this format. First, it is divided into the three broad types of activities that can either generate or use cash (operating, investing, and financing). Second, we have already put three amounts into the statement (the $380,000 increase in cash from the end of 2003 to the end of 2004, and the beginning and ending cash balances). If nothing else, accounting is neat and tidy, and the cash flow statement epitomizes this fact. The cash flow statement is one of the few accounting reports for which we know the result before we start to prepare it. In the case of Pipkin Limited, we determined the change in cash by looking at the comparative balance sheets (Exhibit 10–3). Remember, the more important purpose of the statement of cash flows is not to disclose what the change in cash was, but to disclose what caused the change.

Step 2 Determine the net change in each account on the balance sheet:

See Exhibit 10–6. Notice that the increase (decrease) column adds up exactly like the balance sheet, and the net change in assets must equal the net change in liabilities and equity.

Step 3 Determine the method to use for the operating activities section:

We will first examine the direct method and then the indirect method to prepare the operating activities section of the cash flow statement.

PIPKIN LIMITED
Balance Sheets
December 31, 2004, and December 31, 2003
(in thousands)

Assets:	2004	2003	Increase (Decrease)
Current Assets:			
Cash	$ 2,800	$ 2,420	$ 380
Accounts Receivable	2,925	3,112	(187)
Merchandise Inventory	970	866	104
Prepaid Expenses	250	200	50
Total Current Assets	$ 6,945	$ 6,598	$ 347
Property, Plant, and Equipment:			
Land	$ 100	$ 100	$ 0
Buildings	9,554	7,929	$1,625
LESS: Accumulated Amortization	4,597	4,417	180
Buildings, Net	$ 4,957	$ 3,512	$1,445
Equipment	$ 3,359	$ 2,984	$ 375
LESS: Accumulated Amortization	1,955	1,904	51
Equipment, Net	$ 1,404	$ 1,080	$ 324
Total Property, Plant, and Equipment	$ 6,461	$ 4,692	$1,769
Total Assets	$13,406	$11,290	$2,116
Liabilities:			
Current Liabilities:			
Accounts Payable	$ 2,020	$ 1,816	$ 204
Notes Payable	3,400	2,700	700
Total Current Liabilities	$ 5,420	$ 4,516	$ 904
Long-Term Liabilities	2,500	2,000	500
Total Liabilities	$ 7,920	$ 6,516	$1,404
Shareholders' Equity:			
Common Shares	$ 3,400	$ 3,000	$ 400
Retained Earnings	2,086	1,774	312
Total Shareholders' Equity	$ 5,486	$ 4,774	$ 712
Total Liabilities and Shareholders' Equity	$13,406	$11,290	$2,116

Determining Cash Flow from Operating Activities— Direct Method

The *CICA Handbook* indicates that the preferred preparation method for the operating section is the direct method, supplemented. To prepare the direct method, we transform the income statement into a statement of cash receipts and disbursements by reversing the accruals and deferrals used in creating the accrual basis accounting. Does it seem that we are going backwards? We might consider it going forward in a circular pattern. We circle back to the cash view of the business because it presents the reality of cash. If we think of it as reversing the accrual process, it should not be very difficult. To accomplish this feat, we examine the income statement along with the current assets and current liabilities on the comparative balance sheets.

We begin by assembling our information and examining the format that we must use to create the direct method. Exhibit 10–7 contains the basic form for the direct method operating activities.

> **PIPKIN LIMITED**
> **Partial Statement of Cash Flows**
> **For the Year Ended December 31, 2004**
> **(in thousands)**
>
> | | | |
> |---|---:|---:|
> | Cash Flows from Operating Activities: | | |
> | Cash Received from Customers | | $? |
> | Cash Paid for: | | |
> | Merchandise | $? | |
> | Operating Expenses | ? | |
> | Interest | ? | |
> | Income Taxes | ? | |
> | Net Cash Provided (Used) by Operating Activities | | $? |

We must determine five values to complete the operating section. These five values correspond to the revenue and expense items on the income statement, excluding noncash items. If the income statement listed more items, the statement of cash flows could also list more values.

1. **Cash received from customers**—To determine the cash that customers paid, we must examine Sales and Accounts Receivable. Sales made during the period increase Accounts Receivable, and cash paid by customers decreases it. We can formulate the following mathematical relationship between sales, cash, and accounts receivable (A/R):

$$\text{Beginning A/R} + \text{Sales} - \text{Customers' Cash Payments} = \text{Ending A/R}$$

Anytime we know all but one item in an equation, we can solve for the unknown. We know the beginning and ending balances of Accounts Receivable from the comparative balance sheets and Sales from the income statement. Therefore we can determine the amount of cash collected from customers as follows:

$$\text{Beginning A/R} + \text{Sales} - \text{Customers' Cash Payments} = \text{Ending A/R}$$
$$\$3,112 + \$15,158 - \text{Customers' Cash Payments} = \$2,925$$
$$\text{Customers' Cash Payments} = \$3,112 + \$15,158 - \$2,925$$
$$\text{Customers' Cash Payments} = \$15,345$$

Another way to view this equation is as follows:

$$\text{Sales} +/- \text{Change in Accounts Receivable} = \text{Customers' Cash Payments}$$

If the balance in the accounts receivable is rising, this indicates that a portion of sales is not being collected in cash. Therefore, increases in accounts receivable reduce cash inflows while decreases in accounts receivable increase cash flow. Notice how the change in accounts receivable is inversely related to the effect it has on cash flows. The relationship holds for all types of assets, not just accounts receivable. For example, if inventory or buildings or any other asset increases, this will reduce a company's cash flow. For Pipkin Limited, the opposite is occurring. The balance in the accounts receivable account is falling by $187 ($3,112 – $2,925), and this means that a greater proportion of accounts receivable is being collected, thereby improving cash flows. We can calculate the customers' cash payments as follows:

$$\$15,158 + \$187 = \$15,345$$

2. **Cash paid for merchandise**—To determine the cash paid for merchandise, we must look at the relationship between Cost of Goods Sold, Inventory, and Accounts Payable. Purchases of new merchandise increase the Inventory account, and the cost of product sold decreases it. Purchases of new merchandise increase the Accounts Payable account, and payment of cash for purchases decreases it. We can establish the following mathematical relationship among Cost of Goods Sold, Inventory, Accounts Payable (A/P), and cash paid for merchandise:

   Beginning Inventory + Purchases − Cost of Goods Sold = Ending Inventory

   and

   Beginning A/P + Purchases − Cash Paid for Merchandise = Ending A/P

   By substituting information, we can determine the cash paid for merchandise:

   Beginning Inventory + Purchases − Cost of Goods Sold = Ending Inventory
   $$\$866 + \text{Purchases} - \$11,151 = \$970$$
   $$\text{Purchases} = \$970 - \$866 + \$11,151$$
   $$\text{Purchases} = \$11,255$$

   Beginning A/P + Purchases − Cash Paid
   for Merchandise = Ending A/P
   $$\$1,816 + \$11,255 - \text{Cash Paid for Merchandise} = \$2,020$$
   $$\text{Cash Paid for Merchandise} = \$1,816 + \$11,255 - \$2,020$$
   $$\text{Cash Paid for Merchandise} = \$11,051$$

   Again, an alternative way to view the above is to combine the income statement item with the changes in related balance sheet accounts to calculate the related cash flow.

   Cost of Goods Sold +/− Change in Inventory +/− Change in Accounts Payable
   = Cash Paid for Merchandise

   In this case, with regard to the balance sheet account changes, we are dealing with a change in an asset and a change in a liability account. Recall that changes in asset accounts are inversely related to their effect on cash flows. Liability account changes, on the other hand, are directly related to cash flow effects. For example, if a bank loan account balance rises, this increases cash flow, whereas if it falls because a portion of it was paid down, cash flow will also fall. For Pipkin Limited, there is an increase in inventory of $104($970 − $866), which lowers cash flow. There is an increase in accounts payable of $204 ($2,020 − $1,816), which increases cash flow. Since we are calculating a cash outflow amount for cash paid for merchandise, this can be calculated as follows:

   $$\$11,151 + \$104 - \$204 = \$11,051$$

3. **Cash paid for operating expenses**—To determine the cash paid for operating expenses, we examine the Operating Expenses on the income statement and Prepaid Expenses and Accrued Expenses Payable on the balance sheet. When we incur operating expenses, we frequently either pay them in advance (such as insurance or rent) or pay them after the fact (such as supplies, utilities, and wages). Prepaid Expenses is increased by payments of cash and decreased by recognition of the expense on the income statement. Incurring an expense increases Accrued Expenses Payable, and payment of the expense decreases the accrued expense account. We could establish the following mathematical relationships among Operating Expenses, Prepaid Expenses (PP Expenses), Accrued Expenses Payable (AE), and cash paid for operating expenses:

Beginning PP Expenses + Cash Paid for Operating Expenses −
Expense Used = Ending PP Expenses

and

Beginning AE + Expense Used − Cash Paid for Operating Expenses = Ending AE

By substituting information from the balance sheet and income statement, we can determine the cash paid for operating expenses. Because Pipkin Limited has no accrued expenses, we need only make the computation for prepaid expenses.

Beginning PP Expenses + Cash Paid for
Operating Expenses − Expense Used = Ending PP Expenses
$200 + Cash Paid for Operating Expenses − $3,047 = $250
Cash Paid for Operating Expenses = $250 − $200 + $3,047
Cash Paid for Operating Expenses = $3,097

An alternative way to calculate cash paid for operating activities is to combine the related income statement account with the change in the related balance sheet account. In this case:

Operating Expenses +/− Change in Prepaid Expenses +/− Change in Accrued
Expenses Payable = Cash Paid for Operating Expenses

For Pipkin Limited, Prepaid Expenses increased by $50 and there was no Accrued Expenses Payable balance. Like any increase in asset, the $50 increase is a cash outflow. Therefore, we can calculate Cash Paid for Operating Expenses as follows:

$3,047 + $50 = $3,097

4. **Cash paid for interest**—To determine the amount of cash paid for interest, we explore the relationship between Interest Expense and the liability for Accrued Interest. The passage of time without payment triggers interest expense, which increases the Accrued Interest Payable account, and payment of interest decreases the account. We can formulate the following mathematical relationship among Interest Expense, Accrued Interest Expense, and cash payments for interest:

Beginning Accrued Interest Payable +
Interest Expense − Cash Interest Payments = Ending Accrued Interest Payable
$0 + $160 − Cash Interest Payments = $0
Cash Interest Payments = $160

We can therefore conclude that when there is no beginning and ending balance in the Accrued Interest Payable account, the cash paid equals the expense amount.

An alternative way to calculate cash paid for interest is to combine the related income statement account with the change in the related balance sheet account. In this case:

Interest Expense +/− Change in Accrued Interest Payable
= Cash Interest Payments

For Pipkin Limited, there was no Accrued Interest Payable balance. Therefore, we can calculate Cash Interest Payments as follows:

$160 + $0 = $160

5. **Cash paid for income taxes**—To calculate the cash paid for income taxes, we examine the income tax expense and the income taxes payable account. The income taxes payable account is increased by the tax expense for the period and decreased by the cash payments made during the period. We can express the mathematical relationship between the income tax expense, income taxes payable, and the cash paid for income taxes as follows:

Beginning Taxes Payable + Income Tax Expense − Cash Tax Payments
= Ending Taxes Payable
$0 + $120 − Cash Tax Payments = $0
Cash Tax Payments = $120

Similar to the interest expense, Pipkin Limited has no beginning or ending income taxes payable account, so the amount paid in cash for income taxes equals the expense.

An alternative way to calculate cash paid for income taxes is to combine the related income statement account with the change in the related balance sheet account. In this case:

Income Tax Expense +/− Change in Income Taxes Payable
= Cash Paid for Income Taxes

For Pipkin Limited, there was no Income Taxes Payable balance. Therefore, we can calculate Cash Paid for Income Taxes as follows:

$120 + $0 = $120

Now we can insert our calculations into the format and complete Pipkin Limited's direct method net cash flow from operating activities section of the cash flow statement in Exhibit 10–8.

Exhibit 10–8
Basic Format of Direct Method Operating Activities of the Cash Flow Statement

PIPKIN LIMITED
Partial Statement of Cash Flows
For the Year Ended December 31, 2004
(in thousands)

Cash Flows from Operating Activities:		
Cash Received from Customers		$15,345
Cash Paid for:		
Merchandise	$11,051	
Operating Expenses	3,097	
Interest	160	
Income Taxes	120	14,428
Net Cash Provided (Used) by Operating Activities		$ 917

 Discussion Question

10–9. What items from the income statement were included in the direct method operating activities? What items were omitted? Why?

10–10. For each item on the income statement that is included in the direct method operating activities, what balance sheet account changes are added or subtracted in arriving at the related cash flow item?

We can now turn our attention to the indirect method of presenting cash flow from operations.

Determining Cash Flow from Operating Activities— Indirect Method

The indirect method receives its name from its format, which begins with net income and transforms net income into cash flow from operations. We can do this because most items involved in net income, except amortization and gains and losses, are either already cash or are expected to eventually become or use cash. Revenues will eventually become cash inflows, and most expenses (except amortization) will eventually become cash outflows. Over the entire life of the company, net income on the cash basis and accrual basis will equal one another. Therefore, we must adjust the net income figure for any differences between the cash and accrual basis of revenue and expense recognition. In addition, gains and losses recognized on the income statement do not represent cash flows. We also want to remove those activities from the operating section because they were placed into the section by listing net income. In summary, we will remove accrual differences, noncash expenses, and nonoperating activities from net income to arrive at cash flow from operations.

We will begin our trek through the indirect method by looking at the basic format for the indirect method in Exhibit 10–9.

Exhibit 10–9
Basic Format for Pipkin Limited's Indirect Method Operating Section of the Statement of Cash Flows

PIPKIN LIMITED
Partial Statement of Cash Flows
For the Year Ended December 31, 2004
(in thousands)

Cash Flows from Operating Activities:		
Net Income		$449
Adjustments to Reconcile Net Income		
to Net Cash Provided by Operating Activities:		
Amortization Expense	$231	
Gain or Loss on Sale of Assets		
Increase in ?	?	
Decrease in ?	?	
Net Cash Provided (Used) by Operating Activities		$?

As we mentioned, we make three basic types of adjustments to net income. We list these in the following order on the cash flow statement:

1. Add back amortization.
2. Add back losses or subtract gains on the sale of assets or any other investing and financing event.
3. Add or subtract the adjustments for accrual accounting from current assets and current liabilities that represent operating activities. Remember not to include current Marketable Securities, Notes Payable, and the current portion of a long-term loan, because these represent investing and financing activities.

We will utilize information primarily from the income statement, the current assets and current liabilities, and other information pertinent to preparing the report. We need to determine three groups of values:

1. **Amortization**—Because amortization represents a noncash expenditure of converting the cost of long-lived items (buildings and equipment in Pipkin Limited's case) from asset to expense, the deduction for them on the income statement reduces income but not cash. Therefore, we must add the amount of amortization expense for the period to net income in converting it into a cash flow account. Pipkin Limited's income statement (Exhibit 10–4) had amortization expense of $231,000 for the year ($180,000 on buildings and $51,000 on equipment). Thus, our adjustment is $231,000.

   What if amortization were included in cost of goods sold or combined with other expenses? Is it possible to determine how much amortization was expensed? The answer is yes. Provided that no amortizable assets were disposed of, we can look at the change in the Accumulated Amortization accounts or the intangible asset accounts to determine the amounts. First look on the income statement to determine whether there are any gains or losses on the disposal of assets. Pipkin Limited had none for 2004. Next, look at Exhibit 10–6. The net change in the Accumulated Amortization accounts for buildings was $180,000 and for equipment $51,000. This amount matches the information we found on the income statement.

2. **Gains or losses on disposal of assets**—The income statement shows no gains or losses on disposal of assets. Another clue would be finding that the amount of net property, plant, and equipment or intangible assets decreased more than the amount of the amortization.

3. **Changes in current assets or current liabilities**—As we saw with the analysis of the direct method, the change in current assets and current liabilities is directly related to the difference between cash and accrual basis statements. We now look at each account, reproduced in Exhibit 10–10.

   a. **Accounts Receivable**—According to Pipkin Limited's balance sheets, Accounts Receivable decreased $187,000 during 2004. If you refer back to our analysis of cash received from customers in the direct method, the cash received was $15,345,000 compared with sales of $15,158,000. The difference is $187,000. The only way Accounts Receivable can decrease is for the customers' payments to exceed current sales. Conversely, the only way Accounts Receivable can increase is for current sales to exceed customers'

Exhibit 10–10
Current Assets and Current Liabilities Sections of Balance Sheets for Pipkin Limited for 2004 and 2003

PIPKIN LIMITED			
Partial Balance Sheets			
December 31, 2004, and December 31, 2003			
Current Assets and Current Liabilities Only			
(in thousands)			
	2004	**2003**	**Increase (Decrease)**
Current Assets:			
Cash	$2,800	$2,420	$380
Accounts Receivable	2,925	3,112	(187)
Merchandise Inventory	970	866	104
Prepaid Expenses	250	200	50
Total Current Assets	$6,945	$6,598	$347
Current Liabilities:			
Accounts Payable	$2,020	$1,816	$204
Notes Payable	3,400	2,700	700
Total Current Liabilities	$5,420	$4,516	$904

payments. Therefore, we add decreases in Accounts Receivable and subtract increases in Accounts Receivable to convert from the accrual basis to the cash basis. We must add the $187,000 as an adjustment to net income.

b. **Merchandise Inventory**—The inventory account increased by $104,000 during 2004 according to Exhibit 10–6. The increase in inventory requires the use of cash resources. When inventory decreases, we use up inventory purchased in previous periods and conserve current cash. As we saw with the direct method, merchandise inventory is linked to accounts payable. However, with the indirect method, we consider each account independently. Therefore, we add decreases and subtract increases in the inventory account to net income. We must subtract Pipkin Limited's increase in the inventory account.

c. **Prepaid Expenses**—Pipkin Limited increased its Prepaid Expenses by $50,000 during 2004. If you refer to the equation for Prepaid Expenses in the direct method, you can see that cash payments generate increases in the account. If the account increases, the cash payments must exceed the amount of the expense. If the account decreases, the cash payments must be less than the amount of the expense. Therefore, we must add decreases and subtract increases in the Prepaid Expenses account. Pipkin's increase in Prepaid Expenses should be subtracted from net income as part of the adjustments.

d. **Accounts Payable**—Pipkin Limited increased its Accounts Payable by $204,000 during 2004. After examining the equation for the account in the direct method section, you can see that purchases increase the amount of the Accounts Payable and payments reduce it. If the account increases during a period, then the firm purchases more than it pays. Conversely, if the company pays more cash on the liability than it purchases, the account balance will decrease. Therefore, we will add increases and subtract decreases in the account as an adjustment to net income. Notice that increases and decreases in liabilities take the opposite sign of increases and decreases to assets. Pipkin's $204,000 will be added to the net income.

e. **Notes Payable**—Changes in Notes Payable represent financing activities even though it is a current liability.

With these calculations made, we can complete the operating section of the cash flow statement in Exhibit 10–11.

Exhibit 10–11
Basic Format for Pipkin Limited's Indirect Method Operating Section of the Statement of Cash Flows

PIPKIN LIMITED		
Partial Statement of Cash Flows		
For the Year Ended December 31, 2004		
(in thousands)		
Cash Flows from Operating Activities:		
Net Income		$449
Adjustments to Reconcile Net Income		
to Net Cash Provided by Operating Activities:		
Amortization Expense	$231	
Decrease in Accounts Receivable	187	
Increase in Merchandise Inventory	(104)	
Increase in Prepaid Expenses	(50)	
Increase in Accounts Payable	204	468
Net Cash Provided (Used) by Operating Activities		$917

Discussion Questions

10–11. Compare the two amounts of operating activities in Exhibits 10–8 and 10–11. Explain the results.

10–12. How would you use the information given in the direct method? Indirect method? Which do you prefer?

Step 4 Complete the Investing Activities Section:

Determining Cash Flow from Investing Activities

Determining cash flow from investing activities requires analysis of the noncurrent assets plus additional information we collected. Exhibit 10–12 duplicates that section from the company's comparative balance sheets.

Exhibit 10–12
Long-Term Asset Section of Balance Sheets for Pipkin Limited for 2004 and 2003

			Increase
PIPKIN LIMITED			
Partial Balance Sheets			
December 31, 2004, and December 31, 2003			
Long-Term Assets Only			
(in thousands)			
	2004	**2003**	**(Decrease)**
Plant and Equipment:			
Buildings	$9,554	$7,929	$1,625
LESS: Accumulated Amortization	4,597	4,417	180
Buildings, Net	$4,957	$3,512	$1,445
Equipment	$3,359	$2,984	$ 375
LESS: Accumulated Amortization	1,955	1,904	51
Equipment, Net	$1,404	$1,080	$ 324
Total Plant and Equipment	$6,361	$4,592	$1,769

The $1,625,000 increase in the building account and the $375,000 increase in the equipment account make us suspect that Pipkin Limited invested in a new building and new equipment. We can verify this information from the additional information we gathered in Step 2 that indicated the $2,000,000 investment was paid by cash. The only other changes in the plant and equipment accounts represent the amortization for the current year that we examined in the indirect method section on amortization. Pipkin Limited has two investing activities that we can add to the growing cash flow statement in Exhibit 10–13.

Exhibit 10–13
Partial Statement of
Cash Flows for Pipkin
Limited Operating
Activities and Investing
Activities Sections

PIPKIN LIMITED

Partial Statement of Cash Flows

For the Year Ended December 31, 2004

(in thousands)

Cash Flows from Operating Activities:		
Net Income		$449
Adjustments to Reconcile Net Income		
to Net Cash Provided by Operating Activities:		
Amortization Expense	$231	
Decrease in Accounts Receivable	187	
Increase in Merchandise Inventory	(104)	
Increase in Prepaid Expense	(50)	
Increase in Accounts Payable	204	468
Net Cash Provided by Operating Activities		$917
Cash Flows from Investing Activities:		
Purchase of Building	$(1,625)	
Purchase of Equipment	(375)	
Net Cash Used by Investing Activities		(2,000)

Step 5 Complete the Financing Activities Section:

Determining Cash Flow from Financing Activities

By analyzing the liabilities and shareholders' equity sections of the balance sheet, we can determine Pipkin's financing activities. We have duplicated those sections from Pipkin Limited's comparative balance sheets in Exhibit 10–14.

Exhibit 10–14
Long-Term Liabilities
and Shareholders'
Equity Sections of
Balance Sheets for
Pipkin Limited for
2004 and 2003

PIPKIN LIMITED

Partial Balance Sheets

December 31, 2004, and December 31, 2003

Long-Term Liabilities and Shareholders' Equity Only

(in thousands)

	2004	2003	Increase (Decrease)
Notes Payable	$3,400	$2,700	$700
Long-Term Liabilities	2,500	2,000	500
Common Shares	3,400	3,000	400
Retained Earnings	2,086	1,774	312

We must consider the changes in the notes payable from current liabilities, long-term liabilities, and equity accounts. Pipkin Limited increased its Notes Payable by $700,000 and its Long-Term Liabilities by $500,000. In addition, it sold $400,000 of common shares. All of these changes represent cash inflows to the company. But what about the $312,000 change in Retained Earnings? We can examine the composition of Retained Earnings to see what increases and decreases it by referring back to Exhibit 10–6. Net income increases Retained Earnings, and dividends decrease Retained Earnings. We can generate this formula for Retained Earnings (R/E):

Beginning R/E + Net Income − Dividends = Ending R/E
$1,774,000 + $449,000 − Dividends = $2,086,000
Dividends = $2,086,000 − $1,774,000 − $449,000
Dividends = $137,000

We can verify this calculation with the additional information we gathered in Step 1. The dividends represent a financing cash outflow. We can now complete the statement of cash flows in Exhibit 10–15.

Exhibit 10–15
Complete Statement of Cash Flows for Pipkin Limited

PIPKIN LIMITED
Statement of Cash Flows
For the Year Ended December 31, 2004
(in thousands)

Cash Flows from Operating Activities:		
Net Income		$ 449
Adjustments to Reconcile Net Income		
to Net Cash Provided by Operating Activities:		
Amortization Expense	$ 231	
Decrease in Accounts Receivable	187	
Increase in Merchandise Inventory	(104)	
Increase in Prepaid Expense	(50)	
Increase in Accounts Payable	204	468
Net Cash Provided by Operating Activities		$ 917
Cash Flows from Investing Activities:		
Purchase of Building	$(1,625)	
Purchase of Equipment	(375)	
Net Cash Used by Investing Activities		$(2,000)
Cash Flows from Financing Activities:		
Proceeds from Long-Term Loan	$ 500	
Proceeds from Notes Payable	700	
Proceeds from Sale of Common Shares	400	
Payment of Cash Dividends	(137)	
Net Cash Provided by Financing Activities		$ 1,463
Net Increase in Cash during 2004		$ 380
Beginning Cash Balance, January 1, 2004		2,420
Ending Cash Balance, December 31, 2004		$ 2,800

Pipkin Limited's statement of cash flows was fairly simple to create because there were relatively few things to consider in its construction. Statements of cash flows for actual companies can be complicated. But whether simple or complex, all statements of cash flows assume the basic format used for Pipkin Limited.

Disposals of Property, Plant, and Equipment

When these types of assets are sold, an inflow of cash results. The proceeds received upon the sale of such assets should be shown in the investing section of the statement of cash flows. In addition to this, a gain or loss is usually recorded in the income statement. Like amortization, these items do not represent cash flows. To illustrate this, consider a company selling land that cost $100,000 for $180,000.

Obviously a gain of $80,000 would be recorded, but what is the related cash flow? Clearly it is $180,000 and this amount would not change even if the land cost $120,000 and the gain was only $60,000. The gain, therefore, is the difference between the cash inflow of $180,000 and the cost of the land. It is not a cash inflow. So when we prepare the operating activity section using the indirect method, the gain of $80,000 would be deducted from net income to eliminate its effect on net income because it does not represent a cash flow.

Supplemental Schedule

If the indirect method is used, amounts paid for interest and for income taxes must be disclosed at the bottom of the statement of cash flows. Such disclosure is done to allow readers to understand the cash flow relating to these two critical items. Additional information should also be provided that outlines any significant non-cash investing and financing activities. Examples of such transactions include trading an asset for another, buying an asset with borrowed funds, or repaying a loan by issuing shares. In such transactions, no cash exchanges occur but the transaction may have future cash consequences. For example, suppose a company buys a building through mortgage financing. Although this has no major cash flow implications today, future cash flows will be affected since mortgage payments will be made. Readers of the financial statements have to be made aware of these future events.

HOW TO USE THE STATEMENT OF CASH FLOWS

The purpose of the statement of cash flows is to disclose the company's inflows and outflows of cash during a specific time period. One of the most important things the statement shows is what a company invested in during the period and how that investment was financed. Investments in long-lived productive assets produce revenues and, eventually, cash. Operating and financing activities finance investments. How that investment was financed is presented in both the top section of the statement (operating activities) and the bottom section of the statement (financing activities).

To demonstrate this concept, we have extracted the cash flow totals for the three types of activities from Pipkin Limited's statement of cash flows (Exhibit 10–15):

Net cash provided by operating activities	$ 917,000
Net cash used by investing activities	$(2,000,000)
Net cash provided by financing activities	$ 1,463,000

The amounts shown above for Pipkin Limited are typical of most profitable and growing companies. The cash from operations is positive and is generally higher than net income for two reasons: amortization has been added back to net income, and changes in noncash working capital have contributed to cash flows. This is illustrated below:

Net income	$449
Amortization	231
Changes in noncash working capital	237
Net cash provided by operating activities	$917

When analyzing the statement of cash flows, be careful to observe adjustments caused by noncash income statement items. These items, in particular gains, do not necessarily translate into cash flows although they increase net income. Also be aware of the overall effect of the changes in noncash working capital accounts. If these items are not increasing cash flows, it may be indicative of poor management by the company over the collection of accounts receivable, the ordering of inventory, and the payment of accounts payable. Companies should strive to collect accounts receivable as quickly as possible given the normal credit terms granted to customers by the industry. Companies should also strive to order inventory at appropriate times so that the level of inventory is not too high or too low. Finally, accounts payable should be paid on the due date and not before that date to better utilize the company's cash.

For most companies, the investing activities section of the statement of cash flows will show a total outflow of cash. This indicates that the company is growing and replacing property, plant, and equipment. When this subtotal shows a negative amount, it indicates that the company may be short of cash and is seeking funds by selling its long-term assets.

Pipkin Limited invested $2,000,000 in a building and equipment during 2004. It made the investment to enhance the way the company conducts its business by upgrading its manufacturing facilities, allowing entry into new markets, or developing new products. Although we cannot assess whether this investment was good or bad, we can determine how the company financed it.

Pipkin Limited or any company has only two sources of available cash. A company either generates cash internally (from profitable operations) or obtains cash from external sources (borrowing, or selling shares). Pipkin Limited generated about 46 percent of the cash required for the investment internally (from operating activities) and the balance from outside sources (financing activities). With that in mind, focus on this important concept: **In the long run, all investments must be financed through operations, because the only renewable source of cash is operations.** A firm can borrow only a finite amount of cash, can sell only a finite amount of shares, and can sell only a few of its assets or it will have none. Operations provide a renewable source of cash limited only by the firm's ability to operate profitably.

Now you can see why the statement of cash flows is an economic decision maker's most valuable tool in determining how a company finances its investments. By carefully examining it, users can obtain insights into many aspects of a company's operations. The statement of cash flows, in combination with the three financial statements introduced earlier in this text (income statement, statement of owners' equity [or retained earnings], and balance sheet), provides important information upon which economic decision makers rely. In the next chapter we will explore other methods of analyzing the financial statements to make decisions for and about a company.

SUMMARY

Accountants developed the statement of cash flows to give financial statement users information about the cash flows of companies during a particular period. Information necessary for the development of a statement of cash flows can be found on a company's comparative balance sheets and the income statement of the period. A company may choose whether to calculate operating cash flows by the direct or indirect method.

The statement of cash flows provides information about cash flows used by or provided by three major functions (or activities) of the firm: operating, investing, and financing. Operating cash flows represent cash provided from revenue-producing activities and are similar to cash basis net income. Healthy companies have positive operating cash flows. To compute operating activities cash flow, analyze the income statement, current assets, and current liabilities.

Investing cash flows represent cash inflows and outflows from the long-term assets the firm buys and sells. Typical transactions that are classified as investing activities are the purchase and sale of property, plant, and equipment or long-term investments in other companies. Growing companies normally have negative investing cash flows.

The financing activities section of the statement of cash flows shows what types of external financing the company used to provide funds. Information showing the results of financing activities can be found in the long-term liability section and the equity section of the balance sheet.

The statement of cash flows furnishes valuable information about the cash inflows and outflows of a business during a particular period. It provides an explanation of the changes in cash from the beginning to the end of a period. Therefore, the statement of cash flows can be considered a financial statement analysis tool as well as a financial statement.

KEY TERMS

direct method, p. 358
financing activities, p. 357
indirect method, p. 358
investing activities, p. 357

operating activities, p. 356
statement of cash flows, p. 354
working capital, p. 354

REVIEW THE FACTS

1. When did the present format of the statement of cash flows come into existence?
2. What is the main purpose of the statement of cash flows?
3. Name the two methods of preparing the statement of cash flows. Which method is more commonly used by publicly traded companies?
4. What are the three major classifications of activities presented on the statement of cash flows?
5. In what category are the cash flows related to interest and dividends received and interest paid usually reported?
6. Provide examples of an inflow of cash and an outflow of cash for each of the three categories of business activity shown on the statement of cash flows.
7. Distinguish between the direct method and the indirect method of presenting operating cash flows.
8. What is the starting point for calculation of cash flows from operating activities using the indirect method?
9. Where are the items included in operating activities reported in the financial statements?
10. Where are the items included in investing activities reported in the financial statements?
11. Where are the items included in financing activities reported in the financial statements?
12. Which section(s) of the statement of cash flows tells the user how much cash the company used to acquire amortizable assets?
13. Which section(s) of the statement of cash flows tells the user how investments made by the company were financed?

APPLY WHAT YOU HAVE LEARNED

LO 1: Cash Flow Terminology

1. Presented below is a list of items relating to the concepts discussed in this chapter, followed by definitions of those items in scrambled order:

a. Operating activities
b. Indirect method
c. Amortization expense
d. Comparative financial statements

e. Financing activities
f. Working capital
g. Direct method
h. Investing activities

1. _b_ Provides a reconciliation of accrual net income to the cash provided by or used by operating activities
2. _d_ Accounting reports providing information from two or more consecutive periods at once
3. _a_ Activities centred on the actual day-to-day business transactions of a company
4. _f_ Current assets less current liabilities
5. _e_ Business activities related to long-term assets
6. _g_ Provides detail as to the individual sources and uses of cash associated with operating activities
7. _c_ An item that reduces reported net income but does not require the use of cash
8. _h_ Activities such as the issuance of debt or equity and the payment of dividends

REQUIRED:
Match the letter next to each item on the list with the appropriate definition. Each letter will be used only once.

LO 2: Identification of Activities

2. Listed below are the three broad types of activities that can either generate or use cash in any business, followed by descriptions of various items.

a. Operating activities
b. Investing activities

c. Financing activities

1. _b_ Payment of dividends
2. _a_ Amortization
3. _a_ Purchase of merchandise inventory
4. _a_ Purchase of vehicles
5. _b_ Repayment of 90-day loans
6. _b_ Issuing common shares
7. _a_ Payment of wages to employees
8. _a_ Payment of taxes
9. _c_ Cash from sale of property and equipment
10. _c_ Loans to other companies
11. _a_ Adjustments for changes in current asset and current liability items
12. _c_ Cash from selling investments in other companies

REQUIRED:
Classify each of the items listed above by placing the letter of the appropriate activity category in the space provided.

LO 2: Identification of Activities

3. Listed below are the three broad types of activities that can either generate or use cash in any business, followed by descriptions of various items.

a. Operating activities   **c.** Financing activities
b. Investing activities

1. _a_ Amortization expense
2. _b_ Purchase of a building
3. _a_ Sale of merchandise inventory
4. _c_ Sale of shares
5. _b_ Repayment of 30-day loans
6. _c_ Purchase of one's own shares
7. _a_ Payment of rent on office space
8. _a_ Payment of insurance on factory equipment
9. _b_ Cash from sale of land
10. _c_ Purchase of shares in other companies
11. _c_ Cash from the sale of bonds held for investment
12. _a_ Cash from the collection of accounts receivable

REQUIRED:
Classify each of the items listed above by placing the letter of the appropriate activity category in the space provided.

LO 2: Identification of Sources and Uses—Indirect Method

4. Following are the changes in some of Sam Cagle Limited's assets, liabilities, and equities from December 31, 2003, to December 31, 2004:

1. _____ Accounts payable decreased.
2. _____ Property and equipment increased.
3. _____ Accounts receivable increased.
4. _____ Long-term notes payable decreased.
5. _____ Prepaid expenses decreased.
6. _____ Short-term notes payable increased.
7. _____ Taxes payable decreased.
8. _____ Common shares increased.
9. _____ Wages payable increased.
10. _____ Merchandise inventory decreased.

REQUIRED:
The company is in the process of preparing the operating activities section of its statement of cash flows for 2004. Some of the items above will be included and others will not. Place the letter *I* in the space next to each item that should be considered an inflow of cash in the operating activities section, and place the letter *O* in the space next to each item that should be considered an outflow of cash in the operating activities section. Place the letter *N* next to any item not included in the operating activities section.

LO 3: Operating Activities Section—Indirect Method

5. Presented below are partial comparative balance sheets of Jackson Limited at December 31, 2004 and 2003:

JACKSON LIMITED
Partial Balance Sheets
December 31, 2004, and December 31, 2003
Current Assets and Current Liabilities Only
(in thousands)

	2004	2003	Increase (Decrease)
Current Assets:			
Cash	$3,400	$2,920	$ 480
Accounts Receivable	1,825	2,212	(387)
Merchandise Inventory	1,170	966	204
Prepaid Expenses	240	270	(30)
Total Current Assets	$6,635	$6,368	$ 267
Current Liabilities:			
Accounts Payable	$2,321	$1,740	$ 581
Notes Payable	3,100	3,300	(200)
Total Current Liabilities	$5,421	$5,040	$ 381

Additional Information: Net income for 2004 was $406,000. Included in the operating expenses for the year was amortization expense of $175,000.

REQUIRED:
Prepare the operating activities section of Jackson Limited's statement of cash flows for 2004 using the indirect method.

LO 3: Operating Activities Section—Indirect Method

6. Presented below are partial comparative balance sheets of Scotia Limited at December 31, 2004 and 2003:

SCOTIA LIMITED
Partial Balance Sheets
December 31, 2004, and December 31, 2003
Current Assets and Current Liabilities Only
(in thousands)

	2004	2003	Increase (Decrease)
Current Assets:			
Cash	$2,110	$2,650	$ (540)
Accounts Receivable	1,254	977	277
Merchandise Inventory	730	856	(126)
Prepaid Expenses	127	114	13
Total Current Assets	$4,221	$4,597	$(376)
Current Liabilities:			
Accounts Payable	$1,054	$1,330	$ (276)
Notes Payable	2,100	1,750	350
Total Current Liabilities	$3,154	$3,080	$ 74

Additional Information: Net income for 2004 was $86,900. Included in the operating expenses for the year was amortization expense of $102,000.

REQUIRED:

Prepare the operating activities section of Scotia Limited's statement of cash flows for 2004 using the indirect method.

LO 3: Operating Activities Section—Indirect Method

7. Athabasca Limited's worksheet for the preparation of its 2004 statement of cash flows included the following:

	January 1	December 31
Accounts Receivable	$78,000	$71,000
Prepaid Insurance	48,000	36,000
Inventory	56,000	75,000

Athabasca Limited reported net income of $450,000 for the year.

REQUIRED:

Prepare the cash flow from operating activities section of Athabasca Limited's statement of cash flows using the indirect method.

LO 4: Investing Activities Section

8. In preparing its cash flow statement for the year ended December 31, 2004, Mavis Limited gathered the following data:

Gain on sale of machinery	$18,000
Proceeds from sale of machinery	60,000
Purchase of Fred Inc. bonds (face value $100,000)	80,000
Dividends declared	75,000
Dividends paid	40,000
Proceeds from issuing common shares of Mavis Limited	50,000

REQUIRED:

Prepare the cash flow from investing section of the cash flow statement for Mavis Limited.

LO 4: Investing Activities Section

9. In preparing its cash flow statement for the year ended December 31, 2004, Nash Limited gathered the following data:

Loss on sale of machinery	$ 24,000
Proceeds from sale of machinery	40,000
Purchase of Alco, Inc. bonds (face value $800,000)	980,000
Dividends declared	95,000
Dividends paid	96,000
Purchase of company's own common shares	80,000

REQUIRED:

Prepare the cash flow from investing section of the cash flow statement for Nash Limited.

LO 4: Investing Activities Section

10. In preparing its cash flow statement for the year ended December 31, 2004, Rambler Limited gathered the following data:

Loss on sale of equipment	$ 4,000
Proceeds from sale of equipment	20,000
Purchase of equipment	980,000
Dividends received	35,000
Dividends paid	28,000
Payment of bank loan	60,000

REQUIRED:

Prepare the cash flow from investing section of the cash flow statement for Rambler Limited.

LO 4: Financing Activities Section

11. In preparing its cash flow statement for the year ended December 31, 2004, Reo Limited gathered the following data:

Gain on sale of equipment	$ 4,000
Proceeds from sale of equipment	30,000
Proceeds from sale of common shares	890,000
Dividends declared	35,000
Dividends paid	28,000
Proceeds from bank loan	200,000
Payment of bank loan	60,000

REQUIRED:

Prepare the cash flow from financing section of the cash flow statement for Reo Limited.

LO 4: Financing Activities Section

12. In preparing its cash flow statement for the year ended December 31, 2004, Diamond Limited gathered the following data:

Loss on sale of equipment	$ 54,000
Proceeds from sale of equipment	390,000
Proceeds from sale of preferred shares	200,000
Dividends received	95,000
Dividends paid	80,000
Proceeds from bank loan	300,000
Payment of loan interest	20,000
Repayment of bank loan	120,000

REQUIRED:

Prepare the cash flow from financing section of the cash flow statement for Diamond Limited.

LO 4:   Financing Activities Section

13. In preparing its cash flow statement for the year ended December 31, 2004, Cirrus Limited gathered the following data:

Gain on sale of equipment	$ 27,000
Proceeds from sale of equipment	115,000
Proceeds from sale of preferred shares	100,000
Purchase of land	65,000
Dividends paid	75,000
Proceeds from sale of common shares	500,000
Proceeds from bank loan	300,000
Payment of loan interest	100,000
Repayment of bank loan	400,000

REQUIRED:

Prepare the cash flow from financing section of the cash flow statement for Cirrus Limited.

LO 4:   Concepts of Cash Flow Statements

14. Presented below is Rock Limited's statement of cash flows for the year ended December 31, 2004.

ROCK LIMITED
Statement of Cash Flows
For the Year Ended December 31, 2004
(in thousands)

Cash Flows from Operating Activities:		
Net Income		$ 389
Adjustments to Reconcile Net Income		
to Net Cash Provided by Operating Activities:		
Amortization Expense	$ 131	
Increase in Accounts Receivable	(287)	
Increase in Merchandise Inventory	(104)	
Increase in Prepaid Expense	(70)	
Decrease in Accounts Payable	(4)	(334)
Net Cash Provided by Operating Activities		$ 55
Cash Flows from Investing Activities:		
Purchase of Building	$(1,255)	
Purchase of Equipment	(304)	
Net Cash Used by Investing Activities		$(1,559)
Cash Flows from Financing Activities:		
Proceeds from Long-Term Loan	$ 800	
Proceeds from Sale of Common Shares	300	
Payment of Cash Dividends	(100)	
Net Cash Provided by Financing Activities		$ 1,000
Net Decrease in Cash during 2004		$ (504)
Cash Balance, January 1, 2004		1,000
Cash Balance, December 31, 2004		$ 496

REQUIRED:

Respond to the following questions:

a. For which of the three broad types of activities did Rock Limited use the majority of its cash during 2004?

b. What does your answer to the previous question tell you about Rock Limited?

c. From which of the three broad types of activities did Rock Limited obtain the majority of its cash during 2004?

d. Is the activity you identified in the previous requirement an appropriate source of cash in the long run? Explain your reasoning.

LO 4: Concepts of Cash Flow Statements

15. Presented below is McDougle Limited's statement of cash flows for the year ended December 31, 2004:

McDOUGLE LIMITED
Statement of Cash Flows
For the Year Ended December 31, 2004
(in thousands)

Cash Flows from Operating Activities:		
Net Income		$ 1,608
Adjustments to Reconcile Net Income		
to Net Cash Provided by Operating Activities:		
Amortization Expense	$ 218	
Increase in Accounts Receivable	(341)	
Decrease in Merchandise Inventory	81	
Increase in Prepaid Expense	(100)	
Increase in Accounts Payable	154	12
Net Cash Provided by Operating Activities		$ 1,620
Cash Flows from Investing Activities:		
Purchase of Building	$(1,000)	
Purchase of Equipment	(200)	
Net Cash Used by Investing Activities		$(1,200)
Cash Flows from Financing Activities:		
Repayment of Long-Term Loan	$ (350)	
Proceeds from Sale of Common Shares	350	
Payment of Cash Dividends	(100)	
Net Cash Used by Financing Activities		$ (100)
Net Increase in Cash during 2004		$ 320
Cash Balance, January 1, 2004		430
Cash Balance, December 31, 2004		$ 750

REQUIRED:

Respond to the following questions:

a. For which of the three types of activities did McDougle Limited use the majority of its cash during 2004?

b. What does your answer to the previous question tell you about McDougle Limited?

c. From which of the three types of activities did McDougle Limited obtain the majority of its cash during 2004?

d. Is the activity you identified in the previous requirement an appropriate source of cash in the long run? Explain your reasoning.

LO 4: Preparation of Cash Flow Statement

16. Use the balance sheets, income statement, and the additional information provided below to complete this problem.

HOOPLE LIMITED
Balance Sheets
At December 31, 2004, and December 31, 2003
(in thousands)

		2004		2003
ASSETS:				
Current Assets:				
Cash		$ 1,618		$1,220
Accounts Receivable		1,925		2,112
Merchandise Inventory		1,070		966
Prepaid Expenses		188		149
Total Current Assets		$ 4,801		$4,447
Plant and Equipment:				
Buildings	$4,818		$3,292	
LESS: Accumulated Amortization	(361)		(300)	
Buildings, Net		$ 4,457		$2,992
Equipment	$1,434		$1,145	
LESS: Accumulated Amortization	(141)		(100)	
Equipment, Net		$ 1,293		$1,045
Total Plant and Equipment		$ 5,750		$4,037
Total Assets		$10,551		$8,484
LIABILITIES:				
Current Liabilities:				
Accounts Payable		$ 1,818		$1,686
Notes Payable		900		1,100
Total Current Liabilities		$ 2,718		$2,786
Long-Term Loan		2,500		2,000
Total Liabilities		$ 5,218		$4,786
SHAREHOLDERS' EQUITY:				
Common Shares		$ 3,390		$2,041
Retained Earnings		1,943		1,657
Total Shareholders' Equity		$ 5,333		$3,698
Total Liabilities and				
Shareholders' Equity		$10,551		$8,484

HOOPLE LIMITED
Income Statement
For the Year Ended December 31, 2004
(in thousands)

Net Sales		$11,228
LESS: Cost of Goods Sold		7,751
Gross Profit on Sales		$ 3,477
LESS: Operating Expenses:		
Amortization—Buildings and Equipment	$ 102	
Other Selling and Administrative	2,667	
Total Expenses		2,769
Operating Income		$ 708
LESS: Interest Expense		(168)
Income Before Taxes		$ 540
Income Taxes		(114)
Net Income		$ 426

Additional Information: There were no sales of plant and equipment during the year, and the company paid dividends of $140,000 to shareholders during the year.

REQUIRED:

a. Prepare Hoople Limited's statement of cash flows for the year ended December 31, 2004, using the direct method for operating activities.

b. In which of the three categories of activities did Hoople Limited use the majority of its cash during 2004?

c. What does your answer to the previous question tell you about Hoople Limited?

d. From which of the three types of activities did Hoople Limited obtain the majority of its cash during 2004?

e. Is the activity you identified in the previous requirement an appropriate source of cash in the long run? Explain your reasoning.

LO 4: Preparation of Cash Flow Statement

17. Use the Hoople Limited financial statements in Problem 16 to complete the following requirements.

REQUIRED:

a. Prepare Hoople Limited's statement of cash flows for the year ended December 31, 2004, using the indirect method for operating activities.

b. Why is amortization expense added back in the statement of cash flows created in part a?

LO 4: Preparation of Cash Flow Statement

18. Use the balance sheets, income statement, and the additional information presented below to complete this problem.

MOOSE JAW LIMITED
Balance Sheets
At December 31, 2004, and December 31, 2003
(in thousands)

		2004		2003
ASSETS:				
Current Assets:				
Cash		$ 529		$ 660
Accounts Receivable		1,006		1,011
Merchandise Inventory		396		452
Prepaid Expenses		38		62
Total Current Assets		$ 1,969		$ 2,185
Plant and Equipment:				
Buildings	$2,000		$1,681	
LESS: Accumulated Amortization	(176)		(146)	
Buildings, Net		$ 1,824		$ 1,535
Equipment	$ 809		$ 609	
LESS: Accumulated Amortization	(76)		(61)	
Equipment, Net		$ 733		$ 548
Total Plant and Equipment		$ 2,557		$ 2,083
Total Assets		$ 4,526		$ 4,268
LIABILITIES:				
Current Liabilities:				
Accounts Payable		$ 726		$ 809
Notes Payable		750		600
Total Current Liabilities		$ 1,476		$ 1,409
Long-Term Loan		1,500		1,200
Total Liabilities		$ 2,976		$ 2,609
SHAREHOLDERS' EQUITY:				
Common Shares		$ 1,300		$ 1,000
Retained Earnings		250		659
Total Shareholders' Equity		$ 1,550		$1,659
Total Liabilities and				
Shareholders' Equity		$ 4,526		$ 4,268

MOOSE JAW LIMITED
Income Statement
For the Year Ended December 31, 2004
(in thousands)

Sales		$ 6,391
Less: Cost of Goods Sold		4,474
Gross Profit on Sales		$ 1,917
Less: Operating Expenses:		
Amortization—Buildings and Equipment	$ 45	
Other Selling and Administrative	2,066	
Total Expenses		2,111
Operating Income		$ (194)
Less: Interest Expense		145
Income Before Taxes		$ (339)
Income Taxes		0
Net Loss		$ (339)

Additional Information: There were no sales of plant and equipment during the year, and the company paid dividends to shareholders during the year of $70,000.

REQUIRED:

a. Prepare Moose Jaw Limited's statement of cash flows for the year ended December 31, 2004, using the indirect method for operating activities.

b. In which of the three broad activities did Moose Jaw Limited use the majority of its cash during 2004?

c. What does your answer to the previous question tell you about Moose Jaw Limited?

d. In which of the three broad activities did Moose Jaw Limited obtain the majority of its cash during 2004?

e. Is the activity you identified in the previous requirement an appropriate source of cash in the long run? Explain your reasoning.

f. Prepare Moose Jaw Limited's statement of retained earnings for 2004.

LO 4: Preparation of Cash Flow Statement

19. Use Moose Jaw Limited financial statements in Problem 18 to complete the following requirements.

REQUIRED:

a. Prepare Moose Jaw Limited's statement of cash flows for the year ended December 31, 2004, using the direct method for operating activities.

b. Why are changes in non-cash working capital items not listed on the statement of cash flows created in part a?

LO 4: Analysis of Cash Flow Information

20. Presented below are the totals from the main three sections of Bourassa Construction Limited's most recent statement of cash flows:

Net cash provided by operating activities	$ 1,812,000
Net cash used by investing activities	$(1,280,000)
Net cash used by financing activities	$ (153,000)

REQUIRED:

a. What do these totals tell you about the company?

b. What additional information would you want to see before you analyzed the company's ability to generate positive cash flow in the future?

c. Did the company have a net income or loss for the period? What additional information would you want before trying to predict the company's net income for the next period?

LO 4: Analysis of Cash Flow Information

21. Presented below are the totals from the main three sections of Coleman Limited's most recent statement of cash flows:

Net cash used by operating activities	$ (835,000)
Net cash used by investing activities	$(1,280,000)
Net cash provided by financing activities	$ 2,153,000

REQUIRED:

a. What do these totals tell you about the company?

b. What additional information would you want to see before you analyzed the company's ability to generate positive cash flow in the future?

c. Did the company have a net income or loss for the period? What additional information would you want before trying to predict the company's net income for the next period?

LO 4: Analysis of Cash Flow Information

22. Presented below are the totals from the main three sections of Faulkner Limited's most recent statement of cash flows:

Net cash used by operating activities	$(1,409,000)
Net cash provided by investing activities	$ 1,980,000
Net cash used by financing activities	$ (303,000)

REQUIRED:

a. What do these totals tell you about Faulkner Limited?

b. What additional information would you want to see before you analyzed Faulkner Limited's ability to generate positive cash flow in the future?

LO 4: Discussion

23. Remember, tools are developed to solve problems. This chapter is titled "The Statement of Cash Flows: Bringing the Focus Back to Cash."

REQUIRED:

a. Explain in your own words what caused the focus of financial statements to shift to something other than cash.

b. Describe how the statement of cash flows serves as a tool to bring the focus of economic decision makers back to cash.

LO 4: Discussion—Direct Method versus Indirect Method

24. Compare the two methods for preparing the statement of cash flows, the direct method and the indirect method. Which sections are different and which sections are the same?

LO 4: Amortization and Purchases of Machinery

25. Skaggs Company Limited is preparing a statement of cash flows for the year ended December 31, 2004. Selected beginning and ending account balances are as follows:

	Beginning	Ending
Machinery	$450,000	$475,500
Accumulated Amortization—Machinery	95,000	129,000
Loss on sale of machinery	—	2,000

During the year, the company received $44,500 for a machine that cost $49,500 and purchased other items of machinery.

REQUIRED:

a. Compute the amortization on machinery for the year.
b. Compute the amount of machinery purchases for the year.

LO 4: Amortization and Purchases of Machinery

26. Miles Company Limited is preparing a statement of cash flows for the year ended December 31, 2004. Selected beginning and ending account balances are as follows:

	Beginning	Ending
Machinery	$250,000	$280,000
Accumulated Amortization—Machinery	65,000	89,000
Gain on sale of machinery	—	2,000

During the year, the company received $50,000 for a machine that cost $65,000 and purchased other items of machinery.

REQUIRED:

a. Compute the amortization on machinery for the year.
b. Compute the amount of machinery purchases for the year.

LO 4: Amortization and Purchases of Equipment

27. Bennett Limited is preparing a statement of cash flows for the year ended December 31, 2004. Selected beginning and ending account balances are as follows:

	Beginning	Ending
Computers	$300,000	$390,000
Accumulated Amortization—Computers	165,000	215,000
Gain on sale of computers	—	12,000

During the year, the company received $20,000 for a computer that cost $40,000 and purchased other computer items.

REQUIRED:

a. Compute the amortization on computers for the year.
b. Compute the amount of computer purchases for the year.

LO 4: Operating Activities—Direct Method

28. Foster Limited gathered the following information from its accounting records:

Collections from customers	$450,000
Payments to suppliers	150,000
Payments for income taxes	75,000
Interest received from investments	5,000
Payments to employees	64,000
Payments for interest	85,000
Amortization expense	50,000

REQUIRED:

Prepare the operating section of the cash flow statement for Foster Limited using the direct method.

LO 4: Operating Activities—Direct Method

29. Galway Company Limited gathered the following information from its accounting records:

Collections of accounts receivable	$350,000
Cash sales	85,000
Payments to suppliers	260,000
Payments for income taxes	45,000
Interest received from investments	15,000
Payments to employees	95,000
Payments for interest	68,000
Amortization expense	25,000

REQUIRED:

Prepare the operating section of the cash flow statement for the company using the direct method.

LO 4: Operating Activities—Direct Method

30. Porter Company Limited gathered the following information from its accounting records:

Proceeds from issuing common shares	$200,000
Payments for dividends	100,000
Collections of accounts receivable	870,000
Cash sales	385,000
Payments to suppliers on account	738,000
Cash purchases	250,000
Payments for income taxes	245,000
Interest received from investments	95,000
Payments to employees	460,000
Payments for interest	35,000
Amortization expense	125,000

REQUIRED:

Prepare the operating section of the cash flow statement for the company using the direct method.

LO 4: Statement of Cash Flows—Direct Method

31. The following information is from the records of Wolf Company Limited for the year ended December 31, 2004.

- Loaned $2,000 to Jones Limited
- Sold Wolf Company Limited common shares for $10,000 cash
- Purchased equipment for $20,000 cash
- Cash sales to customers were $95,000
- Sales on account were $0
- Sold equipment for $4,000 cash
- Paid cash to employees for wages, $9,500
- Paid cash for merchandise, $29,000
- Paid a $2,000 cash dividend
- Borrowed $6,000 from British Columbia Bank
- Purchased Bell Canada shares for $5,000
- Received a cash dividend of $200 from Bell Canada
- Paid cash for other expenses, $8,000
- Made a loan payment, to British Columbia Bank, of $2,200, which included $200 interest

REQUIRED:
Prepare a statement of cash flows for Wolf Company Limited for the year ended December 31, 2004.

LO 4: Statement of Cash Flows—Direct Method

32. The following information is from the records of RoJo Company Limited for the year ended December 31, 2004.

- Purchased equipment for cash of $8,000
- Cash sales to customers were $75,000
- Sold RoJo Company Limited common shares for $6,000 cash
- Loaned $1,000 to Jordan Limited
- Sales on account were $0
- Sold equipment for $1,000 cash
- Paid cash to employees for wages, $4,500
- Borrowed $5,000 from Royal Bank
- Paid cash for merchandise, $32,000
- Paid a $500 cash dividend
- Made a loan payment, to Royal Bank, of $1,500, which included $100 interest
- Purchased Petro-Canada shares for $2,000
- Received a cash dividend of $100 from Petro-Canada
- Paid cash for other expenses, $3,000

REQUIRED:
Prepare a statement of cash flows for RoJo Company Limited for the year ended December 31, 2004.

LO 4: Statement of Cash Flows—Direct Method

33. The following information is from the records of Campbell River Limited for the year ended December 31, 2004.

- Sales on account were $0
- Paid cash to employees for wages, $7,000

- Purchased equipment for $3,000 cash
- Cash sales to customers were $80,000
- Sold Campbell River Limited shares for $9,000 cash
- Loaned $2,000 to Pippen Limited
- Paid cash for merchandise, $24,000
- Sold equipment for cash of $2,000
- Borrowed $8,000 from Scotia Bank
- Paid a $100 cash dividend
- Made a loan payment, to Scotia Bank, of $3,000, which included $500 interest
- Purchased Nortel shares for $1,000
- Received a cash dividend of $50 from Nortel
- Paid cash for other expenses, $2,000

REQUIRED:
Prepare a statement of cash flows for Campbell River Limited for the year ended December 31, 2004.

ANNUAL REPORT PROJECT

34. After this assignment you will be able to complete Section V of the annual report project. For the section on cash flows you should complete the following requirements.

a. List the total for operating, investing, and financing cash flows for each of the years shown in the report's statement of cash flows.

b. Examine the operating cash flows. Have the operating cash flows been positive? Have the operating cash flows increased or decreased in the years presented? Are the operating cash flows sufficient to pay principal and interest on debt and meet other cash requirements?

c. Examine investing cash flows. For each line presented in the investing section, discuss how the line relates to another part of the annual report. Include the page number where you found the information. The Management Discussion and Analysis may be a very good place to find this information.

d. Examine the financing cash flows. For each line presented in this section, trace the amount or find a discussion of the amount elsewhere in the report. Document by page reference where you found the information.

e. What method is used to prepare the cash flow statement, direct or indirect?

11

Financial Statement Analysis

*Y*our fledgling business has begun to grow, and a major retailer recently approached you wanting to place a very large order. To produce the order and wait for the retailer to pay you will require a substantial amount of cash. (Now you understand all that discussion about the necessity of cash!) Your first meeting with the local bank's loan officer went well; however, she indicated that you must provide her with detailed financial statements so that she could "run the ratios." She further explained that if you passed the ratio tests, the bank would probably make the loan. Your accountant will help you prepare the financial statements, but how will you know whether your business can pass these tests? Should your accountant compute the ratios before you go to the bank? Better yet, are there any banks that do not require these ratio tests?

Financial reporting is an essential source of information for economic decision makers, and financial statements are a central component of financial reporting. In the appendix to Chapter 1, we explored the information provided in the annual report. Gathering and reading this kind of information forms the first step in analyzing the information to make it useful in the decision-making process.

Financial statement analysis is the process of looking beyond the face of the financial statements to gain additional insight into a company. Financial statement analysis involves many different factors, including trend analysis and ratio analysis. Your study of the statement of cash flows in Chapter 10 was also a type of financial statement analysis, for the statement of cash flows analyzes what caused the change in cash from one period to the next. ■

trend analysis A technique whereby an analyst tries to determine the amount of changes in key financial amounts over time to see if a pattern of change emerges.

ratio analysis A technique for analyzing the relationship between two items from a company's financial statements for a given period.

In this chapter, we explore two forms of financial statement analysis—trend analysis and ratio analysis—and show you how to use the results in proper combination with other information to make economic decisions. With **trend analysis,** the analyst tries to determine the amount of changes in key financial amounts over time to see if a pattern of change emerges. **Ratio analysis** is a technique for analyzing the relationship between two items from a company's financial statements for a given period. These items may be on the same financial statement, or they may come from different financial statements. The ratios discussed in this chapter are based on items from the balance sheet and the income statement.

LEARNING OBJECTIVES

After completing your work on this chapter, you should be able to do the following:

1. Identify the three major categories of users of financial statement analysis and describe the objectives of each.
2. Gather information to evaluate the political climate and general economic conditions, and describe the ways in which each can affect business.
3. Locate sources of information about specific industries.
4. Describe the purpose of trend analysis and ratio analysis, and explain the three primary characteristics that analysis helps users evaluate.
5. Calculate financial ratios designed to measure a company's profitability, liquidity, and solvency.
6. Evaluate a company's ratios using a comparison to industry averages.
7. Use ratio values from consecutive time periods to evaluate the profitability, liquidity, and solvency of a business.
8. State the limitations of ratio analysis.

WHO PERFORMS FINANCIAL STATEMENT ANALYSIS AND WHY?

financial statement analysis The process of looking beyond the face of the financial statements to gather more information.

Several different types of economic decision makers perform **financial statement analysis**, and because their objectives vary, their perspectives on the results of that analysis will differ. Our focus in this chapter will be on three types of economic decision makers:

1. Creditors (short-term and long-term)
2. Equity investors (present and potential)
3. Company management

Independent auditors, government agencies, prospective employees, and others also are interested in analyzing a company's financial statements, but we will concentrate on these three important categories of users. First, we examine their objectives, and later in this chapter, we will see how ratio analysis meets their need for information about a company's performance.

Objectives of Creditors

Creditors lend money to a company on either a short-term or a long-term basis. Do not confuse the concepts of current assets or liabilities with short-term or long-term lending. For financial statement purposes, the "current" designation describes assets or liabilities that are due within one year or one operating cycle, whichever is longer. For lenders, short-term lending is for loans of less than three years and long-term lending is for more than three years.

There are two major types of *short-term creditors*. One group, called trade creditors, provides goods and services to a business and expects payment within whatever time period is customary in the industry (usually between 30 and 60 days). Trade creditors seldom charge interest. Because the credit they extend to a company is essentially an interest-free loan, they analyze a company's financial statements to determine whether that company pays its bills on time and will be able to pay promptly in the future.

Lending institutions offer commercial loans to support the day-to-day operations of a business in exchange for a short-term note from the business. Unlike trade creditors, banks charge interest. The objectives of these two groups of short-term creditors, however, are quite similar. Both want to be assured of receiving prompt payments from the company.

Long-term creditors also seek assurance of receiving prompt payments, but from a different perspective. These creditors—generally banks and corporate bondholders—lend money to companies for relatively long periods of time. Therefore, in analyzing a company's financial statements, their principal objectives are to determine whether the company will be able to make its periodic interest payments and to repay the loan when required.

When we explore the information resulting from ratio analysis later in the chapter, we will see how it is used by both short-term and long-term creditors. However, creditors are only one class of users of this information.

Objectives of Equity Investors

Equity investors are those who have purchased or might purchase an ownership interest in a company through share ownership or partnership. Investors expect a return on their investment. Recall from our discussion in Chapter 4 that return on investment for a corporate equity investor has two components:

1. Dividends: the distribution of earnings from a corporation to its owners (shareholders)
2. Share appreciation: the increase in the selling price of a share in the stock market between the time it is purchased and the time it is sold

When analyzing a company's financial statements, present and potential equity investors want to determine whether the company will be able to distribute dividends in the future and whether its share price will rise in value. Both these future activities depend on the company's ability to generate income and cash in the future. Cash dividends can be paid only if a company has sufficient cash and sufficient retained earnings, both of which depend on future generation of earnings. Further, generation of earnings is widely considered to be the single most important factor affecting a company's share price appreciation over time.

Both creditors and equity investors are external decision makers who use ratio analysis. However, ratio analysis is also a useful tool for internal decision makers—namely, a company's management.

Objectives of Management

Management is responsible for a company's day-to-day operation. Because they are decision makers, they share some objectives of external parties, but because they are internal, they also have other, different objectives in performing financial statement analysis.

In the context of this chapter, management has two major objectives in analyzing its own company's financial statements. The first is to put those statements in the best possible light before presenting them to important external parties. This is a natural and legitimate objective, since a company's relationship with creditors and shareholders is vital. However, management's natural desire to analyze the company's financial statements with a view toward impressing external parties favourably can lead to managing the financial statements rather than managing the business.

 ## Discussion Questions

11–1. What do you think the phrase "managing the financial statements rather than managing the business" means?

11–2. Are there any ethical boundaries in managing the financial statements?

Management's second objective in analyzing the company's financial statements is to monitor the overall performance of the business in much the same manner as creditors and investors. The company's financial statements, of course, provide managers with important information for making business decisions, but because managers are internal parties, they can obtain additional, internally generated information. At times, managers focus on management accounting information when they evaluate their company's performance, but we will limit our discussion in this chapter to publicly available financial accounting information.

Now that you understand the basic objectives of the three primary users of financial statement analysis, we can explore important factors that affect company performance and that should be considered by anyone undertaking financial statement analysis.

GATHERING BACKGROUND INFORMATION— AN IMPORTANT FIRST STEP

In the appendix to Chapter 1, we discussed how to find background information on companies. Anyone who wants to do a thorough analysis of a company's financial statements should consult the sources suggested in that appendix and gather enough background information on the company to put its financial statement information in proper context. The assignment in the Chapter 5 Annual Report Project (p. 170) helps you analyze a firm's internal environment.

Since businesses do not operate in a vacuum, it is also important to gather background information about a company's external environment. Because ratio analysis is based on financial statement information, conclusions drawn from its results should also consider general economic conditions, political events, and industry outlook.

General Economic Conditions and Expectations

The general economic environment in which a company operates affects its business activity and therefore its financial results. For a company producing goods bought by the general public, bright economic conditions generally enhance sales. For a company manufacturing and selling equipment to other companies, an economy that encourages business growth is an important factor. So first we must consider general economic conditions and expectations when evaluating the performance and overall financial position of a business.

The health of the Canadian economy receives widespread daily news coverage. Popular business periodicals such as *Canadian Business* and *Investment Executive*, and newspapers such as the *National Post* and *The Globe and Mail* inform their readers about current economic conditions. Statistical data on measures of economic health (e.g., gross national product, producer price index) are available in such books as *The Economic Indicators Handbook*.

Economic decision makers not only evaluate past performance of businesses; they also attempt to predict future performance. Business periodicals are good sources for information about anticipated changes in economic conditions. Business analysts, economists, and politicians often voice their views on television, on radio, and in print. Remember, though, all of these "expert" predictions of the future of the Canadian economy are, at best, educated guesses. Use this information carefully!

Although general economic conditions certainly affect a company's performance, a company's poor performance should not be excused because the economy is in a recession. Neither should a company's exceptional performance be dismissed as simply the product of a healthy economy. Economic conditions provide one context within which we evaluate the results of business activity. Other external factors must also be considered.

Political Events and Political Climate

Political events can certainly have an impact on a company's profitability. The terrorist attack on the World Trade Center on September 11, 2001, caused the bankruptcy of airline companies and severely depressed hotel and resort revenues for months following the attack.

Political parties take credit when the general economy improves and blame each other when it declines. That is the nature of politics. The truth is that both improvement and decline in the general economy result from many interrelated and complex factors. Indeed, the factors affecting the general economy are so complicated and intertwined that no political party can control the economy enough to take credit or blame. Still, there is no question that what goes on in politics, both domestic and foreign, has a significant influence on the general economy as well as on the world of business. The actions taken by Parliament and the cabinet on such matters as the amount of government regulation, income taxes, health care, and welfare reform will have an enormous impact on the general economy. And we know that changes in the general economy will affect the level of business activity.

In Canada, the political climate is generally reflected in public opinion. For the past two decades, the public has scrutinized companies' positions on social and environmental issues. The concept of being "politically correct" arose from such public scrutiny. As we discussed in Chapter 1, a wise firm pays close attention to its social responsibility and frequently describes its corporate citizenship in its annual report. A growing number of investors have resolved to invest their money only in companies that have a genuine commitment to responsible behaviour. This trend has generated a broader sense of social responsibility in Canadian corporations.

Where, then, can you find accurate, objective information about a company's corporate citizenship? Your library most likely has publications intended to give you this information, but the evaluations you read will reflect the writer's views of corporate social responsibility, which may not coincide with your own. We suggest that instead of naively accepting such appraisals, you carefully consider the perspective of each author.

Thus far we have explored the impact of both economic and political conditions on business activity. In addition to considering these factors when using financial information, we must consider the outlook for the industry in which the company operates.

Industry Outlook

The third factor to consider when using financial information is the industry in which a company operates, for industry affiliation may define the company's prospects for future growth.

Industry opportunities and challenges are key considerations in evaluating a company's outlook. For example, a company in an industry that is facing an overall decline in demand may be powerless to take any action to encourage its own future growth. We saw this when the demand for personal computers waned in 2000 and the profitability of computer manufacturers fell dramatically.

Government action is not the only force that produces industry-wide effects. Technological change often spurs spectacular growth within an industry. The field of telecommunications, for instance, has undergone a revolution in the past decade. Just a short time ago, the fax machine was an expensive luxury—a form of communication reserved for "big business." Today, most computers come from the factory with internal faxes and many individuals have complete computer systems connected to the Internet.

Often a technological change that opens the doors of opportunity in one industry closes them in another. For example, the development of personal computers has virtually wiped out opportunities for expansion among companies producing typewriters. But remember that each threat produces opportunity. Adaptable companies will change the product mix to seize upon new opportunities and discontinue product lines that no longer have markets. So when considering a company's outlook for the future, it is important to learn what lies ahead for the entire industry and to see how the company has planned to meet any environmental threats.

 Discussion Question

11–3. Changes in society, family structures, and the way people behave and interact have had dramatic impact on business. Cite two examples of such changes, identify industries they have affected, and describe how they did so.

Not only does a company's industry affiliation affect the opportunities it faces, but it may also define the challenges ahead. For example, a few decades ago, companies did not have to consider the environmental impact of their actions. Now with more environmental legislation in existence, businesses must be aware of how these new rules affect the way they operate their business.

The flip side of government regulation is deregulation. When government suddenly discontinues its regulation and frees the market, it has an impact on all companies operating within the deregulated industry. For example, when the federal government deregulated the telecom industry, all telephone companies were affected, and many mergers occurred.

 Discussion Questions

11–4. Identify two industries and describe their similarities and differences.

11–5. If you were offered an upper-level management position in two companies—one from each of the industries you identified in your response to Discussion Question 11–4—which would you take? Why?

11–6. If you had $2,000 to invest and your only options were the common shares of two companies—one from each of the industries you identified in your response to Discussion Question 11–4—which would you choose? Explain your reasoning.

Where do you look for information about a particular industry? Several sources are available.

The *Financial Post* publishes various industry reports. Statistics Canada publishes volumes of information about specific industries. Other government-sponsored websites such as Strategis at http://strategis.ic.gc.ca can also provide a great deal of information about Canadian industries. When accessing information about an industry, you must know what the SIC (standard industrial classification) code for that industry is. Typically, the website will provide this information. It should be noted that the SIC system will soon be replaced with a North American classification system known as NAICS (North American Industry Classification System).

We have now explored the importance of background information and suggested how you can gather data on economic conditions, political events, and industry outlook. The impact of each of these factors on a company's past performance and its prospects should be considered when doing any type of financial statement analysis, for these impacts provide the context within which financial information should be evaluated.

Now we turn to the heart of this chapter—trend analysis and ratio analysis.

TREND ANALYSIS

horizontal analysis The study of percentage changes in comparative financial statements.

One form of trend analysis is **horizontal analysis**. This method of analysis compares the change in accounts shown on the financial statements from one year to the next and expresses that change as a percentage. For example, what does the following tell you?

	2004	2003	% Change
Sales	100,000	80,000	25.0%
Cost of goods sold	50,000	35,000	42.9%

You can conclude from the above that the cost of goods sold is increasing faster than sales. We do not know the exact reason for this but just knowing this trend will encourage us to find the answers to other questions. For example, we should also want to know if the volume of product sales also rose by 25%. If so, then there was no price increase per unit (because the only reason for the change was volume, not price), but there was an increase in the cost per unit of inventory purchased. This increased cost was not passed on to customers.

Another method of trend analysis is called **vertical analysis** or **common size financial statements**. This method involves converting the amounts on a financial statement into percentages of a major element on the statement, which is 100 percent. For example, when analyzing a balance sheet, all amounts included on it would be expressed as a percentage of total assets. When using this method on the income statement, items would be expressed as a percentage of revenues. This method allows for a rational comparison of performance between companies of differing sizes. Shown below is a vertical analysis of the balance sheets of two companies.

vertical analysis The analysis of a financial statement that reveals the relationship of each statement item to the total, which is 100 percent. Common size financial statements are a type of vertical analysis.

	Company #1	%	Company #2	%
Current Assets:				
Cash	$ 10,000	2	$ 800,000	23
Accounts Receivable	30,000	6	500,000	14
Merchandise Inventory	40,000	9	700,000	20
Total Current Assets	$ 80,000	17	$2,000,000	57
Property, Plant and Equipment	400,000	83	1,500,000	43
Total Assets	$480,000	100	$3,500,000	100
Current Liabilities:				
Accounts payable	$ 40,000	8	$ 110,000	3
Notes payable	5,000	1	400,000	11
Total Current Liabilities	$ 45,000	9	$ 510,000	14
Long-Term Debt	250,000	52	1,000,000	29
Total Liabilities	$295,000	61	$1,510,000	43
Shareholders' Equity	185,000	39	1,990,000	57
Total Liabilities and				
Shareholders' Equity	$480,000	100	$3,500,000	100

You can conclude a number of things from the percentages shown above. For example, Company #1 has financed its assets with a greater portion of debt. This is probably because its property plant and equipment is newer or because the company owns rather than rents land and buildings. We also know that Company #2 has a significant amount of cash reserves relative to its assets, and that a portion of this will be used soon to pay off a large notes payable balance.

Vertical and horizontal analysis can also be combined. For example, we could have calculated percentages for each company above for two years and then calculated the percentage change in each percentage for the year.

RATIO ANALYSIS: CALCULATING THE RATIOS

Before we compute any ratios, you need to understand that the absolute numbers resulting from the calculations are of little value in themselves. It is the analysis and interpretation of the numbers—the art of ratio analysis—that produces the desired information. To be truly useful to economic decision makers, a company's ratios need to be compared to other information, such as the ratio values for industry averages or the company's ratios in past years. After introducing all the ratios in this section of the chapter, we will make these comparisons and interpret the findings in the next section.

Ratio analysis, as we explained at the beginning of the chapter, is a method of analyzing the relationship between two items from a company's financial statements for a given period. You will recall that we said important relationships may exist between two items on the same financial statement or between two items from different financial statements. All the ratios we present here are based on information from the balance sheet and the income statement. Some use items from the same financial statement, while others use one item from each statement.

As we introduce each ratio, we will explore what information it offers and show how it is calculated. The 13 ratios we have selected for presentation are representative ratios only. There are many more ratios than these.

One other item needs to be addressed before we begin computing and comparing ratios: There is a lack of consistency among analysts in the way they calculate various ratios. Even when the name of the ratio is the same from one analyst to the next, the financial statement items the two analysts used to calculate that ratio may have been different. This inconsistency often makes it very difficult to compare ratios calculated by different analysts or financial publications.

A variety of ratios are computed by decision makers analyzing financial statements. These ratios are used to glean information about a company's past performance and current financial position that will help the decision maker predict future results of business activity. The ratios presented in this chapter are used to measure either profitability, liquidity, or solvency—three characteristics important to those assessing a company's well-being. In addition, as each characteristic is described, we will discuss which users are most interested in it and why it is of concern to them.

The Company We Will Analyze

In this chapter we are going to analyze the financial statements of Sobeys Inc., one of the largest grocery chains in Canada. Selected portions of Sobey's 2001 annual report are presented in the Appendix at the end of this text. Information about the grocery industry in Canada can be obtained through a number of sources, such as business periodicals or trade journals. Most articles from these sources can be obtained through computerized databases at most libraries. Another extremely important source of information is a company's web site, where various statements by the company regarding its financial performance can be found along with the financial statements on both a quarterly and annual basis. It is also quite common for companies to place analyst conference calls and interview information on the web site as well.

Our analysis of Sobeys will include a comparison with Loblaw Companies Limited, which is the largest grocer in Canada with a market share in excess of 35 percent. In 1998 this company purchased Provigo Inc., which was the third-largest grocer in the country. Also in that same year, the fourth-largest grocer, Sobeys, acquired the second-largest grocer, the Oshawa Group. By 2002, Loblaw Companies Limited and Sobeys Inc. dominated 50 percent of the grocery industry in Canada. These are the only two grocers that operate in all provinces. Loblaw operates grocery stores under the following names: Fortinos, Loblaws, Provigo, SuperValu, Your Independent Grocer, Atlantic Superstore, and The Real Canadian Superstore. Sobeys operates IGA, Price Chopper, Knechtel, and Foodland grocery stores, as well as SERCA, Canada's largest provider of food to restaurants, hotels, and institutions.

In addition to these two large national companies, four regional grocers also operated: Canada Safeway (in Western Canada), Metro Inc. (in Quebec), A&P Canada (in Eastern Canada) and Overwaitea Food Group (in British Columbia).

Rumours always circulate in the industry about possible mergers or alliances between some of the regional grocers in order for them to compete more effectively with the national chains. Other possibilities include takeovers by the national chains of regional chains, although doing this might not be allowed. Government regulators concerned with too much concentration by any particular company could prevent such takeovers. A more likely possibility is the introduction of new competitors into the Canadian market, in particular Wal-Mart and warehouse clubs like Costco.

The grocery industry is not as susceptible as other industries to large variations in the demand for its products. Significant amounts of sales growth are not expected in this industry. Two types of growth are measured for grocery store chains: growth from "same store" sales and growth from opening new outlets.

Severe price competition exists, and the way to profitability often lies with management's ability to provide good service and control costs. Cost controls would aim at efficient inventory management and proper staff utilization.

Some trends that are occurring in the industry include the move to larger outlets or superstores. Currently in Canada, the average grocery store has 28,000 to 32,000 square feet compared with the US average of 40,000 square feet. Some outlets as large as 140,000 square feet will be opened soon. Another trend adopted by some grocers is offering ancillary services by renting space in their stores to banks, dry cleaners, and even fitness clubs in an effort to attract more customers. Other services can also be offered by the grocery store itself, such as photofinishing and pharmacy services. For a number of years, the larger grocery chains have sold private labels, which usually sell at higher margins. This trend is expected to continue. Finally, through the use of membership cards, grocers attempt to track more effectively the buying patterns and needs of their customers.

Information About a Specific Company

The first place to look for financial information about a company is in its annual report. Other information can also be found on the company's web site, in periodicals and industry publications, and from analyst's reports prepared by brokerage firms.

In reviewing the 2001 annual report for Sobeys Inc., in particular the CEO's Message and the Management Discussion and Analysis, we can learn the following key information about the company for the year ended May 5, 2001:

- The year end of the company is May 5, 2001. The year end for the previous year was May 6, 2000. The year-end dates vary because the company, like many retailers, ends the year on a Saturday, making it easier to count inventory on the following day when some outlets may not be open.
- 1,351 stores are operated, of which 949 are franchised.
- Approximately 80% of the company's sales were from food distribution operations (grocery stores) with the remainder from food service operations (SERCA).
- The food service operating margins decreased from 1.63 percent to 1.44 percent in fiscal 2001.
- In fiscal 2001, sales rose by 5.7 percent with same store sales increasing by 3.7 percent. Total square footage grew by 3.8 percent.
- In fiscal 2001, 51 new stores were opened and another 92 were modernized.

- $250 million worth of common shares were issued in November 2000: 9,174,312 common shares were issued at $27.25 per share. The funds raised were used to pay down debt.
- In November 2000 the company's information system failed to work, and in Ontario and the Atlantic region, inventory shortages occurred. The enterprise-wide system that failed to operate during this peak time was abandoned. The resulting pre-tax loss was $89.1 million.
- Three major capital infrastructure projects were undertaken to modernize SERCA's Ontario distribution network.
- A new management team, including a new CEO, was put in place during fiscal 2001.
- In an effort to improve cash flows, the company entered into a securitization agreement with a banking syndicate to sell accounts receivable. By the end of fiscal 2001, $150 million had been received from the syndicate.
- Because of the acquisition of the Oshawa Group in 1998, the company has a significant amount of debt.
- In an effort to better meet customer needs, the company is moving away from short-term volume-based agreements with suppliers to multi-year alliances.
- Formal employee satisfaction surveys are being conducted to help identify organizational strengths and weaknesses.
- Open market areas at the front of stores offer customers a fresh range of products by clustering produce, bakery, seafood, meat, and deli areas together.
- In 2002, the earnings per share is expected to grow by 30 percent, and total sales are expected to exceed $12 billion.
- By the end of fiscal 2002, over 50 stores will have in-store TD Canada Trust banks.
- In fiscal 2002, $550–$600 million will be spent on capital expenditures and total square footage is expected to grow by 5 percent.

Measuring Profitability

profitability The ease with which a company generates income.

profitability ratios A set of ratios that measures a firm's past performance and helps predict its future profitability level.

Profitability is the ease with which a company generates income. If a company generates a high level of income very easily, it is said to have high profitability. All companies must maintain at least a minimum level of profitability to meet their obligations, such as servicing long-term debt and paying dividends to shareholders. **Profitability ratios** measure a firm's past performance and help predict its future profitability level. Therefore, present and potential shareholders and long-term creditors use these ratios to evaluate investments. Similarly, managers use them to monitor and evaluate their company's performance.

Analysts must utilize profitability ratios carefully. Managers have two potential reasons to boost these ratios and make the company appear very profitable. First, they may want to make the company's financial results look more appealing to external decision makers. Second, their own compensation may be directly tied to these profitability ratios, for often managers receive bonuses based on the level of profitability achieved by the company. Do shareholders and creditors also want the company to be profitable? Yes, but profitability ratios are based on short-term results (usually one year), and the only way to boost them is to attain the highest possible profit for any given year. That in itself seems satisfactory, however:

A preoccupation with short-term profits is detrimental to the long-term value of a business!

Shareholders and creditors, then, should generally take a longer-term view of the company's health than can be measured by profitability alone.

As you look at the profitability ratios in this section, focus both on what they should reveal about a company and on how they might encourage shortsighted behaviour by management. It is quite common for managers to slant business decisions toward those that make the ratios "look better" to the decision makers who are using their company's financial statements.

 Discussion Question

11–7. Give an example of a management decision that would be made differently depending on whether the decision maker is considering the short-term or long-term well-being of the company. Explain the impact of the two different perspectives on the outcome of the decision.

return on assets ratio
A profitability ratio that measures how efficiently the company uses its assets to produce profits.

Return on Assets Ratio   The **return on assets ratio** (sometimes called the return on total assets) measures how efficiently the company uses its assets to produce profits. After all, the reason companies invest in assets is to produce revenue and ultimately profit (net income). Air Canada, for example, invests in aircraft and other assets for the express purpose of producing income. Air Canada's creditors (particularly long-term), shareholders, and management are all interested in knowing how efficiently the aircraft and other assets are being used to produce the company's income. The return on assets ratio is one approach to measuring that efficiency. It is computed as follows:

$$\text{Return on assets} = \frac{\text{Net income before taxes}}{\text{Total assets}}$$

Because Sobeys places goodwill amortization (note that this was the last year that goodwill could be amortized) near the bottom of the income statement, there is no subtotal called net income before taxes. To arrive at that amount, we need to take net income and add to it the income tax expense.

For 2001, the return on assets is:

$$\frac{\$42.0 + \$40.6}{\$2,917.6} = 0.0283, \text{ or } 2.83\%$$

For 2000, the return on assets is:

$$\frac{\$80.2 + \$77.5}{\$2,891.0} = 0.0545, \text{ or } 5.45\%$$

Clearly the return on assets fell in 2001. Why? Because of lower net income before income taxes, but why was this lower? Because of restructuring costs incurred primarily from the decision to discontinue the enterprise-wide systems initiative.

If a company has a low return on its assets, how would it determine the cause of the problem and improve the situation? The answer to that question lies in the next two profitability ratios we will examine, because they are actually the two components of the return on assets ratio.

profit margin before income tax ratio A profitability ratio that measures the earnings produced from a given level of revenues by comparing net income before income tax to the revenue figure.

Profit Margin Before Income Tax Ratio

The **profit margin before income tax ratio** has the same numerator as the return on assets ratio. The denominator for this ratio is total sales for the period. By comparing net income to sales, we can determine the amount of income produced by a given level of revenue. We calculate the profit margin before income tax as follows:

$$\text{Profit margin before income tax} = \frac{\text{Net income before taxes}}{\text{Sales}}$$

Both components of the profit margin before tax are drawn from the income statement. This ratio indicates the contribution of sales to the overall profitability of the company—it shows how much net income is generated from a dollar of sales.

Sobeys Inc. profit margin before income taxes for 2001 is:

$$\frac{\$42.0 + \$40.6}{\$11,370.5} = 0.0073, \text{ or } 0.73\%$$

For 2000, the profit margin before income taxes is:

$$\frac{\$80.2 + \$77.5}{\$11,006.1} = 0.0143, \text{ or } 1.43\%$$

Again, we see a decrease in this ratio primarily due to the decrease in the numerator arising from lower net income. In general, the amount of profit as a percentage of sales is very low in the grocery industry because of severe pressure to keep prices competitive.

Discussion Question

11–8. What situations might cause a company to have a low profit margin before income tax?

Profit margin before income tax is just one component of the return on assets ratio; the second component—total asset turnover—is equally important.

total asset turnover ratio A profitability ratio that indicates the amount of revenues produced for a given level of assets used.

Total Asset Turnover Ratio

The **total asset turnover ratio** shows the amount of sales produced for a given level of assets used. The purpose of this ratio is similar to that of the return on total assets ratio except that it indicates how effectively the company uses its total assets to generate sales rather than net income. Total asset turnover has the same denominator as the return on assets ratio, but the numerator is total sales for the period. We calculate total asset turnover as follows:

$$\text{Total asset turnover} = \frac{\text{Sales}}{\text{Total assets}}$$

The total asset turnover for Sobeys Inc. for 2001 is:

$$\frac{\$11,370.5}{\$2,917.6} = 3.8972, \text{ or } 3.90 \text{ times}$$

For 2000, the total asset turnover is:

$$\frac{\$11,006.1}{\$2,891.0} = 3.8070, \text{ or } 3.80 \text{ times}$$

The turnover ratio has improved slightly in 2001 due primarily to the increase in sales. Notice that this ratio is expressed in "times" rather than as a percentage. In general, turnover ratios should not be too high or too low. If this ratio is too high, it may mean that a company has assets that are aging and should be replaced. If the ratio is too low, it indicates that the assets of the company are not as productive in generating sales.

Compared to other industries, grocery retailers have high asset turnovers. Although they do not make much profit on each sale, they do a good job of generating sales—they operate high-volume, low-margin businesses.

Now that we have explored both components of the return on assets ratio, we can look more closely at the relationship among the three ratios:

$$\text{Return on Assets} = \text{Profit margin before taxes} \times \text{Total asset turnover}$$

$$\frac{\text{Net income before taxes}}{\text{Total assets}} = \frac{\text{Net income before taxes}}{\text{Sales}} \times \frac{\text{Sales}}{\text{Total assets}}$$

Notice that the return on assets can be calculated by multiplying the profit margin before taxes by the total asset turnover. For 2001, Sobeys' return on assets can be calculated by multiplying the profit margin before taxes of 0.73% by the total asset turnover of 3.90 (0.73% × 3.90 = 2.83% with some slight rounding). For 2000, this can be calculated as 1.43% × 3.80 = 5.45% (with some slight rounding).

If a company's return on assets is low, both its profit margin before income tax and its total asset turnover should be investigated—separately—to determine the source of the problem. After each component is analyzed, the company will be in a position to focus on areas needing improvement.

Discussion Questions

11–9. Offer two separate suggestions as to how a company can make its total asset turnover ratio higher.

11–10. A company wishing to boost its return on assets ratio could focus its efforts on either component—profit margin before income tax or total asset turnover ratio. Which component do you think would be easier to improve? Explain how you came to your conclusion.

Rather than relying on any single measure of profitability, wise financial statement users turn to several different ratios. We now explore two more profitability ratios.

Profit Margin After Income Tax Ratio   As its name suggests, this ratio is only slightly different from the profit margin measure already discussed. The **profit margin after income tax ratio** indicates the amount of after-tax net income generated by a dollar of sales. This difference is subtle, but it may be important in some analyses. The profit margin after income tax is calculated as follows:

$$\text{Profit margin after income tax} = \frac{\text{Net income after taxes}}{\text{Sales}}$$

profit margin after income tax ratio   A profitability ratio that measures the earnings produced from a given level of revenues by comparing net income after income tax with the revenue figure.

For 2001, Sobeys' profit margin after income tax can be calculated as follows:

$$\frac{\$42.0}{\$11,370.5} = 0.0037, \text{ or } 0.37\%$$

For 2000, the profit margin before income taxes is:

$$\frac{\$80.2}{\$11,006.1} = 0.0073, \text{ or } 0.73\%$$

These ratios indicate the same trend although with lower values than the preceding profit margin before income tax ratio did.

Whether profit margin is computed before or after taxes, the result is a useful measure of profitability. The profit margin gives an indication of how much better the company is at setting higher prices for its products than its competitors are. It also measures whether the company is controlling its expenses relative to sales compared to its competitors.

return on equity ratio
A profitability ratio that measures the after-tax net income generated from a given level of investment by a company's owners.

Return on Equity Ratio   The **return on equity ratio** demonstrates profitability by comparing a company's after-tax net income to the amount of investment by the company's owners. Equity represents the owners' claims to the assets of the business. Return on equity indicates how much after-tax income was generated for a given level of equity. The return on equity ratio is calculated as follows:

$$\text{Return on equity} = \frac{\text{Net income after taxes}}{\text{Equity}}$$

The numerator of this ratio is drawn from the income statement and the denominator is taken from the balance sheet.

In 2001, Sobeys Inc. had a return on equity of:

$$\frac{\$42.0}{\$1,089.8} = 0.0385, \text{ or } 3.85\%$$

For 2000, the return on equity was:

$$\frac{\$80.2}{\$817.7} = 0.0981, \text{ or } 9.81\%$$

The decline in the return on equity in 2001 is due in part to the lower net income discussed before, but it is also due to the higher level of equity. During fiscal 2001, $250 million worth of common shares were issued, and this caused a major increase in equity and a lowering of the return on equity. Retained earnings also rose because the company was profitable. The deferred foreign exchange gain, which is a component of equity, is immaterial to our analysis. This account represents the cumulative exchange gains and losses that the company has experienced from operating foreign operations.

Before covering other ratios, ask yourself why a company's return on assets would be any different from its return on equity. For Sobeys Inc. in 2001, the return on assets was lower than the return on equity. Why? Because the company has more assets than equity. If a company had no liabilities, the assets and equity would be equal and these two return ratios would also be equal. Therefore, the spread between the return on asset ratio and the return on equity ratio will widen as a company takes on more liabilities.

When a company chooses to finance its assets with liabilities, it is using leverage. Leverage is simply the process of using borrowed funds. Normally, when a company does this, management hopes that the interest rate on the borrowed funds will be less than the rate of return earned by the borrowed funds. The difference between these two rates accrues to the equity holders, thereby improving their return. For example, assume that a company has $200 in assets that were financed half with debt ($100) and half with equity ($100). Assume that the return on assets (before considering interest) was 10 percent or $20. Assume that the interest rate on the debt was 6 percent or $6. The net income of the company would be $20 − $6 = $14. The return on equity would be 14 percent ($14 of net income divided by equity of $100). Why was the return on equity 4 percent greater than the return on assets? Because the difference between the return on assets of 10 percent (which the borrowed funds helped to finance), and the interest rate on the debt of 6 percent is 4 percent. This 4 percent accrued to the owners. The more debt that is obtained, the greater the difference between return on equity and the return on assets.

Does this mean that companies should strive to increase debt? Not necessarily. What would happen in our example above if the return on assets fell to 5 percent and interest rates rose to 8 percent? In this case, leverage would not be advantageous and would make the return on equity lower than the return on assets. To illustrate, the assets would earn $200 × 5% = $10. Net income would be $10 less interest of $8 ($100 × 8%) for a total of $2. The return on equity would be only 2 percent compared to the return on assets of 5 percent indicating that leverage was not useful in this case.

Measuring Liquidity

An asset's liquidity describes the ease with which it can be converted to cash. A company's liquidity refers to its ability to generate the cash needed to meet its short-term obligations. Clearly, all economic decision makers must consider a firm's liquidity, for if a company cannot meet its current obligations, it may not be around long enough to be profitable in the long run. Short-term creditors and company's management, however, tend to be the information users who pay most careful attention to liquidity.

Over time many ratios have been developed specifically to measure liquidity. The **liquidity ratios** we have chosen to discuss take different approaches to evaluating a firm's ability to generate sufficient cash to meet its short-term obligations. Several of them consider current assets and current liabilities. Recall that a current asset is one that is either already cash or is expected to become cash within one year, and a current liability is any obligation that must be paid within one year. If we are interested in liquidity, certainly we would expect to find helpful information in these two balance sheet categories.

liquidity ratios A set of ratios developed to measure a firm's ability to generate sufficient cash in the short run to retire short-term liabilities.

current ratio A liquidity ratio that measures a company's ability to meet short-term obligations by comparing current assets to current liabilities.

Current Ratio The **current ratio** is probably the most widely used measure of a company's liquidity. It compares current assets to current liabilities, offering a measure of the company's ability to meet its short-term financial obligations with cash generated from current assets. The current ratio is calculated as follows:

$$\text{Current ratio} = \frac{\text{Current assets}}{\text{Current liabilities}}$$

This ratio indicates the amount of current assets for each dollar of current liabilities. Sobeys Inc. current ratio for 2001 can be calculated as follows:

$$\frac{\$1,061.9}{\$1,143.6} = 0.9286, \text{ or } 0.93 \text{ to } 1$$

For fiscal 2000, the current ratio is:

$$\frac{\$1,068.9}{\$1,270.4} = 0.8414, \text{ or } 0.84 \text{ to } 1$$

The company's liquidity has increased in 2001 primarily because of a decrease in current liabilities (mainly accounts payable). You should notice, however, that in both years, the current ratio was below a value of 1. Does this mean that the company does not have an ability to pay off its current liabilities with its current assets? Does this mean that the company does not have enough liquidity? No. In fact, for a grocery store chain, we should expect to see a current ratio below 1. Why? Consider the nature of the current assets. These consist primarily of cash, accounts receivable, and inventory. For Sobeys, a large balance of cash does not need to be maintained because cash flow is steady, since the demand for groceries does not fluctuate. Any excess cash can then be used to open new stores or to renovate existing stores. Accounts receivable, which relates primarily to SERCA, would otherwise be negligible because consumers do not usually buy groceries on credit. Lastly, inventory levels are not excessive because of the perishable nature of groceries. As a result of these circumstances, the current assets of grocery stores are relatively lower than they would be for other types of businesses. On the other hand, accounts payable balances for grocery stores would consist of amounts owed to suppliers within 30 to 60 days. Compared to other businesses, the accounts payable for a grocery store would be relatively the same. Therefore, because of the lower current assets compared to current liabilities, grocery store operators should be expected to have lower current ratios, which is exactly what we see with Sobeys.

In other industries, a current ratio below 1 could be disastrous. On average, the current ratio is usually above 2:1 in most industries.

 ## Discussion Question

11–11. If Sobeys Inc. were to borrow money to retire current liabilities, it would have to pay interest on the borrowed funds. What effect (if any) would the additional interest expense have on the following ratios:

a. profit margin before income tax?

b. profit margin after income tax?

c. return on assets?

d. return on equity?

e. total asset turnover?

Quick Ratio What would happen to the current ratio of a manufacturing company if a downturn in the economy were experienced? Accounts receivable would rise as customers took longer to pay, but there would be a corresponding increase in accounts payable as the company would also take longer to pay its suppliers. Inventories would pile up as production outgrew sales. To maintain cash balances, second mortgages would be taken out. The effect of these activities on the balance sheet would be an increase in current assets caused mainly by the increased inventories and an increase in long-term liabilities. This in turn would lead to an increase in the current ratio. If one interpreted such a rise in the current ratio as an increase in liquidity, that interpretation would be very wrong. To mitigate this type of conclusion from arising, analysts and, in particular, bankers try to assess the liquidity

quick ratio or **acid-test ratio**
A liquidity ratio that is similar to the current ratio, but a more stringent test of liquidity, because only current assets considered to be highly liquid (quickly converted to cash) are included in the calculation.

of a business by calculating the **quick ratio**. This ratio, which is sometimes called the **acid-test ratio,** is similar to the current ratio. It is a more stringent test of liquidity, however, because it considers only current assets that are highly liquid (quickly convertible into cash) in the numerator. Some variation exists as to what assets are included in the quick ratio calculation because the definition of "highly liquid" is quite subjective. We calculate the quick ratio as follows:

$$\text{Quick ratio} = \frac{\text{Cash} + \text{Receivables} + \text{Marketable (Trading) Securities}}{\text{Current liabilities}}$$

In the numerator of our equation, cash is obviously liquid. We also assume accounts receivable and notes receivable will be quickly converted to cash. However, if a company knows that any account receivable or note receivable will not be quickly converted, it should not include that item in the calculation of this ratio. Marketable securities held in a company's trading portfolio are highly liquid and often represent excess cash that the company plans to use in the near future. The denominator of the quick ratio is identical to the one used for the current ratio.

 ## Discussion Question

11-12. Besides the three assets—cash, receivables, and marketable securities—considered in our version of the quick ratio, what other current assets might a company have?

The quick ratio for Sobeys Inc. in fiscal 2001 is:

$$\frac{\$82.4 + \$346.2 + \$1.7}{\$1,143.6} = 0.3762, \text{ or } 0.38 \text{ to } 1$$

For fiscal 2000, the current ratio is:

$$\frac{\$53.1 + \$420.0 + \$1.7}{\$1,270.4} = 0.3737, \text{ or } 0.37 \text{ to } 1$$

As expected, the value of these ratios is lower than we calculated for the current ratio, but there is no noticeable deterioration in the liquidity of the company over these two years.

 ## Discussion Question

11-13. How would holding an excessive amount of inventory affect the following ratios:
  a. profit margin before income tax?
  b. profit margin after income tax?
  c. return on assets?
  d. return on equity?
  e. current ratio?
  f. quick ratio?
  g. total asset turnover?

receivables turnover ratio
A liquidity ratio that measures how quickly a company collects its accounts receivable.

Receivables Turnover Ratio The **receivables turnover ratio** measures the liquidity of accounts receivable. Accounts receivable is the amount a company is owed by its customers, and it is often a sizable current asset. Companies need to convert accounts receivable to cash as quickly as possible because they represent interest-free loans to customers. Most companies routinely sell to their customers on a credit basis.

The receivables turnover ratio indicates how quickly a company collects its receivables. The calculation for receivables turnover is:

$$\text{Receivables turnover} = \frac{\text{Sales}}{\text{Accounts receivable}}$$

The sales figure is drawn from the income statement, and accounts receivable is found on the balance sheet.

The receivables turnover for Sobeys Inc. for fiscal 2001 is:

$$\frac{\$11,370.5}{\$346.2} = 32.8437, \text{ or } 32.84 \text{ times}$$

For 2000, the receivables turnover is:

$$\frac{\$11,006.1}{\$420.0} = 26.2050, \text{ or } 26.21 \text{ times}$$

Since the receivables turnover ratio measures the speed at which accounts receivable are collected, we can conclude that receivables were collected more quickly in 2001 than in 2000. It should be noted, however, that compared to most companies, Sobeys has a high receivables turnover ratio because its accounts receivable are quite low. This, of course, is due to the fact that most people do not buy groceries on credit. A large portion of the accounts receivable would relate to the food service business operated by Sobeys through SERCA.

If we wanted to know how long it took to collect the average receivable, we could divide the number of days per year by the receivables turnover. For example, in fiscal 2001, it took Sobeys, on average, 11 days to collect accounts receivable:

$$\frac{365 \text{ days}}{32.84} = 11.11 \text{ days}$$

This compares with 14 days in fiscal 2000. Remember, however, that this number is made artificially low because the sales amount used in determining the receivables turnover ratio was not just credit sales but all sales.

$$\frac{365 \text{ days}}{26.21} = 13.92 \text{ days}$$

As with any turnover ratio, management does not want the receivables turnover ratio to be too high (it might indicate that credit policies are too tight) or too low (it would indicate a collection problem). With regard to Sobeys, the receivables turnover can really be evaluated only if it is compared to the turnover ratio of its competitors. Comparing it to the prior year is also useful and indicates, as noted above, an improvement in the speed at which receivables are collected.

The final liquidity ratio we present is quite similar in nature to the receivables turnover.

inventory turnover ratio
A liquidity ratio that indicates how long a company holds its inventory.

Inventory Turnover Ratio Like the receivables turnover ratio, the **inventory turnover ratio** is a measure of the liquidity of one specific asset—in this case, inventory. This ratio indicates the number of times total merchandise inventory is purchased and sold during a period. The calculation of inventory turnover is as follows:

$$\text{Inventory turnover} = \frac{\text{Cost of sales}}{\text{Inventory}}$$

We normally find the cost of sales expense on the income statement and the inventory asset on the balance sheet.

Unfortunately, companies can "lump" together the cost of goods sold with other expenses, and Sobeys has done this. This practice is common and prevents analysts from comparing sales with related cost of goods sold. When faced with this dilemma, all we can do is use the cost of goods sold and administrative expenses amount as the numerator in this ratio. The inventory turnover ratio for Sobeys in 2001 would therefore be:

$$\frac{\$11,006.4}{\$509.3} = 21.6108, \text{ or } 21.61 \text{ times}$$

In 2000, the corresponding amount would be:

$$\frac{\$10,642.5}{485.5} = 21.9207, \text{ or } 21.92 \text{ times}$$

The values calculated above indicate that almost 22 times per year, Sobeys sells the inventory it typically has on hand. These values are normal for this industry. The turnover did not change significantly nor should it, because the demand for a grocery store's products should not change dramatically and neither should the level of inventory maintained. In industries where the demand for a company's products can fluctuate dramatically, if the turnover ratio rises significantly, it may indicate inventory shortage problems and if the turnover ratio falls, it indicates that inventories are selling slowly and may be obsolete.

As we did with the receivables turnover ratio, we can take the inventory turnover ratio and divide it into the number of days in a year to determine how many days on average it takes to sell inventory on hand. For Sobeys' fiscal 2001, the average time that inventory is held can be calculated as follows:

$$\frac{365 \text{ days}}{21.61} = 16.89 \text{ days}$$

For fiscal 2000, the corresponding calculation is:

$$\frac{365 \text{ days}}{21.92} = 16.65 \text{ days}$$

Please note that the relationship between all liquidity ratios should be considered when properly analyzing financial statements. For example, assume that a company's current ratio is rising despite a decrease in cash. At the same time the receivables turnover ratio is falling while the inventory turnover ratio has remained unchanged. What is happening? The company is collecting accounts receivable at a slower rate. The receivable and inventory turnover ratios exist to provide us with more insight into the activity of these two major components of working capital.

Measuring Solvency

solvency A company's ability to meet the obligations created by its long-term debt.

solvency ratios A set of ratios developed to measure a firm's ability to meet its long-term debt obligations.

Solvency is the third important characteristic that decision makers use as an indication of companies' financial well-being. **Solvency** is a company's ability to meet the obligations created by its long-term debt. Obligations resulting from debt include both paying back the amount borrowed and paying interest on the debt. A set of **solvency ratios** has been developed to measure firms' solvency. Some of these ratios focus on the overall level of debt a company carries, while others measure a company's ability to make interest payments. A solvency ratio focusing on ability to make interest payments is similar in purpose to a liquidity ratio.

Solvency ratios are of most interest to shareholders, long-term creditors, and, of course, company management. There are numerous solvency ratios; we will look at three of the ones most widely used.

debt ratio A solvency ratio that indicates what proportion of a company's assets is financed by debt.

Debt Ratio   The **debt ratio** measures what proportion of a company's assets is financed by debt. All of a company's assets are claimed by either creditors or owners. This can be demonstrated by looking once again at the accounting (business) equation:

$$\text{Assets} = \text{Liabilities} + \text{Owners' Equity}$$
$$100\% = \text{Some \%} + \text{Some \%}$$

Calculation of the debt ratio illustrates the percentage of assets that are supported by debt financing. Creditors and shareholders watch the debt ratio from their individual perspectives and tend to get nervous if they perceive it to be out of balance. The format of the debt ratio may vary somewhat. We will calculate it as follows:

$$\text{Debt ratio} = \frac{\text{Total liabilities}}{\text{Total assets}}$$

Both the items necessary to calculate the debt ratio can be found on the balance sheet.

Sobeys Inc. 2001 debt ratio is:

$$\frac{\$1,827.8}{\$2,917.6} = 0.6265, \text{ or } 62.65\%$$

The debt ratio for fiscal 2000 can be calculated as follows:

$$\frac{\$2,073.3}{\$2,891.0} = 0.7172, \text{ or } 71.72\%$$

As we can see from the above, the total amount of assets did not change significantly in 2001 but the amount of liabilities did decrease. This was due to the paying down of bank loans (in part from funds raised by issuing common shares). Consequently, the ratio fell. Is this trend good for a company? It depends. If the rate of interest on borrowed funds exceeds the return that these funds earn, then a company should pay down its debt as quickly as possible. The reverse would also be true. If a company can borrow funds at a low interest rate and invest these funds to earn a rate of return that would exceed the interest rate, then more debt should be obtained. In Sobeys case, Note 6 to the financial statements provides details on the rate of interest paid on bank loans, etc. Because these rates exceed the return on assets calculated above, the company is taking steps to pay down this debt. Therefore the reduction in the value of the debt ratio in 2001 is a positive sign.

 Discussion Question

11–14. If a company has a higher debt ratio than that of its competitors, is this a good thing?

The debt ratio indicates the relationship between the amount of liabilities and the assets held by a company. The next solvency ratio we examine considers a company's liabilities in relation to shareholders' equity.

debt to equity ratio
A solvency ratio indicating the relationship between creditors' claims to a company's assets and the owners' claims to those assets.

Debt to Equity Ratio

The **debt to equity ratio** is a solvency ratio indicating the relationship between creditors' claims to the company's assets (liabilities) and owners' claims to those assets (equity).

As is obvious from its name, the debt to equity ratio is calculated as:

$$\text{Debt to equity ratio} = \frac{\text{Total liabilities}}{\text{Equity}}$$

Both the items necessary to calculate the debt to equity ratio can be found on the balance sheet. The numerator is the same as for the debt ratio.

Sobeys Inc. debt to equity ratio for fiscal 2001 can be calculated as:

$$\frac{\$1,827.8}{\$1,089.8} = 1.6772, \text{ or } 1.68 \text{ to } 1$$

For 2000, the corresponding calculations are:

$$\frac{\$2,073.3}{\$817.7} = 2.5355, \text{ or } 2.54 \text{ to } 1$$

The results of the debt to equity ratio mirror those of the debt ratio and indicate exactly the same trend. The debt is being reduced by proceeds received from issuing shares.

Both the debt ratio and the debt to equity ratio focus on the overall debt load carried by a company. The last solvency ratio we will examine indicates a company's ability to meet the obligations associated with its debt.

coverage ratio or **times interest earned ratio**
A solvency ratio that provides an indication of a company's ability to make its periodic interest payments.

Coverage Ratio

The **coverage ratio,** also called the **times interest earned ratio,** indicates a company's ability to make its periodic interest payments. It compares the amount of income available for interest payments to the interest requirements. Creditors use this ratio to assess the risk associated with lending money to a business. The formula used to calculate this ratio is:

$$\text{Coverage ratio} = \frac{\text{Earnings before interest expense and income taxes}}{\text{Interest expense}}$$

The numerator consists of earnings before interest and tax expense because this figure represents the amount of earnings available for periodic interest payments. To arrive at this amount, we need to add interest expense to earnings before taxes on the income statement. Interest expense is usually found on the income statement.

Sobeys Inc. coverage ratio for 2001 is calculated as follows:

$$\frac{\$42.0 + \$73.8 + \$40.6}{\$73.8} = 2.1192, \text{ or } 2.12 \text{ times}$$

For fiscal 2000, the coverage ratio is:

$$\frac{\$80.2 + \$89.0 + \$77.5}{\$89.0} = 2.7719, \text{ or } 2.77 \text{ times}$$

We can see that the interest coverage has declined in 2001 due mainly to the lower amount of net income. However, it should be noted that interest expense was also falling as debt was being paid down.

Discussion Questions

11–15. Can we always find the amount of interest expense for the reporting period in the annual report? Why?

11–16. Name at least three places the interest expense might be found in an annual report.

Measuring Valuation

Studies have shown that a strong correlation exists between the earnings of a company and the performance of its share price. A common technique for determining if a share is expensive or cheap is to compare the share price of a company to its earnings per share. A ratio calculating this is called the **price earnings ratio** and is calculated as follows:

price earnings ratio A ratio of the market price of a common share to the company's earnings per share. It measures the value that the stock market places on $1 of a company's earnings.

$$\text{Price earnings ratio} = \frac{\text{Price of a common share at the balance sheet date}}{\text{Earnings per share}}$$

Normally, the basic earnings per share is used for this calculation. If the value of this ratio is high compared to those of its competitors, it might indicate that the share price is expensive. If the value is low, the share price is relatively cheap. However, just because a share is cheap does not mean that it is worth buying. It may be cheap for a very good reason. Likewise, a well-run growing company may have a high price earnings ratio compared to its competitors but this may be justified.

To calculate Sobeys Inc.'s price earnings ratio for 2001, we need to find the market price of the share at May 5, 2001. Since this is a Saturday and the stock market is not open on that day, we used instead the share price at the close of trading on May 4, 2001, which was $23. We then divide this value by the earnings per share, which is shown at the bottom of the income statement. The May 5, 2001, price earnings ratio is:

$$\frac{\$23}{\$0.69} = 33.3333, \text{ or } 33 \text{ times}$$

For 2000, the year end date was May 6 and the closing share price on May 5, 2000 was $21. Sobey's Inc's May 6, 2000, price earnings ratio was:

$$\frac{\$21}{\$1.43} = 14.6853, \text{ or } 15 \text{ times}$$

Notice that the price earnings ratio rises when income falls. The question we have to ask ourselves is whether, at $23 per share, Sobeys shares are worth buying in May 2001. We will consider this question later after comparing these ratio values to industry averages.

Analysts use ratio analysis to evaluate the company's current levels of profitability, liquidity, and solvency. Ratios can send up red flags that warn management, creditors, and investors of trouble ahead. An unprofitable company becomes illiquid because it cannot generate profits and cash, a situation which eventually leads to insolvency. Insolvency then leads to bankruptcy. When red flags appear, management can initiate corrective action to prevent future troubles. Exhibit 11–1 summarizes the calculations and purpose of the profitability, liquidity, and solvency ratios discussed in this chapter, along with the price earnings ratio.

Discussion Questions

11–17. Assume you had to decide to invest in one of two companies with no information other than values of four of their financial ratios. Which four would you want to know? Explain the reasons for your choices.

11–18. Martino Company and Patco Corporation are in the same line of business. However, Martino uses straight-line amortization, whereas Patco uses an accelerated amortization method. If this is the only difference in the business activity of the two companies, how should their financial ratios compare at the end of their first year of operations? Explain the effect of the difference in amortization methods on each of the 13 ratios described in this chapter.

Exhibit 11–1
Summary of Key Ratios

Ratio	Calculation	Purpose of Ratio
Profitability Ratios		
1. Return on Assets	$\dfrac{\text{Net income before taxes}}{\text{Total assets}}$	Measures the return earned on investment in assets.
2. Profit Margin Before Income Tax	$\dfrac{\text{Net income before taxes}}{\text{Sales}}$	Measures the pretax earnings produced from a given level of revenues.
3. Total Asset Turnover	$\dfrac{\text{Sales}}{\text{Total assets}}$	Indicates the firm's ability to generate revenues from a given level of assets.
4. Profit Margin After Income Tax	$\dfrac{\text{Net income after taxes}}{\text{Sales}}$	Measures the amount of after-tax net income generated by a dollar of sales.
5. Return on Equity	$\dfrac{\text{Net income after taxes}}{\text{Equity}}$	Measures the after-tax income generated from a given level of equity.
Liquidity Ratios		
6. Current Ratio	$\dfrac{\text{Current assets}}{\text{Current liabilities}}$	Indicates a company's ability to meet short-term obligations.
7. Quick Ratio	$\dfrac{\text{Cash} + \text{Accounts receivable} + \text{Notes receivable}}{\text{Current liabilities}}$	Measures short-term liquidity more stringently than the current ratio does.
8. Receivables Turnover	$\dfrac{\text{Sales}}{\text{Accounts receivable}}$	Indicates how quickly a company collects its receivables.
9. Inventory Turnover	$\dfrac{\text{Cost of sales}}{\text{Inventory}}$	Indicates how long a company holds its inventory.
Solvency Ratios		
10. Debt Ratio	$\dfrac{\text{Total liabilities}}{\text{Total assets}}$	Measures the proportion of assets financed by debt.
11. Debt to Equity Ratio	$\dfrac{\text{Total liabilities}}{\text{Equity}}$	Directly compares the amount of debt financing to the amount of equity financing.
12. Coverage Ratio	$\dfrac{\text{Earnings before interest expense and income taxes}}{\text{Interest expense}}$	Indicates a company's ability to make its periodic interest payments.
Valuation Ratios		
13. Price Earnings Ratio	$\dfrac{\text{Price of common share}}{\text{Earnings per share}}$	Measures relationship between earnings and share price

RATIO ANALYSIS: USING THE RATIOS

We have calculated 13 ratios based on the financial statements included in Sobeys Inc.'s 2001 annual report. Financial ratios are bits of data that become valuable information when used in comparison to prior years' ratios or to industry averages. This kind of interpretation is what we referred to earlier as the "art of ratio analysis." In this section of the chapter, we compare Sobeys' ratios to industry average ratios and to those of Sobeys' major competitor, Loblaws.

Let us compare Sobeys' ratios with those of its largest competitor and also with industry average ratios obtained from Statistics Canada.

Exhibit 11–2
Comparative
Profitability Ratios

Profitability Ratios	Sobeys Inc. May 5, 2001	Loblaw Cos. Ltd. December 30, 2000	Industry Average
Return on Assets	2.83%	8.76%	10.1%
Profit Margin Before Income Tax	0.73%	3.93%	1.2%
Total Asset Turnover	3.90 times	2.23 times	Not Available
Profit Margin After Income Tax	0.37%	2.35%	1.1%
Return on Equity	3.85%	15.1%	16.3%

Based on the comparative profitability ratios in Exhibit 11-2, Sobeys Inc. is below average, but this is due mainly to the non-recurring restructuring costs of $89.1 million. Since this amount is tax deductible, it did save Sobeys taxes of $39.9 million, so the net loss from restructuring was $89.1 − $39.9 = $49.2 million. This is roughly equal to the net income for the entire year of $42.0 million. If this restructuring cost had not occurred, any ratio with net income in the numerator would have doubled, bringing Sobeys Inc. ratio values closer to those of Loblaw and the industry average. It should be noted that the return on assets for both Sobeys and Loblaw is below the industry average. This is probably due to the fact that when these companies merged with the Oshawa Group and Provigo respectively in 1998, the assets of the acquired companies would have been placed on the balance sheets of Sobeys and Loblaw at cost (market value on the date of acquisition). Therefore, these companies have, on average, newer assets on their books, and this would make the numerator in an asset turnover ratio larger and decrease the value of the ratio overall. One bright spot in the profitability ratios is the total asset turnover ratio, which indicates that Sobeys generates more revenue for each dollar of assets held than does Loblaw.

 Discussion Questions

11-19. Sobeys Inc.'s return on equity is larger than its return on assets. Why?

11-20. Which of the following groups do you think would be interested in Sobeys Inc.'s return on equity ratio?

   a. trade creditors

   b. other short-term creditors (banks)

   c. long-term creditors

   d. shareholders

   e. management

   Explain your reasoning.

Exhibit 11–3
Comparative Liquidity
Ratios

Liquidity Ratios	Sobeys Inc. May 5, 2001	Loblaw Cos. Ltd. December 30, 2000	Industry Average
Current Ratio	0.93 to 1	0.91 to 1	0.65 to 1
Quick Ratio	0.38 to 1	0.32 to 1	Not Available
Receivables Turnover	32.84 times	52.81 times	30.0 times
Inventory Turnover	21.61 times	14.40 times	17.22 times

Based on the comparative liquidity ratios in Exhibit 11.3, there are no significant differences in the current or quick ratios. If anything, both Sobeys and Loblaw appear to have better liquidity than the industry as a whole. The receivables turnover is better at Loblaw because it has a relatively lower level of accounts receivable than Sobeys. This is due to Sobeys' food service arm, SERCA, which sells to institutions on credit. Certainly the turnover rate is sufficiently high, so concern about the collectibility of accounts receivable is not warranted. Sobeys' inventory turnover rate is higher than Loblaw's and the industry average, and this is an indication of good inventory management.

 Discussion Questions

11–21. Which of the following groups do you think would be interested in Sobeys Inc.'s inventory turnover ratio?

    a. trade creditor

    b. other short-term creditors (banks)

    c. long-term creditors

    d. shareholders

    Explain your reasoning.

11–22. What would a company do to improve its inventory turnover ratio?

11–23. What would a company do to improve its receivables turnover ratio?

Exhibit 11–4
Comparative Solvency
Ratios

Solvency Ratios	Sobeys Inc. May 5, 2001	Loblaw Cos. Ltd. December 30, 2000	Industry Average
Debt Ratio	62.65%	65.38%	60%
Debt to Equity Ratio	1.68 to 1	1.89 to 1	0.90 to 1
Coverage Ratio	2.12 times	5.59 times	5.76 times

Based on the comparative solvency ratios in Exhibit 11-4, both Sobeys and Loblaw have a higher debt to equity ratio than the industry average. This is due to the acquisitions of the Oshawa Group and Provigo. However, because of the lower level of income, Sobeys' coverage ratio is below that of Loblaw or the industry average.

Discussion Questions

11–24. If Sobeys Inc.'s coverage ratio was 0.212 instead of 2.12 and you were the company's banker, would you be concerned? Why or why not?

11–25. Which of the following groups might be concerned if a company's debt to equity ratio were higher than the industry average?

   a. trade creditors

   b. other short-term creditors

   c. long-term creditors

   d. shareholders

Explain the reasons for their concern.

Exhibit 11–5
Comparative Valuation Ratios

Solvency Ratios	Sobeys Inc. May 5, 2001	Loblaw Cos. Ltd. December 30, 2000	Industry Average
Price Earnings	33 times	27 times	Not available

Refer to the solvency ratios in Exhibit 11-5. Sobeys' higher price earnings ratio indicates that relative to its earnings, the price of Sobeys' shares appears higher than that of Loblaw. Whenever the ratios of a company like Loblaw show greater profitability than another company like Sobeys, the price earnings ratio of the more profitable company is usually higher. In this case it isn't because the market realizes that Sobeys' income will be higher next year when no restructuring expense will be recorded. Recall that the restructuring expense was about equal to net income, so if it does not recur in fiscal 2002, and all else remains equal, one would expect that net income will double and the price earnings ratio will be cut in half to 16 or 17 times earnings. If this were to happen, Sobeys' shares would look cheap compared to Loblaw's with a price earnings ratio of 27 times. In this case, it is now Loblaw's stock that is trading at a higher price earnings multiple. Two companies can have almost identical ratios and the market will still prefer to buy one share rather than the other. This is true with Loblaw at this point. The market clearly preferred it to Sobeys. Why? Because Loblaw had more growth and stability. From 2000 to 2001, Loblaw revenue rose faster than Sobeys', and its earnings per share increased rather than decreased.

Discussion Question

11–26. For which ratios is a higher statistic better? For which ratios is a lower statistic better?

Drawing Conclusions

At their respective year ends, Sobeys' stock was trading at $23 per share while Loblaw's was trading at $50.50 per share. If you were going to invest in the shares of either of these companies which one would you pick? You may be tempted to choose Loblaw because of its superior profitability ratios, but one must realize that Sobeys' ratios were lower due to the nonrecurring restructuring costs of $49.2 million. If these restructuring costs had not occurred, net income would have doubled and the price earnings ratio would have been cut in half to 16.5. Taking this into consideration and comparing it to the higher Loblaws' price earnings ratio of 27 times, one should have concluded that Sobey's share price was cheap and a better buy than Loblaw's shares.

By the end of 2002, Sobeys' shares were trading at over $39 while Loblaw's were trading at over $54. Sobeys' share price had risen by over 69 percent compared to a 7 percent increase for Loblaw's.

Before concluding our analysis of Sobeys, we should realize that share prices are not based just on historical information but also on decisions made by management on a daily basis. If you look closely at Note 16 to the financial statements in Sobeys 2001 annual report, you will see a note on segmented information. Such a note provides the reader with key information about the operating segments of a business. In this case, notice the relationship between the operating income and sales of the food distribution segment and the food service segment. The food distribution segment's operating income as a percentage of sales is 2.5% (232.7 ÷ $9,161.0 = 2.5%). The food service segment's operating income as a percentage of sales is 1.4% ($31.9 ÷ $2,209.5 = 1.4%). Clearly, the food service segment, SERCA, is not as profitable as the grocery store chains. Knowing this, management sold SERCA in late 2001. The proceeds from the sale of this division will allow the company to pay off a portion of its debt, thereby reducing interest expenses further and increasing net income. Another consequence of paying down the debt will be a reduction in the debt to equity ratio and an increase in the interest coverage ratio. Such a move will also allow management to focus on its core business and improve operating efficiencies.

LIMITATIONS OF RATIO ANALYSIS

Ratio analysis is an excellent tool for gathering additional information about a company, but it does have its limitations.

1. *Attempting to predict the future using past results depends on the predictive value of the information we use.* Changes in the general economy, in the economy of the particular industry being studied, and in the company's management present some of the uncertainties that can cause past results to be an unreliable predictor of the future.
2. *The financial statements used to compute the ratios are based on historical cost.* In a time of rapidly changing prices, comparison between years may be difficult.
3. *Figures from the balance sheet (i.e., assets, liabilities) used to calculate the ratios are year-end numbers.* Because most businesses have their fiscal year end in the slowest part of the year, the balances in such accounts as receivables, payables, and inventory at year end may not be representative of the rest of the year. Some analysts suggest using averages (i.e., average current assets for the year). However, even when this approach is taken, the problem is not eliminated, for averages are typically based on year-end numbers from two consecutive years.
4. *Industry peculiarities create difficulty in comparing the ratios of a company in one industry with those of a company in another industry.* Even comparison of companies within an industry may not be reasonable at times because

different companies use different accounting methods (e.g., amortization methods).

5. *Lack of uniformity concerning what is to be included in the numerators and denominators of specific ratios makes comparison to published industry averages extremely difficult.*

Perhaps the greatest single limitation of ratio analysis is that people tend to place too much reliance on the ratios. Financial ratios should not be viewed as a magical checklist in the evaluation process. Ratio analysis only enriches all the other information that decision makers should consider when making credit, investment, and similar types of decisions.

SUMMARY

In response to the need to reduce uncertainty in the decision-making process, analysts developed several techniques to assist economic decision makers as they evaluate financial statement information. Creditors (short-term and long-term), equity investors (present and potential), and company management comprise the three major categories of financial statement users. Because their objectives vary, their perspectives on the results of financial statement analysis will differ.

Three external factors—general economic conditions and expectations, political events and political climate, and industry outlook—affect business performance and should be considered when evaluating results of any type of financial statement analysis.

One important method of financial statement analysis is ratio analysis, a technique for analyzing the relationship between two items from a company's financial statements for a given period. We compute ratios by dividing the dollar amount of one item from the financial statements by the dollar amount of the other item from the statements. Another method is trend analysis, which looks at one ratio or financial statistic over time to determine if an upward or downward trend exists.

Analysts have developed a great many ratios to help economic decision makers assess a company's financial health. Because not all ratios are relevant in a given decision situation, decision makers must take care to select appropriate ratios to analyze. Ratio values, in and of themselves, have very little meaning. They become meaningful only when compared to other relevant information, such as industry averages or the company's ratio values from other years.

We broadly classify financial ratios as profitability ratios, liquidity ratios, solvency ratios, and valuation ratios. Profitability ratios attempt to measure the ease with which companies generate income. Liquidity ratios measure a company's ability to generate positive cash flow in the short run to pay off short-term liabilities. Solvency ratios attempt to measure a company's ability to meet the obligations created by its long-term debt. Valuation ratios attempt to relate a company's earnings performance to its share price. Individual ratios are listed in Exhibit 11–1.

Each of the these ratios provides valuable information for both internal and external decision makers. Ratio analysis does have its limitations. Placing too much reliance on the financial statements and the ratios derived from them without putting the information in the proper political, economic, and industry perspective can lead to poor decisions. Ratio analysis is an important financial analysis tool. Like the other tools we have discussed throughout this book, it must be used wisely and in the proper context.

KEY TERMS

coverage ratio or times interest
 earned ratio, p. 413
current ratio, p. 407
debt ratio, p. 412
debt to equity ratio, p. 413
financial statement analysis, p. 393
horizontal analysis, p. 398
inventory turnover ratio, p. 410
liquidity ratios, p. 407
price earnings ratio   414
profit margin after income
 tax ratio, p. 405
profit margin before income
 tax ratio, p. 404

profitability, p. 402
profitability ratios, p. 402
quick ratio or acid-test ratio, p. 408
ratio analysis, p. 393
receivables turnover ratio, p. 409
return on assets ratio, p. 403
return on equity ratio, p. 406
solvency, p. 411
solvency ratios, p. 411
total asset turnover ratio, p. 404
trend analysis, p. 393
vertical analysis or common size
 financial statements, p. 399

REVIEW THE FACTS

1. What is the purpose of financial statement analysis?
2. List the three financial statement user groups discussed in the chapter and describe what each group hopes to learn from financial statement analysis.
3. Describe the three types of external factors that warn users of financial information to consider, and explain how each factor can impact a company's performance.
4. From which financial statements are components of the ratios discussed in the chapter drawn?
5. Define profitability.
6. List the profitability ratios discussed in the chapter. For each one, describe the calculation used and the purpose of the ratio.
7. What are the two component ratios of the return on assets?
8. Define liquidity.
9. List the liquidity ratios discussed in the chapter. For each one, describe the calculation used and the purpose of the ratio.
10. What is the difference between the current ratio and the quick ratio? What is the purpose in examining both?
11. Define solvency.
12. List the three solvency ratios discussed in the chapter. For each one, describe the calculation used and the purpose of the ratio.
13. How are the debt ratio and the coverage ratio related?
14. What information can be gathered from calculating a company's coverage ratio?
15. Briefly describe how the price earnings ratio can be used.
16. Describe what additional information can be gleaned from an industry comparison of a company's ratios.
17. What is the purpose of conducting a comparison between a company's ratio values and those of the preceding year?
18. Describe the five limitations of ratio analysis discussed in the chapter.

APPLY WHAT YOU HAVE LEARNED

LO 1: Discussion

1. Identify the three major categories of financial statement analysis users and describe the basic objectives of each group.

LO 2: Discussion

2. Discuss how one goes about gathering background information on a company.

LO 4: Matching

3. Listed below are items relating to the concepts presented in this chapter, followed by definitions of those items in scrambled order.

a. Financial statement analysis	g. Profitability
b. Ratio analysis	h. Profitability ratios
c. Short-term creditors	i. Liquidity
d. Long-term creditors	j. Liquidity ratios
e. Shareholders	k. Solvency
f. Management	l. Solvency ratios

1. __j.__ Designed to measure a firm's ability to generate sufficient cash to meet its short-term obligations.
2. __b.__ A method for analyzing the relationship between two items from a company's financial statements for a given period.
3. __h.__ Designed to measure the ease with which a company generates income.
4. __l.__ Focus on interest payments and the overall debt load a company carries.
5. __a.__ Looking beyond the face of the financial statements to gather additional information.
6. __e.__ Those who own an equity interest in a corporation.
7. __i.__ The ease with which an item, such as an asset, can be converted into cash.
8. __c.__ Trade creditors and lending institutions such as banks.
9. __k.__ A company's ability to meet the obligations created by its long-term debt.
10. __d.__ Bondholders and lending institutions such as banks.
11. __g.__ The ease with which companies generate income.
12. __f.__ A group or groups of people responsible for a company's day-to-day operations.

REQUIRED:
Match the letter next to each item in the list with the appropriate definition. Each letter will be used only once.

LO 4: Matching

4. Listed below are all the ratios discussed in this chapter, followed by explanations of what the ratios are designed to measure in scrambled order.

a. Return on assets
b. Profit margin before income tax
c. Profit margin after income tax
d. Total asset turnover
e. Current ratio
f. Quick ratio
g. Price earnings ratio
h. Debt ratio
i. Coverage ratio
j. Return on equity
k. Receivables turnover
l. Inventory turnover
m. Debt to equity ratio

1. _e_ Most common ratio used to measure a company's ability to meet short-term obligations.
2. _i_ Measures a company's ability to make periodic interest payments.
3. _a_ Measures the return earned on investment in assets.
4. _f_ A more stringent test of short-term liquidity than the current ratio.
5. _b_ Measures the pretax earnings produced from a given level of revenues.
6. _c_ Measures the amount of after-tax net income generated by a dollar of sales.
7. _g_ Measures the relationship between a company's share price and its earnings per share.
8. _h_ Indicates the proportion of assets financed by debt.
9. _d_ Measures a company's ability to generate revenues from a given level of assets.
10. _m_ Compares the amount of debt financing with the amount of equity financing.
11. _j_ Measures how much after-tax income was generated for a given level of equity investment.
12. _l_ Indicates how long a company holds its inventory.
13. _k_ Measures how quickly a company collects amounts owed to it by its customers.

REQUIRED:
Match the letter next to each item on the list with the appropriate explanation. Each letter will be used only once.

LO 4: Matching

5. Listed below are all the ratios discussed in this chapter.

1. _____ Return on assets
2. _____ Debt ratio
3. _____ Profit margin before income tax
4. _____ Quick ratio
5. _____ Total asset turnover
6. _____ Current ratio
7. _____ Coverage ratio
8. _____ Return on equity
9. _____ Receivables turnover
10. _____ Price earnings ratio
11. _____ Inventory turnover
12. _____ Debt to equity ratio
13. _____ Profit margin after income tax

REQUIRED:
Identify each of the 13 ratios as a profitability ratio (P), a liquidity ratio (L), a solvency ratio (S), or a valuation ratio (V) by assigning it the appropriate letter.

LO 5: Ratio Computation

6. Presented below are partial comparative balance sheets of Mikey Limited at December 31, 2004 and 2003:

MIKEY LIMITED
Partial Balance Sheets
December 31, 2004, and December 31, 2003
Current Assets and Current Liabilities Only
(in thousands)

	2004	2003
Current Assets:		
Cash	$3,400	$2,920
Accounts Receivable	1,825	2,212
Merchandise Inventory	1,170	966
Prepaid Expenses	240	270
Total Current Assets	$6,635	$6,368
Current Liabilities:		
Accounts Payable	$2,321	$1,740
Notes Payable	3,100	3,300
Total Current Liabilities	$5,421	$5,040

REQUIRED:

a. Calculate Mikey Limited's current ratios for 2004 and 2003.
b. Calculate Mikey Limited's quick ratios for 2004 and 2003.
c. Which financial statement users are most interested in these two sets of ratios? Explain why the ratios are considered important to these users.
d. Assume that the average company in Mikey Limited's industry has a current ratio of 2:1 and a quick ratio of 1.25:1. If you were evaluating Mikey Limited's liquidity, what could you learn by comparing Mikey Limited's ratios to the industry averages?

LO 5: Ratio Computation

7. Presented below are partial comparative balance sheets of Harold Company Limited at December 31, 2004 and 2003:

HAROLD COMPANY LIMITED
Partial Balance Sheets
December 31, 2004, and December 31, 2003
Current Assets and Current Liabilities Only
(in thousands)

	2004	2003
Current Assets:		
Cash	$2,110	$2,650
Accounts Receivable	1,254	977
Merchandise Inventory	730	856
Prepaid Expenses	127	114
Total Current Assets	$4,221	$4,597
Current Liabilities:		
Accounts Payable	$1,054	$1,330
Notes Payable	2,100	1,750
Total Current Liabilities	$3,154	$3,080

REQUIRED:

a. Calculate Harold Company Limited's current ratios for 2004 and 2003.
b. Calculate Harold Company Limited's quick ratios for 2004 and 2003.
c. Which financial statement users are most interested in these two sets of ratios? Explain why the ratios are considered important to these users.
d. Assume that the average company in Harold Company Limited's industry has a current ratio of 2.5:1 and a quick ratio of 1:1. If you were evaluating Harold's liquidity, what could you learn by comparing Harold Company Limited's ratios to those of the industry averages?
e. What, if anything, could you determine by comparing Harold Company Limited's current ratio and quick ratio for 2003 with the same ratios for 2004? Explain your reasoning.

LO 7: Liquidity Evaluation

8. A five-year comparative analysis of Sagal Limited's current ratio and quick ratio is as follows:

	2000	2001	2002	2003	2004
Current ratio	1.24	1.95	2.55	3.68	4.13
Quick ratio	1.20	1.06	0.96	0.77	0.51

REQUIRED:

a. What does this analysis tell you about the overall liquidity of Sagal Limited over the five-year period?
b. What does this analysis tell you about what has happened to the composition of Sagal Limited's current assets over the five-year period?

LO 7: Liquidity Evaluation

9. A five-year comparative analysis of Carnegie Limited's current ratio and quick ratio is as follows:

	2000	2001	2002	2003	2004
Current ratio	4.24	3.95	2.95	2.68	1.93
Quick ratio	0.51	0.86	1.03	1.33	1.68

REQUIRED:

a. What does this analysis tell you about the overall liquidity of Carnegie Limited over the five-year period?
b. What does this analysis tell you about what has happened to the composition of Carnegie Limited's current assets over the five-year period?

LO 7: Profitability Evaluation

10. A five-year comparative analysis of Morone Limited's profit margin before tax and profit margin after tax is as follows:

	2000	2001	2002	2003	2004
Profit margin before tax	3.68	4.61	6.88	7.96	9.87
Profit margin after tax	2.22	2.95	4.41	5.27	7.09

REQUIRED:

a. What does this analysis indicate about Morone Limited's performance over the five-year period?

b. Which of the following groups would be interested in this analysis? Include in your answer a brief discussion of how you think each of them would interpret this analysis.

   (1) Trade creditors

   (2) Long-term creditors

   (3) Shareholders

LO 7: Profitability Evaluation

11. A five-year comparative analysis of Manley Limited's profit margin before tax and profit margin after tax is as follows:

	2000	2001	2002	2003	2004
Profit margin before tax	11.28	9.16	8.48	7.01	5.78
Profit margin after tax	9.33	8.59	6.14	5.72	3.89

REQUIRED:

a. What does this analysis indicate about Manley Limited's performance over the five-year period?

b. Which of the following groups would be interested in this analysis? Include in your answer a brief discussion of how you think each of them would interpret this analysis.

   (1) Trade creditors

   (2) Long-term creditors

   (3) Shareholders

LO 7: Capital Structure Evaluation

12. A five-year comparative analysis of Smythe Limited's debt to equity ratio and debt ratio is as follows:

	2000	2001	2002	2003	2004
Debt to equity ratio	2.75	2.50	2.25	1.50	1.00
Debt ratio	73.33	71.43	69.23	60.00	50.00

REQUIRED:

a. What does this analysis indicate about Smythe Limited's capital structure over the five-year period?

b. Which of the following groups would be interested in this analysis? Include in your answer a brief discussion of how you think each of them would interpret this analysis.

   (1) Trade creditors

   (2) Long-term creditors

   (3) Shareholders

LO 7: Capital Structure Evaluation

13. A five-year comparative analysis of Bausch Corporation's debt to equity ratio and debt ratio is as follows:

	2000	2001	2002	2003	2004
Debt to equity ratio	1.50	1.15	2.65	2.25	1.90
Debt ratio	60.00	53.49	72.60	69.23	65.52

REQUIRED:

a. What does this analysis indicate about Corporation's capital structure over the five-year period?

b. Which of the following groups would be interested in this analysis? Include in your answer a brief discussion of how you think each of them would interpret this analysis.

  (1) Trade creditors

  (2) Long-term creditors

  (3) Shareholders

LO 5: Ratio Computation

14. Presented below are the comparative balance sheets for Whipple Limited at December 31, 2004 and 2003. Also included is Whipple Limited's income statement for the year ended December 31, 2004.

WHIPPLE LIMITED
Balance Sheets
December 31, 2004, and December 31, 2003
(in thousands)

	2004	2003
ASSETS:		
Current Assets:		
Cash	$ 1,618	$1,220
Accounts Receivable	1,925	2,112
Merchandise Inventory	1,070	966
Prepaid Expenses	188	149
Total Current Assets	$ 4,801	$4,447
Plant and Equipment:		
Buildings, Net	$ 4,457	$2,992
Equipment, Net	1,293	1,045
Total Plant and Equipment	$ 5,750	$4,037
Total Assets	$10,551	$8,484
LIABILITIES:		
Current Liabilities:		
Accounts Payable	$ 1,818	$1,686
Notes Payable	900	1,100
Total Current Liabilities	$ 2,718	$2,786
Long-Term Liabilities	2,500	2,000
Total Liabilities	$ 5,218	$4,786
SHAREHOLDERS' EQUITY:		
Common Shares	$ 3,390	$2,041
Retained Earnings	1,943	1,657
Total Shareholders' Equity	$ 5,333	$3,698
Total Liabilities and Shareholders' Equity	$10,551	$8,484

WHIPPLE LIMITED
Income Statement
For the Year Ended December 31, 2004
(in thousands)

Sales Revenue		$11,228
LESS: Cost of Goods Sold		7,751
Gross Profit on Sales		$ 3,477
LESS: Operating Expenses:		
Amortization—Buildings and Equipment	$ 102	
Other Selling and Administrative	2,667	
Total Expenses		2,769
Income Before Interest and Taxes		$ 708
LESS: Interest Expense		168
Income Before Taxes		$ 540
Income Taxes		114
Net Income		$ 426

REQUIRED:
Calculate the following ratios for 2004:

(1) Return on assets
(2) Profit margin before income tax
(3) Total asset turnover
(4) Profit margin after income tax
(5) Return on equity
(6) Current ratio
(7) Quick ratio
(8) Receivables turnover
(9) Inventory turnover
(10) Debt ratio
(11) Debt to equity
(12) Coverage ratio

LO 5: Ratio Computation

15. Presented below are the comparative balance sheets for Earlywine Limited at December 31, 2004 and 2003, and the income statements for the years ended December 31, 2004 and 2003.

EARLYWINE LIMITED
Income Statements
For the Years Ended December 31, 2004 and 2003
(in thousands)

	2004	2003
Sales Revenue	$9,228	$8,765
LESS: Cost of Goods Sold	6,751	6,097
Gross Profit on Sales	$2,477	$2,668
LESS: Operating Expenses:		
Amortization—Buildings and Equipment	$ 80	$ 56
Other Selling and Administrative	1,667	1,442
Total Expenses	$1,747	$1,498
Income Before Interest and Taxes	$ 730	$1,170
LESS: Interest Expense	98	89
Income Before Taxes	$ 632	$1,081
Income Taxes	190	357
Net Income	$ 442	$ 724

EARLYWINE LIMITED
Balance Sheets
December 31, 2004, and December 31, 2003
(in thousands)

	2004	2003
ASSETS:		
Current Assets:		
Cash	$1,292	$ 980
Accounts Receivable	1,068	1,112
Merchandise Inventory	970	906
Prepaid Expenses	88	109
Total Current Assets	$3,418	$3,107
Plant and Equipment:		
Buildings, Net	$3,457	$2,442
Equipment, Net	993	945
Total Plant and Equipment	$4,450	$3,387
Total Assets	$7,868	$6,494
LIABILITIES:		
Current Liabilities:		
Accounts Payable	$ 998	$ 786
Notes Payable	600	500
Total Current Liabilities	$1,598	$1,286
Long-Term Liabilities	837	467
Total Liabilities	$2,435	$1,753
SHAREHOLDERS' EQUITY:		
Common Shares	$2,490	$2,000
Retained Earnings	2,943	2,741
Total Shareholders' Equity	$5,433	$4,741
Total Liabilities and Shareholders' Equity	$7,868	$6,494

REQUIRED:

a. Calculate the following ratios for 2004 and 2003:

(1) Return on assets
(2) Profit margin before income tax
(3) Total asset turnover
(4) Profit margin after income tax
(5) Return on equity
(6) Current ratio
(7) Quick ratio
(8) Receivables turnover
(9) Inventory turnover
(10) Debt ratio
(11) Debt to equity ratio
(12) Coverage ratio

b. Using the ratios you calculated in the previous requirement, complete the following comparison of Earlywine Limited's ratios to those of its entire industry and companies of comparable asset size for 2004.

	Total Industry	Assets Between $5 Million and $10 Million	Earlywine
Current ratio	1.46	1.95	
Quick ratio	0.93	1.11	
Coverage ratio	5.63	5.16	
Total asset turnover	1.76	1.42	
Inventory turnover	5.73	5.47	
Receivables turnover	7.83	6.54	
Debt to equity ratio	1.94	1.93	
Debt ratio	65.99	65.87	
Return on assets	9.30	10.40	
Return on equity	6.12	5.85	
Profit margin before tax	6.27	5.88	
Profit margin after tax	4.99	4.61	

c. Analyze the industry comparison you completed in the previous requirement as follows:
   (1) Identify any ratios you think do not warrant further analysis. Be sure to explain why any particular ratio is not going to be analyzed further.
   (2) For those ratios you felt deserved further analysis, assess whether Earlywine Limited's ratios are better or worse relative to both the entire industry and companies of comparable asset size.

LO 5: Ratio Analysis

16. Presented below is a comparison of Harry Limited's ratios for the years 2000 to 2004.

	2000	2001	2002	2003	2004
Current ratio	1.77	1.91	2.93	2.41	3.12
Quick ratio	1.40	1.26	1.08	0.94	0.79
Coverage ratio	6.90	6.91	5.76	5.24	3.49
Total asset turnover	1.46	1.40	1.17	1.08	0.99
Inventory turnover	8.88	8.24	8.11	6.46	4.45
Receivables turnover	8.93	7.41	6.52	5.87	5.34
Debt to equity ratio	0.96	1.22	1.97	2.21	2.54
Debt ratio	48.97	54.95	66.33	68.85	71.75
Return on assets	9.28	8.44	8.20	7.68	6.21
Return on equity	8.31	8.06	7.22	6.38	4.77
Profit margin before tax	10.00	9.45	8.27	7.78	4.12
Profit margin after tax	8.66	7.90	7.14	6.52	2.28

REQUIRED:
Analyze the five-year company comparison as follows:
a. Identify any ratios you think do not warrant further analysis. Be sure to explain why any particular ratio is not going to be analyzed further.
b. For each ratio you felt deserved further analysis, assess whether it has improved or worsened over the five-year period.
c. Based on your analysis of the five-year company comparison, comment briefly on the trend of Harry Limited's performance over the five-year period.

Applications 17 to 21 are based on the following comparative financial statements of Atkinson and Company Limited.

ATKINSON AND COMPANY LIMITED
Balance Sheets
December 31, 2004, and December 31, 2003
(in thousands)

	2004		2003
ASSETS:			
Current Assets:			
Cash	$ 2,240		$1,936
Accounts Receivable	2,340		2,490
Merchandise Inventory	776		693
Prepaid Expenses	200		160
Total Current Assets	$ 5,556		$5,279
Plant and Equipment:			
Buildings	$7,723		$6,423
LESS: Accumulated Amortization	3,677		3,534
Buildings, Net			$2,889
Equipment	$2,687		$2,387
LESS: Accumulated Amortization	1,564		1,523
Equipment, Net	1,123		864
Total Plant and Equipment	$ 5,169		$3,753
Total Assets	$10,725		$9,032
LIABILITIES:			
Current Liabilities:			
Accounts Payable	$ 1,616		$1,080
Notes Payable	2,720		2,920
Total Current Liabilities	$ 4,336		$4,000
Long-Term Liabilities	2,000		1,600
Total Liabilities	$ 6,336		$5,600
SHAREHOLDERS' EQUITY:			
Common Shares	$ 3,000		$2,400
Retained Earnings	1,389		1,032
Total Shareholders' Equity	$ 4,389		$3,432
Total Liabilities and Shareholders' Equity	$10,725		$9,032

ATKINSON AND COMPANY LIMITED
Income Statements
For the Years Ended December 31, 2004 and 2003
(in thousands)

	2004		2003	
Sales Revenue		$14,745		$12,908
LESS: Cost of Goods Sold		10,213		8,761
Gross Profit on Sales		$ 4,532		$ 4,147
LESS: Operating Expenses:				
Advertising and Sales Commissions	$1,022		$ 546	
General and Administrative	2,721		2,451	
Total Expenses		3,743		2,997
Income Before Interest and Taxes		$ 789		$ 1,150
LESS: Interest Expense		172		137
Income Before Taxes		$ 617		$ 1,013
LESS: Income Taxes		123		355
Net Income		$ 494		$ 658

LO 5: Calculating Ratios

17. Using the Atkinson and Company Limited's financial statements, calculate the following ratios for 2004 and 2003:

1. Return on assets
2. Profit margin before income tax
3. Total asset turnover
4. Profit margin after income tax
5. Return on equity
6. Current ratio
7. Quick ratio
8. Receivables turnover
9. Inventory turnover
10. Debt ratio
11. Debt to equity ratio
12. Coverage ratio

LO 6: Comparing Ratios to Industry Averages

18. Presented below is a partially completed comparison of Atkinson and Company Limited's ratios to those of its entire industry and companies of comparable asset size for 2004.

	Total Industry	Assets Between $10 Million and $25 Million	Atkinson
Current ratio	2.24	1.95	
Quick ratio	1.33	1.31	
Coverage ratio	5.43	3.16	
Total asset turnover	1.76	1.42	
Inventory turnover	5.78	5.77	
Receivables turnover	7.83	6.54	
Debt to equity ratio	2.28	1.94	
Debt ratio	69.51	65.99	
Return on assets	9.30	10.40	
Return on equity	16.12	15.85	
Profit margin before tax	6.67	3.88	
Profit margin after tax	4.49	2.61	

REQUIRED:

a. Complete the industry comparison by calculating each of Atkinson and Company Limited's ratios for 2004 and recording them in the space provided. (Note: If you have completed Application 17, you have already done the calculations. Just use the ratios you have already calculated.)

b. Analyze the industry comparison you did in the previous requirement as follows:

   (1) Identify any ratios you think do not warrant further analysis. Be sure to explain why any particular ratio is not going to be analyzed further.

   (2) For those ratios you felt deserved further analysis, assess whether Atkinson and Company Limited's ratios are better or worse relative to both the entire industry and companies of comparable asset size.

   (3) Based on your analysis of the industry comparison, comment briefly on how you think Atkinson and Company Limited compares to other companies in its industry.

LO 5: Calculating Ratios

19. Presented below is a partially completed comparison of Atkinson and Company Limited's ratios for the years 2000 to 2004.

	2000	2001	2002	2003	2004
Current ratio	2.07	2.62	1.79		
Quick ratio	1.00	1.09	1.01		
Coverage ratio	6.31	5.44	4.48		
Total asset turnover	1.11	1.86	1.34		
Inventory turnover	10.88	11.37	11.81		
Receivables turnover	4.80	4.99	5.10		
Debt to equity ratio	1.22	1.65	1.61		
Debt ratio	54.95	62.26	61.69		
Return on assets	5.22	6.11	5.34		
Return on equity	10.98	11.62	11.05		
Profit margin before tax	4.68	4.12	4.44		
Profit margin after tax	3.06	3.16	3.31		

REQUIRED:

a. Complete the five-year company comparison by calculating each of Atkinson and Company Limited's ratios for 2003 and 2004 and recording them in the space provided. (Note: If you have completed Application 17 you have already done the calculations. Just use the ratios you have already calculated.)

b. Analyze the five-year company comparison you completed in the previous requirement as follows:

(1) Identify any ratios you think do not warrant further analysis. Be sure to explain why any particular ratio is not going to be analyzed further.

(2) For each ratio you felt deserved further analysis, assess whether it has improved or got worse over the five-year period.

(3) Based on your analysis of the five-year company comparison, comment briefly on the trend of Atkinson and Company Limited's performance over the five-year period.

Comprehensive

20. This chapter focused on ratio analysis performed on the income statement and the balance sheet. For this reason, the financial statements for Atkinson and Company Limited did not include a statement of cash flows. To assess the company's overall performance in 2004, however, you should also look at its statement of cash flows.

REQUIRED:

a. Using the 2003 and 2004 comparative balance sheets and the income statement for 2004, prepare Atkinson and Company Limited's 2004 statement of cash flows.

b. Which of the three broad activities (operating, investing, and financing) provided Atkinson and Company Limited with the majority of its cash during 2004?

c. Briefly discuss whether the activity you identified in the previous requirement is an appropriate source of cash in the long run.

d. In which of the three broad activities (operating, investing, and financing) did Atkinson and Company Limited use most of its cash during 2004?

e. Briefly discuss what your answer to the previous requirement reveals about Atkinson and Company Limited.

Comprehensive

21. This chapter focused on ratio analysis performed on the income statement and the balance sheet. For this reason, the financial statements for Atkinson and Company Limited did not include a statement of retained earnings. To assess the company's overall performance in 2004, however, you should also look at the company's statement of retained earnings.

REQUIRED:

a. Using the 2003 and 2004 comparative balance sheets and the income statement for 2004, prepare Atkinson and Company Limited's 2004 statement of retained earnings.

b. Briefly discuss how the statement of retained earnings demonstrates articulation among Atkinson and Company Limited's financial statements.

LO 8: Limitations of Ratio Analysis

22. The chapter discussed several limitations of ratio analysis, namely:

1. Using past results to predict future performance
2. Using historical cost as a basis for ratios
3. Using year-end balances as either the numerator or denominator for many ratios
4. Industry peculiarities
5. Lack of uniformity in defining the numerators and denominators used in calculating ratios
6. Giving too much credence to ratio analysis

REQUIRED:
Explain why each of the six items listed above limit the usefulness of ratio analysis.

ANNUAL REPORT PROJECT

23. With the work you have done during the term, you can now complete the last two sections of your project. Refer to the work you did on the project in Chapter 9 to compute your company's ratios to complete Part VI.

REQUIRED:

Part VII Summary and Conclusion

a. Compute the 13 basic ratios presented in Chapter 11 for the last two years and present them in tabular form.

b. Evaluate your company's profitability, liquidity, and solvency by comparing them to industry averages.

c. Prepare a summary of your conclusions about your company using the price earnings ratio and all of the information you have gathered during the term. Part of your conclusion should include a recommendation whether or not to invest in this company.

d. Assemble your entire report, place in an appropriate folder, and submit it to your professor.

Appendix: Sobeys 2001 Annual Report

BUILDING SUSTAINABLE WORTH

Financial and Operating Overview

- Reached consolidated sales of $11.37 billion, a new high. Same store sales increased 3.7%.
- Exceeded $70 million integration synergy target by year-end.
- Discontinued further development of enterprise-wide information system, taking an associated restructuring charge of $89.1 million ($49.2 million after tax).
- Achieved a record $110.3 million or $1.81 per share in earnings before restructuring charges and goodwill amortization.
- Issued $250 million of common shares in November 2000.
- Invested $505 million in company-wide capital expenditures; opened 51 new or replacement stores, expanded or modernized another 92 stores.
- Completed consolidation and modernization of SERCA's Ontario distribution network.
- Launched New National Merchandising Structure and Program.
- Improved debt to capital ratio, from 53.1% to 38.5%.

At Sobeys we have a clear vision: to be the most worthwhile experience in the marketplace ... period. Delivering that experience takes motivated people with real commitment to customer service, franchised dealers committed to serving their communities, engaged suppliers who share a steadfast focus on identifying and meeting consumer needs, and well-informed shareholders who understand, believe and invest in Sobeys' long-term growth strategy. As the feature section of this year's annual report explains, consistently meeting the expectations of each of these important stakeholder groups is the key to Building Sustainable Worth.

SOBEYS INC. AT A GLANCE

- IGA
- Garden Market IGA
- IGA Extra
- Sobeys
- Price Chopper
- Serca
- Foodland
- Needs & Green Gables
- Lawton's
- Thrifty Food
- Food Town
- Boni Choix

Market Presence

- Corporate Stores	402
- Franchised Stores	949
- Distribution Centres	27
- Foodservice Operations	20

Northern & Western

Northwest Territories

Food Town	2
Total	**2**

British Columbia

IGA	3
Garden Market IGA	3
Total	**6**

Alberta

Garden Market IGA	47
IGA	53
Food Town	15
Total	**115**

Saskatchewan

Garden Market IGA	5
IGA	13
Food Town	15
Thrifty Foods	2
Total	**35**

Manitoba

Garden Market IGA	13
IGA	20
Food Town	19
Price Chopper	1
Total	**53**

Ontario

Garden Market IGA	6
IGA	135
Sobeys	34
Knechtel	59
Foodland	43
Price Chopper	57
Price Check	22
Food Town	53
Total	**409**

Quebec

IGA	230
IGA Extra	4
Sobeys	10
Boni Choix	114
Les Marches Tradition	21
Total	**388**

Atlantic

New Brunswick

Sobeys	23
Foodland	3
Needs and Green Gables	15
Lofood	7
Lawtons	9
Total	**57**

Nova Scotia

Sobeys	41
Foodland	17
Needs and Green Gables	66
Lofood	5
Lawtons	35
Total	**164**

Prince Edward Island

Sobeys	5
Needs and Green Gables	4
Lofood	2
Lawtons	1
Total	**12**

Newfoundland

Sobeys	16
Foodland	37
Needs and Green Gables	36
Lawtons	21
Total	**110**

CHAIRMAN'S MESSAGE

"Bill has assembled an outstanding leadership group and we are counting on this team, along with Bill, to advance our company with the focus and commitment that we have already seen produce early and encouraging results.

We have an extensive and well-positioned food distribution and food service network. Our ability to satisfy an even modestly larger share of our customers' requirements represents a huge opportunity for Sobeys"

David F. Sobey
Chairman of the Board

This past year was one of important change and challenge for Sobeys Inc. As a public company now three years old, we find ourselves well positioned to capitalize on the promise and potential so apparent at the time of the acquisition of the Oshawa Group. Our efforts this past year have focused on getting our company, our leadership and our people well prepared to advance through our "Next Stage of Development".

In November 2000, Bill McEwan was appointed President & Chief Executive Officer. Doug Stewart fulfilled his 10-year mandate, having served the last five years as Chief Executive Officer of Sobeys Inc. John Sobey retired as President and Chief Operating Officer of Sobeys Inc. after 31 years with the company.

On behalf of the Board, I would like to thank Doug and John for their great contributions to the company over their years of service. I also want to thank the Board of Directors for their valued counsel and acknowledge the strong contribution of Hugh Farrington, who recently retired from the Board of Directors.

Bill McEwan joins Sobeys with over 25 years experience in the retail food distribution and consumer products industries. His leadership, planning, operational, merchandising and communication skills will serve him and Sobeys well going forward.

I have great confidence that our new leadership team will build our business on a strengthened foundation and continue Sobeys' great tradition as a leading Canadian food distributor.

Sincerely,

(signed)

David F. Sobey   July 6, 2001

Chairman

CEO's Message

"We are very well positioned for growth. Our efforts going forward must focus on poising our organization to capitalize on the full breadth of our opportunity. We have established clarity of purpose, a new leadership team, and the focus and discipline required to advance our winning strategy."

Bill McEwan
Chief Executive Officer

This is my first letter to shareholders since joining Sobeys as your new CEO in November of last year. Over the first several months on the job I have been delighted to confirm my beliefs, as a former competitor and supplier, that Sobeys is indeed a wonderful organization, with great people and extraordinary opportunities for growth.

I consider myself fortunate for having been afforded the privilege to lead our company through its next stage of development. And I appreciate this early opportunity to openly share our challenges, our successes, our strengths and our immediate priorities. It's important that you know our vision for Sobeys, as well as our fresh approach to "building sustainable worth" for all our constituents; that is, our customers, our people and franchisees, our suppliers and our shareholders.

Building on Initiative

It has been clear to me for some time that Sobeys is one of those special organizations with a genuine feel for the rhythm of the food business. About 60 years ago, Frank Sobey was the first merchant in Atlantic Canada to introduce customers to the benefits of "cash and carry" grocery shopping. That took foresight and courage—back in an era when doing business that way was truly foreign to consumers.

The initiative demonstrated by the acquisition of the Oshawa Group food distribution business with its $8 billion in sales to fortify Sobeys' position in a consolidating industry, is further evidence of an organization committed to aggressive, intelligent and strategic growth. That transaction created Canada's second largest retail food distribution organization with over 1,300 stores and thousands of wholesale customers in 10 provinces. Additionally, SERCA is Canada's largest and only national foodservice distribution company.

We are very well positioned for growth. Our efforts now are focused on poising our organization to capitalize on the full breadth of our opportunity.

A Foundation to Build On

During the past year, after adjusting for the extra week last fiscal year, Sobeys Inc. sales rose 5.3% to reach $11.37 billion from $11.0 billion the year before. Comparable store sales grew 3.7%, while total store square footage grew 3.8% to 20.7 million square feet. Operating income was $264.6 million, or 2.33% of sales on the strength of higher sales volumes, better margins and lower operating expenses associated with the achievement of our $70 million operating synergy target for the integration of the Oshawa Group.

That's good progress but, despite these gains, results fell well short of our expectations. The greatest impact on earnings resulted from a major five-day information systems disruption that occurred in late November 2000. Our Ontario and Atlantic corporate stores and Lumsden Brothers wholesale business suffered unprecedented out-of-stocks during the peak five-to six-week selling season prior to Christmas. As a direct result of the disruption, earnings before restructuring charges for the year were $1.50 per share, well short of our $1.72 per share target. The disruption led to a comprehensive evaluation of our enterprise-wide systems initiative and the subsequent decision to abandon further development and implementation. In conjunction with this decision, Sobeys announced a one-time after-tax charge of $49.2 million or $0.81 per share.

While Sobeys posted a respectable operating performance during the past year—including an earnings increase of 13.7% prior to the one-time charge—we are not performing to potential. Our next stage of development is upon us and we have established clarity of purpose, a new Leadership team and the focus and discipline required to advance our winning strategy. But only superior execution will deliver superior results.

Building Sustainable Worth

It starts with a determination that our overall purpose is to build sustainable worth. It requires a clear understanding that creating shareholder worth—while the ultimate measure of success for any public company—can only be the result, not the sole purpose, of our strategy.

Our customers must, first and foremost, be provided with a shopping experience that is worthwhile to them.

Our employees, franchisees and affiliates must feel that our company is a workplace worthy of their personal commitment.

Our suppliers must see the working relationships with our organization as worthy of their best talent and resources—where investments of their time, expertise and money are worthwhile.

When our customers, our people and franchisees, and our suppliers feel that the experience with Sobeys is "worth it" … shareholders worth will grow at Sobeys.

Building Sustainable Worth—the theme of this year's report—recognizes that our success depends on meeting the needs of each of these important stakeholder groups. The feature section of this report outlines how we are building sustainable worth.

Leading the Transformation

My first order of business was to secure the leadership required to take us forward. Over the past several months we have assembled the strongest possible Senior Executive team available … period.

It is a talented, realigned and fully engaged leadership team—our Leadership Committee.

Wayne Wagner has served as President Operations, Western Region for 14 years and is now joined by Eugene Duynstee, President Operations, Ontario Region; Marc Poulin, President Operations, Quebec Region; and John Lynn, formerly Executive Vice President, Support Services and now President Operations, Atlantic Region. Gary Seaman is President, SERCA Foodservice.

Glenn Hynes, formerly Senior Vice President Planning and Business Intelligence was appointed Executive Vice President and CFO in June of this year.

Duncan Reith joined the company in January, 2001 as Executive Vice President and Chief Merchandising Officer.

Jim Dickson, Partner, Stewart McKelvey Stirling Scales, joined the company in June, 2001 as Executive Vice President Corporate Services, General Counsel and Secretary.

Together, the Leadership Committee will lead the continued transformation and growth of Sobeys.

Our second imperative—which might seem too obvious to mention—is to do a better job of remembering what business we are in. Our core business is food. We exist to consistently provide our customers with superior food and related products and services supported and enabled by appropriate processes, services and technology.

One of the first decisions I had to face, upon joining Sobeys, was the future of our proposed enterprise-wide information system. It soon became very clear that we were going down a path that was creating a tremendous disruption and distraction for the organization—one that, in the end, wasn't going to provide us with a sustainable solution for the long term. The decision to move forward with more flexible and adaptable technology developed to support our focus on our core business was vital.

Accordingly, our third imperative has been to realign the structure of the organization and properly deploy our people and resources to support our business initiatives rather than servicing a disconnected, unsustainable corporate initiative.

Six Immediate Priorities

We will deliver early success and a sustainable future by focusing with urgent commitment on six important priority initiatives.

First, we have completed comprehensive regional market overviews, which have identified specific growth opportunities for our three major banners based on extensive demographic and competitive analysis of every local market in our business. This doesn't mean we are ready to act on all our opportunities overnight. But going forward, we know exactly where we want to grow our market presence and can now more effectively allocate our capital resources. We are poised to take advantage of priority market opportunities.

Second, we completed the integration of our Ontario foodservice operations. In September 2000, SERCA opened a state-of-the-art, 265,000 sq. ft. distribution centre in Mississauga, Ontario, a critical step in the consolidation and modernization of SERCA's Ontario network.

Third, we have completed a national distribution and logistics plan to reduce our cost of moving product from source to our customers while at the same time improving overall service levels. Our centralized operational support teams, working with regionally managed distribution centre operations, have identified significant warehouse and transportation cost reduction opportunities that are being aggressively pursued and secured. We have already begun to realize a higher level of synergy from Sobeys' two state-of-the art distribution centres in southern Ontario. The expansion of the Milton, Ontario distribution centre and the opening of a new 420,000 sq. ft. multi-temperature warehouse in Whitby, Ontario have allowed us to retire outdated facilities and save more than $10 million a year in future operating expenses. These facilities provide the capacity we need to support our expanding store network. On July 1, 2001 we transitioned operational management of the Milton facility from a third party to Sobeys management. This change alone will account for $3.8 million in savings per year going forward.

Fourth is our national merchandising strategy and improved structure that shifts the focus from strictly negotiating volume purchases of product to more intelligently meeting the needs of our consumers. Under Duncan Reith's leadership we recently launched our new vendor engagement program to simplify our national and regional merchandising processes. We are focused on delivering a stronger merchandising and selling "attitude" by establishing more productive vendor relationships, utilizing business intelligence on consumer trends, sharing best practices across the operating regions and capitalizing on common buying and national vendor programs. We will be easier to do business with, we will optimize our overall store sizes and market presence, and our sales, profitability and customer satisfaction will grow.

Fifth is the development of an information technology strategic plan to support and enable our operations across the country. We have established an IT framework and governance structure that will better position the IT organization to support and enable our business initiatives. With this framework in place, IT is positioned to support our business efforts and requirements more productively.

Sixth is an ambitious plan to simplify the overall organization and better focus our energy and resources on worth-creating and cost-reducing activities. The Leadership Committee is driving this initiative to eliminate redundant or waste-creating processes, re-deploy our talented people, and promote quick adoption of best practices company-wide.

I have traveled to all of our markets these past several months and I am personally committed to facilitating best practice adoption as too logical to ignore.

The Year Ahead

Irrespective of the fortunes of the overall Canadian economy, we expect to achieve significant growth in each of our regions during the current fiscal year. We are aiming for greater than 30% growth in earnings per share in fiscal 2002 based on rising same-store sales growth, additional sales from $550–$600 million in company-wide capital spending and significant margin enhancement through the initiatives mentioned in this letter.

Longer term, we are well positioned to continue building sustainable worth for all of our stakeholders. We have an extensive and well-positioned retail food distribution network. With Garden Market IGA, Sobeys, Price Chopper and the other arrows in our quiver, we will be targeting the distinct needs of different consumer groups in each of our markets as never before. As we continue to strengthen our market presence, our sales, profitability and customer satisfaction will grow.

At the same time, it is important to remember that, through SERCA, we are also the country's largest and only national foodservice company—one that is uniquely equipped to both meet the coast-to-coast needs of major customers in a consolidating industry as well as the requirements of small and medium size accounts. All told, we are at the consumer's table—meals inside and outside the home—more than any other food provider in Canada.

Our People

I would like to acknowledge the outstanding contribution of Pierre Croteau, who passed away in April 2001 after a courageous battle with cancer. Pierre was the highly respected President Operations, Quebec Region, whose commitment and leadership skills were well known throughout the grocery industry.

Finally, I would like to thank the more than 32,000 employees and franchisees across the country, whose efforts have allowed us to deliver solid operating results in fiscal 2001 while preparing a stronger foundation for success in the years ahead. There is much opportunity and many more challenges ahead, but with their continued enthusiasm and support, I know we have what it takes to make Sobeys a consistently worthwhile experience for all of its stakeholders, for many years to come.

Sincerely,

(signed)

Bill McEwan   July 6, 2001

Every public company exists to create shareholder value. But at Sobeys, our efforts to build sustainable worth depend on meeting the needs of a wider group of constituents, starting, first and foremost, with our customers. Our vision is to make Sobeys the most worthwhile shopping experience in the marketplace by accurately identifying customers' preferences and efficiently meeting their needs. It takes skilled and dedicated people to do that, and the kind of motivation that only comes by making Sobeys a company worthy of their commitment. We also work openly and collaboratively with our suppliers to improve our offerings, lower costs and create a working relationship that is worthy of their very best resources. And finally, building sustainable worth depends on clear and consistent communication with each of our stakeholder groups, including the investors whose continued interest and support is critical to our success.

Our Customers

With 1,351 stores in 10 provinces, thousands of wholesale customers and the country's only national foodservice operation, Sobeys has the largest end-to-end food presence in Canada.

But making the most of that position demands a sincere commitment to serving our customers and earning the opportunity to satisfy a greater share of their everyday requirements. We have begun to use consumer data more intelligently, not to simply sell more product off the shelves, but to tell us what our customers really want. We are also reconfiguring our stores to create the freshest possible experience while adding a thoughtful combination of complementary services. Our aim is to make Sobeys the most worthwhile experience for our customers ... consistently.

Determining the optimum product and service offerings for each of our banners is a key first step to overall customer satisfaction. Our Sobeys banner stores are designed to provide time-pressed shoppers with industry leading fresh departments, a select range of conveniences such as in-store pharmacy and wellness centers, extended-hour banking and the highest standards of personal service. Price Chopper, our 20,000 to 45,000 sq. ft. discount format, delivers everyday low prices to the more price sensitive segment of the market with a simplified operating approach. Garden Market IGA, our mid-size stores for neighbourhood communities, delivers an unsurpassed fresh market experience and personalized service in a comfortably sized store that appeals to the vast majority of shoppers.

Our People

Across the country we enjoy an enviable reputation for personalized service and a strong connection to the communities served through our corporate and franchised stores. It's a competitive strength that's earned through the skill and dedication of our people, and it's one that we must never take for granted.

We know there is a direct correlation between employee satisfaction and shareholder value. And that well-trained people, who enjoy what they do and whose values are congruent with those of the organization, are vital. We have never been more dedicated to fostering a workplace environment that is worthy of our employees and franchisees commitment.

Central to such efforts is open, consistent communication. During the past few months, our senior management has met with employees throughout the company to find out what makes them feel satisfied and proud about their work. The result of this discovery process is a grass-roots consensus of the company's core values that is being integrated into our communications surrounding a wide range of initiatives—from recruitment and training to reward and recognition programs.

Just as our ability to deliver compelling store offerings to our customers is critical for success, we are equally committed to measuring the effectiveness of our "employee proposition". That's why we are beginning to conduct formal employee satisfaction surveys that will help identify organizational strengths and weaknesses, assess the linkage between performance and incentive compensation plans and, above all, provide a yardstick with which to measure our progress going forward.

Our Suppliers

An often forgotten but always vital element in the pursuit of customer satisfaction is the retailers' supplier. Whether it's a provider of products, services, information, financing or technology, our goal is to make their relationship with Sobeys worth the very best of their time, talent and resources. Realizing that objective starts with a significant reengineering of our approach to procurement and merchandising.

Traditionally, Sobeys' buying strategies have been designed to maximize economies of scale and achieve volume targets. While those objectives are still important, our next stage of development requires an important shift in focus toward the customer as the starting point. That's why we are moving from short-term volume based agreements to multi-year alliances with key suppliers, where success is measured not only in volume but also by our mutual ability to profitably increase our share of customers' total requirements.

Our new approach to category management is an essential part of this process. Once a separate function, we have moved category management away from bookshelf plans to everyday interaction between newly empowered category managers and their suppliers. Together, we are working more effectively to deliver what our customers are looking for – at the right time, and at the right price … consistently. In the process, we are making it easier to do business with Sobeys.

Our Shareholders

Ultimately, the success of any public company is measured by its ability to build worth for its investors. Sobeys is committed to growing long-term shareholder worth, but equally important, we have committed ourselves to sharing the company's strategy for growth, and the measurement of our progress, along the way.

That commitment starts with a 5.5% target for top-line growth in fiscal 2002, fueled by a combination of same store sales increases and additional revenues associated with planned company-wide capital investment of more than $550 million during the next year.

We are also calling for an increase in earnings per share (EPS) greater than 30% in fiscal 2002. It's an aggressive target, but it will be achieved through specific margin enhancement and sustainable cost reduction initiatives.

Reaching these financial targets depends on meeting a greater percentage of our customers' daily needs. We aim to do that through a range of initiatives that will sharpen our banner position market-by-market and constantly improve our offering to customers.

Capable and engaged employees are equally vital to success. By establishing an employee satisfaction survey, we are creating a baseline from which to measure the effectiveness of our worthiness as a workplace going forward.

Finally, we will work more closely with our vendors to deliver a precise mix of products and services that sustains and enhances customer satisfaction. By re-engineering our procurement and merchandising programs, we are determined to make Sobeys worth the very best of their efforts.

- With an established market presence from coast to coast, our same store sales growth and new investment will deliver total revenue of over $12.0 billion in fiscal 2002.
- Operating earnings are expected to increase significantly in the years ahead as the result of specific performance improvement initiatives in procurement, merchandising, marketing and distribution.
- Sobeys is well positioned for growth as one of two national players in a consolidating industry. In fiscal 2002, company wide capital spending is expected to reach a record $550 to $600 million.

Growth in Store

Sobeys is a leading retail food and foodservice organization in Canada with annual sales in excess of $11 billion, 1,351 stores in 10 provinces, thousands of wholesale customers and the country's only national foodservice operation. But our growth has just begun. Here are a few reasons investors like what's in store at Sobeys.

Solid Fundamentals

Sobeys has a proven ability to grow—organically and through acquisition. Sales have grown from $3.20 billion in 1998 to $11.37 billion in 2001, operating profits continue to grow, and infrastructure investments over the past two years have established a platform for continued growth.

Strong Leadership

Sobeys leadership is determined to build sustainable worth for all our constituents—customers, people and franchisees, suppliers and shareholders—by operating the best retail food and foodservice businesses in Canada. The talent, focus and winning plan are all in place.

Accelerating Earnings

Forecast fiscal 2002 earnings per share growth of greater than 30% over fiscal 2001. Action plans to generate sustained operating cost savings and secure margin expansion have been identified and are being implemented.

Record Reinvestment

Enterprise-wide capital investment in retail food and foodservice operations is planned to exceed $1 billion over the next two years, modernizing our current store network and expanding in opportunity markets with new stores.

Attractive Valuation

Sobeys' common shares (symbol SBY on the Toronto Stock Exchange) are currently valued at less than 13 times forward earnings with a PEG (price earnings to growth rate) ratio of 0.4 times.

FISCAL 2002 OBJECTIVES

Sobeys' vision is to be the most worthwhile experience for all our constituents—customers, people and franchisees, suppliers and shareholders—by operating the best retail food and foodservice businesses in Canada. Sobeys is focused on superior execution. In order to measure our performance, management has established the following key metrics and fiscal 2002 objectives.

	Fiscal 2002 Objective
Revenue ($ in billions)	$12.0+
Operating Earnings per Share Growth	30%+
National Share of Requirements[1]	20.5%
Employee Satisfaction Index[2]	125
Supplier Rating[3]	1st Quartile

(1) **National Share of Requirements** is the measurement of the percentage of all households' total grocery requirements that are satisfied by our retail stores.

(2) Starting with a base index of 100 in fiscal 2001, through independent employee surveys, the **Employee Satisfaction Index** measures progression in employee satisfaction.

(3) **Supplier Rating** is an independent comprehensive survey of how Sobeys ranks with its suppliers on key performance criteria versus our retail peer group.

MANAGEMENT'S DISCUSSION AND ANALYSIS

The following is a discussion and analysis of the consolidated financial results of Sobeys Inc. ("Sobeys" or "the Company") for the fiscal year ended May 5, 2001 as compared to the fiscal year ended May 6, 2000. As part of this discussion, an assessment is made as to the consolidated operating performance, the outlook of each business segment, the financial condition of the Company, liquidity and capital resources, and the impact of risks. This discussion contains forward-looking statements and should be read in conjunction with the Company's discussion regarding forward-looking statements found on page A-21. This discussion should also be read in conjunction with the consolidated financial statements, including the notes that accompany them, found on pages A-23 to A-35.

Financial Overview

The following table illustrates selected items from the consolidated statements of earnings as a percentage of total sales.

Percentage of total sales (except per share amounts)	F2001	F2000
Sales	100.0%	100.0%
Cost of sales, selling and administrative expenses	96.8	96.7
Depreciation	0.9	0.9
Operating income (before goodwill charges)	2.3	2.4
Interest expense	0.6	0.8
Restructuring charge	0.8	—
Earnings before the following items:	0.9	1.6
Income taxes (recovery):		
Restructuring	(0.4)	—
Other operations	0.7	0.7
Goodwill charges	0.2	0.2
Net earnings	0.4	0.7
Earnings per share (before restructuring charge)	$ 1.50	$ 1.43
Net earnings per share	$ 0.69	$ 1.43

It is important to note, when comparing fiscal 2001 results to the previous year, that fiscal 2001 contained 52 weeks of operations compared to 53 weeks in fiscal 2000. Accordingly, fiscal 2001 results are not directly comparable to the prior year's results.

Highlights

In fiscal 2001, Sobeys achieved sales of $11.37 billion, an increase of $364.4 million or 3.3% over fiscal 2000, with all regions contributing to this increase. Adjusting for the additional week of sales in fiscal 2000, sales growth was 5.3% over last year. Same-store sales increased 3.7%, primarily as a result of store improvements resulting from the capital expenditure program, and food price inflation.

Earnings per share (before restructuring charge) increased to $1.50 from $1.43 per share in fiscal 2000. Earnings (before restructuring charge and goodwill amortization) equalled $110.3 million or $1.81 per share in fiscal 2001 as compared to $99.1 million or $1.77 per share in the preceding year. The restructuring charge of $89.1 million ($49.2 million after-tax) reflects the Company's decision on January 24, 2001 to discontinue further development and implementation of its enterprise-wide systems initiative. Subsequent to this decision, the system was phased out of 30 corporate stores in Ontario and over time will be phased out of operation in Sobeys Atlantic Region. The operations of Sobeys Quebec, Sobeys West, SERCA, and the remaining 379 stores in Ontario had not been converted to the system.

On November 16, 2000, Sobeys issued 9,174,312 common shares for net proceeds of $245.9 million. These proceeds were used for the reduction of outstanding bank credit facilities and for the Company's capital expenditure program. It is also important to note that fiscal 2001 per share calculations include the dilutive effect of the share issuance on November 16, 2000 based on a weighted average number of shares outstanding of 60.8 million versus 56.0 million shares in fiscal 2000.

In fiscal 2001, the Company opened or replaced 51 stores including 8 Sobeys (fiscal 2000—3), 12 IGA (fiscal 2000—14), 5 Garden Market IGA / IGA extra (fiscal 2000—6), 7 Price Chopper (fiscal 2000—12) and 19 other banner stores. The capital expenditure program also included the renovation or expansion of 92 stores, including 4 Sobeys (fiscal 2000—9), and 39 IGA (2000—50) and 19 Garden Market IGA / IGA extra banner stores (fiscal 2000—8). Company-wide capital expenditures totalled $505 million in fiscal 2001 for the expansion and modernization of the Company's store and distribution network. At fiscal year-end 2001, the Company operated 1,351 stores (comprised of 402 corporate stores and 949 franchised stores). The Company's total square footage increased by 751,514 square feet to 20.7 million square feet, an increase of 3.8% over fiscal 2000.

Fiscal 2001 Fourth Quarter Review

Fourth quarter sales were $2.84 billion versus $2.85 billion in fourth quarter of the previous year. Fourth quarter 2001 contained 13 weeks as opposed to 14 weeks in fiscal 2000. This extra week in fiscal 2000 represented $204 million in sales. Adjusting for the additional week, fourth quarter sales increased 7.3% over the previous year. Same-store sales for the quarter grew 4.0%.

Fourth quarter EBITDA (earnings before interest, taxes, depreciation and amortization) totalled $96.1 million, a slight increase of $0.7 million over the fourth quarter last year. As a percentage of sales, EBITDA equaled 3.38%, an increase of 4 basis points over the 3.34% recorded in the fourth quarter of last year. The fourth quarter included an increase in equipment lease expense over the fourth quarter of fiscal 2000, as well as an increase in legal costs to defend a now resolved lawsuit commenced in Ontario by a number of IGA franchisees. The lawsuit was resolved in April 2001 without payment of damages by Sobeys.

Net earnings for the fourth quarter of $25.4 million (39¢ per share) increased $2.3 million or 10% over the fourth quarter last year.

Financial Information by Quarter

(in millions, except per share information)	Q4 May 5, 2001	Q3 Feb. 3, 2001	Q2 Nov. 4, 2000	Q1 Aug. 5, 2000	Q4 May 6, 2000	Q3 Jan. 29, 2000	Q2 Oct. 30, 1999	Q1 July 31, 1999
Operations								
Revenue	$2,842.6	$2,818.8	$2,853.1	$2,856.0	$2,854.6	$2,665.3	$2,721.4	$2,764.8
Earnings from continuing operations, before goodwill and restructuring charge	30.2	19.5	27.9	32.7	27.8	23.1	22.3	25.9
Goodwill amortization	4.8	4.6	4.7	5.0	4.7	4.6	4.7	4.9
Restructuring charge		49.2						
Net earnings (loss)	$ 25.4	$ (34.3)	$ 23.2	$ 27.7	$ 23.1	$ 18.5	$ 17.6	$ 21.0
Per Share Information (basic & fully diluted)								
Earnings from continuing operations, before goodwill and restructuring charge	$ 0.46	$ 0.30	$ 0.49	$ 0.58	$ 0.49	$ 0.41	$ 0.39	$ 0.47
Goodwill amortization	0.07	0.07	0.08	0.09	0.08	0.08	0.08	0.09
Restructuring charge		0.76						
Net earnings (loss)	$ 0.39	$ (0.53)	$ 0.41	$ 0.49	$ 0.41	$ 0.33	$ 0.31	$ 0.38
Weighted average number of common shares outstanding (millions)	65.8	64.6	56.4	56.3	56.3	56.3	55.7	55.6

Results of Consolidated Operations

Revenue

Operating Revenue by Segment ($ in millions)	2001	2000*	Change ($)	Change (%)
Food distribution	9,161.0	8,936.2	224.8	2.5
Foodservice	2,209.5	2,069.9	139.6	6.7
Total revenue	11,370.5	11,006.1	364.4	3.3

*Fiscal 2000 contained 53 weeks of operations.

Consolidated revenue in fiscal 2001 reached $11.37 billion, a 3.3% increase over fiscal 2000. On a proforma basis, excluding the additional week of sales ($204 million) in the previous fiscal year, the year-over-year sales growth rate was 5.3%. Food price inflation, at 3.0%, was a factor with respect to sales growth in 2001 versus 0.4% in the prior year. Sobeys, for the most part, attributes additional sales growth to same-store sales growth of 3.7% and sales generated by increased retail square footage resulting from the company-wide capital expenditure program. Sobeys recorded increased sales performance in all regions, but did not recognize its full sales potential due to a third quarter system and business disruption that affected its Atlantic Canada operations, Ontario corporate stores, and Lumsden Brothers wholesale operation. Same-store sales performance in Atlantic Canada, although positive, lagged the other regions significantly as a result of the disruption.

Operating Income

Operating Income by Segment ($ in millions)	2001	2000*	Change ($)	Change (%)
Food distribution	232.7	231.8	0.9	0.4
Foodservice	31.9	33.8	(1.9)	(5.6)
Total operating income	264.6	265.6	(1.0)	(0.4)

*Fiscal 2000 contained 53 weeks of operations.

The Company's operating income declined 0.4% from fiscal 2000 to $264.6 million. Operating margin fell to 2.33%, from 2.41% in fiscal 2000. Trading margin (EBITDA/sales—or earnings before interest, taxes, depreciation and amortization divided by sales) decreased to 3.20% from 3.30% in fiscal 2000. The decrease in operating income, operating margin, and trading margin was largely reflective of two non-recurring items: first, a one-time, five-day database and system disruption in the third quarter, which forced "work-around" procedures and resulted in unprecedented out-of-stocks in the Atlantic and Ontario corporate stores; and second, transitional operating costs incurred for the Ontario food distribution and foodservice operations resulting from three major capital infrastructure projects.

EBITDA in the Sobeys Atlantic region, Ontario corporate stores, and Lumsden Brothers wholesale operation collectively declined due to the impact of the enterprise-wide systems and business disruption, as previously noted. Excluding the Sobeys Atlantic Region and 30 Ontario corporate stores, all other regions along with the foodservice division reported EBITDA growth above fiscal 2000 levels and met Company expectations.

The Company's food distribution and foodservice operations experienced operating costs above usual levels with respect to three major capital projects in Ontario: a 420,000 square foot distribution centre in Whitby; an expanded Milton distribution centre; and a 265,000 square foot distribution centre in Mississauga. These facilities have resulted in improved service levels, order picking accuracy, and on-time deliveries. However, the Company has not yet achieved targeted operating cost levels as one-time operating costs have been incurred to ensure Sobeys' customers and franchisees were well served throughout the transition period. The transitional operating costs incurred in the Ontario food distribution and foodservice operations also impacted fiscal 2001 EBITDA.

Effective July 1, 2001, Sobeys ended a third-party facility management agreement in respect of the operation of the Company's Milton, Ontario distribution centre. Sobeys management has projected $3.8 million in annual cost savings resulting from the transition of the facility to Sobeys management.

Depreciation and Goodwill

Depreciation expense increased by 1.5% to $99.5 million in fiscal 2001 as a result of the increase in capital assets acquired through the capital expenditure program. Expressed as a percentage of sales, depreciation was relatively unchanged from the prior year at 0.9% of sales. Total depreciation and goodwill charges amounted to $118.6 million or 1.0% of sales in fiscal 2001 compared to $116.9 million or 1.1% of sales in fiscal 2000.

Financing Costs

Interest expense in fiscal 2001 was $73.8 million, compared to $89.0 million recorded in fiscal 2000, representing a 17.1% year-over-year decline. Interest on long-term debt decreased $16.3 million while interest on short-term debt increased by $1.1 million from the prior fiscal year. The overall decrease in interest expense can, for the most part, be attributed to the debt reduction program outlined in the Recapitalization Plan portion of the discussion.

Tax Rate

The effective tax rate before restructuring and goodwill charges was 42.2%, a 1.7% reduction from fiscal 2000. The decrease was a result of a 1.0% reduction in statutory tax rates and a slight shift in taxable income into jurisdictions with lower statutory tax rates.

Sobeys expects its fiscal 2002 effective tax rate before goodwill charges to be 40.4%. The expected reduction from fiscal 2001 is the result of decreasing statutory tax rates.

Net Earnings

Earnings (before restructuring charge) increased to $91.2 million ($1.50 per share) from the $80.2 million ($1.43 per share) recorded in fiscal 2000, a year-over-year earnings increase of 13.7%. Including the after-tax restructuring charge of $49.2 million, net earnings of $42.0 million ($0.69 per share) represented a $38.2 million decrease from the $80.2 million ($1.43 per share) achieved in fiscal 2000. As noted previously, fiscal 2001 per share calculations include the 5% dilution effect of the issuance of 9,174,312 common shares on November 16, 2000.

Earnings growth (before the restructuring charge) of 13.7% was primarily reflective of the 17.1% decrease in interest expense and the decrease in the Company's effective tax rate.

Segmented Results

Sobeys operates principally in two business segments: Food Distribution, which represented 80.6% of Sobeys' total fiscal 2001 sales and 87.9% of total operating income, and Foodservice (SERCA), which represented 19.4% of total fiscal 2001 sales and 12.1% of operating income.

Food Distribution

Sales

Food Distribution sales reached $9.16 billion in fiscal 2001, a 2.5% increase from $8.94 billion in fiscal 2000. The extra week in fiscal 2000 accounted for approximately $168 million of sales from food distribution. On a proforma basis, allowing for the additional week in fiscal 2000, the year-over-year sales growth rate was 4.4%. The benefits of higher same-store sales of 3.7% and revenues from new retail space resulting from the company-wide capital expenditure program accounted for the growth in sales over the prior year. After adjusting for the effects of Canadian food price inflation, real comparable sales for all banners rose by 0.7%. Total store square footage increased to 20.7 million square feet from 20.0 million square feet in the prior year.

At the end of fiscal 2001, Sobeys operated a total of 1,351 stores, comprised of 402 corporate stores and 949 franchised stores. The Company's stores operate under a range of corporate and franchise retail banners that includes IGA, Garden Market IGA, IGA extra, Sobeys, Foodland, Price Chopper, Le Marchés Tradition, Boni Choix, Knechtel, Lofood, Needs, Green Gables, Food Town, and Lawton's Drugs.

Banners	Corporate stores	Franchised stores	Totals	Average store size (sq. ft.)
IGA	21	442	463	17,762
Garden Market IGA / IGA extra	26	52	78	30,033
Sobeys	129	—	129	37,725
Foodland	3	97	100	8,541
Price Chopper	2	56	58	25,135
Knechtel	2	57	59	10,971
Lawton's Drugs	60	6	66	6,037
Food Town	1	103	104	5,025
Lofood	14	—	14	14,379
Needs & Green Gables	120	1	121	2,172
Boni Choix	—	114	114	5,202
Other banners	24	21	45	7,927
Totals	402	949	1,351	15,342

At the end of fiscal 2001, the proportion of total store square footage by region was: Atlantic, 21.1%; Quebec, 29.1%; Ontario, 33.1%; and Western, 16.7%. The 2002 capital expenditure program includes plans to grow total store square footage by 5%.

Operating Income

In fiscal 2001, food distribution operating margin (EBIT before goodwill / sales) decreased to 2.54% compared to 2.59% of sales in fiscal 2000. Food distribution operating income increased $0.9 million from fiscal 2000 to reach $232.7 million in fiscal 2001. The impact of ongoing cost reduction, distribution efficiencies, migration of best practices across the regions as well as the benefits of National Merchandising are expected to enhance operating results in fiscal 2002.

Foodservice

Sales

Sales for fiscal 2001 reached $2.21 billion (2000—$2.07 billion), a 6.7% increase from the previous year or an increase of 8.8% when adjusted for the additional week of sales in fiscal 2000. On a proforma basis, excluding the additional week in the previous year and sales associated with the August 2000 acquisition of Dellixo Foodservice in Quebec, the sales growth rate was 5.8%.

Operating Income

In fiscal 2001, foodservice operating margin decreased to 1.44% from 1.63% in the previous year. Foodservice operating income (EBIT before goodwill charges) decreased $1.9 million from fiscal 2000 to $31.9 million in fiscal 2001. A new 265,000 square foot distribution centre in Mississauga, Ontario opened and began to ship products in the second quarter of fiscal 2001, which impacted operating costs. In fiscal 2001, the Company completed the consolidation of the SERCA Ontario distribution network, reducing the number of distribution centres from 11 to 5.

Liquidity and Capital Resources

The Company's financial position continued to strengthen in fiscal 2001 and this trend is expected to continue in fiscal 2002. The total debt-to-equity ratio improved to 0.6:1 at fiscal 2001 year end from 1.1:1 at the prior year-end. This favourable trend was primarily a result of the Company's Recapitalization Plan, which resulted in the retirement of $197.7 million in long-term debt.

In addition, key debt ratios strengthened during the year. Total debt (includes on-balance sheet borrowings of $683.5 million and $150.0 million off-balance sheet receivables securitization) to EBITDA declined from 2.55 times at May 6, 2000 to 2.29 times at the end of fiscal 2001. Debt (as previously defined) to total capital also improved—from 53.1% to 43.3% at May 2001 while EBITDA to total interest expense coverage grew to 4.93 times from 4.09 times in the prior year.

Short-term liquidity improved during the year as short-term borrowings declined from $71.4 million at May 5, 2000 to $25.0 million at the end of fiscal 2001. Cash flows from operating activities decreased from $306.2 million in fiscal 2000 to $82.5 million in fiscal 2001 primarily as a result of a ($180.2) million net change in other current items in fiscal 2001 versus $44.3 million in fiscal 2000. A portion of the net change in other current items was related to one-time items that were not operational in nature, but were related to third-party franchisee financing arrangements that were not finalized by year-end and restructuring liabilities relating to the Oshawa acquisition which decreased during the year. Cash flows used in investing activities increased to $193.2 million in fiscal 2001 versus $144.9 million in the prior year due to a combination of lower proceeds on disposal of property and equipment and higher investment in deferred charges. Cash flows generated by financing activities represented a $140.0 million source of funds in fiscal 2001 as compared to a $182.2 million use of funds in fiscal 2000. This significant increase was due to funds generated by the Company's Recapitalization Plan.

In fiscal 2001, company-wide capital expenditures increased by $119 million to $505 million. The Company constructed a total of 51 new and replacement stores and renovated and expanded 92 existing stores during the year. Capital spending for fiscal 2001 was financed through funds from operations, net proceeds from the November 16, 2000 equity issue, existing bank credit lines, third-party loans, franchisee spending, and sale-leasebacks to related parties.

The Company continues to focus on growth plans through a combination of new store openings and renovations, as well as growth through acquisitions where appropriate. Company-wide capital spending is expected to total $550–$600 million in fiscal 2002, supported by $320 million in on-balance sheet financing, $120 million in third-party lease financing with the remainder funded by the Company's franchisees, and third-party developers.

Debt

At year-end, the Company maintained bank credit facilities that were $275 million in excess of borrowings. Short-term debt, comprised of bank loans and bankers' acceptances, amounted to $25.0 million (2000—$71.4 million) at year-end. Long-term debt, comprised of $495.0 million due within the next five years and $163.5 million of other long-term debt with varying maturities, totalled $658.5 million (2000—$856.2 million) at year-end. The fair value of long-term debt, excluding capital leases, is estimated to be $688.0 million.

In December 2000, Standard & Poor's issued its initial rating on Sobeys, with a BBB− (stable trend) rate level. On January 25, 2001, DBRS reaffirmed its BBB rating on Sobeys; however, it changed its trend from stable to negative.

Recapitalization Plan

As a result of Sobeys' $1.5 billion acquisition of The Oshawa Group Limited in December 1998, the Company incurred approximately $1.0 billion of bank debt. The transaction created a highly levered capital structure that relied heavily on shorter-term bank debt. Moreover, given the short time frame required to complete the acquisition, the bank debt was secured and quite restrictive. Sobeys' management reached the decision to subsequently refinance its debt based on the following objectives: to achieve diversified funding, to access public debt markets, to shift the majority of debt from a secured to an unsecured basis, to reduce the overall after-tax cost of debt, to achieve increased operating and financial flexibility, to remove restrictive conditions contained in the existing credit facilities, and to maximize shareholder value.

On June 22, 2000, Sobeys filed a short-form shelf prospectus with securities regulators to establish an unsecured medium-term note program (MTN) to permit the issuance of up to $500 million in MTNs from time to time over the following two years. On June 29, 2000, Sobeys refinanced $810 million in secured bank debt by: issuing $175 million Series A MTNs, with an interest rate of 7.65%, maturing November 1, 2005; securitizing $210 million in trade and other receivables; and negotiating a non-revolving $250 million unsecured bank credit facility to be repaid over 5 years and a $300 million revolving unsecured bank credit facility. On October 2, 2000, the Company issued $100 million Series B three-year MTNs at an effective interest rate of 7.05%. On November 16, 2000, the Company issued 9,174,312 common shares at $27.25 per share for gross proceeds of $250 million.

As a result of this recapitalization, at fiscal year-end 2001, the Company's new capital structure facilitated access to public debt and securitization markets, established two new unsecured bank credit facilities with less restrictive financial covenants, and achieved off-balance sheet funding via trade receivables securitization. The reduction in annual borrowing costs as a result of this recapitalization plan amounts to approximately $9 million pre-tax or $0.08 per share. The effect of the recapitalization plan on interest coverage and debt-to-capitalization ratios has been positive.

Accounting Policy Changes Implemented in Fiscal 2001

The Canadian Institute of Chartered Accountants ("CICA") issued two new accounting standards in the past year, Section 3465 "Income Taxes" and Section 3461 "Employee Future Benefits," effective for fiscal years beginning on or after January 1, 2000. Effective May 7, 2000 the Company adopted both standards retroactively without restatement of prior periods. The cumulative effect of initial adoption was reported as a decrease in retained earnings of $1.2 million and $3.4 million, respectively. The implementation of section 3461 resulted in an increase in future tax assets of $24.4 million and an increase in goodwill of $26.2 million, net of amortization, relating to the purchase of The Oshawa Group Limited during fiscal 1999.

Accounting Policy Changes Subsequent to Fiscal 2001

The CICA has issued accounting standard, Section 1751 "Interim Financial Statements," effective for interim periods in fiscal years commencing on or after January 1, 2001. This standard requires that the Company expand disclosure on its quarterly consolidated financial statements. The Company intends to adopt this standard in the first quarter of 2002 (three months ended August 4, 2001).

Risk and Risk Management

Given the mature structure of the Canadian food distribution industry, the most significant operating risk to the Company is the potential for reduced revenues and profit margins as a result of intense competition. To mitigate this risk, the Company's strategy is to be geographically diversified with a national presence, to be market-driven, to be focused on superior execution, and to be supported by cost-effective operations. The Company has entered into an agreement with a third-party consultant to assist in the development of a cost-reduction plan and operational policies, which will be applied throughout the Company. This plan and related policies are expected to have a positive impact on the ability of the Company to face operational risks in a competitive environment.

Sobeys revenues are diversified by region with no one region or division (Atlantic, Quebec, Ontario, Western, foodservice) contributing more than 26% of total sales. This ensures a balance of earnings should competition in a particular region intensify or the outlook for an area change. Management is committed to controlling operating risks through continual innovation (store format and positioning, retail brand development, customer loyalty initiatives), and through the realization of lower costs from increasing economies of scale.

Sobeys has adopted a number of key financial policies to manage financial risk. In the ordinary course of managing its debt, the Company has entered into various interest rate swaps, which are referred to in our financial statements. The Company has fixed the interest rate on $75.0 million of its debt at 6.2% for one year and has fixed the interest rate on $292.1 million of its debt at 6.8% for four years by utilizing interest exchange agreements.

Inflationary risk is not considered to have a material effect on the financial condition or performance of the Company. Any inflationary pressures are mitigated by adjusting merchandising practices to reflect changes in consumers' buying habits.

Sobeys is self-insured for limited risks while maintaining comprehensive loss prevention and management programs to mitigate retained risks. The range of non-insured related risk exposure is not expected to be material to the overall operations of the Company. The Company conducts an ongoing comprehensive environmental monitoring process and is unaware of any significant environmental liabilities.

Information Technology

As a result of the January 24, 2001 decision to abandon the enterprise-wide software and systems initiative, the Company plans to eventually phase out the existing software system in the Atlantic region, continue to use and enhance existing legacy systems, undertake a company-wide master data and data warehousing initiative, and assess core application enhancements. The Company's IT strategy includes ongoing evaluation of available product options to ensure that information technology will continue to support and enable Sobeys Inc. operations.

Outlook

Looking forward to fiscal 2002, management believes the Company is well positioned for growth. Sobeys intends to build sustainable worth for all its constituents primarily through the realization of operating cost savings, margin expansion through customer-focused category management, distribution efficiencies, ongoing capital cost savings, and other productivity enhancements.

We are aiming for greater-than-30% growth in earnings per share in fiscal 2002 and revenues of over $12 billion. Our key fiscal 2002 objectives are found on page A-12 of this report.

Forward-Looking Statements

Certain forward-looking statements are included in this annual report concerning capital expenditures, cost reduction, and operating improvements. Such statements are subject to inherent uncertainties and risks, including but not limited to: general business and economic conditions in the Company's operating regions; pricing pressures and other competitive factors; results of the Company's ongoing efforts to reduce costs; and the availability and terms of financing. Consequently, actual results and events may vary significantly from those included in or contemplated or implied by such statements.

MANAGEMENT'S RESPONSIBILITY FOR FINANCIAL REPORTING

Preparation of the consolidated financial statements accompanying this annual report and the presentation of all other information in the report are the responsibility of management. The financial statements have been prepared in accordance with appropriate and generally accepted accounting principles and reflect management's best estimates and judgements. All other financial information in the report is consistent with that contained in the financial statements.

The Board of Directors, through its Audit Committee, oversees management in carrying out its responsibilities for financial reporting and systems of internal control. The Audit Committee, which is chaired by and includes non-management directors, meets regularly with financial management and external auditors to satisfy itself as to the reliability and integrity of financial information and the safeguarding of assets. The Audit Committee reports its findings to the Board of Directors for consideration in approving the annual financial statements to be issued to shareholders. The external auditors have full and free access to the Audit Committee.

(signed)   (signed)

Bill McEwan   R. Glenn Hynes, C.A.
President and   Executive Vice President and
Chief Executive Officer   Chief Financial Officer
June 27, 2001   June 27, 2001

AUDITORS' REPORT

To the Shareholders of Sobeys Inc.

We have audited the consolidated balance sheets of Sobeys Inc. as at May 5, 2001 and May 6, 2000, and the consolidated statements of earnings, retained earnings, and cash flows for the years then ended. These financial statements are the responsibility of the Company's management. Our responsibility is to express an opinion on these financial statements based on our audits.

We conducted our audits in accordance with Canadian generally accepted auditing standards. Those standards require that we plan and perform an audit to obtain reasonable assurance whether the financial statements are free of material misstatement. An audit includes examining, on a test basis, evidence supporting the amounts and disclosures in the financial statements. An audit also includes assessing the accounting principles used and significant estimates made by management, as well as evaluating the overall financial statement presentation.

In our opinion, these consolidated financial statements present fairly, in all material respects, the financial position of the Company as at May 5, 2001 and May 6, 2000 and the results of its operations and its cash flows for the years then ended in accordance with Canadian generally accepted accounting principles.

(signed)   (signed)

New Glasgow, Nova Scotia   Grant Thornton LLP
June 8, 2001   Chartered Accountants

Consolidated Balance Sheet

As at May 5, 2001 (in millions)	2001	2000
Assets		
Current		
Cash	$ 82.4	$ 53.1
Short-term investments, at cost (*quoted market value $2.7; 2000 $2.6*)	1.7	1.7
Receivables	346.2	420.0
Inventories	509.3	485.5
Prepaid expenses	41.4	41.0
Income taxes recoverable	22.3	8.3
Future tax provision (*Note 10*)	16.7	—
Current portion mortgages and loans receivable	41.9	59.3
	1,061.9	1,068.9
Mortgages and loans receivable (*Note 2*)	115.4	103.6
Property and equipment (*Note 3*)	859.4	882.9
Goodwill (less accumulated amortization of $50.2; 2000 $30.2)	723.5	714.9
Future tax provision (*Note 10*)	46.7	—
Deferred income tax	—	32.0
Deferred charges (*Note 4*)	110.7	88.7
	$2,917.6	$2,891.0
Liabilities		
Current		
Bank loans (*Note 5*)	$ —	$ 6.4
Bankers' acceptances (*Note 5*)	25.0	65.0
Accounts payable and accrued charges	1,069.4	1,129.1
Long-term debt due within one year	49.2	69.9
	1,143.6	1,270.4
Long-term debt (*Note 6*)	609.3	786.3
Employee future benefit obligation (*Note 17*)	60.8	—
Deferred revenue	14.1	16.6
	1,827.8	2,073.3
Shareholders' Equity		
Capital stock (*Note 8*)	896.1	647.3
Deferred foreign exchange translation gain	1.2	0.6
Retained earnings	192.5	169.8
	1,089.8	817.7
	$2,917.6	$2,891.0

See accompanying notes to consolidated financial statements.

On behalf of the Board

(signed)   (signed)

Director   Director

Consolidated Statement of Retained Earnings

Year Ended May 5, 2001 (in millions)	2001 (52 weeks)	2000 (53 weeks)
Balance, beginning of year	$169.8	$103.0
Adjustment relating to employee future benefits (*Note 1*)	(3.4)	—
Adjustment relating to change in accounting of future tax assets and liabilities (*Note 1*)	(1.2)	—
Net earnings	42.0	80.2
	207.2	183.2
Dividends paid	14.7	13.4
Balance, end of year	$192.5	$169.8

See accompanying notes to consolidated financial statements.

Consolidated Statement of Earnings

Year Ended May 5, 2001 (in millions)	2001 (52 weeks)	2000 (53 weeks)
Sales	$11,370.5	$11,006.1
Cost of sales, selling and administrative expenses	11,006.4	10,642.5
Depreciation	99.5	98.0
Operating Income	264.6	265.6
Interest expense		
Long-term debt	63.5	79.8
Short-term debt	10.3	9.2
	73.8	89.0
	190.8	176.6
Restructuring (*Note 9*)	(89.1)	—
Earnings before the following items	101.7	176.6
Income taxes (*Note 10*)		
Restructuring (*Note 9*)		
Future income tax benefit	(39.9)	—
Other operations		
Current income tax expense	32.4	46.0
Future income tax expense	48.1	31.5
	40.6	77.5
Earnings before goodwill charges	61.1	99.1
Goodwill charges (*Note 1*)	19.1	18.9
Net earnings	$ 42.0	$ 80.2
Earnings per share, basic and fully diluted (*Note 11*)		
Earnings before goodwill charges	$ 1.00	$ 1.77
Net earnings	$ 0.69	$ 1.43

See accompanying notes to consolidated financial statements.

Consolidated Statement of Cash Flows

Year Ended May 5, 2001 (in millions)	2001 (52 weeks)	2000 (53 weeks)
Operations		
Net earnings	$ 42.0	$ 80.2
Items not affecting cash (*Note 12*)	174.2	181.7
Net restructuring charges not affecting cash	35.2	—
	251.4	261.9
Net change in other current items as a result of restructuring	11.3	—
Operating cash flow	262.7	261.9
Net change in other current items	(180.2)	44.3
Cash flows from (used in) operating activities	82.5	306.2
Investment		
Property and equipment	(207.8)	(207.3)
Proceeds on disposal of property and equipment	56.9	94.9
Long-term investments and advances	5.7	(3.9)
Increase in deferred costs	(47.8)	(29.3)
Business acquisitions, net of cash acquired	(2.5)	(0.1)
Employee future benefits obligation	1.7	—
Increase in deferred foreign currency translation gains	0.6	0.8
Cash flows from (used in) investing activities	(193.2)	(144.9)
Financing		
Bank loans	(6.4)	(1.1)
Bankers' acceptances	(40.0)	(50.0)
Issue of long-term debt	553.2	10.7
Repayment of long-term debt	(750.9)	(128.4)
Revolving securitization	150.0	—
Reduction (increase) of share purchase loan	(4.1)	—
Issue of capital stock	252.9	0.1
Payment of dividends	(14.7)	(13.4)
Cash flows from (used in) financing activities	140.0	(182.1)
Increase (decrease) in cash	29.3	(20.8)
Cash, beginning of year	54.8	75.6
Cash, end of year	$ 84.1	$ 54.8
Operating cash flow per share (*Note 11*)	$ 4.32	$ 4.68

Cash is defined as cash and short-term investments.
See accompanying notes to consolidated financial statements.

(In millions except share capital) May 5, 2001

1. SUMMARY OF SIGNIFICANT ACCOUNTING POLICIES

Principles of consolidation

These consolidated financial statements include the accounts of the Company and all subsidiary companies.

Depreciation

Depreciation is recorded on a straight-line basis over the estimated useful lives of the assets as follows:

Equipment and vehicles	3–10 years
Buildings	15–40 years
Leasehold improvements	7–10 years

Inventories

Warehouse inventories are valued at the lower of cost and net realizable value with cost being determined substantially on a first-in, first-out basis. Retail inventories are valued at the lower of cost and net realizable value less normal profit margins as determined by the retail method of inventory valuation.

Leases

Leases meeting certain criteria are accounted for as capital leases. The imputed interest is charged against income and the capitalized value is depreciated on a straight-line basis over its estimated useful life. Obligations under capital leases are reduced by rental payments net of imputed interest. All other leases are accounted for as operating leases with rental payments being expensed as incurred.

Goodwill

Goodwill represents the excess of the purchase price of the business acquired over the fair value of the underlying net tangible assets acquired at the date of acquisition. Goodwill is amortized on a straight-line basis over its estimated life of 40 years. Goodwill charges are net of income tax recovery of $0.9 (2000 $0.8). The Company evaluates the carrying value of goodwill by considering whether the amortization of the goodwill balance over its remaining life can be recovered through undiscounted future operating cash flows of the acquired operation(s).

Interest capitalization

Interest related to the period of construction is capitalized as part of the cost of the related property and equipment. The amount of interest capitalized to construction in progress in the current year was $0.8 (2000 $0.8).

Deferred revenue

Deferred revenue consists of a long-term purchase agreement and rental revenue arising from the sale of subsidiaries. Deferred revenue is being taken into income over the term of the related agreement and leases.

Foreign currency

Assets and liabilities of self-sustaining foreign investments are translated at exchange rates prevailing at the balance sheet date. The revenues and expenses of the foreign operations are translated at average exchange rates prevailing during the year. The gains and losses on translation are deferred and included as a separate component of shareholders' equity titled "deferred foreign exchange translation gain."

Development and store opening expenses

Development and opening expenses of new stores and store conversions are written off during the first year of operation.

Accounting estimates

The preparation of consolidated financial statements in conformity with generally accepted accounting principles requires management to make estimates and assumptions that affect the amounts reported in the consolidated financial statements and accompanying notes. These estimates are based on management's best knowledge of current events and actions that the Company may undertake in the future.

Employee future benefits

Effective May 7, 2000, the Company changed its method of accounting for employee future benefits to conform with the recommendations of the Canadian Institute of Chartered Accountants. This change has been applied on a retroactive basis without restatement of prior years. Accordingly, opening retained earnings has decreased by $3.4, accrued benefit obligations have increased by $59.1, goodwill has increased by $26.2 (net of amortization), and future tax assets have increased by $24.4.

Future tax provision

Effective May 7, 2000, the Company adopted the Canadian Institute of Chartered Accountants new handbook section 3465, relating to a new method of accounting for deferred income taxes. This change has been applied retroactively through an adjustment to retained earnings of $1.2 and prior periods have not been restated as permitted under the standard. The difference between the tax basis of assets and liabilities and their carrying value on the balance sheet has been used to calculate future tax assets and liabilities. The future tax assets and liabilities have been measured using the substantially enacted tax rates that will be in effect when the differences are expected to reverse.

2. MORTGAGES AND LOANS RECEIVABLE

	2001	2000
Loans receivable	$104.2	$97.0
Mortgages receivable	10.5	5.5
Other	0.7	1.1
	$115.4	$103.6

Loans receivable

Loans receivable represent long-term financing to certain retail associates. These loans are primarily secured by inventory, fixtures and equipment, bear interest at rates which fluctuate with prime, and have repayment terms up to 10 years. The carrying amount of the loans receivable approximates fair value based on the variable interest rates charged on the loans and the operating relationship of the associates with the Company.

The loans and mortgages receivable are net of current portions of $41.9 (2000 $59.3).

3. PROPERTY AND EQUIPMENT

	Cost	Accumulated Depreciation	2001 Net Book Value
Land	$ 75.0	$ —	$ 75.0
Land held for development	69.6	—	69.6
Building	270.5	92.1	178.4
Equipment	1,098.0	737.8	360.2
Leasehold improvements	207.4	112.7	94.7
Construction in progress	68.5	—	68.5
Assets under capital lease	18.4	5.4	13.0
	$1,807.4	$948.0	$859.4

	Cost	Accumulated Depreciation	2000 Net Book Value
Land	$ 82.9	$ —	$ 82.9
Land held for development	60.0	—	60.0
Building	297.8	94.8	203.0
Equipment	1,050.0	699.3	350.7
Leasehold improvements	183.9	99.6	84.3
Information system development	74.7	—	74.7
Construction in progress	22.3	—	22.3
Assets under capital lease	8.2	3.2	5.0
	$1,779.8	$896.9	$882.9

4. DEFERRED CHARGES

	Cost	Accumulated Amortization	2001 Closing Value
Deferred store marketing	$ 42.2	$ 3.9	$ 38.3
Deferred financing costs	26.8	12.2	14.6
Deferred purchase agreements	22.9	6.6	16.3
Transitional pension asset	15.5	—	15.5
Other	26.5	0.5	26.0
Total	$133.9	$23.2	$110.7

5. BANK LOANS AND BANKERS' ACCEPTANCES

Under the terms of a credit agreement entered into between the Company and a banking syndicate arranged by the Bank of Nova Scotia, a revolving term credit facility of $300.0 was established. This unsecured facility will expire on June 28, 2001, however various provisions of the agreement provide the Company with the ability to extend the facility for a minimum period of two years.

Interest is payable on this facility at rates which fluctuate with changes in the prime rate.

6. LONG-TERM DEBT

	2001	2000
First mortgage loans, average interest rate 9.1% due 2001–2021	$ 37.5	$ 30.1
Medium term note, interest rate of 7.6%, due November 1, 2005	175.0	—
Medium term note, interest rate of 7.0%, due October 2, 2003	100.0	—
Bank loans, average interest rate 6.8%, due June 29, 2005	220.0	691.5
Debentures, average interest rate 10.7%, due 2008–2013	88.5	102.8
Notes payable and other debt at interest rates fluctuating with the prime rate	23.9	21.2
	644.9	845.6
Capital lease obligations, due 2001–2011, net of imputed interest	13.6	10.6
	658.5	856.2
Less amount due within one year	49.2	69.9
	$609.3	$786.3

Included in first mortgage loans is U.S. dollar denominated debt with a Canadian dollar equivalent of $8.4 (2000 $8.8).

Debentures and first mortgage loans are secured by land and buildings and specific charges on certain assets. As additional security, the Company has provided a fixed and floating charge over all assets, subject to permitted encumbrances, a general assignment of book debts and the assignment of proceeds of insurance policies.

During the year a short-form prospectus was filed providing for the issuance of up to $500.0 in unsecured medium term notes. The Company also negotiated a new unsecured $550.0 credit facility consisting of $250.0 of non-revolving debt to be repaid over five years, plus a $300.0 revolving line of credit.

Debt retirement payments and capital lease obligations in each of the next five fiscal years are:

	Long-term debt	Capital leases
2002	$ 47.1	$2.1
2003	46.8	1.8
2004	146.9	1.8
2005	47.0	1.6
2006	241.0	1.6

Operating leases

The net aggregate, annual, minimum rent payable under operating leases for fiscal 2002 is approximately $139.1 ($221.8 gross less expected sub-lease income of $82.7). The net commitments over the next five fiscal years are:

	Net lease obligation
2002	$139.1
2003	133.0
2004	115.3
2005	110.0
2006	105.4

7. ACCOUNTS RECEIVABLE SECURITIZATION

On June 29, 2000, the Company entered into a revolving securitization program, whereby some accounts receivable were sold to a banking syndicate under terms that transfer significant risks and rewards of ownership. The transaction was recognized as a sale and the accounts receivable were removed from the consolidated balance sheet.

As at May 5, 2001, the Company had received $150.0 from the banking syndicate. The Company has retained interest of $116.0 which is included in receivables.

8. CAPITAL STOCK

Authorized	Number of shares
Preferred shares, par value of $25 each, issuable in a series as a class	500,000,000
Preferred shares, without par value, issuable in a series as a class	500,000,000
Common shares without par value	500,000,000

Issued and outstanding	Number of shares		Capital stock (in millions)	
	2001	2000	2001	2000
Common shares, without par value	65,778,957	56,303,261	$912.5	$659.6
Loans receivable from officers and employees under share purchase plan			(16.4)	(12.3)
Total capital stock			$896.1	$647.3

On November 16, 2000, the Company issued 9,174,312 common shares for net proceeds of $245.9.

During the current fiscal year, 298,795 common shares of Sobeys Inc. were issued under the Company's share purchase plan to certain officers and employees for $7.0.

Loans receivable from officers and employees of $16.4 under the Company's share purchase plan are classified as a reduction of Shareholders' Equity. Loan repayments will result in a corresponding increase in Capital Stock. The loans are non-interest bearing and non-recourse and are secured by 826,683 common shares of Sobeys Inc.

9. RESTRUCTURING AND INTEGRATION CHARGE

On January 24, 2001, the Company announced its decision to discontinue further development and implementation of its enterprise-wide systems initiative. This resulted in a pre-tax restructuring expense of $89.1 ($49.2 after tax). The system will be eventually phased out of operation in Sobeys Atlantic Region and has been phased out of 30 corporate Sobeys stores in Ontario. The operations of Sobeys Quebec, Sobeys West, Serca Foodservice and the remaining 379 stores in Ontario had not been converted to the enterprise-wide system. The amount remaining in liabilities at May 5, 2001 is $11.3. The restructuring activities associated with this event are expected to be completed over time.

Subsequent to the acquisition of The Oshawa Group Limited in December 30, 1998, the Company commenced a comprehensive review of its strategic direction, facilities, and staffing levels of all operations of the combined organizations. This integration initiative was undertaken to create operating efficiencies, cost savings, and revenue enhancement opportunities. This project, which was substantially completed in April 1999, brought together the operating groups of both business units and generated a new business plan for the future. In connection with the integration initiative, the Company recorded a $85.1 charge ($47.1 after tax) in the fourth quarter of fiscal 1999 for restructuring and integration. The amount remaining in liabilities at May 5, 2001 is $16.7 (2000 $56.5). The restructuring activities associated with this event are expected to be completed during the next fiscal year.

10. INCOME TAXES

Income tax expense varies from the amount that would be computed by applying the combined federal and provincial statutory tax rate as a result of the following:

	2001	2000
Income tax expense according to combined statutory rate of 40.3% (2000—42.8%)	$68.8	$67.3
Increase (reduction) in income taxes resulting from:		
Adjustment to future tax assets and liabilities for substantially enacted changes in tax laws and reduction in capital gains inclusion rate	1.5	—
Non-taxable gains	(0.9)	—
Non-deductible goodwill amortization	7.7	7.4
Large corporation tax	2.5	2.2
Total income taxes (before restructuring)	79.6	76.9
Restructuring	(39.9)	—
Total	$39.7	$76.9

May 5, 2001 income tax expense attributable to net income consists of:

	Current	Future	Total
Operations	$32.4	$48.1	$80.5
Restructuring	—	(39.9)	(39.9)
Goodwill	—	(0.9)	(0.9)
	$32.4	$ 7.3	$39.7

The tax effect of temporary differences that give rise to significant portions of the future tax provision at May 5, 2001, are presented below:

Employee future benefit obligation	$27.0
Restructuring provisions	16.7
Pension contributions	(13.6)
Deferred cost	(14.8)
Tax loss carry forward	56.2
Other	(8.1)
	$63.4

Future tax provision—current	$16.7
Future tax provision—non current	46.7
	$63.4

11. EARNINGS AND CASH FLOW PER SHARE

Earnings and cash flow per share amounts are calculated on the weighted average number of shares outstanding (2001—60,754,767; 2000—55,988,892).

	2001	2000
Earnings before restructuring and goodwill charges	$110.3	$99.1
Goodwill charges (net of income taxes)	19.1	18.9
Earnings before restructuring charge	91.2	80.2
Restructuring charge	(49.2)	—
Net earnings	$ 42.0	$80.2
Earnings per share is comprised of the following:		
Earnings before restructuring and goodwill charges	$ 1.81	$ 1.77
Goodwill charges (net of income taxes)	(0.31)	(0.34)
Earnings before restructuring charge	1.50	1.43
Restructuring charge	(0.81)	—
Net earnings	$ 0.69	$ 1.43

12. SUPPLEMENTARY CASH FLOW INFORMATION

a) Items not affecting cash	2001	2000
Depreciation	$ 99.5	$ 98.0
Goodwill amortization	20.0	19.6
Deferred income taxes	—	55.4
Future tax provision	31.7	—
(Gain) loss on disposal of assets	(0.2)	0.3
Amortization of deferred items	23.2	8.4
	$174.2	$181.7

b) Other items	2001	2000
Net interest paid	$ 78.1	$ 95.3
Net income taxes paid	$ 63.8	$ 20.2

13. RELATED PARTY TRANSACTIONS

The Company leased certain real property from related parties, at fair market value, during the year. The aggregate net payments under these leases amounted to approximately $51.2 (2000 $48.2). The Company was charged expenses of $0.8 (2000 $0.3) by related parties.

The Company sold real property to related parties, at fair market value, during the year. The aggregate proceeds were $11.9. At May 5, 2001, mortgage receivables of $9.0 were owing from related parties.

14. FINANCIAL INSTRUMENTS

Credit risk

There is no significant concentration of credit risk. The credit risk exposure is considered normal for the business.

Other financial instruments

The book value of cash, receivables, income taxes recoverable, loans and mortgages receivable, bank loans, bankers' acceptances and accounts payable and accrued charges approximate fair values at May 5, 2001. The fair value of marketable securities is $2.7.

The total fair value of long-term debt is estimated to be $688.0. The fair value of variable rate long-term debt is assumed to approximate its carrying amount.

The fair value of other long-term debt has been estimated by discounting future cash flows at a rate offered for debt of similar maturities and credit quality.

Interest rate swaps

The Company has fixed the interest rate on $75.0 of its debt at 6.2% for one year and has fixed the interest rate on $292.1 of its debt at 6.8% for four years by utilizing interest exchange agreements.

Interest rate risk

The majority of the Company debt is at fixed rates. Accordingly, there is limited exposure to interest rate risk.

15. CONTINGENT LIABILITIES

Guarantees and commitments

The Company has undertaken to provide cash to meet any obligations which Sobey Leased Properties Limited (a wholly owned subsidiary of the majority shareholders of Sobeys, Empire Company Limited) is unable or fails to meet until all of its debentures have been paid in full in accordance with their terms. Any deficiency payment made by the Company will be by purchase of fully-paid non-assessable 5% redeemable, non-voting preference shares of that company. The aggregated outstanding principal amounts of these debentures at May 5, 2001 is $44.7.

At May 5, 2001, the Company was contingently liable for letters of credit issued in the aggregate amount of $22.5.

The Company has guaranteed certain bank loans contracted by franchisees. As at May 5, 2001, these loans amounted to approximately $14.7.

There are various claims and litigation, which the Company is involved with, arising out of the ordinary course of business operations. The Company's management does not consider the exposure to such litigation to be material, although this cannot be predicted with certainty.

16. SEGMENTED INFORMATION

	2001	2000
Sales		
Food distribution	$9,161.0	$8,936.2
Foodservice	2,209.5	2,069.9
	11,370.5	11,006.1
Operating income		
Food distribution	232.7	231.8
Foodservice	31.9	33.8
	264.6	265.6
Identifiable assets		
Food distribution	1,828.0	1,810.1
Foodservice	366.1	366.0
Goodwill	723.5	714.9
	2,917.6	2,891.0
Depreciation		
Food distribution	87.0	86.5
Foodservice	12.5	11.5
	99.5	98.0
Capital expenditures		
Food distribution	193.7	192.6
Foodservice	14.1	14.7
	$ 207.8	$ 207.3

The Company operates principally in two business segments, food distribution and foodservice. The food distribution segment consists of the distribution of food products through a retail network in all provinces of Canada. The foodservice segment distributes foodservice products to primarily hospitality, institutional, and commercial customers throughout Canada.

17. EMPLOYEE FUTURE BENEFITS

The Company has a number of defined benefit and defined contribution plans providing pension and other retirement benefits to most of its employees.

Defined contribution plans
The total expense for the Company's defined contribution plans is as follows:

	2001	2000
	7.7	5.7

Defined benefit plans

Information about the Company's defined benefit plans, in aggregate, is as follows:

	Pension Benefit Plans 2001	Other Benefit Plans 2001
Accrued benefit obligation		
Balance at beginning of year	$195.9	$ 59.1
Current service cost	4.3	1.5
Interest cost	14.4	4.1
Employee contributions	0.3	0.0
Plan amendments	0.4	0.0
Benefits paid	(15.7)	(3.9)
Curtailment	0.1	0.0
Actuarial loss	6.7	1.0
Balance at end of year	$206.4	$ 61.8
Plan assets		
Market value at beginning of year	$205.6	$ —
Actual return on plan assets	11.3	0.0
Employer contributions	8.0	3.9
Employee contributions	0.3	0.0
Benefits paid	(15.7)	(3.9)
Market value at end of year	$209.5	$ —
Funded status		
Surplus (deficit)	$3.1	$(61.8)
Unamortized past service cost	0.4	—
Unamortized actuarial loss	12.0	1.0
Accrued benefit asset (liability)	$ 15.5	$(60.8)
Expense		
Current service cost	$4.3	$ 1.5
Interest cost	14.4	4.1
Expected return on plan assets	(16.6)	0.0
	$ 2.1	$ 5.6

Included in the accrued benefit obligation at year-end are the following amounts in respect of plans that are not funded:

	Pension Benefit Plans 2001	Other Benefit Plans 2001
Accrued benefit obligation	$16.0	$61.8

The significant actuarial assumptions adopted in measuring the Company's accrued benefit obligations are as follows (weighted-average assumptions as of May 5, 2001):

	Pension Benefit Plans 2001	Other Benefit Plans 2001
Discount rate	7.35%	7.35%
Expected long-term rate of return on plan assets	8.00%	
Rate of compensation increase	4.00%	

For measurement purposes, a 4.5% to 5.0% annual rate of increase in the per capita cost of covered health care benefits was assumed, a rate that is expected to be slightly in excess of inflation. The average remaining service period of the active employees covered by the pension benefit plans and other benefit plans is 13 and 17 years, respectively.

18. COMPARATIVE FIGURES

Comparative figures have been reclassified, where necessary, to reflect the current year's presentation.

Glossary of Accounting Terms

accelerated amortization methods Those methods that record more amortization expense in the early years of an asset's life and less in the later years. (p. 227)

account A record that contains the history of all increases and decreases of an accounting element. (p. 175)

accounting cycle The sequence of steps repeated in each accounting period to enable the firm to analyze, record, classify, and summarize the transactions into financial statements. (p. 172)

accounting information Raw data concerning transactions that have been transformed into financial numbers that can be used by economic decision makers. (p. 38)

accounting system The overall format used to gather data from source transactions to create the books and records that are used to prepare the financial statements of a business entity. (p. 179)

accrual basis accounting A method of accounting in which revenues are recognized when they are earned, regardless of when the associated cash is collected. The expenses incurred in generating the revenue are recognized when the benefit is derived rather than when the associated cash is paid. (p. 48)

accruals Adjustments made to record items that should be included on the income statement but have not yet been recorded. (p. 145)

accrue As used in accounting, to come into being as a legally enforceable claim. (p. 48)

accrued expenses Expenses appropriately recognized under accrual accounting in one income statement period although the associated cash will be paid in a later income statement period. (p. 145)

accrued revenues Revenues appropriately recognized under accrual accounting in one income statement period although the associated cash will be received in a later income statement period. (p. 145)

accumulated amortization The total amount of cost that has been systematically converted to expense since a long-lived asset was first purchased. (p. 149)

adjustments Changes made in recorded amounts of revenues and expenses in order to follow the guidelines of accrual accounting. (p. 145)

amortizable base   The total amount of amortization expense that is allowed to be claimed for an asset during its useful life. The amortizable base is the cost of the asset less its residual value. (p. 143)

amortization   The systematic and rational conversion of a long-lived asset's cost from asset to expense in the income statement periods benefited. (p. 143)

amortization expense   The amount of cost associated with a long-lived asset converted to expense in a given income statement period. (p. 143)

articulation   The links among the financial statements. (p. 138)

assets   An accounting element that is one of the three components of a balance sheet. Assets are economic resources controlled by an entity as a result of past transactions or events—that is, what a company has. (p. 66)

audit   Examination by an independent accountant of enough of a company's records to determine whether the financial statements have been prepared in accordance with GAAP and demonstrate a fair representation of the company's financial status. (p. 17)

authorized shares   The maximum number of shares a corporation has been given permission to issue under its corporate chart (p. 72)

average cost method   The inventory cost flow method that assigns an average cost to the units of inventory on hand at the time of each sale. (p. 278)

balance sheet   A financial statement providing information about an entity's present condition. Reports what a company possesses (assets) and who has claim to those possessions (liabilities and owners' equity). (p. 65)

basic earnings per share   A simple calculation of earnings per common share based on shares outstanding on the balance sheet date. (p. 335)

beginning inventory   The amount of merchandise inventory (units or dollars) on hand at the beginning of the income statement period. (p. 265)

book inventory   The amount of ending inventory (units and dollars) resulting from transactions recorded by a perpetual inventory system. (p. 270)

bond   An interest-bearing debt instrument that allows corporations to borrow large amounts of funds for long periods of time and creates a liability for the borrower. (p. 101)

business   Depending on the context, the area of commerce or trade, an individual company, or the process of producing and distributing goods and services. (p. 2)

business segment   A portion of the business for which assets, results of operations, and activities can be separately identified. (p. 333)

Canadian Institute of Chartered Accountants (CICA)   In Canada, the primary body responsible for setting generally accepted accounting principles. (p. 16)

capital   A factor of production that includes the buildings, machinery, and tools used to produce goods and services. Also sometimes used to refer to the money used to buy those items. (p. 3)

capital cost allowance (CCA)   Amortization method that taxpayers use to calculate amortization expense for tax purposes. (p. 227)

cash basis accounting   A basis of accounting in which cash is the major criterion used in measuring revenue and expense for a given income statement period. Revenue is recognized when the associated cash is received, and expense is recognized when the associated cash is paid. (p. 45)

cash flow   The movement of cash in and out of a company. (p. 36)

chart of accounts   A list of all the accounts used by a business entity. The list usually contains the name of the account and the account number. (p. 175)

classified balance sheet   A balance sheet showing assets and liabilities categorized into current and long-term items. (p. 325)

collateral   Something of value that will be forfeited if a borrower fails to make payments as agreed. (p. 98)

commercial borrowing The process that businesses go through to obtain financing. (p. 95)

common share A share of ownership in a corporation. Each share represents one vote in the election of the board of directors and other pertinent corporate matters. (p. 72)

common size financial statements See definition of *vertical analysis*. (p. 399)

comparative financial statements Financial statements showing results from two or more consecutive periods. (p. 337)

compound journal entry Any entry recorded in the general journal that contains more than two accounts. (p. 182)

conservatism A characteristic of reliability. In times of uncertainty, it is better to underestimate the wealth and income of a business than to overestimate it. (p. 41)

consumer borrowing Loans obtained by individuals to buy homes, cars, or other personal property. (p. 95)

contributed capital Total amount invested in a corporation by its shareholders. (p. 72)

contributed surplus The excess paid by shareholders for shares over the par value of the shares. Contributed surplus can also arise from increases in equity arising from the cancellation of shares. (p. 73)

convertible securities Debt or equity securities that can be converted into the company's common shares. (p. 335)

corporation One of the three forms of business organization. The only form that is legally considered to be an entity separate from its owners. (p. 9)

cost/benefit analysis Deals with the trade-off between the rewards of selecting a given alternative and the sacrifices required to obtain those rewards. (p. 34)

cost of goods manufactured The cost of converting raw materials into finished goods in a manufacturing firm. The cost is equivalent to purchases in a manufacturing firm. (p. 267)

cost of goods sold The cost of the product sold as the primary business activity of a company. Also called cost of products sold or cost of sales. (p. 126)

cost of goods sold (COGS) The cost of the merchandise inventory no longer on hand and assumed sold during the period. Also called cost of sales. (p. 265)

coverage ratio or **times interest earned ratio** A solvency ratio that provides an indication of a company's ability to make its periodic interest payments. (p. 413)

credit A term that means "to lend," appearing on the right side of a general ledger account. (p. 180)

current assets Assets that are either cash or will become cash within one year. (p. 325)

current liabilities Liabilities that must be settled within one year. (p. 327)

current ratio A liquidity ratio that measures a company's ability to meet short-term obligations by comparing current assets to current liabilities. (p. 407)

date of declaration The date upon which a corporation announces plans to distribute a dividend. At this point, the corporation becomes legally obligated to make the distribution: A liability is created. (p. 136)

date of payment The date a corporate dividend is actually paid. The payment date is generally announced on the date of declaration. (p. 137)

date of record Owners of the shares on this day are the ones who will receive the dividend announced on the date of declaration. (p. 136)

debenture An unsecured bond payable. (p. 101)

debit A term that means "to owe," appearing on the left side of a general ledger account. (p. 180)

debt financing Acquiring funds for business operations by borrowing. Debt financing is one type of external financing. (p. 94)

debt ratio A solvency ratio that indicates what proportion of a company's assets is financed by debt. (p. 412)

debt to equity ratio A solvency ratio indicating the relationship between creditors' claims to a company's assets and the owners' claim to those assets. (p. 413)

default A failure to repay a loan as agreed. (p. 96)

deferrals Situations in which cash is either received or paid, but the income statement effect is delayed until some later period.

Deferred revenues are recorded as liabilities, and deferred expenses are recorded as assets. (p. 145)

diluted earnings per share   A calculation of earnings per common share, including all potentially dilutive securities. (p. 335)

direct method   The format of a statement of cash flows that provides detail about the individual sources and uses of cash associated with operating activities. (p. 358)

discontinued operations   The disposal of a business segment. One of the nonrecurring items shown net of tax on the income statement. (p. 333)

discount   If a bond's selling price is below its par value, the bond is being sold at a discount. This will occur if the market or effective interest rate is higher than the stated rate on the bond. (p. 105)

discounted note   A loan arrangement in which the bank deducts the interest from the proceeds of the loan. Also called a *non-interest-bearing* note. (p. 100)

dividends   A distribution of earnings from a corporation to its owners. Dividends are most commonly distributed in the form of cash. (p. 72)

double-declining-balance method   An accelerated amortization method in which amortization expense is twice the straight-line percentage multiplied by the book value of the asset. (p. 227)

drawings   Distributions to the owners of proprietorships and partnerships. Also called withdrawals. (p. 133)

earned equity   The total amount a company has earned since its beginning, less any amounts distributed to the owner(s). In a corporation, this amount is called retained earnings. (p. 66)

earnings per share (EPS)   A calculation indicating how much of a company's total earnings is attributable to each common share. (p. 335)

effective interest rate   The rate of interest actually earned by a lender. This amount will be different from the nominal interest rate if a bond is bought at a discount or premium, or a note is discounted. Also called yield rate or market interest rate. (p. 100)

ending inventory   The amount of inventory (in units or dollars) still on hand at the end of an accounting period. (p. 265)

entrepreneurship   The factor of production that brings the other three factors—natural resources, labour, and capital—together to form a business. (p. 3)

equity   An accounting element that is one of the three components of a balance sheet. Equity is the ownership interest in the assets of a profit-oriented enterprise after its liabilities have been deducted. Also called net assets. (p. 66)

equity financing   Acquiring funds for business operations by giving up ownership interest in the company. For a corporation, this means issuing capital stock. Equity financing is one type of external financing. (p. 94)

expense   An accounting element representing the outflow of assets resulting from an entity's ongoing major or central operations. This is the sacrifice required to attain the rewards (revenues) of doing business. (p. 43)

external decision makers   Economic decision makers outside a company who make decisions about the company. The accounting information they use to make those decisions is limited to what the company provides to them. (p. 35)

external financing   Acquiring funds from outside the company. Equity and debt financing are the two major types of external financing. (p. 94)

extraordinary item   A gain or loss that is both unusual in nature and infrequent in occurrence. One of the nonrecurring items shown net of tax on the income statement. (p. 334)

factors of production   The four major items needed to support economic activity: natural resources, labour, capital, and entrepreneurship. (p. 3)

feedback value   A primary characteristic of relevance. To be useful, accounting must provide decision makers with information that allows them to assess the progress of an investment. (p. 40)

financial accounting   The branch of accounting developed to meet the informational needs of external decision makers. (p. 36)

financial reporting   Financial disclosures provided to economic decision makers that include both quantitative (numerical) information and qualitative (descriptive) information. (p. 20)

financial statement analysis   The process of looking beyond the face of the financial statements to gather more information. (p. 393)

financing activities   Business activities, such as the issuance of debt or equity and the payment of dividends, that focus on the external financing of the company. (p. 357)

finished goods inventory   The inventory ready to sell in a manufacturing company. Equivalent to the merchandise inventory in a merchandising firm. (p. 267)

first in, first out (FIFO)   The inventory flow concept based on the assumption that the first units of inventory purchased are the first ones sold. (p. 271)

functional obsolescence   Occurs when an asset can no longer perform the function for which it was purchased. (p. 235)

gains   Net inflows resulting from peripheral activities of a company. An example is the sale of an asset for more than its book value. (p. 235)

general journal   A book of original entry in which are recorded all transactions not otherwise recorded in a special journal. (p. 174)

general ledger   A book of final entry that includes a record for each account listed in the chart of accounts. (p. 175)

generally accepted accounting principles (GAAP)   Guidelines for presentation of financial accounting information designed to serve external decision makers' need for consistent and comparable information. (p. 15)

goods available for sale (GAFS)   The total amount of merchandise inventory a company has available to sell in a given income statement period. (p. 265)

gross margin   An item shown on a multistep income statement, calculated as: Sales − Cost of Goods Sold. Also called gross profit. (p. 128)

gross margin or **gross profit**   The excess of benefit received over the sacrifice made to complete a sale. Gross profit considers only the cost of the item sold; it does not consider the other costs of operations. (p. 5)

historical cost   Total of all costs required to bring an asset to a productive state. (p. 226)

horizontal analysis   The study of percentage changes in comparative financial statements. (p. 398)

income statement   A financial statement providing information about an entity's past performance. Its purpose is to measure the results of the entity's operations for some specific time period. Also called the statement of earnings or the statement of results of operations. (p. 124)

indenture   The legal agreement made between a bond issuer and a bondholder that states repayment terms and other details. (p. 102)

indirect method   The format of the statement of cash flows that begins with a reconciliation of accrual net income to the cash provided by or used by operating activities. (p. 358)

information   Data that have been transformed so that they are useful in the decision-making process. (p. 38)

intangible assets   Assets consisting of contractual rights such as patents, copyrights, and trademarks. (p. 327)

interest   The cost to the borrower of using someone else's money. Also, what can be earned by lending money to someone else. (p. 96)

internal decision makers   Economic decision makers within a company who make decisions for the company. They have access to much or all of the accounting information generated within the company. (p. 35)

internal financing   Providing funds for the operation of a company through the earnings process of that company. (p. 94)

inventory turnover ratio   A liquidity ratio that indicates how long a company holds its inventory. (p. 410)

investing activities   Business activities related to long-term assets. Examples are the purchase and sale of property, plant, and equipment. (p. 357)

investment bankers   Intermediaries between the corporation issuing shares and the investors who ultimately purchase the shares. Also called underwriters. (p. 77)

investments   Assets that represent long-term ownership in subsidiaries, or the shares or bonds of other companies. (p. 327)

investments by owners   That part of owners' equity generated by the receipt of cash (or other assets) from the owners. (p. 66)

issued shares   Shares that have been distributed to the owners of the corporation in exchange for cash or other assets. (p. 72)

journal   A book of original entry in which is kept a chronological record of the transactions of a business entity. (p. 174)

labour   The mental and physical efforts of all workers performing tasks required to produce and sell goods and services. This factor of production is also called the human resource factor. (p. 3)

last in, first out (LIFO)   The inventory flow concept based on the assumption that the last units of inventory purchased are the first ones sold. (p. 271)

liabilities   An accounting element that is one of the three components of a balance sheet. Liabilities are obligations arising from past transactions or events that may be settled through the transfer or use of assets, provision of services, or other yielding of economic benefits in the future—that is, what a company owes. (p. 66)

liquidity   An item's nearness to cash. (p. 326)

liquidity ratios   A set of ratios developed to measure a firm's ability to generate sufficient cash in the short run to retire short-term liabilities. (p. 407)

long-term assets   Assets that are expected to benefit the company for longer than one year. (p. 329)

long-term financing   Any financing in which repayment extends beyond three years. This type of financing supports the long-range goals of the company. (p. 94)

long-term liabilities   Amounts that are not due for settlement until at least one year from now. (p. 327)

losses   Net outflows resulting from peripheral activities of a company. An example is the sale of an asset for less than its book value. (p. 235)

management accounting   The branch of accounting developed to meet the informational needs of internal decision makers. (p. 36)

manufacturing   The business activity that converts purchased raw materials into some tangible, physical product. (p. 11)

market economy   A type of economy in which all or most of the factors of production are privately owned and that relies on competition in the marketplace to determine the most efficient way to allocate the economy's resources. (p. 4)

matching principle   Accounting principle that relates the expenses to the revenues of a particular income statement period. Once it is determined in which period a revenue should be recognized, the expenses that helped to generate the revenue are matched to that same period. (p. 142)

materiality   Something that will influence the judgment of a reasonable person. (p. 39)

merchandise inventory   The physical units (goods) a company buys to resell as part of its business operation. Also called inventory. (p. 265)

merchandising   The business activity involving the selling of finished goods produced by other businesses. (p. 11)

mortgage   A document that states the agreement between a lender and a borrower who has secured the loan by offering something of value as collateral. (p. 98)

moving average cost method   The inventory cost flow method that assigns an average cost to the units of inventory on hand at the time of each sale in a perpetual inventory system. (p. 283)

multistep income statement An income statement format that highlights gross margin and operating income. (p. 128)

natural resources Land and the materials that come from the land, such as timber, mineral deposits, oil deposits, and water. One of the factors of production. (p. 3)

net book value The original cost of a long-lived asset less its accumulated amortization. This item is often shown on the balance sheet. (p. 149)

net cash flow The difference between cash inflows and cash outflows; it can be either positive or negative. (p. 36)

net income The amount of profit that remains after all costs have been considered. The net reward of doing business for a specific time period. Also called earnings or net earnings (p. 125)

net loss The difference between revenues and expenses of a period in which expenses are greater than revenues. (p. 125)

net of tax The proper presentation format for nonrecurring items shown below income from continuing operations on the income statement. (p. 332)

neutrality A primary characteristic of reliability. To be useful, accounting information must be free of bias. (p. 41)

nominal interest rate The interest rate set by the issuers of bonds, stated as a percentage of the par value of the bonds. Also called the contract rate, coupon rate, or stated rate. (p. 102)

non-interest-bearing note See definition of *discounted note*. (p. 100)

nonrecurring item Results of activities that cannot be expected to occur again, and therefore should not be used to predict future performance. (p. 330)

normal balance The balance of the account derived from the type of entry (debit or credit) that increases the account. (p. 180)

note payable An agreement between a lender and a borrower that creates a liability for the borrower. (p. 97)

Ontario Securities Commission (OSC) The Ontario agency empowered to set reporting standards for all companies that trade shares on the Toronto Stock Exchange (p. 16)

operating activities Activities that result in cash inflows and outflows generated from the normal course of business. (p. 356)

operating cycle The length of time it takes for an entity to complete one revenue-producing cycle from purchase of goods to collection of cash. (p. 325)

operating income Income produced by the major business activity of the company. An item shown on the multistep income statement. Also called income from operations. (p. 128)

opportunity cost The benefit or benefits forgone by not selecting a particular alternative. Once an alternative is selected in a decision situation, the benefits of all rejected alternatives become part of the opportunity cost of the alternative selected. (p. 34)

outstanding shares Shares of stock actually held by shareholders. The number may be different than that for issued shares because a corporation may reacquire its own shares. (p. 72)

partnership A business form similar to a proprietorship, but having two or more owners. (p. 7)

par value (for bonds) The amount that must be paid back upon maturity of a bond. Also called face value or maturity value. (p. 102)

par value (for shares) An arbitrary amount assigned to each share of stock by the incorporators at the time of incorporation. (p. 72)

period Length of time (usually a month, quarter, or year) for which activity is being reported on an income statement. (p. 125)

periodic inventory system An inventory system in which all inventory and cost of goods sold calculations are done at the end of the income statement period. (p. 267)

periodicity The assumption that the economic activities of an entity can be traced to some specific time period and results of those activities can be reported for any arbitrary time period chosen. (p. 42)

permanent (or real) accounts The general ledger accounts that are never closed. The permanent accounts include assets, liabilities, and equity accounts except for owner withdrawals and dividends. (p. 179)

perpetual inventory system An inventory system in which both the physical count of inventory units and the cost classification (asset or expense) are updated when a transaction involves inventory. (p. 268)

post-closing trial balance A trial balance prepared after all closing entries have been posted that proves that the only accounts remaining in the general ledger are the permanent accounts and that the accounting equation remains in balance. (p. 179)

predictive value A primary characteristic of relevance. To be useful, accounting must provide information to decision makers that can be used to predict the future and timing of cash flows. (p. 40)

preferred shares A share of ownership in a corporation that has preference over common shares as to dividends and as to assets upon liquidation of the corporation. Usually preferred shares do not have voting rights. (p. 74)

premium If a bond's selling price is above its par value, the bond is being sold at a premium. This will occur if the market or effective interest rate is lower than the stated rate on the bond. (p. 105)

prepaid expenses Expenses created when cash is paid before any benefit is received. Because the benefit to be derived is in the future, the item is recorded as an asset. Later, when the benefit is received from the item, it will be recognized as an expense. (p. 146)

price earnings ratio Ratio of the market price of a common share to the company's earnings per share. It measures the value that the stock market places on $1 of a company's earnings. (p. 414)

primary stock market The business activity involved in the initial issue of shares from a corporation. (p. 77)

principal In the case of notes and mortgages, the amount of funds actually borrowed. (p. 98)

profit The excess of benefit over sacrifice. A less formal name for net income or net profit. (p. 4)

profitability The ease with which a company generates income. (p. 402)

profitability ratios A set of ratios that measure a firm's past performance and help predict its future profitability level. (p. 402)

profit margin after income tax ratio A profitability ratio that measures the earnings produced from a given level of revenues by comparing net income after income tax with the revenue figure. (p. 405)

profit margin before income tax ratio A profitability ratio that measures the earnings produced from a given level of revenues by comparing net income before income tax to the revenue figure. (p. 404)

promissory note A legal promise to repay a loan. (p. 98)

prospectus A description of an upcoming bond issue that is provided as information for potential investors. (p. 105)

purchases The amount of merchandise inventory bought during the income statement period. (p. 265)

quick ratio or **acid-test ratio** A liquidity ratio that is similar to the current ratio, but is a more stringent test of liquidity because only current assets considered to be highly liquid (quickly converted to cash) are included in the calculation. (p. 408)

ratio analysis A technique for analyzing the relationship between two items from a company's financial statements for a given period. (p. 393)

raw materials inventory The inventory of raw materials to be transferred into production in a manufacturing company. (p. 267)

realization Actual receipt of cash or payment of cash. Once cash has been collected or a transaction is complete, it is considered to be realized. (p. 45)

receivable Money due to an entity from an enforceable claim. (p. 48)

receivables turnover ratio A liquidity ratio that measures how quickly a company collects its accounts receivable. (p. 409)

recognition The process of recording an event in the accounting records and reporting it on the financial statements. (p. 43)

relevance One of the two primary qualitative characteristics of useful accounting information. It means the information must have a bearing on a particular decision situation. (p. 40)

reliability One of the two primary qualitative characteristics of useful accounting information. It means the information must be reasonably accurate. (p. 40)

representational faithfulness A primary characteristic of reliability. To be useful, accounting information must reasonably report what actually happened. (p. 40)

residual value The estimated value of an asset when it has reached the end of its useful life. Also called salvage or scrap value. (p. 144)

retained earnings The sum of all earnings of a corporation minus the amount of dividends declared. (p. 72)

return on assets ratio A profitability ratio that measures how efficiently the company uses its assets to produce profits. (p. 403)

return on equity ratio A profitability ratio that measures the after-tax net income generated from a given level of investment by a company's owners. (p. 406)

revenue An accounting element representing the inflows of assets as a result of an entity's ongoing major or central operations. This is the reward of doing business. (p. 43)

sales revenue The revenue generated from the sale of a tangible product as a major business activity. Also called sales. (p. 128)

secondary stock market The business activity focusing on trades of shares among investors subsequent to the initial issue. (p. 77)

selling price The amount received when bonds are issued or sold. This amount is affected by the difference between the nominal interest rate and the market rate. Selling price is usually stated as a percentage of the bond's par value. Also called the market price (p. 102)

separate entity assumption The assumption that economic activity can be identified with a particular economic entity and that the results of activities for each entity will be recorded separately. (p. 8)

service A business activity that does not deal with tangible products, but rather provides some sort of service as its major operation. (p. 12)

share dividend A dividend paid in the corporation's own shares. (p. 135)

shareholder A person who owns shares in a corporation. (p. 9)

short-term financing Financing secured to support an operation's day-to-day activities. Repayment is usually required within three years. (p. 94)

single-step income statement A format of the income statement that gathers all revenues into "total revenues" and all expenses into "total expenses." Net income is calculated as a subtraction of total expenses from total revenues. (p. 127)

sole proprietorship An unincorporated business that is owned by one person. Also called a proprietorship. (p. 6)

solvency A company's ability to meet the obligations created by its long-term debt. (p. 411)

solvency ratios A set of ratios developed to measure a firm's ability to meet its long-term debt obligations. (p. 411)

special journal A book of original entry designed to record a specific type of transaction. (p. 174)

specific identification The method of inventory cost flow that identifies each item sold by a company. (p. 274)

stakeholder Anyone who is affected by the way a company conducts its business. (p. 5)

statement of cash flows A financial statement that provides information about the causes of a change in a company's cash balance from the beginning to the end of a specific period. (p. 354)

statement of owners' equity   The financial statement that reports activity in the capital accounts of proprietorships and partnerships and in the retained earnings account of corporations. The statement of owners' equity serves as a bridge between the income statement and the balance sheet. Also called statement of partners' equity for a partnership. (p. 130)

statement of partners' equity   A statement of owners' equity for a partnership. (p. 131)

statement of retained earnings   A corporate financial statement that shows the changes in retained earnings during a particular period. (p. 132)

straight-line amortization   A method of calculating periodic amortization. The amortizable base of an asset is divided by its estimated useful life. The result is the amount of amortization expense to be recognized in each year of the item's estimated useful life: (Cost − Residual Value)/N = Annual Amortization Expense. (p. 144)

syndicate   A group of underwriters working together to get a large bond issue sold to the public. (p. 104)

T-account   An account form that represents the general ledger account with only two columns. (p. 181)

tangible property   Property used in a business, such as buildings, equipment, machinery, furniture, and fixtures. (p. 226)

technological obsolescence   Occurs when an asset is no longer compatible with current technology. (p. 235)

temporary (or nominal) accounts   The general ledger accounts that are closed to a zero balance at the end of the fiscal year as the net income or net loss is transferred to the appropriate equity account. Temporary accounts include revenues, expenses, gains, losses, owner withdrawals, and dividend accounts. (p. 178)

timeliness   A primary characteristic of relevance. To be useful, accounting information must be provided in time to influence a particular decision. (p. 46)

total asset turnover ratio   A profitability ratio that indicates the amount of revenues produced for a given level of assets used. (p. 404)

trend analysis   A technique whereby an analyst tries to determine the amount of changes in key financial amounts over time to see if a pattern of change emerges. (p. 393)

trial balance   The listing of the general ledger account balances that proves that the general ledger and, therefore, the accounting equation are in balance. (p. 176)

underwriters   Professionals in the field of investment banking. Also called investment bankers. (p. 77)

unearned revenues   Revenues created when cash is received before the revenue is earned. Because the cash received has not yet been earned, an obligation is created and a liability is recorded. Later, when the cash is deemed to have been earned, it will be recognized as a revenue. (p. 146)

units of production amortization method   A straight-line amortization method that uses production activity as the base to assign amortization expense. (p. 229)

verifiability   A primary characteristic of reliability. Information is considered verifiable if several individuals, working independently, would arrive at similar conclusions using the same data. (p. 40)

vertical analysis   The analysis of a financial statement that reveals the relationship of each statement item to the total, which is 100 percent. Common size financial statements are a type of vertical analysis. (p. 399)

working capital   The difference between current assets and current liabilities. (p. 354)

work-in-process inventory   The cost of raw materials, labour, and other expenses associated with unfinished units during the process of converting raw materials into finished goods for a manufacturing company. (p. 267)

worksheet   A tool used by the accountant to accumulate the necessary information used to prepare the financial statements. (p. 176)

Index

Closing entries, preparing and posting, 178–79
Collateral, 98
Commercial borrowing, 95
Common shares, 72
    cash dividends on, 135–36
Common size financial statements, 399
Comparative financial statements, 337–39
Compound journal entry, 182
Computers, effect on accounting, 201
Consumer borrowing, 95
Conservatism of accounting information, 41
Contract rate, 102
Contributed capital, 72
Contributed surplus, 73
Convertible securities, 335
Corporate officers, 70–71
Corporate reporting, *see* Annual report
Corporate secretary, 71
Corporation(s)
    advantages, 9, 10
    articulation, 141–42
    balance sheet for, 69–70
    board of directors, 70
    capital structure, 72–76
    defined, 9
    disadvantages, 9–10
    dividends, 134–35
    financial statements of, 141–42
    organizational structure, 70–71
    public, 76
    statement of owners' equity, 132
    shareholders, 70
Cost/benefit analysis, 34
Cost flow assumptions, 273–75
    periodic inventory system, 278–79
    specific identification, 274–75
    under perpetual inventory system, 280–85
Cost of goods manufactured, 267
Cost of goods sold (COGS), 126, 265
Coupon rate, 102
Coverage ratio, 413
Credit, 180
Credit unions, 95
Current ratio, 407–408
Currency, translating, 13
Current assets, 325
Current liabilities, 327
Customer's promise to pay, 51

D
Date of declaration, dividends, 136
Date of payment, dividends, 137
Date of record, dividends, 136
Debenture, 101
Debit, 180

Debt financing, 94
Debt investments, compared to equity investments, 109–110
Debt ratio, 412
Debt to equity ratio, 413
Decision makers
    external, 35–36
    internal, 35
    understandability and, 52–53
Decision-making
    accounting information, 38–39
    cash flow, 36
    cost/benefit analysis, 34
    defined, 33
    economic, 35–38
    financial accounting, 36
    management accounting, 36
    net cash flow, 36
    opportunity cost, 34
    reality vs. measurement of reality, 41–45
    trade-off, 33–34
Default on a loan, 96
Deferrals, prepaid expenses, 145–46
Diluted earnings per share, 335
Direct method, 358, 363–68
Discount, 105
    cash, 291
Discounted note, 100
Discontinued operations, 332–34
Dividends, 72, 134–35
    cash, on common shares, 135–36
    cash, on preferred shares, 138
    dates, 136–37
Double-declining-balance amortization, 227, 231–32
    recording long-lived assets, 247–48
Double-entry system, 15
Double taxation, 9
Drawings, 133
    partnership, 133–34

E
Earned equity, 66
Earnings
    retained, 72
statement of, 132
Earnings per share (EPS), 335–37
    basic, 335
    calculating, 335–36
    diluted, 335
    income statement presentation, 336–37
Ending inventory, 265
Entrepreneurship, 3
Equity, 66
Equity financing, 94